THE  GLOBAL SOLUT

Every 4LTR Press solution includes:

 +  +  +

| Visually Engaging Textbook | Online Study Tools | Tear-out Review Cards | Interactive eBook |

STUDENT RESOURCES:

- Interactive eBook
- Auto-Graded Quizzes
- Flashcards
- E-Lectures
- Glossary
- Internet Exercises
- Games
- PowerPoint® Slides
- Videos
- Video Quizzing
- Global Economic Watch Blog
- Interactive Maps
- Student Review Cards

Students sign in at **www.cengagebrain.com**

INSTRUCTOR RESOURCES:

- All Student Resources
- Engagement Tracker
- First Day of Class Instructions
- Instructor's Manual
- Test Bank
- PowerPoint® Slides
- Instructor Prep Cards

Learning Management System Integration Available!

Instructors sign in at **www.cengage.com/login**

"4LTR Press rocks. You understand my brain and my budget."

– **Samantha Jerabek**, Student, *University of Cincinnati*

SOUTH-WESTERN
CENGAGE Learning

GLOBAL2
Mike W. Peng

SVP, Learning Acquisitions & Solutions
  Planning: Jack W. Calhoun

Publisher: Erin Joyner

Sr. Acquisitions Editor: Michele Rhoades

Vice President, 4LTR Press: Neil Marquardt

Developmental Editor: Dana Freeman,
  B-books, Ltd.

Product Development Manager, 4LTR Press:
  Steven E. Joos

Associate Project Manager, 4LTR Press:
  Pierce Denny

Marketing Manager: Jonathan Monahan

Marketing Manager, 4LTR Press:
  Courtney Sheldon

Sr. Marketing Communications Manager:
  Jim Overly

Production Director: Amy McGuire,
  B-books, Ltd.

Sr. Content Project Manager:
  Tamborah Moore

Media Editor: Rob Ellington

Manufacturing Planner: Ron Montgomery

Production Service: B-books, Ltd.

Rights Acquisitions Specialist:
  Deanna Ettinger

Photo Researcher: Charlotte Goldman

Text Permissions Researcher: Tom Wilcox,
  PreMediaGlobal

Sr. Art Director: Tippy McIntosh

Internal Designer: Craig Ramsdell,
  Ramsdell Design

Cover Designer: KeDesign, Mason, OH

Cover Image: © Ocean/Corbis

For product information and technology assistance, contact us at **Cengage Learning Customer & Sales Support, 1-800-354-9706**

For permission to use material from this text or product, submit all requests online at **www.cengage.com/permissions**. Further permissions questions can be emailed to **permissionrequest@cengage.com**.

Library of Congress Control Number: 2011942795

Student Edition ISBN-13: 978-1-111-82175-3
Student Edition ISBN-10: 1-111-82175-5

South-Western
5191 Natorp Boulevard
Mason, OH 45040
USA

Cengage Learning products are represented in Canada by Nelson Education, Ltd.

For your course and learning solutions, visit **www.cengage.com**. Purchase any of our products at your local college store or at our preferred online store **www.CengageBrain.com**.

Design Photography Credits:
Microphone: © Ryan McVay/Photodisc/Getty Images, PengAtlas Globe: © iStockphoto.com/Henrik Jonsson, By the Numbers Letters: © iStockphoto.com/German, By the Numbers Background: © iStockphoto.com/nicholas belton

Cover and Page i Photography Credits:
Inside Front Cover: © iStockphoto.com/sdominick, © iStockphoto.com/alexsl, © iStockphoto.com/A-Digit; Page i: © iStockphoto.com/CostinT, © iStockphoto.com/photovideostock, © iStockphoto.com/Leontura; Back Cover: © iStockphoto.com/René Mansi

Printed in the United States of America
1 2 3 4 5 6 7 15 14 13 12 11

Mike W. Peng is the O. P. Jindal Chair of Global Business Strategy at the Jindal School of Management, University of Texas at Dallas. He is also Executive Director of the Center for Global Business, which he founded. At UT Dallas, he has been the number-one contributor to the 45 top academic journals tracked by *Financial Times*, which ranked UT Dallas as a top 20 school in research worldwide and its MBA and EMBA programs increasingly in the top tier.

Professor Peng holds a bachelor's degree from Winona State University, Minnesota, and a PhD degree from the University of Washington, Seattle. He previously served on the faculty at Ohio State University, Chinese University of Hong Kong, and University of Hawaii. He has held visiting or courtesy appointments in Australia (University of Sydney and Queensland University of Technology), Britain (University of Nottingham), China (China Europe International Business School, Shanghai Jiaotong University, Renmin University, Sun Yat-sen University, Tongji University, and Xi'an Jiaotong University), Denmark (Copenhagen Business School), Hong Kong (Chinese University of Hong Kong, Hong Kong Baptist University, Hong Kong Polytechnic University, and University of Hong Kong), the United States (University of Memphis, University of Michigan, Seattle Pacific University, and Western Washington University), and Vietnam (Foreign Trade University).

Professor Peng is one of the most prolific and influential scholars in international business (IB). During the decade 1996–2006, he was a top seven contributor to IB's number-one journal, *Journal of International Business Studies*. His research is also among the most widely cited—both the United Nations and the World Bank have cited his work. He has authored over 90 articles in leading journals. Since *GLOBAL*'s launch, he has published not only in top IB journals, such as the *Academy of Management Journal, Journal of International Business Studies*, and *Strategic Management Journal*, but also in leading outlets in operations (*Journal of Operations Management*), entrepreneurship (*Journal of Business Venturing*), and human resources (*International Journal of Human Resource Management*).

Professor Peng's market leading textbooks, *Global Strategy, Global Business*, and *GLOBAL*, are studied in over 30 countries, and have been translated into Chinese, Spanish, and Portuguese. A European adaptation, *International Business* (with Klaus Meyer), has been successfully launched.

Professor Peng has served on numerous editorial boards. He recently completed a term as Editor-in-Chief of the *Asia Pacific Journal of Management*, during which he managed the doubling of submissions and the successful bid to gain entry into the Social Sciences Citation Index (SSCI).

Professor Peng is also an active consultant, trainer, and keynote speaker. He has provided on-the-job training to over 300 professors. He has consulted and been a keynote speaker for multinational enterprises (such as AstraZeneca, Berlitz, KOSTA, Nationwide, SAFRAN, and Texas Instruments), nonprofit organizations (such as Greater Dallas Asian American Chamber of Commerce and World Affairs Council of Dallas-Fort Worth), educational and funding organizations (such as Harvard University Kennedy School of Government, National Science Foundation, and University of Memphis), and national and international organizations (such as the US-China Business Council, US Navy, and The World Bank).

Professor Peng has attracted close to $1 million in external funding. His honors include a National Science Foundation CAREER Grant, a US Small Business Administration Best Paper Award, a (lifetime) Distinguished Scholar Award from the Southwestern Academy of Management, and a (lifetime) Scholarly Contribution Award from the International Association for Chinese Management Research. He has been quoted in *The Economist, Newsweek, Smart Business Dallas, The Exporter Magazine, The World Journal, Business Times* (Singapore), *Sing Tao Daily* (Vancouver), *Brasil Econômico* (São Paulo), and Voice of America.

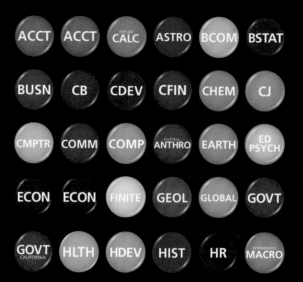

ONE APPROACH.
70 UNIQUE SOLUTIONS.

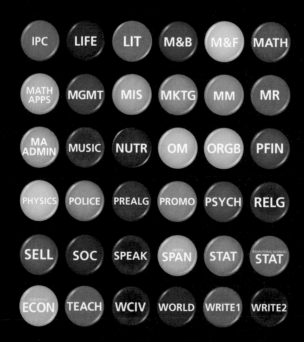

www.cengage.com/4ltrpress

BRIEF Contents

PengAtlas Map

© iStockphoto.com/iofoto

Contents

CONTENTS

© iStockphoto.com/Geoffrey Holman / © iStockphoto.com/blackred / © iStockphoto.com/R.R.

© iStockphoto.com/Олег Дорошин

© iStockphoto.com/photovideostock
© iStockphoto.com/Terry Hankins / © iStockphoto.com/Martin Tanner
© iStockphoto.com/Ravi Tahilramani

PengAtlas Map

USE THE TOOLS.

- Rip out the Review Cards in the back of your book to study.

Or Visit CourseMate to:

- Read, search, highlight, and take notes in the Interactive eBook
- Review Flashcards (Print or Online) to master key terms
- Test yourself with Auto-Graded Quizzes
- Bring concepts to life with Games, Videos, and Animations!

Go to CourseMate for GLOBAL to begin using these tools.
Access at **www.cengagebrain.com**

Complete the Speak Up
survey in CourseMate at
www.cengagebrain.com

f Follow us at
www.facebook.com/4ltrpress

GLOBALIZING Business

CHAPTER 1

Avon Fights Recession—One Lipstick at a Time

When numerous mighty, masculine companies in the banking and automobile industries fell left and right during the recent Great Recession of 2008–2009, Avon Products, Inc. (NYSE: AVP), a self-styled "company for women," rose to new heights around the world. Avon is a leading global beauty products company with 42,000 employees and with $11 billion in annual revenue. As the world's largest direct seller, Avon markets "smart value" products to women in more than 100 countries through 5.8 million independent sales representatives often affectionately known as "Avon ladies." Today, not all Avon representatives are women, and Avon has officially dropped the "lady" title for them. They are simply called "representatives," because Avon has been increasingly recruiting men to hawk its products. In 2008, while numerous companies in most industries lost money, Avon's revenue *grew* 5% (in local currency), to a record $10.7 billion. The growth continued in 2009 and 2010: Its revenue in 2010 (at $11 billion) grew 6% and its profit increased 7% from 2009. The active number of representatives jumped 11% worldwide. In the United States alone, Avon recruited 200,000 more representatives in 2009. At a time most companies struggled for survival and forgot about dividends, Avon proudly declared regular quarterly dividends. In an otherwise bleak environment, investors noticed Avon's enviable performance, pushing its share price from $14.40 on March 9, 2009, to $30.91 on May 3, 2011.

Founded in 1886, Avon pioneered direct selling. In its long history, Avon, chased by competitors such as Mary Kay and Tupperware, has had its fair share of ups and downs. So why has its performance been so outstanding lately? Obviously, the severity of the recent recession has rewritten a number of taken-for-granted "rules of the game" concerning job security, employment, and

AP Images/M. Spencer Green

LEARNING OBJECTIVES

After studying this chapter, you should be able to:

LO1 *explain the concepts of international business and global business.*

LO2 *give three reasons why it is important to study global business.*

LO3 *articulate the fundamental question that the study of global business seeks to answer and two perspectives from which to answer it.*

LO4 *identify three ways of understanding what globalization is.*

LO5 *state the size of the global economy and its broad trends.*

careers. Direct selling has always been a way (mostly for women) to earn supplemental income. It has now become even more important for an increasing number of both women and men who have lost their jobs. Even currently employed individuals increasingly join direct selling, in case their jobs disappear. Burned by the recession, individuals who feel the need to "recession-proof" their income find direct selling to be a great new line of work. According to Richard Berry, director of the UK Direct Selling Association:

Direct selling is almost uniquely immune to economic trends. When you have a recession and people want a low-cost way of making an extra income, direct selling is a great option. The reason our members tend not to suffer from a drop in consumer demand is that the products they sell are low-cost household and personal products, all of which are the last thing to suffer a downturn in demand.

Additionally, with essentially no entry barrier, laid-off bankers and stay-at-home moms are all rushing in. Competition is tough. Why has Avon been doing so well? Avon's iconic brand certainly helps. Its massive army of Avon Ladies and Avon Dudes ensures unrivaled reach around the globe. Another reason for Avon's success is that a new generation of representatives find that they do not have to go door-to-door if they do not want to. Instead, they can take catalogs to church events, school functions, or sorority sisters' gatherings. They often operate on the "party-plan" model, pitching their wares at neighborhood potlucks and dessert parties. They are typically networked, using eBay, Twitter, and Blackberry to creatively expand their business. Direct selling is not a get-rich-quick scheme. Representatives have to work hard. In the United States, the average revenue for a party is $400, of which the representative makes 25%. So to be successful, representatives have to party a lot.

Throughout its history, Avon has emphasized social responsibility. More than 120 years ago, the very idea that women could run their own entrepreneurial businesses selling products in their communities and recruiting others to do the same was revolutionary. Today, this idea of empowering women continues to be revolutionary in some parts of the world where women are discriminated against. Avon is one of the world's largest microfinance lenders for women, extending some $1 billion in credit to help women (and some men) start their new ventures. This is because every time a representative joins Avon, a small loan is provided to cover the initial products up front. This is especially valuable and rare in a world where credit is drying up.

In addition, direct selling can be a low-risk way of experimenting with entrepreneurial ideas, even some would-be entrepreneurs may eventually move away from direct selling. This is because direct selling gives individuals an idea of how they like selling, how good they are at it, and how they manage their time, inventory, and finances to maximize profit—without necessarily having to quit current jobs, if they have jobs. For unemployed individuals, another benefit of direct selling is that it gets them out in the community, while the unemployed typically have a tendency to shy away from social engagements. One expert noted:

If you are out of work, you can become out of touch. Direct selling gives you another point of contact with people. You never know what's going to land in your lap if you're out there meeting people.

Avon's chairman and CEO, Andrea Jung, proudly noted in her message to Avon's website visitors that Avon is "a true force for good, improving and changing the lives of others as we continue to fulfill our vision as the company for women." As governments, companies, and individuals around the world struggle to find ways to tame recession, Avon may indeed provide a glimmer of hope—one lipstick at a time.

Sources: E. Dugan, "Door-to-door sales revive in Britain," *BusinessWeek*, 8 July 2009, available online at http://www.businessweek.com; K. Klein, "The entrepreneurs born of recession," *BusinessWeek*, 13 March 2009, available online at http://www.businessweek.com; J. Cousins, "Avon Lady ranks boom in downturn," *Shanghai Daily*, 28 June 2009, available online at http://www.shanghaidaily.com; J. Quinn, "Avon Lady reborn in the USA," *Telegraph*, 5 July 2009, available online at http://www.telegraph.co.uk; H. Woldu, "Mary Kay in China," in M. W. Peng, *Global Business*, 2nd ed. (Cincinnati: South-Western Cengage Learning) 590–592; www.avoncompany.com [accessed 3 May 2011].

How do firms such as Avon Products compete around the globe? How can Avon's direct-selling competitors such as Mary Kay and Tupperware strengthen their competitive advantage to keep up? How can beauty products competitors that market through traditional channels, such as Procter & Gamble (P&G), Unilever, and Kao, fight back? What determines the success and failure of these firms—and numerous others—around the world during a tumultuous time brought on by the recent recession? This book will address these and other important questions on global business.

International business (IB)
(1) A business (or firm) that engages in international (cross-border) economic activities or (2) the action of doing business abroad.

Multinational enterprise (MNE)
A firm that engages in foreign direct investment and operates in multiple countries.

Foreign direct investment (FDI)
Investment in, controlling, and managing value-added activities in other countries.

LO1 Explain the concepts of international business and global business.

LO2 Give three reasons why it is important to study global business.

WHAT IS GLOBAL BUSINESS AND WHY STUDY IT?

Traditionally, **international business (IB)** is defined as a business (or firm) that engages in international (cross-border) economic activities. It can also refer to the action of doing business abroad. The previous generation of IB textbooks almost always takes the foreign entrant's perspective. Consequently, such books deal with issues such as how to enter foreign markets and how to select alliance partners. The most frequently discussed foreign entrant is the **multinational enterprise (MNE)**, defined as a firm that engages in **foreign direct investment (FDI)** by directly investing in, controlling, and managing value-added activities in other countries.[1] MNEs and their cross-border activities are important, but they cover only one side of IB—the foreign side. Students educated by these books often come away with the impression that the other side of IB—namely, domestic firms—does not exist. But domestic firms do not just sit around in the face of foreign entrants such as MNEs. Domestic firms actively compete and/or collaborate with foreign entrants.[2] In other words, focusing on the foreign entrant side captures only one side of the coin.

There are *two* key words in IB: international (I) and business (B). However, previous textbooks all focus on the international aspect (the foreign entrant) to the extent that the business part (which also includes domestic business) almost disappears. This is unfortunate because IB is fundamentally about B in addition to being I. To put it differently, the IB course in the undergraduate and MBA curricula at numerous business schools is probably the *only* course with the word "business" in the course title. All other courses you take are labeled management, marketing, finance, and so on, representing one functional area but not the overall picture of business. Does it matter? Of course! It means that your IB course is an *integrative* course that has the potential to provide you with an overall business perspective (as opposed to a functional view) grounded in a global environment. Consequently, it makes sense that your textbook should give you both the I and B parts, not just the I part.

To cover both the I and B parts, **global business** is defined in this book as business around the globe—thus the title of this book: *GLOBAL*. For the B part, the activities include *both* international (cross-border) activities covered by traditional IB books and domestic (non-IB) business activities. Such deliberate blurring of the traditional boundaries separating international and domestic

business is increasingly important today, because many previously national (domestic) markets are now globalized. For example, not long ago, competition among college business textbook publishers was primarily on a nation-by-nation basis. South-Western Cengage Learning (our publisher), Prentice Hall, and McGraw-Hill primarily competed in the United States. A different set of publishers competed in other countries. As a result, textbooks studied by British students would be authored by British professors and published by British publishers, textbooks studied by Brazilian students would be authored by Brazilian professors and published by Brazilian publishers, and so on. Now South-Western Cengage Learning (under British and Canadian ownership), Pearson Prentice Hall (under British ownership), and McGraw-Hill (still under US ownership) have significantly globalized their competition, thanks to rising demand for high-quality business textbooks in English. Around the globe, they are competing against each other in many markets, publishing in multiple languages. For instance, *GLOBAL*'s sister books, *Global Business* and *Global Strategy*, are published by different subsidiaries in Chinese, Spanish, and Portuguese in addition to English, reaching customers in over 30 countries. Despite such worldwide spread of competition, in each market—down to each school—textbook publishers have to compete locally to win adoption from every class every semester. Overall, it becomes difficult to tell in this competition what is international and what is domestic. Thus "global" is a better word to capture the essence of this competition.

GLOBAL also differs from other books on IB because most focus on competition in developed economies. Here, by contrast, you'll find extensive space devoted

> ## There are two key words in IB: international (I) and business (B).

Global business
Business around the globe.

EXHIBIT 1.1 The Contributions of Emerging Economies Relative to Developed Economies (World %)

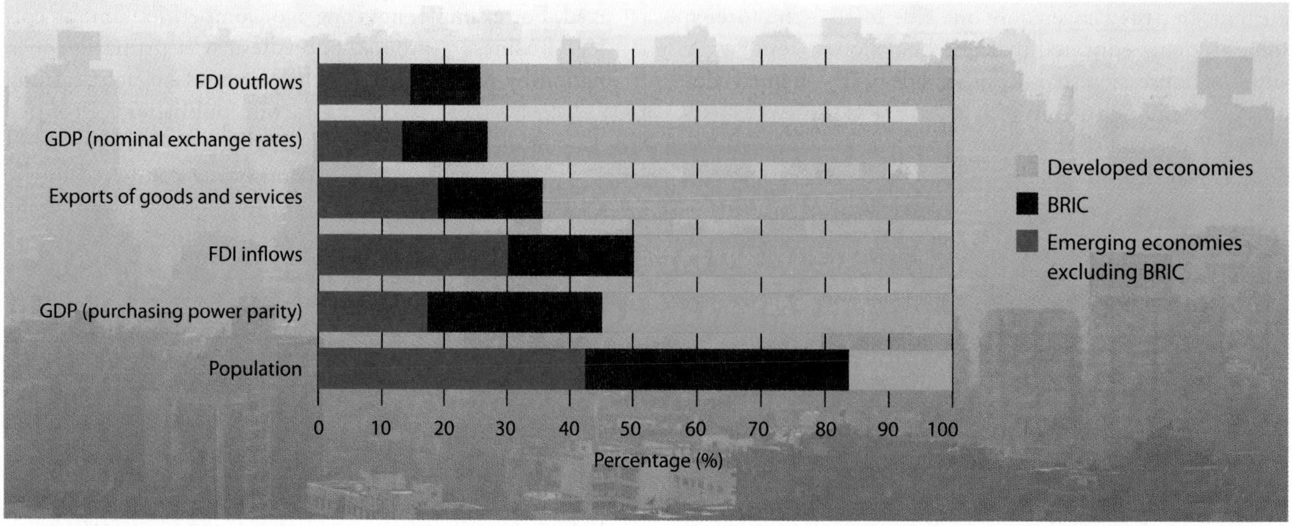

FDI outflows
GDP (nominal exchange rates)
Exports of goods and services
FDI inflows
GDP (purchasing power parity)
Population
0 10 20 30 40 50 60 70 80 90 100
Percentage (%)
Developed economies
BRIC
Emerging economies excluding BRIC

© iStockphoto.com/Ugurhan Betin

Sources: Data extracted from International Monetary Fund, *World Economic Outlook: Sustaining the Recovery* (Washington: IMF) 162; United Nations, *World Investment Report 2010* (New York and Geneva: UN) xiii; World Bank, World Development Indicators database (Washington: World Bank). All data refer to 2010.

to competitive battles waged throughout **emerging economies**, a term that has gradually replaced the term "developing countries" since the 1990s.[3] Another commonly used term is **emerging markets** (see PengAtlas Map 1). How important are emerging economies? PengAtlas Map 2 illustrates that 11 of 19 countries that consist of the **Group of 20 (G-20)** are emerging economies (the 20th member is the European Union [EU]). Exhibit 1.1 shows that emerging economies now collectively contribute approximately 45% of the global **gross domestic product (GDP)**. GDP is the sum of value added by resident firms, households, and governments operating in an economy.

Emerging economy (or emerging market)
A developing country.

Group of 20 (G-20)
The group of 19 major countries plus the European Union (EU) whose leaders meet on a regular basis to solve global economic problems.

Gross domestic product (GDP)
The sum of value added by resident firms, households, and governments operating in an economy.

Purchasing power parity (PPP)
A conversion that determines the equivalent amount of goods and services different currencies can purchase. This conversion is usually used to capture the differences in cost of living in different countries.

Triad
Three regions of developed economies (North America, Western Europe, and Japan).

Base of the pyramid
The vast majority of humanity, about five billion people, who make less than $2,000 a year on a per capita basis.

Note that this percentage is adjusted for **purchasing power parity (PPP)**, a conversion that determines the equivalent amount of goods and services that different currencies can purchase and that is used to capture the differences in cost of living in different countries. Using official (nominal) exchange rates without adjusting for PPP, emerging economies contribute approximately 26% of the global GDP. Why is there such a huge difference between the two measures? Because the cost of living (such as housing and haircuts) in emerging economies is lower than that in developed economies. For example, one dollar spent in Mexico can buy a lot more than one dollar spent in the United States.

The global economy can be viewed as a pyramid shown in Exhibit 1.2. The top consists of about 1 billion people with per capita annual income greater than $20,000. These are mostly people who live in the developed economies of the **Triad**, which consists of North America, Western Europe, and Japan. Another billion people, making $2,000 to $20,000 a year, make up the second tier. The vast majority of humanity—about five billion people—make less than $2,000 a year and comprise the **base of the pyramid**. Most MNEs (and most traditional IB books) focus on the top and second tiers and end up ignoring the base of the pyramid.[4] An increasing number of such low-income countries have shown increasingly more economic opportunities as income levels have risen. Today's students—and tomorrow's business leaders—will ignore these opportunities at the base of the pyramid at their own peril. This book will help ensure that you will not ignore these opportunities (see the Closing Case).

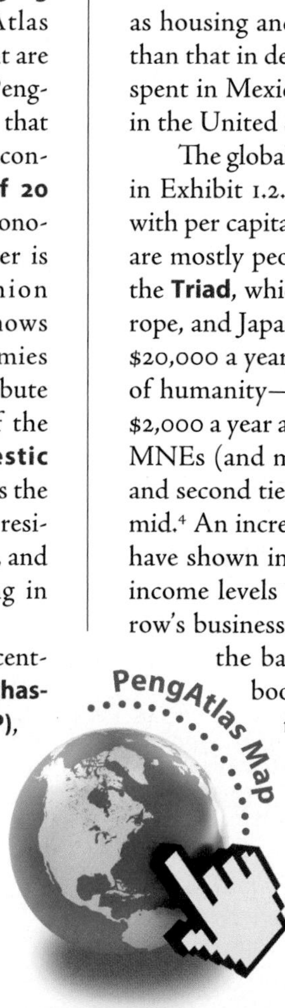

PengAtlas Map

Global business (or IB) is one of the most exciting, challenging, and relevant subjects offered by business schools. There are at least three compelling reasons why you should study it—and study hard (Exhibit 1.3). First, mastering global business knowledge helps advance your

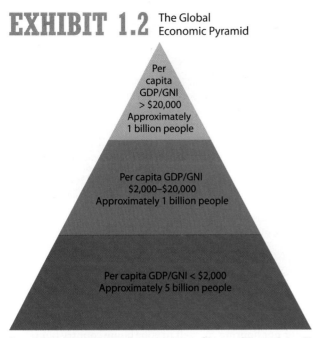

EXHIBIT 1.2 The Global Economic Pyramid

Per capita GDP/GNI > $20,000
Approximately 1 billion people

Per capita GDP/GNI $2,000–$20,000
Approximately 1 billion people

Per capita GDP/GNI < $2,000
Approximately 5 billion people

Source: C. K. Prahalad and S. Hart, "The fortune at the bottom of the pyramid," *Strategy+Business* 26 (2002): 54–67 and S. Hart, *Capitalism at the Crossroads* (Philadelphia: Wharton School Publishing, 2005) 111.

employability and your career in an increasingly competitive global economy. An ignorant individual is unlikely to emerge as a winner in global competition.

Second, expertise in global business is often a prerequisite to join the top ranks of large firms, something many ambitious students aspire to. It is now increasingly difficult, if not impossible, to find top managers at large firms who do not possess significant global competence. Eventually you will need hands-on global experience, not merely knowledge acquired from this course.[5] However, in order to set yourself apart as an ideal candidate to be selected for an executive position, you'll need to demonstrate that you are interested in global business and have mastered knowledge of it during your education. This is especially true if you expect to gain experience as an **expatriate manager** (or "**expat**" for short)—a manager who works abroad (see Chapter 13 for details).

Thanks to globalization, low-level jobs not only command lower salaries but are also more vulnerable. On the other hand, top-level jobs, especially those held by expats, are both financially rewarding and relatively secure. Expats

EXHIBIT 1.3 Why Study Global Business?

- Advancing your employability and your career in the global economy

- Better preparation for possible expatriate assignments abroad

- Stronger competence in interacting with foreign suppliers, partners, and competitors and in working for foreign-owned employers in your own country

often command a significant **international premium** in compensation—a significant pay raise when working overseas. In US firms, their total compensation package is approximately $250,000 to $300,000 (including benefits; not all is take-home pay). For example, if a 2,000-employee ball bearing factory in Lima, Ohio, is shut down and the MNE sets up a similar factory in Lima, Peru, only about 10 to 20 jobs would be saved. Yes, you guessed it: Those jobs would consist of a few top-level positions such as the CEO, CFO, CIO, factory director, and chief engineer who will be sent by the MNE as expats to Peru to start up operations there. Because it is regarded as a "hardship" assignment, the MNE has to give them many more perks in Peru than it did in Ohio. How about company-subsidized luxury housing plus maid services, free tuition for children in American or international schools in Peru, and all-expenses-paid vacations for the whole family to see their loved ones in Ohio? Moreover, these expats do not live in Peru forever. When they return to the United States after a tour of duty (usually two to three years), if their current employer does not provide attractive career opportunities, they are often hired away by competitor firms. This is because competitor firms are also interested in globalizing their business by tapping into the expertise and experience of these former expats. And, yes, competitor firms will have to pay them even more to hire away these internationally experienced managers.

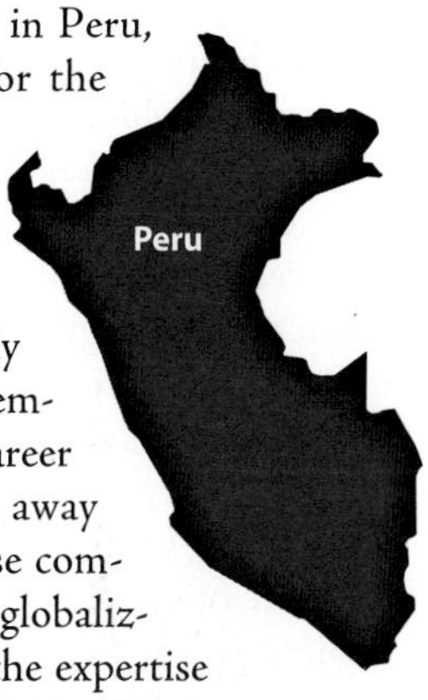

Peru

This hypothetical example is designed to motivate you to study hard so that someday, you may become one of these sought-after, globe-trotting managers. But, even if you don't want to be an expat, we assume that you don't want to join the ranks of the unemployed due to factory closings and business failures.

Lastly, even if you do not aspire to compete for the top job at a large firm or work overseas, and even if you work at a small firm or are self-employed, you may find yourself dealing with foreign-owned suppliers and buyers, competing with foreign-invested firms in your home market, and perhaps even selling and investing overseas. Alternatively, you may find yourself working for a foreign-owned firm, your domestic employer may be acquired by a foreign player, or your unit may be ordered to shut down for global consolidation. Any of these is a very likely scenario, because approximately 80 million people worldwide, including 18 million Chinese, 6 million Americans, and 1 million British, are employed by foreign-owned firms. Understanding how global business decisions

Expatriate manager (expat)
A manager who works outside his or her native country.

International premium
A significant pay raise commanded by expatriates when working overseas.

7

are made may facilitate your own career in such firms. If there is a strategic rationale to downsize your unit, you would want to be able to figure this out and be the first one to post your resume on Monster.com. In other words, it is your career that is at stake. Don't be the last to know! In short, in this age of global competition, "how do you keep from being Bangalored or Shanghaied" (that is, having your job outsourced to India or China)?[6] A good place to start is to study hard and do well in your IB course.

> **LO3** *Articulate the fundamental question that the study of global business seeks to answer and two perspectives from which to answer it.*

A UNIFIED FRAMEWORK

Global business is a vast subject area. It is one of the few courses that will make you appreciate why your university requires you to take a number of seemingly unrelated courses in general education. We will draw on major social sciences such as economics, geography, history, political science, psychology, and sociology. We will also draw on a number of business disciplines such as finance, marketing, and strategy. The study of global business is thus very interdisciplinary.[7] It is easy to lose sight of the forest while scrutinizing various trees or even branches. The subject is not difficult, and most students find it to be fun. The number one student complaint is about the overwhelming amount of information. This is also *my* number one complaint as your author: you may have to read and learn this material, but I have to bring it all together in a way that is understandable and in a compact book that does not go on for 900 pages. To make your learning more focused, more manageable, and hopefully more fun, in this section we will develop a unified framework (shown in Exhibit 1.4).

One Fundamental Question

What is it that we do in global business? Why is it so important that practically every student in business schools around the world is either required or recommended to take this course? While there are certainly a lot of questions to raise, a relentless interest in what determines the success and failure of firms around the globe serves to focus the energy of our field. Global business is fundamentally

> ## What determines the success and failure of firms around the globe?

> **Institution-based view**
> *A leading perspective in global business that suggests that firm performance is, at least in part, determined by the institutional frameworks governing firm behavior around the world.*

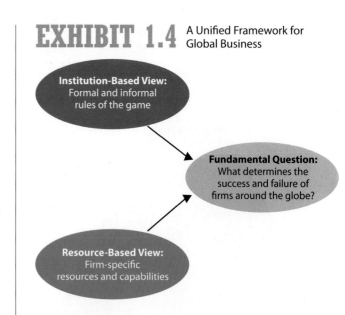

EXHIBIT 1.4   A Unified Framework for Global Business

Institution-Based View: Formal and informal rules of the game

Resource-Based View: Firm-specific resources and capabilities

Fundamental Question: What determines the success and failure of firms around the globe?

© Cengage Learning 2013

about not limiting yourself to your home country but treating the entire global economy as your potential playground (or battlefield). Some firms may be successful domestically but fail miserably when they venture abroad. Other firms successfully translate their strengths from their home market to other countries. If you were to lead your firm's efforts to enter a particular foreign market, wouldn't you want to find out what drives the success and failure of other firms in that market?

Overall, the focus on firm performance around the globe defines the field of global business (or IB) more than anything else. Numerous other questions and topics all relate in one way or the other to this most fundamental question. Therefore, all of the chapters in this book will be centered on this fundamental question: *What determines the success and failure of firms around the globe?*[8] *GLOBAL* is the first global business (or IB) textbook to develop its chapters with a consistent theme in mind. Why is this unified framework important? It will enable you to see the global business forest as well as its trees. Each chapter will introduce you to new materials (trees), but you will always be able to relate it back to the fundamental question. As we proceed through the book, we will look at this question from two different core perspectives: an institution-based view and a resource-based view.[9]

First Core Perspective: An Institution-Based View

An **institution-based view** suggests that the success and failure of firms are enabled and constrained by institutions.[10]

By **institutions**, we mean the rules of the game. Doing business around the globe requires intimate knowledge about both formal rules (such as laws) and informal rules (such as values) that govern competition in various countries. If you establish a firm in a given country, you will work within the **institutional framework**, or the formal and informal institutions that govern individual and firm behavior in that country. Firms that do not do their homework and thus remain ignorant of the rules of the game in a certain country are not likely to emerge as winners.

Formal institutions, or formal rules of the game, include laws and regulations. For example, Hong Kong's laws and regulations treat all foreign firms, whether from neighboring mainland China (whose firms are still technically regarded as "non-domestic") or far-away Chile, the same as they treat indigenous Hong Kong firms. This equal treatment enhances the potential odds for the success of foreign firms. It is thus not surprising that Hong Kong attracts a lot of outside firms. Other rules of the game, which may discriminate against foreign firms, would undermine the chances for foreign entrants. India's recent attraction as a site for foreign investment in information technology (IT) and business process outsourcing (BPO) was only possible after it changed its FDI regulations from confrontational to accommodating. Prior to 1991, India's rules severely discriminated against foreign firms. As a result, few foreign firms bothered to show up there, and the few that did had a hard time. For example, in the 1970s, the Indian government demanded that Coca-Cola either hand over the recipe for its secret syrup, which it did not even share with the US government, or get out of India. Painfully, Coca-Cola chose to leave India. Its return to India since the 1990s speaks volumes about the changing rules of the game in India.

Informal institutions, or informal rules of the game, include cultures, ethics, and norms. These are not established by laws and regulations, yet they play an important role in shaping the success and failure of firms around the globe. For example, individualistic societies, particularly the English-speaking countries such as Australia, Britain, and the United States, tend to have a relatively higher level of entrepreneurship as reflected in the number of business start-ups. Why? Because the act of founding a new firm tends to deviate from the social norm of working for someone else, a norm that is not as strong as in collectivistic societies. Conversely, collectivistic societies such as Japan often have a hard time fostering entrepreneurship. Most people there refuse to stick their neck out to found new businesses because it is contrary to the norm.

Overall, an institution-based view suggests that institutions, or the formal and informal rules of the game, shed a great deal of light on what drives firm performance around the globe.

Second Core Perspective: A Resource-Based View

The institution-based view suggests that the success and failure of firms around the globe are largely determined by their environment. This is certainly correct. Indeed, India did not attract much FDI prior to 1991, and Japan does not nurture a lot of internationally competitive start-ups. However, insightful as this perspective is, there is a major drawback. If we push this view to its logical extreme, then firm performance around the globe would be *entirely* determined by environment. The validity of this extreme version is certainly questionable.

The **resource-based view** has emerged to overcome this drawback.[11] While the institution-based

Institutions
Formal and informal rules of the game.

Institutional framework
Formal and informal institutions that govern individual and firm behavior.

Formal institutions
Institutions such as laws, regulations, and rules.

Informal institutions
Institutions such as norms, cultures, and ethics.

Resource-based view
A leading perspective in global business that suggests that firm performance is, at least in part, determined by its internal resources and capabilities.

Hong Kong's laws and regulations treat all foreign firms the same as they treat domestic firms. This equal treatment enhances the odds for the success of foreign firms.

view primarily deals with the *external* environment, the resource-based view focuses on a firm's *internal* resources and capabilities. It starts with a simple observation: In harsh, unattractive environments, most firms either suffer or exit. However, a few superstars thrive in these environments against all odds. For example, despite the former Soviet Union's obvious hostility toward the United States during the Cold War, PepsiCo began successfully operating in the former Soviet Union in the 1970s (!). Most consumer products firms struggle in the recent recession, and some have dropped out of business. But a small number of players, such as Avon, have been raking in profits year after year (see the Opening Case). Although the demise of Detroit—thanks to General Motors' and Chrysler's bankruptcies—had been widely reported, Ford, which is also based in Detroit, had turned itself into the world's most profitable automaker by 2010.[12] How can these firms succeed in highly unattractive and often hostile environments? A short answer is that PepsiCo, Avon, and Ford must have certain valuable and unique *firm-specific* resources and capabilities that are not shared by competitors in the same environments.

Doing business outside one's home country is challenging. Foreign firms have to overcome a **liability of foreignness**, which is the *inherent* disadvantage that foreign firms experience in host countries because of their non-native status.[13] Just think about all the differences in regulations, languages, cultures, and norms. Against such significant odds, the primary weapon foreign firms employ is *overwhelming* resources and capabilities that not only offset the liability of foreignness but also offer them significant competitive advantage. Today, many of us take it for granted that Coca-Cola is the best-selling soft drink in Mexico, and that Microsoft Word is the market-leading word processing software around the world. We really shouldn't. Why? Because it is *not* natural for these foreign firms to dominate non-native markets. These firms must possess some very rare and powerful firm-specific resources and capabilities that drive these remarkable success stories and are the envy of their rivals around the globe.

> *Identify three ways of understanding what globalization is.*

WHAT IS GLOBALIZATION?

Globalization, generally speaking, is the close integration of countries and peoples of the world. This abstract five-syllable word is now frequently heard and debated. Those who approve of globalization count its con-

Liability of foreignness
The inherent disadvantage that foreign firms experience in host countries because of their non-native status.

Globalization
The close integration of countries and peoples of the world.

tributions to include greater economic growth and standards of living, increased technology sharing, and more extensive cultural integration. Critics argue that globalization causes global recession, undermines wages in rich countries, exploits workers in poor countries, and gives MNEs too much power. This section outlines three views on globalization, recommends the pendulum view, and introduces the idea of semiglobalization.

Three Views on Globalization

Depending on what sources you read, globalization could be

- a new force sweeping through the world in recent times,
- a long-run historical evolution since the dawn of human history, or
- a pendulum that swings from one extreme to another from time to time.

An understanding of these views helps put the debate about globalization in perspective. First, opponents of globalization suggest that it is a new phenomenon beginning in the late 20th century, driven by recent technological innovations and a Western ideology focused on exploiting and dominating the world through MNEs. The arguments against globalization focus on an ideal world free of environmental stress, social injustice, and sweatshop labor but present few clear alternatives to the present economic order. Advocates and anti-globalization protesters often argue that globalization needs to be slowed down, if not stopped.

A second view contends that globalization has always been part of human history. Historians debate whether globalization started 2,000 or 8,000 years ago. MNEs existed for more than two millennia, with their earliest traces discovered in Phoenician, Assyrian, and Roman times.[14] International competition from low-cost countries is nothing new. In the first century A.D., the Roman emperor Tiberius was so concerned about the massive quantity of low-cost Chinese silk imports that he imposed the world's first known import quota of textiles.[15] In a nutshell, globalization is nothing new and will always exist.

© iStockphoto.com/Hedda Gjerpen

The Romans were the first to impose import quotas.

A third view suggests that globalization is the "closer integration of the countries and peoples of the world which has been brought about by the enormous reduction of the costs of transportation and communication and the breaking down of artificial barriers to the flows of goods, services, capital, knowledge, and (to a lesser extent) people across borders."[16] Globalization is neither recent nor one-directional. It is, more accurately, a process similar to the swing of a pendulum.

The Pendulum View on Globalization

The third view, the pendulum view, probably makes the most sense, because it can help us understand the ups and downs of globalization. The current era of globalization originated in the aftermath of World War II, when major Western nations committed to global trade and investment. However, between the 1950s and the 1970s, this view was not widely shared. Communist countries, such as the former Soviet Union and China, sought to develop self-sufficiency. Many non-communist developing countries such as Argentina, Brazil, India, and Mexico focused on fostering and protecting domestic industries. But refusing to participate in global trade and investment ended up breeding uncompetitive industries. In contrast, four developing economies in Asia—namely, Hong Kong, Singapore, South Korea, and Taiwan—earned their stripes as the "Four Tigers" by participating in the global economy. They became the *only* economies once recognized as less developed (low-income) by the World Bank to have subsequently achieved developed (high-income) status.

Inspired by the Four Tigers, more and more countries and regions—such as China in the late 1970s, Latin America in the mid 1980s, Central and Eastern Europe in the late 1980s, and India in the 1990s—realized that joining the world economy was a must. As these countries started to emerge as new players in the world economy, they became collectively known as "emerging economies." As a result, globalization rapidly accelerated in the 1990s.

The pendulum view suggests, however, that globalization is unable to keep going in one direction. Rapid globalization in the 1990s saw some significant backlash. First, the rapid growth of globalization led to the historically inaccurate view that globalization is new. Second, it created fear among many people in developed economies that they would lose jobs. Emerging economies not only seem to attract many low-end manufacturing jobs away from developed economies, but also increasingly appear to threaten some high-end jobs. Finally, some factions in emerging economies complained against the onslaught of MNEs, alleging that they not only destroy local companies but also local cultures, values, and the environment.

While small-scale acts of vandalizing McDonald's restaurants are reported in several countries, the December 1999 anti-globalization protests in Seattle and the September 2001 terrorist attacks in New York and Washington are undoubtedly the most visible and most extreme acts of anti-globalization forces at work. As a result of these attacks, international travel was curtailed, and global trade and investment flows slowed in the early 2000s. Then in the mid 2000s, worldwide GDP, cross-border trade, and per capita GDP all soared to historically high levels. More than half of the world GDP growth now comes from emerging economies (see Exhibit 1.1). In particular, **BRIC**, a newly coined acronym for the emerging economies of Brazil, Russia, India, and China, has become a new buzzword. More recently (since 2008), devastated by the skyrocketing oil prices and the subprime mess, the world was engulfed in a global economic crisis now known as the Great Recession (see Exhibit 1.5 on page 13). This

BRIC
A newly coined acronym for the emerging economies of Brazil, Russia, India, and China.

Risk Management Lessons for Global Business From Japan's Earthquake

On March 11, 2011, Japan suffered from a triple disaster—a 9.0 earthquake (its worst in recorded history), followed by a 20-foot tsunami, followed by a nuclear power plant accident that emitted harmful radiation. As a result, several lessons in risk management quickly emerged.

First, despite its obsession about safety, the nuclear power industry was under prepared for the truly rare, low-probability events (known as the "black swan" events in the jargon). Reactor risk modeling, like financial risk modeling, was inadequate to account for the worst-case disaster at the Fukushima nuclear power plant.

Second, while the nuclear power industry had industry-specific problems, the overall risk management for the Japanese economy was commendable. Even as the reactors smoked, they were protected by the world's highest sea walls. No skyscrapers tumbled. No trains running 150 miles per hour derailed. The drills and preparations that were meticulously conducted during "peace time" worked after the first wave of the disaster struck and saved numerous lives.

Third, from a global standpoint, many non-Japanese firms that relied on made-in-Japan products were ill-prepared for such a sudden and major breakdown of the supply chain. Despite the widely noted migration of manufacturing jobs to low-cost countries such as China and Malaysia, Japan has remained an export powerhouse. In 2010, it was the world's fourth largest exporter (after China, Germany, and the United States) with $765 billion exports. For example, Japan produces approximately one fifth of the world's semiconductors and 40% of electronic components. While low-end products tend to be made overseas, "Japan has higher and higher market share of specialty materials as you go up the value chain," noted one expert. For example, Boeing outsourced 35% of the work on its newest 787 Dreamliner to Japanese manufacturers. Among them, Mitsubishi Heavy Industries built the 787's wings and no one else could do the job—Boeing had no Plan B. On March 17, General Motors closed two US-based factories for a week due to a lack of components arriving from Japan. For planes, cars, and laptops assembled outside of Japan, the made-in-Japan components may represent a relatively small amount, but they tend to be mission-critical. "If the Japanese cannot supply," noted another expert, "then no one is going to get their iPad 2" because no smart factory can build an iPad 2 with only 97% of the parts. Thanks to the "lean manufacturing" movement that also originated from Japan a generation ago, inventory levels at many factories around the world are now kept down to days' and even hours' worth. When "just-in-time" delivery fails, the supply chain can easily break down. Surprisingly, only about 10% of firms have detailed contingency plans to deal with severe chain disruptions. As the true magnitude regarding the disaster's impact remained unclear, firms suffering from the excruciating shortage of components from Japan could only hope (1) that the current disaster would be quickly over, and (2) that they would do better when dealing with the next disaster in global business.

Sources: "Downsides of just-in-time inventory," *Bloomberg Businessweek*, March 28, 2011: 17–18; "Facing up to nuclear risk," *Bloomberg Businessweek*, March 21, 2011: 13–14; "Now, a weak link in the global supply chain," *Bloomberg Businessweek*, March 21, 2011: 18–19; "The cataclysm this time," *Bloomberg Businessweek*, March 21, 2011: 11–13.

© Kiyoshi Ota/Bloomberg via Getty Images

recession was characterized by a painful financial meltdown and numerous government bailouts. Rightly or wrongly, many people blamed globalization for the crisis.

After unprecedented intervention throughout developed economies whose governments ended up being the largest shareholders of many banks, there is growing confidence that the global economy has turned the corner and that the global recession is now at an end. However, economic recovery is likely to be slow in developed economies, whereas emerging economies have rebounded faster.[17] The recession reminds all firms and managers of the importance of **risk management**—the identification and assessment of risks and the preparation to minimize the impact of high-risk, unfortunate events (see In Focus).[18] As a technique to prepare and plan for multiple scenarios

Risk management
The identification and assessment of risks and the preparation to minimize the impact of high-risk, unfortunate events.

EXHIBIT 1.5 Symptoms of the Global Economic Crisis, 2008–2009

- The bursting of a real estate bubble
- The liquidity and solvency problems for major banks
- The refusal by consumers and companies to spend on consumption or investment
- Plummeting global output, trade, and investment
- Skyrocketing unemployment
- Rapid contagion around the world due to the closely interconnected nature of the global economy

(such as high risk or low risk), **scenario planning** is now used by many firms around the world.[19] As far as the direction of globalization is concerned, the recovery may see more protectionist measures, since various governments, in their stimulus packages and job creation schemes, emphasize "buy national" (such as the "buy American" policy in the United States and the promotion of "indigenous innovation" in China) and "hire locals." In short, the pendulum is swinging back.

The effort to understand globalization brings to mind the story of the six blind men trying to figure out the shape and form of an elephant based on what part of the animal each touched. One man thinks it is a wall, another calls it a spear, a third argues it is a snake, and the others believe it to be a tree, a fan, and a rope. Like the proverbial elephant, globalization is rarely comprehended as a whole. The suddenness and ferocity of the recent economic crisis surprised everybody—ranging from central bankers to academic experts. Our task is more challenging than that of the blind men who were studying a standing animal. Our beast—globalization—does not stand still and is often rapidly moving back and forth (!). Yet, we try to live with it, avoid being crushed by it, and even attempt to profit from it. Overall, relative to the other two views, the view of globalization as a pendulum is more balanced and more realistic. In other words, globalization has both rosy and dark sides, and it changes over time.

Semiglobalization

Despite the debate over it, globalization is not complete. Do we really live in a globalized world? Are selling and investing abroad just as easy as at home? Obviously not. Most measures of market integration, such as trade and FDI, have recently scaled new heights but still fall far short of pointing to a single, globally integrated market. In other words, what we have may be labeled **semiglobalization**, which is more complex than extremes of total isolation and total globalization. Semiglobalization suggests that barriers to market integration at borders are high, but not high enough to completely insulate countries from each other.[20]

Semiglobalization calls for more than one way of doing business around the globe. Total isolation on a nation-state basis would suggest localization—a strategy of treating each country as a unique market. So an MNE marketing products to 100 countries will need to come up with 100 versions of local cars or drinks. This approach is clearly too costly. Total globalization, on the other hand, would lead to standardization, or a strategy of treating the entire world as one market. The MNE in our previous example can just market one version of "world car" or "world drink." The world obviously is not that simple. Between total isolation and total globalization, semiglobalization has no single, right strategy, resulting in a wide variety of experimentations. Overall, (semi)globalization is neither to be opposed as a menace nor to be celebrated as a panacea; it is to be *engaged*.

> **LO5** State the size of the global economy and its broad trends.

GLOBAL BUSINESS AND THE GLOBALIZATION DEBATE

The challenge confronting a new generation of business leaders in the 21st century is enormous. At the dawn of the 21st century, globalization's seemingly inevitable forward direction took a turn, revealing globalization to be more of a pendulum than a one-way march. This directly affects you as a future business leader, as a consumer, and as a citizen. At least two sets of sudden, high-profile events occurred that have had significant ramifications for business around the world: anti-globalization protests and terrorist attacks. First, large-scale anti-globalization protests began in December 1999, when over 50,000 protesters blocked downtown Seattle in an attempt to derail a ministerial meeting of the World Trade Organization (WTO). The demonstrators were protesting against

Scenario planning
A technique to prepare and plan for multiple scenarios (either high or low risk).

Semiglobalization
A perspective that suggests that barriers to market integration at borders are high but not high enough to completely insulate countries from each other.

a wide range of issues, including job losses resulting from foreign competition, downward pressure on wages for unskilled workers, and environmental destruction. Since Seattle, anti-globalization protesters have turned up at just about every major globalization meeting. It is obvious that numerous individuals in many countries believe that globalization has detrimental effects on living standards and the environment. As shown throughout this book, neither the pro-globalization nor the anti-globalization forces have won the debate on globalization.[21]

The terrorist attacks in New York and Washington on September 11, 2001, and more recent terrorist attacks elsewhere in the world are the second set of events. After the attacks in the United States, terrorists struck Afghanistan, Britain, India, Indonesia, Iraq, Pakistan, and Spain. Terrorism, which used to be "a random political risk of relatively insignificant proportions,"[22] is now a leading concern for business leaders around the globe. Heightened risk of terrorism has reduced freedom of international movement as various countries curtailed visas and immigration; enhanced security checks at airports, seaports, and land border crossing points; and cancelled or scaled down trade and FDI deals, especially in high-risk regions such as the Middle East.

The challenge that faces you, then, involves a complex set of issues surrounding the benefits and costs of globalization as well as threats and hindrances to global business caused by terrorism. This book will provide you with a roadmap to help you navigate that challenge. At this critical juncture in global business, first, you must have a basic understanding of the world economy. Second, you must critically examine your own personal views and biases associated with globalization. This section helps you do both.

A Glance at the Global Economy

The global economy at the beginning of the 21st century is an approximately $60 trillion economy (total global GDP calculated at official, nominal exchange rates). While there is no need to memorize a lot of statistics, it is useful to remember this $60 trillion figure to put things in perspective.

A frequent observation in the globalization debate is the enormous size of MNEs. If the largest MNE, Wal-Mart, were an independent country, it would be the 22nd largest economy—its sales are smaller than Indonesia's GDP but larger than Poland's. The sales of the largest EU-based MNE, Royal Dutch Shell, are larger than the GDP of each of the following EU member countries: Norway, Denmark, Greece, and Ireland. The sales of the largest Asia Pacific–based MNE, Toyota, are greater than the GDP of each of the following Asia Pacific countries: Malaysia, Singapore, and New Zealand. Today, over 77,000 MNEs control at least 770,000 subsidiaries overseas.[23] Total annual sales for the largest 500 MNEs exceed $20 trillion (about one third of global output). Exhibit 1.6 documents the change in the makeup of the 500 largest MNEs. In general, MNEs from the Triad dominate the list. About one third of these firms have generally been US firms, and the United States has experienced some reduction in numbers recently. The European Union has maintained a reasonably steady share of about one third of these firms. From its heyday in the 1990s, Japan has experienced the most dramatic variation (roughly corresponding to its economic boom and bust with several years of delay).

Among MNEs from emerging economies, those from China have come on strong.[24] Beijing is now headquarters to 41 *Fortune* Global 500 firms, more than New

EXHIBIT 1.6 Recent Changes in the *Fortune* Global 500

	Number of Global 500 Companies					
	2005	2006	2007	2008	2009	2010
Developed economies						
United States	170	162	153	140	139	133
European Union	165	165	170	163	161	149
Japan	70	67	64	68	71	68
Switzerland	12	13	14	15	15	15
Canada	14	16	14	14	11	11
Australia	8	8	8	9	8	8
Emerging economies						
China	20	24	29	37	46	61
India	6	6	7	7	8	8
Brazil	4	5	5	6	7	7
Russia	5	4	5	8	6	7
BRIC	35	39	46	58	67	83

Source: The most recent *Fortune* Global 500 list (for 2010) is published in *Fortune*, July 25, 2011. Older data were accessed online on July 7, 2011 at www.money.cnn.com/magazines/fortune/global500/2010/countries/US.html

York's 22. Clearly, Western rivals cannot afford to ignore these new MNEs, and students reading this book need to pay attention to these emerging multinationals.

The Globalization Debate and You

As a future business leader, you are not a detached reader. The globalization debate directly affects *your* future.[25] Therefore, it is imperative that you participate in the globalization debate instead of letting other people make decisions on globalization that will significantly affect your career, your consumption, and your country. It is important to know your own biases when joining the debate. By the very act of taking an IB course and reading this book, you probably already have some pro-globalization biases compared to non-business majors elsewhere on campus

EXHIBIT 1.7 Views on Globalization

Overall, do you think globalization is *good* for...	General public	Business students
...US consumers like you?	68%	96%
...US companies?	63%	77%
...the US economy?	64%	88%
...strengthening poor countries' economies?	75%	82%

Sources: A. Bernstein, "Backlash against globalization," *BusinessWeek*, 24 April 2000: 43; M. W. Peng and H. Shin, "How do future business leaders view globalization?," *Thunderbird International Business Review* 50, no. 3 (2008): 179. All differences are statistically significant.

Business students tend to focus more on the economic gains of globalization and be less concerned with its darker sides.

and the general public in your country. You are not alone. In the last several decades, most executives, policy makers, and scholars in both developed and emerging economies, who are generally held to be the elite in these societies, are biased toward acknowledging the benefits of globalization. Although it is long known that globalization carries both benefits and costs, many of the elite have failed to take into sufficient account the social, political, and environmental costs associated with globalization. However, that the elite share certain perspectives on globalization does *not* mean that most other members of the society share the same views. Unfortunately, many of the elite fail to understand the limits of their beliefs and mistakenly assume that the rest of the world thinks like them.

To the extent that powerful economic and political institutions are largely controlled by the elite in almost every country, it is not surprising that some anti-globalization groups, feeling powerless, end up resorting to unconventional tactics such as mass protests to make their point.

Many of the opponents of globalization are **nongovernmental organizations (NGOs)**, such as environmentalists, human rights activists, and consumer groups. Ignoring them would be a grave failure when doing business around the globe. Instead of viewing NGOs as opponents, many firms view them as partners. NGOs do raise a valid point when they insist that firms, especially MNEs, should have a broader concern for the various stakeholders affected by the MNEs' actions around the world. At present, this view is increasingly moving from the peripheral to the mainstream (see Chapter 14).

It is certainly interesting and perhaps alarming to note that as would-be business leaders who will shape the global economy in the future, current business school students already exhibit values and beliefs in favor of globalization similar to those held by executives, policy makers, and scholars and different from those held by the general public. Shown in Exhibit 1.7, US business students have significantly more positive (almost one-sided) views toward globalization than the general public has. While these data are based on US business students, my teaching and lecturing around the world suggest that most business students—regardless of their nationality—seem to share such positive views on globalization. This is not surprising. Both self-selection to study business

Nongovernmental organizations (NGOs)
Organizations that are not affiliated with governments. Such organizations include environmentalist groups, human rights activists, and consumer groups.

and socialization within the curriculum, in which free trade is widely regarded as positive, may lead to certain attitudes in favor of globalization. Consequently, business students tend to focus more on the economic gains of globalization and be less concerned with its darker sides.

Current and would-be business leaders need to be aware of their own biases embodied in such one-sided views toward globalization. Since business schools aspire to train future business leaders by indoctrinating students with the dominant values managers hold, these results suggest that business schools may have largely succeeded in this mission. However, to the extent that current managers (and professors) have strategic blind spots, these findings are potentially alarming. They reveal that business students already share these blind spots. Despite possible self-selection in choosing to major in business, there is no denying that student values are shaped, at least in part, by the educational experience business schools provide. Knowing such limitations, business school professors and students need to work especially hard to break out of this mental straitjacket.

In order to combat the widespread tendency to have one-sided, rosy views, a significant portion of this book is devoted to the numerous debates that surround globalization.[26] Beyond this chapter, which illustrates a big debate in itself, debates are systematically introduced in *every* chapter to provoke more critical thinking and discussion. Virtually all textbooks uncritically present knowledge "as is" and ignore the fact that the field is alive with numerous debates. No doubt, debates drive practice and research forward. Therefore, it is imperative that you be exposed to cutting-edge debates and encouraged to form your own views. In addition, ethics is emphasized throughout the book. A featured Ethical Dilemma can be found in every chapter. Two whole chapters are devoted to ethics, norms, and cultures (Chapter 3) and corporate social responsibility (Chapter 14).

ORGANIZATION OF THE BOOK

This book has three parts. Part I is *foundations*. Following this chapter, Chapters 2, 3, and 4 deal with the two leading perspectives: institution-based and resource-based views. Part II covers *tools*, focusing on trade (Chapter 5), foreign investment (Chapter 6), foreign exchange (Chapter 7), and global and regional integration (Chapter 8). Part III focuses on *managing* around the world. We start with the internationalization of small, entrepreneurial firms (Chapter 9), followed by ways to enter foreign markets (Chapter 10), to make alliances and acquisitions work (Chapter 11), to strategize, structure, and learn (Chapter 12), to manage human resources (Chapter 13), and finally to manage corporate social responsibility (Chapter 14).

ETHICAL DILEMMA
GE INNOVATES FROM THE BASE OF THE PYRAMID

Although the 133-year-old General Electric (GE) is usually regarded as a model of management excellence, the recent recession has been brutal. A recent *Economist* article on GE used the following unflattering title: "Losing Its Magic Touch"—for a good reason. Since 2008, GE has slashed its dividends by two thirds, lost a prized AAA credit rating, and seen $269 billion wiped off its stock market value due to concerns about the quality of some loans made by its financial services unit, GE Capital.

One glimmer of hope out of GE's recent mess is a new initiative called "reverse innovation," which has attracted GE chairman and CEO Jeff Immelt's personal attention. MNEs such as GE historically innovate new products in developed economies, and then localize these products by tweaking them for customers in emerging economies. Unfortunately, a lot of these expensive products, with well-off customers at the top of the global economic pyramid in mind, flop at the base of the pyramid not only because of their price tag, but also because of their lack of consideration for the specific needs and wants of local customers. Being the exact opposite, reverse innovation turns innovative products created for emerging economies into low-cost offerings for developed economies.

Take a look at GE's conventional ultrasound machines, originally developed in the United States and Japan and sold for between $100,000 and $350,000. In China, these expensive, bulky devices sold poorly because not every sophisticated hospital imaging center could afford them. GE's team in China realized that more than 80% of China's population relies on rural hospitals or clinics that are poorly funded. Conventional ultrasound machines are simply out of reach for these facilities. Patients thus have to travel to urban hospitals to access ultrasound. However, transportation to urban hospitals, especially for the sick and the pregnant, is challenging. Since most Chinese patients could not come to the ultrasound machines, the machines, thus, have to go to the patients. Scaling down its existing bulky, expensive, and complex ultrasound machines was not going to serve that demand.

GM realized that it needed a revolutionary product—a compact, portable ultrasound machine. In 2002, GE in China launched its first compact ultrasound, which combined a regular laptop computer with sophisticated software. The machine sold for only $30,000. In 2008, GE introduced a new model that sold for $15,000, less than 15% of the price tag of its high-end conventional ultrasound models. While portable ultrasounds have naturally become a hit in China, especially in rural clinics, they have also generated dramatic growth throughout the world, including developed economies. These machines combine a new dimension previously unavailable to ultrasound machines—portability—with an unbeatable price, in developed economies where containing health care cost is increasingly paramount. Before the global recession hit in 2008, portable ultrasounds were a $278 million global product line for GE, growing at 50% to 60% annually. Even in the midst of a severe global recession, this product line has been growing 25% annually in China.

GE's experience in developing portable ultrasound machines in China is not alone. For rural India, GE has pioneered a $1,000 handheld electrocardiogram (ECG) device that brings down the cost by a margin of 60% to 80%. In the Czech Republic, GE developed an aircraft engine for small planes that slashes its cost by half. This allows GE to challenge Pratt & Whitney's dominance of the small turboprop market in developed economies.

Such outstanding performance in and out of emerging economies, in combination with GE's dismal recent experience in developed economies, has rapidly transformed GE's mental map of the world (Exhibit 1.8). Ten years ago, it focused on the Triad and paid relatively minor attention to the "rest of the world." Now strategic attention is on emerging economies and other resource-rich regions, and the Triad becomes the "rest of the world." In an October 2009 *Harvard Business Review* article, Immelt wrote:

EXHIBIT 1.8   GE's Mental Map of the World

2000	2010
• United States • Europe • Japan • Rest of the world	• People-rich regions, such as China and India • Resource-rich regions, such as the Middle East, Australia, Brazil, Canada, and Russia • Rest of the world, such as the United States, Europe, and Japan

Source: Extracted from J. Immelt, V. Govindarajan, and C. Trimble, "How GE is disrupting itself" *Harvard Business Review* (October 2009) 56–65.

To be honest, the company is also embracing reverse innovation for defensive reasons. If GE doesn't come up with innovations in poor countries and take them global, new competitors from the developing world—like Mindray, Suzlon, Goldwind, and Haier—will.... GE has tremendous respect for traditional rivals like Siemens, Philips, and Rolls-Royce. But it knows how to compete with them; they will never destroy GE. By introducing products that create a new price-performance paradigm, however, the emerging giants very well could. Reverse innovation isn't optional; it's oxygen.

Sources: "General Electric: Losing its magic touch," *Economist*, 21 March 2009, 73–75; "Frugal healing," *Economist*, 22 January 2011, 73–74; "Life should be cheap," *Economist*, 22 January 2011,16; J. Immelt, V. Govindarajan, and C. Trimble, "How GE is disrupting itself," *Harvard Business Review* (October 2009): 56–65; C. K. Prahalad and R. Mashelkar, "Innovation's holy grail," *Harvard Business Review* (July 2010): 132–141.

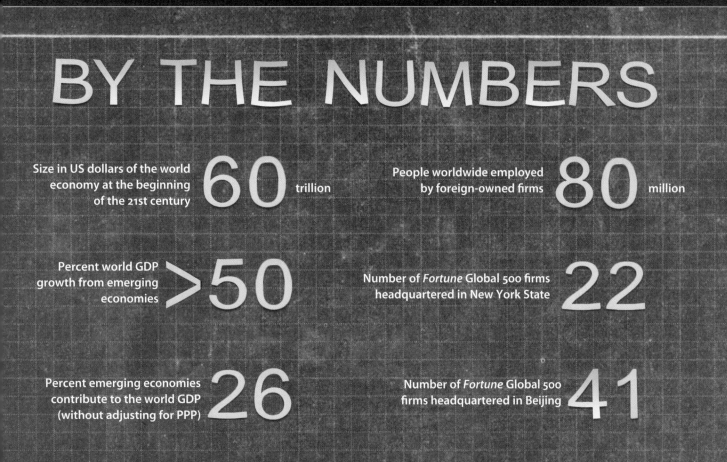

BY THE NUMBERS

Size in US dollars of the world economy at the beginning of the 21st century   **60** trillion

People worldwide employed by foreign-owned firms   **80** million

Percent world GDP growth from emerging economies   **>50**

Number of *Fortune* Global 500 firms headquartered in New York State   **22**

Percent emerging economies contribute to the world GDP (without adjusting for PPP)   **26**

Number of *Fortune* Global 500 firms headquartered in Beijing   **41**

Understanding Politics, LAWS, & Economics

CHAPTER 2

Adam Smith Versus Deng Xiaoping

Adam Smith would probably turn in his grave if he heard that in 2008, the fundamental principle of his theory first published in 1776 in *The Wealth of Nations*, *laissez faire* (the idea that governments should be hands-off when managing the economy), would be severely challenged. Most strikingly, these challenges came from the United States and Great Britain—the two countries so deeply in love with Adam Smith that they had often preached "free market principles" around the world until recently.

To be sure, the times were tough: Financial markets were melting down, banks were failing left and right, and consumer and investor confidence were reaching all-time lows since the Great Depression. However, the solutions turned the unthinkable into a new orthodoxy. Labeled "radical intervention" or even "financial socialism," the solutions centered on nationalization of failing banks and financial services firms. Yet, for over three decades

(since the 1980s), privatization—the complete opposite of nationalization—had been largely in the air.

On October 3, 2008, the Emergency Economic Stabilization Act, commonly known as the $700 billion bank bail-out plan or the Paulson plan (named after then-US Treasury Secretary Henry Paulson in the George W. Bush Administration), was passed. The Congressional debate prior to its passage was ferocious, because critics argued that this would clearly violate the enshrined free market principle of non-intervention. On October 15, Paulson announced the first step of implementation, by injecting $125 billion into eight banks: Bank of America, JPMorgan Chase, Citigroup, and Wells

LEARNING OBJECTIVES
After studying this chapter, you should be able to:

LO1 *identify two types of institutions.*

LO2 *explain how institutions reduce uncertainty.*

LO3 *identify the two core propositions underpinning an institution-based view of global business.*

LO4 *list the differences between democracy and totalitarianism.*

LO5 *list the differences among civil law, common law, and theocratic law.*

LO6 *articulate the importance of property rights and intellectual property rights.*

LO7 *list the differences among market economy, command economy, and mixed economy.*

LO8 *explain why it is important to understand the different institutions when doing business abroad.*

ley $10 billion each, and Bank of New York and State Street between $2 billion and $3 billion each. In return, the US government, having turned these banks into (partially) state-owned enterprises (SOEs), would take non-voting preference shares paying 5% interest. This action was so at odds with the free market tradition in the United States that its principal architect, Paulson, admitted that it was "objectionable." In Paulson's own words at a press conference:

Government owning a stake in any private US company is objectionable to most Americans, me included. Yet the alternative of leaving businesses and consumers without access to financing is totally unacceptable.

Similarly, on October 8, 2008, the UK government announced a £400 billion ($692 billion) rescue package to inject cash into UK banks. The justification was that if the government had not acted, UK banks faced the real risk of collapse. So used to being lectured by the British about "free markets," other EU governments were reluctant to believe this initially. But they quickly followed UK actions by bailing out their own troubled banks. By the end of 2008, governments in most developed economies became the largest shareholders in their financial industries, reversing three decades of deregulation and privatization.

No doubt, these actions will be recorded as an important turning point in economic history, triggering a fundamental rethink regarding the merits of private ownership and state ownership. The once-cherished assumptions about the superiority of the US economic model, centered on more market forces and less government intervention, are now in doubt. Recently, French Presi-

dent Nicolas Sarkozy announced that such "laissez faire capitalism is over." The irony was that he had been elected in 2007 on a campaign platform promising to practice more "Anglo-Saxon capitalism" in France.

"Forget Adam Smith. Whatever Works." This is the title of a *BusinessWeek* article in October 2008. On October 11, Federal Reserve Bank of Dallas President Richard Fisher gave a speech at the Group of Seven (G-7) finance ministers meeting in Washington, and borrowed a line from the late Chinese leader Deng Xiaoping: "Regardless of whether it is a white cat or a black cat, as long as it can catch mice, it is a good cat."

Of course, Deng in the early 1980s popularized his pragmatic "cat theory" in an effort to transform China from a command economy to a market economy. Interestingly, nearly three decades later, the "cat theory" was being invoked in a totally *opposite* direction. The upshot is that to the same extent that a pure command economy does not exist, a pure free market economy does not exist either. No doubt the post-bailout United States and Great Britain can still be labeled "market economies," but it is prudent to drop the "F" word. In other words, let's drop the "free" from the term "free market economies."

Sources: "Forget Adam Smith. Whatever works." *BusinessWeek*, 27 October 2008, 22–24; "Business in America," *Economist*, 30 May 2009, special report; "Is Sarkozy a closet socialist?" *Economist*, 15 November 2008, 61–62; "US injection lifts confidence," *Financial Times*, 15 October 2008, 1; "Whatever it took," *Financial Times*, 15 October 2008, 11; M. W. Peng, G. Bruton, and C. Stan, "Theories of the (state-owned) firm," working paper, University of Texas at Dallas, 2011; R. Reich, "Government in your business," *Harvard Business Review*, July–August 2009: 94–99.

What are the benefits and costs of private ownership? What are the pros and cons of state ownership? What are the political ideologies behind such ownership arrangements? Why are the stakes so high? As the Opening Case illustrates, these decisions are affected by institutions, popularly known as the "rules of the game" (first introduced in Chapter 1). As economic players, firms play by these rules. However, institutions are not static and they may change, as evidenced by the 2008 bailouts. Such **institutional transitions** are "fundamental and comprehensive changes introduced to the formal and informal rules of the game that affect firms as players."[1]

Overall, the success and failure of firms around the globe are to a large extent determined by firms' ability to understand and take advantage of the different rules of the game. This calls for firms to constantly monitor, decode, and adapt to the changing rules of the game in order to survive and prosper. As a result, such an institution-based view has emerged as a leading perspective on global business.[2] This chapter first introduces the institution-based view. Then, we focus on *formal*

institutions (such as political systems, legal systems, and economic systems). *Informal* institutions (such as cultures, ethics, and norms) will be discussed in Chapter 3.

> **Identify two types of institutions.**

UNDERSTANDING INSTITUTIONS

A popular metaphor for institutions is the "rules of the game," but what exactly are institutions? Douglass North, a Nobel laureate in economics, more formally defines institutions as "the humanly devised constraints that structure human interaction."[3] An institutional framework is made up of both the formal and informal institutions governing individual and firm behavior. Richard Scott, a leading sociologist, identifies three pillars that support these institutions: regulatory, normative, and cognitive.[4]

Formal institutions include laws, regulations, and rules, as shown in Exhibit 2.1. Their primary supportive pillar, the **regulatory pillar**, is the coercive power of governments. For example, out of patriotic duty, many individuals may pay taxes. However, many individuals pay taxes out of fear—if they did not pay and got caught, they would go to jail. In other words, it is the coercive power of governments'

Institutional transitions
Fundamental and comprehensive changes introduced to the formal and informal rules of the game that affect organizations as players.

Regulatory pillar
The coercive power of governments exercised through laws, regulations, and rules.

tax laws that forms the regulatory pillar to compel many individuals to pay taxes.

On the other hand, informal institutions include norms, cultures, and ethics. Informal institutions are supported by two pillars: normative and cognitive. The **normative pillar** refers to how the values, beliefs, and actions—collectively known as norms—of other relevant players influence the behavior of focal individuals and firms. For example, a recent norm among Western firms is the rush to invest in China and India. This norm has prompted many Western firms to imitate each other without a clear understanding of how to make such moves work. Cautious managers who resist such herding are often confronted by board members, investors, and reporters with the question "Why don't you invest in China and India?" In other words, "Why don't you follow the norm?"

The **cognitive pillar** is the second support for informal institutions. It refers to the internalized (or taken-for-granted) values and beliefs that guide individual and firm behavior. For example, whistleblowers reported Enron's wrongdoing out of a belief in what is right and wrong. While most employees may not feel comfortable with organizational wrongdoing, the social norm in the firm is not to rock the boat. Essentially, whistleblowers choose to follow their internalized personal beliefs on what is right by overcoming the social norms that encourage silence. In Enron's case, the normative pillar suggests being quiet, whereas the whistleblowers' actions are supported by their strong cognitive pillar regarding what is right and wrong.

Formal and informal institutional forces stem primarily from home countries and host countries. In addition, international and regional organizations such as the World Trade Organization (WTO), the International Monetary Fund (IMF), and the European Union (EU) may also influence firm conduct in terms of do's and don'ts. See Chapters 7 and 8 for more details.

LO2 **Explain how institutions reduce uncertainty.**

WHAT DO INSTITUTIONS DO?

While institutions do many things, their key role is to *reduce uncertainty*. Specifically, institutions influence the decision-making process of both individuals and firms by signaling what conduct is legitimate and acceptable and what is not. Basically, institutions constrain the range of acceptable actions. Why is it so important to reduce uncertainty? Because uncertainty can be potentially devastating. Political uncertainty such as an uprising may render long-range planning obsolete. Economic uncertainty such as failure to carry out transactions as spelled out in contracts may result in economic losses. See the Closing Case for the ongoing political and economic uncertainty in the Middle East.

Uncertainty surrounding economic transactions can lead to **transaction costs**, which are the costs associated with economic transactions or, more broadly, the costs of doing business. Oliver Williamson, a Nobel laureate in economics, makes the comparison to frictions in mechanical systems: "Do the gears mesh, are the parts lubricated, is there needless slippage or other loss of energy?" He goes on to suggest that transaction costs can be regarded as "the economic counterpart of frictions: Do the parties to exchange operate harmoniously, or are there frequent misunderstandings and conflicts?"[5]

An important source of transaction costs is **opportunism**, defined as the act of seeking self-interest with guile. Examples include misleading, cheating, and confusing other parties in transactions that will increase transaction

EXHIBIT 2.1 Dimensions of Institutions

Degree of formality	Examples	Supportive pillars
Formal institutions	Laws Regulations Rules	Regulatory (coercive)
Informal institutions	Norms Cultures Ethics	Normative Cognitive

Normative pillar
The mechanisms through which norms influence individual and firm behavior.

Cognitive pillar
The internalized, taken-for-granted values and beliefs that guide individual and firm behavior.

Transaction costs
The costs associated with economic transactions or, more broadly, the costs of doing business.

Opportunism
The act of seeking self-interest with guile.

© iStockphoto.com/Feng Yu

© iStockphoto.com/xyno

costs. Attempting to reduce such transaction costs, institutional frameworks increase certainty by spelling out the rules of the game so that violations (such as failure to fulfill a contract) can be mitigated with relative ease (such as through formal courts and arbitration).

Without stable institutional frameworks, transaction costs may become prohibitively high, to the extent that certain transactions simply would not take place. For example, due to the unrest in Libya, most multinational oil companies have evacuated foreign personnel and shut down production in the country since February 2011 (see the Closing Case). Conceptually, this is a case of transaction costs being too high.

Institutions are not static. Institutional transitions in some emerging economies are so pervasive that these countries are simply called "transition economies" (a *subset* of "emerging economies"). Examples include those countries that are moving from central planning to market competition, such as China, Poland, and Russia (see In Focus). Institutional transitions in these countries as well as other emerging economies such as Brazil, India, and South Africa create both huge challenges and tremendous opportunities for domestic and international firms. For example, a Swedish manager working for IKEA in Russia complained that "Russia is a bit of a rollercoaster, you don't know exactly what will happen tomorrow."[6] See In Focus for more on Russia.

Having outlined the definitions of various institutions and their supportive pillars as well as the key role of institutions in uncertainty reduction, next we will introduce the first core perspective on global business: an institution-based view.

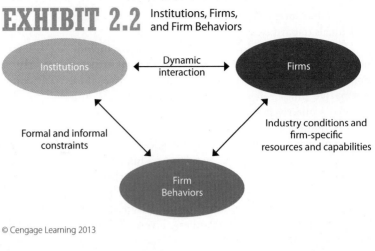

EXHIBIT 2.2 Institutions, Firms, and Firm Behaviors

Institutions ↔ Dynamic interaction ↔ Firms

Formal and informal constraints

Industry conditions and firm-specific resources and capabilities

Firm Behaviors

© Cengage Learning 2013

EXHIBIT 2.3 Two Core Propositions of the Institution-Based View

1 Managers and firms *rationally* pursue their interests and make choices within the formal and informal constraints in a given institutional framework.

2 While formal and informal institutions combine to govern firm behavior, in situations where formal constraints are unclear or fail, informal constraints will play a *larger* role in reducing uncertainty and providing constancy to managers and firms.

© iStockphoto.com/blackred

Identify the two core propositions underpinning an institution-based view of global business.

AN INSTITUTION-BASED VIEW OF GLOBAL BUSINESS

An institution-based view of global business, as shown in Exhibit 2.2, focuses on the dynamic interaction between institutions and firms and considers firm behavior as the outcome of such an interaction. Specifically, firm behavior is often a reflection of the formal and informal constraints of a particular institutional framework. In short, institutions matter.

How do institutions matter? The institution-based view suggests two core propositions (see Exhibit 2.3). First, managers and firms *rationally* pursue their interests and make choices within institutional constraints. At the state-owned railways in China and India, which are not affected by international competition, managers are eager to ask for help from the government and reluctant to improve ser-

vice. In contrast, managers in Chinese and Indian IT industries have to excel in the game of market responsiveness and innovation because rules of the game in these industries are defined by the global heavyweights. Both strategies are perfectly rational.

Second, while formal and informal institutions combine to govern firm behavior, informal constraints play a *larger* role in reducing uncertainty and providing constancy for managers and firms in situations where formal constraints are unclear or fail. For example, when the former Soviet Union collapsed and with it the formal regime, the growth of many entrepreneurial firms was facilitated by informal constraints based on personal relationships and connections (called *blat* in Russian) among managers and officials.

Many observers have the impression that relying on informal connections is relevant only to firms in emerging economies and that firms in developed economies pursue only market-based strategies. This is far from the truth. Even in developed economies, formal rules make up only a small (though important) part of institutional constraints, and informal constraints are pervasive. Just as firms compete in product markets, firms also fiercely compete in the political marketplace characterized by informal relationships. Basically, if a firm cannot be a market leader, it may still beat the competition on other grounds—namely, the nonmarket, political environment. In September 2008, a

IN FOCUS

The Russia Puzzle

Russia is not the Soviet Union. But what is it? Since the collapse of the former Soviet Union in 1991, Russia has undergone a series of extraordinary institutional transitions. It changed from a communist totalitarian state into a democracy with regular elections. Its centrally planned economy was transformed into a capitalist economy of mostly private firms. Yet, Russia has remained a huge puzzle to policy makers, scholars, and managers both in Russia and abroad, thus provoking a constant debate.

Politically, does Russia really have a democracy? In 2004, Russia was *downgraded* from "Partly Free" to "Not Free"—on a 1–3 scale of "Free," "Partly Free," and "Not Free"—by Freedom House, a leading nongovernmental organization (NGO) promoting political freedom (see PengAtlas Map 3). This was driven by Russia's recent steady drift toward more authoritarian rule under then-president Vladimir Putin. Yet, Russia under Putin between 2000 and 2008 grew 7% annually, whereas Russia under Boris Yeltsin during the 1990s, when it was "Partly Free," experienced a catastrophic economic decline. Most Russians, who were economically better off in the 2000s, do not seem to mind living in a "less democratic" country (relative to what Russia was in the 1990s).

Legally, establishing the rule of law that respects private property is one of the main goals of Russia's institutional transitions. In a society whereby nobody had any significant private property until recently, how a small number of individuals became super-rich oligarchs (tycoons) almost overnight is intriguing. By 2003, the top ten families or groups owned 60% of Russia's total market capitalization. Should the government protect private property if it is acquired through illegitimate or "gray" means? Most oligarchs obtained their wealth during the chaotic 1990s. The government thus faces a dilemma: Redistributing wealth by confiscating assets from the oligarchs creates more uncertainty, whereas respecting and protecting the property rights of the oligarchs results in more resentment among the population. Thus far, except when a few oligarchs, notably Mikhail Khodorkovsky, threatened to politically challenge the government, the government sided with the oligarchs. Not surprisingly, oligarchs have emerged as a strong force in favor of property rights protection.

Where exactly is Russia heading? The key to solving this puzzle is to understand Putin (who became prime minister in 2008) and his chosen successor, President Dmitry Medvedev. While Russia becomes economically richer and stronger (thanks to high oil prices), the government is bolder and more assertive in foreign affairs. At home, the government is also sliding back to more authoritarian ways. But, one argument goes, if the government delivers economic growth or at least survives the recent downturn, so what?

In addition, other experts note that despite its former superpower status, Russia has become a "normal," middle-income country. With GDP per capita around $8,000, Russia in 2012 is at a level similar to that of Argentina in 1991 and Mexico in 1999. Democracies in this income range are rough around the edges. They tend to

have corrupt governments, high income inequality, concentrated corporate ownership, and turbulent economic performance. In all these aspects, Russia may be quite "normal." However, these flaws are not necessarily incompatible with further progress down the road. For example, consumers in normal, middle-income countries naturally demand bank loans, credit cards, and mortgages, which have only appeared recently in Russia and created lucrative opportunities for Russian and foreign firms.

Because Russia is so large and complex, news from Russia is often simultaneously both good and bad. For example, IKEA, a leading Swedish furniture retailer, aggressively entered Russia in 2000, investing $4 billion in a decade during which Russia's yuppies became known as the "IKEA Generation." However, even as one of the largest foreign investors, IKEA has been frustrated by corruption, especially at the local level. In 2009, IKEA put on hold all new investment in Russia.

At the same time, despite such bad news, overall, big political risks seem reasonably remote. With the Middle East up in flames, Russia's stability as an oil producer shines. More foreign firms are now rushing in. As the R in BRIC, Russia is simply too big and too rich to ignore. Disposable household income in Russia is one third higher than Brazil's, four times China's, and ten times India's. However, the Russian economy seems overly dependent on raw materials exports (such as oil, gas, and minerals). The global collapse of demand, due to the 2008–2009 crisis, is hurting Russia. Yet, the new government, under President Medvedev, has the ambition to transform Russia into a more innovation-driven economy. Overall, solving the Russia puzzle has a direct bearing on firms' assessment of the risks of operating in Russia relative to the risks of operating in other countries such as BIC in BRIC.

Sources: "Dreams of an iPad economy for Russia," *Bloomberg Businessweek*, 7 February 2011, 11–12; "IKEA in Russia," *BusinessWeek*, 13 July 2009, 33; "The peril and promise of investing in Russia," *BusinessWeek*, 5 October 2009, 48–51; "Enigma variations," *Economist*, 29 November 2008, 3–18; S. Guriev and A. Rachinsky, "The role of oligarchs in Russian capitalism," *Journal of Economic Perspectives*, 19 (2005): 131–150; S. Puffer and D. McCarthy, "Can Russia's state-managed, network capitalism be competitive?" *Journal of World Business*, 42 (2007): 1–13; A. Shleifer and D. Treisman, "A normal country," *Journal of Economic Perspectives*, 19 (2005): 151–174; Freedom House, "Russia's democratic development in peril," press release, July 2004, available online at http://www.freedomhouse.org [accessed July 2011].

PengAtlas Map

failing Merrill Lynch was able to sell itself to Bank of America for $50 billion. Supported by US government officials, this mega deal was arranged over 48 hours (shorter than the time most people take to decide on which car to buy), and the negotiations took place *inside* the Federal Reserve building in New York. In contrast, Lehman Brothers failed to secure government support and had to file for bankruptcy. Overall, the skillful use of a country's institutional frameworks to acquire advantage is at the heart of the institution-based view.

While there are numerous formal and informal institutions, in this chapter we focus on *formal* institutions. (Informal institutions will be covered in Chapter 3.) Chief among formal institutions are political systems, legal systems, and economic systems. We introduce each in turn.

© Yoshikazu Tsuno/AFP/Getty Images

List the differences between democracy and totalitarianism.

POLITICAL SYSTEMS

A **political system** refers to the rules of the game on how a country is governed politically. At the broadest level, there are two primary political systems: democracy and totalitarianism. This section first outlines these two systems and then discusses their ramifications for political risk.

Democracy

Democracy is a political system in which citizens elect representatives to govern the country on their behalf. Usually, the political party with the majority of votes wins and forms a government. Democracy was pioneered by the Athenians in ancient Greece. In today's world, Great Britain has the longest experience of running a democracy, and India has the largest democracy (by population).

A fundamental aspect of democracy that is relevant to global business is an individual's right to freedom of expression and organization. For example, starting up a firm is an act of economic expression, essentially telling the rest of the world: "I want to be my own boss! And I want to make some money!" In most modern democracies, the right to organize economically has been ex-

Political system
The rules of the game on how a country is governed politically.

Democracy
A political system in which citizens elect representatives to govern the country on their behalf.

Totalitarianism (or dictatorship)
A political system in which one person or party exercises absolute political control over the population.

tended not only to domestic individuals and firms but also to *foreign* individuals and firms that come to do business. While those of us fortunate enough to have been brought up in a democracy take the right to establish a firm for granted, we should be reminded that this may not necessarily be the case under other political systems. Before the 1980s, if someone dared to formally establish a private firm in the former Soviet Union, he or she would have been arrested and *shot* by the authorities.[7]

Totalitarianism

On the opposite end of the political spectrum from democracy is **totalitarianism** (also known as **dictatorship**), which is defined as a political system in which one person or party exercises absolute political control over the population. There are four major types of totalitarianism:

- *Communist totalitarianism* centers on a communist party. This system was embraced throughout Central and Eastern Europe and the former Soviet Union until the late 1980s. It is still practiced in China, Cuba, Laos, North Korea, and Vietnam.

- *Right-wing totalitarianism* is characterized by its intense hatred of communism. One party, typically backed by the military, restricts political freedom because its members believe that such freedom would lead to communism. In the decades following World War II, South Africa, South Korea, Taiwan, and most Latin American countries practiced right-wing totalitarianism. Most of these countries have recently become democracies.

- *Theocratic totalitarianism* refers to the monopolization of political power in the hands of one religious party or group. Iran and Saudi Arabia are leading examples. Another example is Afghanistan under Taliban rule until 2001, when US forces removed that group from formal power.

- *Tribal totalitarianism* refers to one tribe or ethnic group (which may or may not be the majority of the population) monopolizing political power and oppressing other tribes or ethnic groups. Rwanda's bloodbath in the 1990s was due to some of the most brutal practices of tribal totalitarianism.

Political Risk

While the degree of hostility toward business varies among different types of totalitarianism (some can be more pro-business than others), totalitarianism in general is not as good for business as democracy. Totalitarian countries often experience wars, riots, protests, chaos, and breakdowns (see the Closing Case). As a result, these countries often suffer from a high level of **political risk**, which is a risk associated with political changes that may negatively impact domestic and foreign firms.

Firms operating in democracies also confront political risk, but such risk is qualitatively different than that in totalitarian countries. For example, Quebec's possible independence from the rest of Canada creates some political risk. Although firms highly exposed in Quebec experience some drop in their stock price, there is no general collapse of stock price in Canada or flight of capital out of Canada.[8] Investors are confident that, should Quebec become independent, the Canadian democracy is mature enough to manage the secession process in a relatively non-disruptive way.

Historically speaking, no two democracies have gone to war with each other. Obviously, when two countries are at each other's throats, we can forget about doing business between them. In this regard, the recent advance of democracy and retreat of totalitarianism is highly beneficial for global business. It is not a coincidence that globalization took off in the 1990s, a period during which both communist and right-wing totalitarianism significantly lost its power and democracy expanded around the world (see Chapter 1).

Canada

List the differences among civil law, common law, and theocratic law.

Articulate the importance of property rights and intellectual property rights.

LEGAL SYSTEMS

A **legal system** refers to the rules of the game on how a country's laws are enacted and enforced. By specifying the do's and don'ts, a legal system reduces transaction costs by minimizing uncertainty and combating opportunism. This section first introduces three different legal traditions and then discusses crucial issues associated with property rights and intellectual property.

Civil Law, Common Law, and Theocratic Law

Laws in different countries typically are not enacted from scratch but are often transplanted—voluntarily or otherwise—from three legal traditions (or legal families): civil law, common law, and theocratic law. Each is introduced here.

Civil law was derived from Roman law and strengthened by Napoleon's France. It is "the oldest, the most influential, and the most widely distributed around the world."[9] It uses comprehensive statutes and codes as a primary means to form legal judgments. Over 80 countries practice civil law.

Common law, which is English in origin, is shaped by precedents and traditions from previous judicial decisions. Common law has spread to all English-speaking countries, most of which were at one time British colonies. Relative to civil law, common law has more flexibility because judges have to resolve specific disputes based on their *interpretation* of the law, and such interpretation may give new meaning to the law, which will in turn shape future cases. Civil law has less flexibility because judges have the power only to *apply* the law. Thus civil law is less confrontational because comprehensive statutes and codes serve to guide judges. Common law, on the other hand, is more confrontational because plaintiffs and defendants, through their lawyers, must argue and help judges to favorably interpret the law largely based on precedents.

The third legal family is **theocratic law**, a legal system based

Political risk
Risk associated with political changes that may negatively impact domestic and foreign firms.

Legal system
The rules of the game on how a country's laws are enacted and enforced.

Civil law
A legal tradition that uses comprehensive statutes and codes as a primary means to form legal judgments.

Common law
A legal tradition that is shaped by precedents from previous judicial decisions.

Theocratic law
A legal system based on religious teachings.

on religious teachings. Examples include Jewish and Islamic laws. Although Jewish law is followed by some elements of the Israeli population, it is *not* formally embraced by the Israeli government. Islamic law is the only surviving example of a theocratic legal system that is formally practiced by some governments, including those in Iran and Saudi Arabia. Despite the popular characterization of Islam as anti-business, it is important to note that Mohammed was a merchant trader and the tenets of Islam are pro-business in general. However, the holy book of Islam, the Koran, does advise against *certain* business practices. In Saudi Arabia, McDonald's operates "ladies only" restaurants in order to comply with the Koran's ban on direct, face-to-face contact between unrelated men and women (who often wear a veil) in public. Moreover, banks in Saudi Arabia have to maintain two retail branches: one staffed by men for male customers and another staffed by women for female customers. This requirement obviously increases

ber, for example, the United States was a "developing" or "emerging" economy 100 years ago.) While there are many answers, a leading answer, most forcefully put forward by Peruvian economist Hernando de Soto, focuses on the protection of property rights.[10] In developed economies, every parcel of land, every building, and every trademark is represented in a property document that entitles the owner to derive income and benefits from it. That property document is also important when violators are prosecuted through legal means.

When a legal system is stable and predictable, tangible property also makes other, less tangible economic activities possible. For example, property can be used as collateral for credit. The single most important source of funds for new start-ups in the United States is the mortgage of entrepreneurs' houses. But this cannot be done without documented right to the property. If you live in a house but cannot produce a title document specifying that you are the

> # What the developing world lacks and desperately needs is formal protection of property rights in order to facilitate economic growth.

property, overhead, and personnel costs. To reduce costs, some foreign banks such as HSBC staff their back office operations with both male and female employees who work side by side.

Overall, legal systems are a crucial component of the institutional framework because they form the first regulatory pillar that supports institutions. They directly impose do's and don'ts on businesses around the globe. A legal system has numerous components. Two of these, property rights and intellectual property, are discussed next.

Property Rights

One fundamental economic function that a legal system serves is to protect **property rights**, which are the legal rights to use an economic property (resource) and to derive income and benefits from it. A legal system fills this economic role whether it is civil, common, or theocratic. Examples of property include homes, offices, and factories. (Ideas are also property, but these will be discussed separately in the next section.)

What difference do property rights supported by a functioning legal system make? A lot. Why did developed economies become developed? (Remem-

legal owner of the house (which is a very common situation throughout the developing world, especially in "shanty towns"), no bank in the world will allow you to use your house as collateral for credit. To start up a new firm without property as collateral, borrowers end up securing funds from family members, friends, and other acquaintances through *informal* means. But funds through informal means are almost certainly more limited than funds that could have been provided formally by banks. Insecure property rights are why, in general, the average firm size in the developing world is smaller than that in the developed world. Insecure property rights also result in using technologies that employ little fixed capital and do not entail long-term investment (such as R&D). These characteristics of firms in developing economies do not bode well in global competition where leading firms reap benefits from economies of scale, capital-intensive technologies, and sustained investment in

Property rights
Legal rights to use an economic property (resource) and to derive income and benefits from it.

R&D. What the developing world lacks and desperately needs is formal protection of property rights in order to facilitate economic growth.

Intellectual Property Rights

While the term "property" traditionally refers to *tangible* pieces of property such as land, **intellectual property** specifically refers to *intangible* property that is the result of intellectual activity (such as the content of books, videos, and websites). **Intellectual property rights (IPR)** are legal rights associated with the ownership of intellectual property. IPR primarily include rights associated with patents, copyrights, and trademarks.

- **Patents** are legal rights awarded by government authorities to inventors of new products or processes. The inventors are given exclusive (monopoly) rights to derive income from such inventions through activities such as manufacturing, licensing, or selling.

- **Copyrights** are the exclusive legal rights of authors and publishers to publish and disseminate their work. For example, the book you are reading now is protected by copyright.

- **Trademarks** are the exclusive legal rights of firms to use specific names, brands, and designs to differentiate their products from others.

IPR need to be asserted and enforced through a *formal* system designed to provide an incentive for people and firms to innovate.[11] To be effective, the system must also punish violators. But the intangible nature of IPR makes enforcement difficult. **Piracy**, or unauthorized use of IPR, is widespread around the world. Acts of piracy range from unauthorized sharing of music files to deliberate counterfeiting of branded products.

Overall, an institution-based view suggests that the key to understanding IPR violation is realizing that IPR violators are not amoral monsters but ordinary people and firms. When filling out a survey on "What is your dream career?" no high school graduate anywhere in the world will answer "Counterfeiting." Nevertheless, thousands of individuals and firms *voluntarily* choose to be involved in this business worldwide. Why? Because IPR protection is weak in many countries. For example, counterfeiters in China will be criminally prosecuted only if their profits exceed approximately $10,000. No counterfeiters are dumb enough to keep records to show that they make that much money. If caught, they can usually get away by paying a small fine. Stronger IPR protection may significantly reduce the incentive to be involved in piracy and counterfeiting. IPR reforms currently being discussed in China, for example, propose criminalizing *all* counterfeiting activities regardless of the amount of profits.

ECONOMIC SYSTEMS

Market, Command, and Mixed Economies

An **economic system** refers to the rules of the game on how a country is governed economically. A pure **market economy** is characterized by the "invisible hand" of market forces first noted in 1776 by Adam Smith in *The Wealth of Nations*. The government takes a *laissez faire* (hands-off) approach. Theoretically, all factors of production should thus be privately owned. The government performs only functions the private sector cannot perform, such as providing roads and defense.

A pure **command economy** is defined by a government taking, in the words of Lenin, the "commanding height" in the economy. Theoretically, all factors of production should be state-owned and state-controlled, and all supply, demand, and pricing are planned by the government. During the heydays of communism, the former Soviet Union and China approached such an ideal.

A **mixed economy**, by definition, has elements of both a market economy and a command economy. It boils down to the relative distribution of market forces versus command forces. In practice, no country has ever completely embraced Adam Smith's ideal *laissez faire* approach. Question: Which economy has the highest degree of economic freedom (the lowest degree of government intervention in the economy)? Hint: It is *not* the United States. Answer: A series of surveys report that it is Hong Kong (the post-1997

Intellectual property
Intangible property that results from intellectual activity (such as the content of books, videos, and websites).

Intellectual property rights (IPR)
Legal rights associated with the ownership of intellectual property.

Patents
Exclusive legal rights of inventors to derive income from their inventions through activities such as manufacturing, licensing, or selling.

Copyrights
Exclusive legal rights of authors and publishers to publish and disseminate their work.

Trademarks
Exclusive legal rights of firms to use specific names, brands, and designs to differentiate their products from others.

Piracy
The unauthorized use of intellectual property rights.

Economic system
The rules of the game on how a country is governed economically.

Market economy
An economy that is characterized by the "invisible hand" of market forces.

Command economy
An economy in which theoretically all factors of production are state-owned and state-controlled, and all supply, demand, and pricing are planned by the government.

Mixed economy
An economy that has elements of both a market economy and a command economy.

handover to Chinese sovereignty does not make a difference).[12] The crucial point here is that there is still some noticeable government intervention in the economy, even in Hong Kong. During the aftermath of the 1997 economic crisis when the share price of all Hong Kong firms took a nose dive, the Hong Kong government took a highly controversial course of action. It used government funds to purchase 10% of the shares of all the blue chip firms listed in the Hang Seng index. This action slowed down the sliding of share prices and stabilized the economy, but it turned all the blue chip firms into state-owned enterprises (SOEs)—at least 10% owned by the state. In 2008, US and European governments did something similar, nationalizing a large chunk of their failing banks and financial services firms via bailouts and turning them into SOEs (see the Opening Case and the Debate).

Likewise, no country has ever had a complete command economy, not even in the Eastern Bloc during the Cold War. Poland never nationalized its agriculture. Hungarians were known to have second (and private!) jobs, while all of them theoretically worked only for the state. Black markets hawking agricultural produce and small merchandise existed in practically all former communist countries. While the former Soviet Union and Central and Eastern European countries have recently rejected communism, even ongoing practitioners of communism such as China and Vietnam have embraced market reforms. Cuba has a lot of foreign-invested hotels. Even North Korea is now interested in attracting foreign investment.

Overall, the economic system of most countries is a mixed economy. In practice, when we say a country has a market economy, it is really a shorthand version for a country that organizes its economy *mostly* (but not completely) by market forces and that still has certain elements of a command economy. China, France, Russia, Sweden, and the United States all claim to have a market economy now, but the meaning is different in each country. In other words, free markets are not totally free. It boils down to a matter of degree.

Adam Smith

What Drives Economic Development?

Regardless of the economic system used, developing the economy is one of the aims for most governments. The differences in economic development around the globe are striking (see PengAtlas Map 4). As Exhibit 2.4 shows, per capita income in Norway is $76,450 but only $110 in Burundi. Why are some countries so developed (rich), while others are so underdeveloped (poor)? Scholars and policy makers have debated this very important question since Adam Smith. We will look at three possible positions one can take in this debate.

One side argues that rich countries tend to have a smarter and harder working population driven by a stronger motivation for economic success, such as the Protestant work ethic identified by Max Weber over a century ago. Still, it is difficult to imagine that Norwegians are, on average, nearly *770 times* smarter and harder working than Burundians. This line of thinking, bordering on racism, is no longer acceptable in the 21st century.

A second voice in this debate suggests that rich countries tend to be well endowed with natural resources. But one can easily point out that some poor countries also possess rich natural resources, while some rich countries are very poor in natural resources. The Democratic Republic of Congo (formerly Zaire) is rich in diamonds, oil and natural gas, water, timber, and other minerals, while Japan lacks significant natural resources. In addition, some countries are believed to be cursed by their poor geographic location, which may be landlocked and/or located near the hot equator zone and infested with tropical diseases. This

EXHIBIT 2.4
Top Ten and Bottom Ten Countries by Per Capita Gross National Income (GNI) (see also PengAtlas Map 4)

Richest ten	US$	Poorest ten	US$
Norway	$76,450	Mozambique	$320
Switzerland	$59,880	Rwanda	$320
Denmark	$54,910	Niger	$280
Ireland	$48,140	Sierra Leone	$260
Sweden	$46,060	Malawi	$250
United States	$46,040	Eritrea	$230
Netherlands	$45,820	Ethiopia	$220
Finland	$44,400	Liberia	$150
United Kingdom	$42,740	Democratic Republic of Congo (Zaire)	$140
Austria	$42,700	Burundi	$110

Source: The World Bank, *World Development Report 2009: Reshaping Economic Geography* (Washington: The World Bank, 2009). GNI is gross domestic product (GDP) plus net receipts of primary income (compensation of employees and property income) from nonresident sources.

DEBATE
ETHICAL DILEMMA

Private Ownership Versus State Ownership

Private ownership is good. State (or public) ownership is bad. Although crude, these two statements fairly accurately summarize the intellectual and political reasoning behind three decades of privatization around the world since the early 1980s. As providers of capital, private owners are otherwise known as capitalists, and their central role in the economic system gives birth to the term "capitalism." State ownership emphasizes the social and public nature of economic ownership, and leads to the coinage of the term "socialism." Both forms of ownership have their pros and cons. The debate is which form of ownership is better—whether the pros outweigh the cons.

The debate on private versus state ownership underpins much of the global economic evolution since the early 20th century. It was the failure of capitalism, most disastrously embodied in the Great Depression (1929–1933), that made the Soviet-style socialism centered on state ownership shine. Numerous elites in developing countries and a nontrivial number of scholars in developed economies noticed this. As a result, in postwar decades, state ownership was on the march, and private ownership was in decline. State ownership was not only extensive throughout the former Eastern Bloc (the former Soviet Union, Central and Eastern Europe, and China), but was also widely embraced throughout developed economies in Western Europe.

However, SOEs typically suffered from a lack of accountability and a lack of concern for economic efficiency. SOEs were known to feature relatively equal pay between the executives and the rank and file. Since extra work did not translate into extra pay, employees had little incentive to improve their work. Given the generally low pay and the non-demanding work environment, former Soviet SOE employees summed it well: "They pretend to pay us, and we pretend to work."

As Britain's prime minister, Margaret Thatcher privatized a majority of British SOEs in the 1980s. Very soon, SOEs throughout Central and Eastern Europe followed suit. After the former Soviet Union collapsed, the new Russian government unleashed some of the most aggressive privatization schemes in the 1990s. Eventually, the privatization movement became global, reaching Brazil, India, China, Vietnam, and many other countries. In no small part, such a global movement was championed by the **Washington Consensus**, spearheaded by two Washington-based international organizations: the International Monetary Fund (IMF) and the World Bank. A core value of the Washington Consensus is the unquestioned belief in the superiority of private ownership over state ownership. The widespread privatization movement suggested that the Washington Consensus clearly won the day—or it seemed.

Unfortunately, the pendulum suddenly swung back in 2008 (see the Opening Case). During the unprecedented recession, major governments in developed economies, led by the US government, bailed out numerous failing private firms using public funds, effectively turning them into SOEs. As a result, all the arguments in favor of private ownership and "free market" capitalism collapsed. Since SOEs had such a dreadful reputation (essentially a "dirty word"), the US government has refused to acknowledge that it has SOEs. Instead, it admits that the United States has "government-sponsored enterprises" (GSEs). These GSEs include General Motors (GM), whose new nickname is Government Motors, and Citigroup, which has become Citigovernment.

Critics argue that despite noble goals to rescue the economy, protect jobs, and fight recession, government bailouts serve to heighten **moral hazard**—recklessness when people and organizations (including firms and governments) do not have to face the full consequences of their actions. In other words, capitalism without the risk of failure becomes socialism. It is long known that executives in SOEs face a "soft budget constraint" in that they can always dip into state coffers to cover their losses. When executives in private firms who make risky decisions find out that their firms will not go under (thanks to generous bailouts) if the decisions turn sour, they are likely to embrace more risk in the future. In other words, bailouts foster a kind of "heads I win, tails you lose" thinking among executives regarding state coffers and taxpayer dollars. Per Proposition 1 (Exhibit 2.3), these executives are being perfectly rational: Taking on risks, if successful, will enrich their private firms, their owners (shareholders), and themselves; if unsuccessful, Uncle Sam will come to the rescue. Having bailed out failing private firms once, governments that not long ago were the strongest champions of "free markets" now increasingly find it hard to draw the line. Although the worst fear about the recession is now over, debate continues to rage. So stay tuned.

Sources: P. Bernstein, "The moral hazard economy," *Harvard Business Review* (July 2009): 101–102; S. Harrington, "Moral hazard and the meltdown," *Wall Street Journal*, 23 May 2009; M. W. Peng, *Business Strategies in Transition Economies* (Thousand Oaks, CA: Sage, 2000); M. W. Peng, G. Bruton, and C. Stan, "Theories of the (state-owned) firm," working paper, University of Texas at Dallas (2011).

Washington Consensus
A view centered on the unquestioned belief in the superiority of private ownership over state ownership in economic policy making, which is often spearheaded by two Washington-based international organizations: the International Monetary Fund and the World Bank.

Moral hazard
Recklessness when people and organizations (including firms and governments) do not have to face the full consequences of their actions.

argument is not convincing either, because some land-locked countries (such as Switzerland) are phenomenally well developed and some countries near the equator (such as Singapore) have accomplished enviable growth. Geography is important, but it is not destiny.

A third side of the debate argues that institutions are "the basic determinants of the performance of an economy."[13] In short, rich countries are rich because they have developed better market-supporting institutional frameworks. Consider these points:

+ The presence of formal, market-supporting institutions encourages individuals to specialize and firms to grow in size. This is the "division of labor" thesis first advanced by Adam Smith (see Chapter 5). Specialization is economically advantageous because firms are able to capture the gains from transactions with distant, foreign countries. For example, as China's market institutions progress, many Chinese firms have grown substantially.

+ A lack of strong, formal, market-supporting institutions forces individuals to trade on an informal basis with a small neighboring group. This forces firms to remain small and local in nature, as are most firms in Africa. Over 40% of Africa's economy is reportedly informal, the highest proportion in the world.[14]

+ Formal, market-supporting institutions that protect property rights fuel more innovation, entrepreneurship, and thus economic growth. While spontaneous innovation has existed throughout history, why has its pace accelerated significantly since the Industrial Revolution starting in the 1700s? A big factor was the Statute of Monopolies enacted in Great Britain in 1624, which was the world's first patent law to formally protect the IPR of inventors and make innovation financially lucrative.[15] This law has been imitated around the world. Its impact is still felt today, as we now expect continuous innovation to be the norm. Think of the doubling of computing power every couple of years. This would not have happened had there not been a system of IPR protection that protects and rewards innovation.

These arguments, of course, are the backbone of the institution-based view of global business, which has clearly won this debate.

Explain why it is important to understand the different institutions when doing business abroad.

MANAGEMENT SAVVY

Focusing on *formal* institutions, this chapter has sketched the contours of an institution-based view of global business. How does the institution-based view help us answer our fundamental question of utmost concern to managers around the globe: What determines the success and failure

of firms around the globe? In a nutshell, this chapter suggests that firm performance is determined, at least in part, by the institutional frameworks governing firm behavior. It is the growth of the firm that, in the aggregate, leads to the growth of the economy. Not surprisingly, most developed economies are supported by strong, effective, and market-supporting formal institutions and most underdeveloped economies are pulled back by weak, ineffective, and market-depressing formal institutions. In other words, when markets work smoothly in developed economies, formal market-supporting institutions are almost invisible and taken for granted. However, when markets work poorly, the absence of strong formal institutions may become conspicuous.

For managers doing business around the globe, this chapter suggests two broad implications for action (see Exhibit 2.5). First, managerial choices are made rationally within the constraints of a given institutional framework. Therefore, managers aiming to enter a new country need to do their homework by having a thorough understanding of the formal institutions affecting their business. The rules for doing business in a democratic market economy are certainly different from the rules in a totalitarian command economy. In short, "When in Rome, do as the Romans do." While this is a good start, managers also need to understand *why* "Romans" do things in a certain way by studying the formal institutions governing "Roman" behavior. A superficial understanding may not get you very far and may even be misleading or dangerous.

Second, while this chapter has focused on the role of formal institutions, managers should follow the advice of the second proposition of the institution-based view: In situations where formal constraints are unclear or fail, informal constraints such as relationship norms will play a *larger* role in reducing uncertainty. If, for example, you are doing business in a country with a strong propensity for informal, relational exchanges, it may not be a good idea to insist on formalizing the contract right away; such a plan could backfire. Because such countries often have relatively weak legal systems, personal relationship building is often used to substitute for the lack of strong legal protection. Attitudes such as "business first, relationship afterwards" (have a drink *after* the negotiation) may clash with the norm that puts things the other way around (lavish entertainment first, talk about business later). We often hear that, because of their culture, the Chinese prefer to cultivate personal relationships (*guanxi*) first. This is *not* entirely

EXHIBIT 2.5 Implications for Action

- When entering a new country, do your homework and have a thorough understanding of the formal institutions governing firm behavior.
- When doing business in countries with a strong propensity for informal relational exchanges, insisting on formalizing the contract right away may backfire.

true. Investing in personal relationships up front may simply be the initial cost one has to pay if interested in eventually doing business together, given the absence of a strong and credible legal and regulatory regime in China. In other words, the value on personal relationships has as much to do with the absence of institutional constraints as it does with cultural norms. In fact, personal relationships are key

to business in a broad range of countries from Argentina to Zimbabwe, each with *different* cultural traditions. So the interest in cultivating what the Chinese call *guanxi*, the Russians call *blat*, or the Vietnamese call *guan he* is not likely to be driven by culture alone but more likely by these countries' common lack of formal market-supporting institutions.

ETHICAL DILEMMA

MANAGING POLITICAL RISK IN THE MIDDLE EAST: A FOCUS ON LIBYA

The Middle East is not known for political stability. Yet, multinational oil companies typically have to work with totalitarian governments in this oil-rich region if these multinationals desire to have a presence there. A crucial question is: What should these firms do when political risk in the region, or in a particular country, rises?

In 2011, this question has turned from being a theoretical one to a highly practical one. This is because starting in Tunisia, a series of protests and uprisings have engulfed the region since January 2011. While revolutions in Tunisia, Egypt, and Libya have captured significant media attention, what has been less reported (at least in the West) is the protests and uprisings in Algeria, Bahrain, Jordan, Kuwait, Lebanon, Morocco, Oman, Saudi Arabia, Syria, and Yemen. The spring of 2011 has quickly earned a special name, the Arab Spring, which will be recorded as a turning point in the history of the Middle East.

Nowhere are the decisions made by multinational executives more hair-raising than in Libya. Before 2011, Libya was Africa's third largest and the world's 17th largest oil producer, pumping out 1.6 million barrels (about 2% of world total) a day. Over 85% of its crude oil was exported. About a third of it went to Italy, 14% to Germany, 10% each to France and China, and 5% to the United States. Libya's state-owned National Oil Corporation (NOC) accounted for approximately 50% of the oil output, and the rest was produced by ENI of Italy; Statoil of Norway; Repsol of Spain; Wintershall (a subsidiary of BASF) of Germany; OMV of Austria; Gazprom of Russia; Sinopec of China; and ConocoPhillips, Occidental Petroleum, Marathon, and Hess of the United States. In addition, BP of Britain, Shell of the Netherlands, and ExxonMobil of the United States had signed leases but were still in exploration stages and were not producing oil when violence broke out.

The high-stakes drama in Libya started in February 2011, when protesters and government forces clashed. The confrontation quickly turned violent. It became a civil war between the rebel-controlled East (centered on Benghazi) and the government-controlled West (centered on Tripoli, the capital). As violence escalated, foreign governments ordered evacuations of their nationals, and so did multinational oil companies. Multinationals either completely shut down their production or left the remaining Libyans to run the uncertain operations.

In March 2011, in the face of a humanitarian disaster that would be unleashed by government forces approaching Benghazi, air strikes were launched by allied forces. Spearheaded by French, UK, and US forces in the initial salvos, the allied forces eventually included militaries from 17 countries. There are 13 from NATO countries, three from the Arab League (Jordan, Qatar, and United Arab Emirates), and one country that is neither a member of NATO nor

The two recent revolutions in Tunisia and Egypt were quick and had relatively few casualties. They lasted a couple of weeks and resulted in the departure of their dictators at a cost of about 200 deaths in Tunisia and 800 in Egypt. International forces did not intervene militarily. However, the civil war in Libya, now involving allied air strikes, has been significantly longer and more bloody, costing at least 10,000 casualties as of May 2011. The hope of early wins and Colonel Muammar Qaddafi's departure has evaporated. Among the allies, bickering over the lack of a clearly defined objective and exit strategy started from the beginning. Both the rebels and the pro-Qaddafi forces seem ready to dig in for the long haul.

While the decision to evacuate expatriates (foreign nationals) and shut down production was relatively straightforward, oil company executives, caught in the middle of all of the above, are scratching their heads regarding what to do *next*. Attacks on oil fields by the rebels, by the pro-Qaddafi forces, and by the allies have all been reported but seldom confirmed. Executives not only have fiduciary (required by law) responsibility to safeguard shareholders' assets, but also moral and ethical responsibility to look after employees and their families. Most of the employees are Libyan and have not been evacuated. About the remaining assets and employees in Libya, the CEO of Austria's OMV told reporters in April 2011, "We have no precise information at all; we have no official contact at all; we are dependent on random contact."

Italy's ENI, a big player in Libya, has to walk a fine line between the rebels and the regime. While ENI has shut down most production and has been talking with the rebels, it is still supplying natural gas to the government-controlled Tripoli. ENI is presumably doing this to both hedge its bets while the Qaddafi regime hangs on and also to fulfill some of its ethical responsibility to its gas clients stuck in a war zone. When the Italian government has called for Qaddafi's ouster and Italian fighters are dropping bombs on government forces, ENI's balancing act is extraordinarily challenging, and ENI "risks angering both sides no matter what they do," according to an expert.

US firms ConocoPhillips, Marathon, and Hess have taken a different approach, which is totally passive. They keep plans and opinions to themselves. Typical of an "ostrich" approach, a ConocoPhillips spokesman in April 2011 told reporters, "We do not have anyone available to discuss Libya." While nobody knows how the conflict will end and how long it will take, multinationals with abandoned assets and lost revenue in Libya cannot afford not to have any future plans. Stay tuned for how close these plans are to realities as the high drama unfolds.

Sources: "Islam and the Arab revolutions," *Economist*, 2 April 2011, 11; "The colonel is not beaten ..." *Economist*, 2 April 2011, 41, 43; "Where has Libya's oil gone?" *Bloomberg Businessweek*, 18

Emphasizing Cultures, ETHICS, & Norms

CHAPTER 3

OPENING CASE

Partying in Saudi Arabia

The Swiss unit of French engineering giant Alstom builds infrastructure projects, especially power stations, all over the world. As is typical for engineering and construction firms, Alstom often sends its engineers out on short-term expatriate assignments for a few months. These construction projects are typically in remote locations far away from major cities, and the engineers have to become accustomed to working with a local workforce and living in the local community. They thus have to learn to adapt—quickly.

Cultural differences often become most evident when people enjoy social events ranging from lunch meetings to parties. A Swiss Alstom engineer recalls his experience when partying with colleagues in Saudi Arabia:

Once there was a farewell for someone from the building site. On this occasion, there was a little celebration. We were told, at midday, that there would be a party after work. We waited and were wondering what would happen, where they would do it, and if they would bring something. There were neither chairs nor tables. Around 2 PM, they came with huge aluminum tablets, the size of a wagon wheel, filled up with rice, and in the middle a huge piece of mutton, grilled mutton. Finally, three or four of these tablets were on the floor of the workshop. They just put them on the floor! Of course we had cleaned up before. They came dressed in their celebratory dresses, and we expected some sort of ceremony. But they just sat down on the floor in the white gowns, around the tablets, and started eating.

The [Swiss] colleague who was with me was a vegetarian. He said, "I won't squat on the floor like that, and I won't eat anything either." Everyone had a piece of mutton in his hand—it was incredible. One would hold the mutton, and another pulled out a chunk and passed it to me: "Here, mutton, that's good, you must eat!" We had no plates, nothing. Everyone grabbed

LEARNING OBJECTIVES
After studying this chapter, you should be able to:

LO1 explain where informal institutions come from.

LO2 define culture and articulate its two main manifestations.

LO3 articulate three ways to understand cultural differences.

LO4 explain why understanding cultural differences is crucial for global business.

LO5 explain why ethics is important.

LO6 identify ways to combat corruption.

LO7 identify norms associated with strategic responses when firms deal with ethical challenges.

LO8 explain how you can acquire cross-cultural literacy.

from the party bowl, and scooped out a handful of rice. And now, my mate said: "I won't squat on the floor like that," and I said, "Come on, let's just sit down. You don't have to eat mutton, but you can at least do as if you are."

Our Saudi colleagues were very happy that we were there, and that they could invite us for this meal. It was important to them that we would participate. We had known these people from work, but still, initially, the atmosphere was a bit uncomfortable. We didn't know how to behave. But then, after we sat down, and meat was passed around, it became real interesting. We talked and relaxed. My mate also sat down and afterwards he said he enjoyed it very much. The English vocabulary of those people was quite limited, so we had to talk "with hands and feet." Even so, we

were chatting about work, what kind of rice this was, and what was in the rice. It was typical Saudi rice with raisins and the taste was quite fantastic. We couldn't talk much, the language barrier was just there. But then we picked up a few bits of Arabic, and the next morning we could say "Good morning" in Arabic. Every day a word more, they had immense joy hearing us speak Arabic.

Source: N. Felix, "Dann hat man es gewusst, und dann war gut," in M. Spisak and H. Stalder (eds.), *In der Fremde* (Bern, Switzerland: Haupt, 2007) 29–37. The original was in German, and was translated by Professor Klaus Meyer (University of Bath, UK). © Haupt Bern. Reproduced with permission.

Why does partying in Saudi Arabia involve picking meat from the same piece of mutton and scooping rice from the same bowl all using bare hands? Why did one Swiss colleague initially feel uncomfortable? Why did the other Swiss colleague (the author) have a different attitude when participating in this "strange" party? Why did the Saudi colleagues have immense joy when hearing Swiss colleagues speak a few words of Arabic? After the party, will the Swiss and Saudi colleagues work more closely and effectively? More fundamentally, what informal institutions govern individual behavior and firm behavior in different countries?

This chapter continues our coverage on the institution-based view, which began with formal institutions in Chapter 2. Now we will focus on informal institutions represented by cultures, ethics, and norms. As informal institutions, cultures, ethics, and norms play an important part in shaping the success and failure of firms around the globe. Remember that the institution-based view suggests two propositions. First, managers and firms rationally pursue their interests within a given institutional framework. Second, in situations where formal institutions are unclear or fail, informal institutions play a larger role in reducing uncertainty. The first proposition deals with both formal and informal institutions. But the second proposition hinges on the informal institutions we are about to discuss. As the Opening Case shows, informal institutions are about more than just how to wine and dine properly. Informal institutions can facilitate better relationships among people who come from different cultural backgrounds, which is why they deserve a great deal of our attention.

LO1 *Explain where informal institutions come from.*

WHERE DO INFORMAL INSTITUTIONS COME FROM?

Recall that any institutional framework consists of both formal and informal institutions. While formal institutions such as politics, laws, and economics (see Chapter 2) are important, they only make up a small (although important) part of the rules of the game that govern individual and firm behavior. As pervasive features of every economy, informal institutions can be found almost *everywhere*.

Where do informal institutions come from? They come from socially transmitted information and are a part of the heritage that we call cultures, ethics, and norms. Those within a society tend to perceive their own culture, ethics, and norms as "natural, rational, and morally right."[1] This self-centered mentality is known as **ethnocentrism**. For example, many Americans believe in "American exceptionalism," a view that holds the United States to be exceptionally well endowed to lead the

Ethnocentrism
A self-centered mentality held by a group of people who perceive their own culture, ethics, and norms as natural, rational, and morally right.

© iStockphoto.com/iofoto

world. The Chinese call China *zhong guo*, which literally means "the country in the middle" or "middle kingdom."

Recall from Chapter 2 that informal institutions are underpinned by the normative and cognitive pillars, while formal institutions are supported by the regulatory pillar. While the regulatory pillar clearly specifies the do's and don'ts, informal institutions, by definition, are more elusive. Yet, they are no less important. Thus it is imperative that we pay attention to three different informal institutions: culture, ethics, and norms.

LO2 Define culture and articulate its two main manifestations.

CULTURE

Out of many informal institutions, culture is probably the most frequently discussed. Before we can discuss its two major components—language and religion—first we must define culture.

Definition of Culture

Although hundreds of definitions of culture have appeared, we will use the definition proposed by the world's foremost cross-cultural expert, Geert Hofstede, a Dutch professor. He defines **culture** as "the collective programming of the mind which distinguishes the members of one group or category of people from another."[2] Before proceeding, it is important to make two points to minimize confusion. First, although it is customary to talk about American culture or Brazilian culture, no strict one-to-one correspondence between cultures and nation-states exists. Many subcultures exist within multiethnic countries such as Belgium, Brazil, China, India, Indonesia, Russia, South Africa, Switzerland, and the United States (see In Focus). Second, culture has many layers, such as regional, ethnic, and religious. Even firms may have a specific organizational culture. Companies such as GE, Huawei, IKEA, and Toyota are well known for their distinctive corporate cultures (see the Closing Case on Siemens). Acknowledging the validity of these two points, we will, however, follow Hofstede by using the term "culture" to discuss *national* culture unless otherwise noted. While this is a matter of expediency, it is also a reflection of the institutional realities of the world with about 200 nation-states.[3]

Culture is made up of numerous elements. Although culture is too complex to dissect in the space we have here, we will highlight two major components of culture that impact global business: language and religion.

Language

Approximately 6,000 languages are spoken in the world. In terms of the number of native speakers, Chinese is the world's most widely spoken language (20% of the world population). English is a distant second (6% of the world population), followed closely by Hindi (5%) and Spanish (5%). Yet, the dominance of English as a global business language, or **lingua franca**, is unmistakable.[4] This is driven by two factors. First, English-speaking countries contribute the largest share (approximately 40%) of global output. Such economic dominance not only drives trade and investment ties between English-speaking countries and the rest of the world, but also generates a constant stream of products and services marketed in English. Think about the ubiquitous Hollywood movies, *Economist* magazine, and Google's search engine.

Second, recent globalization has called for the use of one common language. For firms headquartered in English-speaking countries as well as Scandinavia and the Netherlands (where English is widely taught and spoken), using English to manage operations around the globe poses little difficulty. However, settling on a global language for the entire firm is problematic for firms headquartered in Latin countries (such as Italy) or Asian countries (such as Japan), in which English is not widely spoken. Yet, even in these firms, it is still difficult to insist on a language other than English as the global corporate *lingua franca*. Around the world, non-native speakers of English who can master English increasingly command a premium in jobs and compensation, and this fuels a rising interest in English. For example, consider the Taiwanese-born Hollywood director Ang Lee, Icelandic-born singer Björk, and Colombian-born pop star Shakira.

On the other hand, the dominance of English may also lead to a disadvantage. Although native speakers of English have a great deal of advantage in global business, an expatriate manager who does not know the local language misses a lot of cultural subtleties and can only interact with locals fluent in English (see the Opening Case). Weak (or no) ability in foreign languages makes it difficult or even impossible to detect translation errors, which may result in embarrassments. For example, Rolls-Royce's Silver Mist was translated into German as "Silver Excrement." Coors Beer translated its slogan, "Turn it loose!" into Spanish as "Drink Coors and get

Shakira

Culture
The collective programming of the mind which distinguishes the members of one group or category of people from another.

Lingua franca
A global business language.

IN F☉CUS

Marketing to Hispanics in the United States

According to the US Census Bureau definition, Hispanics are individuals of Latin American descent living in the United States who may be of any race or ethnic group (such as white or black). With approximately 45 million people (15% of the US population), Hispanics represent the largest minority group in the United States. To put things in perspective, the US Hispanic population is larger than the population of Australia, Denmark, Finland, Norway, and Sweden *combined*. The print media advertising revenues for the US Hispanic market, $1.5 billion, have now surpassed the advertising revenues for the total UK magazine market.

How to effectively market products and services to this sizable group of customers is a leading challenge among many marketers. Although most US Hispanics speak some English, Spanish is likely to remain their language of preference. Approximately 38% of Hispanics surveyed report English-language ads to be less effective than Spanish-language ads in terms of recall. Approximately half of US Hispanics who watch TV during prime time watch Spanish language programming. The Spanish-language TV network, Univision, is now the fifth largest TV network in the United States, behind ABC, CBS, Fox, and NBC.

The typical debate in *international* marketing, standardization versus localization, is relevant here *within* a country. Direct translation of English-language campaigns is often ineffective, because it often misses the emotional and culturally relevant elements. Savvy marketers thus call for "transcreation." For instance, Taco Bell's tagline "Think outside the bun" evolved into a Hispanic adaption: "*No solo de pan vive el hombre*" ("A man does not live by bread alone"). Volkswagen completely changed its "Drivers Wanted" English slogan, and marketed to US Hispanics with a new slogan, "*Agarra Calle*" ("Hit the Road"), with a specific, Spanish-language website agarracalle.com. When marketing its minivans on TV, Chrysler showed a grandfather figure engaged in a puppet show at a child's birthday party—a traditional way for Hispanics to entertain children.

Interestingly, although about 60% of the US Hispanic population can trace their roots to Mexican heritage, direct importation of ads used in Mexico may not necessarily be successful either. The reasons are twofold. First, the US Hispanic culture, with influences from numerous other Latin American countries, is much more diverse than the Mexican culture. Second, mainstream (Anglo) media in the United States has asserted substantial influence on US Hispanics. A case in point is that 40% of Spanish-dominant Hispanics regularly watch English-language TV programming.

Overall, US Hispanics possess a distinctive cultural identity that is neither mainstream (Anglo) American nor pure Mexican. One size does not fit all. Any firm interested in marketing products and services to the "US market" needs to use both caution and creativity when marketing to Hispanics.

Sources: N. Singh and B. Bartikowski, "A cross-cultural analysis of print advertising targeted to Hispanic and non-Hispanic American consumers," *Thunderbird International Business Review*, 51 (2009): 151–164; *Advertising and Marketing Review*, 2009, Hispanic marketing, available online at http://www.admarketreview.com; US Census Bureau, 2011, Hispanics in the United States, available online at http://www.census.gov.

© Ariel Skelley/Blend Images/Jupiterimages

diarrhea!" Chevrolet marketed its Nova car in Latin America with disastrous results—"*No va*" means "no go" in Spanish.[5] To avoid such embarrassments, you will be better off if you can pick up at least one foreign language during your university studies.

Religion

Religion is another major manifestation of culture. Approximately 85% of the world's population report having some

PengAtlas Map

religious belief. PengAtlas Map 5 shows the geographical distribution of different religious heritages. The four leading religions are Christianity (approximately 1.7 billion adherents), Islam (1 billion), Hinduism (750 million), and Buddhism (350 million). Of course, not everybody claiming to be an adherent actively practices a religion. For instance, some Christians may go to church only *once* every year—at Christmas.

Because religious differences have led to numerous challenges, knowledge about religions is crucial

36

Part I: Laying Foundations

EXHIBIT 3.1 High-Context Versus Low-Context Cultures

| High Context | Chinese | Korean | Japanese | Arab | | Spanish | American, British, Canadian | Scandinavian | German, Swiss | Low Context |

© Cengage Learning 2013

even for *non*-religious managers. For example, in Christian countries, the Christmas season represents the peak in shopping and consumption. Half of toy sales for a given year in the United States occur during the month before Christmas. Since American kids consume half of the world's toys and virtually all toys are made outside the United States (mostly in Asia), this means 25% of the world toy output is sold in one country in a month, thus creating severe production, distribution, and coordination challenges. For toy makers and stores, missing the boat from Asia, whose transit time is at least two weeks, can literally devastate an entire holiday season and probably the entire year.

> **Articulate three ways to understand cultural differences.**

> **Explain why understanding cultural differences is crucial for global business.**

CLASSIFYING CULTURAL DIFFERENCES

Before reading this chapter, every reader already knows that cultures are different. There is no controversy in stating that the Indian culture is different from the Russian culture. But, how are the Indian and Russian cultures *systematically* different? This section outlines three different ways to systematically understand cultural differences: (1) the context approach, (2) the cluster approach, and (3) the dimension approach.

The Context Approach

Of the three main approaches to understanding cultural difference, the context approach is the most straightforward because it relies on a single dimension: context.[6] **Context** is the background against which interaction takes place. Exhibit 3.1 outlines a spectrum of countries along the dimension of low versus high context. In **low-context cultures** such as North American and Western European countries, communication is usually taken at face value without much reliance on unspoken conditions or assumptions, which are features of context. In other words, "no" means "no." On the other hand, in **high-context cultures** such as Arab and Asian countries, communication relies heavily on unspoken conditions or assumptions, which are

as important as the words used. "No" does not necessarily mean "no," and you must rely much more on the context in order to understand just what "no" means.

Why is context important? Failure to understand the differences in interaction styles may lead to misunderstandings. For example, in Japan, a high-context culture, negotiators prefer not to flatly say "no" to a business request. They will say something like "We will study it" or "We will get back to you later." Their negotiation partners are supposed to understand the context of these unenthusiastic responses and interpret them as essentially "no," even though the word "no" is never explicitly said. By contrast, lawyers in the United States, a low-context culture, are included in negotiations to essentially help remove the context—a contract should be as straightforward as possible, and there should be no room for parties to read between the lines. But negotiators from high-context cultures such as China often prefer *not* to involve lawyers until the very last phase of contract drafting. In high-context cultures, initial rounds of negotiations are supposed to create the context for mutual trust and friendship. For individuals brought up in high-context cultures, decoding the context and acting accordingly becomes second nature. Straightforward communication and confrontation, typical in low-context cultures, often baffle them.

The Cluster Approach

The cluster approach groups countries that share similar cultures together as one **cluster.** Exhibit 3.2 on the next page shows three influential sets of clusters. This table is the first time these three major systems of cultural clusters are compiled side by side. Viewing them together can allow us to see their similarities and differences. The first is the Ronen and Shenkar clusters, proposed by management professors Simcha Ronen and Oded Shenkar.[7] In alphabetical order, these clusters are Anglo, Arabic, Far Eastern, Germanic, Latin American, Latin European,

Context
The background against which interaction takes place.

Low-context culture
A culture in which communication is usually taken at face value without much reliance on unspoken conditions or assumptions.

High-context culture
A culture in which communication relies heavily on the underlying unspoken conditions or assumptions, which are as important as the words used.

Cluster
A group of countries that have similar cultures.

EXHIBIT 3.2 Cultural Clusters

Ronen and Shenkar Clusters	GLOBE Clusters	Huntington Civilizations
Anglo	Anglo	Western (1)
Arabic	Middle East	Islamic
Far East	Confucian Asia	Confucian (Sinic)
Germanic	Germanic Europe	Western (2)
Latin America	Latin America	Latin American
Latin Europe	Latin Europe	Western (3)
Near Eastern	Southern Asia	Hindu
Nordic	Nordic Europe	Western (4)
Central and Eastern Europe	Eastern Europe	Slavic-Orthodox
Sub-Saharan Africa	Sub-Saharan Africa	African
Independents: Brazil, India, Israel, Japan		Japanese

Sources: R. House, P. Hanges, M. Javidan, P. Dorfman, and V. Gupta, eds., *Culture, Leadership, and Organizations: The GLOBE Study of 62 Societies* (Thousand Oaks, CA: Sage, 2004); S. Huntington, *The Clash of Civilizations and the Remaking of World Order* (New York: Simon & Schuster, 1996); M. W. Peng, C. Hill, and D. Wang, "Schumpeterian dynamics versus Williamsonian considerations," *Journal of Management Studies* 37 (2000): 167–184; S. Ronen and O. Shenkar, "Clustering countries on attitudinal dimension," *Academy of Management Review* 10 (1985): 435–454. For Western civilization, Huntington does not use such labels as Western 1, 2, 3, and 4 as in the table. They were added by the present author to establish some rough correspondence with the respective Ronen and Shenkar and GLOBE clusters.

Near Eastern, and Nordic. Ronen and Shenkar originally classified these eight clusters, which cover 44 countries. They classified Brazil, India, Israel, and Japan as independents. Upon consultation with Shenkar, my colleagues and I more recently added Central and Eastern Europe and sub-Saharan Africa as two new clusters.[8]

The second set of clusters is called the GLOBE clusters, named after the Global Leadership and Organizational Behavior Effectiveness project led by management professor Robert House.[9] The GLOBE project identifies ten clusters and covers 62 countries. Five of the clusters use labels identical to the Ronen and Shenkar clusters. The GLOBE's Anglo, Germanic Europe, Latin America, Latin Europe, and Nordic Europe clusters roughly (but not completely) correspond with the respective Ronen and Shenkar clusters. But Ronen and Shenkar's Latin America cluster does not include Brazil (which is regarded as an independent), whereas GLOBE's includes Brazil. In addition, GLOBE has the clusters of Confucian Asia, Eastern Europe, Middle East, Southern Asia, and sub-Saharan Africa.

The third set of clusters is the Huntington civilizations, popularized by political scientist Samuel Huntington. Huntington includes eight civilizations, in theory covering *every* country. A **civilization** is "the highest cultural grouping of people and the broadest level of cultural identity people have."[10] Huntington divides the world into eight

Civilization
The highest cultural grouping of people and the broadest level of cultural identity people have.

civilizations: African, Confucian (Sinic), Hindu, Islamic, Japanese, Latin American, Slavic-Orthodox, and Western. While this classification shares a number of similarities with the Ronen and Shenkar and GLOBE clusters, Huntington's Western civilization is a very broad cluster that is subdivided into Anglo, Germanic, Latin European, and Nordic clusters by Ronen and Shenkar and by GLOBE. In addition to such an uncontroversial classification scheme, Huntington has advanced a highly controversial idea that Western civilization will clash with the Islamic and Confucian civilizations in the years to come. Incidents such as 9/11, the 2003 war in Iraq, and more recently the 2011 air attacks launched by Western allies on Libya, have often been cited as evidence of such a clash.

For our purposes, we do not need to debate the validity of Huntington's provocative thesis of the "clash of civilizations"; we will leave that debate to your political science or international relations classes. However, we do need to appreciate the underlying idea that people and firms are more comfortable doing business with other countries within the same cluster/civilization. Having a common language, history, and religion as well as common customs reduces the liability of foreignness when operating in another country but within the same cluster/civilization (see Chapter 1). For example, Hollywood movies are more likely to succeed in English-speaking countries. Most foreign investors in China are from Hong Kong and Taiwan; they are not very "foreign." Brazilian firms enjoy doing business in Africa's Angola and Mozambique, which are also Portuguese-speaking countries.

EXHIBIT 3.3 Hofstede Dimensions of Culture

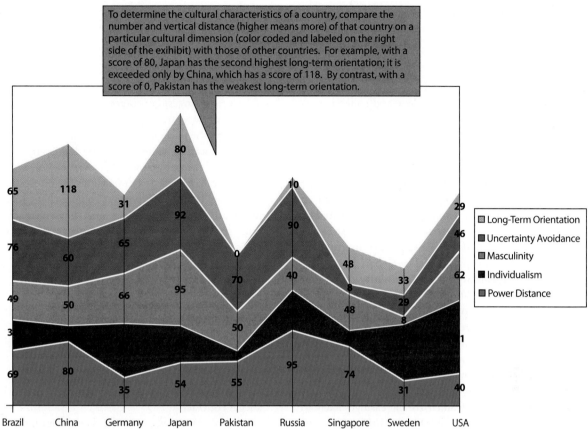

To determine the cultural characteristics of a country, compare the number and vertical distance (higher means more) of that country on a particular cultural dimension (color coded and labeled on the right side of the exihibit) with those of other countries. For example, with a score of 80, Japan has the second highest long-term orientation; it is exceeded only by China, which has a score of 118. By contrast, with a score of 0, Pakistan has the weakest long-term orientation.

Legend:
- Long-Term Orientation
- Uncertainty Avoidance
- Masculinity
- Individualism
- Power Distance

Countries: Brazil, China, Germany, Japan, Pakistan, Russia, Singapore, Sweden, USA

Sources: G. Hofstede, "Cultural constraints in management theories," *Academy of Management Executive* 7, no. 1 (1993): 81–94 and G. Hosftede, *Cultures and Organizations: Software of the Mind* (New York: McGraw-Hill, 1997) 25, 26, 53, 84, 113, 166. For updates, see http://www.geerthofstede.com.

The Dimension Approach

While both the context and cluster approaches are interesting, the dimension approach is more influential. The reasons for such influence are probably twofold. First, insightful as the context approach is, it represents only one dimension. What about other dimensions? Second, the cluster approach has relatively little to offer regarding differences of countries *within* one cluster. For example, what are the differences between Argentina and Chile, both of which belong to the same Latin America cluster according to Ronen and Shenkar and GLOBE? By focusing on multiple dimensions of cultural differences both within and across clusters, the dimension approach aims to overcome these limitations. While there are several competing frameworks, the work of Hofstede and his colleagues is by far the most influential and thus our focus here.

Hofstede and his colleagues have proposed five dimensions, illustrated in Exhibit 3.3. First, **power distance** is the extent to which less powerful members within a country expect and accept that power is distributed unequally. For example, in high power distance Brazil, the richest 10% of the population pockets approximately 50% of the national in-

come, and everybody accepts this as the way it is. In low power distance Sweden, the richest 10% only obtains 22% of the national income.[11] Major differences occur even within the same cluster. For example, in the United States, subordinates often address their bosses by their first names, a reflection of a relatively low power distance. While your boss, Mary or Joe, still has the power to fire you, the distance appears to be shorter than if you have to address this person as Mrs. Y or Dr. Z. In low power distance American universities, all faculty members, including the lowest-ranked assistant professors, are commonly addressed as "Professor A." In high power distance British universities, only full professors are allowed to be called "Professor B" (everybody else is called "Dr. C" or "Ms. D" if D does not have a PhD). German universities are perhaps most extreme: Full professors with PhDs need to be honored as "Prof. Dr. X."

Second, **individualism** refers to the idea that an

Power distance
The extent to which less powerful members within a culture expect and accept that power is distributed unequally.

Individualism
The idea that the identity of an individual is fundamentally his or her own.

individual's identity is fundamentally his or her own, whereas **collectivism** refers to the idea that an individual's identity is fundamentally tied to the identity of his or her collective group, be it a family, village, or company. In individualistic societies, led by the United States, ties between individuals are relatively loose and individual achievement and freedom are highly valued. In collectivist societies such as many countries in Africa, Asia, and Latin America, ties between individuals are relatively close and collective accomplishments are often sought after. In Chinese restaurants, most dishes are served "family style" to be shared by all the people around the table. In American restaurants, most dishes are served "individual style" to be enjoyed only by the particular persons who order them. Shown in our Opening Case, some Swiss engineers who came from an individualistic culture were astonished at a party hosted by their collectivistic colleagues in Saudi Arabia, where everybody would pick meat from the same piece of mutton and scoop rice from the same party bowl using bare hands.

Third, the **masculinity** versus **femininity** dimension refers to sex role differentiation. In every traditional society, men tend to have occupations, such as politician, soldier, or executive, which reward assertiveness. Women, on the other hand, usually work in caring professions such as teaching and nursing in addition to being homemakers. High-masculinity societies (led by Japan) continue to maintain a sharp role differentiation along gender lines. In low-masculinity societies (led by Sweden), women are increasingly likely to become politicians, scientists, and soldiers (think about the movie *GI Jane*), and men frequently assume the role of nurses, teachers, and househusbands.

Fourth, **uncertainty avoidance** refers to the extent to which members in a culture accept or avoid ambiguous situations and uncertainty. Members of high uncertainty avoidance cultures (led by Greece) place a premium on job security and retirement benefits. They also tend to resist change, which often creates uncertainty. Low uncertainty avoidance cultures (led by Singapore) are characterized by a greater willingness to take risks and less resistance to change.

Finally, **long-term orientation** emphasizes perseverance and savings for future betterment. China, which has the world's longest continuous written history of approximately 4,000 years and the highest contemporary savings rate, leads the pack. On the other hand, members of short-term orientation societies (led by Pakistan) prefer quick results and instant gratification.

Overall, Hofstede's dimensions are interesting and informative. It is also important to note that Hofstede's dimensions are not perfect and have attracted some criticisms.[12] However, it is fair to suggest that these dimensions represent a *starting point* for us as we try to figure out the role of culture in global business.

Culture and Global Business

A great deal of global business activity is consistent with the context, cluster, and dimension approaches to cultural differences. For instance, the average length of contracts is longer in low-context countries such as Germany than in high-context countries such as Vietnam, where a lot of agreements are unspoken and not necessarily put in a legal contract.

Also, as pointed out by the cluster approach, firms are a lot more serious in preparation when doing business with countries in other clusters compared to how they deal with fellow countries within the same cluster. Countless new books in English have recently been published on how to do business in China. Two decades ago, gurus wrote about how to do business in Japan. Evidently, there is a huge demand for English-speaking business people to read such books before heading to China and Japan. But has anyone ever seen a book in English on how to do business in Canada?

Hofstede's dimension approach can be illustrated by numerous real-world examples. For instance, managers in

Collectivism
The idea that an individual's identity is fundamentally tied to the identity of his or her collective group.

Masculinity
A relatively strong form of societal-level sex-role differentiation whereby men tend to have occupations that reward assertiveness and women tend to work in caring professions.

Femininity
A relatively weak form of societal-level sex-role differentiation whereby more women occupy positions that reward assertiveness and more men work in caring professions.

Uncertainty avoidance
The extent to which members of a culture accept or avoid ambiguous situations and uncertainty.

Long-term orientation
A perspective that emphasizes perseverance and savings for future betterment.

The dimensional approach may help explain the 2011 Greek protests against reduced job security and retirement benefits. Greece is considered a "high uncertainty avoidance culture," which means its people will generally resist change and the uncertainty it brings

high power distance countries such as France and Italy have a greater tendency for centralized authority. Although widely practiced in low power distance Western countries, asking for feedback and participation from subordinates—known as empowerment—is often regarded as a sign of weak leadership and low integrity in high power distance countries such as Egypt, Russia, and Turkey.

Individualism and collectivism also affect business activities. Individualist US firms may often try to differentiate themselves, whereas collectivist Japanese firms tend to follow each other. Because entrepreneurs stick their necks out by founding new firms, individualistic societies tend to foster a relatively higher level of entrepreneurship.

Likewise, masculinity and femininity affect managerial behavior. The stereotypical manager in high-masculinity societies is "assertive, decisive, and aggressive," and the

force, typical of a country with a relatively higher level of femininity. Yet, its US division reportedly tolerated sexual discrimination and sexual harassment behaviors. In 1998, Mitsubishi paid $34 million to settle these charges in the United States.

LO5 *Explain why ethics is important.*

LO6 *Identify ways to combat corruption.*

ETHICS

Cross-cultural differences can be interesting. But they can also be unethical, all depending on the institutional frameworks in which firms are embedded. This is discussed next.

Sensitivity to cultural differences does not guarantee success but can at least avoid blunders.

---

word "aggressive" carries positive connotations. In contrast, high-femininity societies generally consider "aggressive" a negative term, and managers are "less visible, intuitive rather than decisive, and accustomed to seeking consensus."[13]

Managers in low uncertainty avoidance countries such as Britain rely more on experience and training, whereas managers in high uncertainty avoidance countries such as China rely more on rules. In addition, cultures with a long-term orientation are likely to nurture firms with long horizons. For example, Japan's Matsushita has a 250-year plan, which was put together in the 1930s.[14] While this is certainly an extreme case, Japanese and Korean firms tend to focus more on the long term. In comparison, Western firms often focus on relatively short-term profits (often on a *quarterly* basis).

Overall, there is strong evidence for the importance of culture. Sensitivity to cultural differences does not guarantee success but can at least avoid blunders. For instance, a Chinese manufacturer exported to the West a premium brand of battery called White Elephant without knowing the meaning of this phrase in Western culture. In another example, when a French manager (a man) was transferred to a US subsidiary and met his American secretary (a woman) for the first time, he greeted her with an effusive cheek-to-cheek kiss, a harmless "Hello" in France. However, the secretary later filed a complaint for sexual harassment. More seriously, Mitsubishi Motors encountered major problems when operating in the United States. While Japan leads the world in masculinity, the company's US facilities had more female participation in the labor

Definition and Impact of Ethics

Ethics refers to the principles, standards, and norms of conduct that govern individual and firm behavior. Ethics is not only an important part of informal institutions but is also deeply reflected in formal laws and regulations. To the extent that laws reflect a society's minimum standards of conduct, there is a substantial overlap between what is ethical and what is legal as well as between what is unethical and what is illegal. However, in some cases, what is legal may be unethical. For example, mass lay-offs are legal, but are widely viewed as unethical by people in many countries.

Recent scandals have pushed ethics to the forefront of global business discussions. Numerous firms have introduced a **code of conduct**—a set of guidelines for making ethical decisions. But firms' ethical motivations are still subject to debate. Three views have emerged:

- A *negative view* suggests that firms may simply jump onto the ethics bandwagon under social pressure to *appear* more legitimate without necessarily becoming better.
- A *positive view* maintains that some (although not all) firms may be self-motivated to do it right regardless of social pressure.
- An *instrumental view* believes that good ethics may simply be a useful instrument to help make money.

Ethics
The principles, standards, and norms of conduct that govern individual and firm behavior.

Code of conduct
A set of guidelines for making ethical decisions.

Perhaps the best way to appreciate the value of ethics is to examine what happens after some crisis. As a reservoir of goodwill, the value of an ethical reputation is *magnified* during a time of crisis. One study found that any US firm engulfed in crisis (such as the *Exxon Valdez* oil spill) takes an average hit of 8% of their market value in the first week. After ten weeks, however, firms in the study with positive ethical reputations actually saw their stock value *rise* 5%, whereas the stock of those without such reputations dropped 15%.[15] Ironically, catastrophes may allow more ethical firms to shine. The upshot seems to be that ethics pays.

Managing Ethics Overseas

Managing ethics overseas is challenging because what is ethical in one country may be unethical elsewhere. There are two schools of thought.[16] First, **ethical relativism** follows the cliché, "When in Rome, do as the Romans do." If Muslim countries discriminate against women, so what? Likewise, if industry rivals in China can fix prices, who cares? Isn't that what "Romans" do in "Rome"? Second, **ethical imperialism** refers to the absolute belief that "There is only one set of Ethics (with a capital E), and we have it." Americans are especially renowned for believing that their ethical values should be applied universally. For example, since sexual discrimination and price fixing are wrong in the United States, they must be wrong everywhere. In practice, however, neither of these schools of thought is realistic. At the extreme, ethical relativism would have to accept any local practice, whereas ethical imperialism may cause resentment and backlash among locals.

Three middle-of-the-road guiding principles have been proposed by Thomas Donaldson, a business ethicist. These are shown in Exhibit 3.4. First, respect for human dignity and basic rights—such as concern for health, safety, and the need for education rather than working at a young age—should determine the absolute, minimal ethical thresholds for *all* operations around the world.

Second, firms should respect local traditions. If a firm bans giving gifts, it can forget about doing business in China and Japan, where gift giving is part of the business norm. While hiring employees' children and relatives instead of more qualified applicants is illegal in the United States under equal opportunity laws, it is rou-

tine practice for Indian companies and is expected to strengthen employee loyalty. What should US companies setting up subsidiaries in India do? Donaldson advises that such nepotism is not necessarily wrong, at least not in India.

Finally, respect for institutional context calls for a careful understanding of local institutions. Codes of conduct banning bribery are not very useful unless accompanied by guidelines for the scale and scope of appropriate gift giving/receiving. Citigroup allows employees to accept noncash gifts whose nominal value is less than $100. The *Economist* allows its journalists to accept any gift that can be consumed in a single day; a bottle of wine is acceptable, but a case of wine is not.[17] Overall, these three principles, although far from perfect, can help managers make decisions about which they may feel relatively comfortable.

Ethics and Corruption

Ethics helps to combat **corruption**, often defined as the abuse of public power for private benefits usually in the form of bribery, in cash or in kind.[18] Competition should be based on products and services, but corruption distorts that basis, causing misallocation of resources and slowing economic development. Transparency International, headquartered in Berlin, Germany, is probably the most influential anti-corruption nongovernmental organization (NGO). It found a strong correlation between a high level of corruption and a low level of economic development. In other words, corruption and poverty go together. Some evidence indicates that corruption discourages foreign direct investment (FDI). If the level of corruption in Singapore, which is very low, were to increase to the mid-range level in Mexico, it reportedly would have the same negative effect on FDI inflows as raising the tax rate by 50%.[19]

Around the world, the amount of bribes paid is estimated to be $1 trillion, which is about 1/60th (or 1.7%) of global GDP.[20] In the global fight against corruption,

© iStockphoto.com/Jin Kim

Ethical relativism
A perspective that suggests that all ethical standards are relative.

Ethical imperialism
The absolute belief that "there is only one set of Ethics (with a capital E), and we have it."

Corruption
The abuse of public power for private benefits, usually in the form of bribery.

EXHIBIT 3.4 Managing Ethics Overseas: Three Approaches

- Respect for human dignity and basic rights
- Respect for local traditions
- Respect for institutional context

Sources: T. Donaldson, "Values in tension: Ethics away from home," *Harvard Business Review* (September-October 1996): 4–11 and J. Weiss, *Business Ethics*, 4th ed. (Cincinnati: South-Western Thomson, 2006).

EXHIBIT 3.5 Strategic Responses to Ethical Challenges

Strategic Responses	Strategic Behaviors	Examples in the Text
Reactive	Deny responsibility; do less than required	Ford Pinto safety (the 1970s)
Defensive	Admit responsibility but fight it; do the least that is required	Nike sweatshops (the early 1990s)
Accommodative	Accept responsibility; do all that is required	Toyota recalls (2009–2011); Ford Explorer rollovers (the 2000s)
Proactive	Anticipate responsibility; do more than is required	BMW recycling (the 1990s)

the Foreign Corrupt Practices Act (FCPA) was enacted by the US Congress in 1977 and bans bribery of foreign officials. Many US firms complain that the act has unfairly restricted them. They also point out that overseas bribery expenses were often tax deductible (!) in many EU countries such as Austria, France, and Germany until the late 1990s. Even with the FCPA, however, there is no evidence that US firms are inherently more ethical than others. The FCPA itself was triggered in the 1970s by investigations of many corrupt US firms. Even the FCPA makes exceptions for small grease payments to get through customs abroad. Most alarmingly, the World Bank reported that despite over three decades of FCPA enforcement, US firms "exhibit systematically *higher* levels of corruption" than other firms in the Organization for Economic Co-operation and Development (OECD).[21]

Overall, the FCPA can be regarded as an institutional weapon in the global fight against corruption. Despite the FCPA's formal *regulatory* teeth, for a long time it had neither a *normative* pillar nor a *cognitive* pillar. Until recently, the norm among many other OECD firms was to pay bribes first and get tax deductions later, a clear sign of ethical relativism (see the Closing Case on Siemens). Only in 1997 did the OECD Convention on Combating Bribery of Foreign Public Officials commit all 30 member countries (essentially all developed economies) to criminalize bribery. The regulation went into force in 1999. A more ambitious campaign is the UN Convention against Corruption, signed by 106 countries in 2003 and activated in 2005. If every country criminalizes bribery and every firm resists corruption, their combined power will eradicate it.[22] But this will not happen unless FCPA-type legislation is institutionalized and *enforced* in every country.

> **LO7** *Identify norms associated with strategic responses when firms deal with ethical challenges.*

NORMS AND ETHICAL CHALLENGES

As an important informal institution, **norms** are the prevailing practices of relevant players—the proverbial "everybody else"—that affect the focal individuals and firms. How firms strategically respond to ethical challenges is often driven, at least in part, by norms. Four broad strategic responses are (1) reactive strategy, (2) defensive strategy, (3) accommodative strategy, and (4) proactive strategy. These are illustrated in Exhibit 3.5.

A **reactive strategy** is passive. Firms do not feel compelled to act when problems arise, and denial is usually the first line of defense. In the absence of formal regulation, the need to take action is neither internalized through cognitive beliefs nor embodied in any practicable norm. For example, in the early 1970s, Ford marketed the Pinto car even though the company knew the gas tank had a fatal design flaw that made the car susceptible to exploding in rear-end collisions. Citing high costs, Ford decided against adding an $11-per-car improvement. Sure enough, accidents happened and people were burned and killed in Pintos. Ford refused to recall the Pinto until 1978. Then, under intense formal pressures from the government and informal pressures from the media and consumer groups, Ford belatedly recalled all 1.5 million Pintos.

A **defensive strategy** focuses on regulatory compliance. In the early 1990s, media and activist groups charged Nike with running sweatshops, although there was no existing regulation prohibiting sweatshops. Nike's initial response was "We don't make shoes," because Nike did not directly own and manage the factories. Its contractors in Indonesia and Vietnam were in charge. This response, however, failed to convey that Nike felt any ethical responsibility. Only when several senators began to suggest legislative solutions—regulations with which Nike would need to comply—did Nike become more serious.

In an **accommodative strategy**, accepting responsibility becomes an organizational norm, and cognitive beliefs and values are increasingly internalized. These normative and cognitive values may be shared by a number of

Norms
The prevailing practices of relevant players that affect the focal individuals and firms.

Reactive strategy
A response to an ethical challenge that often involves denial and belated action to correct problems.

Defensive strategy
A response to an ethical challenge that focuses on regulatory compliance.

Accommodative strategy
A response to an ethical challenge that involves accepting responsibility.

Are Cultures Converging or Diverging?

Every culture evolves and changes. But what is the *direction* of change? This question is the center of a great debate.

CONVERGENCE In this age of globalization, one side of the debate argues that there is a great deal of convergence, especially toward more modern, Western values such as individualism and consumerism. As evidence, convergence gurus point out the worldwide interest in Western products, such as Blackberry, iPad, Kindle, Levi's jeans, McDonald's, and MTV, especially among the youth.

DIVERGENCE Another side of the debate suggests that Westernization in consumption does not necessarily mean Westernization in values. In a most extreme example, on the night of September 10, 2001, the 9/11 terrorists drank American soft drinks, ate American pizzas, and enjoyed American movies—and then went on to kill thousands of Americans the next day. In another example, the increasing popularity of Asian foods (such as tofu and sushi) and games (such as Pokémon and Bakugan) in the West does not necessarily mean that Westerners are converging toward Asian values. In short, the world may continue to be characterized by cultural divergence.

A middle-of-the-road group makes two points. First, the end of the Cold War, the rise of the Internet, and the ascendance of English as the language of global business all offer evidence of some cultural convergence, at least on the surface and among the youth. For example, younger Chinese, Japanese, and Russian managers are typically more individualistic and less collectivistic than the average citizen of their respective countries. Second, deep down, cultural divergence may continue to be the norm. So perhaps a better term is "crossvergence," which acknowledges the validity of both sides of the debate. This idea suggests that when marketing products and services to younger customers around the world, a more global approach featuring uniform content and image may work, whereas local adaptation may be a must when dealing with older, more tradition-bound consumers.

Sources: National Commission on Terrorist Attacks on the United States, *The 9/11 Report* (New York: St Martin's, 2004) 364; M. Chen and D. Miller, "West meets East," *Academy of Management Perspectives* (November 2010): 17–24; H. Lin and S. Hou, "Managerial lessons from the East," *Academy of Management Perspectives* (November 2010): 6–16.

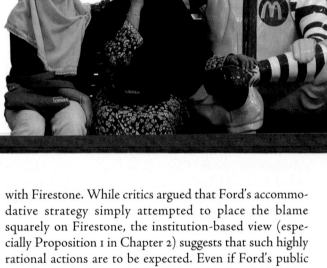

firms, leading to new industry norms. In other words, higher levels of ethical and moral responsibility, beyond simply the minimum of what is legally required, are accepted standards. During 2009 and 2010, Toyota initially was reluctant to recall 12 million vehicles, some of which had a tendency to suffer from unintended acceleration. In early 2011, Toyota recalled an additional 1.7 million vehicles for fuel leaks. This time, Toyota became more accommodative, aggressively carrying out recalls before they turned into a bigger mess.[23]

Companies can change their strategic response. Ford evidently learned the painful lesson from its Pinto fire fiasco in the 1970s. When Ford Explorer vehicles equipped with Firestone tires had a large number of fatal rollover accidents in 2000, Ford aggressively initiated a speedy recall, launched a media campaign featuring its CEO, and discontinued the 100-year-old relationship with Firestone. While critics argued that Ford's accommodative strategy simply attempted to place the blame squarely on Firestone, the institution-based view (especially Proposition 1 in Chapter 2) suggests that such highly rational actions are to be expected. Even if Ford's public relations campaign was only window dressing designed to make the company look good to the public, it publicized a set of ethical criteria against which the company could be judged and opened doors for more scrutiny by concerned stakeholders. It is probably fair to say that Ford was a better corporate citizen in 2000 than it was in 1975.

Finally, firms that take a **proactive strategy** anticipate institutional changes and do more than is required. In 1990, the German government proposed a "take-back" policy, requiring automakers to design cars whose components can be taken back by the same manufacturers for recycling. With this policy in mind, BMW anticipated its emerging responsibility and not only designed easier-to-disassemble cars but also enlisted the few high-quality dismantler firms as part of an exclusive recycling infrastructure.

Proactive strategy
A strategy that anticipates ethical challenges and addresses them before they happen.

Further, BMW actively participated in public discussions and succeeded in establishing its approach as the German national standard for automobile disassembly. Other automakers were thus required to follow BMW's lead. However, the other automakers had to fight over smaller, lower-quality dismantlers or develop in-house dismantling infrastructures from scratch. Through such a proactive strategy, BMW set a new industry standard for environmentally friendly norms in both car design and recycling. Overall, while there is probably a certain element of window dressing in proactive strategies, the fact that proactive firms are going beyond the current regulatory requirements is indicative of the normative and cognitive beliefs held by many managers at these firms on the importance of doing the right thing.

Explain how you can acquire cross-cultural literacy.

MANAGEMENT SAVVY

The institution-based view emphasizes the importance of informal institutions—cultures, ethics, and norms—as the soil in which business around the globe either thrives or stagnates. How does this perspective answer our funda-

EXHIBIT 3.6   Implications for Action

- Be prepared.
- Slow down.
- Establish trust.
- Understand the importance of language.
- Respect cultural differences.
- Understand that no culture is inherently superior in all aspects.

tions governing their behavior. For example, the two Swiss colleagues in the Opening Case would probably be less shocked if they had enough knowledge about the collectivistic nature of the Saudi (and Arabic) culture, which is different from the individualistic Western culture. Most of us probably did not realize that feeling free to say "no" when offered food or drink reflects a cultural underpinning of individualism. Refusing a friendly cup of coffee (or a friendly piece of mutton at a party) from a Saudi businessman may be considered an affront that should be avoided. Finally, *skills* are good practices based on awareness and knowledge of other cultures (see Exhibit 3.6).

While skills can be taught in a classroom, the most effective way to learn them is total immersion in a foreign culture. Even for gifted individuals, learning a new language

> **The best managers expect norms to shift over time and constantly decipher the changes in the informal rules of the game in order to take advantage of new opportunities.**

mental question: What determines the success and failure of firms around the globe? The institution-based view argues that firm performance is determined, at least in part, by the informal cultures, ethics, and norms governing firm behavior.

This emphasis on informal institutions suggests two broad implications for savvy managers around the globe. First, managers should enhance their **cultural intelligence**, defined as an individual's ability to understand and adjust to new cultures. Acquisition of cultural intelligence passes through three phases: awareness, knowledge, and skills. *Awareness* refers to the recognition of both the pros and cons of your own cultural mental software and the appreciation of people from other cultures. *Knowledge* refers to the ability to identify the symbols, rituals, and taboos in other cultures. Knowledge is also known as cross-cultural literacy. While you may not share (or may disagree) with their values, you will at least have a road map of the informal institu-

and culture well enough to function at a managerial level will take at least several months of full-time studies. Most employers do not give their expatriates that much time to learn before sending them abroad. Most expatriates are thus inadequately prepared, and the costs for firms, individuals, and families are tremendous (see Chapter 13). This means that you, a student studying this book, are advised to invest in your own career by picking up at least one foreign language, spending one semester (or year) abroad, and reaching out to make some international friends who are taking classes with you and perhaps even sitting next to you. Such an investment during university studies will make you stand out among the crowd and propel your future career to new heights.

Savvy managers should also be aware of the prevailing norms and their

Cultural intelligence
An individual's ability to understand and adjust to new cultures.

transitions globally. The norms around the globe in the 21st century are more culturally sensitive and more ethically demanding than, say, in the 1970s. This is not to suggest that every local norm needs to be followed. Failing to understand the changing norms or adapting to them in an insensitive and unethical way may lead to unsatisfactory or, worse, disastrous results. The best managers expect norms to shift over time and constantly decipher the changes in the informal rules of the game in order to take advantage of new opportunities. How BMW managers have proactively shaped the automobile recycling norms in Germany serves as a case in point. Firms that fail to realize the passing of old norms and adapt accordingly are likely to fall behind or even go out of business.

ETHICAL DILEMMA

SIEMENS NEEDS TO CLEAN UP AROUND THE GLOBE

Founded in 1847, Siemens, headquartered in Munich and Berlin, is an engineering conglomerate whose revenues in 2010 reached $103 billion from 190 countries. As a global firm with over 400,000 employees, Siemens is not only subject to German regulations, but also subject to regulations in many countries, especially in the United States since its shares have been publicly listed on the New York Stock Exchange since 2001.

In the late 2000s, Siemens found itself engulfed in a sea of scandals around the globe. In November 2007, Siemens disclosed in its Form 6-K to the US Securities and Exchange Commission (SEC) that authorities around the world were conducting investigations of Siemens "regarding allegations of public corruption, including criminal breaches of fiduciary duty including embezzlement, as well as bribery, money laundering, and tax evasion, among others." According to the report, authorities from the following countries/regions were involved:

Germany

- Brazil
- China
- Czech Republic
- European Union/ European Commission
- Germany
- Greece
- Hungary
- Indonesia
- Italy
- Japan
- Mexico
- New Zealand
- Norway
- Poland
- South Africa
- Switzerland
- Turkey
- United States

In the same report, Siemens disclosed that its internal investigation uncovered $1.9 billion in questionable payments made to outsiders by the company from 2000 to 2006. In its own words:

These payments raise concerns in particular under the Foreign Corrupt Practices Act (FCPA) of the United States, anti-corruption legislation in Germany, and similar legislation in other countries. The payments identified were recorded as deductible business expenses in prior periods [2000–2006] in determining income tax provisions . . . the Company's investigation determined that certain of these payments were non-deductible under tax regulations of Germany and other jurisdictions.

In December 2008, Siemens pleaded guilty to corruption charges and settled with

the US and German governments for a combined total of $1.6 billion in fines, including $800 million to US authorities. This represented the largest fine ever imposed in an FCPA case since the act was passed by Congress in 1977. Siemens was alleged to have bribed officials in Africa, Asia, Europe, the Middle East, and the Americas approximately 4,200 times to the tune of $1.4 billion between 2000 and 2006 with the goal of winning contracts abroad. Linda Thomsen of the SEC noted in a press release:

The scope of the bribery scheme is astonishing, and the tone set at the top at Siemens was a corporate culture in which bribery was tolerated and even rewarded at the highest levels of the company. The SEC portion of the Siemens settlement, $350 million in disgorgement, is by far the largest settlement amount ever obtained by the SEC under the FCPA. To put this in context, the largest prior SEC FCPA settlement was reached in 2007 and was for $33 million. The SEC settlement with Siemens is more than ten times that amount.

Joseph Persichini, Assistant Director of the Federal Bureau of Investigation (FBI), noted:

A massive, willful, and carefully orchestrated criminal corruption scheme. Their actions were not an anomaly. They were standard operating procedures for corporate

executives who viewed bribery as a business strategy.

However, the settlement stopped the case from going to trial in both the United States and Germany—although authorities in other countries may still pursue a court trial (for example, the Greek government in 2011 threatened to pursue Siemens in court). When asked why, despite such strong words, the US government had not pressed criminal charges against the company or its executives, Persichini said that Siemens had cooperated fully in the investigation, engaged in significant reforms, and hired a former German finance minister as an independent compliance monitor for the next four years. "In this case, one weighed all the factors," he said, "This was the right disposition. And the court agreed with our proposal."

During 2006–2008, in response to the scandals, Siemens undertook a number of measures: Its supervisory board established a compliance committee, its managing board engaged an external attorney to provide a protected communication channel for employees and third parties, the company appointed a chief compliance officer, marketed a compliance hotline to employees, and adopted a Global Amnesty Program for employees who voluntarily provided useful information regarding their wrongdoing. In an effort to distance itself from the scandals, Siemens in July 2007 broke convention from internal promotion and hired a non-German outsider—an Austrain executive, Peter Löscher, from pharmaceutical giant Merck—as CEO. In December 2008, after its guilty plea, Siemens released a statement, in which it noted that the US authorities recognized its "extraordinary cooperation" with the investigation as well as its recent compliance efforts. Siemens also noted that the US Defense Logistics Agency confirmed that "Siemens remains a responsible contractor for US government business." Gerhard Cromme, chairman of Siemens' supervisory board, noted in the statement:

United States

Siemens is closing a painful chapter in its history... For Siemens, the corruption cases in Germany and the United States are now over. Today marks the end of an unprecedented two-year effort to resolve extremely serious matters for the company. Based on robust leadership processes, Siemens has established a sustainable culture of compliance.... We regret what happened in the past. But we have learned from it and taken appropriate measures. Siemens is now a stronger company.

Talk is cheap, according to critics. Many critics are suspicious of whether the new measures would transform a "bad barrel." Within one week of the settlement, Siemens announced in late December 2008 that it won a $2.1 billion contract in Iraq for high-efficiency gas turbines. This would be one of the biggest orders Siemens ever booked in the Middle East. Critics are naturally suspicious of deals like this.

Since his arrival in 2007, the new CEO, in an effort to change the organizational culture, replaced almost the entire executive team and switched half of the middle managers. In an interview, Löscher called the bribery scandal "a catalytic event." He continued:

It would not have been possible to achieve what we achieved at this speed without this event, which made us question how to do things.... In hindsight, it is an extremely positive caesura point.

Sources: "How Siemens got its geist back," *Bloomberg Businessweek*, 31 January 2011, 18–20; "Siemens wins big Iraq contract after global corruption scandal," *Deutsche Well*, 22 December 2008, available online at http://www.dw-world.de; "Siemens makes $1.3 billion in plea deals," *Los Angeles Times*, 16 December 2008, available online at http://articles.latimes.com; M. Halper, "Siemens guilty of US corruption," *Managing Automation*, 16 December 2008, available online at http://www.managingautomation.com; Siemens AG, *Form 6-K Report of Foreign Private Issuer* (New York: SEC, 8 November 2007); www.siemens.com.

BY THE NUMBERS

6,000 approximate number of languages spoken in the world

1.7 approximate number of people (in billions) who adhere to Christianity

20 percent of world population that speaks Chinese (as a native language)

1 approximate number of people (in billions) who adhere to Islam

6 percent of world population that speaks English (as a native language)

250 number of years covered by Matsushita's business plan

1 estimated amount of bribes (in trillions of dollars) paid worldwide

Leveraging Resources & CAPABILITIES

CHAPTER 4

Saturna Capital: A Leading Company in Islamic Finance

Saturna Capital Corporation, adviser to both the Saturna Investment Trust and the Amana Mutual Funds Trust, is one of the world's most successful companies in the rapidly growing and specialized activity of Islamic investing. Saturna currently manages approximately $2.6 billion in assets, representing a tenfold increase since the beginning of 2005. The vast majority of these assets are invested in equities according to Islamic finance principles, which prohibit the use of interest and forbid investments in firms involved in alcohol, tobacco, and gambling activities. Indeed, the Amana Mutual Funds Trust's two largest equity mutual funds, the Amana Trust Income Fund (AMANX) and the Amana Trust Growth Fund (AMAGX), are recognized as the largest in the world that invest according to *sharia* (Islamic law).

Considering its unlikely location, Saturna's success within the global market of Islamic finance is even more remarkable. Its corporate headquarters is in the small city of Bellingham, Washington (population: 67,200), located about midway between the much larger cities of Seattle, Washington, and Vancouver, British Columbia. Saturna is named for one of the larger islands in northern Puget Sound's beautiful San Juan archipelago, easily visible from Bellingham. Furthermore, it is a relatively small company— operating with only about 40 employees. Therefore, Saturna provides an apt example of a firm's ability to transcend geographical barriers and compete on a global scale through persistent leverage of core competence.

In the mid-1980s, when Saturna's founder Nicholas Kaiser was initially approached by a group of Muslim investors with the idea for an Islamic mutual fund, Islamic investing was certainly off the radar screen of major financial players in the United States. In fact, the group's idea had already been rejected by one well-established

LEARNING OBJECTIVES

After studying this chapter, you should be able to:

LO1 define resources and capabilities.

LO2 explain how value is created from a firm's resources and capabilities.

LO3 articulate the difference between keeping an activity in-house and outsourcing it.

LO4 explain what a VRIO framework is.

LO5 explain how to use a VRIO framework to understand a firm's resources and capabilities.

LO6 identify four things you need to do as part of a successful career and business strategy.

© The Studio Dog/Photodisc/Jupiterimages

...... It was Kaiser's openness to learning about *sharia*-compliant investment principles and his willingness to enter uncharted territory that allowed him, as a non-Muslim, native-born American, to acquire a skill set that would prove to complement his portfolio management expertise. Today, Saturna is the beneficiary of the corporate-wide transfer of his highly developed knowledge of Islamic investing, which allows the company to compete successfully in an important global market.

To some extent, Saturna's rapid growth mirrors the rapid growth of the Islamic financial industry. By some estimates, the industry more than doubled in size during the last decade with the growth driven by, among other things, a surge in oil-related wealth. Nevertheless, Saturna's growth has markedly exceeded that of the industry as a whole—that includes hundreds of financial institutions located in major financial capitals that also compete for clients who want to invest in accordance with Islamic law. Saturna's competitors include such corporate behemoths as HSBC, Citicorp, Deutsche Bank, and UBS, as well as large banks headquartered in the Persian Gulf region and Southeast Asia, where the majority of the world's Muslims live.

In light of what many may see as formidable competitive disadvantages related to its location and relatively small size, how does one explain Saturna's remarkable success? One of the most compelling explanations is Kaiser's exceptional talent as an investment manager. The Amana Trust Income and Amana Trust Growth mutual funds are consistently ranked in the top of their peer categories for long-term performance, despite being measured against funds with no restrictions on where they can invest. While avoiding investments in banks and other financial companies (because they charge interest) proved fortuitous in the aftermath of the collapse of financial stocks in 2008, such limitations can handicap overall financial performance.

Saturna's outstanding corporate governance also undoubtedly contributes to its success. In particular, it has a sterling reputation for financial integrity, including vigilance in complying with mutual fund regulations. Its commitment to upholding the ethical principles of its investors is supported by its board of directors, mostly consisting of prominent Muslim community leaders, as well as its use of *sharia* scholars as advisors regarding its compliance with Islamic laws of investing. Saturna's director of Islamic investing, Monem Salam, serves as a vital interface between the company and the population of potential Muslim investors. Both a devout Muslim and an MBA graduate, Salam is very effective in ensuring that Saturna's investments meet the needs of its Muslim clientele as well as communicating Saturna's remarkable performance to potential investors.

The investment management business is ultimately about serving the needs of customers. Besides providing industry-leading financial returns, Saturna dedicates considerable resources to providing value-added services for its current customers and to the broader American Muslim community. For example, Saturna will estimate *zakah* (the percentage of investment earnings to set aside for charitable giving according to *sharia*) on behalf of investors in affiliated accounts. It also creates a worksheet to help investors save for *hajj* (a Muslim's obligatory pilgrimage to Mecca).

Perhaps the most impressive evidence of Saturna's success is the fact that many Amana Fund shareowners are not Muslim. They are quite happy to abide by the Islamic law and appreciate Saturna's uncompromising standards of customer service. Saturna and the dedicated efforts of its employees clearly demonstrate how a small firm in an unlikely location can cultivate a culture of principled financial operations and leverage a niche market strategy to earn respect and recognition in a global industry.

Sources: This case was written by Professor Steven Globerman (Kaiser Professor of International Business, Western Washington University). It is based on the author's interviews with Nick Kaiser; D. Kathman, 2009, Nick Kaiser, Saturna Capital, *Morningstar Advisor*, January 30.

Why is Saturna able to outcompete its much larger and more visible rivals in a global industry? What is so special about this company? The answer is that there must be certain resources and capabilities specific to Saturna that are not shared by its competitors. This insight has been developed into a resource-based view (see Chapter 1), which has emerged as one of the two core perspectives on global business.[1]

One leading tool in global business is **SWOT analysis**. A SWOT analysis determines a firm's strengths (S), weaknesses (W), opportunities (O), and threats (T). The institution-based view of global business we discussed in Chapters 2 and 3 deals with the *external* opportunities and threats, enabled and constrained by formal and informal rules of the game. The resource-based view, on the other hand, concentrates on a firm's *internal* strengths and weaknesses. In this chapter, we first define resources and capabilities. Then we discuss the value chain analysis, concentrating on the decision to keep an activity in-house or outsource it. We then focus on the VRIO framework centered on value (V), rarity (R), imitability (I), and organization (O).

SWOT analysis
An analytical tool for determining a firm's strengths (S), weaknesses (W), opportunities (O), and threats (T).

© iStockphoto.com/photovideostock

UNDERSTANDING RESOURCES AND CAPABILITIES

A basic proposition of the resource-based view is that a firm consists of a bundle of productive resources and capabilities. **Resources** are defined as "the tangible and intangible assets a firm uses to choose and implement its strategies."[2] There is some debate regarding the definition of capabilities. Some scholars define them as a firm's capacity to dynamically deploy resources, suggesting a potentially crucial distinction between resources and capabilities and resulting in a "dynamic capabilities" view.[3]

While scholars may debate the fine distinctions between resources and capabilities, these distinctions are likely to "become badly blurred" in practice.[4] For example, is Saturna's ability to successfully invest in firms that comply with Islamic finance principles a resource or capability? How about its ability to attract non-Muslim investors? For current and would-be managers, the key is to understand how these attributes help improve firm performance, not to figure out whether they should be labeled as resources or capabilities. Therefore, in this book, we will use the terms "resources" and "capabilities" *interchangeably* and often in *parallel*. In other words, **capabilities** are defined here the same as resources.

All firms, even the smallest ones, possess a variety of resources and capabilities. How do we meaningfully classify such diversity? A useful way is to separate the resources and capabilities into two categories: tangible and intangible (Exhibit 4.1). **Tangible resources and capabilities** are assets that are observable and easily quantified. They can be broadly organized in three subcategories.

First, *financial resources and capabilities* refer to the depth of a firm's financial pockets. Examples include the ability to generate internal funds and raise external capital. Saturna's ability to tap into the pool of funds from Muslim investors, discussed in the Opening Case, is such an example.

Second, *physical resources and capabilities* include plants, offices, equipment, their geographic locations, and access to raw materials and distribution channels. For example, it makes sense to attribute Amazon's success to its online savvy, as many people do. But a crucial reason why Amazon has emerged as the largest bookseller is that it has built some of the largest *brick-and-mortar* (physical) book warehouses in key locations throughout the United States.

Third, *technological resources and capabilities* are skills and assets that generate leading-edge products and services supported by patents, trademarks, copyrights, and trade secrets. For instance, over 60% of Canon's current products, including popular digital cameras and digital copiers, have been introduced during the past two years.

Intangible resources and capabilities are, by definition, harder to observe and more difficult (if not impossible) to quantify than tangible ones (see Exhibit 4.1). Yet, it is widely acknowledged that they must exist because no firm is likely to generate competitive advantage by relying on tangible resources and capabilities alone. We discuss three types of intangible assets.

First, *human resources and capabilities* include the knowledge, trust, and talents embedded within a firm that are not captured by its tangible systems and structures. For example, Dallas-based Southwest Airlines' dedicated employees are widely noted as a leading force behind its enviable performance.

Second, *innovation resources and capabilities* include a firm's assets and skills to research and develop new products and services as well as to create or restructure a production path or service organization. Apple, for instance, is renowned for its cool innovations.

Third, *reputational resources and capabilities* are a firm's abilities to develop and leverage its reputation as a solid provider of goods/services, an attractive employer, and/or a socially responsible corporate citizen. Reputation can be regarded as an outcome of a competitive process in which firms signal their attributes to constituents. For example, South-Western Cengage Learning's market-leading "global" books—*Global Business*, *Global Strategy*, and *GLOBAL* (this book)—enjoy a great reputation around the world and are studied by students in over 30 countries.

It is important to note that all resources and capabilities discussed here are

Resources (or capabilities)
The tangible and intangible assets a firm uses to choose and implement its strategies.

Tangible resources and capabilities
Assets that are observable and easily quantified.

Intangible resources and capabilities
Assets that are hard to observe and difficult (if not impossible) to quantify.

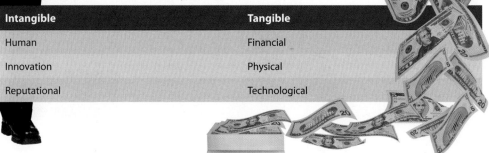

EXHIBIT 4.1 Examples of Resources and Capabilities

Intangible	Tangible
Human	Financial
Innovation	Physical
Reputational	Technological

© C Squared Studios/Photodisc/Getty Images / © iStockphoto.com/Andrew Dernie

merely *examples* and that they do not constitute an exhaustive list. As firms forge ahead, discovery and leveraging of new resources and capabilities are likely.

RESOURCES, CAPABILITIES, AND THE VALUE CHAIN

If a firm is a bundle of resources and capabilities, how do they come together to add value? A value chain analysis allows us to answer this question. Most value is created through a series of activities known as a **value chain**. The value chain, illustrated in Panel A of Exhibit 4.2, consists of steps in the process of turning inputs into outputs. Value is added at each stage of the chain, from R&D to marketing. The stages of the chain involve both primary activities (such as assembling a product) and support activities (such as creating an infrastructure to distribute it).[5] Movement along the chain is described as a stream. Activities that occur early in the process such as design are thought of as *upstream* activities, while later stages such as marketing are considered *downstream*.

Each activity requires a number of resources and capabilities. Value chain analysis forces managers to think about resources and capabilities at a very micro, activity-based level. Given that no firm is likely to have enough resources and capabilities to be good at all primary and support activities, the key is to examine whether the firm has resources and capabilities to perform a *particular activity* in a manner superior to competitors—a process known as **benchmarking** in SWOT analysis. If managers find that their firm's particular activity is unsatisfactory, a two-stage decision model can remedy the situation, as shown in Exhibit 4.3. In the first stage, managers ask: "Do we really need to perform this activity in-house?" Exhibit 4.4 introduces a framework to take a hard look at this question. The answer boils down to two factors: whether an activity is industry specific or common across industries and whether this activity is proprietary (firm specific) or not. So an activity that falls in Cell 2 of Exhibit 4.4 would be answered "No, we don't need to perform this activity in-house," because the activity has a

Value chain
A series of activities used in the production of goods and services that make a product or service more valuable.

Benchmarking
Examining whether a firm has resources and capabilities to perform a particular activity in a manner superior to competitors.

EXHIBIT 4.2 The Value Chain

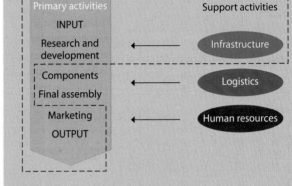

Panel A. An Example of Value Chain with Firm Boundaries

Primary activities
- INPUT
- Research and development
- Components
- Final assembly
- Marketing
- OUTPUT

Support activities
- Infrastructure
- Logistics
- Human resources

Panel B. An Example of Value Chain with Some Outsourcing

Primary activities
- INPUT
- Research and development
- Components
- Final assembly
- Marketing
- OUTPUT

Support activities
- Infrastructure
- Logistics
- Human resources

Note: Dashed lines represent firm boundaries.

© Cengage Learning 2013

© Inspirestock/Jupiterimages

EXHIBIT 4.3 A Two-Stage Decision Model in Value Chain Analysis

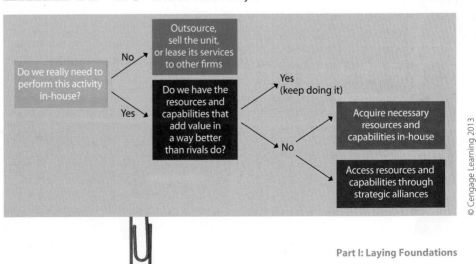

Do we really need to perform this activity in-house?

- No → Outsource, sell the unit, or lease its services to other firms
- Yes → Do we have the resources and capabilities that add value in a way better than rivals do?
  - Yes (keep doing it)
  - No → Acquire necessary resources and capabilities in-house
  - No → Access resources and capabilities through strategic alliances

© Cengage Learning 2013

EXHIBIT 4.4 In-House Versus Outsource

Commoditization versus proprietary nature of the activity

Industry specificity

	Industry specific	Common across industries	
High commoditization	Cell 1 Outsource	Cell 2 Outsource	
Proprietary (firm specific)	Cell 3 In-House	Cell 4 ???	

Note: At present, there are no clear guidelines for Cell 4, where firms either choose to perform activities in-house or outsource.

© Cengage Learning 2013

EXHIBIT 4.5 Location, Location, Location

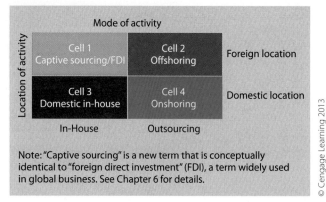

Mode of activity

Location of activity

	In-House	Outsourcing	
Foreign location	Cell 1 Captive sourcing/FDI	Cell 2 Offshoring	
Domestic location	Cell 3 Domestic in-house	Cell 4 Onshoring	

Note: "Captive sourcing" is a new term that is conceptually identical to "foreign direct investment" (FDI), a term widely used in global business. See Chapter 6 for details.

© Cengage Learning 2013

great deal of commonality across industries and little need for keeping it proprietary. As a product loses its ability to command high prices and high margins through market competition, it undergoes a process known as **commoditization**—that is, becoming a commodity that does not command high prices. The answer may also be "No" if the activity is in Cell 1, which is industry specific but also with a high level of commoditization. In this case, the firm may want to outsource the activity, sell the unit involved, or lease the unit's services to other firms (see Exhibit 4.3). This is because operating multiple stages of activities in the value chain may be inefficient and costly.

Think about steel, definitely a crucial component for automobiles. The question for automakers is: "Do we need to make steel ourselves?" The requirements for steel are common across end-user industries—that is, the steel for automakers is essentially the same for construction, defense, and other steel-consuming end users (ignoring minor technical differences for the sake of our discussion). While it is imperative for automakers to keep the auto-making activity (especially engine and final assembly) proprietary (Cell 3 in Exhibit 4.4), there is no need to make steel in-house. Therefore, although many automakers such as Ford and GM were historically involved in steelmaking, none of them does it now. In other words, steelmaking is outsourced and steel commoditized.

Outsourcing is defined as turning over an activity to an outside supplier that will perform the activity on behalf of the focal firm. Many consumer products companies such as Nike that possess strong capabilities in upstream activities (such as design) and downstream activities (such as marketing) have outsourced manufacturing to suppliers in low-cost countries. Not only is manufacturing often outsourced, there is a recent trend toward outsourcing a number of service activities such as information technology (IT), human resources, and logistics. What drives this trend? Many firms previously considered certain activities to be a special part of their industries. (Think about airline

reservations and bank call centers.) Now they believe that these activities have relatively generic attributes that can be shared across firms or industries. Of course, this changing viewpoint is fueled by the rise of specialized service providers such as Infosys in IT, Foxconn in contract manufacturing, and DHL and UPS in logistics. These specialist firms argue that such activities can be broken off from the various client firms (just as steelmaking was broken off from automakers decades ago) and leveraged to serve multiple clients with greater economies of scale. For client firms, such outsourcing results in "leaner and meaner" organizations that can focus on core activities better (see Panel B in Exhibit 4.2).

If the answer to the question "Do we really need to perform this activity in-house?" is "Yes" (Cell 3 in Exhibit 4.4), but the firm's current resources and capabilities are not up to the task (Exhibit 4.3), then there are two second-stage choices. First, the firm may want to acquire and develop capabilities in-house so that it can perform this particular activity better. Or, it may go with the second option if it does not have enough skills to develop these capabilities in-house and access them through strategic alliances. For example, neither Sony nor Ericsson was strong enough on its own to elbow into the competitive mobile handset market, so they formed a joint venture named Sony Ericsson to penetrate it.

Conspicuously absent in both Exhibits 4.3 and 4.4 is the *geographic* dimension—domestic versus foreign locations. Because the two terms "outsourcing" and "offshoring" have emerged rather recently, there is a great deal of confusion, especially among some journalists who often casually (and erroneously) equate the two. To minimize confusion, we go from two terms in Exhibit 4.4 (in-house versus outsource) to four terms in Exhibit 4.5

Commoditization
A process of market competition through which unique products that command high prices and high margins gradually lose their ability to do so, thus becoming commodities.

Outsourcing
Turning over an organizational activity to an outside supplier that will perform it on behalf of the focal firm.

EXHIBIT 4.6 The VRIO Framework and Firm Performance

Is a resource or capability . . .					Competitive implications	Firm performance
Valuable?	Rare?	Costly to imitate?	Exploited by organization?			
No	—	—	No	➡ Competitive disadvantage	Below average
Yes	No	—	Yes	➡ Competitive parity	Average
Yes	Yes	No	Yes	➡ Temporary competitive advantage	Above average
Yes	Yes	Yes	Yes	➡ Sustained competitive advantage	Persistently above average

Sources: J. Barney, *Gaining and Sustaining Competitive Advantage*, 2nd ed. (Upper Saddle River, NJ: Prentice Hall, 2002) 173; R. Hoskisson, M. Hitt, and R. D. Ireland, *Competing for Advantage* (Cincinnati: Thomson South-Western, 2004) 118.

© iStockphoto.com/Alex Slobodkin

based on locations and modes. They are (1) **offshoring** (international/foreign outsourcing); (2) **onshoring** (or **inshoring**) (domestic outsourcing); (3) **captive sourcing** (setting up subsidiaries abroad—the work is done in-house but the location is foreign); and (4) domestic in-house activity.

Outsourcing—especially offshoring—has no shortage of controversies and confusion (see Debate). Despite the set of new labels, we need to be aware that "offshoring" and "onshoring" (or "inshoring") are simply international and domestic variants of outsourcing, respectively. While offshoring low-cost IT work to India, the Philippines, and other emerging economies has become widely practiced, interestingly, eastern Germany; northern France; and Appalachian, Great Plains, and southern regions of the United States have emerged as new hotbeds for inshoring.[6] In job-starved regions such as Michigan, high-quality IT workers may accept wages 35% lower than at headquarters, and government incentives are available. Another term "captive sourcing" is conceptually identical to foreign direct investment (FDI),[7] which is nothing new in the world of global business (see Chapters 1 and 6 for details).

One interesting lesson we can take away from Exhibit 4.5 is that value-adding activities may be geographically dispersed around the world, even for a single firm, to take advantage of the best locations and modes to perform certain activities. For example, a Dell laptop may be designed in the United States (domestic in-house activity), its components may be produced in Taiwan (offshoring) as well as the United States (onshoring), and its final assembly may be in Malaysia (captive sourcing/FDI). When customers call for help, the call center may be with an outside service provider in India, Ireland, Jamaica, or the Philippines (offshoring).

Overall, a value chain analysis enables managers to ascertain a firm's strengths and weaknesses on an activity-by-activity basis, *relative to rivals*, in a SWOT analysis. The recent proliferation of new labels is intimidating, causing some gurus to claim that "twenty-first century offshoring really is different."[8] In reality, we still see the time-honored SWOT analysis at work behind the new vocabulary. The next section introduces a framework on how to do this.

> **Explain what a VRIO framework is.**

> **Explain how to use a VRIO framework to understand a firm's resources and capabilities.**

ANALYZING RESOURCES AND CAPABILITIES WITH A VRIO FRAMEWORK

The resource-based view focuses on the value (V), rarity (R), imitability (I), and organizational (O) aspects of resources and capabilities, leading to a **VRIO framework**.[9] Looking at a firm from the perspective of these four important aspects has a number of ramifications for competitive advantage. They are summarized in Exhibit 4.6.

Value

Do firm resources and capabilities add value? Value chain analysis suggests that this is the most fundamental question to ask. Only value-adding resources can possibly lead to competitive advantage, whereas non-value-adding capabilities may lead to competitive *disadvantage*. As the competitive landscape changes, what was previously a value-adding resource and capability may become obsolete. The evolution of IBM is a case in point. IBM historically excelled in making hardware, including tabulating machines in the 1930s, mainframes in the 1960s, and personal

Offshoring
Outsourcing to an international or foreign firm.

Onshoring (or inshoring)
Outsourcing to a domestic firm.

Captive sourcing
Setting up subsidiaries abroad so that the work done is in-house but the location is foreign. Also known as foreign direct investment (FDI).

VRIO framework
The resource-based framework that focuses on the value (V), rarity (R), imitability (I), and organizational (O) aspects of resources and capabilities.

Part I: Laying Foundations

DEBATE
ETHICAL DILEMMA

For and Against Offshoring

Offshoring—or, more specifically, international outsourcing—has emerged as a leading corporate movement in the 21st century. Outsourcing low-end manufacturing to countries such as China and Mexico is now widely practiced. But increased outsourcing of more high-end services, particularly IT services and all sorts of **business process outsourcing (BPO)**, to countries such as India is controversial. Because digitization and commoditization of service work is enabled only by the very recent rise of the Internet and the reduction of international communication costs, their long-term impact is not known. Thus, it is debatable whether such offshoring proves to be a long-term benefit or hindrance to Western firms and economies.

FOR Proponents argue that offshoring creates enormous value for firms and economies. Western firms are able to tap into low-cost yet high-quality labor, translating into significant cost savings. Firms can also focus on their core capabilities, which may add more value than dealing with non-core (and often uncompetitive) activities. In turn, offshoring service providers, such as Infosys and Wipro, develop *their* core competencies in IT/BPO. A McKinsey study that focused on offshoring between the United States and India reported that for every dollar spent by US firms in India, the US firms save 58 cents (see Exhibit 4.7). Overall, $1.46 of new wealth is created, of which the US economy captures $1.13 through cost savings and increased exports to India. India captures the other 33 cents through profits, wages, and additional taxes. While acknowledging that some US employees may lose their jobs, proponents suggest that on balance, offshoring is a win-win solution for both US and Indian firms and their economies.

AGAINST Critics make three points on strategic, economic, and political grounds. Strategically, if "even core functions like engineering, R&D, manufacturing, and marketing can—and often should—be moved outside," what is left of the firm? US firms have gone down this path before—in manufacturing—with disastrous results. In the 1960s, Radio Corporation of America (RCA) invented the color TV and then outsourced its production to Japan, a low-cost country at that time. Fast forward to the 2000s and the United States no longer has any US-owned color TV producers. Critics argue that offshoring nurtures rivals. Why are Indian IT/BPO firms now emerging as strong rivals? It is in part because they built up their capabilities doing work for EDS and IBM in the 1990s, particularly by working to help the IT industry prevent the "millennium bug" (or Y2K) problem.

Economically, critics question whether developed economies, on the whole, actually gain more. While shareholders and corporate highflyers embrace offshoring, it increasingly results in job losses in high-end areas such as design, R&D, and IT/BPO. While white-collar individuals who lose jobs will naturally hate it, the net impact on developed economies may still be negative.

Finally, critics make the political argument that many large Western firms are unethical and are interested only in the cheapest and most exploitable labor. Not only is work commoditized, people are degraded as tradable commodities that can be jettisoned. As a result, large firms that outsource work to emerging economies are often accused of destroying jobs at home, ignoring corporate social responsibility, violating customer privacy (for example, by sending medical records, tax returns, and credit card numbers to be processed overseas), and in some cases undermining national security. Not surprisingly, the debate often becomes emotional and explosive when such accusations are made.

For firms in developed economies, where this debate primarily takes place, the choice is not really offshoring versus non-offshoring, but where to draw the line on offshoring. There is relatively little debate in emerging economies because they clearly stand to gain from offshoring. Taking a page from the Indian playbook, the Philippines, with numerous English-speaking professionals, is trying to eat some of India's lunch. Northeast China, where Japanese is widely taught, is positioning itself as an ideal location for call centers for Japan. Central and Eastern Europe gravitates toward serving Western Europe. Central and South American countries want to grab call center contracts for the large Hispanic market in the United States.

Sources: M. Gottfredson, R. Puryear, and S. Phillips, "Strategic sourcing," *Harvard Business Review* (February 2005): 132; M. W. Peng, 2009, *Global Strategy*, 2nd ed. Cincinnati: South-Western Cengage Learning.

Business process outsourcing (BPO)
The outsourcing of business processes such as loan origination, credit card processing, and call center operations.

EXHIBIT 4.7 Benefit of $1 US Spending on Offshoring to India

Benefit to the United States	$	Benefit to India	$
Savings accruing to US investors/customers	0.58	Labor	0.10
Exports of US goods/services to providers in India	0.05	Profits retained in India	0.10
Profit transfer by US-owned operations in India back to the United States	0.04	Suppliers	0.09
Net direct benefit retained in the United States	0.67	Central government taxes	0.03
Value from US labor re-employed	0.46	State government taxes	0.01
Net benefit to the United States	1.13	*Net benefit to India*	0.33

Source: D. Farrell, "Offshoring: Value creation through economic change," *Journal of Management Studies* (2005) 42: 675–683. Copyright © 2005 Blackwell Publishing. All rights reserved. Reproduced by permission. Farrell is director of the McKinsey Global Institute, and she refers to a McKinsey study.

computers (PCs) in the 1980s. However, as competition for hardware heated up, IBM's core capabilities in hardware not only added little value but also increased core rigidities that hindered its efforts to move into new areas. Since the 1990s, under two new CEOs, IBM has focused on more lucrative software and services and has developed new value-adding capabilities. Now the company is an on-demand computing *service* provider for corporations. As part of this new strategy, IBM sold its PC division to China's Lenovo.

The relationship between valuable resources and capabilities and a firm's performance is straightforward. Non-value-adding resources and capabilities, such as IBM's historical expertise in hardware, may become weaknesses instead of strengths. If firms are unable to get rid of non-value-adding resources and capabilities, they are likely to suffer below-average performance. In the worst case, they may become extinct, a fate IBM narrowly skirted during the 1990s.

Rarity

Simply possessing valuable resources and capabilities may not be enough. The next question is: How rare are the valuable resources and capabilities? At best, valuable but common resources and capabilities will lead to competitive parity but no advantage. Consider the identical aircraft made by Boeing and Airbus and used by Southwest, Ryanair, and most other airlines. The aircraft are certainly valuable, but they are not rare. Airlines have to compete on how they use the same aircraft differently. The same is true for bar codes, enterprise resource planning (ERP) software, and radio frequency identification (RFID) tags. Their developers are too willing to sell them everywhere, thus undermining their novelty value—in other words, rarity.

Resources and capabilities must, therefore, be both valuable and *rare* to have the potential to provide some temporary competitive advantage. Western IT firms increasingly rely on intellectual property (IP) to provide streams of revenue through patent licensing. For example, IBM now earns $1 billion a year from its IP portfolio, and has topped the list for the most patents for 18 straight years. In 2010, it was awarded 5,896 US patents, becoming the first company to exceed 5,000 patents in a single year.[10] Still, there is always a danger that firms' licensees (or their licensees' employees) may use the technology for purposes other than those originally intended. While blatant patent infringement is illegal, smart reverse engineering (inventing around a given patent) is legal.

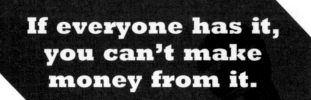

If everyone has it, you can't make money from it.

Causal ambiguity
The difficulty of identifying the actual cause of a firm's successful performance.

However cliché, rarity boils down to a simple point: If everyone has it, you can't make money from it.[11] For example, the quality of Detroit automakers (the Big Three) is now comparable with the best Asian and European rivals. But high quality is now expected by car buyers and is no longer rare, so it provides no advantage. Case in point: Even in their home country, the Big Three's quality improvements have not translated into stronger sales. Embarrassingly, both GM and Chrysler, despite the decent quality of their cars, had to declare bankruptcy and be bailed out by the US government in 2009.

Imitability

Valuable and rare resources and capabilities can be a source of competitive advantage only if they are also difficult to imitate by competitors. While it is relatively easier to imitate a firm's *tangible* resources such as plants, it is a lot more challenging and often impossible to imitate *intangible* capabilities such as tacit knowledge, superior motivation, and managerial talents.

Imitation is difficult. Why? In two words: **causal ambiguity**, which means the difficulty of identifying the actual cause of a firm's successful performance. What exactly has caused Barbie to be the queen of toys for over 50 years? Barbie has no shortage of competitors and imitators such as Bratz. In the past five decades, every self-respecting toymaker has allegedly been learning from Barbie's maker Mattel. Yet, Barbie's attractiveness to girls from San Francisco to Shanghai has remained (see In Focus).

A natural question is: How can Barbie (or actually Mattel) do it? Usually, a number of resources and capabilities will be nominated, including Barbie's embodiment of traditional feminine value, her flexibility to take on new professions such as flight attendant and aerobics instructor as they were invented, and her reassuring brand in troubled economic times. While all of these resources and capabilities are plausible, what *exactly* is it? Knowing the answer to this question is not only intriguing to scholars and students, it can also be hugely profitable for Mattel's rivals. Unfortunately, outsiders usually have a hard time understanding what a firm does inside its boundaries. We can try, as many rivals have, to identify Mattel's secret sauce for success by drawing up a long list of possible reasons labeled as resources and capabilities in our classroom discussion. But in the final analysis, as outsiders we are not sure.

What is even more fascinating for scholars and students and frustrating for rivals is that even managers of a focal firm such as Mattel often do not know exactly what contributes to their success. When interviewed, they can usually generate a long list of what they do well, such as a strong organizational culture, a relentless drive, and many

IN FOCUS

Barbie at 50

Frowned upon by feminists but fought over by five-year-olds, Barbie has been a victim of controversy as much as fashion ever since her birth 50 years ago in March 1959. The charge sheet against the pint-sized piece of plastic is long. She teaches the supremacy of looks over substance; she stereotypes outdated gender roles; she celebrates an impossible body ideal; and she spreads platinum hair, plastic limbs, and a nauseating shade of pink into households from Honolulu to Hamburg.

Yet, could it be that Barbie, far from being a relic from another era, is in fact a woman for our troubled economic times? For a start, she may benefit from having a strong, reassuring brand in a downturn. Although global Barbie sales fell by 9% in 2008, battering profits at Mattel, her maker, Barbie topped the 2008 survey by America's National Retail Federation of the most popular girls' toys, relegating even the Nintendo Wii to fifth place. And she has just seen off her hipper rivals, the Bratz. After a long legal battle, a federal judge recently ordered their maker, MGA, to transfer the trademark rights to Mattel.* Barbie is once again

the queen of the toy shop. In previous recessions, toy sales held up reasonably well, as parents cut back elsewhere.

As the recession deepens, Barbie's conservative values are also back in vogue. Amid concern about rampant individualism and excess, she evokes a simpler, gentler era. And since *staying in* is the new *going out*, little girls will have more time for old-fashioned play.

Barbie also embodies career flexibility, a valuable attribute in difficult times. Having started out as a fashion model in a black-and-white striped bathing suit, she tiptoed into other professions as fast as they were invented. She was a flight attendant in the 1960s as mass aviation took off, an aerobics instructor with leg-warmers in the 1980s, and even a black presidential candidate four years before Barack Obama. Time for a new Barbie, dressed as a distressed-debt investor?

Source: "Barbie at 50: In the pink," *Economist*, 7 March 2009, 72. © Economist Newspaper Group. Reprinted by permission.

* In 2001, MGA launched the Bratz dolls. In 2004, Mattel sued, and in 2008 a jury ruled that Mattel, not MGA, owns the Bratz line because Bratz's designer worked for Mattel when he created Bratz. Retailers quickly stopped ordering Bratz, whose sales collapsed.

---

other attributes. To make matters worse, different managers of the same firm may have different lists. When probed as to which resource or capability is "it," they usually suggest that it is all of the above in *combination*. This is probably one of the most interesting (and most frustrating!) aspects of the resource-based view: If insiders have a hard time figuring out what unambiguously contributes to their firm's performance, it is not surprising that outsiders' efforts in understanding and imitating these capabilities are usually flawed and often fail.

Overall, valuable and rare but imitable resources and capabilities may give firms some temporary competitive advantage, leading to above-average performance for some time. But such advantage is not likely to be sustainable. As the Barbie example shows, only valuable, rare, and *hard-to-imitate* resources and capabilities may potentially lead to sustained competitive advantage.

Organization

Even valuable, rare, and hard-to-imitate resources and capabilities may not give a firm sustained competitive advantage if the firm is not properly organized. Although highly paid movie stars represent some of the most valuable, rare, and hard-to-imitate resources, *most* movies flop. More generally, the question of organization asks: How should a firm, such as a movie studio, be organized to develop and leverage the full potential of its resources and capabilities?

Numerous components within a firm are relevant to the question of organization.[12] In a movie studio, these components include talent for finding good ideas, photography crews, musicians, singers, makeup specialists, animation artists, and managers on the business side who deal with sponsors, distributors, and local sites. These components are often called **complementary assets** because it is difficult to generate box office hits by themselves. In the last movie you saw, did you remember the name of the makeup artist? Of course not—you probably only remember the stars. However, stars alone cannot generate hit movies. It is the *combination* of star resources and complementary assets that create hit movies. "It may be that not just a few resources and capabilities enable a firm to gain a competitive advantage but that literally thousands of these organizational attributes, bundled together, generate such advantage."[13]

Another idea is **social complexity**, which refers to the intricate and interdependent ways that firms are typically organized. Many multinationals consist of thousands of people scattered throughout many different countries. How they overcome cultural differences and achieve organizational goals is profoundly complex. It is often the invisible relationships among employees around

Complementary assets
The combination of numerous resources and assets that enable a firm to gain a competitive advantage.

Social complexity
The socially intricate and interdependent ways that firms are typically organized.

the world that add value. Such organizationally embedded capabilities are thus very difficult for rivals to imitate. This emphasis on social complexity refutes what is half-jokingly called the "Lego" view of the firm, in which a firm can be assembled and disassembled from modules of technology and people, like Lego toy blocks. By treating employees as identical and replaceable blocks, the Lego view fails to realize that the social capital associated with complex relationships and knowledge permeating many firms can be a source of competitive advantage.

Overall, only valuable, rare, and hard-to-imitate resources and capabilities that are organizationally embedded and exploited can possibly lead to persistently above-average performance. Because resources and capabilities cannot be evaluated in isolation, the VRIO framework presents four interconnected and increasingly difficult hurdles for them to become a source of sustainable competitive advantage. In other words, V, R, I, and O come together as one *package*.

> **Identify four things you need to do as part of a successful career and business strategy.**

MANAGEMENT SAVVY

How does the resource-based view answer the big question in global business: What determines the success and failure of firms around the globe? The answer is straightforward. Fundamentally, some firms outperform others because winners possess some valuable, rare, hard-to-imitate, and organizationally embedded resources and capabilities that their competitors do not have. This view is especially insightful when we see firms such as Saturna and Mattel persistently succeed while others struggle in difficult industries.

Shown in Exhibit 4.8, the resource-based view suggests four implications for action. First, the proposition that firms "compete on resources and capabilities" is not novel. The subtlety comes when managers attempt, via the VRIO framework, to distinguish resources and capabilities that are valuable, rare, hard to imitate, and organizationally embedded from those that do not share these attributes. In other words, the VRIO framework can greatly aid the time-honored SWOT analysis, especially the S (strengths) and W (weaknesses) parts. Managers, who cannot pay attention to every resource and capability, must have some sense of what *really* matters. When evaluating their firms' capabilities, managers commonly fail to assess how their capabilities compare with those of their rivals. As a result, most firms end up having a mixed bag of both good and mediocre capabilities. Using the VRIO framework, a value chain analysis helps managers make decisions on what capabilities to focus on in-house and what to outsource. Increasingly, what really matters is not tangible resources that are relatively easy to imitate but intangible capabilities that are harder for rivals to wrap their arms around. Therefore, managers need to identify, develop, and leverage valuable, rare, hard-to-imitate, and organizationally embedded resources and capabilities, which are often intangible. It is thus not surprising that capabilities not meeting these criteria are increasingly outsourced.

Second, relentless imitation or benchmarking, while important, is not likely to be successful in the long run. Follower firms have a tendency to mimic the most visible, the most obvious, and, consequently, the *least* important practices of winning firms. Follower firms that meticulously replicate every resource possessed by winning firms at best can hope to attain competitive parity. Firms endowed with sufficient resources to imitate others may be better off developing their own unique capabilities. The best-performing firms such as Saturna and Mattel often create new ways of adding value.

Third, even a sustainable competitive advantage will not last forever, particularly in today's global competition. All a firm can hope for is a competitive advantage that can be sustained for as long as possible. Over time, all advantages may erode. As noted earlier, each of IBM's product-related advantages associated with tabulating machines, mainframes, and PCs was sustained for a period of time. But, eventually, these advantages disappeared. Therefore, the lesson for all firms, including current market leaders, is to develop strategic *foresight*—over-the-horizon radar is a good metaphor. Such strategic foresight enables firms to anticipate future needs and move early to identify, develop, and leverage resources and capabilities for future competition.

Finally, here is a very personal and relevant implication for action. As a student who is probably studying this book in a developed (read: high-wage and thus high-cost!) country such as the United States, you may be wondering: What do I get out of this? How do I cope with the frightening future of global competition? There are two lessons you can draw. First, the whole debate on offshoring, a part of the larger debate on globalization, is very relevant and directly affects your future as a manager, a consumer, and a citizen (see Chapter 1). So don't be a couch potato. Be

EXHIBIT 4.8 Implications for Action

- Managers need to build firm strengths based on the VRIO framework.
- Relentless imitation or benchmarking, while important, is not likely to be a successful strategy.
- Managers need to build up resources and capabilities for future competition.
- Students need to make themselves into "untouchables" whose jobs cannot be easily outsourced.

active, get involved, and be prepared, because it is not only their debate, it is *yours* as well. Second, be very serious about the VRIO framework of the resource-based view. While the resource-based view has been developed to advise firms, there is no reason you cannot develop that into a resource-based view of the *individual*. In other words, you can use the VRIO framework to make yourself into an "untouchable"—a person whose job cannot be outsourced, as defined by Thomas Friedman in *The World Is Flat*

(2005). An untouchable individual's job cannot be outsourced because he or she possesses valuable, rare, and hard-to-imitate capabilities that are indispensable to an employer. This won't be easy. But you really don't want to be mediocre. A generation ago, parents told their kids: Eat your food—kids in China and India are starving. Now, Friedman would advise you: Study this book and leverage your education—students in China and India are starving for your job.[14]

CLOSING CASE

ETHICAL DILEMMA

WHY AMAZON'S KINDLE CANNOT BE MADE IN THE UNITED STATES

The Amazon Kindle is a revolutionary e-reader device developed by Amazon's Lab126 unit based in California. Kindle 1 first retailed for $399. It sold out in its first six *hours* when it debuted in November 2007. In October 2009, Amazon unleashed Kindle 2 with a more attractive price tag: $259. July 2010 saw the launch of Kindle 3, which retailed at only $139. In 2011, Amazon announced that digital books were outselling its traditional print books for the first time ever on its site, with an average of 115 Kindle editions being sold for every 100 print books. For such a cutting-edge, high-tech product, unfortunately, no US-based manufacturer is able to make it in the United States. Its components are made in China, Taiwan, and South Korea, and its final assembly is in China.

Why Kindle cannot be made in its home country has become "Exhibit A" in the debate about the future of the US economy. Since no US-based manufacturer has the capabilities to produce Kindle at home, Amazon has no choice but to outsource Kindle's production to Asia. Critics argue that after decades of outsourcing production to low-cost countries, US firms have not only lost millions of low-skill jobs, but also abilities to make the next generation of high-tech, high-value goods. In addition to Kindle, the not-made-in-USA list includes electric-car batteries, light-emitting diodes, and carbon-fiber components of Boeing's 787 Dreamliner.

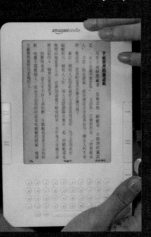

The common belief is that as long as US firms control upstream R&D and design activities and downstream branding, marketing, and distribution services in a value chain, their competitiveness would remain unchallenged in global competition. Outsourcing basic manufacturing will not be a grave problem. However, critics argue that when a large chunk of value-adding activities, such as manufacturing, is taken out of a country, employment opportunities for these activities shrink, experienced people change careers, and smart students avoid these "dead-end" fields. Eventually, a critical mass of capabilities is lost and will be no longer able to support upstream and downstream activities, which will be forced to migrate overseas too.

Consider the migration of PC production. Original equipment manufacturers (OEMs) in Asia, for sure, offered compelling low-cost solutions to US firms. US firms, initially, did not feel threatened. However, product innovation for new gadgets and process innovation in manufacturing are intertwined. PC designers need to frequently interact with manufacturing engineers in order to optimize the design. While the loss of US-based manufacturing makes US design engineers less able to handle complex new designs, the influx of jobs for manufacturing engineers in Asia makes Asian design engineers more capable. Thus, the erosion of PC manufacturing capabilities leads to the erosion of PC design skills. Ferocious product market competition often forces US firms then to relinquish the de-

sign function to their Asian suppliers, which then become original design manufacturers (ODMs). Of course, one solution is to jettison a US PC brand all together, as evidenced by IBM's sale of its PC division to China's Lenovo. Lenovo thus becomes an original brand manufacturer (OBM). Today for all the remaining US-owned PC brands, with the exception of Apple, every laptop is not only manufactured but also designed in Asia. Competing with them are a bunch of PC brands from Taiwan, such as Acer, BenQ, ASUS, Advantech, HTC, and MSI, in addition to Lenovo from China and Samsung and LG from South Korea.

Nevertheless, the migration of PC production still fits the theory of product life cycle (that is, US-based firms manufactured and designed PCs first, and then gradually the production and design functions migrated to Asia). The theory of product life cycle seems no longer valid in the case of Amazon Kindle. US-based firms simply do not have a chance to manufacture it, which does not generate a single US manufacturing job at a time when the US unemployment rate is sky-high. If US firms do not participate in the first phase manufacturing of the new technology, it is easy to see that they will not be in the running for all that will follow. In the $30 billion global solar industry, the United States has a chance to be a contender in manufacturing. But odds are not great. This is because the United States produces just 5% of the world's solar panel cells, while China is already the number one player, making 35%.

General Electric (GE) CEO Jeff Immelt has recently admitted that GE has probably gone too far in outsourcing. He has labeled the notion that the United States could remain an economic superpower by relying solely on services and consumption "flat wrong." Recently, Ford chairman Bill Ford, Dow Chemical CEO Andrew Liveris, and former Intel CEO Andy Grove have openly called for "industrial policy," an unpopular term (in the United States at least) that is otherwise known as government intervention by picking winners. However, by bailing out Detroit and rescuing Wall Street, the Obama administration has been dragged into "industrial policy" without much of a clear long-term policy. At a time global competition is heating up, how to beef up the manufacturing (and other) capabilities of US firms in order to enhance US competitiveness undoubtedly remains job number one for numerous executives and policymakers.

Sources: "Can the future be built in America?" *BusinessWeek*, 21 September 2009, 46–51; "Amazon doubles down on the Kindle," *Bloomberg Businessweek*, 2 August 2010, 38–39; A. Grove, "How to make an American job," *Bloomberg Businessweek*, 5 July 2010, 48–53; "Amazon Kindle book sales soar," *PC World*, 27 January 2011, available online at www.pcworld.com; L. Pierce, "Big losses in ecosystem niches," *Strategic Management Journal*, 30, (2009): 323–347; G. Pisano and W. Shih, "Restoring American competitiveness," *Harvard Business Review* (July–August 2009): 114–125; C. Weigelt, "The impact of outsourcing new technologies on integrative capabilities and performance," *Strategic Management Journal*, 30 (2009): 595–616.

TRADING Internationally

CHAPTER 5

OPENING CASE

Why Are German Exports So Competitive?

Until 2009, Germany had been the world's export champion for a long time. Although China snatched the world's export champion title in 2009, Germany's export volume (approximately $1.4 trillion a year) routinely outperforms other powerhouses such as the United States and Japan. On the road, BMW and Mercedes cars visibly set global standards. In information technology (IT), SAP is king of the hill for enterprise resource planning (ERP). Adidas shoes and Nivea skincare products are favored by many around the world. In addition to these high-profile firms, Germany also has a lot of less visible but equally successful firms in their respective domains. These typically small- and medium-sized *Mittelstand* firms account for 40% of German exports. Krones (beverage bottling and packaging systems), Heidenhain (encoders for manufacturing equipment), and Dorma (moveable walls) may not be household

names, but they hold up to 90% of the worldwide market share in their niches. Also, consider Neumann microphones, which have captured songs from singers ranging from Elvis Presley to Céline Dion. These tiny microphones can last 22 years before they need repair. But they don't come cheap: A top-of-the-line, made-in-Germany Neumann microphone costs $6,450 (!).

In a world dominated by price-chopping Wal-Mart stores and their suppliers, which often produce in China, why do German exports that typically compete in the high end win the hearts, minds, and wallets of so many customers around the world? What is unique about German exports? German products and firms are world renowned for their excellent engineering, superb craftsmanship, and obsession with perfection. Although manufacturing only contributes 30% of Germany's GDP, manufacturing products enjoy

© OLIVER LANG/AFP/Getty Images

LEARNING OBJECTIVES
After studying this chapter, you should be able to:

LO1 *use the resource-based and institution-based views to explain why nations trade.*

LO2 *outline the classical and modern theories of international trade.*

LO3 *explain the importance of political realities governing international trade.*

LO4 *identify factors that should be considered when your firm participates in international trade.*

a lion's share of Germany's exports.* Not surprisingly, these exports center on engineering-driven products, such as automobiles, machinery, and chemical goods. Overall, German exports are not cheap, but they are often "worth it."

While these positive country-of-origin images associated with German exports are well known to practically every reader of this book, what is *not* appreciated, typically, is the formal and informal rules that are behind Germany's export prowess. Formally, the German government has sought to avoid large-scale deindustrialization (otherwise known as loss of manufacturing jobs) and encouraged firms to produce at home. In an effort to push more unemployed to seek jobs, the German government has trimmed unemployment benefits. The unique "co-determination" scheme implemented after World War II has allowed labor union representatives to occupy half of the seats on firms' supervisory boards, and they naturally are not interested in voting for outsourcing jobs to lower-cost countries. In the face of relentless global cost competition and relatively inflexible labor markets, German managers have been holding down wage increases. German wages have been more or less frozen since the mid-1990s.

Hovering between 1% and 2% in much of the 2000s (before 2008), German economic growth was slow. In part this was due to relatively modest consumer spending. Informally, Germans often tell visitors that saving is a national obsession that goes far back into their history. The post-WWI Great Depression and post-WWII devastation are often pointed to as sources for such an understandable thrifty habit. Between 2000 and 2008, consumer spending remained flat in Germany, and it has declined since the 2008–2009 crisis.

Powerful industrial infrastructure and modest domestic consumption combine to suggest that exports are often the only source of German economic growth. And what a growth engine German exports are. Between 2000 and 2008, exports grew by 80%, resulting in a hefty trade *surplus* of 8% of GDP in 2008—in contrast, the US trade *deficit* was 6% of GDP, and Spain's was 10%.

Such an outstanding export performance is also helped by Germany's trading partners. Nine out of the top ten importers of German products are within the European Union (EU) (led by France), and the United States is the second largest importer. Prior to the 2008–2009 crisis, most of these countries experienced a consumption binge and import boom fueled by cheap credit. So in a way, rather like China and Japan, Germany has earned its surplus by living off the consumption overindulgence of its export customers. Unfortunately, Germany's export success has irritated some of its EU trading partners within the euro zone, which have failed to hold down wages but cannot resort to currency devaluation.

Then the 2008–2009 crisis hit, and virtually all the top ten importers cut back on their spending. The collapse of demand has caused a collapse of German exports, forcing the entire German economy to shrink—a 6% drop of GDP for 2009. There is some soul searching both inside and outside of Germany on whether the country has relied too much on exports. In October 2009, German chancellor Angela Merkel, after her reelection for the second term, responded to such critics in a major speech:

Germany's strength lies largely in the fact that the Federal Republic is a center of industry and that it is an export nation. . . All those who now say we have depended too much on exports are undermining our biggest source of prosperity and must be rebuffed.

* The typical impression that services are underdeveloped in Germany is wrong: 69% of its GDP is contributed by services (and agriculture has another 1%); Germany is the world's third largest exporter of commercial services (behind the United States and Britain). To avoid confusion, we use the term "German exports" to refer to "manufacturing exports" here.

Sources: "German exports remain key," *BusinessWeek*, 15 October 2009, available online at http://www.bloomberg.com; "The export model sputters," *Economist*, 9 May 2009, 53–54; "The lives of others," *Economist*, 8 August 2009, 65–66; "Unbalanced Germany," *Economist*, 8 August 2009, 10; "Mittel-management," *Economist*, 27 November 2010, 74; B. Venohr and K. Meyer, "Uncommon common sense," *Business Strategy Review* (Spring 2009): 39–43.

Germany

Export
To sell abroad.

Import
To buy from abroad.

Merchandise trade
Tangible products being bought and sold.

Service trade
Intangible services being bought and sold.

Why are German exports so competitive in the world? How does international trade contribute to Germany's economic growth and prosperity? Why has its export success irritated some of its trading partners?

International trade is the oldest and still the most important building block of international business. It has never failed to generate debate. We begin by addressing a crucial question: Why do nations trade? Then we outline how the two core perspectives introduced in earlier chapters—namely, the resource-based and institution-based views—

can help answer this question. The remainder of the chapter deals with the theories and realities of international trade. As before, debates and implications for action follow.

Use the resource-based and institution-based views to explain why nations trade.

WHY DO NATIONS TRADE?

Internationally, trade means **export** (sell abroad) and **import** (buy from abroad). International trade consists of both merchandise trade and service trade. **Merchandise trade** is the buying and selling of tangible products, while **service trade** is the buying and selling of intangible services.

International trade is far more complex than domestic trade. So why do nations go through the trouble of trading internationally? Without getting into details, we can safely say that there must be economic gains from trade. More

© Cengage Learning 2013

EXHIBIT 5.1
World Merchandise Exports, 2007–2010
(1st quarter in 2005 =100)

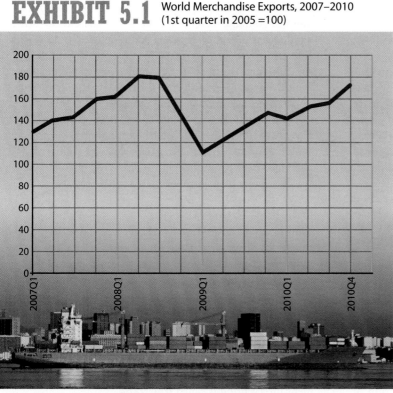

Source: World Trade Organization, 2011, available online at http://www.wto.org/english/news_e/news11_e/rese_14mar11_e.htm [accessed 25 March 2011]. Reproduced by permission.

© iStockphoto.com/luoman

importantly, such gains must be shared by *both* sides. Otherwise, there would be no willing exporters and importers. In other words, international trade is a *win-win* deal. The top ten exporting and importing nations can be found in PengAtlas Maps 6 and 7. Overall, world trade growth (averaging about 6% during 1996–2007) routinely outpaced GDP growth (averaging 3% during the same period). Thanks to the global recession, world merchandise exports suffered from an 11% decrease in 2008. Recovery started in 2009. In 2010, merchandise exports increased by 22% in value (Exhibit 5.1).

Why are there gains from trade? How do nations benefit from such gains? The remainder of this chapter will answer these questions. But before proceeding, it is important to realize that it is misleading to say that *nations* trade. A more accurate expression would be that *firms* from different nations trade.[1] Unless different governments directly buy and sell from each other (such as arms sales), the majority of trade is conducted by firms that pay little attention to country-level ramifications. For example, Wal-Mart imports large quantities of goods into the United States and does not export much. Wal-Mart thus di-

rectly contributes to the US trade deficit. A **trade deficit** occurs when a nation imports more than it exports, so the US government does not like this type of activity. But in most countries, governments cannot tell firms such as Wal-Mart what to do (and not to do) unless those firms engage in illegal activities. Likewise, when we discuss US–China trade, we are really referring to thousands of US firms buying from and selling to China, which also has thousands of firms buying from and selling to the United States. Unlike the United States, China has a **trade surplus**, which occurs when a nation exports more than it imports. The aggregation of such buying (importing) and selling (exporting) by both sides leads to the country-level **balance of trade**—namely, whether a country has a trade surplus or deficit. Overall, we need to be aware that when we ask "Why do nations trade?" we are really asking "Why do *firms* from different nations trade?"

Having acknowledged the limitations of the expression that *nations* trade, we will still use it. Why? Because it has been commonly used and also serves as a short-hand version of the more accurate but more cumbersome "firms from different nations trade." This clarification does enable us to use the two *firm-level* perspectives introduced earlier—the resource-based and institution-based views—to shed light on why nations trade.

Recall from Chapter 4 that valuable, rare, inimitable, and organizationally derived (VRIO) products determine a firm's competitive advantage. Applying this insight, we can suggest that valuable, rare, and inimitable products generated by organizationally strong firms in one nation such as Germany can lead to the competitive advantage of its exports (see the Opening Case).[2] Further, recall from Chapters 2 and 3 that numerous politically and culturally derived rules of the game, known as institutions, constrain individual and firm behavior. Institutions can either limit or facilitate trade. For example, although American movies dominate the world market, Canada, France, and South Korea use regulations to limit the market share of American movies in order

Institutions can either limit or facilitate trade.

PengAtlas Map

Trade deficit
An economic condition in which a nation imports more than it exports.

Trade surplus
An economic condition in which a nation exports more than it imports.

Balance of trade
The country-level trade surplus or deficit.

to protect their domestic movie industries. On the other hand, we also see the rise of rules that facilitate trade, such as those promoted by the World Trade Organization (see Chapter 8).

Overall, why are there economic gains from international trade? According to the resource-based view, it is because some firms in one nation generate exports that are valuable, unique, and hard to imitate and that firms from other nations find it beneficial to import.[3] How do nations benefit from such gains? According to the institution-based view, different rules governing trade are designed to determine how such gains are shared (or not shared). The remainder of this chapter expands on these two perspectives.

> **LO2** Outline the classical and modern theories of international trade.

THEORIES OF INTERNATIONAL TRADE

Theories of international trade provide one of the oldest, richest, and most influential bodies of economic literature. Although the publication of Adam Smith's *The Wealth of Nations* in 1776 is usually considered the foundation of modern economics, theories of international trade predate Adam Smith. In fact, Adam Smith wrote *The Wealth of Nations* to challenge an earlier theory: mercantilism. This section introduces six major theories of international trade: (1) mercantilism, (2) absolute advantage, (3) comparative advantage, (4) product life cycle, (5) strategic trade, and (6) national competitive advantage of industries. The first three are often regarded as classical trade theories, and the last three are viewed as modern trade theories.

Mercantilism

Widely practiced during the 17th and 18th centuries, the theory of **mercantilism** viewed international trade as a zero-sum game. It suggested that the wealth of the world (measured in gold and silver at that time) was fixed, so a nation that exported more than it imported would enjoy the net inflows of gold and silver and become richer. On the other hand, a nation experiencing a trade deficit would see its gold and silver flowing out and, consequently, would become poorer. The upshot? Self-sufficiency would be best.

Although mercantilism is the oldest theory in international trade, it is not an extinct dinosaur. Very much alive, mercantilism is the direct intellectual ancestor of modern-day **protectionism**, which is the idea that governments should actively protect domestic industries from imports and vigorously promote exports. Even today, many modern governments may still be mercantilist at heart.

Absolute Advantage

The theory of absolute advantage, advocated by Adam Smith in 1776, opened the floodgates for the free trade movement that is still going on today. Smith argued that in the aggregate, the "invisible hand" of the free market—not government—should determine the scale and scope of economic activities. By trying to be self-sufficient and to (inefficiently) produce a wide range of goods, mercantilist policies *reduce* the wealth of a nation in the long run. The idea that free market forces should determine the buying and selling of goods and services with little or no government intervention is called **free trade**.

Specifically, Smith proposed a **theory of absolute advantage**: With free trade, a nation gains by specializing in economic activities in which it has an absolute advantage. What is absolute advantage? A nation that is more efficient than anyone else in the production of any good or service is said to have an **absolute advantage** in the production of that good or service. For instance, Smith argued that Portugal enjoyed an absolute advantage over England in producing grapes and wines because Portugal had better soil, water, and weather. Likewise, England had an absolute advantage over Portugal in raising sheep and producing wool. It cost England more to grow grapes: An acre of land that could raise sheep and produce fine wool would only produce an inferior grape and a lower quality wine.

Everyone has heard of port wine, one of Portugal's most famous exports, but who has heard of any world-famous English wines? Smith recommended that England specialize in sheep and wool, that Portugal specialize in grapes and wines, and that they trade with each other. Here are two of Smith's greatest insights. First, by specializing in the production of goods for which each has an absolute advantage, both can produce more. Second, both can benefit more by trading. By specializing, England produces more wool than it can

Portugal

England

© Cengage Learning 2013

use, and Portugal produces more wine than it can drink. When both countries trade, England gets more (and better) wine and Portugal more (and better) wool than either country could produce on its own. In other words, international trade is not a zero-sum game as mercantilism suggests. It is a *win-win* game.

How can this be? Smith's England–Portugal example offers a general sense, but let us use a specific example with hypothetical numbers (see Exhibits 5.2 and 5.3). For the sake of simplicity, assume that there are only two nations in the world: China and the United States. They perform only two economic activities: growing wheat and making aircraft. Production of wheat or aircraft, naturally, requires resources such as labor, land, and technology. Assume that both countries are equally endowed with 800 units of resources. Between the two activities, the United States has an absolute advantage in the production of aircraft: It takes 20 resources to produce an aircraft (for which China needs 40 resources), and the total US capacity is 40 aircraft if it does not produce wheat (point D in Exhibit 5.2). China has an absolute advan-

EXHIBIT 5.2 Absolute Advantage

tage in the production of wheat: It takes 20 resources to produce 1,000 tons of wheat (for which the United States needs 80 resources), and the total Chinese capacity is 40,000 tons of wheat if it does not make aircraft (point A). It is important to note that the United States can grow wheat and China can make aircraft, albeit inefficiently. Both nations need wheat and aircraft. Without trade, each nation would have to produce *both* by spending half of their resources on each—China at point B (20,000 tons of wheat and

EXHIBIT 5.3 Absolute Advantage

Know

Total units of resources = 800 for each country		Wheat	Aircraft
1. Resources required to produce 1,000 tons of wheat and one aircraft	China US	20 resources 80 resources	40 resources 20 resources
2. Production and consumption with no specialization and without trade (each country devotes *half* of its resources to each activity)	China (point B) US (point C) *Total production*	20,000 tons 5,000 tons *25,000 tons*	10 aircraft 20 aircraft *30 aircraft*
3. Production with specialization (China specializes in wheat and produces no aircraft, and the United States specializes in aircraft and produces no wheat)	China (point A) US (point D) *Total production*	40,000 tons 0 *40,000 tons*	0 40 aircraft *40 aircraft*
4. Consumption after each country trades one fourth of its output while producing at points A and D, respectively (scenario 3 above)	China US *Total consumption*	30,000 tons 10,000 tons *40,000 tons*	10 aircraft 30 aircraft *40 aircraft*
5. *Gains* from trade: Increase in consumption as a result of specialization and trade (scenario 4 versus scenario 2 above)	China US	+10,000 tons +5,000 tons	0 +10 aircraft

© Cengage Learning 2013

ten aircraft) and the United States at point C (5,000 tons of wheat and 20 aircraft). Interestingly, if they stay at points A and D, respectively, and trade one quarter of their output with each other (that is, 10,000 tons of Chinese wheat with ten American aircraft), these two countries, and by implication the global economy, both produce more and consume more (see Exhibit 5.3). In other words, the numbers show that there are *net* gains from trade based on absolute advantage.

Comparative Advantage

According to Adam Smith, each nation should look for absolute advantage. However, what can nations do when they do *not* possess absolute advantage? Continuing our two-country example of China and the United States, what if China is absolutely inefficient compared to the United States in the production of *both* wheat and aircraft (which is the real case today)? What should they do? Obviously, the theory of absolute advantage runs into a dead end.

British economist David Ricardo responded to Smith in 1817 by developing a **theory of comparative advantage**. This theory suggests that even though the United States has an absolute advantage in both wheat and aircraft over China, as long as China is not equally less efficient in the production of both goods, China can still choose to specialize in the production of one good (such as wheat) in which it has comparative advantage. **Comparative advantage** is defined as the relative (not absolute) advantage in one economic activity that one nation enjoys in comparison with other nations. Exhibits 5.4 and 5.5 show that China's comparative advantage lies in its *relatively less inefficient* production of wheat. If China devotes all resources to wheat, it can produce 10,000 tons, which is four fifths of the 12,500 tons that the United States can produce. However, at a maximum, China can produce only 20 aircraft, which is merely half of the 40 aircraft that the United States can make. By letting China specialize in the production of wheat and import-

ing some wheat from China, the United States is able to leverage its strengths by devoting its resources to aircraft. For example, if the United States devotes four fifths of its resources to aircraft and one fifth to wheat (point C in Exhibit 5.4), if China concentrates 100% of its resources on wheat (point E), and if the two trade with each other, then both countries produce and consume more than what they would produce and consume if they inefficiently devoted half of their resources to each activity (see Exhibit 5.5).

Again, the numbers show that there are *net* gains from trade—this time from comparative advantage. One crucial concept here is **opportunity cost**, which refers to the cost of pursuing one activity at the expense of another activity, given the alternatives. For the United States, the opportunity cost of concentrating on wheat at point A in Exhibit 5.4 is tremendous relative to producing aircraft at point D

EXHIBIT 5.4 Comparative Advantage

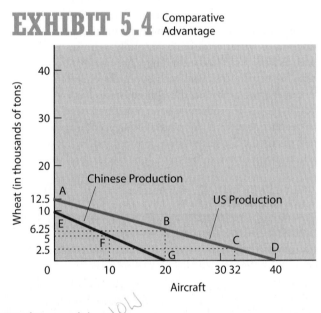

EXHIBIT 5.5 Comparative Advantage

KNOW

Total units of resources = 800 for each country		Wheat	Aircraft
1. Resources required to produce 1,000 tons of wheat and one aircraft	China US	80 resources 64 resources	40 resources 20 resources
2. Production and consumption with no specialization and without trade (each country devotes *half* of its resources to each activity)	China (point F) US (point B) *Total production*	5,000 tons 6,250 tons *11,250 tons*	10 aircraft 20 aircraft *30 aircraft*
3. Production with specialization (China devotes all resources to wheat, and the United States devotes one fifth of its resources to wheat and four fifths of its resources to aircraft)	China (point E) US (point C) *Total production*	10,000 tons 2,500 tons *12,500 tons*	0 32 aircraft *32 aircraft*
4. Consumption after China trades 4,000 tons of wheat for 11 US aircraft while producing at points E and C, respectively (scenario 3 above)	China US *Total consumption*	6,000 tons 6,500 tons *12,500 tons*	11 aircraft 21 aircraft *32 aircraft*
5. *Gains* from trade: Increase in consumption as a result of specialization and trade (scenario 4 versus scenario 2 above)	China US	+1,000 tons +250 tons	+1 aircraft +1 aircraft

Theory of comparative advantage
A theory that suggests that a nation gains by specializing in production of one good in which it has comparative advantage.

Comparative advantage
The relative (not absolute) advantage in one economic activity that one nation enjoys in comparison with other nations.

Opportunity cost
The cost of pursuing one activity at the expense of another activity.

IN FOCUS

Brazil's Comparative Advantage in Agriculture

A pine tree in a forest in Finland needs 50 years before it can be felled to make paper. A eucalyptus tree in coastal Brazil is ready in seven. Grapes in France can only be harvested once a year. Grapes in northeastern Brazil can bear fruit twice a year. Chicken and hog farmers in Canada have to consume energy to heat the barns. Their competitors in Brazil need no energy to heat their animals' dwellings. Blessed by an abundant supply of sun, soil, and water, Brazil is the world's number one exporter in beef, coffee, oranges, poultry, soybeans, and sugar. While Brazil's agricultural prowess may be the envy of many countries, in Brazil it has become a source of frustration. For much of the 20th century, the Brazilian government sought to deviate from Brazil's dependence on agriculture-based commodities and to industrialize, often with little regard to comparative or competitive advantage. The government's favorite policy was protectionism, which often did not succeed.

Brazil's market opening since the 1990s has led more Brazilians to realize that the country's comparative advantage indeed lies in

agriculture. One commodity that can potentially transform the low prestige associated with agricultural products is sugar cane-based ethanol. Brazil is a world leader in the production of ethanol, which has been mandated as an additive to gasoline used in cars since the 1970s. A system to distribute ethanol to gas stations, an oddity in the eyes of the rest of the world until recently, now looks like a national treasure that is the envy of the world. At present, no light vehicle in Brazil is allowed to run on pure gasoline. Since 2007, the mandatory blend for car fuels is at least 25% ethanol. Brazil currently produces 18 billion liters of ethanol, of which it exports 4 billion—more than half of worldwide exports. Ethanol now accounts for 40% of the fuel used by cars in Brazil. As the global ethanol trade is estimated to rise 25-fold by 2020, Brazil's comparative advantage in agricultural products is destined to shine more brightly.

Sources: "The economy of heat," *Economist*, 14 April 2007, 8–9; L. F. Monteiro, "Is God Brazilian?" Presentation at the Strategic Management Society Conference on Latin America, Rio de Janeiro, 11 March 2011; "Biofuels: The promise and the risks," *World Development Report 2008* (Washington: World Bank) 70–71.

---

because it is only 25% more productive in wheat than China but is 100% more productive in aircraft.

Relative to absolute advantage, the theory of comparative advantage seems counterintuitive. But comparative advantage is actually far more realistic and useful when applied in the real world than is absolute advantage. Why? While it is easy to identify an absolute advantage in a highly simplified, two-country world (like the one in Exhibit 5.2), how can each nation decide what to specialize in when there are over 200 nations in the world? It is simply too challenging to ascertain that one nation is absolutely better than all others in one activity. Is the United States *absolutely* better than not only China but also all other 200 nations in aircraft production? European nations that produce Airbus planes obviously beg to differ. The theory of comparative advantage suggests that even without an absolute advantage, the United States can still specialize profitably in aircraft as long as it is relatively more efficient than others. This insight has greatly lowered the threshold for specialization because absolute advantage is no longer required.

Where do absolute and comparative advantages come from? In a word: productivity. Smith looked at *absolute* productivity differences, and Ricardo emphasized *relative* pro-

ductivity differences. In this sense, absolute advantage is really a special case of comparative advantage. But what leads to such productivity differences? In the early 20th century, Swedish economists Eli Heckscher and Bertil Ohlin argued that absolute and comparative advantages stem from different **factor endowments**—the extent to which different countries possess various factors of production such as labor, land, and technology. This **factor endowment theory** (or **Heckscher–Ohlin theory**) proposed that nations will develop comparative advantages based on their *locally abundant* factors. For example, Brazil has abundant land, water, and warm weather—factors that enable it to become an agricultural powerhouse (see In Focus).

Product Life Cycle

The three classical theories—mercantilism, absolute advantage, and comparative advantage—all paint a *static* picture: If England has an absolute or comparative advantage in

Factor endowments
The extent to which different countries possess various factors of production such as labor, land, and technology.

Factor endowment theory (or Heckscher–Ohlin theory)
A theory that suggests that nations will develop comparative advantages based on their locally abundant factors.

© IStockphoto.com/Justin Horrocks / © IStockphoto.com/Luciana Bueno Santos

textiles, which it does mostly because of its factor endowments such as favorable weather and soil, it should keep making textiles. But factor endowments and trade patterns change over time, so the assumption that trade is static does not always hold in the real world. Adam Smith's England, over 200 years ago, was a major exporter of textiles, but today England's textile industry is rather insignificant. So what happened? While one may argue that the weather in England has changed and the soil has become less fertile for sheep (and wool), it is difficult to believe that weather and soil have changed so much in 200 years, which is a relatively short period for long-run climatic changes. Now consider another example that has nothing to do with weather or soil change. Since the 1980s, the United States has changed from a net exporter to a net importer of personal computers (PCs), while Malaysia has gone from being a net importer to a net exporter. Why have patterns of trade in PCs changed over time? Classical theories would have a hard time answering this intriguing question.

In 1966, American economist Raymond Vernon developed the **product life cycle theory**, which is the first *dynamic* theory to account for changes in the patterns of trade over time. Vernon divided the world into three categories: lead innovation nation (which, according to him, is typically the United States), other developed nations, and developing nations. Further, every product has three life cycle stages: new, maturing, and standardized. Shown in Exhibit 5.6, the first stage involves production of a new product (such as a TV) that commands a price premium. Such production will concentrate in the United States, which exports to other developed nations. In the second, maturing stage, demand and ability to produce grow in other developed nations such as Australia and Italy, so it becomes worthwhile to produce there. In the third stage, the previously new product is standardized (or commoditized). Thus, much production will now move to low-cost developing nations that export to developed nations. In other words,

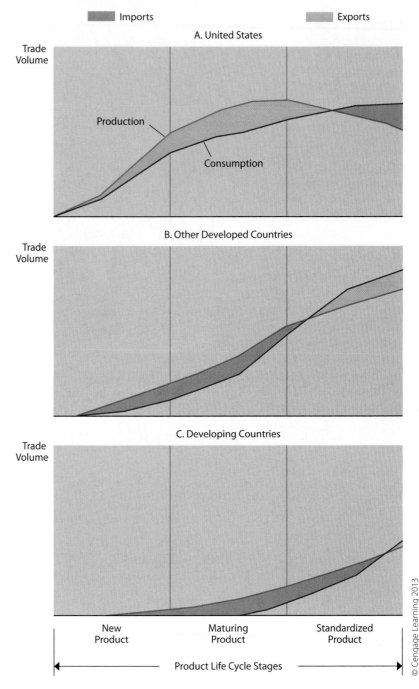

EXHIBIT 5.6 Theory of Product Life Cycles

Imports Exports

A. United States

Trade Volume

Production
Consumption

B. Other Developed Countries

Trade Volume

C. Developing Countries

Trade Volume

New Product | Maturing Product | Standardized Product

Product Life Cycle Stages

© Cengage Learning 2013

comparative advantage may change over time.

While this theory was first proposed in the 1960s, some later events such as the migration of PC production have supported its prediction. However, this theory has been criticized on two accounts. First, it assumes that the United States will always be the lead innovation nation for new products. This may be increasingly invalid. For example, the fanciest mobile (cell) phones are now routinely pioneered in Asia and Europe. Second, this theory assumes a stage-by-stage migration of production, taking at least several years, if not decades. In reality, however, an increasing number of firms now launch new products such as iPods *simultaneously* around the globe.

Product life cycle theory
A theory that suggests that patterns of trade change over time as production shifts and as the product moves from new to maturing to standardized stages.

EXHIBIT 5.7 Entering the Very Large, Super-Jumbo Market?

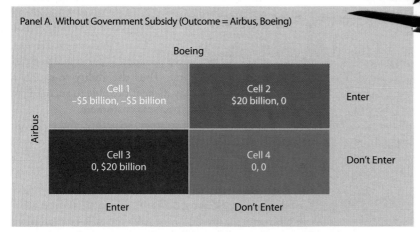

Panel A. Without Government Subsidy (Outcome = Airbus, Boeing)

	Boeing	
	Enter	Don't Enter
Airbus Enter	Cell 1 −$5 billion, −$5 billion	Cell 2 $20 billion, 0
Airbus Don't Enter	Cell 3 0, $20 billion	Cell 4 0, 0

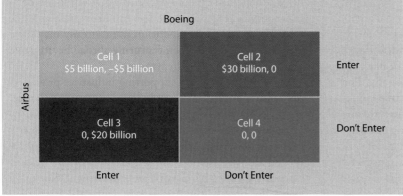

Panel B. With $10 Billion Subsidy From European Governments (Outcome = Airbus, Boeing)

	Boeing	
	Enter	Don't Enter
Airbus Enter	Cell 1 $5 billion, −$5 billion	Cell 2 $30 billion, 0
Airbus Don't Enter	Cell 3 0, $20 billion	Cell 4 0, 0

Strategic Trade

Except for mercantilism, none of the theories discussed above say anything about the role of governments. Since the days of Adam Smith, government intervention is usually regarded by economists as destroying value because, they contend, it distorts free trade. But government intervention is extensive and is not going away. In fact, thanks to the global recession, government intervention has been increasing around the world since 2008. Can government intervention actually add value? Since the 1970s, a new theory, strategic trade theory, has been developed to address this question.

Strategic trade theory suggests that strategic intervention by governments in certain industries can enhance their odds for international success. What are these industries? They tend to be highly capital-intensive industries with high barriers to entry, where domestic firms may have little chance of entering and competing without government assistance. These industries also feature substantial **first-mover advantages**—advantages that first entrants enjoy and do not share with late entrants. A leading example is the commercial aircraft industry. Founded in 1915 and strengthened by large military orders during World

War II, Boeing has long dominated this industry. In the jumbo jet segment, Boeing's first-mover advantages associated with its 400-seat 747, first launched in the late 1960s, are still significant today. Alarmed by such US dominance, British, French, German, and Spanish governments realized in the late 1960s that if they did not intervene, individual European aerospace firms might be driven out of business by US rivals. So these European governments agreed to launch and subsidize Airbus. In four decades, Airbus has risen from scratch to splitting the global market 50-50 with Boeing.

How do European governments help Airbus? Let us use the super-jumbo aircraft, which is larger than the Boeing 747, as an example. Both Airbus and Boeing are interested in entering this market. However, the demand in the next 20 years is only about 400 to 500 aircraft and a firm needs to sell at least 300 just to break even, which means that only one firm can be supported profitably. Shown in Exhibit 5.7 (Panel A), the outcome will be disastrous if both enter because each will lose $5 billion (Cell 1). If one enters and the other does not, the entrant will make $20 billion (Cells 2 and 3). It is also possible that both will choose not to enter (Cell 4). If a number of European governments promise Airbus a subsidiary of, say, $10 billion if it enters, then the picture changes to Panel B. Regardless of what Boeing does, Airbus finds it lucrative to enter. In Cell 1, if Boeing enters, it will lose $5 billion as before, whereas Airbus will make $5 billion ($10 billion subsidy minus $5 billion loss). So Boeing has no incentive to enter. Therefore, the more likely outcome is Cell 2, where Airbus enters and enjoys a profit of $30 billion. Therefore, the subsidy has given Airbus a *strategic* advantage, and the policy to assist Airbus is known as a **strategic trade policy**. This has indeed been the case, as the 550-seat A380 entered service in 2007 and became a formidable competitor for the Boeing 747.

strategic trade theory
A theory that suggests that strategic intervention by governments in certain industries can enhance their odds for international success.

First-mover advantage
Advantage that first entrants enjoy and do not share with late entrants.

Strategic trade policy
Economic policy that provides companies a strategic advantage through government subsidies.

Strategic trade theorists do not advocate a mercantilist policy to promote all industries. They propose to help only a few strategically important industries, such as those centered on clean energy like electric cars and batteries.[4] Still, this theory has been criticized on two accounts. First, many scholars and policy makers are uncomfortable with government intervention. What if governments are not sophisticated and objective enough to do this job? Second, many industries claim that they are strategically important. For example, after 9/11, American farmers successfully argued that agriculture is a strategic industry because the food supply needs to be guarded against terrorists and extracted more subsidies. Overall, where to draw the line between strategic and non-strategic industries is tricky.

National Competitive Advantage of Industries

The most recent theory is known as the **theory of national competitive advantage of industries.** This is popularly known as the **diamond theory** because its principal architect, Harvard strategy professor Michael Porter, presents it in a diamond-shaped diagram, as shown in Exhibit 5.8.[5] This theory focuses on why certain *industries* (but not others) within a nation are competitive internationally. For example, while Japanese electronics and automobile industries are global winners, Japanese service industries are notoriously inefficient. Porter is interested in finding out why.

Porter argues that the competitive advantage of certain industries in different nations depends on four aspects, which form a diamond. First, he starts with factor endowments, which refer to the natural and human resources as noted by the Heckscher–Ohlin theory. Some countries (such as Saudi Arabia) are rich in natural resources but short on population, while others (such as Singapore) have a well-educated population but few natural resources. Not surprisingly, Saudi Arabia exports oil, and Singapore exports semiconductors (which need abundant skilled labor). While building on these insights from previous theories, Porter argues that factor endowments are not enough.

Second, tough domestic demand propels firms to scale new heights. Why are American movies so competitive worldwide? One reason may be the level of extraordinary demand in the US market for exciting movies. Endeavoring to satisfy domestic demand, US movie studios unleash *High School Musical* and then *High School Musical 2* and *3* or *Spider-Man* and then *Spider-Man 2* and *3*, each time packing in more excitement. Most movies—in fact, most products—are created to satisfy domestic demand first. Thus the ability to satisfy a tough domestic crowd may make it possible to successfully deal with less demanding overseas customers.

Third, domestic firm strategy, structure, and rivalry in one industry play a huge role in its international success or failure. One reason the Japanese electronics industry is so competitive globally is because its *domestic* rivalry is probably the most intense in the world. If the 20 or so models of digital cameras or camcorders available in a typical American electronics store frustrate you, you will be even more frustrated when shopping for these items in Japan because the average store there carries about 200 models (!). Most firms producing such a bewildering range of models do not make money. However, the few top firms such as Canon that win the tough competition domestically may have a relatively easier time when venturing abroad because overseas competition is less demanding.

Finally, related and supporting industries provide the foundation upon which key industries can excel. In the absence of strong related and supporting industries such as engines, avionics, and materials, an aerospace industry cannot become globally competitive. Each of these related and supporting industries requires years (and often decades) of hard work and investment. For instance, inspired by the Airbus experience, the Chinese, Korean, and Japanese governments poured money into their own aerospace industries. Eventually, they all realized that Europe's long history and excellence in a series of critically related and supporting industries made it possible for Airbus to succeed. A lack

© Cengage Learning 2013

Theory of national competitive advantage of industries (or diamond theory)
A theory that suggests that the competitive advantage of certain industries in different nations depends on four aspects that form a diamond when diagrammed.

EXHIBIT 5.8 National Competitive Advantage of Industries: The Porter Diamond

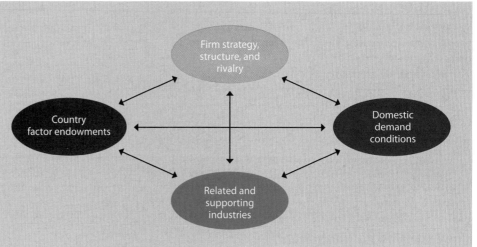

Source: M. Porter, "The competitive advantage of nations," *Harvard Business Review* (March-April 1990): 77. Reprinted with permission.

Part II: Acquiring Tools

of such industries made it unrealistic for the Chinese, Korean, and Japanese aerospace industries to succeed in making commercial aircraft.

Overall, Porter argues that the dynamic interaction of these four aspects explains what is behind the competitive advantage of leading industries in different nations. This theory is the first *multilevel* theory to realistically connect firms, industries, and nations, whereas previous theories work on only one or two levels. However, it has not been comprehensively tested. Some critics argue that the diamond places too much emphasis on domestic conditions. The recent rise of India's IT industry suggests that its international success is not entirely driven by domestic demand, which is relatively tiny compared with overseas demand—it is overseas demand that matters a lot more in this case.

Evaluating Theories of International Trade

In case you are tired after studying the six theories, you have to appreciate that we have just gone through over 300 years of research, debates, and policy changes around the world in about eight pages (!). As a student, that is not a small accomplishment. Exhibit 5.9 enables you to see the big picture. While you review it, keep the following four points in mind.

First, the classical pro-free trade theories seem like common sense today, but they were *revolutionary* in the late

EXHIBIT 5.9 Theories of International Trade: A Summary

Classical theories	Main points	Strengths and influences	Weaknesses and debates
Mercantilism	• International trade is a zero-sum game; trade deficits are dangerous • Governments should protect domestic industries and promote exports	• Forerunner of modern-day protectionism	• Inefficient allocation of resources • Reduces the wealth of the nation in the long run
Absolute advantage	• Nations should specialize in economic activities in which they have an absolute advantage and trade with others • By specializing and trading, each nation produces more and consumes more • The wealth of all trading nations and the world increases	• Birth of modern economics • Forerunner of the free trade movement • Defeats mercantilism, at least intellectually	• When one nation is absolutely inferior to another, the theory is unable to provide any advice • When there are many nations, it may be difficult to find an absolute advantage
Comparative advantage	• Nations should specialize in economic activities in which they have a comparative advantage and trade with others • Even if one nation is absolutely inferior to another, the two nations can still gainfully trade • Factor endowments underpin comparative advantage	• More realistic guidance to nations (and their firms) interested in trade but having no absolute advantage • Explains patterns of trade based on factor endowments	• Relatively static, assuming that comparative advantage and factor endowments do not change over time

Modern theories			
Product life cycle	• Comparative advantage first resides in the lead innovation nation, which exports to other nations • Production migrates to other advanced nations and then developing nations in different product life cycle stages	• First theory to incorporate dynamic changes in patterns of trade • More realistic with trade in industrial products in the 20th century	• The United States may not always be the lead innovation nation • Many new products are now launched simultaneously around the world
Strategic trade	• Strategic intervention by governments may help domestic firms reap first-mover advantages in certain industries • First-mover firms, aided by governments, may have better odds at winning internationally	• More realistic and positively incorporates the role of governments in trade • Provides direct policy advice	• Ideological resistance from many free trade scholars and policy makers • Invites all kinds of industries to claim they are strategic
National competitive advantage of industries	• Competitive advantage of different industries in a nation depends on the four interacting aspects of a diamond • The four aspects are (1) factor endowments; (2) domestic demand; (3) firm strategy, structure, and rivalry; and (4) related and supporting industries	• Most recent, most complex, and most realistic among various theories • As a multilevel theory, it directly connects firms, industries, and nations	• Has not been comprehensively tested • Overseas (not only domestic) demand may stimulate the competitiveness of certain industries

1700s and early 1800s when the world was dominated by mercantilistic thinking. Second, all theories simplify to make their point. Classical theories rely on highly simplistic assumptions of a model consisting of only two nations and two goods. Third, the theories also assume perfect **resource mobility**—the assumption that a resource used in producing for one industry can be shifted and put to use in another industry (for example, one resource removed from wheat production can be moved to make aircraft). In reality, not all resources can be moved. Farm hands, for example, will probably have a hard time assembling modern aircraft. Finally, classical theories assume no foreign exchange issues and zero transportation costs. So is free trade still as beneficial as Smith and Ricardo suggested in the real world of many countries, numerous goods, imperfect resource mobility, fluctuating exchange rates, high transportation costs, and product life cycle changes? The answer is still *Yes!* Worldwide data support the *basic* arguments for free trade.[6] (See the Debate feature for disagreements.)

Instead of relying on simple factor analysis, modern theories rely on more realistic product life cycles, first-mover advantages, and the diamond to explain and predict patterns of trade. Overall, classical and modern theories have significantly contributed to today's ever deepening trade links around the world. Yet, the victory of pro-free trade theories is not complete. The political realities, outlined next, indicate that mercantilism is still alive and well.

> **LO3** *Explain the importance of political realities governing international trade.*

REALITIES OF INTERNATIONAL TRADE

Although most theories support free trade, plenty of trade barriers exist. Although some trade barriers are being dismantled, many will remain. Let us examine why this is the case. To do so, we will first discuss the two broad types of trade barriers: tariff barriers and non-tariff barriers.

Tariff Barriers

A **tariff barrier** is a means of discouraging imports by placing a tariff (tax) on imported goods. As a major tariff barrier, an **import tariff** is a tax imposed on a good brought in from another country. Exhibit 5.10 uses rice tariffs in Japan to show *unambiguously* that net losses, known as **deadweight costs**, occur when import tariffs are imposed.

Resource mobility
The assumption that a resource used in producing a product in one industry can be shifted and put to use in another industry.

Tariff barrier
A means of discouraging imports by placing a tariff (tax) on imported goods.

Import tariff
A tax imposed on imports.

Deadweight costs
Net losses that occur in an economy as the result of tariffs.

- Panel A: In the absence of international trade, the domestic price is P_1 and domestic rice farmers produce Q_1, determined by the intersection of domestic supply and demand curves.

- Panel B: Because Japanese rice price P_1 is higher than world price P_2, foreign farmers export to Japan. Japanese farmers reduce output to Q_2. Japanese consumers enjoy more rice at Q_3 at a much lower price P_2.

- Panel C: The government imposes an import tariff, effectively raising the price from P_2 to P_3. Japanese farmers increase production from Q_2 to Q_4, and consumers pay more at P_3 and consume less by reducing consumption from Q_3 to Q_5. Imports fall from Q_2Q_3 in Panel B to Q_4Q_5 in Panel C.

Classical theorists such as Smith and Ricardo would have advised Japan to enjoy the gains from trade in Panel B. But political realities land Japan in Panel C, which, by limiting trade, introduces total inefficiency represented by the area consisting of A, B, C, and D. However, Japanese rice farmers gain the area of A, and the government pockets tariff revenues in the area of C. Therefore:

$$\text{Net losses} = \text{Total inefficiency} - \text{Net gain}$$
$$\text{(deadweight)} = \text{Area} (A + B + C + D) - \text{Area} (A + C)$$
$$= \text{Area} (B + D)$$

The net losses (areas B and D) represent unambiguous economic inefficiency to the nation as a whole. Japan is not alone in this regard. In 2010, an Apple iPad that retailed for $600 in the United States cost $1,000 (!) in Brazil, after adding a 60% import tariff.[7] In 2009, the United States slapped a 35% import tariff on tires made in China. Brazilian iPad lovers and American tire buyers have to pay more, and some may be unable to afford the products. While not being able to get your hands on an iPad will have no tangible damage, some economically struggling US drivers who should have replaced their worn-out tires may be forced to delay replacing their tires—and some may be *killed* should they be involved in accidents before they are able to afford the now more expensive tires.[8]

Given the well-known net losses, why are tariffs imposed? The answer boils down to the political realities. Although everybody in a country suffers because of higher prices, it is very costly to politically organize individuals and firms that are geographically scattered to advance the case for free trade. On the other hand, certain special interest groups tend to be geographically concentrated and skillfully organized to advance their interest. Although farmers represent less than 5% of the Japanese population, they represent a disproportionate number of votes in the Diet (Japanese parliament).[9] Why? Diet districts were drawn up in the aftermath of World War II, when most Japanese lived in rural areas. Although the majority of the population now lives in urban areas, such districts were never re-zoned. Thus when the powerful farm lobby speaks, the Japanese government listens.

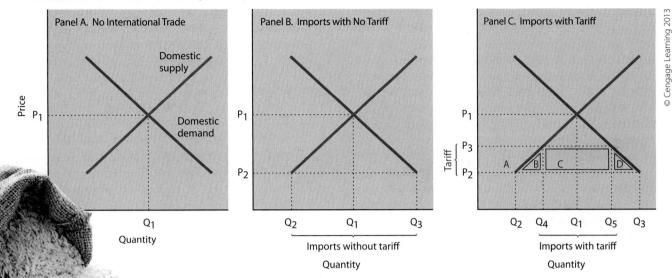

EXHIBIT 5.10 Tariff on Rice Imports in Japan

Panel A. No International Trade

Price — P_1 — Domestic supply — Domestic demand — Quantity — Q_1

Panel B. Imports with No Tariff

P_1 — P_2 — Q_2 — Q_1 — Q_3 — Imports without tariff — Quantity

Panel C. Imports with Tariff

Tariff — P_1 — P_3 — P_2 — A B C D — Q_2 — Q_4 — Q_1 — Q_5 — Q_3 — Imports with tariff — Quantity

© Cengage Learning 2013

P_1: Japanese domestic price without imports. P_2: World price (and Japanese domestic price with no tariff). P_3: Japanese domestic price with import tariff.

Non-Tariff Barriers

Today, tariff barriers are often criticized around the world, and non-tariff barriers are now increasingly the weapon of choice in trade wars. A **non-tariff barrier (NTB)** discourages imports using means other than tariffs on imported goods. NTBs include subsidies, import quotas, export restraints, local content requirements, administrative policies, and antidumping duties.

Subsidies, as noted earlier, are government payments to domestic firms. Much like their Japanese counterparts, European farmers are masters of extracting subsidies even though they constitute only 2% of the EU population. The EU's Common Agricultural Policy (CAP) costs European taxpayers $47 billion a year, eating up 40% of the EU budget.

Import quotas are restrictions on the quantity of goods that can be brought into a country. Import quotas are worse than tariffs because foreign goods can still be imported if tariffs are paid. Quotas are thus the most straightforward denial of absolute or comparative advantage. For example, between 2003 and 2009, Australia annually exported 770,000 head of live cattle to Indonesia, to the delight of Indonesian beef lovers. However, since 2009, import permits suddenly became harder to obtain. A quota of only 500,000 head of imported cattle was set for 2011.[10] For Indonesia, a densely populated island nation, importing beef from the sparsely populated cattle country next door would tap into

Australia's comparative advantage and would be win-win for both countries. But with the shrinking quota, Aussie cattle exporters are devastated, and Indonesian beef lovers have to put up with skyrocketing prices—and some of them may have to quit eating beef at all.

Because import quotas are protectionist pure and simple, they force countries to shoulder certain political costs in today's largely pro-free trade environment. In response, **voluntary export restraints (VERs)** have been developed to show that, on the surface, exporting countries *voluntarily* agree to restrict their exports. In essence, though, VERs are export quotas. One of the most (in)famous examples is the set of VERs that the Japanese government agreed to in the early 1980s to restrict US-bound automobile exports. The VERs, of course, were a euphemism because the Japanese did not really volunteer to restrict their exports. Only when faced with concrete protectionist threats did the Japanese reluctantly agree.

Another NTB is **local content requirements**, which are rules stipulating that a certain proportion of the value of the goods made in one country must originate from that country. The Japanese automobile VERs are again a case in point. Starting in the mid 1980s,

Non-tariff barrier (NTB)
A means of discouraging imports using means other than taxes on imported goods.

Subsidy
A government payment to domestic firms.

Import quota
A restriction on the quantity of goods that may be brought into a country.

Voluntary export restraint (VER)
An international agreement that shows that an exporting country voluntarily agrees to restrict its exports.

Local content requirement
A rule that stipulates that a certain proportion of the value of a good must originate from the domestic market.

because of VERs, Japanese automakers switched to producing cars in the United States through foreign direct investment. Initially, such factories were "screwdriver plants," because a majority of components were imported from Japan and only screwdrivers were needed to tighten the bolts. To deal with this issue, many countries impose local content requirements, mandating that a domestically produced product will still be treated as an "import" subject to tariffs and NTBs unless a certain fraction of its value (such as the 51% specified by the Buy America Act) is produced locally.

Administrative policies are bureaucratic rules that make it harder to import foreign goods. For example, Singapore bans the import of regular chewing gum because the government is concerned about the mess from the improper disposal of used gum. Only gums with documented health benefits can be imported. Further, customers will have to give their names to the seller so that the authorities can hold someone accountable in case of a chewing gum mess. The Brazilian government ordered Petrobras to buy 70% of its equipment from Brazil. The Russian government recently complained that Aeroflot, the country's flag carrier, flies a nearly all Western fleet made by Boeing and Airbus, and threatened to use administrative measures to force Aeroflot to buy Russian aircraft if it did not change its purchase behavior.

Finally, the arsenal of trade weapons also includes **antidumping duties** levied on imports that have been "dumped," or sold below cost in order to unfairly drive domestic firms out of business. See the Debate feature in Chapter 10 for some specific examples.

Economic Arguments Against Free Trade

Overall, trade barriers reduce or eliminate international trade. While certain domestic industries and firms benefit, the entire country—or at least a majority of its consumers—tends to suffer. Given these well-known negative aspects, why do people make arguments against free trade? This section outlines economic arguments against free trade, and the next section deals with political arguments. Two prominent economic arguments against free trade are: (1) the need to protect domestic industries and (2) the need to shield infant industries.

The oldest and most frequently used economic argument against free trade is the urge to protect domestic industries, firms, and jobs from allegedly "unfair" foreign competition—in short, protectionism. Calls for protection are not limited to commodity producers. Highly talented individuals, such as American mathematicians and Japanese sumo wrestlers, have also called for protection. Foreign math PhDs grab 40% of US math jobs, and recent US math PhDs face a jobless rate of 12%. Many American math PhDs have thus called for protection of their jobs. Similarly, Japanese sumo wrestlers insist that foreign sumo wrestlers should not be allowed to throw their weight around in Japan.

The second argument is the infant industry argument. Young domestic firms need government protection. Otherwise, they stand no chance of surviving and will be crushed by mature foreign rivals. It is thus imperative that governments level the playing field by assisting infant industries. While this argument is sometimes legitimate, governments and firms have a tendency to abuse it. Some protected infant industries may never grow up—why bother? When Airbus was a true infant in the 1960s, it no doubt deserved some subsidies. However, by the 2000s, Airbus had become a giant that could take on Boeing. (In some years, Airbus has outsold Boeing.) Nevertheless, Airbus continues to ask for subsidies, which European governments continue to provide.

Political Arguments Against Free Trade

Political arguments against free trade are based on advancing a nation's political, social, and environmental agenda regardless of possible economic gains from trade. These arguments include national security, consumer protection, foreign policy, and environmental and social responsibility.

First, national security concerns are often invoked to protect defense-related industries. France has always insisted on maintaining an independent defense industry to produce nuclear weapons, aircraft carriers, and combat jets. While the French can purchase such weapons at much lower costs from the United States, which is eager to sell them, the French answer has usually been "No, thanks!"

Second, consumer protection has frequently been used as an argument for nations to erect trade barriers (see the Closing Case). For example, American hormone-treated beef was banned by the European Union in the 1990s because of the alleged health risks. Even though

France

Administrative policy
A bureaucratic rule that makes it harder to import foreign goods.

Antidumping duty
A cost levied on imports that have been "dumped," or sold below cost to unfairly drive domestic firms out of business.

Foreign math PhDs grab 40% of US math jobs.

Classical Theories Versus New Realities

Smith and Ricardo would probably turn in their graves if they heard that one of today's hottest trade debates—over trade deficit—still echoes the old debate between mercantilists and free traders. Nowhere is the debate more ferocious than in the United States, which runs the world's largest trade deficit. In 2010, it reached $634 billion (4% of GDP). It was lower than the $760 billion peak (6% of GDP) in 2006. In 2009, the deficit was "only" $400 billion (3% of GDP), mostly due to rapid falls in imports as the recession cut into US consumer spending. At present, the deficit is still very high. *Should this level of trade deficit be of concern?*

NO Armed with classical theories, free traders argue that the deficit is not a grave concern and that international trade is not about competition. They argue that the United States and its trading partners mutually benefit by developing a deeper division of labor based on comparative advantage. Former Treasury secretary Paul O'Neill went so far as to say that trade deficit was "an antiquated theoretical construct."

YES Critics strongly disagree. They argue that international trade *is* about competition—about markets, jobs, and incomes. In 2009, President Obama announced the goal of doubling US exports within the next five years. Highlighting the importance of exports, Boeing CEO Jim McNerney said: "Every time a Boeing 777 lands in China, it lands with about 4 million parts reflecting the workmanship of some 11,000 small, medium, and large suppliers." Trade deficits have always been blamed on the particular country with which the United States runs the largest deficit, such as Japan in the 1980s. Because the US trade deficit with China reached $273 billion in 2010 (more than one third of the total deficit), the recent trade deficit debate is otherwise known as the China trade debate (Exhibit 5.11), which is often emotionally charged.

While the China trade debate is primarily about *merchandise* trade and unskilled manufacturing jobs that classical theories talk about, another debate (mostly on India) is about *service* trade and high-skill jobs in high technology such as IT. Classical theorists argue that the United States and India trade by tapping into each other's comparative advantage: India leverages its abundant, high-skill, and low-wage labor, and Americans channel their energy and resources to higher-skill, higher-paying jobs. While regrettably certain Americans will lose jobs, the nation as a whole benefits—so the theory goes.

But, not so fast!, argued retired MIT economics professor Paul Samuelson. In an influential paper, Samuelson suggested that India can innovate in an area, such as IT, where the United States traditionally enjoys comparative advantage. Indian innovation can reduce the price of US software exports and curtail the wage of US IT workers. Despite the availability of cheaper goods (which is a plus), the net effect may be that the United States is *worse* off as a whole. Now even Samuelson, who won a Nobel Prize for his research on the gains from international trade, is not so sure about comparative advantage—one of the founding pillars of modern economics.

Jagdish Bhagwati, an Indian-born, Columbia University

China

EXHIBIT 5.11 Debate on the US Trade Deficit with China

US trade deficit with China is a huge problem	US trade deficit with China is not a huge problem
Naïve trader versus unfair protectionist (in China) The United States is a naïve trader with open markets. China has "unfairly" protected its markets.	*Market reformer versus unfair protectionist (in America)* China's markets are already unusually open. Its trade volume (merchandise and services) is 75% of GDP, whereas the US volume is only 25%.
Greedy exporters Unscrupulous Chinese exporters are eager to gut US manufacturing jobs and drive US rivals out of business.	*Eager foreign investors* Two-thirds of Chinese exports are generated by foreign-invested firms in China, and numerous US firms have invested in and benefited from such operations in China.
The demon who has caused deflation Cheap imports sold at the China price push down prices and cause deflation.	*Thank China (and Wal-Mart) for low prices* Every consumer benefits from cheap prices brought from China by US firms such as Wal-Mart.
Intellectual property (IP) violator China is a blatant violator of IP rights, and US firms lose $2 billion a year.	*Inevitable step in development* True, but (1) the United States did that in the 19th century (to the British), and (2) IP protection will improve in China.
Currency manipulator* The yuan is severely undervalued (maybe up to 40%), giving Chinese exports an unfair advantage in being priced at an artificially low level.	*Currency issue is not relevant* The yuan is somewhat undervalued, but (1) US and other foreign firms producing in China benefit, and (2) yuan appreciation will not eradicate the US trade deficit.
Something has to be done If the Chinese don't do it our way (especially the US demand to raise the value of yuan), the United States should introduce drastic measures (such as slapping 20% to 30% tariffs on all Chinese imports).	*Remember the gains from trade argued by classical theories?* Since 2000, US exports to China grew 330% versus only 29% to the rest of the world. Tariffs will certainly trigger China's retaliation and protests at the WTO, which China may win. In addition, tariffs will not bring back US jobs, which will simply go to Mexico or Malaysia.

* The currency issue will be discussed in more detail in Chapter 7.

Sources: "Five ways forward with China," *Bloomberg Businessweek*, 28 June 2010, 4–5; "The runaway trade giant," *BusinessWeek*, 24 April 2006, 30–33; "The dragon comes calling," *Economist*, 3 September 2005, 24–25; "Top trading partners," US Census Bureau, 2011, available online at http://www.census.gov (accessed 25 March 2011); "US exports to China," *China Business Review*, July 2010, 46–49.

trade expert, and his colleagues countered Samuelson by arguing that classical pro–free trade theories still hold. Bhagwati and colleagues wrote:

Imagine that you are exporting aircraft, and new producers of aircraft emerge abroad. That will lower the price of your aircraft, and your gains from trade will diminish. You have to be naïve to believe that this can never happen. But you have to be even more naïve to think that the policy response to the reduced gains from trade is to give up the remaining gains as well. The critical policy question we must address is: When external developments, such as the growth of skills in China and India, for instance, do diminish the gains from trade to the US, is the harm to the US going to be reduced or increased if the US turns into Fortress America? The answer is: The US will only increase its anguish if it closes its markets.

India

According to Bhagwati and colleagues, the threat posed by Indian innovation is vastly exaggerated, and offshoring is too small to matter much. Although approximately 3.4 million US jobs may be outsourced by 2015, the US economy in any given year destroys 30 million jobs and creates slightly more, thus dwarfing the effect of offshoring. Further, higher-level jobs will replace those lost to offshoring. But here is a huge problem in the middle of the jobless recovery from the Great Recession: Will there be enough such jobs?

"America's trade deficit: Expect some storm damage," *BusinessWeek*, 3 October 2005, 31; N. Easton, "Why free trade matters to companies like Caterpillar," *Fortune*, 26 July 2010, 40; P. Samuelson, "Where Ricardo and Mill rebut and confirm arguments of mainstream economists supporting globalization," *Journal of Economic Perspectives* 18, no. 4 (2004), 135–146; J. Bhagwati, A. Panagariya, and T. Sribivasan, "The muddles over outsourcing," *Journal of Economic Perspectives* 18, no. 4 (2004), 93–114; J. Bhagwati and A. Panagariya, "Trading opinions about free trade," *BusinessWeek*, 27 December 2004, 20.

the United States won a WTO battle on this, the European Union still has refused to remove the ban.

Third, trade intervention is often used to meet foreign policy objectives. **Trade embargoes** are politically motivated trade sanctions against foreign countries to signal displeasure. For example, the United States has enforced embargoes against Iran, Sudan, and Syria. In 2009, DHL paid a record fine of $9.4 million for sending illegal shipments to these countries. According to a US Treasury Department statement, DHL "may have conferred a significant economic advantage to these sanctioned countries that potentially created extraordinarily adverse harm." What are such dangerous shipments? Condoms, Tiffany jewelry, and radar detectors for cars, according to the same Treasury Department statement.[11]

Finally, environmental and social responsibility can be used as political arguments to initiate trade intervention against certain countries. In a "shrimp-turtle" case, the United States banned shrimp imports from India, Malaysia, Pakistan, and Thailand. Although the shrimp were not harvested from US waters, they were caught using a technique that also accidentally trapped and killed sea turtles, an endangered species protected by the United States. India, Malaysia, Pakistan, and Thailand were upset and brought the case to the WTO, alleging that the United States invoked an environmental law as a trade barrier.

the context of international trade: What determines the success and failure of firms' exports around the globe? The two core perspectives lead to two answers. Fundamentally, the various economic theories underpin the resource-based view, suggesting that successful exports are valuable, unique, and hard-to-imitate products generated by certain firms from a nation. However, the political realities stress the explanatory and predictive power of the institution-based view: As rules of the game, laws and regulations promoted by various special interest groups can protect certain domestic industries, firms, and individuals; erect trade barriers; and make the nation as a whole worse off.

Listed in Exhibit 5.12, three implications for action emerge. First, location, location, location! In international trade, a savvy manager's first job is to leverage the comparative advantage of world-class locations. For instance, as managers aggressively tapped into Argentina's comparative advantage in wine production, its wine exports grew from $6 million in 1987 to $500 million in 2010.

Second, comparative advantage is not fixed. Managers need to constantly monitor and nurture the current comparative advantage of a location and take advantage of new promising locations. Managers who fail to realize when a location no longer has a comparative advantage are likely to fall behind. For example, numerous German managers have moved production out of Germany, citing the country's reduced comparative advantage in basic manufacturing.

LO4 *Identify factors that should be considered when your firm participates in international trade.*

Trade embargo
A politically motivated trade sanction against foreign countries to signal displeasure.

MANAGEMENT SAVVY

How does this chapter answer the big question in global business, adapted for

EXHIBIT 5.12 Implications for Action

- Discover and leverage comparative advantage of world-class locations.
- Monitor and nurture the current comparative advantage of certain locations, and take advantage of new locations.
- Be politically active to demonstrate, safeguard, and advance the gains from international trade.

However, they still concentrate top-notch, high-end manufacturing in Germany, leveraging its excellence in engineering (see the Opening Case).

Third, managers need to be politically savvy if they appreciate the gains from trade. While managers at many uncompetitive firms have long mastered the game of using politicians to gain protection, managers at competitive firms tend to shy away from politics. But they often fail to realize that free trade is *not* free—it requires constant efforts to demonstrate and advance the gains from such trade. For example, the US-China Business Council, a pro-free trade (in particular, pro-China trade) group consisting of 250 large US corporations, has frequently spoken out in defense of trade with China.[12]

ETHICAL DILEMMA

CANADA AND THE UNITED STATES FIGHT OVER PIGS

Sharing the world's longest undefended border, Canada and the United States are the best of friends. Their bilateral trading relationship is the world's largest, with $560 billion in volume. The two-way traffic that crosses the Ambassador Bridge between Windsor, Ontario, and Detroit, Michigan, equals all US exports to Japan. About 76% of Canada's exports (approximately one quarter of its GDP) go to its southern neighbor, making it the largest exporter to the United States. Canadian products command approximately 20% of the US import market share. In comparison, China, the second largest exporter to the United States, commands only slightly over 10%. Canada is also the largest importer of US products, absorbing about one quarter of US exports. The United States ran a $28 billion trade deficit with Canada in 2010. Despite such a close relationship, the two countries fight like "cats and dogs" in trade disputes. Most recently, they have traded blows over pigs.

In an effort to tighten food labeling, the Obama administration in 2009 implemented the Mandatory Country of Origin Labeling (COOL) legislation, requiring US firms to track and notify customers of the country of origin of meat and other agricultural products at each major stage of production, including at the retail level. Unfortunately, such a seemingly innocent move in the name of protecting consumers provoked fierce protests from Canada. In a normal year, Canada would export approximately $3 billion in hogs (live pigs) to the United States. In 2009, such exports suffered from a disastrous 60% drop.

The reason is that many young Canadian pigs are exported to the United States, where they are mixed and raised together with indigenous US pigs for fattening and slaughter. After several months, separating the (immigrant) Canadian pigs from the (native-born) US pigs is challenging and costly. The US Department of Agriculture (USDA) estimates that it will cost the food industry $2.5 billion to comply with the new rules. When facing such hassles, several major US pork producers, including the top five that account for more than half of all pork sold in the United States (Cargill, Hormel, JBS SA, Seaboard, and Smithfield), simply stopped buying hogs from Canada or gradually phased out such purchases. In addition to damaging livestock exports, processed meat products from Canada, including the legendary Canadian bacon, were also broadly affected.

Starting in May 2009, the two governments negotiated. While the United States modified some rules to alleviate Canadian concerns, the negotiations eventually broke down. Canada's frustrated Trade Minister Stockwell Day said in October 2009:

The US requirements are so onerous that they affect the ability of our hog and cattle exporters to compete fairly in the US market. The US law leaves the Canadian government with no choice but to escalate its first formal trade dispute with the Obama administration by pressing charges at the WTO.

In response, US Trade Representative Ron Kirk and Agriculture Secretary Tom Vilsack in a joint statement in October 2009 argued:

We believe that our implementation of COOL provides information to consumers in a manner consistent with our WTO commitments. Countries have agreed since long before the existence of the WTO that country-of-origin labeling is a legitimate policy. It is common for other countries to require that goods be labeled as to their origin.

The COOL pig fight is not the only dispute between Canada and the United States. Canada's other trade grievances include "Buy American" purchasing rules and generous US biofuel tax breaks for paper mills. While Canada and the United States fight over item by item in their long list of trade grievances, a useful mental exercise is to ask: What if these two friendly nations stopped trading all together? Normally, scholars studying this intriguing question would have to use simulation methods based on hypothetical data to entertain what would happen if they stopped trading. Thanks to 9/11, such an unthinkable scenario did take place.

Immediately after the terrorist attacks on September 11, 2001, the United States closed all airports, seaports, and land crossings with Canada (and Mexico). The world's largest bilateral trading relationship literally shut down. When the borders reopened days later, US officials undertook intensive inspections of commercial traffic that, among other things, delayed truck carriers for up to 18 hours. An exhaustive study found that Canadian exports to the United States in the fourth quarter of 2001 were 20% lower than they would have been in the absence of the border security consequences of 9/11. Even by 2005, exports from Canada were $12 billion less than they would otherwise have been had 9/11 and the US security responses not occurred. By the same time (2005), US exports to Canada resumed their normal level.

In other words, Canadian exporters will suffer disproportionate damage due to any unilateral tightening of the border by the United States—whether for post-9/11 security reasons or for food safety reasons at present. As Canadian hog producers struggle with the recession, the high Canadian dollar, a spike in feed costs, and widespread swine flu fears, it remains to be seen whether cool heads will prevail when fighting over COOL.

Sources: "Official: Canada will win COOL dispute," *Capital Press*, 13 January 2011, available online at http://www.capitalpress.com; I. Fergusen, *United States–Canada Trade and Economic Relationship* (Washington: Congressional Research Service, 2006); "Canada turns to WTO over US label law," *Globe and Mail*, 8 October 2009, B7; S. Globerman and P. Storer, *The Impacts of 9/11 on Canada–US Trade* (Toronto: University of Toronto Press, 2008); "US-COOL dispute proceeds by WTO," *Pig Progress*, 8 October 2009, available online at http://www.pigprogress.net; "Trade in goods with Canada," US Census Bureau, 2011, available online at http://www.census.gov.

Investing Abroad DIRECTLY

CHAPTER 6

South African Firms Invest Abroad

Since apartheid was removed in 1994, South Africa has brewed a series of multinationals that are increasingly active abroad. While most readers of this book probably have heard about De Beers diamonds, how many of you have heard of Dimension Data, MTN, Old Mutual, SABMiller, Sasol, and Standard Bank? If you have not heard of them, watch out, as they may soon come to a city near you (if they have not already arrived).

Naturally, South African firms frequently begin foreign expansion by entering sub-Saharan African countries. In fact, South Africa, as a source country for foreign investment, is the number one foreign investor in sub-Saharan Africa with more than $8.5 billion plowed into the region. South African Breweries (SAB) first pioneered the concept of the pan-African beer market and then went on to become the global titan known as SABMiller—after acquiring Miller Brewing Company of the United States in 2002.

As an early mover in cellular (mobile) phones, telecom provider MTN was one of a handful of companies to defy conventional wisdom and prove that Africa could be a huge market for mobile services. Retailers such as Massmart, Shoprite, and Game are bringing Western-style shopping to Malawi, Mozambique, Nigeria, Uganda, and others. Standard Bank has charged into 16 African countries that previously often lacked even basic financial services. "Africa is the next China," one South African businessman noted. South African firms have every intention to enjoy first-mover advantages there.

After a short time cutting their teeth in Africa, many South African firms spread their wings beyond the shores of Africa. In the early 1990s, SAB moved into China and Central and Eastern Europe, establishing strong positions in major emerging economies ahead of global rivals. Since becoming SABMiller, it has

© Nadine Hutton/Bloomberg via Getty Images

LEARNING OBJECTIVES
After studying this chapter, you should be able to:

LO1 *identify and define the key terms associated with foreign direct investment (FDI).*

LO2 *use the resource-based and institution-based views to explain why FDI takes place.*

LO3 *explain how FDI results in ownership advantages.*

LO4 *identify the ways your firm can acquire and neutralize location advantages.*

LO5 *list the benefits of internalization.*

LO6 *identify different political views on FDI and understand its benefits and costs to host and home countries.*

LO7 *list three things you need to do as your firm considers FDI.*

further globalized. It is now the second largest brewer in South
America. Old Mutual, South Africa's biggest financial services firm, bought Sweden's oldest insurance house in 2005. Dimension Data (Didata), an IT firm, competes in over 30 countries. Sasol, a chemicals and energy firm, operates in more than 20 countries.

What explains such a surge of internationalization from South Africa? From an institution-based view, the lifting of anti-apartheid sanctions by other countries and the generally open trade and investment environment worldwide have made such global expansion possible. From a resource-based standpoint, since South Africa represents 10% of Africa's population but 45% of its GDP, winning firms in South Africa not surprisingly have a competitive edge in other less competitive African countries. Capabilities that

serve African customers well can then be leveraged to more effectively compete in more distant emerging economies such as China, Central and Eastern Europe, and South America. "South Africans do well when they go elsewhere," noted another expert, "because they're not afraid, having done well in the most difficult continent on earth."

Sources: "Africa's dynamo," *BusinessWeek*, 15 December 2008, 51–56; "Going global," *Economist*, 15 July 2006, 59–60; "Africa's new Big Man," *Economist*, 18 April 2009, 11; "The price of freedom," *Economist*, 5 June 2010: special report; United Nations (UN), *World Investment Report 2010* (New York and Geneva: UN, 2010).

Why are South African firms increasingly interested in foreign direct investment (FDI)? Recall from Chapter 1 that FDI is defined as putting money into activities that control and manage value-added activities in other countries. Is it because of the push of intense competition at home? The pull of lucrative markets abroad? Or both? Also recall from Chapter 1 that firms that engage in FDI are known as multinational enterprises (MNEs). On a worldwide basis, FDI has been experiencing a modest recovery after the setback unleashed by the Great Recession of 2008–2009. Cautious optimism is now in the air.

This chapter starts by first defining key terms related to FDI. Then we address a crucial question: Why do firms engage in FDI? We outline how the core perspectives introduced earlier—namely, resource-based and institution-based views—can help answer this question.[1] We then look at a debate over whether countries should welcome certain FDI. Finally, we outline factors a firm should address as it considers engaging in FDI.

> **Identify and define the key terms associated with foreign direct investment (FDI).**

UNDERSTANDING THE FDI VOCABULARY

Part of FDI's complexity is associated with its vocabulary. This section will try to reduce the complexity by setting the terms straight.

Foreign portfolio investment (FPI)
Holding securities, such as stocks and bonds, of firms in other countries but without a controlling interest.

Management control rights
The rights to appoint key managers and establish control mechanisms.

Horizontal FDI
A type of FDI in which a firm produces the same products or offers the same services in a host country as at home.

The Key Word Is *Direct*

International investment happens primarily in two ways: FDI and **foreign portfolio investment (FPI)**. FPI refers to holding securities, such as stocks and bonds, of companies in countries outside one's own but does not entail the active management of foreign

assets. Essentially, FPI is foreign *indirect* investment. In contrast, the key word in FDI is *direct*—the direct, hands-on management of foreign assets. Some of you reading this book may have some FPIs—that is, you own some foreign stocks and bonds. However, as a student taking this course, it is by definition impossible that you are also engaging in FDI at the same time, because that requires you to be a manager who is getting your feet wet actively managing foreign operations rather than just learning about them.

For statistical purposes, the United Nations defines FDI as an equity stake of 10% or more in a foreign-based enterprise. A lower percentage invested in a foreign firm is considered FPI. Without a sufficiently large equity, it is difficult to exercise **management control rights**—the rights to appoint key managers and establish control mechanisms. Many firms invest abroad for the explicit purpose of managing foreign operations, and they need a large equity, sometimes up to 100%, to be able to do that.

Horizontal and Vertical FDI

FDI can be horizontal or vertical. Recall the value chain from Chapter 4, whereby firms perform value-adding activities stage by stage in a vertical fashion, from upstream to downstream. When a firm takes the same activity at the same value-chain stage from its home country and *duplicates* it in a host country through FDI, we call this horizontal FDI (see Exhibit 6.1). For example, BMW assembles cars in Germany. Through horizontal FDI, it does the same thing in host countries such as Thailand and the United States. Overall, **horizontal FDI** refers to producing the same products or offering the same services in a host country as firms do at home.

If a firm moves upstream or downstream in different value chain stages in a host country through FDI, we label

© iStockphoto.com/Joshua Blake

this **vertical FDI** (see Exhibit 6.2). For example, if BMW (hypothetically) only assembled cars and did not manufacture components in Germany but entered into components manufacturing through FDI in Russia (an earlier activity in the value chain), this would be **upstream vertical FDI**. Likewise, if BMW did not engage in car distribution in Germany but invested in car dealerships in Egypt (a later activity in the value chain), it would be **downstream vertical FDI**.

FDI Flow and Stock

Other words often associated with FDI are "flow" and "stock." **FDI flow** is the amount of FDI moving in a given period (usually a year) in a certain direction. **FDI inflow** usually refers to FDI moving into a country in a year, and **FDI outflow** typically refers to FDI moving out of a country in a year. Peng-Atlas Map 8 illustrates the top ten economies for FDI inflows and outflows. **FDI stock** is the total accumulation of inbound FDI in a country or outbound FDI from a country. Hypothetically, between two countries A and B, if firms from A undertake $10 billion of FDI in B in Year 1 and another $10 billion in Year 2, then we can say that in each of these two years, B receives annual FDI *inflows* of $10 billion and, correspondingly, A generates annual FDI

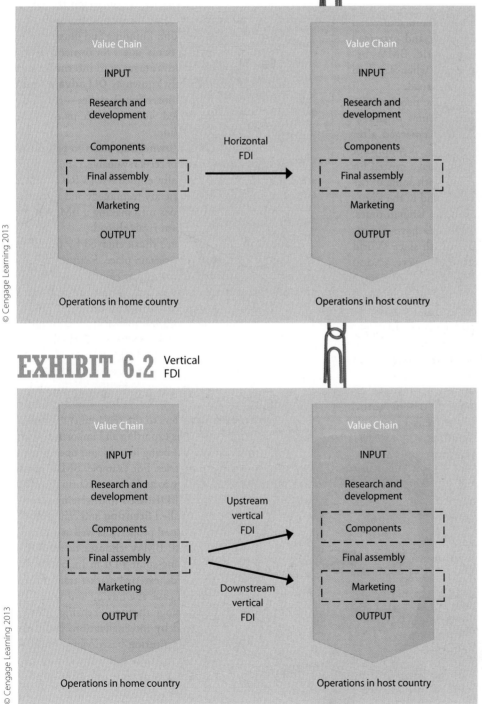

EXHIBIT 6.1 Horizontal FDI

EXHIBIT 6.2 Vertical FDI

Vertical FDI
A type of FDI in which a firm moves upstream or downstream in different value chain stages in a host country.

Upstream vertical FDI
A type of vertical FDI in which a firm engages in an upstream stage of the value chain.

Downstream vertical FDI
A type of vertical FDI in which a firm engages in a downstream stage of the value chain.

FDI flow
The amount of FDI moving in a given period (usually a year) in a certain direction.

FDI inflow
FDI moving into a country in a year.

FDI outflow
FDI moving out of a country in a year.

FDI stock
The total accumulation of inbound FDI in a country or outbound FDI from a country across a given period of time (usually several years).

outflows of $10 billion. If we assume that firms from no other countries undertake FDI in country B and prior to Year 1 no FDI was possible, then the total *stock* of FDI in B by the end of Year 2 is $20 billion. Essentially, flow is a snapshot of a given point in time, and stock represents the cumulative volume.

MNE Versus Non-MNE

An MNE, by definition, is a firm that engages in FDI when doing business abroad. Note that non-MNE firms can also do business abroad by exporting and importing, licensing and franchising, outsourcing, or engaging in FPI. What sets MNEs apart from non-MNEs is FDI. An exporter has to undertake FDI in order to become an MNE. In other words, BMW would not be an MNE if it manufactured all of its cars in Germany and exported them around the world. BMW became an MNE only when it started to directly invest abroad.

Although some people argue that MNEs are a new organizational form that emerged after World War II, that is simply not the case. MNEs have existed for at least 2,000 years, with some of the earliest examples found in the Phoenician, Assyrian, and Roman times. It is true that MNEs have experienced significant growth since World War II. In 1990, there were 37,000 MNEs with 170,000 foreign subsidiaries. As of 2010, some 82,000 MNEs (more than *double* the number in 1990) controlled 790,000 foreign subsidiaries (more than *four times* the number in 1990). The value added of foreign subsidiaries of MNEs rose from 7% of world GDP in 1990 to 11% in 2010.[2] Clearly, there is a proliferation of MNEs lately.

OLI advantages
The advantages of ownership (O), location (L), and internalization (I) that come from engaging in FDI.

Ownership
Possessing and leveraging of certain valuable, rare, hard-to-imitate, and organizationally embedded (VRIO) assets overseas in the context of FDI.

Location
Advantages enjoyed by a firm that derive from the places in which it operates.

Internalization
The replacement of cross-border markets (such as exporting and importing) with one firm (the MNE) located in two or more countries.

Licensing
Buying and selling technology and intellectual property rights.

WHY DO FIRMS BECOME MNEs BY ENGAGING IN FDI?

Having set the terms straight, we need to address a fundamental question: Why do so many firms—ranging from those in the ancient world to today's BMW, Wal-Mart, and Samsung—become MNEs by engaging in FDI? Without getting into details, we can safely say that there must be economic gains from FDI. More importantly, given the tremendous complexities associated with FDI, such gains must significantly outweigh the costs. What are the sources of such gains? The answer, as suggested by British scholar John Dunning and illustrated in Exhibit 6.3, boils down to firms' quest for ownership (O) advantages, location (L) advantages, and internalization (I) advantages—collectively known as **OLI advantages**.[3] The two core perspectives introduced earlier—resource-based and institution-based views—enable us to probe into the heart of this question.

In the context of FDI, **ownership** refers to possession and leveraging by an MNE of certain valuable, rare, hard-to-imitate, and organizationally embedded (VRIO) assets overseas. Owning the proprietary technology and the management know-how that goes into making a BMW helps ensure that the MNE can beat rivals abroad.

Location advantages are those enjoyed by firms because they do business in a certain place. Features unique to a place, such as its natural or labor resources or its location near particular markets, provide certain advantages to firms doing business there. For example, Vietnam has emerged as a convenient location for MNEs that want to diversify away from coastal China with rising labor costs.[4] From a resource-based view, an MNE's pursuit of ownership and location advantages can be regarded as flexing its muscles—its resources and capabilities—in global competition.

Internalization refers to the replacement of cross-border markets (such as exporting and importing) with one firm (the MNE) being located and operating in two or more countries. For example, BMW could sell its technology to an Indonesian firm for a fee; this is a non-FDI-based market entry mode technically called **licensing** and can be done with intellectual property as well as technology. Instead, BMW chooses to assemble cars by having some FDI in Indonesia. In other words, external market transactions (in this case, the buying and selling of technology through licensing) are replaced by internalization. From an institution-based view, internalization is a response to the imperfect rules governing international transactions,

EXHIBIT 6.3 An OLI Framework for Why Firms Engage in FDI

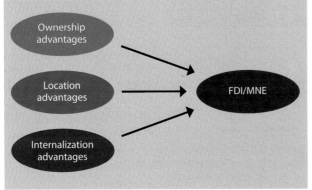

EXHIBIT 6.4 Why Firms Prefer FDI to Licensing

- FDI reduces dissemination risks.
- FDI provides tight control over foreign operations.
- FDI facilitates the transfer of tacit knowledge through "learning by doing."

First, FDI affords a high degree of direct management control that reduces the risk of firm-specific resources and capabilities being appropriated. One of the leading risks abroad is **dissemination risk**, defined as the possibility of unauthorized diffusion of firm-specific know-how. If a foreign company grants a license to a local firm to manufacture or market a product, the licensee (or an employee of the licensee) may disseminate the know-how by using it against the wishes of the foreign company. For example, Pizza Hut found out that its long-time licensee in Thailand disseminated its know-how and established a direct competitor, simply called The Pizza Company, which controlled 70% of the market in Thailand.[5] While owning and managing proprietary assets through FDI does not completely shield firms from dissemination risks (after all, their employees can quit and join competitors), FDI is better because licensing does not provide such management control. Understandably, FDI is extensively used in knowledge-intensive, high-tech industries such as automobiles, electronics, chemicals, and IT.

Second, FDI provides more direct and tighter control over foreign operations. Even when licensees (and their employees) harbor no opportunistic intention to steal secrets, they may not always follow the wishes of the foreign firm that provides the know-how. Without FDI, the foreign firm cannot control its licensee. For example, Starbucks entered South Korea by licensing its format to ESCO. Although ESCO soon opened ten stores, Starbucks felt that ESCO was not aggressive enough in growing the chain. But there was little Starbucks could do. Eventually, Starbucks switched from licensing to FDI, which allowed it to directly promote the aggressive growth of the chain in South Korea.

Finally, certain knowledge (or know-how) calls for FDI as opposed to licensing. Even if there is no

known as **market imperfections** (or **market failure**). Evidently, Indonesian regulations governing the protection of intellectual property such as BMW's proprietary technology do not give BMW sufficient confidence that those rights will be protected. Therefore, internalization is a must.

Overall, firms become MNEs because FDI provides OLI advantages that they otherwise would not obtain. The next three sections explain why this is the case.

LO3 Explain how FDI results in ownership advantages.

OWNERSHIP ADVANTAGES

All investments, including both FDI and FPI, entail ownership of assets. So what is unique about FDI? This section highlights the benefits of direct ownership and compares FDI to licensing when considering market entries abroad.

The Benefits of Ownership

Remember that *direct* is the key word in foreign direct investment. FDI requires a significant equity ownership position. The benefits of direct ownership lie in the *combination* of equity ownership rights and management control rights. Specifically, the ownership rights provide the much-needed management control rights. In contrast, FPI represents essentially insignificant ownership rights and no management control rights. To compete successfully, firms need to deploy overwhelming resources and capabilities to overcome their liabilities of foreignness (see Chapters 1 and 4). FDI provides one of the best ways to facilitate such extension of firm-specific resources and capabilities abroad.

FDI Versus Licensing

Basic choices when entering foreign markets include exporting, licensing, and FDI. Successful exporting may provoke protectionist responses from host countries, thus forcing firms to choose between licensing and FDI. Between licensing and FDI, which is better? Exhibit 6.4 shows three reasons that may compel firms to prefer FDI to licensing.

Market imperfections (or market failure)
The imperfect rules governing international market transactions.

Dissemination risk
The possibility of unauthorized diffusion of firm-specific know-how.

opportunism on the part of licensees and if they follow the wishes of the foreign firm, certain know-how may simply be too difficult to transfer to licensees without FDI. There are two basic categories of knowledge: explicit and tacit. Explicit knowledge is codifiable; that is, it can be written down and transferred without losing much of its richness. Tacit knowledge, on the other hand, is noncodifiable and its acquisition and transfer requires hands-on practice. For example, a driving manual represents a body of explicit knowledge. However, mastering the manual without any road practice does not make you a good driver. Tacit knowledge is more important and harder to transfer and learn—it can only be acquired by doing (in this case, practice driving under the supervision of an experienced driver). Likewise, operating a Wal-Mart store involves a great deal of knowledge, some explicit (often captured in an operational manual) and some tacit. As such, simply giving foreign licensees a copy of the Wal-Mart operational manual will not be enough. Foreign employees will need to learn directly from Wal-Mart personnel by actually doing the job.

From a resource-based standpoint, it is Wal-Mart's tacit knowledge that gives it competitive advantage (see Chapter 4). Wal-Mart owns such crucial tacit knowledge, and it has no incentive to give that knowledge away to licensees without having some management control over how that knowledge is used. Therefore, properly transferring and controlling tacit knowledge calls for FDI. Overall, ownership advantages enable the firm, now becoming an MNE, to more effectively extend, transfer, and leverage firm-specific capabilities abroad.[6]

> *Identify the ways your firm can acquire and neutralize location advantages.*

LOCATION ADVANTAGES

Given the well-known liability of foreignness, foreign locations must offer compelling advantages to make it worthwhile to undertake FDI. We may regard the continuous expansion of international business, such as FDI, as an unending saga in search of location advantages. This section highlights the sources of location advantages and outlines ways to acquire and neutralize those advantages.

Location, Location, Location

Certain locations possess geographical features that are difficult to match by others. For example, although Austria politically and culturally belongs to the West, the country is geographically located in the heart of Central and Eastern Europe (CEE). In fact, Austria's capital, Vienna, is actually *east* of Prague, in the Czech Republic, and Ljubljana, in Slovenia. Not surprisingly, Vienna is an attractive site as MNE regional headquarters for CEE. Similarly, Miami is blessed by its location close to Latin America and the Caribbean. It also has excellent air links with all major cities in North America. Miami thus advertises itself as the "Gateway of the Americas." Locations such as Vienna and Miami naturally attract a lot of FDI.

Beyond natural geographical advantages, location advantages also arise from the clustering of economic activities in certain locations, referred to as **agglomeration** (see In Focus). For instance, the Netherlands grows and processes two thirds of the worldwide exports of cut flowers. Slovakia produces more cars per capita than any other country in the world, thanks to the quest for agglomeration benefits by global automakers. Dallas attracts all the world's major telecom equipment makers and many telecom service providers, making it the Telecom Corridor. Overall, agglomeration advantages stem from:

- **Knowledge spillover**, or the diffusion of knowledge from one firm to others among closely located firms that attempt to hire individuals from competitors.

- Industry demand that creates a skilled labor force whose members may work for different firms without moving out of the region.

- Industry demand that facilitates a pool of specialized suppliers and buyers also located in the region.

Acquiring and Neutralizing Location Advantages

Note that from a resource-based view, location advantages do *not* entirely overlap with country-level advantages such as the factor endowments discussed in Chapter 5. Location advantages refer to the advantages that one firm obtains when operating in a location due to its *firm-specific* capabilities. In 1982, General Motors (GM) ran its Fremont, California, plant into the ground and had to close it. Reopening the same plant in 1984, Toyota initiated its first FDI project in the United States in a joint venture (JV) with GM. Since then, Toyota (together with GM) has leveraged this plant's location advantages by producing award-winning cars that American customers particularly like—the Toyota Corolla and Tacoma. The point is: It is Toyota's unique capabilities, applied to the California location, that literally have saved the plant from its demise. The

© Cengage Learning 2013

Agglomeration
The clustering of economic activities in certain locations.

Knowledge spillover
The diffusion of knowledge from one firm to others among closely located firms that attempt to hire individuals from competitors.

IN FOCUS

Air Capital of the World— Wichita, Kansas

Although the Wichita, Kansas, metro area only has a population of about 600,000 people, the *entire* population of major aerospace companies in the West is represented here: Airbus (North American Wing Design), Boeing (Integrated Defense Systems), Bombardier Aerospace/Learjet, Cessna Aircraft, Raytheon/Beech Aircraft, and Spirit AeroSystems. While Boeing, Cessna, and Raytheon are US-owned, Airbus, Bombardier, and Spirit have come to Wichita via FDI—the latter two companies are Canadian-owned. The city proudly claims itself to be the "Air Capital of the World." Why is Wichita so attractive? In one word, agglomeration (clustering of economic activities). In Wichita, the aerospace industry employs 35,000 workers, and makes up 60% of manufacturing earnings. In Kansas, $22 out of every $100 in earnings comes from this industry.

Wichita's aerospace industry started in the 1920s. Flat land, good winds, and excellent year-round flying weather were initially important. In 1929, Boeing came by acquiring a local start-up. During World War II, Boeing produced numerous military aircraft including the B-29 bomber in Wichita. In postwar decades, Wichita has become one of Boeing's prime engineering, fabrication, assembly, and modification centers. The two US presidential Boeing 747s, known as Air Force One when

Bombardier/Learjet

Cessna

Raytheon/Beach Hawker

the president is on board, were made in Everett, Washington, but modified, equipped, and serviced in Wichita. In addition to large aircraft made by Boeing, Wichita is also the undisputed leader in small aircraft for general aviation (often known as business jets). The top three players—Learjet, Cessna, and Beech—are here. While Cessna and Beech were acquired by US-owned Textron and Raytheon, respectively, Learjet was bought by Canada's Bombardier. Airbus does not manufacture in Wichita. Instead, it set up an R&D center, employing 200 engineers. In 2005, Boeing spun off its commercial aircraft division in Wichita and sold it, for $1.5 billion, to a Canadian company that nobody had heard of in the aerospace industry, Onex Corporation. Although Onex (TSX: OCX) is one of Canada's largest diversified companies with $16 billion annual sales, it had never operated in the aerospace industry before. Onex named its new Wichita-based subsidiary Spirit Aero-Space. Spirit has continued to be a major supplier to Boeing. In addition, exercising the spirit of an independent company, Spirit has also secured new contracts to supply Airbus in Europe.

Sources: R. Whyte, "Competitiveness in the global aircraft industry," Presentation at Wichita State University, 20 May 2006; Wichita Metro Chamber of Commerce, 2011, available online at http://www.wichitakansas.org; http://www.boeing.com; http://www.learjet.com; http://www.cessna.textron.com; http://www.onex.com; http://www.raytheon.com; http://www.wingsoverkansas.com.

California location in itself does not provide location advantages *per se*, as shown by GM's inability to make it work prior to 1982.

Firms do not operate in a vacuum. When one firm enters a foreign country through FDI, its rivals are likely to increase FDI in that host country either to acquire location advantages themselves or to at least neutralize the first mover's location advantages. These actions to imitate and follow competitors are especially likely in **oligopolies**—industries (such as aerospace and semiconductors) populated by a small number of players. The automobile industry is a typical oligopolistic industry. Volkswagen was the first foreign entrant in China, starting production in 1985 and enjoying a market share of 60% in the 1990s. Now, every self-respecting global automaker

Firms do not operate in a vacuum.

has entered China trying to eat some of Volkswagen's lunch. Overall, competitive rivalry and imitation, especially in oligopolistic industries, underscores the importance of acquiring and neutralizing location advantages around the world.

List the benefits of internalization.

INTERNALIZATION ADVANTAGES

Known as internalization, another set of great advantages associated with FDI is the ability to replace the

Oligopoly
An industry populated by a small number of players.

external market relationship with one firm (the MNE) owning, controlling, and managing activities in two or more countries. Internalization is important because of significant imperfections in international market transactions. The institution-based view suggests that markets are governed by rules, regulations, and norms that are designed to reduce uncertainties. Uncertainties introduce transaction costs, or costs associated with doing business (see Chapter 2). This section outlines the necessity of combating market failure and describes the benefits brought by internalization.

Market Failure

International transaction costs tend to be higher than domestic transaction costs. Because laws and regulations are typically enforced on a nation-state basis, enforcement can be an issue on the international level. Suppose two parties from different countries are doing business. If the party from country A behaves opportunistically, the other party from country B will have a hard time enforcing the contract. Suing the other party in a foreign country is not only costly but also uncertain. In the worst case, such imperfections are so grave that markets fail to function, and many firms simply choose not to do business abroad to avoid being burned. High transaction costs can therefore result in market failure in cases where the market imperfections actually prohibit transactions altogether. However, recall from Chapter 5 that there are gains from trade. Not doing business together prevents firms from reaping such gains. In response, MNEs emerge to overcome and combat such market failure through FDI.

Overcoming Market Failure Through FDI

How do MNEs combat market failure through internalization? Let us use an example involving an oil importer, BP in Britain, and an oil exporter, Nigerian National Petroleum Corporation (NNPC) in Nigeria. For the sake of our discussion, assume that BP does all of its business in Britain and NNPC does all of its business in Nigeria; in other words, neither of them is an MNE. BP and NNPC negotiate a contract specifying that NNPC will export a certain amount of crude oil from Nigeria to BP's oil refinery facilities in Britain for a certain amount of money. Shown in Exhibit 6.5, this is both an export contract (from NNPC's perspective) and an import contract (from BP's

standpoint) between two firms. In other words, it is an international market transaction.

An international market transaction between an importer and an exporter like BP and NNPC may suffer from high transaction costs. What is especially costly is the potential opportunism on both sides. For example, NNPC may demand a higher-than-agreed-upon price, citing a variety of reasons such as inflation, natural disasters, or simply rising oil prices after the deal is signed. BP then has to either pay more than the agreed-upon price or refuse to pay and suffer from the huge costs of keeping expensive refinery facilities idle. In other words, NNPC's opportunistic behavior can cause a lot of losses for BP.

Opportunistic behavior can go both ways in a market transaction. In this particular example, BP can also be opportunistic. It may refuse to accept a shipment after its arrival from Nigeria citing unsatisfactory quality, but the real reason may be BP's inability to sell refined oil downstream because gasoline demand is going down. People in Britain are driving less due to skyrocketing oil prices and the recession—the jobless do not need to commute to work. NNPC is thus forced to find a new buyer for a huge tanker load of crude oil on a last-minute, "fire sale" basis with a deep discount, losing a lot of money.

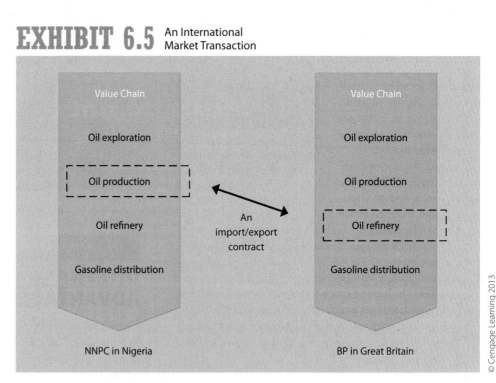

EXHIBIT 6.5 An International Market Transaction

Value Chain

Oil exploration

Oil production

Oil refinery

Gasoline distribution

NNPC in Nigeria

An import/export contract

Value Chain

Oil exploration

Oil production

Oil refinery

Gasoline distribution

BP in Great Britain

© Cengage Learning 2013

Overall, once one side in a market (export/import) transaction behaves opportunistically, the other side will not be happy and will threaten or initiate law suits. Because the legal and regulatory frameworks governing such international transactions are generally not as effective as those governing domestic transactions, the injured party will generally be frustrated, while the opportunistic party can often get away with it. All of these are examples of transaction costs that increase international market inefficiencies and imperfections, ultimately resulting in market failure.

In response, FDI combats such market failure through internalization, which involves replacing the external market with in-house links. The MNE reduces cross-border transaction costs and increases efficiencies by replacing an external market relationship with a single organization spanning both countries.[7] In our example, there are two possibilities for internalization: BP could undertake *upstream* vertical FDI by owning oil production assets in Nigeria, or NNPC could undertake *downstream* vertical FDI by owning oil refinery assets in Great Britain (see Exhibit 6.6). FDI essentially transforms the international trade between two independent firms in two countries to **intrafirm trade** between two subsidiaries in two countries controlled by the same MNE. By coordinating cross-border activities better, the MNE can thus achieve an internalization advantage.

Overall, the motivations for FDI are complex. Based on resource-based and institution-based views, we can see FDI as a reflection of both a firm's motivation to extend its firm-specific capabilities abroad and its responses to overcome market imperfections and failures.

REALITIES OF FDI

The realities of FDI are intertwined with politics. This section starts with three political views on FDI and follows with a discussion of pros and cons of FDI for home and host countries.

Political Views on FDI

There are three primary political views on FDI. First, the **radical view on FDI** is hostile to FDI. Tracing its roots to Marxism, the radical view treats FDI as an instrument of imperialism and a vehicle for exploiting domestic resources, industries, and people by foreign capitalists and firms. Governments embracing the radical view often nationalize MNE assets or simply ban (or discourage) inbound MNEs. Between the 1950s and the early 1980s, the radical view was influential throughout Africa, Asia, Eastern Europe, and Latin America.

On the other hand, the **free market view on FDI** suggests that FDI, unrestricted by government intervention, will enable countries to tap into their absolute or comparative advantages by specializing in the production of certain goods and services. Similar to the win-win logic for international trade as articulated by Adam Smith and David Ricardo (see Chapter 5), free market–based FDI should lead to a win-win situation for both home and host countries. Since the 1980s, a series of countries such as Brazil, China, Hungary, India, Ireland, and Russia have adopted more FDI-friendly policies.

However, a totally free market view does not really

EXHIBIT 6.6
Combating Market Failure Through FDI: One Company (MNE) in Two Countries

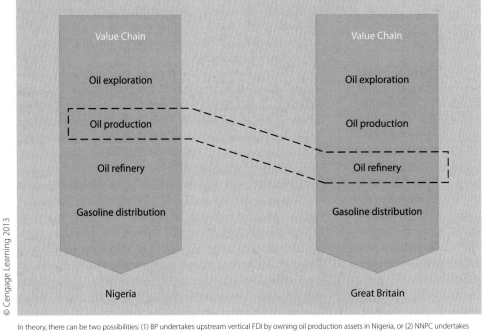

Value Chain — Oil exploration, Oil production, Oil refinery, Gasoline distribution — Nigeria

Value Chain — Oil exploration, Oil production, Oil refinery, Gasoline distribution — Great Britain

© Cengage Learning 2013

In theory, there can be two possibilities: (1) BP undertakes upstream vertical FDI by owning oil production assets in Nigeria, or (2) NNPC undertakes downstream vertical FDI by owning oil refinery assets in Great Britain. In reality, the first scenerio is more likely.

Intrafirm trade
International trade between two subsidiaries in two countries controlled by the same MNE.

Radical view on FDI
A political view that sees FDI as an instrument of imperialism and a vehicle for foreign exploitation.

Free market view on FDI
A political view that holds that FDI, unrestricted by government intervention, will enable countries to tap into their absolute or comparative advantages by specializing in the production of certain goods and services.

exist in practice. Most countries embrace the **pragmatic nationalism view on FDI**, considering both the pros and cons of FDI and approving FDI only when its benefits outweigh its costs. The French government, invoking "economic patriotism," has torpedoed several foreign takeover attempts of French companies. The Chinese government insists that automobile FDI has to take the form of JVs with MNEs so that Chinese automakers can learn from their foreign counterparts.

Overall, more countries in recent years have changed their policies to be more favorable to FDI. Restrictive policies toward FDI succeed only in driving out foreign investors to countries with more favorable policies. Even hard-core countries such as Cuba and North Korea that had a radical view on FDI are now experimenting with some FDI. This general openness is indicative of the emerging pragmatic nationalism in their thinking. In a more recent example, during the 2008–2009 crisis, numerous governments used emergency measures to bail out their firms, and some of these discriminated against MNEs operating in these countries. For example, the Swiss government bailed out UBS and Credit Suisse, but did not help foreign banks with significant operations in Switzerland. The Swiss government of course was not alone. While experts noted that such discriminatory emergency measures pose "a serious threat to open investment,"[8] the governments involved clearly practiced pragmatic nationalism. Pragmatically, no government had the financial resources to bail out both domestic and foreign firms operating in the country. Therefore, even foreign firms (and their governments) may protest, that rescuing domestic firms becomes the only politically feasible action.

Benefits and Costs of FDI to Host Countries

Underpinning pragmatic nationalism is the need to assess the various benefits and costs of FDI to host (recipient) countries and home (source) countries. In a nutshell, Exhibit 6.7 outlines these considerations. This section focuses on *host* countries, and the next section deals with *home* countries.

Cell 1 in Exhibit 6.7 shows four primary benefits to host countries. First, *capital inflow* can help improve a host country's balance of payments. The balance of payments measures a country's payments to and receipts from other countries. Chinese firms undertake FDI by acquiring US-based assets. By bringing more capital into the United States, such FDI helps improve the US balance of payments. (See Chapter 7 for more details.)

Second, *technology*, especially more advanced technology from abroad, can create **technology spillovers** that benefit domestic firms and industries. Technology spillover is the domestic diffusion of foreign technical knowledge and processes. After observing such technology, local rivals may recognize its feasibility and strive to imitate it. This is known as the **demonstration effect**, sometimes also called the **contagion** (or **imitation**) **effect**. It underscores the important role that MNEs play in stimulating competition in host countries.[9]

Third, *advanced management know-how* may be highly valued. In many developing countries, it is often difficult for the development of management know-how to reach a world-class level if it is only domestic and not influenced by FDI.

Finally, FDI creates a total of 80 million *jobs*, which represent approximately 4% of the global workforce.[10] For example, more than 50% of manufacturing employees in Ireland work directly for MNEs. Indirect benefits include jobs created when local suppliers increase hiring and when MNE employees spend money locally, which also results in more jobs.

Cell 2 in Exhibit 6.7 outlines three primary costs of FDI to host countries: loss of sovereignty, adverse effects on competition, and capital outflow. The first concern is the loss of some (but not all) economic sovereignty associated with FDI. Because of FDI, decisions to produce and market products and services in a host country are being made by foreigners. Even if locals serve as heads of MNE subsidiaries, they represent the interest of foreign firms. Will foreigners and foreign firms make decisions that are in the best interest of host countries? This is truly

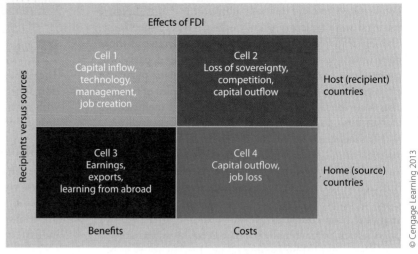

EXHIBIT 6.7 Effects of FDI on Home and Host Countries

Effects of FDI

Recipients versus sources

	Benefits	Costs
Host (recipient) countries	**Cell 1** Capital inflow, technology, management, job creation	**Cell 2** Loss of sovereignty, competition, capital outflow
Home (source) countries	**Cell 3** Earnings, exports, learning from abroad	**Cell 4** Capital outflow, job loss

© Cengage Learning 2013

Pragmatic nationalism view on FDI
A political view that approves FDI only when its benefits outweigh its costs.

Technology spillover
The domestic diffusion of foreign technical knowledge and processes.

Demonstration effect (or contagion or imitation effect)
The effect that occurs when local rivals recognize the feasibility of foreign technology and imitate it.

a million-dollar question. According to the radical view, the answer is "No!" because foreigners and foreign firms are likely to maximize their own profits by exploiting people and resources in host countries. Such deep suspicion of MNEs leads to policies that discourage or even ban FDI. On the other hand, countries embracing free market and pragmatic nationalism views agree that despite some acknowledged differences between foreign and host country interests, the interests of MNEs and host countries overlap sufficiently. Host countries are thus willing to live with some loss of sovereignty (see the Closing Case).

A second concern is associated with the negative effects on local competition. While we have just discussed the positive effects of MNEs on local competition, it is possible that MNEs may drive some domestic firms out of business. Having driven domestic firms out of business, in theory, MNEs may be able to monopolize local markets. While this is a relatively minor concern in developed economies, it is a legitimate concern for less developed economies where MNEs are generally so much larger and financially stronger when compared with local firms. For example, as Coca-Cola and PepsiCo extended their "cola wars" from the United States to countries around the world, they have almost "accidentally" wiped out much of the world's indigenous beverage companies, which are—or were—much smaller.

A third concern is associated with capital outflow. When MNEs make profits in host countries and repatriate (send back) such earnings to headquarters in home countries, host countries experience a net outflow in the capital account in their balance of payments. As a result, some countries have restricted the ability of MNEs to repatriate funds.

Benefits and Costs of FDI to Home Countries

As exporters of capital, technology, management, and, in some cases, jobs, home (source) countries often reap benefits and endure costs associated with FDI that are *opposite* to those experienced by host countries. Cell 3 of Exhibit 6.7 shows three benefits to home countries:

+ repatriated earnings from profits from FDI

+ increased exports of components and services to host countries

+ learning via FDI from operations abroad

Cell 4 in Exhibit 6.7 shows that the costs of FDI to home countries primarily center on capital outflow and job loss. First, since host countries enjoy capital inflow because of FDI, home countries naturally suffer from some capital outflow. Less confident home-country govern-

ments often impose capital controls to prevent or reduce FDI from flowing abroad.

The second concern is now more prominent: job loss. Many MNEs invest abroad while simultaneously curtailing domestic production—that is, they increase employment overseas but lay off domestic employees. As of 2010, US MNEs employed approximately 12 million people in their overseas subsidiaries.[11] However, between 2007 and 2010, about 8.5 million jobs (6% of total employment) were lost in the United States. For instance, since 2006, Ford closed four factories in the United States but invested $3 billion in Mexico to create 2,000 jobs there.[12] It is not surprising that politicians, union members, journalists, and social activists in developed economies such as the United States have increasingly called for restrictions on FDI outflows.

In some parts of the developing world, tension over foreign ownership can turn into political action. Given the recent worldwide trend toward more FDI-friendly policies, many people thought optimistically that nationalization and expropriation against MNE assets were a thing of the past. During 2006, however, the optimists had a rude awakening. In March 2006, Venezuelan president Hugo Chavez ordered Chevron, Royal Dutch, Total, ENI, and other oil and gas MNEs to convert their operations in the country into forced JVs with the state-owned Venezuelan firm PDVSA, and PDVSA would hold at least 60% of the equity. When France's Total and Italy's ENI rejected the terms, the Venezuelan government promptly seized their fields.[13] On May 1, 2006, the Bolivian military seized control of the MNEs' oil fields, and President Evo Morales declared, "The plunder [by MNEs] has ended."[14]

Soon after, Ecuador expropriated the oil fields run by America's Occidental Petroleum.

While the speed of the anti-MNE events in Latin America was surprising, it is important to note that these actions were not sudden, impulsive policy changes. The politicians leading these actions were all democratically elected. These actions were the result of lengthy political debates concerning FDI in the region, and such takeovers were mostly popular among the public. Bolivian president Morales' action in fact fulfilled his campaign promise. Until the 1970s, the treatment and dealings with MNEs among Latin American governments was largely harsh and confrontational. Only in the 1990s when these countries became democratic did they open their oil industries to inbound FDI. So the 180-degree policy reversal is

Bolivia

Welcoming Versus Restricting Sovereign Wealth Fund Investments

A **sovereign wealth fund** (**SWF**) is a state-owned investment fund composed of financial assets such as stocks, bonds, real estate, or other financial instruments funded by foreign exchange assets. Investment funds that we now call SWFs were first created in 1953 by Kuwait. Both the United States and Canada have had their own SWFs (at least at the state and provincial level, such as the Alaska Permanent Fund and Alberta Heritage Fund).

In the recent crisis, SWFs came to the rescue. SWFs now represent approximately 10% of global FDI flows. For example, in November 2007, the Abu Dhabi Investment Authority injected $7.5 billion (4.9% of equity) into Citigroup. In early 2008, China Investment Corporation (CIC) invested $5 billion for a 10% equity stake in Morgan Stanley. As discussed earlier, the equity threshold between FDI and FPI is 10%. While most SWFs make relatively passive FPI, some have become more active, direct investors as they hold larger stakes in recipients.

It is such large-scale investments that have ignited the debate on SWFs. On the one hand, SWFs have brought much-needed cash to rescue desperate Western firms. On the other hand, concerns are raised by host countries, which are typically developed economies. A primary concern is national security in that SWFs may be politically (as opposed to commercially) motivated. Another concern is SWFs' inadequate transparency. Governments in several developed economies, in fear of the "threats" from SWFs, have been erecting measures to defend their companies from SWF takeovers.

As discussed earlier, foreign investment certainly has both benefits and costs to host countries. However, in the absence of any evidence that the costs outweigh benefits, the rush to erect anti-SWF barriers is indicative of protectionist (or, some may argue, even racist) sentiments. For executives at hard-pressed Western firms, it would not seem sensible to ask for government bailouts on the one hand and to reject cash from SWFs on the other hand. Most SWF investment is essentially free cash with few strings attached. For example, CIC, which now holds 10% of Morgan Stanley equity, did not demand a board seat or a management role. For Western policymakers, it makes little sense to spend taxpayers' dollars to bail out failed firms, run huge budget deficits, and then turn away SWFs. Commenting on inbound Chinese investment in the United States (including SWF investment), two experts note:

It seems feckless on the part of US policymakers to stigmatize Chinese investment in the United States based upon imprecise and likely exaggerated estimates of the relevant costs and risks of that investment.

At least some US policymakers agree. In the September/October 2008 issue of *Foreign Affairs*, then-Secretary of the Treasury Henry Paulson commented:

These concerns [on Chinese investment] are misplaced ... the United States would do well to encourage such investment from anywhere in the world—including China— because it represents a vote of confidence in the US economy and it promotes growth, jobs, and productivity in the United States.

Lastly, thanks to the financial crisis in 2008–2009, recent SWF investment in developed economies suffered major losses. Such a "double whammy"—both the political backlash and the economic losses—has severely discouraged SWFs. As a result, the recession put a premium on maintaining a welcoming climate. As part of the efforts to foster such a welcoming climate in times of great political and economic anxiety, both US and Chinese governments confirmed the following in the US–China Strategic and Economic Dialogue (S&ED) on July 28, 2009:

The United States confirms that the Committee on Foreign Investment in the United States (CFIUS) process ensures the consistent and fair treatment of all foreign investment without prejudice to the place of origin. The United States welcomes sovereign wealth fund investment, including that from China. China stresses that investment decisions by its state-owned investment firms will be based solely on commercial grounds.

Beyond bilateral negotiations such as the US–China S&ED, in September 2008, major SWFs of the world at a summit in Santiago, Chile, agreed to a voluntary code of conduct known as the Santiago Principles. These principles are designed to alleviate some of the concerns for host countries of SWF investment and to enhance the transparency of such investment. These principles represent an important milestone of SWFs' evolution.

Sources: V. Fotak and W. Megginson, "Are SWFs welcome now?" *Columbia FDI Perspectives*, No. 9, 21 July 2009, available online at http://www.vcc.columbia.edu; S. Globerman and D.Shapiro, "Economic and strategic considerations surrounding Chinese FDI in the United States," *Asia Pacific Journal of Management*, 26 (2009): 163–183; H. Paulson, "The right way to engage China," *Foreign Affairs*, September/October 2008, available online at http://www.foreignaffairs.org; Sovereign Wealth Fund Institute, "About sovereign wealth fund," 2011, available online at http://www.swfinstitute.org; United Nations (UN), *World Investment Report 2010* (New York and Geneva: UN, 2010) xviii; US Department of the Treasury, 2009, "The First US–China Strategic and Economic Dialogue Economic Track Joint Fact Sheet," 28 July 2009, Washington, DC.

DEBATE
ETHICAL DILEMMA

Sovereign wealth fund (SWF)
A state-owned investment fund composed of financial assets such as stocks, bonds, real estate, or other financial instruments funded by foreign exchange assets.

© iStockphoto.com/Natalia Siverina / © withGod/Shutterstock / © iStockphoto.com/UteHil / © iStockphoto.com/Mark Evans

both surprising, considering how recently these governments welcomed MNEs, and not surprising, considering historical dealings with MNEs in the region. Some argue that the recent actions were driven by industry-specific dynamics: Oil prices skyrocketed so that governments could not resist the urge to raid the cookie jar. But others suggest that these actions represent the swing of a pendulum (see Chapter 1 on the pendulum of globalization).

LO7 *List three things you need to do as your firm considers FDI.*

MANAGEMENT SAVVY

The big question in global business, adapted to the context of FDI, is: What determines the success and failure of FDI around the globe? The answer boils down to two components. First, from a resource-based view, some firms are good at FDI because they leverage ownership, location, and internalization advantages in a way that is valuable, unique, and hard to imitate by rival firms. Second, from an institution-based view, the political realities either enable or constrain FDI from reaching its full economic potential. Therefore, the success and failure of FDI also significantly depends on institutions, or rules of the game, that govern FDI.

Shown in Exhibit 6.8, three implications for action emerge. First, you should carefully assess whether FDI is justified in light of other possibilities such as outsourcing and licensing. This exercise needs to be conducted on an activity-by-activity basis as part of the value chain analysis (see Chapter 4). If ownership and internalization advantages are not deemed critical, then FDI is not recommended.

Second, once a decision to undertake FDI is made, you should pay attention to the old adage, "location, location, location!" The quest for location advantages has to fit with the firm's strategic goals. For example, if a firm is searching for the innovation hot spots, then low-cost locations that do not generate sufficient innovations will not be attractive (see Chapters 10 and 12).

Finally, given the political realities around the world, you should be aware of the institutional constraints. Recent events suggest that savvy MNE managers should not take FDI-friendly policies for granted. Setbacks are likely. During the 2008–2009 crisis, an FDI recession took place in the midst of the Great Recession. The global economic slowdown makes key markets less attractive for investment, and the credit crunch means that firms are less able to invest abroad. Attitudes toward certain forms of FDI (such as sovereign wealth funds discussed in the Debate feature on the previous page) are changing, which could signal changes in the regulatory framework that make it more protectionist. So, at present, despite the modest recovery, the pendulum may be swinging away from FDI (see Chapter 1). In the long run, the interests of MNEs in host countries can best be safeguarded if they accommodate, rather than neglect or dominate, the interests of host countries.

EXHIBIT 6.8 Implications for Action

- Carefully assess whether FDI is justified in light of other foreign entry modes such as outsourcing and licensing.
- Pay careful attention to the location advantages in combination with the firm's strategic goals.
- Be aware of the institutional constraints and enablers governing FDI, and enhance legitimacy in host countries.

CLOSING CASE

ETHICAL DILEMMA
THE FATE OF OPEL

Opel is a wholly owned subsidiary of General Motors (GM) in Germany. Opel was founded in 1863, began making cars in 1899, and was acquired by General Motors in 1929. The GM–Opel relationship survived World War II, during which Opel factories were seized by the Nazis and then bombed by the Allies. Only in 1948 did GM regain control of Opel. In 2008, Opel generated €18 billion in sales and a 7% market share in Western Europe. It had 50,000 employees and eight factories in Europe. About half of the jobs and four factories were in Germany. In addition, Opel ran one factory each in Belgium, Poland, Spain, and the UK—the latter is a Vauxhall plant that produced cars with its own Vauxhall brand. Opel formed the backbone of GM Europe.

Unfortunately, the 80-year-old relationship between GM and Opel experienced some unprecedented turbulence in 2009, during which GM itself declared bankruptcy on June 1. Before June 1, the German federal government, in an effort to protect Opel assets and jobs in the event of a GM bankruptcy, took unprecedented action by offering a €1.5 billion bridge loan to Opel and pushing GM to form

an Opel Trust. The Opel Trust controlled and protected Opel assets during GM's bankruptcy. The board of the trust consisted of representatives from GM, German employees, the German federal government, and the governments of the four German states in which Opel operated. Losing money for a decade, Opel was indeed struggling desperately despite repeated restructuring efforts. In 2008, GM Europe lost $2.8 billion. In the first quarter of 2009, it burned an additional $2 billion with a 25% drop in sales. After June 1, 2009, although the US and Canadian governments bailed GM out by injecting billions of dollars and taking over 61% and 8% of its equity, respectively, there were specific requirements preventing GM from using American and Canadian taxpayer dollars to fund overseas operations such as Opel's. In desperation, GM felt it had to sell Opel to prevent the financial hemorrhage.

Although initially reluctant, GM in September 2009 agreed to support a proposal favored by the German government to sell 55% of Opel's equity to a consortium led by Magna, a Canadian auto parts maker that would take 20% of equity. Magna has two Russian partners—Sberbank and GAZ, Russia's second largest automaker—that would take 35% of equity. German employees would get 10% and GM the remaining 35%. Magna agreed to invest €500 million, while the German government pledged an additional €4.5 billion in state aid loans in addition to the €1.5 billion bridge loan already provided. German Chancellor Angela Merkel extracted a promise from Magna to keep job cuts to a minimum (not exceeding 2,500 jobs) in Germany—a significantly better outcome than a more ruthless restructuring process during which 40% of Opel's German jobs (10,000) might disappear. In part due to her extraordinary efforts to save jobs, Merkel was reelected for a second term in September 2009.

GM was never enthusiastic for the sale to the Magna consortium. Of the four bids GM received, it quickly dropped one from Italy's Fiat and another from China's Beijing Automotive, but strongly favored one from RHJ International, a Belgian private equity firm, which would eventually consider selling Opel back to GM in the future. The Germans saw RHJ as a pawn for GM. From a fair bidding standpoint, the fact that RHJ offered only €275 million, substantially lower than the €400 million offered by the Magna consortium, made it impossible for GM to offer Opel to RHJ and bypass the Magna consortium. To lock in the sale to Magna, the German government also announced that its financing would only support Magna and its partners but not RHJ.

GM had legitimate concerns for the sale to the Magna consortium. It would be hit by a "double whammy." First, GM would lose important passenger car expertise that has fueled a lot of GM's models beyond those carrying the Opel and Vauxhall plates, including many models that are branded as Cadillac, Buick, and Chevrolet. Second, the sale would turn Magna into a major competitor overnight, although the deal forbad Opel from selling in China until 2015 and forbad any entry into the United States. Further, GAZ will take advantage of Opel technology and boost its position in Russia, soon overtaking Germany as Europe's largest car market. RHJ would present none of these strategic headaches.

In October 2009, a significant player previously not involved entered the fray. The European Commissioner for Competition, Neelie Kroes, was pressured by the Belgian, Polish, Spanish, and UK governments that complained that Opel's sale to Magna would result in disproportionate and thus "unfair" job losses in these countries. Kroes wrote to the German government, expressing her

> "...traged, Opel workers took to the streets."

concerns that state aid promised by the German government to the "new Opel" was tied to one bidder and discriminated other EU bidders such as RHJ. The letter demanded that GM and the Opel Trust "be given the opportunity to reconsider the outcome of the bidding process," because state aid "cannot be used to impose political constraints concerning the location of production activities within the EU." After talks between Berlin and the EU, Germany assured that its state aid would be available to any investor with a decent plan. Unfortunately, RHJ had already walked away, so this assurance was entirely theoretical. Satisfied by the assurance, the Eurocrats eventually backed off. They argued that the assurance set a good precedent in the future and that dragging Germany's previously unacceptable behavior into a full-scale probe would push Opel into legal limbo and the firm could collapse.

However, in the middle of such intense politicking and strategizing, in November 2009, GM's board announced a startling shift in direction by cancelling the sale to the Magna consortium and keeping Opel. Outraged, Opel workers took to the streets. German media pointed out that GM might close two factories and lay off 10,000 workers in Germany. The German Minister for Economy and Technology said that "the behavior of GM against the Opel workers as well as against Germany is completely unacceptable." The German government demanded that its €1.5 billion bridge loan be repaid. There were significant concerns about the fate of Opel. Once GM repaid the loan, GM could dissolve Opel Trust and could do whatever it pleased with Opel.

In 2010, GM repaid the German government loan, and announced that its restructuring would cut over 8,000 jobs, including 4,000 in Germany. But the blow of the widely feared plant closing would only fall on one factory in Antwerp, Belgium, which employed 2,600 people. In an effort to save Opel, GM closed the plant by the end of 2010.

Sources: "Green light for Opel?" *BusinessWeek*, 2 November 2009; "Looking for reverse," *Economist*, 29 August 2009, 55; "GM's Opel job cuts," *Huffpost Business*, 20 January 2010, available online at http://www.huffingtonpost.com; "Government denies GM-Opel-Magna scrutiny needed," *Just Auto*, 19 October 2009, available online at http://www.just-auto.com; "GM opts to keep Opel, scraps sale to Magna," *New York Times*, 3 November 2009, available online at http://www.nytimes.com; "At last, GM sets deal to cede control of Opel," *Wall Street Journal*, 11 September 2009, available online at http://online.wsj.com; "GM advances Opel restructuring," *Wall Street Journal*, 7 November 2009, available online at http://online.wsj.com.

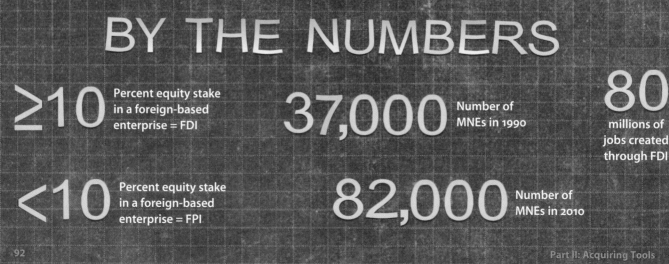

BY THE NUMBERS

≥10 — Percent equity stake in a foreign-based enterprise = FDI

37,000 — Number of MNEs in 1990

80 — millions of jobs created through FDI

<10 — Percent equity stake in a foreign-based enterprise = FPI

82,000 — Number of MNEs in 2010

Dealing with Foreign EXCHANGE

CHAPTER 7

Strong Economies and Strong Currencies in Latin America

Having quickly shaken off the world recession, many countries in Latin America are prospering again. The region's economies grew by an average of 6% in 2010, according to a preliminary estimate by the United Nations Economic Commission for Latin America and the Caribbean. This strong performance, linked in large part to the global commodity boom, has attracted big inflows of foreign cash. With that has come a familiar problem: the region's currencies have soared in value against the dollar, making life uncomfortable for Latin American manufacturers. They find themselves priced out of export markets or struggling to compete with cheap imports. Worried governments are launching a battery of measures to try to restrain the value of their currencies. Will they work?

In January 2011 alone, Chile announced it would buy $12 billion of foreign reserves in the year, and Brazil began requiring its

banks to cover 60% of their bets against the dollar with deposits at the Central Bank that will attract no interest. Peru is buying dollars, too, and similarly extended reserve requirements for banks' sales of foreign exchange. Central banks in Mexico and Colombia are intervening to buy dollars. Chile's announcement prompted an immediate fall in the peso, and other currencies have temporarily stabilized, but there is no guarantee that these measures will be effective in the immediate term.

In part, stronger currencies reflect Latin America's stronger economies. The commodity boom plays to the region's comparative advantage: China and India are gobbling up Brazilian soybeans and iron ore, Chilean copper, and Peruvian silver. Brazil and Colombia have both made big oil discoveries. These countries all have fairly sound economic policies, and their financial systems are

LEARNING OBJECTIVES
After studying this chapter, you should be able to:

LO1 **list the factors that determine foreign exchange rates.**

LO2 **articulate and explain the steps in the evolution of the international monetary system.**

LO3 **identify strategic responses firms can take to deal with foreign exchange movements.**

LO4 **identify three things you need to know about currency when doing business internationally.**

deepening. With money cheap and returns too poor in the rich world, Latin America has become a tempting destination for investors. Guido Mantega, Brazil's finance minister, has blamed the Brazilian real's strength and his country's rising import bill both on loose monetary policy in the United States and China's refusal to allow the yuan to appreciate.

But this is becoming too much of a good thing. The real has appreciated by 38% against the dollar over the past two years (2009–2010), for example. Overall, Latin America posted a current-account surplus of 1.6% of GDP in 2006; in 2011 it is likely to post a deficit of similar magnitude, according to the International Monetary Fund (IMF). There are other signs of overheating: inflation for non-tradable products in Chile is 6.4%, and Brazilian wages are increasing in double-digit rates.

Affected businesses are howling. Chile's wineries need an exchange rate of 530 pesos to the dollar (at the start of January 2011

it was at 484) to be profitable, according to Rene Merino, who represents the industry. In Brazil, São Paulo's industrialists' association claims that "excessive imports" of consumer goods have led to a "dizzying process of deindustrialization," costing 46,000 manufacturing jobs and $10 billion in lost output in the first nine months of 2010.

Uncomfortably strong currencies and overheating economies pose an excruciating dilemma for policymakers. If central bankers raise interest rates to curb inflation, they risk driving up the currency further. But if their interventions in the foreign exchange market drive the currency down, they may boost inflation.

Source: Excerpted from "Waging the currency war," *Economist*, 13 January 2011, available online at http://www.economist.com [accessed 5 April 2011]. © Economist Newspaper Group. Reproduced by permission.

Why is the value of currencies so important in Latin America? What determines foreign exchange rates? How do foreign exchange rates affect trade and investment? What is the role of global institutions such as the IMF? Finally, how can firms respond strategically? This chapter addresses these crucial questions. At the heart of our discussion lie the two core perspectives introduced earlier: the institution-based and resource-based views. Essentially, the institution-based view suggests that domestic and international institutions (such as the IMF) influence foreign exchange rates and affect capital movements. In turn, the resource-based view sheds light on how firms can profit from favorable foreign exchange movements by developing their own firm-specific resources and capabilities.

We start with a basic question: What determines foreign exchange rates? Then, we track the evolution of the international monetary system culminating in the IMF and continue with firms' strategic responses.

> **List the factors that determine foreign exchange rates.**

WHAT DETERMINES FOREIGN EXCHANGE RATES?

Foreign exchange rate
The price of one currency in terms of another.

Appreciation
An increase in the value of the currency.

Depreciation
A loss in the value of the currency.

A **foreign exchange rate** is the price of one currency, such as the dollar ($), in terms of another, such as the euro (€). Exhibit 7.1 provides some examples. An **appreciation** is an increase in the value of the currency, and a **depreciation** is a loss in the value of the currency. This section

South America

© Cengage Learning 2013

addresses a key question: What determines foreign exchange rates?

Basic Supply and Demand

The concept of an exchange rate as the price of a commodity—in this case, a country's currency—helps us understand its determinants. Basic economic theory suggests that a commodity's price is fundamentally determined by its supply and demand. Strong demand will lead to price hikes, and oversupply will result in price drops. Of course, we are dealing with a most unusual commodity here—money—but the basic principles still apply. When the United States sells products to China, US exporters often demand that they be paid in US dollars because the Chinese yuan is useless (or, using the technical term, non-convertible) in the United States. Chinese importers of US products must somehow generate US dollars in order to pay for US imports. The easiest way to generate US dollars is to *export* to the United States, whose buyers pay in US dollars. In this example, the dollar is the common transaction currency involving both US imports and US exports. As a result, the demand for dollars is much stronger than the demand for yuan (while holding the supply constant). A wide variety of users, such as Chinese exporters, Colombian drug dealers, and Swiss bankers, prefer to hold and transact in US dollars, thus fueling the demand for dollars. Such a strong demand explains why the US dollar is the most sought-after currency in the postwar decades (see the Closing Case). At present, about 60% of the world's foreign exchange holdings are in US dollars, followed by 25% in euros, 4% in yens, and 3% in pounds.

The next question is: What determines the supply and demand of foreign exchange? Because foreign exchange involves such a unique commodity, its markets are influenced by not only economic factors but also political and psychological factors. Exhibit 7.2 sketches the five underlying building blocks, which are discussed next.

EXHIBIT 7.1

EXHIBIT 7.1 Examples of Key Currency Exchange Rates

	US Dollar (US$)	Euro (€)	UK Pound (£)	Swiss Franc (SFr)	Mexican Peso	Japanese Yen (¥)	Canadian Dollar (C$)
Canadian Dollar (C$)	0.9612	1.3756	1.5677	1.0466	0.0814	0.0113	—
Japanese Yen (¥)	85.280	122.04	139.09	92.857	7.2226	—	88.722
Mexican Peso	11.807	16.898	19.258	12.856	—	0.13845	12.284
Swiss Franc (SFr)	0.9184	1.3143	1.4979	—	0.0778	0.0108	0.9555
UK Pound (£)	0.6131	0.8774	—	0.6676	0.0519	0.0072	0.6379
Euro (€)	0.6988	—	1.1397	0.7609	0.0592	0.0082	0.7269
US Dollar (US$)	—	1.4311	1.6310	1.0889	0.0847	0.0117	1.0404

Source: These examples are from "Key currency cross rates," *Wall Street Journal*, 6 April 2011, available at http://www.wsj.com [accessed 6 April 2011]. Copyright © 2011 Dow Jones & Company, Inc. All Rights Reserved. Reading *vertically*, the first column means US$1 = C$0.96 = ¥85 = Mexican Peso 11.81 = SFr 0.92 = £0.61 = €0.70. Reading *horizontally*, the last row means €1 = US$1.43; £1 = US$1.63; SFr 1 = US$1.09; Mexican Peso 1 = US$0.08; ¥1 = US$0.01; C$1 = US$1.04.

Relative Price Differences and Purchasing Power Parity

Some countries (such as Switzerland) have famously expensive prices, and others (such as the Philippines) are known to have cheap prices. How do these price differences affect exchange rates? An answer is provided by the theory of purchasing power parity (PPP). Recall from Chapter 1 that PPP is a conversion that determines the equivalent amount of goods and services different currencies can purchase. This conversion is usually used to capture the differences in cost of living between countries. PPP is essentially the "law of one price." The theory suggests that in the absence of trade barriers (such as tariffs), the price for identical products sold in different countries must be the same.

Otherwise, traders may buy low and sell high, eventually driving different prices for identical products to the same level around the world. The PPP theory argues that in the long run, exchange rates should move toward levels that would equalize the prices of an identical basket of goods in any two countries.

One of the most influential (and the most fun-filled) applications of the PPP theory is the Big Mac index, popularized by the *Economist* magazine. The *Economist* compares the cost of a McDonald's Big Mac hamburger in about 120 countries. According to the PPP theory, a Big Mac should cost the same anywhere around the world. In reality, it does not. Exhibit 7.3 on the next page shows that in July 2010, a Big Mac cost $3.73 in the United States and $1.95 in China. But the nominal (official) rate at that time was actually 6.78 yuan to the dollar. According to this calculation, the yuan was 48% undervalued against the dollar—the third most extreme in the Big Mac universe behind Hong Kong and Argentina. Thus, the Big Mac sold in China has the third best "value" in the world. In Hong Kong and Argentina, the Big Mac would cost only $1.90 and $1.78, respectively.

Although the Big Mac index is never a serious exercise, it has been cited by some US politicians as "evidence" that the yuan is artificially undervalued. This claim has been

EXHIBIT 7.2 What Determines Foreign Exchange Rates?

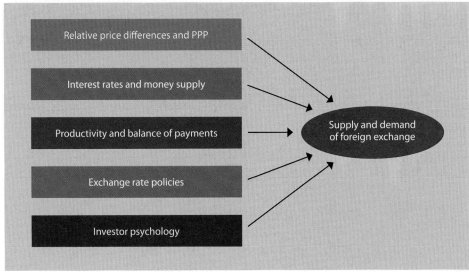

disavowed by the *Economist* itself. Still, we can make three serious observations from the Big Mac index.

- The Big Mac index confirms that prices in some European countries are very expensive. A Big Mac in Norway is the most expensive in the world, costing $7.20 (!).

- Prices in developing countries are cheaper. A Big Mac costs only $2.17 in Thailand. Why? Because a Big Mac is a

© Eriko Sugita/Reuters/Landov

EXHIBIT 7.3 The Big Mac Index

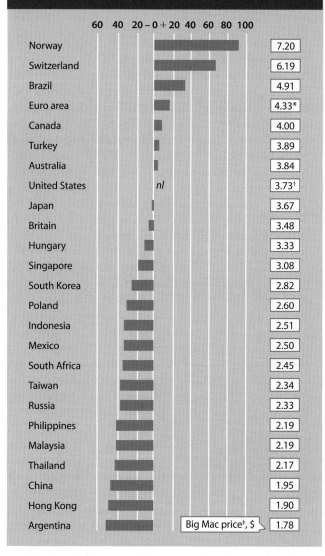

Buns for your buck
Big Mac index, local-currency under(–)/over(+) valuation against the dollar, %

	Big Mac price†, $
Norway	7.20
Switzerland	6.19
Brazil	4.91
Euro area	4.33*
Canada	4.00
Turkey	3.89
Australia	3.84
United States	3.73†
Japan	3.67
Britain	3.48
Hungary	3.33
Singapore	3.08
South Korea	2.82
Poland	2.60
Indonesia	2.51
Mexico	2.50
South Africa	2.45
Taiwan	2.34
Russia	2.33
Philippines	2.19
Malaysia	2.19
Thailand	2.17
China	1.95
Hong Kong	1.90
Argentina	1.78

*Weighted average of member countries; † Average of four cities; ‡ At market exchange rate 21 July 2010; Sources: McDonald's; *Economist*

Source: "Burgernomics: When the chips are down," *Economist*, 24 July 2010, 72. © Economist Newspaper Group. All rights reserved. Reproduced by permission.

product with both traded and non-traded inputs. The costs for traded inputs (such as flour for the bun) are the same, but non-traded inputs (such as labor and real estate) are cheaper in developing countries.

- Although the Big Mac has traded inputs, it is not itself a traded product. No large number of American hamburger lovers would travel to Argentina simply to get the best deal on the Big Mac and then somehow (perhaps in portable freezers?) take large quantities of the made-in-Argentina Big Macs to the United States. If they did, the Big Mac price in Argentina, costing only $1.78 per serving (the lowest in the world), would be driven up and the price in the United States would be pushed down. Remember that prices are determined by supply and demand.

Still, we shouldn't read too much into this index. PPP signals where exchange rates may move *in the long run*. But it does not suggest that the yuan should appreciate by 48% or that the Swiss franc should depreciate by 65% next year. According to the *Economist*, anyone interested in the PPP theory "would be unwise to exclude the Big Mac [index] from their diet, but Super Size servings [of the index] would equally be a mistake."[1]

Interest Rates and Money Supply

While the PPP theory suggests the long-run direction of exchange rate movement, what about the short run? In the short run, variations in interest rates have a powerful effect. If one country's interest rates are high relative to other countries', that country will attract foreign funds. Because inflows of foreign funds usually need to be converted to the home currency, a high interest rate will increase the demand for the home currency, thus enhancing its exchange value. For example, until 2008, Iceland (with high interest rates) had benefitted from the "yen carry trade" undertaken by investors borrowing yen in Japan (where interest rates were next to nothing) and investing in Iceland.[2] The value of the Icelandic krona thus was pushed up.

In addition, a country's rate of inflation relative to that prevailing abroad affects its ability to attract foreign funds and hence its exchange rate. A high level of inflation is essentially too much money chasing too few goods in an economy; technically, it is an expansion of a country's money supply. When a government faces budgetary shortfalls, it may choose to print more currency. More currency tends to stimulate inflation. Inflation, in turn, would cause the currency to depreciate. Why does this chain of events happen? As the supply of a given currency (such as the Mexican peso) increases while the demand stays the same, the per unit value of that currency (such as one peso) goes down. Therefore, the exchange rate is highly sensitive to changes in monetary policy. It responds swiftly to changes in money supply. To avoid losses from holding assets in a depreciated currency, investors sell them for assets denominated in other currencies. Such massive sell-offs may worsen the depreciation. This happened in Britain during the 2008–2009 crisis. Reacting to the Bank of England's loose monetary policy to print more money in order to combat the recession, numerous investors sold off assets held in pound sterling, forcing it to depreciate relative to the euro.

Productivity and Balance of Payments

A rise in a country's productivity relative to that of other countries will improve its competitive position in international trade. This is the basic proposition of the theories of absolute and comparative advantage discussed in Chapter 5. In turn, more FDI will be attracted to the country, fueling demand for its home currency. One recent example is China. All of the China-bound FDI inflows in dollars, euros, and pounds have to be converted to the local currency, boosting the demand for the yuan and hence its value.

Recall from Chapter 5 that changes in productivity will change a country's balance of trade. A country highly productive in manufacturing may generate a merchandise trade surplus, whereas a country less productive in manufacturing may end up with a merchandise trade deficit. These have ramifications for the **balance of payments**, which is officially known as a country's international transaction statement and includes merchandise trade, service trade, and capital movement. Exhibit 7.4 on the next page shows that the United States had a merchandise trade deficit of $647 billion and a service trade surplus of $152 billion in 2010. In addition to merchandise and service trade, we add receipts on US assets abroad (such as repatriated earning from US multinational enterprises [MNEs] in China and dividends paid by Japanese firms to American shareholders), subtract payments on US-based foreign assets (such as repatriated earnings from Canadian MNEs in the United States to Canada or dividends paid by US firms to Dutch shareholders), and government grants and private remittances (such as US foreign aid sent to Iraq or money that Mexican farmhands in America send home). After doing all of the math, we can see that the United States ran a $461 billion current account deficit. Technically, the current account balance consists of exports, minus imports of merchandise and services, plus income on US assets abroad, minus payments on foreign assets in the United States, plus unilateral government transfers and private remittances.

A current account deficit has to be financed by the financial account, which consists of purchases and sales of assets. This is because a country needs to balance its accounts in much the same way as a family deals with its finances. Any deficit in a family budget has to be financed by spending from savings or by borrowing. In a similar fashion, the overall US deficit of $681 billion in 2010 (the net of the $461 billion current account deficit and the $220 billion financial account deficit) was financed largely by borrowing (such as selling US government securities to foreign central banks such as the People's Bank of China).

To make a long story short, a country experiencing a current account surplus will see its currency appreciate. Conversely, a country experiencing a current account deficit will see its currency depreciate. This will not happen overnight but over a span of years and decades. The current movement between the yuan (appreciating) and the dollar (depreciating) illustrated in the Closing Case is but one example. In the 1950s and 1960s, the rise of the dollar was accompanied by a sizable US surplus on merchandise trade. By the 1970s and 1980s, the surplus gradually turned into a deficit. By the 1990s and 2000s, the US current account deficit increased, forcing the dollar to depreciate relative to other currencies such as the yuan, the euro, and the Canadian dollar. Broadly speaking, the value of a country's currency is an embodiment of its economic strengths as reflected in its productivity and balance of payments positions (see the Opening Case). Overall, the recent pressure for the US dollar to depreciate is indicative of the relative decline of US economic strengths compared with its major trading partners (see the Closing Case).

Exchange Rate Policies

There are two major exchange rate policies: floating rate and fixed rate. The **floating** (or **flexible**) **exchange rate policy** is the willingness of a government to let demand and supply conditions determine exchange rates. Governments adopting this policy tend to

Balance of payments
A country's international transaction statement, which includes merchandise trade, service trade, and capital movement.

Floating (or flexible) exchange rate policy
The willingness of a government to let demand and supply conditions determine exchange rates.

EXHIBIT 7.4

The Simplified US Balance of Payments (billion dollars)

I. Current Account	
1. Exports of goods (merchandise)	1,289
2. Imports of goods (merchandise)	−1,936
3. Balance on goods (merchandise trade—lines 1 + 2)	**−647**
4. Exports of services	546
5. Imports of services	−394
6. Balance on services (service trade—lines 4 + 5)	**152**
7. Balance on goods and services (trade deficit/surplus—lines 3 + 6)	**−495**
8. Income receipts on US-owned assets abroad	659
9. Income payments on foreign-owned assets in the United States	−488
10. Government grants and private remittances	−137
11. Balance on current account (current account deficit/surplus—lines 7 + 8 + 9 + 10)	**−461**
II. Financial Account	
12. US-owned assets abroad (increase/financial outflow = −)	−1,025
13. Foreign-owned assets in the United States	1,245
14. Balance on financial account (lines 12 + 13)	**−220**
15. Overall balance of payments (official reserve transactions balance—lines 11 + 14)	**−681**

Source: This is a simplified table adapted from US Department of Commerce, Bureau of Economic Analysis, *US International Transactions: Fourth Quarter and Year 2010*, Table 1, 16 March 2011, Washington: BEA, available online at http://www.bea.gov [accessed 6 April 2011]. This table refers to 2010. The official table has 78 lines. Numbers may not add due to rounding.

believe in the free market and allow it to determine exchange rates, usually on a daily basis via the foreign exchange market. However, few countries adopt a **clean** (or **free**) **float**, which would be a pure market solution. Most countries practice a **dirty** (or **managed**) **float**, with selective government interventions. Of the major currencies, the US, Canadian, and Australian dollars, the yen, and the pound have been under managed float since the 1970s (after the collapse of the Bretton Woods system, which we will discuss in the next section). Since the late 1990s, Brazil, Hungary, Mexico, Poland, South Korea, and numerous other countries have also joined the managed float regime.

The severity of intervention is a matter of degree. Heavier intervention moves the country closer to a fixed exchange rate policy, and less intervention enables a country to approach the free float ideal. A main objective for intervention is to prevent erratic fluctuations that may trigger macroeconomic turbulence. Some countries do not adhere to any particular rates. Others choose **target exchange rates**, which are specified upper and lower bounds within which the exchange rate is allowed to fluctuate. These are also known as **crawling bands**. A country that uses target exchange rates—an approach called "snake in a tube"—will intervene only when the snake (the exchange rate) crawls out of the tube (the upper or lower bounds). Technically, the yuan is now allowed to float, but only within a limited tube (up to 0.5% fluctuation per day) (see the Closing Case).

The second major exchange rate policy is the fixed rate policy. A country adopting a **fixed rate policy** fixes the exchange rate of its

Clean (or free) float
A pure market solution to determine exchange rates.

Dirty (or managed) float
Using selective government intervention to determine exchange rates.

Target exchange rates (or crawling bands)
Specified upper or lower bounds within which an exchange rate is allowed to fluctuate.

Fixed rate policy
Setting the exchange rate of a currency relative to other currencies.

domestic currency relative to other currencies. A specific version of fixed rate policy involves pegging the domestic currency, which means to set the exchange rate of the domestic currency in terms of another currency (the peg). Many developing countries, for example, peg their currencies to the US dollar. There are two benefits to a peg policy. First, a peg stabilizes the import and export prices. Second, many countries with high inflation have pegged their currencies to the dollar in order to restrain domestic inflation because the United States has relatively low inflation.

Investor Psychology

While theories on price differences (PPP), interest rates and money supply, balance of payments, and exchange rate policies predict long-run movements of exchange rates, they often fall short of predicting short-run movements. What then determines short-run movements? They are largely driven by investor psychology, some of which is fickle and thus very hard to predict. Professor Richard Lyons at the University of California, Berkeley, is an expert on exchange rate theories. He was baffled when he observed currency trading firsthand:

As I sat there, my friend traded furiously all day long, racking up over $1 billion in trades each day. This was a world where the standard trade was $10 million, and a $1 million trade was a "skinny one." Despite my belief that exchange rates depend on macroeconomics, only rarely was news of this type his primary concern. Most of the time he was reading tea leaves that were, at least to me, not so clear. . . . It was clear my understanding was incomplete when he looked over, in the midst of his fury, and asked me: "What should I do?" I laughed. Nervously.[3]

Investors—currency traders such as the one Lyons observed, foreign portfolio investors, and average citizens—may move in the same direction at the same time, like a herd, resulting in a **bandwagon effect**. The bandwagon effect seemed to be at play in 2008, when the Icelandic krona lost more than half of its value against the key currencies such as the dollar and the euro. Essentially, a large number of individuals and companies exchanged the krona for the key currencies to minimize their exposure to Iceland's financial crisis—a phenomenon known as **capital flight**. This movement out of the krona pushed down the demand for it, and thus its value. Then, more individuals and companies jumped on the bandwagon, further depressing the exchange rate and making Iceland's crisis worse.

Overall, economics, politics, and psychology are all at play. The stakes are high, yet consensus is rare regarding the determinants of foreign exchange rates. As a result,

predicting the direction of currency movements remains an art or, at best, a highly imprecise science.

Articulate and explain the steps in the evolution of the international monetary system.

EVOLUTION OF THE INTERNATIONAL MONETARY SYSTEM

Having outlined the basic determinants of exchange rates, let us examine the history of the international monetary system, divided into three eras: the gold standard, the Bretton Woods system, and the post–Bretton Woods system.

The Gold Standard (1870–1914)

The **gold standard** was in place from 1870 to 1914 and fixed the value of most major currencies in terms of gold. Gold was used as the **common denominator** for all currencies, which means that all currencies were pegged at a fixed rate to gold. The gold standard was essentially a global peg system with little volatility and a great deal of predictability and stability. To be able to redeem its currency in gold at a fixed price, every central bank needed to maintain gold reserves. The system provided powerful incentives for countries to run current account surpluses, resulting in net inflows of gold.

The Bretton Woods System (1944–1973)

The gold standard was abandoned in 1914 when several World War I combatant countries printed excessive amounts of currency to finance their war efforts. After World War I, especially during the Great Depression (1929–1933), countries engaged in competitive devaluations in an effort to boost exports at the expense of trading partners. But no country could win such a race to the bottom, and the gold standard had to be jettisoned.

Toward the end of World War II, at an allied

Bandwagon effect
The effect of investors moving in the same direction at the same time, like a herd.

Capital flight
A phenomenon in which a large number of individuals and companies exchange domestic currencies for a foreign currency.

Gold standard
A system in which the value of most major currencies was maintained by fixing their prices in terms of gold.

Common denominator
A currency or commodity to which the value of all currencies are pegged.

conference in Bretton Woods, New Hampshire, a new system, known simply as the **Bretton Woods system**, was agreed upon by 44 countries. The system was centered on the US dollar as the new common denominator. All currencies were pegged at a fixed rate to the dollar. Only the dollar was convertible into gold at $35 per ounce. Other currencies were not required to be gold convertible.

The Bretton Woods system propelled the dollar to the commanding heights of the global economy. This system reflected the higher US productivity level and the large trade surplus the United States had with the rest of the world in the first two postwar decades. At the end of World War II, the US economy contributed approximately 70% of the global GDP and was the export engine and growth engine of the world.

The Post–Bretton Woods System (1973–Present)

By the late 1960s and early 1970s, a combination of rising productivity elsewhere and US inflationary policies led to the demise of Bretton Woods. First, in the 1960s, President Lyndon Johnson increased government spending in order to finance both the Vietnam War and the Great Society welfare programs. He did this not by additional taxation but by increasing money supply. These actions led to rising inflation levels and strong pressures for the dollar to depreciate. Second, the United States ran its first post-1945 trade deficit in 1971 as (West) Germany and other countries caught up to the United States in productivity and increased their exports. This pushed the (West) German mark to appreciate and the dollar to depreciate, a situation very similar to the yen–dollar relationship in the 1980s and the current yuan–dollar relationship in the 2000s.

As currency traders bought more German marks, Germany's central bank, the Bundesbank, had to buy billions of dollars to maintain the dollar/mark exchange rate fixed by Bretton Woods. Being stuck with massive amounts of the dollar that were worth less now, Germany unilaterally allowed its currency to float in May 1971.

The Bretton Woods system also became a pain in the neck for the United States because the exchange rate of the dollar was not allowed to unilaterally change. Per Bretton Woods agreements, the US Treasury was obligated to dispense one ounce of gold for every $35 brought to it by a foreign central bank such as the Bundesbank. Consequently, the United States was hemorrhaging gold into the coffers of foreign central banks. In order to stop the flow of gold out of the Treasury, President Richard Nixon unilaterally announced in 1971 that the dollar was no longer convertible into gold. After tense negotiations, the major countries collectively agreed in 1973 to allow their currencies to float, thus ending the Bretton Woods system. In retrospect, the Bretton Woods system had been built on two conditions. First, the US inflation rate had to be low. Second, the United States could not run a trade deficit. When both of these conditions were violated, the system's demise was inevitable.

As a result, today we live with a **post–Bretton Woods system**, which has no official common denominator and is characterized by the diversity of exchange rate systems discussed earlier (various floating systems and fixed rates). Diversity and flexibility are its strengths. Its drawbacks are turbulence and uncertainty. Although the US dollar has not been the official common denominator since the early 1970s, the dollar has retained a significant amount of soft power as a key currency (see the Closing Case). In November 2008 and then in April 2009, in the midst of the worst financial crisis in recent times, leaders of the Group of 20 (G-20) held two summits: first in Washington, DC, and then in London. Both summits called for an overhaul of the world's financial structure. These summits were labeled by the media as an effort to construct "Bretton Woods II."[4] The dust has yet to settle on the outcome of these efforts.

The International Monetary Fund

While the Bretton Woods system is no longer with us, one of its most enduring legacies is the **International Monetary Fund (IMF)**, founded in 1944 as a Bretton Woods institution. (The World Bank is the other Bretton Woods institution.) The IMF's mandate is to promote international monetary cooperation, exchange stability, and orderly exchange arrangements.

Lending is a core responsibility of the IMF, which provides loans to countries experiencing balance-of-payments problems. The IMF can be viewed as a lender of last resort to help member countries out of financial difficulty. Where

Bretton Woods system
A system in which all currencies were pegged at a fixed rate to the US dollar.

Post–Bretton Woods system
A system of flexible exchange rate regimes with no official common denominator.

International Monetary Fund (IMF)
An international organization that was established to promote international monetary cooperation, exchange stability, and orderly exchange arrangements.

does the IMF get its funds? The answer boils down to the same principle as where insurance companies get their funds to pay out insurance claims. Similar to insurance companies collecting premiums from subscribers to accumulate the funds necessary to cover claims, the IMF collects funds from member countries. Each member country is assigned a **quota** that determines its financial contribution to the IMF (technically known as its "subscription"), its capacity to borrow from the IMF, and its voting power. The quota is broadly based on a country's relative size in the global economy.

By definition, the IMF makes loans, not grants. IMF loans usually have to be repaid in one to five years. Although payments have been extended in some cases, no member country has defaulted. An ideal IMF loan scenario would be a balance-of-payments crisis that threatens to severely disrupt a country's financial stability, such as when it imports more than it exports and cannot pay for imports. The IMF could step in and inject funds in the short term to help stabilize the financial system.

While an IMF loan provides short-term financial resources, it also comes with strings attached. Those strings are long-term policy reforms that recipient countries must undertake as conditions of receiving the loan. These conditions usually entail belt tightening and push governments to undertake painful reforms that they otherwise probably would not have undertaken. For example, when the IMF (together with the EU) provided a loan to Greece in 2010, the Greek government agreed to cut pensions and wages for public sector employees by 15% to 20% in order to pay for government debt.[5] Since the 1990s, the IMF has helped Mexico (1994), Russia (1996 and 1998), Asia (Indonesia, South Korea, and Thailand) (1997), Turkey (2001), Brazil (2002), Iceland (2008), Ukraine (2008), Hungary (2008), Greece (2010), and several others. While the IMF has noble goals, its actions are not without criticisms that call for reforms (see Debate).

LO3 *Identify strategic responses firms can take to deal with foreign exchange movements.*

STRATEGIC RESPONSES

From an institution-based view, knowledge about foreign exchange rates and the international monetary system (including the role of the IMF) helps paint a broad picture of the rules of the game that govern financial transactions around the world. Armed with this knowledge, savvy managers need to develop firm-specific resources and capabilities so they can rise to the challenge, or at least avoid having their firms crushed by unfavorable currency movements. This section outlines the strategic responses of two types of firms: financial and non-financial companies.

Strategies for Financial Companies

One of the leading strategic goals for financial companies is to profit from the foreign exchange market. The **foreign exchange market** is where individuals, firms, governments, and banks buy and sell currencies of other countries. Unlike a stock exchange, the foreign exchange market has no central, physical location. This market is truly global and transparent. Buyers and sellers are geographically dispersed but constantly linked, and quoted prices change as often as 20 times a *minute*.[6] Each week, the market opens first in Sydney, then Tokyo, then Hong Kong, and then Singapore. Gradually, Frankfurt, Zurich, Paris, London, New York, Chicago, and San Francisco wake up and come online.

Operating on a 24/7 basis, the foreign exchange market is the largest and

INTERNATIONAL MONETARY FUND

JOHN LIPSKY

CHRISTINE LAGARDE

CAROLINE ATKINSON

International Monetary Fund Managing Director Christine Lagarde holds a news briefing in Washington, DC, on July 6, 2011.

© KEVIN DIETSCH/UPI/Landov

Quota
The weight a member country carries within the IMF, which determines the amount of its financial contribution (technically known as its "subscription"), its capacity to borrow from the IMF, and its voting power.

Foreign exchange market
The market where individuals, firms, governments, and banks buy and sell currencies of other countries.

The IMF's Actions, Criticisms, and Reforms

CRITICISMS The complexity of the IMF's actions means that it cannot please everyone. First, the IMF's critics argue that its lending may *facilitate* more problems because of moral hazard. *Moral hazard* refers to recklessness when people and organizations (including governments) do not have to face the full consequences of their actions. Moral hazard is inherent in all insurance arrangements, including the IMF. Basically, knowing that the IMF would come to the rescue, certain governments may behave more recklessly. For example, between 1958 and 2001, Turkey was rescued by 18 (!) IMF loans.

A second criticism centers on the IMF's lack of accountability. Although the IMF can dictate terms over a host country that is being rescued, none of the IMF officials is democratically elected, and most of them do not have any deep knowledge of the host country. Consequently, they sometimes make disastrous decisions. In 1998, the IMF forced the Indonesian government to drastically cut back on food subsidies for the poor. Riots exploded the next day. Hundreds of people were killed and many properties damaged. Then, the IMF reversed its position by restoring food subsidies. However, in some quarters, the bitterness was all the greater. A lot of protesters argued: If food subsidies could have been continued, why were they taken away in the first place?

A third and perhaps most challenging criticism is that the IMF's "one-size-fits-all" strategy may be inappropriate. Since the 1930s, in order to maintain more employment, most Western governments have abandoned the idea to balance the budget. Deficit spending has been used as a major policy weapon to pull a country out of an economic crisis. Yet the IMF often demands governments in more vulnerable developing countries, in the midst of a major crisis, to balance their budgets by slashing spending (such as cutting food subsidies). These actions often make the crisis far worse than it needs to be. After the IMF came to "rescue" countries affected by the 1997 Asian financial crisis, the unemployment rate was up threefold in Thailand, fourfold in South Korea, and tenfold in Indonesia. Many scholars are surprised that the IMF would pursue its agenda in the absence of conclusive research and with the knowledge of repeated failures.

After a period of relative inactivity in the early 2000s, the IMF went back to action again starting in late 2008, rescuing ten countries, mostly in emerging Europe (Georgia, Hungary, Ukraine, Latvia, Serbia, Belarus, Armenia, and Romania), in five months. Shown in Exhibit 7.5, balancing budgets and raising interest rates were the standard weapons of choice that the IMF would impose on loan recipient countries. In most emerging European countries as well as more developed European countries (such as Iceland [2009] and Greece [2010]), the IMF has still prescribed such bitter "medicines."

REFORMS However, the momentum of the criticisms, the severity of the global crisis, and the desire to better serve the international community have facilitated a series of IMF reforms since 2009. Some of these reforms represent a total (180-degree) change from its previous directions, resulting in an "IMF 2.0" dubbed by *Time*. For example, the IMF now promotes more fiscal spending in order to stimulate the economy and to ease money supply and reduce interest rates, given the primary concern for the global economy is now deflation and recession but not inflation. Obviously, the IMF's change of heart is affected by the tremendous stimulus packages unleashed in developed economies since 2008, which result in skyrocketing budget deficits. If the developed economies can (hopefully) use greater fiscal spending and budget deficits to pull themselves out of a crisis, the IMF simply cannot lecture developing economies that receive its loans to balance their budgets in the middle of a crisis. Then, given the stigma of receiving IMF loans and listening to and then implementing IMF lectures, many countries avoid the IMF until they run out of options. In response, in April 2009, the IMF unleashed a new Flexible Credit Line (FCL), which would be useful for crisis *prevention* by providing the flexibility to draw on it at any time, with no strings attached—a radical contrast to the IMF's past.

Further, the IMF 2.0 is likely to become three times bigger—leaders in the G-20 Summit in London in April 2009 agreed to enhance its funding from $250 billion to $750 billion. Of the $500 billion in new funding, the United States, the European Union, and Japan each is expected to contribute $100 billion. China has signed up for $50 billion. Brazil, India, and Russia has each signed up for $10 billion. However, this is not a done deal, because it is possible that the US Congress may veto the $100 billion spending on "other countries' problems" at a time when the US economy is hurting. Further, injection of substantial funding from emerging economies has led Brazil, Russia, India, and China (BRIC) to call for better representation of these countries. However, enhancing voting rights for BRIC would result in reduced shares for developed economies. Even with the IMF's new proposed change to vote shares, Brazil, with 1.72% of the votes (up from the current 1.38%), will still carry less weight than Belgium (with 1.86%, down from the current 2.09%). Such points of contention continue to rage throughout IMF discussions. Thus, IMF reforms will be a long-term undertaking that will not stop anytime soon.

Sources: "Mission possible," *Economist*, 11 April 2009, 69–71; "New fund, old fundamentals," *Economist*, 2 May 2009, 78; "High stakes," *Economist*, 15 May 2010, 85; A. Ghosh, M. Chamon, C. Crowe, J. Kim, and J. Ostry, "Coping with the crisis: Policy options for emerging market countries," IMF staff position paper (Washington: IMF, 2009); J. Stiglitz, *Globalization and Its Discontents* (New York: Norton, 2002); "International Monetary Fund 2.0," *Time*, 20 April 2009; IMF, http://www.imf.org.

EXHIBIT 7.5 Typical IMF Conditions on Loan Recipient Countries: From 1.0 to 2.0

IMF 1.0	IMF 2.0
• Balance budget by slashing government spending (often cutting social welfare) • Raise interest rates to slow monetary growth and inflation	• Expand fiscal spending by stimulating more economic activity • Ease money supply and reduce interest rates to combat deflation and recession

most active market in the world. On average, the worldwide volume exceeds $2 trillion per *day*. To put this mind-boggling number in perspective, the amount of one single *day* of foreign exchange transactions roughly doubles the amount of worldwide FDI outflows in one *year* and roughly equals close to one quarter of worldwide merchandise exports in one *year*. Specifically, the foreign exchange market has two functions: (1) to service the needs of trade and FDI and (2) to trade in its own commodity—namely, foreign exchange.

There are three primary types of foreign exchange transactions: spot transactions, forward transactions, and swaps. **Spot transactions** are the classic single-shot exchange of one currency for another. For example, Australian tourists visiting Italy go to a bank to exchange their Australian dollars for euros, essentially buying euros with Australian dollars.

Forward transactions allow participants to buy and sell currencies now for future delivery, typically in 30, 90, or 180 days after the date of the transaction. The primary benefit of forward transactions is to protect traders and investors from being exposed to the unfavorable fluctuations of the spot rate, an act known as **currency hedging**. Currency hedging is essentially a way to minimize the foreign exchange risk inherent in all non-spot transactions, which include most trade and FDI deals.[7] Traders and investors expecting to make or receive payments in a foreign currency in the future are concerned that they may be forced to make either a greater payment or receive less in terms of the domestic currency should the spot rate change. For example, if the forward rate of the euro (€/US$) is exactly the same as the spot rate, the euro is flat. If the forward rate of the euro per dollar is *higher* than the spot rate, the euro has a **forward discount**. If the forward rate of the euro per dollar is *lower* than the spot rate, the euro then has a **forward premium**.

Let's apply this to a hypothetical example. Assume that today's exchange rate of €/US$ is 1, that a US firm expects to be paid €1 million six months later, and that the euro is at a 180-day forward discount of 1.1 (or €1/US$1.1). The US firm could take out a forward contract now, and at the end of six months the euro earnings would be converted into $909,091 (€1 million/1.1). Does such a currency-hedging move make sense? Maybe. The move makes sense if the firm knows in advance that the future spot rate will be higher. So in six months if the spot rate is 1.25, then the forward contract provides the US firm with $909,091 instead of $800,000 (€1 million/1.25); the difference is $109,091 (or 14% of $800,000). However, the move would not make sense if after six months the spot rate were actually below 1.1. If the spot rate remained at 1, the firm could have earned $1 million *without* the forward con-

tract, instead of only $909,091 with the contract. This simple example suggests a powerful observation: Currency hedging *requires* firms to have expectations or forecasts of future spot rates relative to forward rates.

Another major type of foreign exchange transactions is a swap. A **currency swap** is the conversion of one currency into another at Time 1, with an agreement to revert it back to the original currency at a specified Time 2 in the future. Deutsche Bank may have an excess balance of pounds but needs dollars now. At the same time, Union Bank of Switzerland (UBS) may have more dollars than it needs at the moment and is looking for more pounds. The two banks can negotiate a swap agreement in which Deutsche Bank agrees to exchange pounds for dollars with UBS today and dollars for pounds at a specific point in the future.

The primary participants of the foreign exchange market are large international banks such as Deutsche Bank, UBS, and Citigroup, which trade among themselves. How do these banks make money by trading money? They make money by capturing the difference between their **offer rate** (the price to sell) and **bid rate** (the price to buy)—the bid rate is *always* lower than the offer rate. In other words, banks buy low and sell high. The difference between the offer rate and the bid rate is technically called the **spread**. For example, Citigroup may quote offer and bid rates for the Swiss franc at $0.5854 and $0.5851, respectively, and the spread is $0.0003—that is, Citigroup is willing to sell one million francs for $585,400 and buy one million francs for $585,100. If Citigroup can simultaneously buy and sell one million francs, it can make $300 (the spread of $0.0003 × one million francs). Given the instantaneous and transparent nature of the

Spot transaction
The classic single-shot exchange of one currency for another.

Forward transaction
A foreign exchange transaction in which participants buy and sell currencies now for future delivery.

Currency hedging
A transaction that protects traders and investors from exposure to the fluctuations of the spot rate.

Forward discount
A condition under which the forward rate of one currency relative to another currency is higher than the spot rate.

Forward premium
A condition under which the forward rate of one currency relative to another currency is lower than the spot rate.

Currency swap
A foreign exchange transaction between two firms in which one currency is converted into another at Time 1, with an agreement to revert it back to the original currency at a specified Time 2 in the future.

Offer rate
The price at which a bank is willing to sell a currency.

Bid rate
The price at which a bank is willing to buy a currency.

Spread
The difference between the offer price and the bid price.

IN FOCUS

Irish Exporters Cope with Currency Fluctuation

A member of the euro area, Ireland has strong exporters that sell not only throughout Europe but also in many other parts of the world. The downside of selling around the world is the complication of having to deal with currency fluctuation. Approximately 50% of the Irish export invoicing is done in either British pound sterling or US dollars, which have fluctuated substantially during the 2008–2009 crisis. While hedging using forward contracts is an obvious coping strategy, many smaller exporters cannot afford the expenses. In addition, hedging is not risk-free. Wrong bets may end up burning firms big time.

To better cope with currency fluctuation, a straightforward mechanism is to insist on payment in euros. As a growing number of buyers of Irish exports have agreed to pay in euros, this strategy seems to have worked. A survey conducted by the Irish Exporters Association found that 38% of buyers in the UK, 18% in North America, 48% in the Middle East, 45% in Asia, 67% in Latin America, and 83% in non-euro-area European countries were willing to pay Irish exporters in euros, thus eliminating the headache of currency fluctuation for Irish exporters. Although this is a small piece of evidence, it does help paint a picture of the euro's rising popularity as a major currency for international trade around the world.

Sources: The Euro Information Website, 2011, http://www.ibiblio.org/theeuro/InformationWebsite.htm; "Exporters get resourceful to fight currency fluctuation," *The Independent*, 21 November, 2009, http://www.independent.ie; Irish Exporters Association, 2011, http://www.irishexporters.ie.

---

electronically linked foreign exchange market around the globe (one new quote in London can reach New York before you finish reading this *sentence*), the opportunities can come and go very quickly. The globally integrated nature of this market leads to three outcomes:

+ a razor-thin spread
+ quick (often literally split-second) decisions on buying and selling
+ ever-increasing volume in order to make more profits

To envision the quick decisions, remember the observation by Lyons mentioned earlier. To get a sense of the ever-increasing volume, recall the daily volume of $2 trillion. In the example above, $300 is obviously peanuts for Citigroup. Do a little math: How much trading in Swiss francs does Citigroup have to do in order to make $1 million in profits for itself?

Strategies for Non-Financial Companies

How do non-financial companies cope with the potential losses they could incur due to fluctuations in the foreign exchange market, broadly known as **currency risks**? There are three primary strategies: (1) invoicing in their own currencies, (2) currency hedging (as discussed above), and (3) strategic hedging. The most basic way is to invoice customers in your own currency. By invoicing in dollars, many US firms have enjoyed such protection from unfavorable foreign exchange movements. As the euro becomes a more powerful currency, firms based in countries that use the euro now increasingly demand that they be paid in euros (see In Focus).

Currency hedging is risky because, as discussed in the previous section, in trying to predict currency movements your bets could be all wrong. **Strategic hedging** means spreading out activities in a number of countries in different currency zones in order to offset any currency losses in one region through gains in

---

Currency risk
The potential for loss associated with fluctuations in the foreign exchange market.

Strategic hedging
Spreading out activities in a number of countries in different currency zones to offset any currency losses in one region through gains in other regions.

> **One new quote in London can reach New York before you finish reading this sentence.**

other regions. Therefore, strategic hedging can be considered as currency diversification. It reduces exposure to unfavorable foreign exchange movements. Strategic hedging is conceptually different from currency hedging. Currency hedging focuses on using forward contracts and swaps to contain currency risks, a financial management activity that can be performed by in-house financial specialists or outside experts (such as currency traders). Strategic hedging refers to dispersing operations geographically—through sourcing or FDI—in multiple currency zones. By definition, this is more strategic because it involves managers from many functional areas such as production, marketing, and sourcing in addition to those from finance. Strategic hedging was one of the key motivations behind Toyota's 1998 decision to set up a new factory in France instead of expanding its existing British operations. Although expanding the British site would have cost less in the short run, France is in the euro zone, which the British have refused to join.

Overall, the importance of foreign exchange management for firms of all stripes interested in doing business abroad cannot be over-stressed. Firms whose performance is otherwise stellar can be devastated by unfavorable currency movements. For example, the Brazilian real appreciated by 38% against the dollar between 2009 and 2010. Brazilian manufacturers thus had a hard time competing with relatively cheap imports (see the Opening Case). On the other hand, thanks to crises in countries such as Greece, Ireland, and Portugal, the euro depreciated sharply against the dollar during the same period. But European exporters such as Daimler-Benz (maker of Mercedes cars) and EADS (manufacturer of Airbus jets) could not be happier.[8]

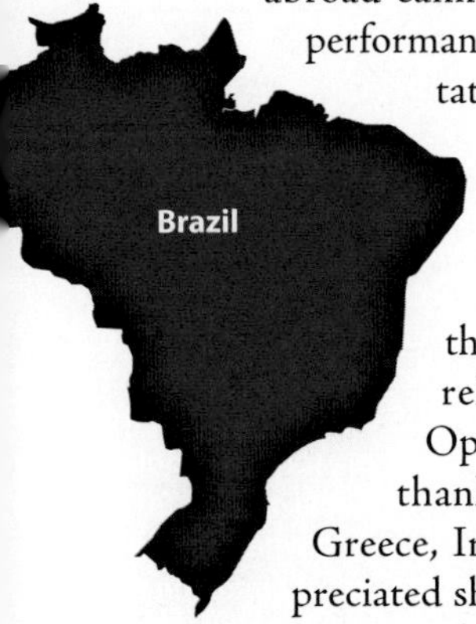

From a resource-based view, it seems imperative that firms develop resources and capabilities that can combat currency risks in addition to striving for excellence in areas such as operations and marketing.[9] Developing such expertise is no small accomplishment because, as noted earlier, predicting currency movements remains an art or at least a highly imprecise science. These challenges mean that firms able to profit from (or at least avoid being crushed by) unfavorable currency movements will possess valuable, rare, and hard-to-imitate capabilities that are the envy of rivals.

LO4 *Identify three things you need to know about currency when doing business internationally.*

MANAGEMENT SAVVY

The big question in global business, adapted to the context of foreign exchange movements, is: What determines the success and failure of currency management around the globe? The answer boils down to two components. First,

from an institution-based standpoint, the changing rules of the game—economic, political, and psychological—enable or constrain firms. As shown in the Closing Case, Wal-Mart's low cost advantage from made-in-China products stems at least in part from the Chinese government's policy to manage its yuan at a favorable level against the dollar. Consequently, Wal-Mart's low cost advantage may be eroded as the yuan appreciates. Second, from a resource-based perspective, how firms develop valuable, unique, and hard-to-imitate capabilities in currency management may make or break them.

Shown in Exhibit 7.6, three implications for action emerge. First, foreign exchange literacy must be fostered. Savvy managers need to pay attention not only to the broad, long-run movements informed by PPP, productivity changes, and balance of payments, but also to the fickle short-run fluctuations triggered by interest rate changes and investor mood swings.

Second, risk analysis of any country must include its currency risks. Previous chapters have advised managers to pay attention to political, regulatory, and cultural risks of various countries. Here, a crucial currency risk dimension is added. An otherwise attractive country may suffer from devaluation of its currency. For example, prior to 2008, foreign and domestic banks in emerging European countries such as Hungary, Latvia, and Poland let numerous home buyers take out mortgage loans denominated in the euro, while a majority of these customers' assets and incomes were in local currencies. Unfortunately, local currencies in these countries were severely devalued in the 2008–2009 crisis, making many home buyers unable to come up with the higher mortgage payments. Banks in the region also suffered from severe losses.[10]

Finally, a country's high currency risks do not necessarily suggest that the country needs to be avoided totally. Instead, it calls for a prudent currency risk management strategy via invoicing in one's own currency, currency hedging, or strategic hedging. Not every firm has the power to invoice in its own currency. Smaller, internationally inexperienced firms may outsource currency hedging to specialists such as currency traders. Strategic hedging may be unrealistic for smaller, inexperienced firms. On the other hand, many larger, internationally experienced firms (such as 3M) choose not to touch currency hedging, citing its unpredictability. Instead, they focus on strategic hedging. Although no one has found a fixed formula, firms without a well thought-out currency management strategy will be caught off guard when currency movements take a nasty turn.

EXHIBIT 7.6 Implications for Action

- Fostering foreign exchange literacy is a must.
- Risk analysis of any country must include an analysis of its currency risks.
- A currency risk management strategy is necessary—via invoicing in one's own currency, currency hedging, or strategic hedging.

ETHICAL DILEMMA

A WEAK DOLLAR VERSUS A STRONG YUAN

The value of the US dollar is a trillion-dollar question (Exhibit 7.7). In terms of international trade competitiveness, a strong dollar may make it harder for US firms to export and to compete on price when combating imports. Conversely, a weak dollar may facilitate more US exports and stem import growth.

The dollar is often compared to China's yuan, which, according to US critics, is pegged to the dollar at an "artificially low" level (maybe up to 40%). A cheap yuan is thus behind the formidable competitiveness of China's exports. The US government argues that the yuan needs to appreciate—or to be made "stronger." However, the issue becomes complicated when one realizes that over 60% of "Chinese exports" are not produced by Chinese-owned firms but by foreign-invested enterprises producing in China. Wal-Mart, for example, sources from 5,000 non-Chinese-owned suppliers manufacturing in China. Therefore, US firms such as Wal-Mart that benefit from the cheap yuan actually do not necessarily support the US government's efforts to let the yuan appreciate.

Officially, China abandoned the yuan's peg at 8.3 yuan per dollar in 2005. While the peg was reintroduced in 2008 to combat the economic crisis, it was abandoned again in June 2010. Since then, the pace of yuan appreciation has gathered steam, reaching 6.5 yuan per dollar in 2011. The appreciation has been carefully managed by the People's Bank of China (PBOC, the central bank), and has not been allowed to rise by 0.5% on any given day.

The debate on the exchange rate between the dollar and the yuan is part of the global debate on the proper valuation of the dollar. In the words of Valéry Giscard d'Estaing, former French president, the dollar enjoys "an exorbitant privilege." US firms are spared

the hassle of having to transact in a foreign currency. The dollar reserves in other countries such as China enable the United States to borrow at a lower cost. The US government can print money at will (known with a euphemism as "quantitative easing"), with negative ramifications around the world.

The dollar's dominance stemmed from US economic strength after World War II. Some critics argue that at present, the dollar punches above its weight, since the US share of global output (20%) and trade (11%) is shrinking. In addition to debating what the "fair" value of the dollar is, a new voice is now calling for *abandoning* the dollar as a reserve currency.* Leading this new movement is China. China is America's number one creditor country, holding about $2.2 trillion in foreign exchange reserves, two-thirds of which are

EXHIBIT 7.7 A Strong Dollar Versus a Weak Dollar

Panel A. A Strong (Appreciating) Dollar

Advantages	*Disadvantages*
• US consumers benefit from low prices on imports • Lower prices on foreign goods help keep US price level and inflation level low • US tourists benefit from lower prices when traveling abroad	• US exporters have a hard time competing on price abroad • US firms have a hard time competing with low-cost imports • Foreign tourists find it more expensive when visiting the United States

Panel B. A Weak (Depreciating) Dollar

Advantages	*Disadvantages*
• US exporters find it easier to compete on price abroad • US firms face less competitive pressure to keep prices low • Foreign tourists benefit from lower prices when visiting the United States	• US consumers face higher prices on imports • Higher prices on imports contribute to a higher price level and inflation level in the United States • US tourists find it more expensive when traveling abroad

denominated in dollars. Since the yuan is not internationally accepted (technically non-convertible), China does not suggest that the yuan be used to replace the dollar. Instead, it has proposed to use Special Drawing Rights (SDRs), already created by the IMF, as a global reserve currency. While this proposal is made in the name of promoting global stability, China is not totally altruistic. Since the US budget deficit has exploded and a ton of new money has been printed to fund stimulus packages, China is deeply worried that a cheapening dollar will be a nasty hit to Chinese holdings of US Treasury bonds. There is some fundamental soul-searching among Beijing's economic mandarins. Their policy of keeping the yuan low versus the dollar to promote exports and then to recycle export earnings to buy US Treasury bonds has backfired. Even the typically timid state-controlled media in China is now full of criticisms of the government's "irresponsible" investment policy, which ends up investing hard-earned dollars from a developing economy to subsidize a very rich economy. China's proposal to dethrone the dollar as a dominant currency, although clearly a long shot, quickly garnered support from Russia and Brazil. In 2009, the United Nations Conference on Trade and Development issued a supportive opinion:

An economy whose currency is used as a reserve currency is not under the same obligation as others to make the necessary macroeconomic or exchange-rate adjustments for avoiding continuing current account

deficits. Thus, the dominance of the dollar as the main means of international payments also played an important role in the build-up of the global imbalances in the run up to the financial crisis.

The United States, on the other hand, has every interest to keep the dollar's status quo as the world's (de facto) reserve currency so that surplus countries will keep buying Treasury bonds—for lack of a better alternative. While China continued to buy new Treasury bonds, it recently took two concrete steps. First, China arranged more than $120 billion in currency swaps with trading partners such as Argentina, Indonesia, Malaysia, and South Korea. The PBOC will make yuan available to pay for imports from these countries if they are short on dollars. Second, China started to use yuan to settle certain transactions with Hong Kong—the first step for the yuan's long march toward international convertibility. By 2011, trade worth $58 billion (385 billion yuan) had been settled in yuan.

* Technically, since the demise of the Bretton Woods system in the early 1970s, the US dollar is no longer the official reserve currency of the world. However, the dollar, due to its soft power, has often been treated as the de facto reserve currency.

Sources: "China's doubts about the dollar," *BusinessWeek*, 8 June 2009, 20; "Learning to crawl," *Economist*, 26 June 2010, 75–76; "Stranger than fiction," *Economist*, 22 January 2011: 85–86; "The rise of the redback," *Economist*, 22 January 2011, 14–15; B. Eichengreen, *Exorbitant Privilege* (New York: Oxford University Press, 2011); "UN panel calls for dollar reserve role to be eliminated," *Wall Street Journal*, 8 September 2009.

BY THE NUMBERS

60 percent of world's foreign exchange holdings in US dollars

4 percent of world's foreign exchange holdings in yens

25 percent of world's foreign exchange holdings in euros

 681 overall US deficit in billions of dollars in 2010

 20 number of times per minute that currency price quotes may change

CHAPTER 8

Capitalizing on Regional Global & INTEGRATION

OPENING CASE

A Day in European Business

It is Tuesday morning at five o'clock. A nearly empty freeway lies ahead of Marcus as he heads for the airport in Munich, Germany. As a manager with European responsibilities, traveling and engaging with other cultures is his daily job.

Marcus is vice president in charge of Northern Europe for an entrepreneurial software company that provides computer-aided design software for use in businesses such as large architectural firms, municipalities, automotive suppliers, aerospace manufacturers, and media and entertainment designers. His responsibilities include defining strategies for the region, budgeting for several European countries, negotiating with new potential business partners, and conducting business reviews with his own local teams, suppliers, and partners.

After parking the car and writing down the exact location (important!), Marcus heads for International Departures. Early morn-

ing departure times are quite reliable, and the flight departs on time. He now has two hours to read the morning news, to get an update on worldwide financials, and to enjoy a cup of tea or two and an unspectacular sandwich.

Arriving at the Warsaw airport, Marcus finds there is less border security than in the past. Since Poland became a member of the European Union (EU) and the signing of the Schengen Agreement, there are no longer any passport controls. Like many business travelers, Marcus has avoided checking his luggage to save time, and ten minutes after deplaning, Marcus is greeted by his local country manager. Unfortunately, Marcus cannot take advantage of the EU's monetary union and still has to use five different wallets. In addition to his "euro wallet" for Germany and other countries that use the euro, he needs one for Swedish krones,

LEARNING OBJECTIVES

After studying this chapter, you should be able to:

LO1 *make the case for global economic integration.*

LO2 *explain the evolution of the GATT and the WTO, including current challenges.*

LO3 *make the case for regional economic integration.*

LO4 *list the accomplishments, benefits, and costs of the European Union.*

LO5 *identify the five organizations that promote regional trade in the Americas and describe their benefits and costs.*

LO6 *identify the three organizations that promote regional trade in the Asia Pacific and describe their benefits and costs.*

LO7 *articulate how regional trade should influence your thinking about global business.*

one for Romanian leu, one for British pounds, and one for Polish zloty, which is what he is carrying today. It is quite a challenge to grab the right wallet leaving home at 4:30 in the morning.

While an experienced driver takes Marcus and his country manager through Warsaw's rush hour traffic, they discuss the latest development at the Polish office. Since joining the EU, the level of professionalism has significantly increased at all levels of management in Poland, and English has become the norm for conversations with local staff. This was not the case when Marcus started doing business in Poland in 2001. Initially, he could only directly communicate with the country manager in English. For the first year, all employees were enrolled in English language training every Friday afternoon. Now this training has paid off, and Marcus can easily talk to everyone in the office directly.

Marcus's first appointment is with a major supplier in the center of Warsaw to discuss opportunities for the coming months. After three hours of PowerPoint presentations, financial reports, and marketing reviews, he is invited for a quick business lunch. Another two hours in the car on the way to his company's Polish office in Lodz are followed by an internal staff meeting with updates by all business unit managers.

Marcus's visits to a country office typically take three days packed with meetings and events to justify the expenses of the journey. Modern technology allows video conferencing at high quality, yet it cannot replace the extremely important human factor in business meetings. Marcus prefers face-to-face discussions where recognizing subtle expressions on the other's face can make a difference between closing a deal and coming home empty handed.

Doing business in different European countries, Marcus faces differences in bureaucracy at almost every step. In Poland, for example, it seems that everything needs to be filed in several copies, stamped, and signed. Notaries hold the "license to print money," because more or less everything related to the administration of a company needs to be signed in the presence of a notary. One of the easiest (and most depressing) ways to discover this is by having a dinner and requesting a receipt. If you ask a waiter for a receipt, after ten minutes he may come back with a huge document (three pages) that needs to be filled out with the company's long tax-ID number, signed several times, and finally stamped by the restaurant before it is accepted. Back home in Germany, Marcus would just take his credit card receipt—that's it.

After a long day, it is time to check in at a business hotel. Besides the construction of highways and roads, this is an area where the progress of economic transition and development of Poland is most visible. In 2001, business travelers in Lodz had only one hotel to choose from. Today, international hotel chains such as Ibis and Radisson provide facilities at very good standards. It is past ten o'clock in the evening when Marcus returns from his business dinner to the hotel, where he prepares for tomorrow—another busy day in European business.

Source: M. W. Peng and K. E. Meyer, *International Business* (London: Cengage Learning EMEA, 2011) 228–229.

Why is Marcus so busy traveling around Europe? Why is there no passport control when his international flight from Munich, Germany, arrives in Warsaw, Poland? Why, despite the widespread use of the euro, does Marcus have to maintain five wallets stuffed with different European currencies? In two words, the answer is economic integration. Economic integration is taking place both regionally and globally. **Regional economic integration** refers to efforts to reduce trade and investment barriers within one region, such as the EU. **Global economic integration**, in turn, refers to efforts to reduce trade and investment barriers around the globe.

This chapter is fundamentally about how the two core perspectives in global business interact. Specifically, how do changes in the rules of the game for global and regional economic integration, as emphasized by the institution-based view, lead firms to better develop and leverage their capabilities as highlighted by the resource-based view? In other words, how do firms around the world capitalize on global and regional economic integration? We start with a description of global economic integration. Then, we introduce regional economic integration. Next, we look at a debate about whether regional integration is a building block or a stumbling block. Finally, we offer some practical tips for managers.

Regional economic integration
Efforts to reduce trade and investment barriers within one region.

Global economic integration
Efforts to reduce trade and investment barriers around the globe.

General Agreement on Tariffs and Trade (GATT)
A multilateral agreement governing the international trade of goods (merchandise).

World Trade Organization (WTO)
The official title of the multilateral trading system and the organization underpinning this system since 1995.

> **Make the case for global economic integration.**

INTEGRATING THE GLOBAL ECONOMY

Current frameworks of regional and global economic integration date back to the end of World War II. The world community was mindful of the mercantilist trade policies in the 1930s, which worsened the Great Depression and eventually led to World War II. Two new developments after the war were initiated to prevent a repeat of these circumstances. Globally, the **General Agreement on Tariffs and Trade (GATT)** was created in 1948 as a multilateral agreement governing the international trade of goods (merchandise). In Europe, regional integration started in 1951. The agreement and ensuing integration proved so successful that they are now considerably expanded. GATT became the **World Trade Organization (WTO)**, which was established in 2005 as the global multilateral trading system and the organization that supports it. Economic integration in Europe led to the EU.

Political Benefits for Global Economic Integration

Recall from Chapters 5 and 6 that, theoretically, economic gains occur when firms from different countries can freely trade and direct. But these insights were not accepted by most governments until the end of World War II. In the late 1920s and early 1930s, virtually all governments tried to protect domestic industries by imposing protectionist policies through tariffs and quotas. Collectively, these beggar-thy-neighbor policies triggered retaliation that further restricted trade. Trade wars eventually turned into World War II.

The postwar urge for global economic integration grew out of the painful lessons of the 1920s and 1930s. While emphasizing economic benefits, global economic integration is *political* in nature. Its fundamental goal is to promote peace (see Exhibit 8.1). Simply put, people who buy and sell from each other are usually reluctant to fight or kill each other. For example, Japan decided to attack Pearl Harbor in 1941 only *after* the United States cut off oil sales to Japan in protest of Japanese aggression in China. Global economic integration also seeks to build confidence. The mercantilist trade policies in the 1930s were triggered by a lack of confidence. So confidence building is key to avoiding the tragedies of the 1930s. Governments, if they are confident that other countries will not raise trade barriers, will not be tempted to do the same.

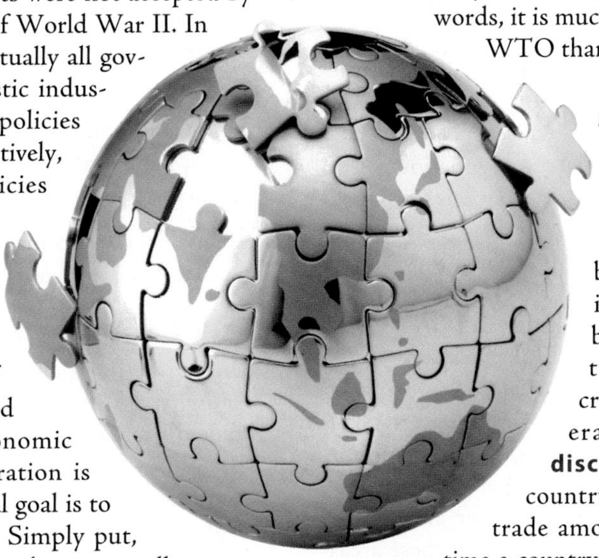

Economic Benefits for Global Economic Integration

There are at least three compelling economic reasons for global economic integration. The first is to handle disputes constructively. The WTO's dispute resolution mechanisms (discussed later in this chapter) are designed to help countries do just this. Although there is an escalation in the number of disputes brought to the WTO, such an increase, according to the WTO, "does not reflect increasing tension in the world. Rather, it reflects the closer economic ties throughout the world, the WTO's expanding membership, and the fact that countries have faith in the system to solve their differences."[1] In other words, it is much better to bring disputes to the WTO than to declare war on each other.

A second benefit is that global economic integration makes life easier for all participants. Officially, the GATT/WTO system is called a **multilateral trading system** because it involves all participating countries (the key word being *multilateral*) and not just two countries (*bilateral*). A crucial principle in the multilateral trading system is **non-discrimination**. Specifically, a country cannot make distinctions in trade among its trading partners. Every time a country lowers a trade barrier, it has to do the same for *all* WTO member countries, except when giving preference to regional partners (an exception we will discuss later). Such non-discrimination makes things easier for all members.

Finally, global economic integration raises incomes, generates jobs, and stimulates economic growth. The WTO estimates that cutting global trade barriers by a third may raise worldwide income by approximately $600 billion. That's equivalent to adding an economy the size of Canada to the world. Benefits are not limited to countries as a whole. Individuals also benefit because more and better jobs are created. In the United States, 12 million people owe their jobs to exports. In China, 18 million people work for foreign-invested firms, which have the highest level of profits and pay among all China-based firms.[2]

Of course, global economic integration has its share of problems. Critics may not be happy with the environmental impact and with the distribution of the benefits from more trade and investment among the haves and have-nots in the world. However, when weighing all of the pros and cons, most governments and people agree that global economic integration generates enormous benefits, ranging from preserving peace to generating jobs.

EXHIBIT 8.1 Benefits of Global Economic Integration

Political benefits
- Promotes peace by promoting trade and investment
- Builds confidence in a multilateral trading system

Economic benefits
- Disputes are handled constructively
- Rules make life easier and discrimination impossible for all participating countries
- Free trade and investment raise incomes and stimulate economic growth

Multilateral trading system
The global system that governs international trade among countries—otherwise known as the GATT/WTO system.

Non-discrimination
A principle that a country cannot make distinctions in trade among its trading partners.

© iStockphoto.com/R.R.

© Cengage Learning 2013

ORGANIZING WORLD TRADE

In this section, we will examine the two principal mechanisms of global economic integration: the GATT and the WTO.

General Agreement on Tariffs and Trade: 1948–1994

The GATT was created in 1948. Unlike the WTO, the GATT was technically an agreement but *not* an organization. Its major contribution was to reduce the level of tariffs by sponsoring rounds of multilateral negotiations. As a result, the average tariff in developed economies dropped from 40% in 1948 to 3% in 2005. Between 1950 and 1995, when the GATT was phased out to become the WTO, world GDP grew about fivefold, but world merchandise exports grew about 100 times (!). During the GATT era, trade growth consistently outpaced GDP growth.

Despite the GATT's phenomenal success in bringing down tariff barriers, by the mid-1980s three concerns had surfaced that made it clear that reforms would be necessary. First, because of the GATT's declared focus on merchandise trade, neither trade in services nor intellectual property (IP) protection was covered. Both of these areas were becoming increasingly important. Second, the many loopholes in merchandise trade needed reforming. The most (in)famous loophole was the Multifiber Arrangement (MFA) designed to *limit* free trade in textiles, a direct violation of the letter and spirit of the GATT. Finally, although the GATT had been successful in reducing tariffs, the global recessions in the 1970s and 1980s led many governments to invoke non-tariff barriers (NTBs) such as subsidies and local content requirements (see Chapter 5). Unlike tariff barriers, which were relatively easy to verify and challenge, NTBs were more subtle but pervasive, thus triggering a growing number of trade disputes. The GATT, however, lacked effective dispute resolution mechanisms. As a result, at the end of the Uruguay Round in 1994, participating countries agreed to upgrade the GATT and launch the WTO.

World Trade Organization: 1995–Present

General Agreement on Trade in Services (GATS)
A WTO agreement governing the international trade of services.

Trade-Related Aspects of Intellectual Property Rights (TRIPS)
A WTO agreement governing intellectual property rights.

Established on January 1, 1995, the WTO is the GATT's successor. This transformation turned the GATT from a provisional treaty serviced by an *ad hoc* secretariat to a full-fledged international organization headquartered in Geneva, Switzerland. Significantly broader in scope than the GATT, the WTO has several new features:

- An agreement governing the international trade of services, the **General Agreement on Trade in Services (GATS)**.

- An agreement governing IP rights, the **Trade-Related Aspects of Intellectual Property Rights (TRIPS)**.

- Trade dispute settlement mechanisms, which allow for the WTO to adjudicate trade disputes among countries in a more effective and less time-consuming way.

- Trade policy reviews, which enable the WTO and other member countries to peer review a country's trade policy.

The next two sections outline the WTO's dispute settlement mechanisms and the Doha Development Agenda.

Trade Dispute Settlement

One of the main objectives for establishing the WTO was to strengthen trade dispute settlement mechanisms. The old GATT mechanisms experienced long delays, blocking by accused countries, and inadequate enforcement. The WTO addresses all three of these problems. First, it sets time limits for a panel, consisting of three neutral countries, to reach a judgment. Second, it removes the power of the accused countries to block any unfavorable decision. WTO decisions will be final. Third, in terms of enforcement, although the WTO has earned the nickname of "the world's supreme court in trade," it does *not* have real enforcement capability. The WTO simply recommends that the losing country change its laws or practices and authorizes the winning country to use tariff retaliation to compel the offending country to comply with the WTO rulings.

Understandably, enforcement by the WTO is controversial because the losing country experiences some loss of sovereignty. Fundamentally, a WTO ruling is a *recommendation* but not an order; no higher-level entity can order a sovereign government to do something against its wishes. In other words, the offending country retains full sovereignty in its decision whether or not to implement a WTO recommendation. Because the WTO has no real power to enforce its rulings, a country that has lost a dispute case can choose one of two options: change its laws or practices to be in compliance, or defy the ruling by doing nothing and suffer trade retaliation by the winning country, known as "punitive duties." Most of the WTO's trade dispute rulings, however, are resolved without resorting to trade retaliation.

© iStockphoto.com/Carmen Martinez Banús

The Doha Round—"The Doha Development Agenda"

In 1999, the WTO intended to start a new round of trade talks in Seattle, but the meeting was sidelined by 30,000 protesters (see Chapter 1). Undeterred by the backlash, WTO member countries went ahead to launch a new round of negotiations in Doha, Qatar, in November 2001. Called the **Doha Round**, it was the only round of trade negotiations sponsored by the WTO.

The Doha Round was significant for two reasons. First, it was launched in the aftermath of the 9/11 attacks. Members had a strong resolve to make global free trade work in order to defeat the terrorist agenda to divide and terrorize the world. Second, this was the first round in the history of GATT/WTO to aim specifically at promoting economic development in developing countries in order to make globalization more inclusive and help the world's poor. Consequently, the official title of the Doha Round was the "Doha Development Agenda." The agenda was ambitious, with four main goals: (1) reduce agricultural subsidies in developed countries to facilitate exports from developing countries; (2) slash tariffs, especially in industries like textiles where developing countries might benefit; (3) free up trade in services; and (4) strengthen IP protection. Note that in the Doha Round, *not* all meetings were held in Doha. Subsequent meetings took place in Cancun, Mexico (2003), Hong Kong (2005), and Geneva (2006 and 2008).

Unfortunately, numerous countries failed to deliver on promises made in Doha. The hot potato turned out to be agriculture. Australia, Argentina, and most developing countries demanded that Japan, the EU, and the United States reduce farm subsidies. Japan rejected any proposal to cut rice tariffs. The EU refused to significantly reduce farm subsidies, which consumed 40% of its budget. The United States actually *increased* farm subsidies. On the other hand, many developing countries, led by India, refused to tighten IP protection, particularly for pharmaceuticals, citing their need for cheap generic drugs to combat diseases such as HIV/AIDS. Overall, developing countries refused to offer concessions in IP and service trade in part because of the failure of Japan, the EU, and the United States to reduce farm subsidies.

Finally, at the Geneva meeting in July 2006, it was evident that member countries could not talk anymore because they were still miles apart from reaching agreement. The Doha Round was thus officially suspended. Labeled "the biggest threat to the postwar [multilateral] trading system" by the *Economist*, the Geneva fiasco of the Doha Round disappointed almost every country involved.[3] Naturally, finger pointing started

immediately. To be fair, no country was totally responsible for Doha's collapse, and all members collectively were culpable. The sheer complexity of reaching an agreement on *everything* among 149 member countries (as of 2006) in the Doha Round was simply mind boggling. (More recently, another round of multilateral negotiations, the Copenhagen Climate Summit, failed to reach any meaningful, binding agreements—see Chapter 14 for details.)

What happens next? Officially, Doha was suspended but not terminated, so it is not dead. After the failed 2006 meeting in Geneva, members held another meeting in Geneva in 2008 but failed again. Efforts again emerged in 2011.[4] But with high levels of unemployment and strong protectionist moods in many parts of the world, chances of getting a Doha deal done are not great. On the other hand, although a global deal may be lost, regional deals are moving "at twice the speed and with half the fuss."[5] The upshot of Doha's failure is a stagnation of multilateralism but an acceleration of regionalism—the topic we turn to next (see Debate).

LO3 *Make the case for regional economic integration.*

INTEGRATING REGIONAL ECONOMIES

There is now a proliferation of regional trade deals. All WTO members but one, Mongolia, are now involved in some regional trade arrangement. This section first introduces the benefits for regional economic integration and follows with a discussion of its major types.

The Pros and Cons of Regional Economic Integration

Similar to global economic integration, the benefits of regional economic integration center on both political and economic dimensions (see Exhibit 8.1). Politically, regional economic integration promotes peace by fostering closer economic ties and building confidence. Only in the last six decades did the Europeans break away from their centuries-old habit of war and violence among themselves. A leading cause of this dramatic behavioral change is economic integration. In addition, regional integration enhances the collective political weight of a region, which has also helped fuel postwar European integration, particularly when dealing with superpowers such as the United States.

Economically, the three benefits associated with regional economic integration are similar to those associated with global economic integration (see Exhibit 8.1).

> **Doha Round**
> *A round of WTO negotiations to reduce agricultural subsidies, slash tariffs, and strengthen intellectual property protection that started in Doha, Qatar, in 2001. Officially known as the "Doha Development Agenda," it was suspended in 2006 due to disagreements.*

Argentina

Australia

Regional Integration: Building Block or Stumbling Block?

BUILDING BLOCK In the absence of global economic integration, regional economic integration is often regarded as the next best thing to facilitate free trade, at least within a region. Some may even argue that regional integration represents building blocks for eventual global integration. For example, the EU now participates in WTO negotiations as one entity, which seems like a building block. Individual EU member countries no longer enter such talks.

STUMBLING BLOCK Another school of thought argues that regional integration has become a stumbling block for global integration. By design, regional integration provides preferential treatment to members and, at the same time, *discriminates* against non-members. Although it is allowed by WTO rules, it is still a form of protectionism centered on us versus them, except "us" is now an expanded group of countries. The proliferation of regional trade deals thus may be alarming.

Of course, all countries party to some regional deals participate in WTO talks, arguing that they are walking on two legs: regional and global. Yet, instead of walking on two legs, critics such as Columbia professor Jagdish Bhagwati argue that "we have wound up on all fours"; in other words, we are crawling with slow progress. This sorry state is triggered by individual countries pursuing their interests in a globally uncoordinated fashion. As regional deals proliferate, non-members feel that they are squeezed out and begin plotting their own regional deals. Very soon, we will end up having a global spaghetti bowl.

Sources: J. Bhagwati, *Free Trade Today* (Princeton: Princeton University Press, 2002) 119; M. W. Peng and K. E. Meyer, "Is Japan being left out," in *International Business* (London: Cengage Learning EMEA, 2011) 281.

First, disputes are handled constructively. Second, consistent rules make life easier and discrimination impossible for participating countries within one region. Third, free trade and investment raise incomes and stimulate economic growth. Regional economic integration may bring additional benefits such as a larger market, simpler standards, reduced distribution costs, and economies of scale for firms based in that region.[6]

However, not everything is rosy in regional integration. A case can be made *against* it. Politically, regional integration is centered on preferential treatments for firms within a region, leading to discrimination against firms outside a region and thus undermining global integration (see Debate). Of course, in practice, global deals such as Doha are so challenging to accomplish that regional deals emerge as realistic alternatives. Economically, regional integration may still result in some loss of sovereignty. For example, the 17 EU members adopting the euro can no longer implement independent monetary policies.

The simultaneous existence of both pros and cons means that some countries are cautious about joining regional economic integration. Norway and Switzerland chose not to join the EU. Even when countries are part of a regional deal, they sometimes choose not to participate in some areas. For example, three EU members—Britain, Denmark, and Sweden—refused to adopt the euro. Overall, different levels of enthusiasm call for different types of regional economic integration, which are outlined next.

Free trade area (FTA)
A group of countries that remove trade barriers among themselves.

Customs union
One step beyond a free trade area, a customs union imposes common external policies on non-participating countries.

Common market
Combining everything a customs union has, a common market additionally permits the free movement of goods and people.

Types of Regional Economic Integration

Exhibit 8.2 shows five main types of regional economic integration. A **free trade area (FTA)** is a group of countries that remove trade barriers among themselves. Each still maintains different external policies regarding non-members, and there is no free movement of people among member countries. An example is NAFTA. A **customs union** is one step beyond an FTA. In addition to all the arrangements of an FTA, a customs union imposes common external policies on non-participants in order to combat trade diversion. Two examples are Andean Community and Mercosur in South America.

A **common market** has everything a customs union has but also permits the free movement of goods and people. Today's EU used to be a common market. An

Switzerland

Norway

© Cengage Learning 2013

EXHIBIT 8.2   Types of Regional Economic Integration

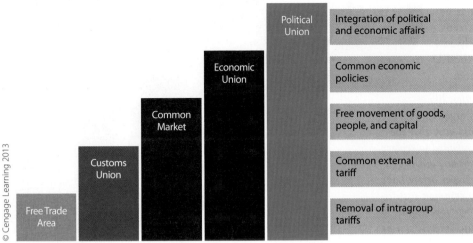

© Cengage Learning 2013

economic union has all the features of a common market, but members also coordinate and harmonize economic policies (monetary, fiscal, and taxation) in order to blend their economies into a single economic entity. Today's EU is an economic union. One possible dimension of an economic union is to establish a **monetary union**, which has been accomplished by 17 EU members through the adoption of the euro (see the next section).

A **political union** is the integration of political and economic affairs of a region. The United States and the former Soviet Union are two examples. The EU at present is not a political union. Overall, each of these five major types is an intensification of the level of regional economic integration from the one before. Next, we look at concrete examples of these arrangements.

> *List the accomplishments, benefits, and costs of the European Union.*

REGIONAL ECONOMIC INTEGRATION IN EUROPE

At present, the most ambitious economic integration has taken place in Europe. The current system of economic integration in Europe is called the **European Union (EU)**. This section outlines its origin and evolution, introduces its current structure, and discusses challenges ahead for the EU.

Origin and Evolution

Although European economic integration is often noted for its economic benefits, its origin was political in nature. More specifically, it was an effort by European statesmen to stop the vicious cycle of hatred and violence. In 1951, Belgium, France, (West) Germany, Italy, Luxembourg, and the Netherlands signed the European Coal and Steel Community (ECSC) Treaty, which was the first step toward what is now the EU. The six founding members were

highly motivated. France and Germany each lost millions of soldiers and civilians in World Wars I and II, not to mention losses in previous major European wars. Reflecting the public mood, statesmen in both countries realized that such killing needed to stop. Italy had the misfortune of being dragged into both world wars (although on a different side in each war) and was devastated whenever France and Germany went to war no matter where it pledged its allegiance. Belgium, the Netherlands, and Luxembourg (Benelux) are small countries geographically sandwiched between France and Germany and were usually wiped out when their two larger neighbors went to war. Naturally, Italy and Benelux would be happy to do anything to stop France and Germany from fighting again. Also, the coal and steel industries traditionally have supplied the raw materials for war. Integrating these two industries among the six members might help prevent future hostilities from breaking out.

In 1957, six member countries of the ECSC signed the Treaty of Rome, which launched the European Economic Community (EEC), later known as the European Community (EC). Starting as an FTA, the EEC/EC progressed to become a customs union and eventually a common market. Over time, more countries joined. In 1991, 12 member countries signed the Treaty on European Union in Maastricht, the Netherlands—in short, the "Maastricht Treaty"—to complete the single market and establish an economic union. The title "European Union" was officially adopted in 1993 when the Maastricht Treaty went into effect. Most recently, the Lisbon Treaty, signed in 2007 and enacted in 2009, amended the Maastricht Treaty that served as a constitutional basis for the EU. Two major changes introduced by the Lisbon Treaty were the appointment of a long-term President of the European Council and a High Representative of the Union for Foreign Affairs and Security Policy.

Economic union
Having all the features of a common market, members also coordinate and harmonize economic policies (in areas such as monetary, fiscal, and taxation) to blend their economies into a single economic entity.

Monetary union
A group of countries that use a common currency.

Political union
The integration of political and economic affairs of a region.

European Union (EU)
The official title of European economic integration since 1993.

The EU Today

Headquartered in Brussels, Belgium, today's EU (see PengAtlas Map 9) has 27 member countries, 500 million citizens, and $15 trillion GDP—approximately 22% of the world's GDP.[7] Here is how the EU describes itself in an official publication:

The European Union is not a federation like the United States. Nor is it simply an organization for cooperation between governments, like the United Nations. Neither is it a state intended to replace existing states, but it is much more than any other organization. The EU is, in fact, unique. Never before have countries voluntarily agreed to set up common institutions to which they delegate some of their sovereignty so that decisions on specific matters of joint interest can be made democratically at a higher, in this case European, level. This pooling of sovereignty is called "European integration."[8]

The EU today is an economic union. Internal trade barriers have been mostly removed. In aviation, the EU now has a single market, which means all European carriers compete on equal terms across the EU, including routes within other European countries. US airlines are not allowed to fly between pairs of cities within Germany, but non-German, EU airlines (such as Ireland's Ryanair) can fly between any pair of German cities. On the ground, it used to take French truck drivers 24 hours to cross the border into Spain due to paperwork requirements and checks. Since 1992, passport and customs control within most (but not all) member countries of the EU has been disbanded, and checkpoints at border crossings are no longer manned (see the Opening Case). The area covered by EU countries became known as the **Schengen** passport-free travel zone, named after Schengen, Luxembourg, where the agreement was signed in 1985. Now, French trucks can move from France to Spain nonstop, similar to how American trucks go from Texas to Oklahoma. At present, 22 of the 27 EU member countries are in the Schengen zone. Five other members are not yet in: Britain and Ireland chose to opt out, and three new members—Bulgaria, Cyprus, and Romania—have yet to meet requirements. (Interestingly, three non-EU member countries, Iceland, Norway, and Switzerland, are also in the Schengen area.)

As an economic union, the EU's proudest accomplishment is the introduction of a common currency, the **euro**, initially in 12 EU countries—known as the **euro zone**—between 1999 and 2002. Because five more countries have joined the euro zone since 2002, 17 countries now use the euro

European Parliament Assembly Room

as their currency. The euro zone accounts for approximately 20% of world GDP (compared with 25% for the United States).

Shown in Exhibit 8.3, adopting the euro has three great benefits. First, it reduces currency conversion costs. Travelers and businesses no longer need to pay numerous processing fees to convert various national currencies for tourist activities or hedging purposes. (Remember the five wallets stuffed with different currencies that Marcus has to carry in the Opening Case?) Second, direct and transparent price comparison is now possible, thus channeling more resources toward more competitive firms. Third, adopting the euro imposes strong macroeconomic disciplines on participating governments. Prior to adopting the euro, different governments determined exchange rates independently. Italy, for example, sharply devalued its lira in 1992 and 1995. While Italian exports became cheaper and more competitive overseas, other EU members, especially France, were furious. Also, when confronting recessions, governments often printed more currency and increased government spending. Such actions cause inflation that can spill over to neighboring countries. By adopting the euro, euro zone countries agree to abolish monetary policy—which involves activities such as manipulating exchange rates and printing more currency—as a tool to solve macroeconomic problems. Overall, the euro has boosted intra-EU trade by approximately 10%. Commanding 25% of global foreign currency reserves, the euro has quickly established itself as the only plausible rival to the dollar.

But there are also significant costs involved in the euro. The first, noted above, is that countries lose the ability to implement independent monetary policy. Especially since 2008, economic life for many EU countries without the option of devaluation is tough (see the Closing Case). The possibility for leaving the euro zone has surfaced in public discussion in some countries.[9] The second cost is the lack of flexibility in implementing fiscal policy in areas such as deficit spending. When a country runs into fiscal difficulties, it may be faced with inflation, high interest rates, and

---

Schengen
A passport-free travel zone within the EU.

Euro
The currency currently used in 17 EU countries.

Euro zone
The 17 EU countries that currently use the euro as the official currency.

© iStockphoto.com/Ababsolutum / © iStockphoto.com/Greg Nicholas

EXHIBIT 8.3 Benefits and Costs of Adopting the Euro

Benefits	Costs
• Reduces currency conversion costs • Facilitates direct price comparison • Imposes monetary disciplines on governments	• Unable to implement independent monetary policy • Limits the flexibility in fiscal policy (in areas such as deficit spending)

a run on its currency. When a number of countries share a common currency, the risks are spread. But some countries can become "free riders." They may not need to fix their own fiscal problems because other, more responsible members will have to shoulder the burden (see the Closing Case).

The EU's Challenges

Politically, the EU and its predecessors—the ECSC, the EEC, and the EC—have delivered more than half a century of peace and prosperity and turned some Cold War enemies into members. Although some people complain about the EU's expenses and bureaucratic meetings, it can be argued that one day spent talking in meetings is one day that member countries are not shooting at one another. Considering that most European countries, until the mid-20th century, were involved in wars as their primary conflict-resolution mechanism, negotiating to resolve differences via EU platforms is not only cheaper but also better in the long run. Economically, the EU has launched a single currency and built a single market in which people, goods, services, and capital—known as the "four freedoms of movement"—can move freely within the core Schengen area (although not throughout the entire EU).

famous term enshrined in the 1957 Treaty of Rome, "ever closer union." Another school of thought, led by the United Kingdom, views the EU as primarily an economic union, which should focus on free trade, pure and simple. The 2010 bailouts to rescue Greece and Ireland have intensified this debate. While Germany reluctantly agreed to lead the efforts to bail out these two financially troubled countries, Germany demanded that the EU-wide "economic governance" be strengthened, and that insolvent countries have to lose some of their economic sovereignty by having their budgets approved (or vetoed) by the EU. While this is viewed as a step toward closer political union, Germany does not share France's political motivation for an "ever closer union," and in fact some German media has called for Germany to withdraw from the euro zone in order to avoid the burden of paying for other countries' problems. However, abandoning the euro is not really realistic for Germany. Thus, Germany's call for tightening the "leash" is motivated by its interest in protecting its own investment in the bailout funds and by its determination to punish the

Germany

There is significant debate about whether the EU should be an economic and political union or just an economic union.

While the accomplishments are enviable in the eyes of other regional organizations, the EU seems to be going through a midlife crisis. Significant challenges lie ahead, especially in terms of internal divisions and enlargement concerns.

Internally, there is a significant debate about whether the EU should be an economic and political union or just an economic union. One school of thought, led by France, argues that an economic union should inevitably evolve toward a political union through which Europe would speak as one voice. Proponents of this view frequently invoke the

insolvent countries so that future governments will have to think twice before running their economies to the ground (see the Closing Case).

There are also significant concerns associated with enlargement. The EU's largest expansion took place in 2004 with the addition of ten new members. Eight of the new members—Estonia, Latvia, Lithuania, Poland, the Czech Republic, Slovakia, Hungary, and Slovenia—were former eastern bloc Central and Eastern Europe (CEE) countries. Three of these—Estonia, Latvia, and Lithuania—were Baltic states that had previously been part of the Soviet Union.

While taking on ten new members was a political triumph, it was also an economic burden. The ten new members constituted 20% of the overall population but contributed only 9% to GDP and had an average GDP per capita that was 46% of the average for the EU.[10] In 2007, Bulgaria and Romania joined the EU and brought down the average further. With low economic growth and high unemployment throughout the EU and severe economic crisis in the so-called PIGS (Portugal, Ireland, Greece, and Spain) countries, many EU citizens are sick and tired of taking on additional burdens to absorb new members.

Another major debate regarding enlargement is Turkey, whose average income is even lower. In addition, its large Muslim population is also a concern for a predominantly Christian EU. If Turkey were to join, its population of 73 million would make it the second most populous EU country behind only Germany, whose population is 83 million. The weight of EU countries in voting is based (mostly) on population. Given the current demographic trends such as high birthrates in Turkey and low birthrates in Germany and other EU countries, if Turkey were to join the EU, it would become the most populous and thus the most powerful member by 2020, commanding the most significant voting power. Turkey's combination of low incomes, high birthrates relative to current EU members, and Muslim majority visibly concern current member countries, especially given the history of Christian-Muslim tension in Europe.

Overall, we can view the EU enlargement as a miniature version of globalization and the "enlargement fatigue" as part of the recent backlash against globalization. Given the accomplishments and challenges, how does the future of the EU look? Since the 2010 crisis in Greece and Ireland, the media is full of speculative calls for splitting the euro zone into a northern group led by Germany and a southern group led by France, or for certain countries (such as PIGS or Germany) to individually abandon the euro. Assuming none of the above actually happens and both the EU and the euro survive, one possible scenario is that there will be an "EU à la carte," where different members pick and choose certain mechanisms to join and other mechanisms to opt out of. Seeking consensus among 27 members during negotiations may be impractical. If every country's representative spent ten minutes on opening remarks, four to five *hours* would be gone before discussions even began. The translation and interpretation among the 23 official languages now cost the EU €1.1 billion ($1.4 billion) a year.[11] Since not every country needs to take part in everything, *ad hoc* groupings of member countries with similar interests are increasingly common and discussions are more efficient. To some extent, "EU à la carte" has already taken place, as evidenced by three countries' refusal to adopt the euro a decade ago and Britain's recent refusal to participate in the euro zone defense fund in 2010 (see the Closing Case).

Identify the five organizations that promote regional trade in the Americas and describe their benefits and costs.

REGIONAL ECONOMIC INTEGRATION IN THE AMERICAS

North America: North American Free Trade Agreement (NAFTA)

The **North American Free Trade Agreement (NAFTA)** is a free trade agreement among Canada, Mexico, and the United States. Because of the very different levels of economic development among the countries involved, when NAFTA was launched in 1994 it was labeled "one of the most radical free trade experiments in history."[12] Politically, the Mexican government was interested in cementing market liberalization reforms by demonstrating its commitment to free trade. Economically, Mexico was interested in securing preferential treatment for 80% of its exports that went to the United States and Canada. Consequently, Mexico signed the NAFTA treaty quite readily. Many Americans, on the other hand, thought it was not the best time to open the borders, as the US unemployment rate was 7% at the time and they feared that American jobs would be further jeopardized by free trade. Texas billionaire H. Ross Perot, a presidential candidate in 1992, described NAFTA's potential destruction of thousands of US jobs as a "giant sucking sound."[13]

As NAFTA went into effect in 1994, tariffs on half of exports and imports among members were removed immediately. In NAFTA's first decade, trade between Canada and the United States grew twice as fast as it did before NAFTA. Expanding even faster, US exports to Mexico grew threefold, from $52 billion to $161 billion. US FDI in Mexico averaged $12 billion a year, three times what India took in. Mexico's US-bound exports grew threefold, and its GDP rose to become the ninth in the world, up from 15th in 1992. In ten years, Mexico's GDP per capita rose 24% to over $4,000 (by 2004), several times that of China.[14]

What about jobs? *Maquiladora* (export assembly) factories blossomed under NAFTA, with jobs peaking at 1.3 million in 2000. Yet, no "giant sucking sound" was heard. Approximately 300,000 US jobs were lost due to NAFTA, but about 100,000 jobs were added. The net loss was small, since the US economy generated 20 million new jobs during the first decade of NAFTA. NAFTA's impact on job

© Cengage Learning 2013

North American Free Trade Agreement (NAFTA)
A free trade agreement among Canada, Mexico, and the United States.

A NAFTA Provision That Took 18 Years to Implement

In 1993 when NAFTA was signed, the United States and Mexico agreed to let their trucks freely cross each other's border. The system until then involved cargo being unloaded on one side of the border and reloaded on to different trucks on the other side—a costly and time-consuming process. However, in the mid-1990s, the Clinton administration went along with the demands made by unions and environmentalists to keep Mexican trucks out, allegedly for safety and environmental reasons. But experts suspected this was really due to protectionist reasons, since US drivers feared losing their jobs. In contrast, the more unionized Canadian truck drivers were allowed to enter.

In 2007, the Bush administration started to run a pilot program to let up to 100 Mexican trucking companies come through. Then, in 2009, the program was cancelled after the Obama administration came into office. In retaliation, Mexico announced additional tariffs on 89 US exports of various sorts, such as 20% on Christmas trees and 45% on grapes. Overall, these tariffs on Mexico-bound exports from the United States hit $2 billion. After intense negotiations, the Obama administration in 2011 decided that the United States should honor its international obligations and not give in to protectionist impulses. Therefore,

one of the last remaining bones of contention in NAFTA, trucking, could finally be resolved satisfactorily.

Sources: "Signs of life," *Economist*, 26 June 2010, 36; "US honors key NAFTA provision finally," *Sign on San Diego*, 16 March 2011, available online at http://www.signonsandiego.com.

---

destruction versus creation in the United States was essentially a wash. But a hard count on jobs misses another pervasive but subtle benefit. NAFTA has allowed US firms to *preserve* more US jobs, because 82% of the components used in Mexican assembly plants are made in the United States, whereas factories in Asia use far fewer US parts. Without NAFTA, entire industries might be lost rather than just the labor-intensive portions.

As NAFTA celebrated its 15th anniversary in 2009, not all is rosy (see In Focus for a recent dispute). Opponents of globalization in both Canada and the United States no longer focus on the negative impact of competition from Mexico but rather on China and India. Despite the impressive gains in their country, many Mexicans feel betrayed by NAFTA. Thanks to Chinese competition, Mexican real wages in manufacturing have stagnated. Many US, Canadian, European, and Japanese multinationals are shifting some of their factory work to China, which has now replaced Mexico as the second largest exporter to the United States (after Canada).[15] About 1,000 *maquiladora* factories have closed down since 2000. NAFTA might have been oversold by its sponsors as a cure-all for Mexico to become the next South Korea, but it can be argued that the Mexican government has not capi-

talized on the tremendous opportunities it has been offered. There is only so much free trade can do; other reforms in infrastructure and education need to keep up.

South America: Andean Community, Mercosur, FTAA, USAN/UNASUR, and CAFTA

Whatever NAFTA's imperfections, it is much more effective than the two customs unions in South America: **Andean Community** and **Mercosur**. Members of the Andean Community (launched in 1969) and Mercosur (launched in 1991) are mostly countries on the *western* and *eastern* sides of the Andean mountains, respectively (see PengAtlas Map 10). There is much mutual suspicion and rivalry between both organizations as well as within each of them. Mercosur is relatively more protectionist and suspicious of the United States, whereas the Andean Community is more pro-free trade. When Colombia and Peru, both Andean Community members,

Andean Community
A customs union in South America that was launched in 1969.

Mercosur
A customs union in South America that was launched in 1991.

signed trade deals with the United States, Venezuela, led by the anti-American president Hugo Chavez, pulled out of the Andean Community in protest and joined Mercosur in 2006.

Neither regional initiative has been effective, in part because only a small part of members' trade is within the union—only about 5% is within the Andean Community and 20% within Mercosur. Their largest trading partner, the United States, lies outside the region. A free trade deal with the United States, not among themselves, would generate the most significant benefits. Emboldened by NAFTA, all Latin American countries except Cuba launched negotiations with Canada and the United States in 1998 for a possible **Free Trade Area of the Americas (FTAA)**. However, by 2005, Argentina, Brazil, Paraguay, Uruguay, and Venezuela had changed their minds and announced that they opposed FTAA, which seems unlikely to be set up.

Instead of pursuing FTAA, Andean Community and Mercosur countries in 2008 agreed to form the **Union of South American Nations** (USAN, more commonly known by its Spanish acronym, **UNASUR**, which refers to *Unión de Naciones Suramericanas*). Inspired by the EU, USAN/UNASUR announced its intention to eventually adopt a common currency, parliament, and passport. A functioning union similar to that of the EU may be possible in 2019.

In the absence of FTAA, one concrete recent accomplishment is the **United States–Dominican Republic–Central America Free Trade Agreement (CAFTA)**, which took effect in 2005. Although small, the five Central American countries—Guatemala, Honduras, El Salvador, Nicaragua, and Costa Rica—plus the Dominican Republic collectively represent the second largest US export market in Latin America. Globally, CAFTA is the tenth largest US export market, importing more US goods and services than Russia, India, and Indonesia *combined*.

REGIONAL ECONOMIC INTEGRATION IN THE ASIA PACIFIC

This section introduces regional integration efforts between Australia and New Zealand, in Southeast Asia, and throughout Asia and the Pacific. They differ from one another in scale and scope.

Australia–New Zealand Closer Economic Relations Trade Agreement (ANZCERTA or CER)

The Australia–New Zealand Closer Economic Relations Trade Agreement (ANZCERTA or CER), launched in 1983, turned the historic rivalry between Australia and New Zealand into a partnership. As an FTA, the CER over time removed tariffs and NTBs. For example, both countries agreed not to charge exporters from the other country for dumping. Citizens from both countries also could freely work and reside in the other country. Mostly due to the relatively high level of geographic proximity and cultural homogeneity, CER has been regarded as a very successful FTA.

Association of Southeast Asian Nations (ASEAN)

Although founded in 1967, the **Association of Southeast Asian Nations (ASEAN)** had not been economically active until 1992. Encouraged by the EU, ASEAN set up the ASEAN Free Trade Area (AFTA) in 1992. Despite some impressive gains, ASEAN suffers from a similar problem faced by Latin American countries: ASEAN's main trading partners—the United States, the EU, Japan, and China—are outside the region. Intra-ASEAN trade usually accounts for less than a quarter of total trade. The benefits of AFTA may thus be limited. In response, ASEAN and China signed an ASEAN–China Free Trade Agreement (ACFTA) in 2002 to be launched by the early 2010s. Given the increasingly strong competition in terms of Chinese exports and China-bound FDI that could have come to ASEAN, ACFTA may potentially turn the rivalry into a partnership. ACFTA is estimated to boost ASEAN's exports to China by 48% and China's exports to ASEAN by 55%, thus raising

Free Trade Area of the Americas (FTAA)
A proposed free trade area for the entire Western Hemisphere.

Union of South American Nations (USAN/UNASUR)
A regional integration mechanism integrating two existing customs unions (Andean Community and Mercosur) in South America.

United States–Dominican Republic–Central America Free Trade Agreement (CAFTA)
A free trade agreement between the United States and five Central American countries and the Dominican Republic.

Association of Southeast Asian Nations (ASEAN)
The organization underpinning regional economic integration in Southeast Asia.

© iStockphoto.com/Nikada

ASEAN's GDP by 0.9% and China's by 0.3%. Similar FTAs are being negotiated with Japan and South Korea.

Asia-Pacific Economic Cooperation (APEC)

While ASEAN was deepening its integration, Australia was afraid that it might be left out and suggested in 1989 that ASEAN and CER countries form the **Asia-Pacific Economic Corporation (APEC)**. Given the lack of a global heavyweight in both ASEAN and CER, Japan was invited and agreed to join. However, ASEAN and CER countries also feared that Japan might dominate the group and create a de facto "yen bloc." Many people remembered how a desire for economic leadership before and during World War II had led Japan to invade many countries in the region, and bitter memories of Japanese wartime atrocities in the region seemed to die hard. At that time, China was far less significant economically than it is now and thus could hardly be expected to counterbalance Japan. Then the United States requested to join APEC, citing its long West Coast to qualify it as a Pacific country. Economically, the United States did not want to be left out of the most dynamically growing region in the world. Politically, the United States was interested in containing Japanese influence in any Asian regional deals. While the United States could certainly serve as a counterweight for Japan, US membership would also change the character of APEC, which had been centered on ASEAN and CER. To make its APEC membership less odd, the United States brought on board two of its NAFTA partners—Canada and Mexico. Canada and Mexico were equally interested in the economic benefits but probably cared less about the US political motives. Once the floodgates for membership were open, Chile, Peru, and Russia all eventually got in, each citing their long Pacific coast lines (!).

Today, APEC's 21 member economies (shown in PengAtlas Map 11) span four continents, are home to 2.6 billion people, and contribute 46% of world trade ($7 trillion), making it the largest regional integration grouping by geographic area. However nice it is to include everyone, APEC may be too big. The goal of free trade by industrialized members no later than 2010 and by developing members no later than 2020 is *not* binding. Essentially as a talking shop, APEC provides a forum for members to make commitments that are largely rhetorical.

> *Articulate how regional trade should influence your thinking about global business.*

MANAGEMENT SAVVY

Of the two major perspectives on global business (institution-based and resource-based views), this chapter has focused

EXHIBIT 8.4 Implications for Action

- Think regional, downplay global.
- Understand the rules of the game and their transitions at both global and regional levels.

on the institution-based view. In order to address the question "What determines success and failure around the globe?" the entire chapter has been devoted to an introduction of the rules of the game as institutions governing global and regional economic integration. How does this knowledge help managers? Managers need to combine the insights from the institution-based view with those from the resource-based view to come up with strategies and solutions on how their firms can capitalize on the opportunities presented by global and regional economic integration. Listed in Exhibit 8.4, two broad implications for action emerge.

First, given the slowdown of multilateralism and the acceleration of regionalism, managers are advised to focus their attention more at regional rather than global levels.[16] To a large extent, they are already doing that. The largest multinational enterprises may have a presence all over the world, but their center of gravity (measured by revenues) is often still their home region (such as within the EU or NAFTA). Thus, they are not really global. Regional strategies make sense because most countries within a region share some cultural, economic, and geographic similarities that can lower the liability of foreignness when moving within the region, as opposed to moving from one region to another. From a resource-based standpoint, most firms are better prepared to compete at a regional rather than a global level.[17] Despite the hoopla associated with global strategies, managers, in short, need to think local and downplay—while not necessarily abandoning—global.

Second, managers also need to understand the rules of the game and their transitions at both global and regional levels. While trade negotiations involve a lot of politics that many managers could hardly care less about, managers who ignore these rules and their transitions do so at their own peril. When the MFA was phased out in 2005, numerous managers at textile firms, who had become comfortable under the MFA's protection, decried the new level of competition and complained about their lack of preparation. In fact, they had 30 *years* to prepare for such an eventuality. When the MFA was signed in 1974, it was agreed that it would be phased out by 2005. The typical attitude of "we don't care about (trade) politics" can lead to a failure in due diligence. The best managers expect their firm's strategies to shift over time, constantly work to decipher the changes in the big picture, and are willing to take advantage of the new opportunities brought by global and regional trade deals.

Asia-Pacific Economic Cooperation (APEC)
The official title for regional economic integration involving 21 member economies around the Pacific.

THE GREEK TRAGEDY
ETHICAL DILEMMA

In 2010, Greece suffered from an economic collapse, which brought about the biggest bailout in EU history. The €110 billion ($146 billion) bailout was jointly funded by the EU and the IMF and called for the Greek government to unleash sweeping reforms to put the country's financial house in order. Public sector pensions and wages were cut 15% to 20%. Value-added and excise taxes were raised twice in 2010. Such shock therapy generated widespread misery and protests. Yet the Greek government, led by American-born Prime Minister George Papandreou, who came to power in 2009, stood firm. The prime minister argued that Greece must "bite the bullet" to avoid a totally tragic ending, such as sovereign debt default (known as "national bankruptcy" in layman's terms).

What led to this mess? An increase in consumer demand and a government spending binge fueled by the 2002 adoption of the euro and the 2004 Olympics. Excessive borrowing and budget deficits exacerbated by low interest rates. Widespread corruption and tax evasion. The shadow (informal) economy that produced no tax revenue was estimated to be at 20% to 30% of GDP. The upshot? Rising wage levels not justified by productivity growth, which ultimately made Greece lose competitiveness in export markets relative to countries like Germany that had held down their wage levels. Another symptom of Greece's economic crisis was skyrocketing government deficit (15% of GDP) and crushing national debt (€300 billion—115% of GDP or $27,000 per citizen). In early 2010, when the bond market realized that Greece was approaching insolvency, the interest for bonds that the Greek government had to pay (technically known as the "bond yield") rose sharply from a more normal 7% to 18%—within one *month*. Facing the unbearable cost to borrow and the inability to service debt, the Greek government had to ask for help from the EU and the IMF. Within one week of the bailout, Greek bond yields decreased to 12%.

While the tragedy was Greek in origin, its script had been in the minds of officials from Greece and other euro zone countries who signed the Stability and Growth Pact (SGP) in 1997. To reduce the hesitation from Germany and other more disciplined countries that they might have to bail out bankrupt members, the SGP committed all euro zone countries to bringing their budget deficit to no more than 3% of GDP. Otherwise, countries could be fined. Essentially, the SGP meant "no bailouts." However, even before the 2008–2009 crisis, Germany and France failed to curtail their deficit to less than 3%. In other words, they were in open defiance of the SGP, essentially free riding. When the recent recession hit, virtually all EU members adopted fiscal stimulus measures to cope. In 2009, the EU fingered not only Greece, but also France, Ireland, Latvia, Malta, and Spain as violators of the SGP, because they ran a budget deficit of more than 3% in 2008. But, it was hard to imagine how the EU could fine these countries, whose governments were already short on cash and would have to run a deficit in order to prevent economic collapse. Overall, the SGP failed: Greece's deficit was more than four times what the SGP allowed.

"The best way to think of it is to think of Greece as a teenager," noted one expert, who continued:

Many Greeks view the state with a combination of a sense of entitlement, mistrust, and dislike similar to that of teenagers vis-à-vis their parents. They expect to be funded without contributing; they often act irresponsibly without care about consequences and expect to be bailed out by the state—but that only increases their sense of dependency, which only increases their feeling of dislike for the state. And, of course, they refuse to grow up. But, like every teenager, they will.

These comments, meant to describe the relationship between Greek citizens and the state, also provide insight into the relationship between Greece and the EU. But the metaphor can only go so far. At the end of the day, Germany is not Greece's parent. Although both countries belong to the "euro family," German citizens and politicians were naturally furious as to why in the middle of their worst postwar economic crisis, they had to foot the largest bill to bail out the profligate Greeks.

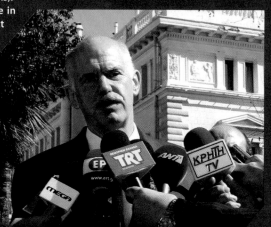

Prime Minister George Papandreou meets the press.

The tragedy was not only Greece's or Germany's, but also the EU's. It severely tested the logic of the EU, whose member countries are not only unequal economically but also differ in their spending and saving habits, and in particular the logic of the euro. Dumping the euro by individual countries was no longer unthinkable and was increasingly discussed in the media. During a crisis, leaving the euro zone would allow Greece to depreciate its own currency, which would enhance its export competiveness. Dumping the euro would also relieve Germany's responsibility to come to the rescue. But here is the catch: A revived Deutsch mark would certainly appreciate and undermine Germany's export competitiveness. In the end, a reluctant Germany—and a reluctant EU—had little alternative. But, the bailout loans would have to be repaid, and thus severe austerity programs, which of course were widely unpopular among the Greeks, became necessary.

In addition to the presumably one-shot deal for Greece, the EU set up a €750 billion ($980 billion) euro zone stabilization fund (including €250 billion from the IMF), which is called "European Stability Mechanism." Germany, which pledged €220 billion, demanded stronger fiscal discipline in the name of better "economic governance" from all members, and threatened sanctions (such as being fined and losing voting rights) if certain member countries failed to meet the necessary criteria. Otherwise, the EU risked becoming a "fiscal transfer union" draining funds from the wealthier and thriftier North to the less wealthy and heavier spending South. Since these proposed new rules could not name any individual countries, they had to apply to all member countries. But then, Germany and France would not agree to being fined or denied a vote. So debates raged, and feelings became more bitter.

At the same time, other PIGS countries (Portugal, Ireland, Greece, and Spain) entered deeper crises one after another. In November 2010, Ireland had to be rescued by €85 billion ($113 billion). In April 2011, Portugal requested to be bailed out. Spain was widely reported to be next. In the meantime, Greece continued to struggle. The *Economist* estimated that even after the bailout, Greek government debt would reach 165% of GDP by 2015. According to the *Economist*, "Greece looks bust." So do other PIGS countries, even after their bailouts. How (bitterly) the tragedy ends remains to be seen.

Greece

Sources: "A more perfect union?" *Bloomberg Businessweek*, 6 December 2010, 11–12; "Germany reaps the euro's reward," *Bloomberg Businessweek*, 19 July 2010, 13–14; "Life amid the ruins," *Bloomberg Businessweek*, 28 June 2010, 52–60; "No easy exit," *Economist*, 4 December 2010, 87–88; "Saving the euro," *Economist*, 20 November 2010, 12; "Bite the bullet," *Economist*, 15 January 2011, 77–78; "Time for Plan B," *Economist*, 15 January 2011, 10.

THE

IN-CROWD

Share your 4LTR Press story on Facebook at
www.facebook.com/4ltrpress for a chance to win.

To learn more about the
In-Crowd opportunity 'like'
us on Facebook.

GROWING & Internationalizing THE Entrepreneurial FIRM

www.voeazul.com.br

OPENING CASE

Azul Takes Off From Brazil

David Neeleman was born in São Paulo to parents who were Mormon missionaries. He spent several years living the life of a well-to-do Brazilian child in the country's Southeast, which typically revolves around beaches, barbecues, and private sports clubs. Many Brazilians lament the contrast between the rich and the poor. But it is less marked now than it was in Neeleman's childhood thanks to a recent spell of growth that has favored the poor in particular. In that, he sees an opportunity. Brazil's middle class is swelling: At the last count there were 97 million people in marketing bracket "C," which means they are rich enough to contemplate getting on an airplane. Neeleman, in turn, has some experience getting people onto planes, having founded JetBlue, an American airline that aims to combine low cost with relatively lavish service.

Neeleman insists that he was "pretty much done with the airline business" last year [2008], when he resigned as chairman of JetBlue, which he had taken from an idea to an IPO and is now valued at $1.6 billion. The previous year [2007] he had ceased to be chief executive after blunders had left passengers stranded during a spell of bad weather.

When he tried to put all this behind him by returning to Brazil, he found airfares that were 70% higher than in America in a country that is considerably poorer, in a market in which the two biggest carriers, TAM and Gol, had a combined share of 85%, and large areas of the country that were scantily served by airlines. All this tempted him back into a business that in the words of Sir Richard Branson, British founder of the Virgin family of carriers, excels at turning billionaires into millionaires.

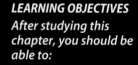

LEARNING OBJECTIVES
After studying this chapter, you should be able to:

LO1 **define entrepreneurship, entrepreneurs, and entrepreneurial firms.**

LO2 **identify the institutions and resources that affect entrepreneurship.**

LO3 **identify three characteristics of a growing entrepreneurial firm.**

LO4 **describe how international strategies for entering foreign markets are different from those for staying in domestic markets.**

LO5 **articulate what you should do to strengthen your**

Making air travel more accessible in a country the size of the continental United States, where infrastructure is weak and many families have been scattered by internal migration, is a noble aim—and potentially a lucrative one. "It sometimes feels like this country is built for 20 million people," says Neeleman, when in fact it has close to 190 million souls. His Brazilian airline Azul (which means blue) was born in December 2008. On some routes, its tickets are cheaper than a bus for the same journey.

In nine months, the company has gone from having no employees to a staff of 1,300. It has 12 planes made by Embraer, a local firm, which pleases the Brazilian government; it will have 14 by the end of 2009. Azul is already the country's third biggest carrier, although it is still a long way behind the big two.

The speed with which Neeleman has taken his new company airborne is perhaps surprising given Brazil's reputation as a bureaucratic place where life is hard for entrepreneurs. In its *Doing Business* survey, the World Bank ranks Brazil 121 places lower than

America on ease of starting a business. According to Neeleman, lots of things that companies need, from capital to telephone lines and computing expertise, are indeed more expensive in Brazil than in America. Labor is not much cheaper when taxes are taken into account. The corporate tax rate is lower than in America but Azul needs an army of accountants to pay it correctly. Customers have less access to credit than American ones do, so Azul has had to perform some of the services of a bank, offering interest-free credit for ten months, and so on.

But the feebler competition and growing market compensate for this. "America has an excess of everything: cars, credit," says Neeleman. "Down here people are getting their first car, first credit card, owning their first home. It feels like the beginning of the cycle."

Source: Excerpted from "Missionary man," *Economist*, 29 August 2009, 58. © Economist Newspaper Group.

How do entrepreneurial firms such as Azul and JetBlue grow? How do they enter international markets? What are the challenges and constraints they face? This chapter deals with these important questions. This is different from many international business (IB) textbooks that typically only cover large firms. To the extent that *every* large firm today started small and that some (although not all) of today's **small and medium-sized enterprises (SMEs)** may become tomorrow's multinational enterprises (MNEs), current and would-be managers will not gain a complete picture of the global business landscape if they only focus on large firms. In addition, since SMEs (in contrast to most large firms, which often have to downsize) generate most jobs now, most students will join SMEs. Some readers of this book will also start up SMEs, thus further necessitating our attention on these numerous "Davids" (such as Azul) instead of on the smaller number of "Goliaths" (such as the big two airlines, TAM and Gol, in Brazil).

This chapter will first define entrepreneurship. Next, we will outline how our two leading perspectives—institution-based and resource-based views—shed light on entrepreneurship. Then, we will introduce the characteristics of a growing entrepreneurial firm and multiple ways to internationalize. In addition, you will encounter a debate about a growing entrepreneurial phenomenon: microfinance. Do's and don'ts follow.

LO1 *Define entrepreneurship, entrepreneurs, and entrepreneurial firms.*

ENTREPRENEURSHIP AND ENTREPRENEURIAL FIRMS

Although entrepreneurship is often associated with smaller and younger firms, no rule bans larger and older firms from being entrepreneurial. So what exactly is entrepreneurship? Recent research suggests that firm size and age are *not* defining characteristics of entrepreneurship. Instead, **entrepreneurship** is defined as "the identification and exploitation of previously unexplored opportunities."[1] Specifically, it is concerned with "the sources of opportunities; the processes of discovery, evaluation, and exploitation of opportunities; and the set of individuals who discover, evaluate, and exploit them."[2] **Entrepreneurs** are founders and owners of new businesses or managers of existing firms, and **international entrepreneurship** is defined as "a combination of innovative, proactive, and risk-seeking behavior that crosses national borders and is intended to create wealth in organizations."[3]

Although SMEs are not the exclusive domain of

Small and medium-sized enterprises (SMEs)
Firms with fewer than 500 employees in the United States and with fewer than 250 employees in the European Union.

Entrepreneurship
The identification and exploitation of previously unexplored opportunities.

Entrepreneurs
Founders and owners of new businesses or managers of existing firms who identify and exploit new opportunities.

International entrepreneurship
A combination of innovative, proactive, and risk-seeking behavior that crosses national borders and is intended to create wealth in organizations.

© iStockphoto.com/Lise Gagne

entrepreneurship, many people often associate entrepreneurship with SMEs because, on average, SMEs tend to be more entrepreneurial than large firms. To minimize confusion, the remainder of this chapter will follow that convention, although it is not totally accurate. That is, while we acknowledge that managers at large firms can be entrepreneurial, we will limit the use of the term "entrepreneur" to owners, founders, and managers of SMEs. Further, we will use the term "entrepreneurial firms" when referring to SMEs. We will refer to firms with more than 500 employees as "large firms."

SMEs are important. Worldwide, they account for over 95% of the number of firms, create approximately 50% of total value added, and generate 60% to 90% of employment, depending on the country. Obviously, entrepreneurship has both rewarding and punishing aspects. Many entrepreneurs will try, and many SMEs will fail (see the Closing Case). Only a small number of entrepreneurs and SMEs will succeed.

LO2 *Identify the institutions and resources that affect entrepreneurship.*

INSTITUTIONS, RESOURCES, AND ENTREPRENEURSHIP

Shown in Exhibit 9.1, both the institution-based view and the resource-based view shed light on entrepreneurship. In this section, we will look at how institutions constrain or facilitate entrepreneurs and how firm-specific (and in many cases entrepreneur-specific) resources and capabilities determine their success and failure.

Institutions and Entrepreneurship

First introduced in Chapters 2 and 3, both formal and informal institutional constraints, as rules of the game, affect entrepreneurship. Although entrepreneurship is thriving around the globe in general, its development is unequal.[4] Whether entrepreneurship is facilitated or retarded significantly depends on formal institutions governing how entrepreneurs start up new firms.[5] A World Bank survey, *Doing Business*, reports some striking differences in government regulations concerning how easy it is to start up new entrepreneurial firms in terms of registration, licensing, and incorporation (Exhibit 9.2 on the next page). Using the relatively straightforward (or even mundane) task of connecting electricity to a newly built commercial building, In Focus illustrates that, in general, governments in developed economies impose fewer procedures (an average of 4.6 procedures for OECD high-income countries) and a lower total cost (free in Japan, and 5.1% of per capita GDP in Germany). On the other hand, entrepreneurs have to put up with harsher hurdles in poor countries. As a class of its own, Burundi imposes a total cost of 430 times its per capita GDP for entrepreneurs to obtain electricity. The number of days to connect electricity is highest in Sierra Leone, where entrepreneurs will wait 441 days.

Overall, it is not surprising that the more entrepreneur friendly these formal institutional requirements are, the more flourishing entrepreneurship is and the more developed the economies become—and vice versa (see PengAtlas Map 12). As a result, more developing economies are now reforming their formal institutions in order to become more entrepreneur friendly. The top ten countries making the most significant entrepreneur-friendly reforms, according to the World Bank's *Doing Business* report, were mostly developing economies—led, for the first time, by a Sub-Saharan African country, Rwanda (see PengAtlas Map 13).

In addition to formal institutions, informal institutions such as cultural values and norms also affect entrepreneurship. For example, because entrepreneurs necessarily take more risk, individualistic and low uncertainty-avoidance societies tend to foster relatively more entrepreneurs, whereas collectivistic and high uncertainty-avoidance societies may result in relatively fewer entrepreneurs. For example, among developed economies, Japan has the lowest rate of start-ups, at one third

EXHIBIT 9.1 Institutions, Resources, and Entrepreneurship

Institution-Based View
Formal institutions
Informal institutions
(both at home and abroad)

Resource-Based View
Value
Rarity
Imitability
Organization

Entrepreneurship
Growth
Innovation
Financing
Internationalization

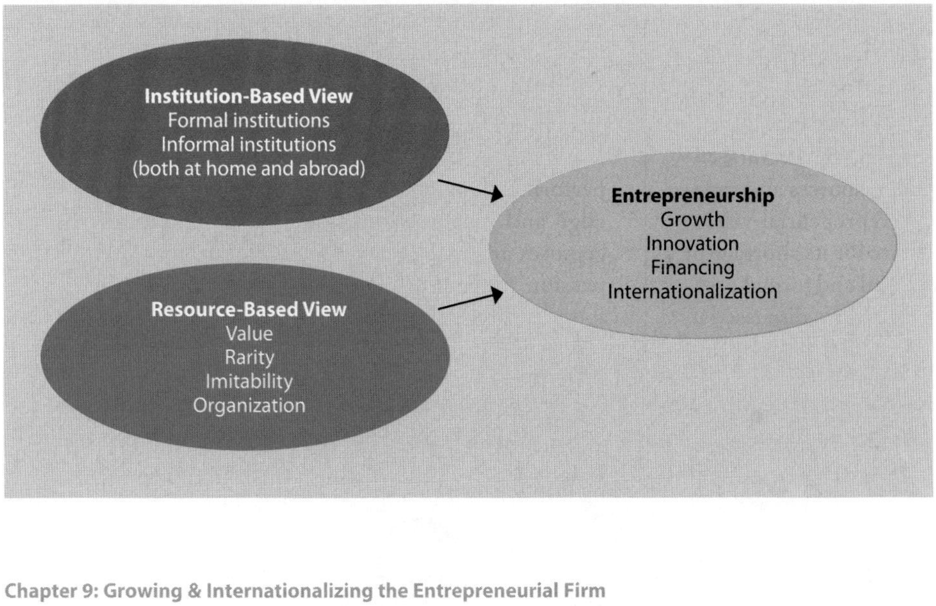

© Cengage Learning 2013

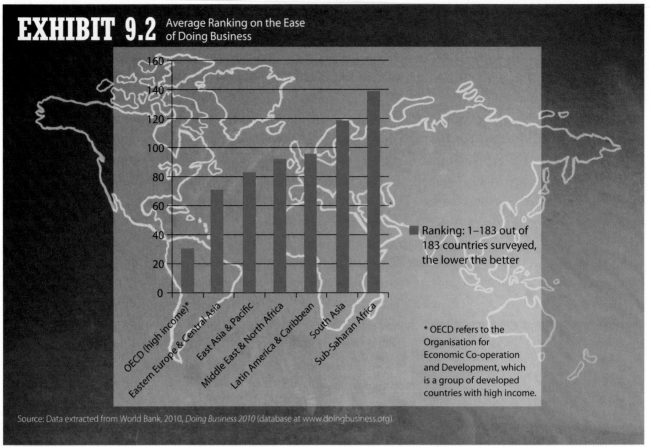

EXHIBIT 9.2 Average Ranking on the Ease of Doing Business

Ranking: 1–183 out of 183 countries surveyed, the lower the better

* OECD refers to the Organisation for Economic Co-operation and Development, which is a group of developed countries with high income.

Source: Data extracted from World Bank, 2010, *Doing Business 2010* (database at www.doingbusiness.org).

---

of America's and half of Europe's.[6] In another example, Russians make heavy use of social networks online, averaging 9.8 hours per month—more than double the world average. While spending that much time online makes sense during the long and cold Russian winter, another important reason is the long-held Russian tradition of relying more on informal information networks for daily life. These informal norms help nurture social network entrepreneurs like Russia's Vkontakte and attract foreign entrants like Facebook.[7] Overall, the institution-based view suggests that both formal and informal institutions matter.[8] Later sections in this chapter will discuss how they matter.

Resources and Entrepreneurship

In addition to being subject to institutional constraints, entrepreneurial firms have a unique set of resources and capabilities.[9] A start-up primarily has entrepreneurial vision, drive, and leadership, which compensate for its shortage of tangible resources such as financial capital and formal organizational structure. The resource-based view, discussed in Chapter 4, sheds considerable light on entrepreneurship, with a focus on its value (V), rarity (R), imitability (I), and organizational (O) aspects (see Exhibit 9.1). Like any

other firm, an entrepreneurial firm must take the VRIO framework into account as it considers how to leverage its resources.

First, entrepreneurial resources must create *value*. For example, by offering cheap fares, convenient schedules, and Wi-Fi and a power port on every seat, Megabus offers superb value to travelers for medium-haul trips that are too far for a leisurely drive but too close to justify the expenses and the increasing hassle to fly. On routes between Chicago and Columbus and between New York and Boston, Megabus is rapidly changing the way Americans—especially the young—travel, so much so that it may help kill plans for the new high-speed rail that after all may not offer that much value (see Chapter 10 Closing Case).[10]

Second, resources must be *rare*. As the cliché goes, "If everybody has it, you can't make money from it." The best-performing entrepreneurs tend to have the rarest knowledge and insights about business opportunities. Math geniuses are few and far between, but the ability to turn a passion for math into profit is truly rare. Google's two founders are such rare geniuses.

Third, resources must be *inimitable*. For example, Amazon's success has prompted a number of online bookstores to directly imitate it. Amazon rapidly built the world's largest book warehouses, which are brick-and-mortar. Ironically for an online

IN FOCUS

Getting Electricity

How long does it take to get electricity, and how much does that cost? The World Bank surveyed the electricity distribution utilities in the largest business city of each of the 140 economies. To ensure that the data are comparable across economies, the respondents were presented with a standard case study:

An entrepreneur would like to connect his newly built warehouse for cold meat storage to electricity. The internal wiring up to the metering point has already been completed by the electrician employed by the construction firm, and the entrepreneur would now like to obtain the final electricity connection from the local distribution utility. The electrician working for the entrepreneur estimates that the warehouse will need a 140 kilo Volt Ampere (kVA) connection.

Selected economies	Direct cost (% of per capita GDP)	Time (days)	Procedures (number)
Japan	0*	105	3*
Hong Kong, China	1.8	101	4
Germany	5.1	17*	3*
Australia	15.4	46	5
United States	16.8	48	5
Singapore	34.2	76	5
United Kingdom	42.2	111	5
Brazil	163.2	36	6
Canada	164.4	133	8**
India	504.9	67	6
China	835.7	118	4
Sierra Leone	1,279.1	441**	8**
Russia	4,521.6	272	8**
Burundi	43,020.5**	158	4
Regional averages			
OECD (high income)	58.3	87.6	4.6
Latin America & Caribbean	526.3	65.4	5.3
Eastern Europe & Central Asia	804.0	156.4	5.8
East Asia & Pacific	1,108.9	91.1	4.8
Middle East & North Africa	1,355.0	78.9	4.8
South Asia	1,695.8	172.5	5.5
Sub-Saharan Africa	6,409.0	162.4	5.2

Source: Data extracted from World Bank, *Doing Business 2010* (database available online at http://www.doingbusiness.org).
* Lowest in the world. ** Highest in the world

company, it is Amazon's best-in-the-breed physical inventories—not its online presence—that are more challenging to imitate.

Fourth, entrepreneurial resources must be *organizationally* embedded. For example, as long as there have been wars, there have been mercenaries ready to fight on behalf of the highest bidder. But only in modern times have private military companies (PMCs) become a global industry.[11] Entrepreneurial PMCs thrive on their organizational capabilities to provide military and security services in dangerous environments, particularly in places like Iraq and Afghanistan where individuals shy away and even national militaries withdraw.

> Identify three characteristics of a growing entrepreneurial firm.

GROWING THE ENTREPRENEURIAL FIRM

This section discusses three major characteristics associated with a growing entrepreneurial firm: (1) growth, (2) innovation, and (3) financing. A fourth characteristic, internationalization, will be highlighted in the next section.

Growth

For many entrepreneurs, like David Neeleman in the Opening Case, the excitement associated with growing a new company is the very thing that attracts them in the first place. Recall from the resource-based view that a firm can be conceptualized as a bundle of resources and capabilities. The growth of an entrepreneurial firm can thus be viewed as an attempt to more fully use currently

EXHIBIT 9.3 Venture Capital Investment as a Percentage of GDP

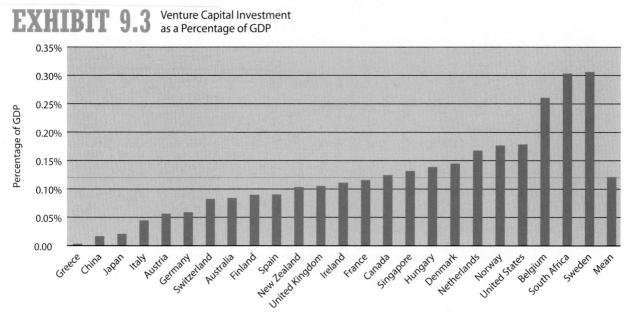

Source: M. Minniti, W. Bygrave, and E. Autio, *Global Entrepreneurship Monitor 2006 Executive Report* (Wellesley, MA: Babson College/GEM, 2006) 49.

under-utilized resources and capabilities. An entrepreneurial firm can leverage its vision, drive, and leadership in order to grow, even though it may be shorter on resources such as financial capital than a larger firm would be.

Innovation

Innovation is at the heart of entrepreneurship. Evidence shows a positive relationship between a high degree of innovation and superior profitability. Innovation allows for a more sustainable basis for competitive advantage. Google's ability to continuously unleash innovations ranging from ever more powerful search engines to free Gmail accounts and Google Scholar references provides a good case in point.

Entrepreneurial firms are uniquely ready for innovation. Owners, managers, and employees at entrepreneurial firms tend to be more innovative and risk-taking than those at large firms. In fact, many SMEs are founded by former employees of large firms who were frustrated by their inability to translate innovative ideas into realities at the large firms. Intel, for example, was founded by three former employees of Fairchild Semiconductor who quit in 1968. Innovators at large firms also have limited ability to personally profit from their innovations because property rights usually belong to the corporation. In contrast, innovators at entrepreneurial firms are better able to reap the financial gains associated with innovation, thus fueling their motivation to charge ahead.

Financing

All start-ups need to raise capital. What are the sources of capital? Three of the "4F" sources of entrepreneurial financing are founders, family, and friends. What is the other "F" source? The answer is . . . *fools* (!). While this is a joke, it strikes a chord in the entrepreneurial world. Given the well-known failure risks of start-ups (a *majority* of them will fail—see the Closing Case), why would anybody other than a fool be willing to invest in a start-up? In reality, most outside strategic investors, who can be wealthy individual investors (often called angels), venture capitalists, banks, foreign entrants, or government agencies, are not fools. They often demand some assurance (such as collateral), examine business plans, and require a strong management team.

Around the world, the extent to which entrepreneurs draw on resources from outside investors (such as venture capitalists) rather than family and friends varies. Exhibit 9.3 shows that Sweden, South Africa, Belgium, and the United States lead the world in venture capital (VC) investment as a percentage of GDP. In contrast, Greece and China have the lowest level of VC investment. Exhibit 9.4 illustrates a different picture: informal investment (mostly by family and friends) as a percentage of GDP. In this case, China leads the world with the highest level of informal investment as a percentage of GDP. In comparison, Brazil and Hungary have the lowest level of informal investment. While there is a lot of noise in such worldwide data, the case of China (second lowest in VC investment and highest in informal investment) is easy to explain: China's lack of formal market-supporting institutions, such as venture capitalists and credit-reporting agencies, requires a high level of informal investment for Chinese entrepreneurs and new ventures, particularly during a time of entrepreneurial boom.[12]

A highly innovative solution, called microfinance, has emerged in response to the lack of financing for entrepreneurial opportunities in many developing countries.

EXHIBIT 9.4   Informal Investment as a Percentage of GDP

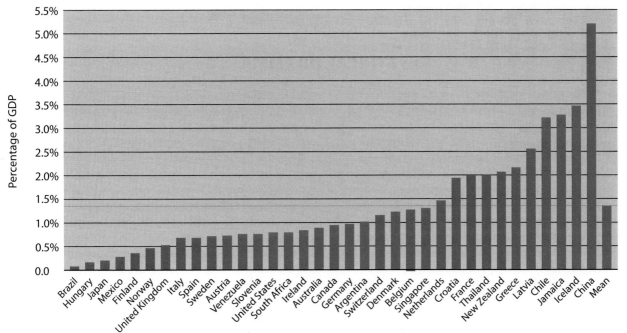

Source: M. Minniti, W. Bygrave, and E. Autio, *Global Entrepreneurship Monitor 2006 Executive Report* (Wellesley, MA: Babson College/GEM, 2006) 53.

Microfinance involves lending small sums ($50–$300) used to start small businesses with the intention of ultimately lifting the entrepreneurs out of poverty. Although microfinance started in the 1970s in countries such as Bangladesh and India, the Debate feature shows that it has now become a global movement and has become controversial lately.

> *Describe how international strategies for entering foreign markets are different from those for staying in domestic markets.*

INTERNATIONALIZING THE ENTREPRENEURIAL FIRM

There is a myth that only large MNEs do business abroad and that SMEs mostly operate domestically. This myth, based on historical stereotypes, is being increasingly challenged as more and more SMEs go international. Further, some start-ups attempt to do business abroad from inception. These are often called **born global firms** (or international new ventures). This section examines how entrepreneurial firms internationalize.

Transaction Costs and Entrepreneurial Opportunities

Compared with domestic transaction costs (the costs of doing business), international transaction costs are qualitatively higher. Some costs are high due to numerous innocent differences in formal institutions and informal norms (see Chapters 2 and 3). Other costs, however, may be due

to a high level of deliberate opportunism that is hard to detect and remedy. For example, when a small business in Texas with $5 million annual revenues receives an unsolicited order of $1 million from an unknown buyer in Alaska, most likely the Texas firm will fill the order and allow the Alaska buyer to pay within 30 or 60 days after receiving the goods—a typical practice among domestic transactions in the United States. But what if this order comes from an unknown buyer (importer in this case) in Azerbaijan? If the Texas firm ships the goods but foreign payment does not arrive on time (after 30, 60, or even more days), it is difficult to assess whether firms in Azerbaijan simply do not have the norm of punctual payment or whether that particular importer is being deliberately opportunistic. If the latter is indeed the case, suing the importer in a court in Azerbaijan, where Azeri is the official language, may be so costly that it is not an option for a small US exporter.

Maybe the Azerbaijani importer is an honest and capable firm with every intention and ability to pay. But because the Texas firm may not be able to ascertain, prior to the transaction, that the Azerbaijani side will pay upon receiving the goods, the Texas firm may simply say, "No, thanks!" Conceptually, this is an example of transaction costs being so high that many firms may choose not to pursue international opportunities. Therefore, entrepreneurial

Microfinance
Lending small sums ($50–$300) used to start small businesses with the intention of ultimately lifting the entrepreneurs out of poverty.

Born global firm
A start-up company that attempts to do business abroad from inception.

DEBATE ETHICAL DILEMMA

Microfinance: Macro Success or Global Mess?

Teach a man to fish, and he'll eat for a lifetime. However, here is a catch: In many poor developing countries, numerous eager fishermen—also known as entrepreneurs—cannot afford a fishing pole. In 1976, Muhammad Yunus, a young economics professor who received his PhD from Vanderbilt University, lent $27 out of his own pocket to a group of poor craftsmen in his native Bangladesh. He also helped found a village-based enterprise called the Grameen Project. It never occurred to Yunus that he would inspire a global movement for entrepreneurial financing, much less that 30 years later, in 2006, he and Grameen Bank, which he founded, would be awarded the Nobel Peace Prize.

Used to buy everything from milk cows to mobile phones (to be used as pay phones by the entire village), microloans can make a huge difference. The poor tend to have neither assets (necessary for collateral) nor credit history, making traditional loans risky. The innovative, simple solution is to lend to women. In lenders' opinion, women, on average, are more likely to use their earnings to support family needs than men, who may be more likely to indulge in drinking, gambling, or drugs. A more sophisticated solution is to organize the women in a village into a collective and lend money to the collective instead of to individuals. Overall, 84% of microloan recipients are women. While interest rates average a hefty 35%, they are still far below the rates charged by local loan sharks. By 2011, more than 7,000 microfinance institutions (MFIs) had served 120 million borrowers around the world.

However, as microfinance grows from periphery to mainstream, not all is rosy. Two ferocious debates have erupted recently. The first debate deals with how to view the initial public offerings (IPOs) of MFIs. The "successful" IPOs of several MFIs have attracted criticisms that these MFIs and their new shareholders, most of whom are wealthy investors from the United States and Europe, have enriched themselves at the expense of very poor people at the base of the lending pyramid. In short, the rich have literally profited from the dirt poor. Is that right?

Second, with the onslaught of the 2008–2009 global crisis, default rates have skyrocketed. Several competitive MFIs may have dumped several microfinance loans to the same uneducated clients. In a microfinance boom, some lending practices have increasingly become competitive and reckless, similar to subprime lending in the West before the financial crisis. Should crops or ventures fail, clients face crushing debt loads. Recovery methods from MFIs sometimes involve intimidation. The Indian government had a list of 85 MFI "victims," who committed suicide. In response, policymakers in some parts of India capped the interest rate at 24% and called on default borrowers to refuse to pay up. Thus, in some parts of India, nearly 80% of borrowers were in default. Because of the high costs of making and collecting payments on millions of tiny loans, MFIs' margins are razor-thin. Such massive defaults quickly pushed some MFIs to go under, and in late 2010 the Indian government reluctantly spent $221 million to bail them out. Sheikh Hasina, Bangladesh's prime minister, charged MFIs with "sucking blood from the poor" and treating the people of Bangladesh as "guinea pigs." She launched an investigation into Grameen Bank's allegedly questionable operations. Although as managing director of Grameen Bank, Yunus was eventually cleared of wrongdoing, microfinance—and its missionary pioneer—has suffered from a crisis of faith.

MFI IPOs	Country	Capital raised	Year
Bank Rakyat Indonesia	Indonesia	$480 million	2003
Equity Bank	Kenya	$88 million	2006
Banco Compartamos	Mexico	$467 million	2007
SKS Microfinance	India	$1.5 billion	2010

Sources: "An IPO for India's top lender to the poor," *Bloomberg Businessweek*, 10 May 2010, 16–17; "In a microfinance boom, echoes of subprime," *Bloomberg Businessweek*, 21 June 2010, 50–51; "Leave well alone," *Economist*, 20 November 2010, 16; "Microcredit missionary," *BusinessWeek*, 26 December 2005, 20; B. Pinkham and P. Nair, *Microfinance: Going global . . . and global public?* Case study, University of Texas at Dallas, 2011; "Saint under siege," *Economist*, 8 January 2011, 75; "Taking tiny loans to the next level," *BusinessWeek*, 27 November 2006, 76–80; "The micromess," *Newsweek*, 20 December 2010, 10; "Under water," *Economist*, 11 December 2010, 56.

EXHIBIT 9.5 — Internationalization Strategies for Entrepreneurial Firms

Entering foreign markets	Staying in domestic markets
• Direct exports • Franchising/licensing • Foreign direct investment (strategic alliances, green-field wholly owned subsidiaries, and/or foreign acquisitions)	• Indirect exports (through export intermediaries) • Supplier of foreign firms • Franchisee or licensee of foreign brands • Alliance partner of foreign direct investors • Harvest and exit (through sell-off to and acquisition by foreign entrants)

© Cengage Learning 2013

opportunities exist to lower transaction costs and bring distant groups of people, firms, and countries together. Exhibit 9.5 shows that while entrepreneurial firms can internationalize by entering foreign markets, they can also add an international dimension without actually going abroad. Next, we discuss how an SME can undertake some of these strategies.

International Strategies for Entering Foreign Markets

SMEs have three broad modes for entering foreign markets: (1) direct exports, (2) licensing/franchising, and (3) foreign direct investment (FDI) (see Chapters 6 and 10 for more details). First, **direct exports** involve the sale of products made by entrepreneurial firms in their home country to customers in other countries. This strategy is attractive because entrepreneurial firms are able to reach foreign customers directly. However, a major drawback is that SMEs may not have enough resources to turn overseas opportunities into profits. Many SMEs reach foreign cus-

tomers through **sporadic (or passive) exporting**, meaning sales prompted by unsolicited inquiries. To actively and systematically pursue export customers would be a different ball game.

Export transactions are complicated. One particular concern is how to overcome the lack of trust between exporters and importers when receiving an order from unknown importers abroad. For example, while the US exporter in Exhibit 9.6 does not trust the Chinese importer, banks on both sides can facilitate this transaction by a **letter of credit (L/C)**, which is a financial contract stating that the importer's bank (Bank of China in this case) will pay a specific sum of money to the exporter upon delivery of the merchandise. It has several steps.

+ The US exporter may question the unknown Chinese importer's assurance that it will promptly pay for the merchandise. An L/C from the highly reputable Bank of China will assure the US exporter that the importer has good creditworthiness and sufficient funds for the transaction. If the US exporter is not sure whether Bank of China is a credible bank, it can consult its own bank, Bank of America, which will confirm that an L/C from Bank of China is as good as gold.

EXHIBIT 9.6 — An Export/Import Transaction

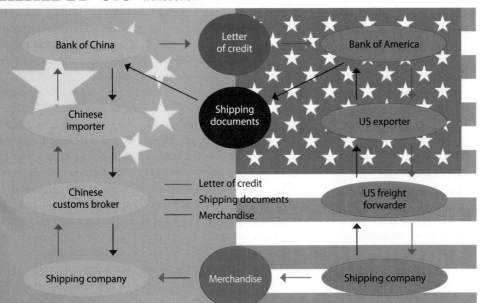

Legend:
— Letter of credit
— Shipping documents
— Merchandise

Direct exports
The sale of products made by firms in their home country to customers in other countries.

Sporadic (or passive) exporting
The sale of products prompted by unsolicited inquiries from abroad.

Letter of credit (L/C)
A financial contract that states that the importer's bank will pay a specific sum of money to the exporter upon delivery of the merchandise.

© iStockphoto.com/best-photo / © iStockphoto.com/Claudio Divizia

- With the assurance through an L/C, the US exporter can release the merchandise, which goes through a US freight forwarder, then a shipping company, and then a Chinese customs broker. Finally, the goods will reach the Chinese importer.

- Once the US exporter has shipped the goods, it will present to Bank of America the L/C from Bank of China and shipping documents. On behalf of the US exporter, Bank of America will then collect payment from Bank of China, which, in turn, will collect payment from the Chinese importer.

In short, instead of having unknown exporters and importers deal with each other, transactions are facilitated by banks on both sides that have known each other quite well because of numerous such dealings. In other words, the L/C reduces transaction costs by reducing the transaction risks.

A second way to enter international markets is through licensing and/or franchising. Usually used in *manufacturing* industries, **licensing** refers to Firm A's agreement to give Firm B the rights to use A's proprietary technology

take a risk because they may suffer a loss of control over how their technology and brand names are used. If a McDonald's (hypothetical) licensee in Finland produces sub-standard products that damage the brand and refuses to improve quality, McDonald's has two difficult choices: (1) sue its licensee in an unfamiliar Finnish court or (2) discontinue the relationship. Either choice is complicated and costly.

A third entry mode is FDI, which was discussed in detail in Chapter 6. FDI may involve strategic alliances with foreign partners (such as joint ventures), green-field wholly owned subsidiaries, and/or foreign acquisitions. FDI has several distinct advantages. By planting some roots abroad, a firm becomes more committed to serving foreign markets. It is physically and psychologically closer to foreign customers. Relative to licensing and franchising, a firm is better able to control how its proprietary technology and brand name are used. However, FDI has a major drawback: its cost and complexity. It requires both a non-trivial sum of capital and a significant managerial commitment. Many SMEs are unable to engage in FDI.

> ## The key differentiator between rapidly and slowly (or non-) internationalizing SMEs seems to be the international experience of the entrepreneurs.

(such as a patent) or trademark (such as a corporate logo) for a royalty fee paid to A by B. Assume (hypothetically) that a US exporter cannot keep up with demand in Turkey. It may consider granting a Turkish firm the license to use its technology and trademark for a fee.

Franchising is essentially the same idea, except it is typically used in *service* industries such as fast food. A great advantage is that SME licensors and franchisors can expand abroad while risking relatively little of their own capital. Foreign firms interested in becoming licensees or franchisees have to put their own capital up front. For example, a McDonald's franchise now costs the franchisee approximately one million dollars. But licensors and franchisors also

Licensing
Firm A's agreement to give Firm B the rights to use A's proprietary technology (such as a patent) or trademark (such as a corporate logo) for a royalty fee paid to A by B. This is typically done in manufacturing industries.

Franchising
Firm A's agreement to give Firm B the rights to use A's proprietary assets for a royalty fee paid to A by B. This is typically done in service industries.

Stage model
Model of internationalization that involves a slow step-by-step (stage-by-stage) process a firm must go through to internationalize its business.

In general, the level of complexity and resources required increases as a firm moves from direct exports to licensing/franchising and finally to FDI. Traditionally, it is thought that most firms will have to go through these different stages and that SMEs (perhaps with few exceptions) are unable to undertake FDI. Known as the **stage model**, this idea posits that SMEs that do eventually internationalize will do so through a slow, stage-by-stage process.

However, enough counter-examples of rapidly internationalizing entrepreneurial firms, known as *born globals*, exist to challenge stage models. Consider Logitech, now a global leader in computer peripherals. It was established by entrepreneurs from Switzerland and the United States, where the firm set up dual headquarters. Research and development (R&D) and manufacturing were initially split between these two countries and then quickly spread to Ireland and Taiwan through FDI. Its first commercial contract was with a Japanese company.

Given that most SMEs still fit the stereotype of slow (or no) internationalization but some entrepreneurial SMEs seem to be born global, a key question is: What leads to rapid internationalization? The key differentiator between rapidly and slowly (or non-) internationalizing SMEs seems to be the international experience of the entrepreneurs.[13] If entrepreneurs have solid previous experience abroad (such as David Neeleman's earlier experience in Brazil as portrayed in the Opening Case), then doing business internationally is not so intimidating. Otherwise, the apprehension associated with the unfamiliar foreign business world may take over, and entrepreneurs will simply want to avoid trouble overseas.

While many entrepreneurial firms have aggressively gone abroad, it is probably true that a majority of SMEs will be unable to do so; they already have enough headaches struggling with the domestic market. However, as discussed next, some SMEs can still internationalize by staying at home.

International Strategies for Staying in Domestic Markets

Exhibit 9.5 also shows a number of strategies for entrepreneurial SMEs to internationalize without leaving their home country. The five main strategies are (1) export indirectly, (2) become suppliers for foreign firms, (3) become licensees or franchisees of foreign brands, (4) become alliance partners of foreign direct investors, or (5) harvest and exit through sell-offs to foreign entrants.

First, whereas direct exports may be lucrative, many SMEs simply do not have the resources to handle such work. But they can still reach overseas customers through **indirect exports**, which involve exporting through domestic-based export intermediaries. **Export intermediaries** perform an important middleman function by linking domestic sellers and overseas buyers who otherwise would not have been connected. Being entrepreneurs themselves, export intermediaries facilitate the internationalization of many SMEs. Intermediaries such as trading companies and export management companies handle about 50% of total exports in Japan and South Korea, 38% in Thailand, and 5% to 10% in the United States.[14]

A second strategy is to become a supplier for a foreign firm that is doing business in the domestic market. For example, when Subway opened restaurants in Northern Ireland, it secured a contract for chilled part-baked bread with a domestic bakery. This relationship was so successful that the bakery now supplies Subway franchisees throughout Europe. SME suppliers thus may be able to internationalize by piggybacking on the larger foreign entrants.

Third, an entrepreneurial firm may consider becoming licensee or franchisee of a foreign brand. Foreign licensors and franchisors provide training and technology transfer—for a fee of course. Consequently, an SME can learn a great deal about how to operate at world-class standards. Further, licensees and franchisees do not have to be permanently under the control of licensors and franchisors. If enough learning has been accomplished and enough capital has been accumulated, it is possible to discontinue the relationship and to reap greater entrepreneurial profits. In Thailand, Minor Group, which had held the Pizza Hut franchise for 20 years, broke away from the relationship.

Its new venture, The Pizza Company, is now the market leader in Thailand.[15]

A fourth strategy is to become an alliance partner of a foreign direct investor. Facing an onslaught of aggressive MNEs, many entrepreneurial firms may not be able to successfully defend their market positions. Then it makes great sense to follow the old adage "If you can't beat them, join them!" While dancing with the giants is tricky, it is better than being crushed by them. (See Chapter 11 for examples of how smaller, domestic firms become alliance partners with MNEs.)

Finally, as a harvest and exit strategy, entrepreneurs may sell an equity stake or the entire firm to foreign entrants. An American couple, originally from Seattle, built a Starbucks-like coffee chain in Britain called Seattle Coffee. When Starbucks entered Britain, the couple sold the chain of 60 stores to Starbucks for a hefty $84 million. In light of the high failure rates of start-ups (see the Closing Case), being acquired by foreign entrants may help preserve the business in the long run.

Articulate what you should do to strengthen your entrepreneurial ability on an international level.

MANAGEMENT SAVVY

What determines the success and failure of entrepreneurial firms around the globe? The answer boils down to two components. First, the institution-based view argues that the larger institutional frameworks explain a great deal about what is behind the differences in entrepreneurial and economic development around the world. Second, the resource-based view posits that it is largely intangible resources such as vision, drive, and willingness to take risks that fuel entrepreneurship around the globe. Overall, the performance of entrepreneurial firms depends on how they take advantage of formal and informal institutional resources and leverage their capabilities at home, abroad, or both.

Two clear implications for action emerge (Exhibit 9.7 on the next page). First, institutions that help entrepreneurship development—both formal and informal—are important. As a result, savvy

Indirect exports
A way for SMEs to reach overseas customers by exporting through domestic-based export intermediaries.

Export intermediary
A firm that acts as a middleman by linking domestic sellers and foreign buyers that otherwise would not have been connected.

entrepreneurs have a vested interest in pushing for more entrepreneur-friendly formal institutions in various countries, such as rules governing how to set up new firms and how to reduce the pain for failed entrepreneurs and their firms (see the Closing Case). Entrepreneurs also need to cultivate strong informal norms granting legitimacy to entrepreneurs. Talking to high school and college students, taking on internships, and providing seed money as angels for new ventures are some of the actions that entrepreneurs can undertake.

Second, when internationalizing, entrepreneurs are advised to be bold. Thanks to globalization, the costs of doing business abroad have fallen recently. But being bold

does not mean being reckless. One specific managerial insight from this chapter is that it is possible to internationalize without actually venturing abroad. When the entrepreneurial firm is not ready to take on higher risk abroad, this more limited involvement may be appropriate. In other words, be bold but not *too* bold.[16]

CLOSING CASE

ETHICAL DILEMMA
BOOM IN BUSTS: GOOD OR BAD?

Corporate bankruptcies* have climbed to new heights in the Great Recession, as firms ranging from huge ones such as General Motors to tiny entrepreneurial outfits are dropping out left and right around the world. Since bankruptcies do not sound good or inspiring, is there anything that we—the government, financial institutions, consumers, taxpayers, or the society at large—can do to prevent widespread bankruptcies?

Efforts to rescue failing firms from bankruptcy stem from an "anti-failure bias" widely shared among entrepreneurs, scholars, journalists, and government officials. Although a majority of entrepreneurial firms fail, this anti-failure bias leads to strong interest in entrepreneurial success (remember how many times Google and Facebook were written up by the press?) and to scant attention devoted to the vast majority of entrepreneurial firms that end up in failure and bankruptcy. However, one perspective suggests that bankruptcies, which are undoubtedly painful to individual entrepreneurs and employees, may be good for society. Consequently, bankruptcy laws need to be reformed to become more entrepreneur friendly by making it easier for entrepreneurs to declare bankruptcies and to move on. Then the financial, human, and physical resources of failed firms can be redeployed in a socially optimal way.

A leading debate is how to treat failed entrepreneurs who file for bankruptcy. Do we let them walk away from debt or punish them? Historically, "entrepreneur-friendly bankruptcy law" is practically an oxymoron, because bankruptcy laws are usually severe and even cruel. The very term "bankruptcy" is derived from a harsh practice: In medieval Italy, if bankrupt entrepreneurs did not pay their debt, debtors would destroy the trading bench (booth) of the

bankrupt—the Italian word for broken bench, "banca rotta," has evolved into the English word "bankruptcy." The pound of flesh demanded by the creditor in Shakespeare's *The Merchant of Venice* is only a slight exaggeration. The world's first bankruptcy law, passed in England in 1542, considered a bankrupt individual a criminal, and penalties ranged from incarceration to a death sentence.

However, recently many governments have realized that entrepreneur-friendly bankruptcy laws can not only lower *exit* barriers, but also lower *entry* barriers for entrepreneurs. Although we are confident that many start-ups will end up in bankruptcy, at present it is impossible to predict which ones will go under. Therefore, from an institution-based standpoint, if entrepreneurship is to be encouraged, there is a need to ease the pain associated with bankruptcy by such means as allowing entrepreneurs to walk away from debt, a legal right that bankrupt US entrepreneurs appreciate. In contrast, until the recent bankruptcy law reforms, bankrupt German entrepreneurs could remain liable for unpaid debt for up to 30 years. Further, German and Japanese managers of bankrupt firms can also be liable for criminal penalties, and under such pressures, numerous bankrupt Japanese entrepreneurs have committed suicide. Not surprisingly, many failed entrepreneurs in Germany and Japan try to avoid business exit despite escalating losses; meanwhile, societal and individual resources cannot be channeled to more productive uses. Therefore, as rules of the "end game," harsh bankruptcy laws become grave exit barriers. They can also create significant entry barriers, as fewer would-be entrepreneurs decide to launch their ventures.

At a societal level, if many would-be entrepreneurs, in fear of failure, abandon their ideas, there will not be a thriving entrepreneurial sector. Given the risks and uncertainties, it is not surprising that many entrepreneurs do not make it the first time. However, if they are given second, third, or more chances, some of them will succeed. For example, approximately 50% of US entrepreneurs who filed bankruptcy resumed a new venture in four years. This high level of entrepreneurialism is, in part, driven by the relatively entrepreneur-friendly bankruptcy laws (such as the provision of Chapter 11 bankruptcy reorganization). On the other hand, a society that severely punishes failed entrepreneurs (such as forcing financially insolvent firms to liquidate instead of offering a US Chapter 11-style reorganization option) is not likely to foster widespread entrepreneurship. Failed entrepreneurs have nevertheless accumulated a great deal of experience and lessons on how to avoid repeating their mistakes; if they drop out of the entrepreneurial game their wisdom will be permanently lost. Overall, worldwide evidence from 29 countries—involving both developed and emerging economies from five continents—has identified a strong linkage between entrepreneur-friendly bankruptcy laws and new firm entries.

institutionally, there is an urgent need to remove some of our anti-failure bias and design entrepreneur-friendly bankruptcy policies so that failed entrepreneurs are given more chances. At a societal level, entrepreneurial failures may be beneficial, since it is through a large number of entrepreneurial experimentations—although many will fail—that winning solutions will emerge and that economies will develop. In short, the boom in busts is not necessarily bad.

* The term "bankruptcies" in this case refers to *corporate* bankruptcies and does not deal with *personal* bankruptcies.

Sources: S. Lee, M. W. Peng, and J. Barney, "Bankruptcy law and entrepreneurship development," *Academy of Management Review*, 32 (2007): 257–272; S. Lee, Y. Yamakawa, and M. W. Peng, "How does bankruptcy law affect entrepreneurship development?" (Washington, DC: US Small Business Administration, 2007) SBA Best Research Papers Collection, available online at http://www.sba.gov/advo/research/rs326tot.pdf; S. Lee, Y. Yamakawa, M. W. Peng, and J. Barney, "How do bankruptcy laws affect entrepreneurship development around the world?" *Journal of Business Venturing* (2011, in press); M. W. Peng, Y. Yamakawa, and S. Lee, "Bankruptcy laws and entrepreneur-friendliness," *Entrepreneurship Theory and Practice*, 34 (2010): 517–530.

BY THE NUMBERS

9.8 hours per month (on average) Russians spend online in social networks

1542 year the world's first bankruptcy law was passed (in Britain)

50 percent total exports handled by trading companies and export management companies in Japan

50 percent of US entrepreneurs who filed bankruptcy and resumed a new venture within four years

 84 millions of dollars Starbucks paid Seattle Coffee for its chain of 60 British stores

Entering Foreign MARKETS

CHAPTER 10

Pearl River Goes Abroad: Exports, Green-Fields, Acquisitions

To many readers of this book, Pearl River is probably the world's largest piano maker that you have never heard of. It is also the fastest growing piano maker in North America, with the largest dealer network in Canada and the United States (over 300 dealers). Its US subsidiary's website proudly announces that Pearl River is "the world's best selling piano." Although some of you may say, "Sorry, I don't play piano, so I don't know anything about leading piano brands," you most likely have heard about Yamaha and Steinway. Therefore, your excuse for not knowing Pearl River would collapse.

The problem is both yours and Pearl River's. Given the relatively low prestige associated with made-in-China goods, you typically will not associate a fine musical instrument such as

piano with a Chinese firm. Pearl River Piano Group (PRPG) is China's largest piano maker and has recently dethroned Japan's Yamaha to become the world champion by volume. Despite PRPG's outstanding capabilities, it is difficult for one firm to change the negative country-of-origin image associated with made-in-China goods.

Founded in 1956 in Guangzhou, China, where the Pearl River flows, Pearl River (the company) exported its very first piano to Hong Kong. Yet, its center of gravity has remained in China. Pianos have become more affordable with rising income, and China's one-child policy has made families willing to invest in their only child's education. As a result, the Chinese now buy half of the pianos produced in the world.

LEARNING OBJECTIVES
After studying this chapter, you should be able to:

LO1 *identify ways in which institutions and resources affect the liability of foreignness.*

LO2 *match the quest for location-specific advantages with strategic goals.*

LO3 *compare and contrast first-mover and late-mover advantages.*

LO4 *list the steps in the comprehensive model of foreign market entries.*

LO5 *explain what you should do to make your firm's entry into a foreign market successful.*

© Li Huang/ColorChinaPhoto/Li Huang/Newscom

If you think life will be easy for the leading firm in the largest market in the world, you are wrong. In fact, life is increasingly hard for PRPG. This is because rising demand has attracted numerous new entrants, many of which compete at the low end in China. More than 140 competitors have pushed PRPG's domestic market share from 70% at its peak a decade ago to about 25% now—although it is still the market leader.

Savage domestic competition has pushed PRPG to increasingly look for overseas opportunities. It now exports to over 80 countries. In North America, PRPG started in the late 1980s by relying on US-based importers. Making its first ever foreign direct investment (FDI), it set up a US-based sales subsidiary, PRPG America, Ltd., in Ontario, California, in 1999. This subsidiary is a green-field subsidiary—namely, a new entity built from scratch. Acknowledging the importance of the US market and the limited international caliber of his own managerial rank, PRPG's CEO, Tong Zhi Cheng, attracted Al Rich, an American with extensive experience in the piano industry, to head the subsidiary. In two years, the green-field subsidiary succeeded in getting Pearl River pianos into about one third of the specialized US retail dealers. In ten years, the Pearl River brand became the undisputed leader in the low end of the upright piano market in North America. Efforts to penetrate the high-end market, however, were still frustrated.

Despite the enviable progress made by PRPG itself in general and by its US subsidiary in particular, the Pearl River brand suffers from all the usual trappings associated with Chinese brands. "We are very cognizant that our pricing provides a strong incentive to buy," Rich noted in a media interview, "but $6,000 is still a lot of money." In an audacious move to overcome buyers' reservations about purchasing a high-end Chinese product, PRPG made its second major FDI move in 2000, by acquiring Ritmüller of Germany.

Ritmüller was founded in 1795 by Wilhelm Ritmüller during the lifetimes of composers Ludvig van Beethoven and Joseph Haydn. It was one of the first piano makers in Germany and one of the most prominent in the world. Unfortunately, during the post-WWII era, Ritmüller's style of small-scale, handicraft-based piano making had a hard time surviving the disruptive, mass-production technologies unleashed by Yamaha and more recently by Pearl River. Prior to being acquired by Pearl River, Ritmüller had become inactive. Today, Ritmüller has entered a new era in its proud history and operates a factory in Germany with full capacity. The entire product line has been reengineered to reflect a new commitment to a classic heritage and standards of excellence. PRPG has commissioned international master piano designers to marry German precision craftsmanship with the latest piano-making technology.

Sources: "The return of the king," *Beijing Review*, 21 May 2009, available online at http://www.bjreview.com; Funding Universe, "Guangzhou Pearl River Piano Group Ltd., Company History," 2009, available online at http://www.fundinguniverse.com; Y. Lu, "Pearl River Piano Group's international strategy," in M. W. Peng, *Global Strategy*, 2nd ed. (Cincinnati: South-Western Cengage Learning, 2009) 437–440; Pearl River Piano Group, 2011, http://www.pearlriverpiano.com; Pearl River USA, 2011, http://www.pearlriverusa.com.

How do firms such as Pearl River enter foreign markets? How do they overcome their liability of foreignness? Why do they enter certain countries but not others? Why do they sometimes export, sometimes set up green-field subsidiaries, and sometimes use acquisitions when entering foreign markets? These are some of the key questions driving this chapter. Entering foreign markets is one of the most important topics in international business. This chapter first draws on the institution-based and resource-based views to discuss ways to overcome the liability of foreignness.[1] Then we focus on three crucial dimensions: Where, *w*hen, and *h*ow—known as the 2W1H dimensions. Our discussion culminates in a comprehensive model, followed by a debate.

disadvantage that foreign firms experience in host countries because of their non-native status. Such a liability is manifested in at least two ways. First, numerous differences in formal and informal institutions govern the rules of the game in different countries. While local firms are already well versed in these rules, foreign firms have to learn the rules quickly. For example, European firms that have subsidiaries operating in the United States are busy learning the new "Buy American" rules in US stimulus packages that would qualify them as "US firms."[2] Many governments ban foreigners from owning assets in certain strategic sectors. Rupert Murdoch (owner of News Corporation) had to become a US citizen in order to acquire US broadcast properties.

Second, although customers in this age of globalization *supposedly* no longer discriminate against foreign firms, the reality is that foreign firms are often still discriminated against, sometimes formally and other times informally. For example, activists in India alleged that both Coca-Cola's and PepsiCo's products contained higher-than-permitted levels of pesticides but did not test any Indian-branded soft drinks, even though pesticide residues are present in virtually all groundwater in India. Although both Coca-Cola and PepsiCo denied these charges, their sales suffered.

Against such significant odds, how do foreign firms crack new markets? The answer boils down to our two core

LO1 *Identify ways in which institutions and resources affect the liability of foreignness.*

OVERCOMING THE LIABILITY OF FOREIGNNESS

Liability of foreignness
The inherent disadvantage that foreign firms experience in host countries because of their non-native status.

It is not easy to succeed in an unfamiliar environment. Recall from Chapter 1 that foreign firms have to overcome a **liability of foreignness**, which is the inherent

IN FOCUS

ETHICAL DILEMMA

Russian Firms Spread Their Wings Abroad

Which emerging economy among BRIC (Brazil, Russia, India, and China) has the largest amount of outward FDI? Surprise! It is neither China nor India. While outward FDI from China and India often grabs media headlines, Russia has the largest stock of outward FDI among all emerging economies (yes, more than China).

After the fall of the Berlin Wall in 1989, Russia suffered a decade of turmoil. Since 1999, the Russian economy staged a spectacular comeback, largely thanks to consistently high prices of its main export items, oil and gas. The 2008–2009 global crisis created another setback. But with the Middle East (think of Libya) up in flames since 2011, the more stable oil and gas production from Russia bodes well for the country's economic performance.

Accumulation of earnings and lucrative opportunities abroad have turned a series of Russian firms into multinational enterprises (MNEs), spreading their wings around the globe. Russian firms active in FDI can be found in three categories: (1) One group targets acquisition targets in Western Europe and North America in an effort to access technological innovations and advanced management know-how. (2) Another group focuses on the "near abroad"—the Commonwealth of Independent States (CIS), whose member countries were all formerly a part of the Soviet Union.

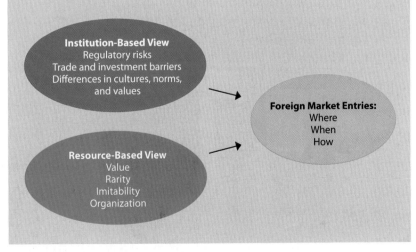

(3) A third group channels funds through offshore financial centers such as Cyprus and the British Virgin Islands and reinvests back in Russia—a process known as capital round-tripping. Experts estimate that about 10% of the Russian outward FDI is involved in round-tripping, leaving the other 90% to be real FDI.

Russian FDI abroad is not without controversies. Host-country governments and the media often voice concern that Russian MNEs, especially large energy companies, may represent the "long arm of the Kremlin." The political hard line recently taken by the Russian government (such as the war with Georgia) heightens such concerns, especially in sensitive, former Soviet Bloc countries such as Hungary, Lithuania, and Poland. Russian MNEs claim that their FDI is solely driven by profit motives. However, host-country governments face the dilemma of how to accommodate the legitimate economic interests of Russian MNEs, harness the FDI dollars they bring, and limit the potential damage when dealing with the bears (or eagles) from Russia.

Sources: A. Panibratov and K. Kalotay, "Russia outward FDI and its policy context," *Columbia FDI Profiles*, No. 1, 2009, available online at http://www.vcc.columbia.edu; M. W. Peng, S. L. Sun, and D. Blevins, "The social responsibility of international business scholars," *Multinational Business Review* 19 (2011): 106-119; United Nations, *World Investment Report 2010* (New York: UN, 2011).

perspectives introduced earlier (see Exhibit 10.1). The institution-based view suggests that firms need to undertake actions deemed legitimate and appropriate by the various formal and informal institutions governing market entries. Differences in formal institutions may lead to regulatory risks due to differences in political, economic, and legal systems (see Chapter 2). There may be numerous trade and investment barriers on a national or regional basis (see Chapters 5, 6, and 8). In addition, the existence of multiple currencies—and currency risks as a result—may be another formal barrier (see Chapter 7). Informally, numerous differences in cultures, norms, and values create another major source of liability of foreignness (see Chapter 3).

EXHIBIT 10.1 Institutions, Resources, and Foreign Market Entries

Institution-Based View
Regulatory risks
Trade and investment barriers
Differences in cultures, norms, and values

Resource-Based View
Value
Rarity
Imitability
Organization

Foreign Market Entries:
Where
When
How

© Cengage Learning 2013

The resource-based view argues that foreign firms need to deploy *overwhelming* resources and capabilities so that after offsetting the liability of foreignness, they still possess competitive advantage.[3] Applying the VRIO framework introduced in Chapter 4 to our Opening Case, we can suggest that Pearl River has some overwhelmingly valuable and rare capabilities in successfully becoming king of the low-end pianos in North America. No rivals are able to imitate Pearl River's combination of excellent quality with attractive pricing. However, thanks to the liability of foreignness (in this case, "Chineseness"), it has a hard time breaking into the high-end market. In response, it has acquired a classic but inactive German brand Ritmüller to reduce such liability of foreignness. Acquiring and integrating a foreign firm requires an enormous amount of organizational capabilities, and many acquisitions fail. Pearl River's organizational capabilities have proven to be a tremendous asset.

Overall, our two core perspectives shed a lot of light on firms' internationalization. For example, In Focus illustrates why there is a recent surge of internationalization undertaken by multinational enterprises (MNEs) from Russia. Next, we investigate the 2W1H dimensions associated with foreign market entries.

Match the quest for location-specific advantages with strategic goals.

WHERE TO ENTER?

Similar to real estate, the motto for international business is "location, location, location." In fact, such a *spatial* perspective (that is, doing business outside of one's home country) is a defining feature of international business.[4] Two sets of considerations drive the location of foreign entries: (1) strategic goals and (2) cultural and institutional distances.

Location-Specific Advantages and Strategic Goals

Favorable locations in certain countries may give firms operating there what are called location-specific advantages. **Location-specific advantages** are the benefits a firm reaps from features specific to a particular place. Certain locations simply possess geographical features that are difficult for others to match. Leading seaports and airports (see PengAtlas Maps 14 and 15) naturally attract a lot of foreign entrants. For example, Dubai, the United Arab Emirates, is an ideal stopping point for air traffic between Europe and Asia, and between Africa and Asia. Two billion people live within four hours of flying time from Dubai, and four billion can be reached within seven hours. Dubai's airport is already the third busiest international airport in terms of passengers behind only London Heathrow and Hong Kong International.[5] Similarly, Rotterdam, the Netherlands, is the main hub for seabound transportation into and out of Europe (see PengAtlas Map 16). More than 500 liner services connect Rotterdam with over 1,000 ports worldwide. Overall, we may regard the continuous expansion of international business as an unending saga in search of location-specific advantages.

We learned in Chapter 6 about agglomeration, or location-specific advantages that arise from the clustering of economic activities in certain locations. The basic idea dates back at least to Alfred Marshall, a British economist who first published it in 1890. Recall that location-specific advantages stem from (1) knowledge spillovers among closely located firms that attempt to hire individuals from competitors, (2) industry demand that creates a skilled labor force whose members may work for different firms without having to move out of the region, and (3) industry demand that facilitates a pool of specialized suppliers and buyers to also locate in the region. For example, due to agglomeration, Dallas has the world's heaviest concentration of telecom companies. US firms such as AT&T, HP, Raytheon, Texas Instruments (TI), and Verizon cluster there.

Location-specific advantages
The benefits a firm reaps from the features specific to a place.

Dallas attracts numerous telecom companies due to agglomeration.

EXHIBIT 10.2 Matching Strategic Goals with Locations

Strategic goal	Location-specific advantage	Examples in the text
Natural resource seeking	Possession of natural resources and related transport and communication infrastructure	Oil in the Middle East, Russia, and Venezuela
Market seeking	Abundance of strong market demand and customers willing to pay	GM in China
Efficiency seeking	Economies of scale and abundance of low-cost factors	Manufacturing in China
Innovation seeking	Abundance of innovative individuals, firms, and universities	IT in the Silicon Valley and Bangalore; telecom in Dallas; aerospace in Russia

© Cengage Learning 2013

Moreover, numerous leading foreign telecom firms such as Alcatel-Lucent, Ericsson, Fujitsu, Huawei, Siemens, and STMicroelectronics have also converged in this region.

Given that different locations offer different benefits, it is imperative that a firm match its strategic goals with potential locations. The four strategic goals are shown in Exhibit 10.2. First, firms seeking *natural resources* have to go to particular foreign locations where those resources are found. For example, the Middle East, Russia, and Venezuela are all rich in oil. Even when the Venezuelan government became more hostile, Western oil firms had to put up with it.

Second, *market-seeking* firms go to countries that have a strong demand for their products and services. For example, China is now the largest car market in the world, and practically all the automakers in the world are now elbowing into this fast-growing market. General Motors (GM) has emerged as the leader. In 2010, GM for the first time sold more cars in China than in the United States.[6]

Third, *efficiency-seeking* firms often single out the most efficient locations featuring a combination of scale economies and low-cost factors. It is the search for efficiency that induced numerous MNEs to enter China. China now manufactures two thirds of the world's photocopiers, shoes, toys, and microwave ovens; one half of DVD players, digital cameras, and textiles; one third of desktop computers; and one quarter of mobile phones, television sets, and steel. Shanghai alone reportedly has a cluster of over 400 of the *Fortune* Global 500 firms. It is important to note that China does not present the absolutely lowest labor costs in the world, and Shanghai is the *highest* cost city in China. However, China's attractiveness lies in its ability to enhance efficiency for foreign entrants by lowering *total* costs.

Finally, *innovation-seeking* firms target countries and regions renowned for generating world-class innovations, such as Silicon Valley and Bangalore (in IT), Dallas (in telecom), and Russia (in aerospace). Such entries can be viewed as "an

option to maintain access to innovations resident in the host country, thus generating information spillovers that may lead to opportunities for future organizational learning and growth."[7] (See Chapter 12 for details.)

It is important to note that location-specific advantages may grow, change, and/or decline, prompting a firm to relocate. If policy makers fail to maintain the institutional attractiveness (for example, by raising taxes) and if companies overcrowd and bid up factor costs such as land and talent, some firms may move out of certain locations previously considered advantageous. For example, Mercedes and BMW proudly projected a 100% "Made in Germany" image until the early 1990s. Now both companies produce in a variety of countries such as Brazil, China, Mexico, South Africa, the United States, and Vietnam and instead boast "Made by Mercedes" and "Made by BMW." Both the relative decline of Germany's location-specific advantages and the rise of other countries' advantages prompted Mercedes and BMW to shift their emphasis from location-specific advantages to firm-specific advantages.

Cultural/Institutional Distances and Foreign Entry Locations

In addition to strategic goals, another set of considerations centers on cultural/institutional distances (see also Chapters 2 and 3). **Cultural distance** is the difference between two cultures along identifiable dimensions such as individualism. Considering culture as an informal part of institutional frameworks governing a particular country, **institutional distance** is "the extent of similarity or dissimilarity between the regulatory, normative, and cognitive institutions of two countries."[8] Broadly speaking, cultural distance is a subset of institutional distance. For example, many Western cosmetics products firms, such as L'Oreal, have shied away from Saudi Arabia, citing its stricter rules of personal behavior. In essence, Saudi Arabia's cultural and institutional distance from Western cultures is too large.

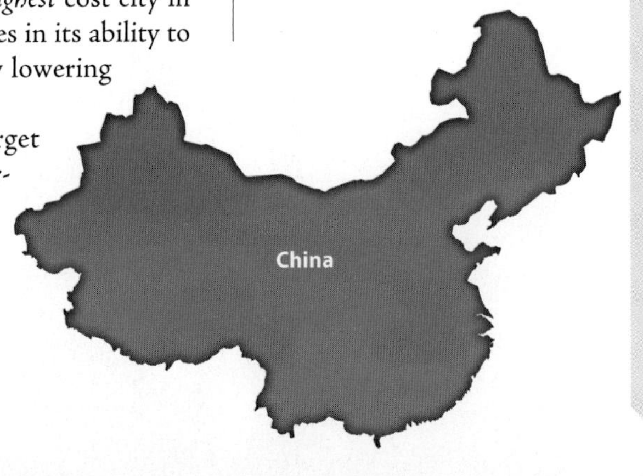

China

Cultural distance
The difference between two cultures along identifiable dimensions such as individualism.

Institutional distance
The extent of similarity or dissimilarity between the regulatory, normative, and cognitive institutions of two countries.

Russia

Sakhalin Island

Two schools of thought have emerged in overcoming these distances. The first is associated with the stage model. According to the stage model first introduced in Chapter 9, firms will enter culturally similar countries during their first stage of internationalization and will then gain more confidence to enter culturally distant countries in later stages. This idea is intuitively appealing: It makes sense for Belgian firms to enter France first and Russian firms to enter Ukraine first to take advantage of common cultural and language traditions. On average, business between countries that share a language is three times greater than between countries without a common language. Firms from common-law countries (English-speaking countries and Britain's former colonies) are more likely to be interested in other common-law countries. Colony–colonizer links boost trade significantly. Overall, certain performance benefits seem to exist when competing in culturally and institutionally adjacent countries.

Citing numerous counter-examples, a second school of thought argues that it is more important to consider strategic goals such as market and efficiency rather than culture and institutions. For example, major Western oil producers on Sakhalin Island, a remote part of the Russian Far East, have no choice but to accept Russia's unfriendly, strong-arm tactics to grab more shares and profits—tactics described as "thuggish ways" by the *Economist*.[9] Because Western oil majors have few alternatives elsewhere, cultural, institutional, and geographic distance in this case does not seem relevant; the oil producers simply have to be there and let the Russians flex their muscles to dictate the terms. Overall, in the complex calculus underpinning entry decisions, location represents only one of several important considerations. As shown next, entry timing and modes are also crucial.

WHEN TO ENTER?

Entry timing refers to whether there are compelling reasons to be an early or late entrant in a particular country. Some firms look for **first-mover advantages**, defined as the benefits that accrue to firms that enter the market first and that later entrants do not enjoy.[10] Speaking of the power of first-mover advantages, "Xerox," "FedEx," and "Google" have now become *verbs* (such as "Google it"). In many African countries, "Colgate" is the generic term for toothpaste. Unilever, a late mover, is disappointed to find out that its African customers call its own toothpaste "the red Colgate" (!). However, first movers may also encounter significant disadvantages which, in turn, become **late-mover advantages**. Exhibit 10.3 shows a number of first- and late-mover advantages.

First movers may gain advantage through proprietary technology. Think about Apple's iPod, iPad, and iPhone. First movers may also make preemptive investments. A number of Japanese MNEs have cherry picked leading local suppliers and distributors in Southeast Asia as new members of the expanded *keiretsu* networks (alliances of Japanese businesses with interlocking business relationships and shareholdings) and have blocked access to the suppliers and distributors by late entrants from the West.[11] In addition, first movers may erect significant entry barriers for late entrants, such as high switching costs due to brand loyalty. Parents who have used a particular brand of disposable diapers (such as Huggies or Pampers) for their first baby often use the same brand for any subsequent babies. Buyers of expensive equipment are likely to stick with the same producers for components, training, and other services for a long time. That is why American, British, French, German, and Russian aerospace firms competed intensely for Poland's first post-Cold War order of fighters—America's F-16 eventually won.

Intense domestic competition may drive some non-dominant firms abroad to avoid clashing with dominant firms head-on in their home market. Matsushita, Toyota,

First-mover advantages
Benefits that accrue to firms that enter the market first and that later entrants do not enjoy.

Late-mover advantages
Benefits that accrue to firms that enter the market later and that early entrants do not enjoy.

American manufacturers competed for Poland's first post-Cold War order of fighter planes, knowing that buyers of expensive equipment tend to be brand loyal.

EXHIBIT 10.3 First-Mover Advantages and Late-Mover Advantages

First-mover advantages	Examples in the text
Proprietary, technological leadership	Apple's iPod, iPad, and iPhone
Preemption of scarce resources	Japanese MNEs in Southeast Asia
Establishment of entry barriers for late entrants	Huggies and Pampers diapers for the firstborn; Poland's F-16 fighter jet contract
Avoidance of clash with dominant firms at home	Sony, Honda, and Epson went to the US market ahead of their Japanese rivals
Relationships with key stakeholders such as governments	Citigroup, JPMorgan Chase, and Metallurgical Corporation of China entered Afghanistan
Late-mover advantages	**Examples in the text**
Opportunity to free ride on first-mover investments	Ericsson won big contracts in Saudi Arabia, free riding on Cisco's efforts
Resolution of technological and market uncertainties	GM and Toyota have patience to wait until the Nissan Leaf resolves uncertainties about the electric car
First mover's difficulty to adapt to market changes	Greyhound is stuck with bus depots, whereas Megabus simply uses curbside stops

© Cengage Learning 2013

and NEC were the market leaders in Japan, but Sony, Honda, and Epson all entered the United States in their respective industries ahead of the leading firms. Finally, first movers may build precious relationships with key stakeholders such as customers and governments. For example, Citigroup, JPMorgan Chase, and Metallurgical Corporation of China have entered Afghanistan, earning a good deal of goodwill from the Afghan government that is interested in wooing more FDI.[12]

The potential advantages of first movers may be counter-balanced by various disadvantages, which are also listed in Exhibit 10.3. Numerous first-mover firms—such as EMI in CT scanners and Netscape in Internet browsers—have lost market dominance in the long run. It is such late-mover firms as General Electric and Microsoft (Internet Explorer) that win. Specifically, late-mover advantages are manifested in three ways. First, late movers may be able to free ride on the huge pioneering investments of first movers. In Saudi Arabia, Cisco invested millions of dollars to rub shoulders with dignitaries, including the king, in order to help officials grasp the promise of the Internet in fueling economic development, only to lose out to late movers such as Ericsson that offered lower cost solutions. For instance, the brand new King Abdullah Economic City awarded an $84 million citywide telecom project to Ericsson, whose bid was more than 20% lower than Cisco's—perhaps in part

because Ericsson did not have to spend the time and money up front involved in convincing Saudi Arabian officials to invest in the project. "We're very proud to have won against a company that did as much advance work as Cisco did," an elated Ericsson executive noted.[13]

Second, first movers face greater technological and market uncertainties. Nissan, for example, has launched the world's first all-electric car, the Leaf, which can run without a single drop of gasoline. However, there are tremendous uncertainties (see Chapter 14 Opening Case). After some of these uncertainties are removed, late movers such as GM and Toyota will join the game with their own all-electric cars.

Finally, as incumbents, first movers may be locked into a given set of fixed assets or reluctant to cannibalize existing product lines in favor of new ones. Late movers may be able to take advantage of the inflexibility of first movers by leapfrogging them. Although Greyhound, the incumbent in intercity bus service in the United States, is financially struggling, it cannot get rid of the expensive bus depots in inner cities that are often ill-maintained and dreadful. Megabus, the new entrant from Britain, simply has not bothered to build and maintain a single bus depot. Instead, Megabus uses curbside stops (like regular city bus stops), which have made travel by bus more appealing to a large number of passengers (see the Closing Case).

Overall, evidence points out both first-mover advantages and late-mover advantages. Unfortunately, a mountain of research is still unable to conclusively recommend a particular entry timing strategy. Although first movers may have an *opportunity* to win, their pioneering status is not a guarantee of success. For example, among the three first movers into the Chinese automobile industry in the early 1980s, Volkswagen has captured significant advantages, Chrysler has had very moderate success, and Peugeot failed and had to exit. Although many of the late movers that entered in the late 1990s are struggling, GM, Honda, and Hyundai have gained significant market shares. It is obvious that entry timing cannot be viewed in isolation and entry timing *per se* is not the sole determinant of success and failure of foreign entries. It is through *interaction* with other strategic variables that entry timing has an impact on performance.

Britain

LO4 List the steps in the comprehensive model of foreign market entries.

HOW TO ENTER?

In this section, we will first consider on what scale—large or small—a firm should enter foreign markets. Then we will look at a comprehensive model for entering foreign markets. The first step is to determine whether to pursue

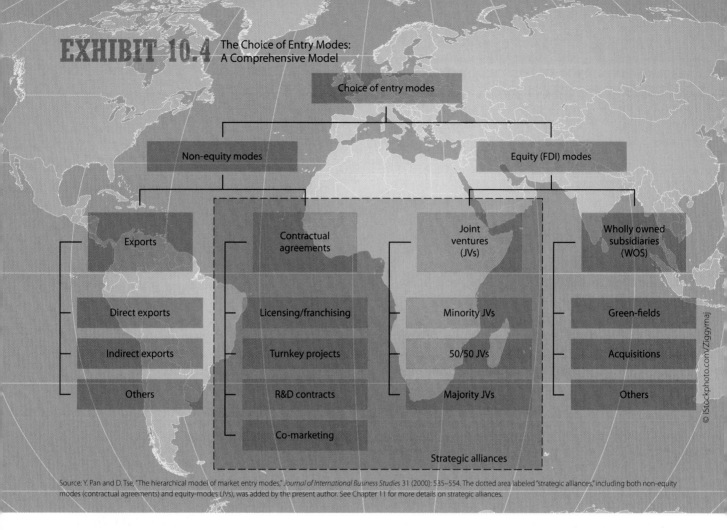

EXHIBIT 10.4 The Choice of Entry Modes: A Comprehensive Model

Source: Y. Pan and D. Tse, "The hierarchical model of market entry modes," *Journal of International Business Studies* 31 (2000): 535–554. The dotted area labeled "strategic alliances," including both non-equity modes (contractual agreements) and equity-modes (JVs), was added by the present author. See Chapter 11 for more details on strategic alliances.

an equity or non-equity mode of entry. As we will see, this crucial decision differentiates MNEs (involving equity modes) from non-MNEs (relying on non-equity modes). Finally, we outline the pros and cons of various equity and non-equity modes.

Scale of Entry: Commitment and Experience

One key dimension in foreign entry decisions is the **scale of entry**, which refers to the amount of resources committed to entering a foreign market. A number of European financial services firms such as ABN Amro, HSBC, and ING Group spent several billion dollars to enter the United States through a series of acquisitions. Such large-scale entries demonstrate a strategic commitment to certain markets. This helps assure local customers and suppliers ("We are here for the long haul!") as well as deter potential entrants.

The drawbacks of such a hard-to-reverse strategic commitment are (1) limited strategic flexibility elsewhere and (2) huge losses if these large-scale bets turn out to be wrong. For example, HSBC's acquisition of House-

hold in order to enter the US subprime mortgage market ended up burning an $11 billion hole on its balance sheet due to the financial market meltdown.

Small-scale entries are less costly. They focus on organizational learning by getting a firm's feet wet—learning by doing—while limiting the downside risk.[14] For example, to enter the market of Islamic finance in which no interest can be charged (according to the Koran), Citibank set up a subsidiary Citibank Islamic Bank. It was designed to experiment with different interpretations of the Koran on how to make money while not committing religious sins. It is simply not possible to acquire such ability outside the Islamic world. The drawback of small-scale entries is a lack of strong commitment, which may lead to difficulties in building market share and capturing first-mover advantages.

Modes of Entry: The First Step—Equity Versus Non-Equity Modes

Managers are unlikely to consider the numerous **modes of entry**, or methods used to enter a foreign market, all at the same time. Given the complexity of entry decisions, it is imperative that managers *prioritize* and consider only a few key variables first and then consider other variables later. The comprehensive model shown in Exhibits 10.4 and 10.5 are helpful.

EXHIBIT 10.5 Modes of Entry: Advantages and Disadvantages

Entry Modes	Advantages	Disadvantages
1. Non-equity modes: Exports		
Direct exports	• Economies of scale in production concentrated in the home country • Better control over distribution	• High transportation costs for bulky products • Marketing distance from customers • Trade barriers and protectionism
Indirect exports	• Concentration of resources on production • No need to directly handle export processes	• Less control over distribution (relative to direct exports) • Inability to learn how to compete overseas
2. Non-equity modes: Contractual agreements		
Licensing/franchising	• Low development costs • Low risk in overseas expansion	• Little control over technology and marketing • May create competitors • Inability to engage in global coordination
Turnkey projects	• Ability to earn returns from process technology in countries where FDI is restricted	• May create efficient competitors • Lack of long-term presence
Research and development (R&D) contracts	• Ability to tap into the best locations for certain innovations at low costs	• Difficult to negotiate and enforce contracts • May nurture innovative competitors • May lose core innovation capabilities
Co-marketing	• Ability to reach more customers	• Limited coordination
3. Equity modes: Partially owned subsidiaries		
Joint ventures	• Sharing costs, risks, and profits • Access to partners' knowledge and assets • Politically acceptable	• Divergent goals and interests of partners • Limited equity and operational control • Difficult to coordinate globally
4. Equity modes: Wholly owned subsidiaries		
Green-field operations	• Complete equity and operational control • Protection of know-how • Ability to coordinate globally	• Potential political problems and risks • High development costs • Add new capacity to industry • Slow entry speed (relative to acquisitions)
Acquisitions	• Same as green-field (above) • Do not add new capacity • Fast entry speed	• Same as green-field (above), except adding new capacity and slow speed • Post-acquisition integration problems

© Cengage Learning 2013

In the first step, considerations for small-scale versus large-scale entries usually boil down to the equity (ownership) issue. **Non-equity modes** include exports and contractual agreements and tend to reflect relatively smaller commitments to overseas markets. **Equity modes**, on the other hand, are indicative of relatively larger, harder-to-reverse commitments. Equity modes call for the establishment of independent organizations overseas (partially or wholly controlled). Non-equity modes do not require such independent establishments. Overall, these modes differ significantly in terms of cost, commitment, risk, return, and control.

The distinction between equity and non-equity modes is not trivial. In fact, it is what defines an MNE: An MNE enters foreign markets via equity modes through FDI. A firm that merely exports/imports with no FDI is usually not regarded as an MNE. As discussed at length in Chapter 6, an MNE, relative to a non-MNE, enjoys the three-pronged advantages of ownership, location, and internalization, col-

lectively known as the OLI advantages. Overall, the first step in entry mode considerations is crucial. A strategic decision has to be made in terms of whether or not to undertake FDI and to become an MNE.

Modes of Entry: The Second Step— Making Actual Selections

During the second step, managers consider variables within *each* group of non-equity and equity modes. If the decision is to export, then the next consideration is direct exports or indirect exports (also discussed in Chapter 9).

Non-equity mode
A mode of entering foreign markets through exports and/or contractual agreements that tends to reflect relatively smaller commitments to overseas markets.

Equity mode
A mode of entering foreign markets through joint ventures and/or wholly owned subsidiaries that indicates a relatively larger, harder-to-reverse commitment.

Dumping and Antidumping

Dumping is defined as an exporter (1) selling abroad below cost and (2) planning to raise prices after eliminating local rivals. Consider the following two scenarios. First, a steel producer in *Indiana* enters a new market, Texas. In Texas, it offers prices lower than those in Indiana, resulting in a 10% market share in Texas. Texas firms have two choices. The first one is to initiate a lawsuit against the Indiana firm for predatory pricing. However, it is difficult to prove (1) that the Indiana firm is selling below cost *and* (2) that its pricing is an attempt to monopolize. Under US antitrust laws, a predation case like this will have no chance of succeeding. Thus, Texas firms are most likely to opt for their second option: to retaliate in kind by offering lower prices to customers in Indiana, leading to lower prices in both Texas and Indiana, which benefit consumers there.

Now, in the second scenario, the invading firm is not from Indiana but *India*. Holding everything else constant, Texas steel firms can argue that the Indian firm is dumping. Under US antidumping laws, Texas steel producers, according to an expert, "would almost certainly obtain legal relief on the very same facts that would not support an antitrust *claim*, let alone antitrust relief." Note that imposing antidumping duties on Indian steel imports reduces the incentive for Texas firms to counter-attack by entering India, resulting in *higher* prices in both Texas and India, where consumers are hurt. These two scenarios are hypothetical but also highly realistic. An Organization for Economic Co-operation and Development (OECD) study in Australia, Canada, the European Union, and the United States reports that 90% of the practices classified as unfair dumping in these countries would never have been questioned under their own antitrust laws if used by a domestic firm in making a domestic sale. Simply filing an antidumping petition (regardless of the outcome), one study finds, may result in a 1% increase of the stock price for US-listed firms (an average of $46 million increase in market value). Evidently, Wall Street knows that Uncle Sam is on your side. In a nutshell, foreign firms are discriminated against by the formal rules of the game.

From an ethical standpoint, Joseph Stiglitz, a Nobel laureate in economics, writes that antidumping duties "are simply naked protectionism" and one country's "fair trade laws" are often known elsewhere as "unfair trade laws." A classic response is: What if, through unfair dumping, foreign rivals drive out local firms and then jack up prices? Given the competitive nature of most industries, it is often difficult (if not impossible) to eliminate all rivals and then recoup losses by charging higher monopoly prices. The fear of foreign monopoly is often exaggerated by special interest groups. One solution is to phase out antidumping laws and use the same standards as used in domestic predatory pricing. Such a waiver of antidumping charges has been in place between Australia and New Zealand, between Canada and the United States, and within the European Union. Thus, a Canadian firm, essentially treated as a US firm, can still be accused of predatory pricing but cannot be accused of dumping in the United States. However, domestically, a predation case is very difficult to make. In such a way, competition can be fostered, aggressiveness rewarded, and dumping legalized.

India

United States

Indiana

Texas

Sources: R. Lipstein, "Using antitrust principles to reform antidumping law," in E. Graham and D. Richardson (eds.), *Global Competition Policy* (Washington: Institute for International Economics, 1997) 405–438; S. Marsh, "Creating barriers for foreign competitors," *Strategic Management Journal* 19 (1998): 25–37; OECD, *Trade and Competition* (Paris: OECD, 1996); J. Stiglitz, *Globalization and Its Discontent* (New York: Norton, 2002) 20.

DEBATE
ETHICAL DILEMMA

Direct exports are the most basic mode of entry, capitalizing on economies of scale in production concentrated in the home country and providing better control over distribution. This strategy essentially treats foreign demand as an extension of domestic demand, and the firm is geared toward designing and producing first and foremost for the domestic market. While direct exports may work if the export volume is small, it is not optimal when the firm has a large number of foreign buyers. Marketing 101 suggests that the firm needs to be closer, both physically and psychologically, to its customers, prompting the firm to consider more intimate overseas involvement such as FDI. In addition, direct exports may provoke protectionism, triggering antidumping actions (see the Debate feature).

As you may recall from Chapter 9, another export strategy is indirect exports—namely, exporting through domestically based export intermediaries. This strategy not only enjoys the economies of scale in domestic production (similar to direct exports) but is also relatively worry free. A significant amount of export trade in commodities such as textiles, woods, and meats, which compete primarily on price, is indirect through intermediaries.[15] Indirect exports have some drawbacks. For example, third parties such as export trading companies may not share the same

Dumping
Exporting products at prices that are below what it costs to manufacture them, with the intent to raise prices after eliminating local rivals.

agendas and objectives as exporters. Exporters choose intermediaries primarily because of information asymmetries concerning risks and uncertainties associated with foreign markets.[16] Intermediaries with international contacts and knowledge essentially make a living by taking advantage of such information asymmetries. They may have a vested interest in making sure that such asymmetries are not reduced. Intermediaries, for example, may repackage the products under their own brand and insist on monopolizing the communication with overseas customers. If the exporter is interested in knowing more about how its products perform overseas, indirect exports would not provide such knowledge.

The next group of non-equity entry modes involves the following types of contractual agreement: (1) licensing or franchising, (2) turnkey projects, (3) research and development contracts, and (4) co-marketing. Recall from Chapter 9 that in licensing/franchising agreements, the licensor/franchisor sells the rights to intellectual property such as patents and know-how to the licensee/franchisee for a royalty fee. The licensor/franchisor, thus, does not have to bear the full costs and risks associated with foreign expansion. On the other hand, the licensor/franchisor does not have tight control over production and marketing.

In **turnkey projects**, clients pay contractors to design and construct new facilities and train personnel. At project completion, contractors hand clients the proverbial key to facilities ready for operations, hence the term "turnkey." This mode allows firms to earn returns from process technology (such as power generation) in countries where FDI is restricted. The drawbacks, however, are twofold. First, if foreign clients are competitors, selling them state-of-the-art technology through turnkey projects may boost their competitiveness. Second, turnkey projects do not allow for a long-term presence after the key is handed to clients. To obtain a longer-term presence, build-operate-transfer agreements are now often used, instead of the traditional build-transfer type of turnkey projects. A **build-operate-transfer (BOT) agreement** is a non-equity mode of entry used to build a longer-term presence by building and then operating a facility for a period of time before transferring operations to a domestic agency or firm. For example, a consortium of German, Italian, and Iranian firms obtained a large-scale BOT power-generation project in Iran. After completion of the construction, the consortium will operate the project for 20 years before transferring it to the Iranian government.

Research and development (R&D) contracts refer to outsourcing agreements in R&D between firms. Firm A agrees to perform certain R&D work for Firm B. Firms thereby tap into the best locations for certain innovations at relatively low costs, such as aerospace research in Russia. However, three drawbacks may emerge. First, given the uncertain and multidimensional nature of R&D, these contracts are often difficult to negotiate and enforce. While delivery time and costs are relatively easy to negoti-ate, quality is often difficult to assess. Second, such contracts may cultivate competitors. A number of Indian IT firms, nurtured by such work, are now on a global offensive to take on their Western rivals. Finally, firms that rely on outsiders to perform a lot of R&D may lose some of their core R&D capabilities in the long run.

Co-marketing refers to efforts among a number of firms to jointly market their products and services. Toy makers and movie studios often collaborate in co-marketing campaigns with fast-food chains such as McDonald's to package toys based on movie characters in kids' meals. Airline alliances such as One World and Star Alliance engage in extensive co-marketing through code sharing. The advantages are the ability to reach more customers. The drawbacks center on limited control and coordination.

Next are equity modes, all of which entail some FDI and transform the firm to an MNE. A **joint venture (JV)** is a corporate child, a new entity jointly created and owned by two or more parent companies. It has three principal forms: Minority JV (less than 50% equity), 50/50 JV (equal equity), and majority JV (more than 50% equity). JVs, such as Shanghai Volkswagen, have three advantages. First, an MNE shares costs, risks, and profits with a local partner, so the MNE possesses a certain degree of control but limits risk exposure. Second, the MNE gains access to knowledge about the host country; the local firm, in turn, benefits from the MNE's technology, capital, and management. Third, JVs may be politically more acceptable in host countries.

In terms of disadvantages, JVs often involve partners from different backgrounds and with different goals, so conflicts are natural. Furthermore, effective equity and operational control may be difficult to achieve since everything has to be negotiated—in some cases, fought over. Finally, the nature of the JV does not give an MNE the tight control over a foreign subsidiary that it may need for global coordination.

Turnkey project
A project in which clients pay contractors to design and construct new facilities and train personnel.

Build-operate-transfer (BOT) agreement
A non-equity mode of entry used to build a longer-term presence by building and then operating a facility for a period of time before transferring operations to a domestic agency or firm.

Research and development (R&D) contract
Outsourcing agreements in R&D between firms.

Co-marketing
Efforts among a number of firms to jointly market their products and services.

Joint venture (JV)
A new corporate entity jointly created and owned by two or more parent companies.

Overall, all sorts of non-equity-based contractual agreements and equity-based JVs can be broadly considered as strategic alliances (within the *dotted area* in Exhibit 10.4); Chapter 11 will discuss them in detail.

The last entry mode is to establish a **wholly owned subsidiary (WOS)**, defined as a subsidiary located in a foreign country that is entirely owned by the parent multinational. There are two primary means to set up a WOS. One is to establish **green-field operations**, building new factories and offices from scratch (on a proverbial piece of "green field" formerly used for agricultural purposes). For example, PRPG America, Ltd., is a wholly owned green-field subsidiary of Pearl River Piano Group of China (see the Opening Case). There are three advantages. First, a green-field WOS gives an MNE complete equity and management control, thus eliminating the headaches associated with JVs. Second, this undivided control leads to better protection of proprietary technology. Third, a WOS allows for centrally coordinated global actions. Sometimes a subsidiary will be ordered to launch actions that by design will *lose* money. In the semiconductor market, TI faced competition from Japanese rivals such as NEC and Toshiba that maintained low prices outside of Japan by charging high prices in Japan and using domestic profits to cross-subsidize overseas expansion. By entering Japan via a WOS and slashing prices there, TI incurred a loss but forced the Japanese firms to defend their profit sanctuary at home, where they had more to lose. This was because Japanese rivals had a much larger market share in Japan, so when the price level in Japan collapsed thanks to the aggressive price cutting unleashed by TI's WOS in the country, NEC and Toshiba would suffer much more significant losses. Consequently, Japanese rivals had to reduce the ferocity of their price wars outside of Japan. Local licensees/franchisees or JV partners are unlikely to accept such a subservient role as being ordered to lose money (!).

In terms of drawbacks, a green-field WOS tends to be expensive and risky, not only financially but also politically. Its conspicuous foreignness may become a target for nationalistic sentiments. Another drawback is that green-field operations add new capacity to an industry, which will make a competitive industry more crowded. For example, think of all the Japanese automobile plants built in the United States, which have severely squeezed the market share of US automakers and forced Chrysler and GM

into bankruptcy. Finally, green-field operations suffer from a slow entry speed of at least one to several years (relative to acquisitions).

The other way to establish a WOS is through an acquisition. Although this is the last mode we discuss here, it represents approximately 70% of worldwide FDI. Acquisition shares all the benefits of green-field WOS but enjoys two additional advantages, namely: (1) adding no new capacity and (2) faster entry speed. In terms of drawbacks, acquisition shares all of the disadvantages of green-field WOS except adding new capacity and slow entry speed. But acquisition has a unique and potentially devastating disadvantage: post-acquisition integration problems. (See Chapter 11 for more details.)

> **LO6** *Explain what you should do to make your firm's entry into a foreign market successful.*

MANAGEMENT SAVVY

Foreign market entries represent a *foundation* for overseas actions. Without these crucial first steps, firms will remain domestic players. The challenges associated with internationalization are daunting, the complexities enormous, and the stakes high. Returning to our fundamental question, we ask: What determines success and failure in foreign market entries? The answer boils down to the two core perspectives: institution-based and resource-based views. Shown in Exhibit 10.6, three implications for action emerge from these perspectives. First, from an institution-based view, managers need to understand the rules of the game, both formal and informal, governing competition in foreign markets. Failure to understand these rules can be costly.

Second, from a resource-based view, managers need to develop overwhelming capabilities to offset the liability of foreignness. For example, over the last two years, which car company has had the highest growth in China, India, and

EXHIBIT 10.6 Implications for Action

- Understand the rules of game—both formal and informal—governing competition in foreign markets.
- Develop overwhelming resources and capabilities to offset the liability of foreignness.
- Match efforts in market entry with strategic goals.

© Cengage Learning 2013

Wholly owned subsidiary (WOS)
A subsidiary located in a foreign country that is entirely owned by the parent multinational.

Green-field operations
Building factories and offices from scratch (on a proverbial piece of "green field" formerly used for agricultural purposes).

"Green-field operations suffer from a slow entry speed."

© iStockphoto.com/Dušan Janković

Russia? It is Hyundai. Hyundai's secret? Its cars come with relatively advanced features such as airbags and anti-lock brakes that local rivals do not include. Relative to more expensive foreign (especially Japanese) rivals, Hyundai cars sell at a more reasonable price. Such an unbeatable combination may eventually enable Hyundai to join the Top Five global automakers.

Finally, managers need to match entries with strategic goals. If the goal is to deter rivals in their home markets through price slashing as TI did in Japan, then be prepared to fight a nasty price war and lose money. If the goal is to generate decent returns, then it may be necessary to withdraw from some tough markets, as when Wal-Mart withdrew from Germany and South Korea.

CLOSING CASE

ENTER THE UNITED STATES BY BUS

If you are a college student in the United States studying in the Midwest or the Northeast, you may have heard of (or may have taken a ride on) Megabus. Its website announces that it is "the first, low-cost, express bus service to offer city-to-city travel for as low as $1 via the Internet." Currently serving 50 US cities from five hubs (Chicago, New York, Philadelphia, Pittsburgh, and Washington, DC), Megabus, according to *Bloomberg Businessweek*, "has fundamentally changed the way Americans—especially the young—travel."

A generation ago, Greyhound was a national icon for intercity travel. Unfortunately, as Americans fell more in love with cars and the cost of airfares dropped further, intercity bus ridership steadily decreased. Further, as inner cities, where the bus depots (terminals) were situated, decayed, bus travel had been associated with the stigma of second-class citizenship, which would be the travel mode of last resort. In 1990, Greyhound filed for Chapter 11 bankruptcy.

Yet, the demand for medium-distance trips that are ideal for intercity bus does not go away. For some of the most travelled routes (such as between Chicago and Detroit and between New York and DC), the distance is too far for a leisurely drive but too close to justify the expense (and increasingly the hassle) of air travel. While Greyhound has been in decline, small, entrepreneurial bus operators, known as the "Chinatown buses," emerged. They started by shuttling passengers (primarily recent Chinese immigrants) between Chinatowns in New York and Boston. Such niche operators quickly grabbed the attention of many college students. Despite four decades of decline, overall US intercity bus ridership spiked in 2006, the year Megabus entered the market.

Although Megabus is a brand new, no-frills entrant into the US market, it is backed by the full strengths of the second largest transport firm in the UK, Stagecoach Group, which employs 18,000 people there. Founded in 1980 and headquartered in Perth, Scotland, Stagecoach operates not only buses, but also trains, trams, and ferries throughout the UK, moving 2.5 million passengers every day. It is listed on the London Stock Exchange (its ticker name is LSE: SGC), where it is a member of the FTSE 250 (the 250 largest firms in the UK, similar to the Fortune 500 group in the US). Megabus is a brand of Stagecoach's wholly owned US subsidiary, Coach USA.

Stagecoach is not a stranger to international forays, having previously operated in Hong Kong, Kenya, Malawi, New Zealand, Portugal, and Sweden. However, these operations turned out to be lackluster and were all sold. For now, the sole international market it focuses on is North America (Megabus entered Canada in 2008).

Although Megabus is clearly a late mover in North America, its future looks bright. So what allows Megabus to turn a declining national trend of bus ridership around? At least four features stand out. First, tickets are super cheap, starting at $1 (!). Megabus uses a yield management system, typically used by airlines, which offers early passengers dirt cheap deals and late passengers higher prices. Although only one or two passengers per trip can get the $1 deal, even the "higher" prices are very competitive. In routes where it competes with Amtrak (the railway), Megabus costs about a tenth of Amtrak. All tickets have to be booked online. This not only eliminates the expenses of maintaining ticket booths, but also attracts a more educated demographic group.

Second, instead of using depots, Megabus follows the Chinatown buses by using curbside stops (like regular city bus stops) to board and disembark passengers. Interestingly, dumping the depot model not only saves a lot of money, but also makes Megabus more attractive, because passengers do not have to spend time in the poorly maintained (and sometimes filthy and unsafe) bus depots.

Third, all Megabus coaches are equipped with Wi-Fi and power outlets, allowing the time on board to be more productive (or more fun). These features, which are typically not available even when flying first class, have made travel by bus totally cool to the online-savvy, younger crowd. Among surveyed passengers, 37% said that Wi-Fi and power outlets were central to their decision to travel by Megabus.

Finally, as gas prices skyrocket and environmental consciousness rises, especially among America's college students, bus travel offers an unbeatable "green" advantage. At eight cents per mile, a bus is four times more fuel-efficient than a car. US curbside carriers, led by Megabus, have already reduced fuel consumption by 11 million gallons a year, equivalent to taking 24,000 cars off the road. While politicians like to talk about the "bright future" of high-speed rail, and the Obama administration has budgeted $10.4 billion to jump-start new rail projects, not a single mile of high-speed rail tracks has been laid as of this writing. At the same time, Megabus has been charging ahead and carrying more than 7 million passengers since its entry, while requiring zero additional investment in infrastructure. Texas, Florida, and California are some of the markets it may enter soon. Given the cost and political headache to build new high-speed rail, *Bloomberg Businessweek* speculated: "The Megabus approach works so well, it may scuttle plans for high-speed rail."

Sources: Megabus, 2011, www.megabus.com; Stagecoach Group, 2011, www.stagecoachgroup .com; "The Megabus effect," *Bloomberg Businessweek*, 11 April 2011: 62–67.

Making Alliances &ACQUISITIONS Work

CHAPTER 11

ETHICAL DILEMMA
Danone and Wahaha: From Alliance to Divorce

In 1996, France's Groupe Danone established five joint ventures (JVs) with China's Wahaha Group. Danone owned 51% of each of these JVs and Wahaha and its employees owned the remainder. Founded in 1987, Wahaha boasts one of the best-known beverage brands in China. By 2006, the total number of JVs between Danone and Wahaha had grown from 5 to 39. A huge financial success for both Danone and Wahaha, their JVs' revenues increased from $100 million in 1996 to $2.25 billion in 2006. These JVs, which cost Danone $170 million, paid Danone a total of $307 million in dividends over the past decade. By 2006, Danone's 39 JV subsidiaries in China, jointly owned and managed by Wahaha, contributed 6% of Danone's total global profits.

In addition to the JVs with Wahaha, Danone also bought stakes in more than seven Chinese food and dairy firms, spending another $170 million (besides what had been spent on Wahaha)

over the past decade in China. In 2006, Danone became the biggest beverage maker by volume in China, ahead of rivals such as Coca-Cola and PepsiCo. At the same time, Wahaha also pursued aggressive growth in China, some of which was beyond the scope of the JVs with Danone. By 2006, Wahaha Group managed 70 subsidiaries scattered throughout China. All these subsidiaries used the same Wahaha brand, but only 39 of them had JV relationships with Danone.

A major dispute erupted concerning Wahaha's other 31 subsidiaries that had no JV relationships with Danone. In 2006, after profits from the 39 JVs jumped 48% to $386 million, Danone wanted to buy Wahaha's other subsidiaries. This would enable Danone to control the Wahaha brand once and for all. This proposal was rejected by Wahaha's founder Zong Qinghou, who served as chairman of the 39 JVs with Danone. Zong viewed this

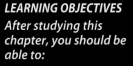

LEARNING OBJECTIVES
After studying this chapter, you should be able to:

define alliances and acquisitions.

articulate how institutions and resources influence alliances and acquisitions.

describe how alliances are formed.

outline how alliances are dissolved.

discuss how alliances perform.

explain why firms undertake acquisitions and what performance problems they tend to encounter.

articulate what you can do to make global alliances and acquisitions successful.

offer as unreasonable because the book value of the non–JV subsidiaries' assets was $700 million with total profits of $130 million, while the price/earnings ratio of Danone's $500 million offer was lower than 4:1. Zong also asserted that the buyout would jeopardize the existence of the Wahaha brand, because Danone would phase it out and promote global brands such as Danone and Evian.

The heart of the dispute stemmed from the master JV agreement between Danone and Wahaha, which granted the subsidiary JVs exclusive rights to produce, distribute, and sell food and beverage products under the Wahaha brand. This meant that every product using the Wahaha brand should be approved by the board of the master JV. Danone thus claimed that the non–JV subsidiaries set up by Zong and his managers were illegally selling products using the Wahaha brand and were making unlawful use of the JVs' distributors and suppliers. However, Zong claimed that the original JV agreement to grant exclusive rights to use the Wahaha brand was never approved by the Chinese trademark office and so was not in force or effect. He further stated that Danone had not made an issue when Wahaha embarked on its expansion and openly used the subsidiary JVs' assets—it seemed that Danone preferred Wahaha to shoulder the risk first. According to Zong, when Wahaha's expansion proved successful, Danone, driven by greed, wanted to reap the fruits. Finally, Zong argued that forcing Wahaha Group to grant the exclusive rights for the Wahaha brand to the JVs with Danone was unfair to Wahaha Group, because Danone was actively investing in other beverage companies around the country and competing with Wahaha. Wahaha pointed out that in human marriage terms, these would be extramarital affairs.

The boardroom dispute spilled into the public domain when Zong publicly criticized Danone in April 2007. In response, Danone issued statements and initiated arbitrations against Wahaha in Stockholm, Sweden. Danone also launched a lawsuit against a company owned by Zong's daughter in the United States, alleging that it was using the Wahaha brand illegally. Outraged, Zong resigned from his board chairman position at all the JVs with Danone. Wahaha's trade union, representing about 10,000 workers of

Wahaha Group, sued Danone in late 2007, demanding $1.36 million in damages. This made the dispute worse, and revenues of the JVs only increased 3% in 2007, during which the industry grew 17% on average.

Between 2007 and 2009, both sides spent most of their energy dealing with over 21 lawsuits and arbitrations in several countries, including not only China and France, but also the British Virgin Islands, Italy, Sweden, and the United States. Even the French president and Chinese minister of commerce called for the two parties to stop lawsuits and to settle. Danone spent $83 million in litigation fees in three years but won no victory. Finally, Danone gave up its 51% share in the JVs and sold it to Wahaha in September 2009. No financial terms were publicly disclosed. A person familiar with the matter said the settlement amount was "slightly below" the figure Danone cited in previously published financial accounts as the value of its Wahaha holdings: $555 million.

From an ethical standpoint, we can wonder whether the divorce was caused by opportunism from the start or by "changed circumstances" as the relationship evolved. Even with the painful divorce, Danone still earned enviable financial returns. A Danone spokesman defended the JV strategy: "If we now have 30% of our sales in emerging markets and we built this in only ten years, it's thanks to this specific [JV] strategy. We have problems with Wahaha. But we prefer to have problems with Wahaha now to not having had Wahaha at all for the last ten years." Wahaha's Zong said in the settlement announcement: "Chinese companies are willing to cooperate and grow with the world's leading peers on the basis of equality and reciprocal benefit."

Sources: This case was written by Professor Sunny Li Sun (University of Missouri–Kansas City) and Professor Hao Chen (Tsinghua University, Beijing). "Chinese drinks giant brands Danone 'espicable' over lawsuit," *China Daily*, 8 June 2007; http://finance.sina.com.cn/focus/2007wahaha; M. W. Peng, S. L. Sun, and H. Chen, "Managing divorce: How to disengage from joint ventures and strategic alliances," *Peking University Business Review* (April 2008); "Danone pulls out of disputed China venture," *Wall Street Journal*, 1 October 2009.

Why did Danone and Wahaha form strategic alliances? Among many forms of alliances, why did they choose joint ventures (JVs)? Why did the JVs fail? Why did Wahaha agree to acquire Danone's equity in the failed JVs? These are some of the key questions we address in this chapter. Alliances and acquisitions are two major strategies for firms around the world, thus necessitating our attention.

This chapter first defines alliances and acquisitions, followed by a discussion on how institution-based and resource-based views shed light on these topics. We then discuss the formation, evolution, and performance of alliances and acquisitions.

Strategic alliances
Voluntary agreements of cooperation between firms.

Contractual (non-equity-based) alliance
An association between firms that is based on a contract and does not involve the sharing of ownership.

LO1 *Define alliances and acquisitions.*

DEFINING ALLIANCES AND ACQUISITIONS

Strategic alliances are voluntary agreements of cooperation between firms. Remember that the dotted area in Exhibit 10.4 in Chapter 10 consists of non-equity-based contractual agreements and equity-based JVs. These can all be broadly considered as strategic alliances. Exhibit 11.1 illustrates this further, depicting alliances as degrees of *compromise* between pure market transactions and acquisitions. **Contractual (non-equity-based) alliances** are associations between firms that are based on contracts and do not involve the sharing of ownership. They include comarketing, research and development (R&D) contracts, turnkey projects, strategic suppliers, strategic distributors,

EXHIBIT 11.1 The Variety of Strategic Alliances

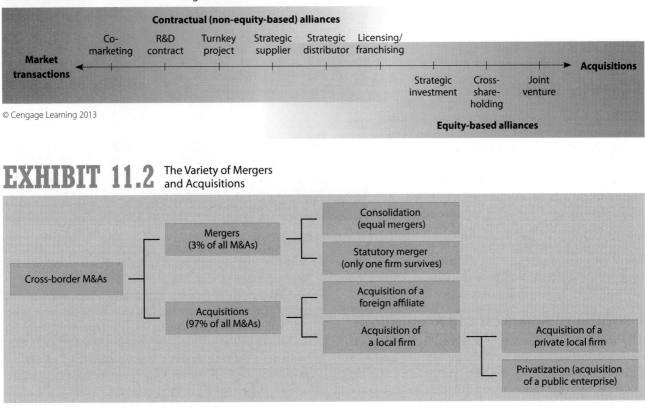

Contractual (non-equity-based) alliances

Market transactions ← Co-marketing | R&D contract | Turnkey project | Strategic supplier | Strategic distributor | Licensing/franchising | Strategic investment | Cross-share-holding | Joint venture → Acquisitions

Equity-based alliances

© Cengage Learning 2013

EXHIBIT 11.2 The Variety of Mergers and Acquisitions

Cross-border M&As
- Mergers (3% of all M&As)
  - Consolidation (equal mergers)
  - Statutory merger (only one firm survives)
- Acquisitions (97% of all M&As)
  - Acquisition of a foreign affiliate
  - Acquisition of a local firm
    - Acquisition of a private local firm
    - Privatization (acquisition of a public enterprise)

Source: United Nations, *World Investment Report 2000* (New York: UNCTAD, 2000) 100.

and licensing/franchising. **Equity-based alliances**, on the other hand, are based on ownership or financial interest between the firms. They include **strategic investment** (one partner invests in another) and **cross-shareholding** (each partner invests in the other). Equity-based alliances also include JVs, which involve the establishment of a new legally independent entity (in other words, a new firm) whose equity is provided by two or more partners.

Although JVs are often used as examples of alliances (as in the Opening Case), *not* all alliances are JVs. A JV is a corporate child produced by two or more parent firms, as is the case with Sony Ericsson. A non-JV, equity-based alliance can be regarded as two firms getting married but not having children. For example, Renault is a strategic investor in Nissan, but both automakers still operate independently. They have *not* given birth to a new car company; if they did, the new company would be a JV.

An **acquisition** is a transfer of the control of operations and management from one firm (target) to another (acquirer), the former becoming a unit of the latter. For example, Volvo is now a unit of China's Geely. A **merger** is the combination of operations and management of two firms to establish a new legal entity. For instance, the merger between South African Brewery and Miller Beer resulted in SABMiller.

Although the phrase "mergers and acquisitions" (M&As) is often used, in reality acquisitions dominate the scene. Only 3% of M&As are mergers. For practical purposes, "M&As" basically mean "acquisitions." Consequently, we will use the two terms "M&As" and "acquisitions" interchangeably. Specifically, we focus on cross-border (international) M&As (Exhibit 11.2). This is not only because of our global interest but also because of (1) the high percentage (about 30%) of international deals among all M&As and (2) the high percentage (about 70%) of M&As among foreign direct investment (FDI) flows.

Equity-based alliance
An association between firms that is based on shared ownership or financial interest.

Strategic investment
A business strategy in which one firm invests in another.

Cross-shareholding
A business strategy in which each partner in an alliance holds stock in the other firm.

Acquisition
The transfer of the control of operations and management from one firm (target) to another (acquirer), the former becoming a unit of the latter.

Merger
The combination of operations and management of two firms to establish a new legal entity.

© iStockphoto.com/Tomislav Forgo

HOW INSTITUTIONS AND RESOURCES AFFECT ALLIANCES AND ACQUISITIONS

What drives alliances? What drives acquisitions? We will now draw on the institution-based and resource-based views to shed light on these important questions. The institution-based view suggests that as rules of the game, institutions influence how a firm chooses between alliances and acquisitions in terms of its strategy.[1] However, rules are not made just for one firm. The resource-based view argues that although a number of firms may be governed by the same set of rules, some excel more than others because of the differences in firm-specific capabilities that make alliances and acquisitions work (see Exhibit 11.3).

Institutions, Alliances, and Acquisitions

Alliances function within a set of formal legal and regulatory frameworks. The impact of these *formal institutions* on alliances and acquisitions can be found along two dimensions: (1) antitrust concerns and (2) entry mode requirements. First, many firms establish alliances with competitors. For example, Siemens and Bosch compete in automotive components and collaborate in household appliances. Antitrust authorities suspect at least some tacit collusion when competitors cooperate. However, because integration within alliances is usually not as tight as acquisitions (which would eliminate one competitor), antitrust authorities are more likely to approve alliances as opposed to acquisitions. A proposed merger of American Airlines and British Airways was blocked by both US and UK antitrust authorities. But the two airlines were allowed to form an alliance that has eventually grown to become the multi-partner OneWorld.

Another way formal institutions affect alliances and acquisitions is through formal requirements on market entry modes. In many countries, governments discourage or simply ban acquisitions to establish wholly owned subsidiaries (WOSs), thereby leaving some sort of alliance with local firms as the only entry choice for FDI. For example, before NAFTA went into effect in 1994, the Mexican government not only limited multinationals' entries to JVs but also dictated a maximum equity position of 49% for the multinational enterprise (MNE).

Recently, two trends have emerged in the entry mode requirements dictated by formal government policies. First is a general trend toward more liberal policies. Many governments that historically approved only JVs as an entry mode (such as those in Mexico and South Korea) now allow WOSs. As a result, JVs have declined and acquisitions have increased in emerging economies.[2] Despite the general movement toward more liberal policies, a second noticeable trend is that many governments still impose considerable requirements, especially when foreign firms acquire domestic assets. The strategically important Chinese automobile assembly industry and the Russian oil industry permit only JVs, thus eliminating acquisitions as a choice. US regulations limit foreign carriers to a maximum 25% of the equity in any US airline, and EU regulations limit non–EU ownership of EU-based airlines to 49%.

Informal institutions also influence alliances and acquisitions. The first set of informal

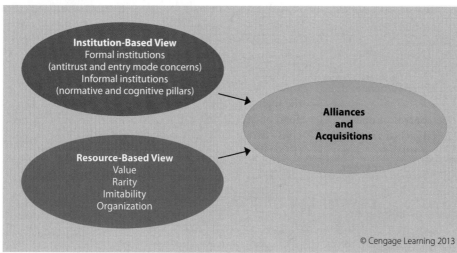

EXHIBIT 11.3 Institutions, Resources, Alliances, and Acquisitions

Institution-Based View
Formal institutions
(antitrust and entry mode concerns)
Informal institutions
(normative and cognitive pillars)

Resource-Based View
Value
Rarity
Imitability
Organization

Alliances and Acquisitions

© Cengage Learning 2013

EXHIBIT 11.4 Strategic Alliances: Advantages and Disadvantages

Advantages	Disadvantages
Reduce costs, risks, and uncertainties	Choosing wrong partners
Access complementary assets and learning opportunities	Potential partner opportunism
Possibility to use alliances as real options	Risk of helping nurture competitors (learning race)

institutions centers on collective norms, supported by a normative pillar. A core idea of the institution-based view is that because firms want to enhance or protect their legitimacy, copying what other reputable organizations are doing—even without knowing the direct performance benefits of doing so—may be a low-cost way to gain legitimacy. Thus, when a firm sees competitors entering alliances, that firm may jump on the alliance bandwagon just to be safe rather than risk ignoring industry trends. When M&As appear to be the trend, even managers with doubts about the wisdom of M&As may nevertheless be tempted to hunt for acquisition targets. Although not every alliance or acquisition decision is driven by imitation, this motivation seems to explain a lot of these activities. The flip side is that many firms rush into alliances and acquisitions without due diligence and then get burned big time.

A second set of informal institutions emphasizes the cognitive pillar, which is centered on internalized, taken-for-granted values and beliefs that guide alliances and acquisitions. For example, Britain's BAE Systems announced that *all* of its future aircraft development programs would involve alliances. Likewise, in the area of acquisitions, Spain's Santander is a firm believer. It has undertaken a total of $70 billion of acquisitions throughout Europe, Latin America, and now North America.[3] Clearly, managers at BAE Systems and Santander believe that such alliances and acquisitions, respectively, are the right (and sometimes the only) thing to do, which have become part of their informal norms and beliefs.

Resources and Alliances

How does the VRIO framework that characterizes the resource-based view influence alliances?

 VALUE Alliances must create value. The three global airline alliance networks—OneWorld, SkyTeam, and Star Alliance—create value by reducing ticket costs by 18% to 28% on two-stage flights compared with separate flights on the same route if the airlines were not allied.[4] Exhibit 11.4 identifies three broad categories of value creation in terms of how advantages outweigh disadvantages. First, alliances may reduce costs, risks, and uncertainties. As Google rises to preeminence, industry rivals such as eBay, Yahoo!, and Microsoft (MSN) are now exploring alliances to counter Google's influence while not taking on excessive risks. Second, alliances allow firms to tap into partners' complementary assets and facilitate

learning. That is how Sony and Ericsson pooled resources together to develop new cell phones via a JV named Sony Ericsson.

Finally, an important advantage of alliances lies in their value as real options. Conceptually, an option is the right (but not obligation) to take some action in the future. Technically, a financial option is an investment instrument permitting its holder, having paid for a small fraction of an asset, the right to increase investment by eventually acquiring the asset if necessary. A **real option** is an investment in real operations as opposed to financial capital.[5] A real options view suggests two propositions:

+ In the first phase, an investor makes a small, initial investment to buy an option, which leads to the right to future investment but is not an obligation to do so.

+ The investor then holds the option until a decision point arrives in the second phase and then decides between exercising the option or abandoning it.

For firms interested in eventually acquiring other companies but uncertain about such moves, working together in alliances affords an insider view to the capabilities of these partners. This is similar to trying on new shoes to see if they fit before buying them. Since acquisitions are not only costly but also very likely to fail, alliances permit firms to *sequentially* increase their investment should they decide to pursue acquisitions. If after working together as partners a firm finds that an acquisition is not a good idea, there is no obligation to pursue it. Overall, alliances have emerged as great instruments of real options because of their flexibility to sequentially scale the investment *up* or *down*.

On the other hand, alliances have a number of nontrivial drawbacks. First, there is always a possibility of being stuck with the wrong partner(s). Firms are advised to choose a prospective partner with caution, preferably a known entity. Yet, the partner should also be sufficiently differentiated to provide some complementary (non-overlapping) capabilities. Many firms find it difficult to evaluate the true intentions and capabilities of their prospective partners until it is too late.

A second disadvantage is potential partner opportunism. While opportunism is likely in any kind of economic relationship, the alliance setting may provide especially strong incentives for some (but not necessarily

Real option
An investment in real operations as opposed to financial capital.

all) partners to be opportunistic. A cooperative relationship always entails some elements of trust that may be easily abused. In the Opening Case, both Danone and Wahaha accused each other of being opportunistic.

 RARITY The ability to successfully manage interfirm relationships—often called **relational (or collaborative) capabilities**—tends to be rare. Managers involved in alliances require relationship skills rarely covered in the traditional business school curriculum, which typically emphasizes competition rather than collaboration. To truly derive benefits from alliances, managers need to foster trust with partners yet be on guard against opportunism.[6]

As much as alliances represent a strategic and economic arrangement, they also constitute a social, psychological, and emotional phenomenon. Words such as "courtship," "marriage," and "divorce" are often used when discussing alliances. Given that the interests of partner firms do not fully overlap and are often in conflict, managers involved in alliances live a precarious existence, trying to represent the interests of their respective firms while attempting to make the complex relationship work. Not surprisingly, sound relational capabilities necessary to successfully manage alliances are in short supply.

 IMITABILITY Imitability occurs at two levels in alliances: (1) firm level and (2) alliance level. At the firm level, alliances between rivals can be dangerous because they may help competitors. By opening their doors to outsiders, alliances make it *easier* to observe and imitate firm-specific capabilities. A **learning race** can arise in which partners aim to learn and imitate each other's tricks as fast as possible. For example, in the late 1980s, McDonald's set up a JV with the Moscow Municipality Government to help the fast-food chain enter Russia. During the 1990s, however, the Moscow mayor set up a rival fast-food chain, The Bistro. The Bistro replicated many of the fast-food giant's products and practices. McDonald's could do little about the situation because nobody sues the mayor in Moscow and hopes to win.

Relational (or collaborative) capability
The ability to successfully manage interfirm relationships.

Learning race
A situation in which alliance partners aim to learn the other firm's "tricks" as fast as possible.

Acquisition premium
The difference between the acquisition price and the market value of target firms.

At the alliance level, another imitability issue is the trust and understanding among partners in successful alliances. Firms without genuine trust and understanding may have a hard time faking it. CFM International, a JV set up by GE and Snecma to produce jet engines in France, has successfully operated for over 30 years. Rivals would have a hard time imitating such a successful relationship.

 ORGANIZATION Some successful alliance relationships are organized in a way that is difficult to replicate. Leo Tolstoy makes the observation in the opening sentence of *Anna Karenina*: "All happy families are alike; each unhappy family is unhappy in its own way." Much the same can be said for business alliances. Each failed alliance has its own mistakes and problems, and firms in unsuccessful alliances (for whatever reason) often find it exceedingly challenging, if not impossible, to organize and manage their interfirm relationships better.

Resources and Acquisitions

 VALUE Do acquisitions create *value*? Overall, their performance record is sobering. As many as 70% of acquisitions reportedly fail.[7] On average, acquiring firms' performance does not improve after acquisitions. Target firms, after being acquired and becoming internal units, often perform worse than when they were independent, stand-alone firms. The only identifiable group of winners is the shareholders of target firms, who may experience on average a 24% increase in their stock value during the period of the transaction. This increase is due to the **acquisition premium**, which is defined as the difference between the acquisition price and the market value of target firms. Shareholders of acquiring firms experience a 4% loss in their stock value during the same period. The combined wealth of shareholders of both acquiring and target firms is only marginally positive, less than 2%.[8] Consider DaimlerChrysler. In 1998, Daimler paid $35 billion for Chrysler with a 40% premium. In 2007, Chrysler was sold to Cerberus Capital Management, a private equity firm, for $7.4 billion, only one fifth of what Daimler paid for it.

 RARITY For acquisitions to add value, one or all of the firms involved must have unique skills that enhance the overall strategy. In other words, the firms must have rare skills to make the acquisition work. In 2004, an executive team at Lenovo, China's leading PC maker, planned to acquire IBM's PC division. Lenovo's board, however, raised a crucial question: If a venerable American technology company had failed to profit from the PC business, did Lenovo have what it takes to do better when managing such a complex global business? The answer was actually "No." The board gave its blessing to the plan only when the acquisition team agreed to acquire the business *and* to recruit top American executives.

 IMITABILITY While many firms undertake acquisitions, a much smaller number of them have mastered the art of post-acquisition integration. Consequently, firms that excel in integration possess *hard-to-imitate* capabilities. For example, each of Northrop Grumman's acquisitions must conform to a carefully orchestrated plan of

EXHIBIT 11.5 Alliance Formation

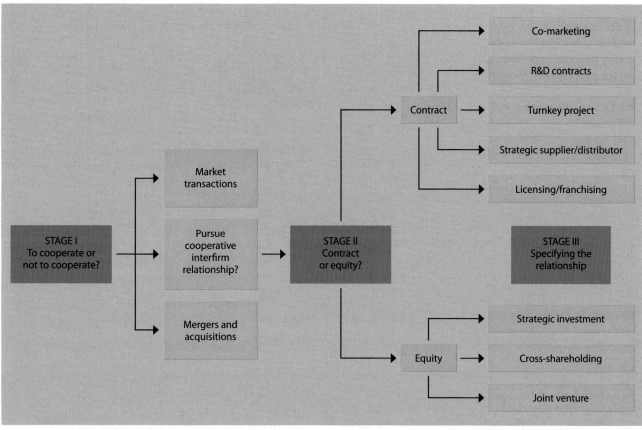

Source: S. Tallman and O. Shenkar, "A managerial decision model of international cooperative venture formation," *Journal of International Business Studies* 25 (1994): 101.

nearly 400 items, from how to issue press releases to which accounting software to use. Unlike its bigger defense rivals such as Boeing and Raytheon, Northrop Grumman thus far has not stumbled with any of its acquisitions.

 ORGANIZATION Fundamentally, whether acquisitions add value boils down to how merged firms are organized to take advantage of the benefits while minimizing the costs. Pre-acquisition analysis often focuses on **strategic fit**, which is the effective matching of complementary strategic capabilities. Yet, many firms do not pay adequate attention to **organizational fit**, which is the similarity in cultures, systems, and structures. On paper, Daimler and Chrysler in 1998 had great strategic fit in terms of complementary product lines and geographic scope, but there was little organizational fit. Despite the official proclamation of a merger of equals, the American unit in DaimlerChrysler saw itself as Occupied Chrysler. American managers resented answering to German managers, and Germans disliked being paid two thirds less than their Chrysler colleagues. These clashes led to a mass exodus of American managers from Chrysler—a common phenomenon in acquired firms. Now with Chrysler's new acquisition by Fiat, whether this new trans-Atlantic marriage will work remains to be seen.

Describe how alliances are formed.

FORMATION OF ALLIANCES

The next few sections discuss in some detail the formation, evolution, and performance of alliances and acquisitions. First: How are alliances formed? A three-stage model in Exhibit 11.5 addresses this process.

In Stage One, a firm must decide if growth can be achieved strictly through market transactions, acquisitions, or cooperative alliances.[9] To grow by pure market transactions, the firm has to confront competitive challenges independently. This is highly demanding, even for resource-rich multinationals. As noted earlier in the chapter, acquisitions have some unique drawbacks, leading many managers to conclude that alliances are the way to go. For example, Dallas-based Sabre Travel Network used alliances to enter Australia, Bahrain, India, Israel, Japan, and Singapore,

In Stage Two, a firm must decide whether to take a contract or an equity approach. As noted in Chapters 6 and 10, the choice

Strategic fit
The effective matching of complementary strategic capabilities between two or more firms.

Organizational fit
The similarity in cultures, systems, and structures between two or more firms.

between contract and equity is crucial. The first driving force is shared capabilities. The more tacit (that is, hard to describe and codify) the capabilities, the greater the preference for equity involvement. Although not the only way, the most effective way to learn *complex* processes is through learning by doing. A good example of this is learning to cook by actually cooking and not by simply reading cookbooks. Many business processes are the same way. A firm that wants to produce cars will find that the codified knowledge found in books or reports is not enough. Much tacit knowledge can only be acquired via learning by doing, preferably with experts as alliance partners.

A second driving force is the importance of direct monitoring and control. Equity relationships allow firms to have some direct control over joint activities on a continuing basis, whereas contractual relationships usually do not. In general, firms that fear their intellectual property may be expropriated prefer equity alliances (and a higher level of equity).

Eventually, in Stage Three, firms need to specify a specific format that is either equity based or contractual (nonequity based), depending on the choice made in Stage Two. Exhibit 11.5 lists the different format options. Since Chapter 10 has already covered this topic as part of the discussion on entry modes, we will not repeat it here.

EXHIBIT 11.6 Alliance Dissolution

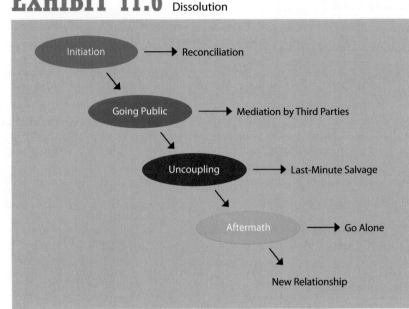

Source: M. W. Peng and O. Shenkar, "Joint venture dissolution as corporate divorce," *Academy of Management Executive* 16, no. 2 (2002): 95.

> **Outline how alliances are dissolved.**

DISSOLUTION OF ALLIANCES

Alliances are often described as corporate marriages and, when terminated, as corporate divorces.[10] Exhibit 11.6 portrays an alliance dissolution model. To apply the metaphor of divorce, we focus on the two-partner alliance. Following the convention in research on human divorce, the party who begins the process of ending the alliance is labeled the **initiator**, while the other party is termed the "partner"—for lack of a better word. We will draw on our Opening Case to explain this process.

The first phase is initiation. The process begins when the initiator starts feeling uncomfortable with the alliance (for whatever reason). Wavering begins as a quiet, unilateral process by the initiator, which was Danone in this case. After repeated demands to modify Wahaha's behavior failed, Danone began to sense that the alliance was probably unsalvageable. At this point, the display of discontent became bolder. Initially, Wahaha, the partner, may simply not "get it." The

Initiator
The party who begins the process of ending the alliance relationship.

initiator's "sudden" dissatisfaction may confuse the partner. As a result, initiation tends to escalate.

The second phase is going public. The party that breaks the news first has a first-mover advantage. By presenting a socially acceptable reason in favor of its cause, this party is able to win sympathy from key stakeholders, such as parent company executives, investors, and journalists. Not surprisingly, the initiator is likely to go public first. Alternatively, the partner may pre-empt by blaming the initiator and establishing the righteousness of its position—this was exactly what Wahaha did. Eventually, both Danone and Wahaha were eager to publicly air their grievances.

The third phase is uncoupling. Like human divorce, alliance dissolution can be friendly or hostile. In uncontested divorces, both sides attribute the separation more to, say, a change in circumstances. For example, Eli Lilly and Ranbaxy, leading pharmaceutical firms in the United States and India, respectively, phased out their JV in India and remained friendly with each other. In contrast, contested divorces involve a party that accuses another. The worst scenario is "death by a thousand cuts" inflicted by one party at every turn. A case in point is the numerous lawsuits and arbitrations filed in many countries by Danone and Wahaha accusing each other of wrongdoing (see the Opening Case).

The last phase is aftermath. Like most divorced individuals, most (but not all) "divorced" firms are likely to search for new partners. Understandably, the new alliance is often negotiated more extensively. One Italian executive reportedly signed *each* of

© iStockphoto.com/Carmen Martinez Banús

the 2,000 pages (!) of an alliance contract.[11] However, excessive formalization may signal a lack of trust—in the same way that pre-nuptial agreements may scare away some prospective human marriage partners.

LO5 **Discuss how alliances perform.**

PERFORMANCE OF ALLIANCES

Although managers naturally focus on alliance performance, opinions vary on how to measure it. A combination of objective measures (such as profit and market share) and subjective measures (such as managerial satisfaction) can be used. Four factors may influence alliance performance: (1) equity, (2) learning and experience, (3) nationality, and (4) relational capabilities.

First, the level of equity may be crucial in how an alliance performs. A greater equity stake may mean that a firm is more committed, which is likely to result in higher performance. Second, whether firms have successfully learned from partners is important when assessing alliance performance. Since learning is abstract, experience is often used as a proxy because it is relatively easy to measure. While experience certainly helps, its impact on performance is not linear. There is a limit beyond which further increase in experience may not enhance performance. Third, nationality may affect performance. For the same reason that marriages where both parties have similar backgrounds are more stable, dissimilarities in national culture may create strains in alliances. Not surprisingly, international alliances tend to have more problems than domestic ones (see the Opening Case). Finally, alliance performance may fundamentally boil down to soft, hard-to-measure relational capabilities. The art of relational capabilities, which are firm-specific and difficult to codify and transfer, may make or break alliances.

Overall, none of these four factors has an unambiguous, direct impact on performance. What has been found is that they may have some *correlations* with performance. It would be naive to think that any of these four single factors would guarantee success. It is their *combination* that jointly increases the odds for the success of strategic alliances.

LO6 *Explain why firms undertake acquisitions and what performance problems they tend to encounter.*

MOTIVES FOR ACQUISITIONS

What drives acquisitions? Exhibit 11.7 shows three potential motives for acquisition: (1) synergistic, (2) hubristic, and (3) managerial motives. All three can be explained by the institution-based and resource-based views. From an institution-based view, synergistic motives for acquisitions are often a response to formal institutional constraints and transitions that affect a company's search for synergy. It is not a coincidence that the number of cross-border acquisitions has skyrocketed in the last two decades. This is the same period during which trade and investment barriers have gone down and FDI has risen. When PepsiCo started doing business in the Soviet Union in 1974, it would not have imagined that in 2011, Russian regulations would permit it to acquire Russia's biggest food products company, Wimm-Bill-Dann.[12]

From a resource-based standpoint, the most important synergistic rationale is to leverage superior resources. Zhejiang Geely Holding Group recently acquired Volvo for $1.5 billion. Superb resources that Volvo possessed but Geely lacked include Volvo's iconic brand, global experience, and world-class safety technology. Attractive resources that Geely enjoyed but Volvo lacked include Geely's familiarity with the Chinese automobile market, the largest in the world. Breakthrough in China will significantly enhance Volvo's economies of scale.[13] Another synergistic rationale is to enhance market power and scale economies. The $3 billion merger between United Airlines and Continental Airlines created the world's largest airline, which enjoys significant pricing power. Such M&As not only eliminate rivals but also reduce redundant assets. Finally, another rationale is to gain access to complementary resources, as evidenced by Lenovo's interest in IBM's worldwide client base.

While all of the synergistic motives, in theory, add value, hubristic and managerial motives reduce value. **Hubris** refers to exaggerated pride or

EXHIBIT 11.7 Motives for Acquisitions

	Institution-Based Issues	Resource-Based Issues
Synergistic motives	• Respond to formal institutional constraints and transitions	• Leverage superior managerial capabilities • Enhance market power and scale economies • Access to complementary resources
Hubristic motives	• Herd behavior—following norms and chasing fads of M&As	• Managers' overconfidence in their capabilities
Managerial motives	• Self-interested actions such as empire building guided by informal norms and cognitions	

Hubris
Exaggerated pride or overconfidence.

© iStockphoto.com/nolimitpictures

© Cengage Learning 2013

EXHIBIT 11.8   Symptoms of Acquisition Failures

	Problems for all M&As	Particular problems for cross-border M&As
Pre-acquisition: Overpayment for targets	• Managers over-estimate their ability to create value • Inadequate pre-acquisition screening • Poor strategic fit	• Lack of familiarity with foreign cultures, institutions, and business systems • Nationalistic concerns against foreign takeovers (political and media levels)
Post-acquisition: Failure in integration	• Poor organizational fit • Failure to address multiple stakeholder groups' concerns	• Clashes of organizational cultures compounded by clashes of national cultures • Nationalistic concerns against foreign takeovers (firm and employee levels)

© Cengage Learning 2013

overconfidence in one's capabilities. Managers of acquiring firms make two strong statements. The first is: "We can manage *your* assets better than you [target firm managers] can!" The second statement is even bolder. Given that purchasing a publicly listed firm requires paying an acquisition premium, managers of an acquiring firm essentially say: "We are smarter than the market!" This attitude is especially dangerous when multiple firms are bidding for the same target. The winning acquirer may suffer from what is called the "winner's curse" in auctions—the winner has overpaid. From an institution-based view, hubristic motives are at play when managers join the acquisition bandwagon. The fact that M&As come in waves speaks volumes about such herd behavior. After a few first-mover firms start making some deals in the industry, waves of late movers, eager to catch up, may rush in, prompted by a "Wow! Get it!" mentality. Not surprisingly, many of those deals turn out to be bust.

While the hubristic motive suggests that some managers may *unknowingly* overpay for targets, some may *knowingly* overpay for targets. Such self-interested actions are fueled by **managerial motives**, defined as a manager's desire for power, prestige, and money, which may lead to decisions that do not benefit the firm overall in the long run. As a result, some managers may deliberately over-diversify their firms through M&As for such personal gains; these are known as agency problems.

PERFORMANCE OF ACQUISITIONS

Why do as many as 70% of acquisitions reportedly fail? Problems can be identified in both pre-acquisition and post-acquisition phases (Exhibit 11.8). During the pre-acquisition phase, executive hubris and/or managerial motives may cause acquiring firms to pay too

Managerial motives
A managers' desire for power, prestige, and money, which may lead to decisions that do not benefit the firm overall in the long run.

much for targets. For example, in 2010, Dell offered $1.15 billion to acquire 3PAR, a data storage systems developer and one of the fastest growing technology companies. HP quickly countered with $1.5 billion. In this bidding war, Dell increased its bid to $1.6 billion, which was accepted by 3PAR. However, this was not the end of the story. A determined HP eventually bagged the deal at $2.3 billion, including paying Dell $72 million for its "break-up" with 3PAR. Given 3PAR's acceptance of Dell's $1.6 billion offer, the implication was that HP eventually paid 44% above market ($2.3 billion – $1.6 billion / $1.6 billion). A natural question is: Was 3PAR worth that much?

Another primary pre-acquisition problem is inadequate screening and failure to achieve strategic fit. For example, Bank of America, in a hurry to make a deal, spent only 48 hours in September 2008 before agreeing to acquire Merrill Lynch for $50 billion. Not surprisingly, failure to do adequate homework (technically, due diligence) led to numerous problems centered on the lack of strategic fit. Consequently, this acquisition was labeled by the *Wall Street Journal* as "a deal from hell."[14]

Acquiring international assets can be even more problematic because institutional and cultural distances can be even larger, and nationalistic concerns over foreign acquisitions may erupt (see the Closing Case). When Japanese firms acquired Rockefeller Center and movie studios in the 1980s and 1990s, the US media reacted with indignation. More recently, in the 2000s, when DP World from the United Arab Emirates and CNOOC from China attempted to acquire US assets, they had to back off due to political backlash.

Numerous integration problems may surface during the post-acquisition phase. Organizational fit is just as important as strategic fit. Many acquiring firms do *not* analyze organizational fit with targets. For example, when Nomura decided to acquire Lehman Brothers' assets in a lightning 24 hours, no consideration was given on the total lack of organizational fit between a hard-charging New York investment

> **Organizational fit is just as important as strategic fit.**

Tata: Clawed by Jaguar and Land Rover

To show off the new Jaguar XJ, Tata Motors in July 2009 rented a gallery in London's fashionable Chelsea district and flew in Jay Leno and other stars. With its muscular new design, the $73,000 car has won rave reviews. Tata, which a year ago paid Ford Motor $2.3 billion for Jaguar Cars and its cousin, Land Rover, seemed to have good reason to be upbeat.

Yet buying Jaguar and Land Rover has so far not worked out well for Ratan Tata, chairman of both the sprawling $64 billion Tata Group and Tata Motors. Unit sales of Jaguar and Land Rover were down 52% for the June 2009 quarter. The brands lost some $1.1 million a day in the same period, pushing the otherwise profitable Tata Motors to a $67 million loss. Tata still needs to spend $1 billion-plus a year in R&D on new models and making power-hungry Jaguars and Land Rovers meet new European emission standards. Among the options: replacing heavy steel with aluminum and more efficient engines such as hybrids. In Mumbai on August 26, 2009, Ratan Tata defended the acquisition as "very much worthwhile," while Tata Motors Vice-Chairman Ravi Kant said on August 31 that the R&D spending would likely continue for five more years.

Funding all this activity has been a headache. Tata this spring rustled up a $480 million loan from the European Investment Bank to help make its cars greener, and it wanted an extra $290 million

© AFP/Getty Images

to cover operating expenses for Jaguar and Land Rover. But Tata needed loan guarantees from the British government. In exchange, Peter Mandelson, the Business Secretary, wanted a seat on the board and the right to fire David Smith, the chief of Jaguar and Land Rover, according to Tata executives. Tata balked, and in August the company gave up on the government and got guarantees from private banks. The British government maintained it could not go forward unless it was assured that UK taxpayers' money would be protected.

Tata was stung by the experience. It lowered inventories, saving $250 million, cut three British factories to single shifts, and eliminated some 2,500 jobs. Unite, a union representing Jaguar and Land Rover workers, agreed to $110 million in cuts such as pay freezes and shorter work hours.

Jaguar and Land Rover won't likely break even before 2011. With less than $300 million in cash on hand, Tata Motors may need to sell equity to raise more funds. The biggest expense is apt to be Land Rover, which may require a major rethink as Americans and Europeans shun SUVs. "Land Rover needs to tweak its entire image," says Paul Newton, a London analyst at research firm IHS Global Insight. "The complication is the huge amounts of money that will take."

Source: Excerpts reprinted from the September 3, 2009 issue of *BusinessWeek* by special permission. © 2009 by Bloomberg L.P.

---

bank and a conservative, seniority-based Japanese firm that still largely practiced lifetime employment (see the Closing Case). Firms may also fail to address the concerns of multiple stakeholders, including employees, unions, and governments (see In Focus). Exhibit 11.9 on the next page humorously portrays one particular challenge. Most firms focus on task issues such as standardizing reporting and pay inadequate attention to people issues, which typically results in low morale and high turnover.

In cross-border M&As, integration difficulties may be much worse because clashes of organizational cultures are compounded by clashes of national cultures. Due to cultural differences, Chinese acquirers such as Geely often have a hard time integrating Western firms such as Volvo. But even when both sides are from the West, cultural conflicts may still erupt. When Four Seasons acquired a hotel in Paris, the simple American request that employees smile at customers was resisted by French employees and laughed at by the local media as "*la culture Mickey Mouse*."

Although acquisitions are often the largest capital expenditures most firms ever make, they frequently are the worst planned and executed activities of all. Unfortunately, while merging firms are sorting out the mess, rivals are likely to launch aggressive attacks. When Lenovo was distracted by its high-profile acquisition of IBM's PC division since 2004, Lenovo's rivals unleashed a series of attacks. As a result, instead of maintaining its status of the world's third largest PC maker with the ambition to become the first, Lenovo's ranking now dropped to the fourth. Adding all of the above together, it is hardly surprising that most M&As fail.

> Articulate what you can do to make global alliances and acquisitions successful.

MANAGEMENT SAVVY

What determines the success and failure in alliances and acquisitions? Our two core perspectives shed light on this

Acquisitions Versus Alliances
Although alliances and acquisitions are alternatives, many firms seem to plunge straight into "merger mania." Between 2005 and 2010, Microsoft, IBM, and HP swallowed 79, 60, and 34 firms, respectively. In many firms, an M&A group reports to the CFO, while a separate unit, headed by the VP or director for business development, deals with alliances. M&As and alliances are thus often undertaken in isolation. A smaller number of firms, such as Eli Lilly, have a separate "office of alliance management." Few firms have established a combined "mergers, acquisitions, *and* alliances" function. In practice, it may be advisable to explicitly compare acquisitions vis-à-vis alliances.

Compared with acquisitions, alliances cost less and allow for opportunities to learn from working with each other before engaging in full-blown acquisitions. While alliances do not preclude acquisitions and may lead to acquisitions, acquisitions are often one-off deals swallowing both the excellent capabilities and mediocre units of target firms, leading to "indigestion" problems. Many acquisitions (such as DaimlerChrysler) probably would have been better off had firms pursued alliances first.

Sources: J. Dyer, P. Kale, and H. Singh, "When to ally and when to acquire," *Harvard Business Review*, July-August (2004): 109–115; H. Yang, S. Sun, Z. Lin, and M. W. Peng, "Behind M&As in China and the United States," *Asia Pacific Journal of Management* 28 (2011): 239–255; H. Yang, Z. Lin, and M. W. Peng, "Behind acquisitions of alliance partners: Exploratory learning and network embeddedness," *Academy of Management Journal* (2011 in press); X. Yin and M. Shanley, "Industry determinants of the 'merger versus alliance' decision," *Academy of Management Review* 33 (2008): 473–491.

big question. The institution-based view argues that alliances and acquisitions depend on a thorough understanding and skillful manipulation of the rules of the game. The resource-based view calls for the development of firm-specific capabilities to make a difference in enhancing alliance and acquisition performance. As two alternatives, neither alliances nor acquisitions should be preordained, and careful analysis of the pros and cons of each should be undertaken before going forward with either one (see Debate).

Consequently, three clear implications for action emerge (see Exhibit 11.10). First, managers need to understand and master the rules of the game—both formal and informal—governing alliances and acquisitions around the world. Lenovo clearly understood and tapped into the Chinese government's support for home-grown multinationals. IBM likewise understood the necessity for the new Lenovo to maintain an American image when it persuaded Lenovo to give up the idea of having dual headquarters in China and the United States and to set up its world headquarters in the United States. This highly symbolic action made it easier to win approval from the US government. In contrast, GE and Honeywell, two US-headquartered firms, proposed to merge and cleared US antitrust scrutiny in 2001. But they failed to anticipate the power of the EU antitrust authorities, which in the end torpedoed the deal. The upshot is that in addition to the economics of alliances and acquisitions, managers need to pay attention to the politics behind such high-stakes strategic moves.

Second, when managing alliances, managers need to pay attention to the soft relational capabilities that often make or break relationships. To the extent that business schools usually provide a good training on hard number-crunching skills, it is time for all of us to beef up on soft but equally important (perhaps even more important) relational capabilities.

Finally, when managing acquisitions, managers are advised not to over-pay for targets and to focus on both strategic and organizational fit. While approaches vary, no firm can afford to take acquisitions, especially the integration phase, lightly (see the Closing Case).

EXHIBIT 11.9 A Challenge in Post-Acquisition Integration

" As you know, some details of the new merger have yet to be resolved. "

Source: *Harvard Business Review* (February 2005): 102. Reprinted with permission.

EXHIBIT 11.10 Implications for Action

- Understand and master the rules of the game governing alliances and acquisitions around the world.
- When managing alliances, pay attention to the soft relationship aspects.
- When managing acquisitions, do not over-pay, focus on both strategic and organizational fit, and thoroughly address integration concerns.

NOMURA INTEGRATES LEHMAN BROTHERS IN ASIA AND EUROPE

Everyone knows Lehman Brothers went bankrupt in September 2008. But what happened to its remains? Britain's Barclay Capital bought Lehman's North America operations for $3.75 billion. Lehman's assets in Asia and Europe were purchased by Japan's Nomura for the bargain-basement price of $200 million. Founded in 1925, Nomura is the oldest and largest securities brokerage and investment banking firm in Japan. Although Nomura had operated in 30 countries prior to its acquisition of Lehman's assets in 2008, it had always been known as a significant but still primarily regional (Asian) player in the big league of the financial services industry. In addition to Lehman, the list of elite investment banking firms in early 2008 would include Goldman Sachs, Morgan Stanley, Bear Stearns, JP Morgan, and Citigroup of the United States, Credit Suisse and UBS of Switzerland, Deutsche Bank of Germany, and ING Group of the Netherlands. No one would include Nomura in this group. Nomura viewed itself primarily as an Asian version of Merrill Lynch.

The tumultuous 2008 led to the collapse of both Bear Stearns (first) and Lehmans Brothers (second), and all of the firms in the big league named above were left in deep financial trouble. To the conservatively managed Nomura, this became the opportunity of a lifetime. Within a lightning 24 hours, CEO Kenichi Watanabe decided to acquire Lehman's remnants in Asia and Europe. Some of the Lehman assets were dirt cheap. For example, its French investment banking operations was sold for only one euro (that is, €1!). Overall, by cherry-picking Lehman's Asia and Europe operations and adding 8,000 employees who tripled Nomura's size outside Japan, Nomura transformed itself into a global heavyweight overnight. The question is: Does Nomura have what it takes to make this acquisition a success?

The answer was a decisive "No!" from Nomura's investors, who drove its shares down by 70% in March 2009. Over the past five years, Nomura had consistently underperformed the Nikkei 225 index, and this acquisition broke a new low record for Nomura. Since the purchase price seemed reasonable and there was little evidence that Nomura over-paid, the biggest challenge is post-acquisition integration, merging a hard-charging New York investment bank with a hierarchical Japanese firm that still largely practices lifetime employment.

Clearly, Lehman's most valuable, rare, and hard-to-imitate asset is its talent. To ensure that Nomura retained most of the ex-Lehman talent, Nomura set aside a compensation pool of $1 billion and guaranteed all ex-Lehman employees who chose to stay with Nomura not only their jobs, but also their 2007 pay level (including bonuses) for three years. About 95% of them accepted Nomura's offer. Given the ferociousness of the financial meltdown in 2008–2009 (which, if you remember, was triggered by Lehman's collapse), many employees at other firms that were not bankrupt lost their jobs. The fact that Nomura guaranteed both jobs and pay levels was widely appreciated by ex-Lehman employees who otherwise would have been devastated and stressed.

Instead, acquiring Lehman introduced significant stress to Nomura's long-held traditions. A leading challenge is pay level. Most senior executives at Lehman made on average $1 million in 2007. While concrete data were not available on specific Nomura executives, media reported that on average, Nomura employees only received *half* the pay of their Lehman counterparts. Not surprisingly, guaranteeing ex-Lehman employees at such an astronomical pay level (viewed from a Nomura perspective) created a major problem among Nomura's Japanese employees. In response, Nomura in 2009 offered its employees in Japan higher pay and bonuses that would start to approach the level ex-Lehman employees were commanding, in exchange for less job security—in other words, they could be fired more easily if they underperformed. So far, about 2,000 Japanese employees accepted the offer, which would link pay to individual and departmental performance rather than the firm as a whole.

Another challenge is the personnel rotation system. Like many leading Japanese firms, Nomura periodically rotates managers to different positions. For example, Yoshihiro Fukuta, who was appointed as head of Nomura International Hong Kong Ltd. in 2008, was rotated back to Tokyo as head of the Internal Audit Division in 2009. While these practices produce well-rounded generalist managers, they generate a rigid hierarchy: a manager in a later cohort year, no matter how superb his performance, is unlikely to supervise a manager in an earlier cohort year. These Nomura practices directly clash with Western norms evidenced by two aspects of Lehman practices: (1) work is increasingly done by specialists who develop deep expertise and (2) superstars are typically on a fast track rocketing ahead. Although the personnel rotation system largely did not apply to Nomura's overseas employees, it resulted in a top echelon that consists entirely of Japanese executives who have gone through the rotations. In an effort to globalize, Nomura's top echelon needs to attract diverse talents, especially those from Lehman. How the rotation system can accommodate the arrival of ex-Lehman employees who had neither the experience nor the stomach for it remains to be seen.

The performance of Nomura's acquisition of Lehman is mixed at this point. For the fiscal year ended in March 2009, Nomura lost $7.5 billion, calling into question the sustainability of paying ex-Lehman employees at such lavish levels. However, ex-Lehman employees indeed delivered some enviable performance. In Asia, Nomura advised 19 high-profile M&A deals in 2009; in 2008, it did two. In Europe, Nomura's equity-trading business jumped from being the 82nd to the third biggest on the London Stock Exchange (Lehman formerly was number one). In 2009, Nomura moved the global headquarters of its investment banking division from Tokyo to London. As the post–acquisition integration intensifies, stay tuned for further transformation of Nomura.

Sources: "Nomura is starting to flex its Lehman muscles," *BusinessWeek*, 28 September 2009; E. Choi, H. Leung, J. Chan, S. Tse, and W. Chu, "How can Nomura be a true global financial company?" case study, University of Hong Kong, 2009; "Nomura's integration of Lehman," *Economist*, 11 July 2009; A. Huo, E. Liu, R. Gampa, and R. Liew, "Nomura's bet on Lehman," case study, University of Hong Kong, 2009; Nomura, 2011, http://www.nomura.com.

Strategizing, Structuring, & Learning AROUND THE World

CHAPTER 12

Kikkoman's Sauce of Success

At the International Trade Fair in Chicago in 1959, visitors were delighted by the salty-savory taste of roast beef marinated in a novel condiment called soy sauce: slices were being given away by young Japanese men. What the nibblers did not know was that the foreigners were not merely demonstration staff but workers at the sauce maker's new American unit, who wanted to see first-hand how American consumers responded to their product. Among them was Yazaburo Mogi, a 24-year-old student at Columbia Business School and the scion of one of the founding families behind Kikkoman, a soy sauce maker that traces its origins to the 17th century.

By the time he reached the top of the firm in 1995, Mr. Mogi was well on his way to transforming it into an international food business and turning an obscure Asian seasoning into a mainstream global product. "We tried to appeal to the non-Japanese, general-market consumer," says Mr. Mogi, who speaks fluent English—a rarity among Japanese bosses. Kikkoman is now the world's largest maker of naturally brewed soy sauce. Foreign sales of its sauce have grown by nearly 10% a year for 25 years. Its distinctive curvy bottle has become commonplace in restaurants and kitchens the world over, alongside other condiments such as Italian olive oil or French mustard. Interbrand, a brand consultancy, ranks Kikkoman among the most recognizable Japanese names in a list otherwise dominated by carmakers and electronics firms.

Indeed, this family-owned Japanese firm is unusual in several ways. In 1973, it became the first Japanese food company to open a factory in America; Mr. Mogi was running the American division by this time. Whereas many Japanese firms eschew mergers and acquisitions, Kikkoman has been active, buying American and Japanese companies in the course of its expansion. In January 2009, Kikkoman adopted a holding-company structure that will make

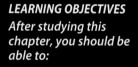

LEARNING OBJECTIVES

After studying this chapter, you should be able to:

LO1 describe the relationship between multinational strategy and structure.

LO2 explain how institutions and resources affect multinational strategy, structure, and learning.

LO3 outline the challenges associated with learning, innovation, and knowledge management.

LO4 list three things you can do to make a multinational firm successful.

acquisitions easier, among other things. Mr. Mogi speaks with pride about corporate governance reforms he has instituted, including succession planning. Since 2004, the firm's presidents have come from outside the founding families. And rather than being centrally run from Tokyo, Kikkoman is known for devolving power to the bosses of its foreign subsidiaries.

Under Mr. Mogi's leadership, Kikkoman's sales have grown to more than $4 billion a year, of which soy sauce accounts for 20%. Most of the firm's revenue now comes from selling other food products in Japan and abroad. Kikkoman is the biggest wholesaler of Asian foodstuffs in America, with similar operations in Europe, China, and Australia. It sells canned fruit and vegetables in Asia under the Del Monte brand, and one of its subsidiaries is Coca-Cola's bottling affiliates in Japan. Foreign sales account for 30% of revenue but 55% of operating profit, three-quarters of which comes from North America. By some measures, Kikkoman is the Japanese firm most dependent on the American market. The recession has hit Kikkoman's profits, but it is relatively well protected. "In a recession, demands shifts from restaurants to household consumption," Mr. Mogi explains, so what his company loses in one market it makes up in the other.

Kikkoman's move into America in the 1950s set the template for the company's foreign expansion. America was the perfect place to venture abroad, says Mr. Mogi. It is open to new things and is willing to incorporate novel ingredients into its cuisine. During his time at business school, Mr. Mogi travelled across America, visiting Asian restaurants. There were very few: in New York he found only eight Japanese eateries. Kikkoman, he realized, had to

adapt its sauce to the local cuisine if it was going to succeed. Kikkoman promoted soy sauce in America by hiring chefs to concoct recipes that incorporated the sauce into classic American dishes. The firm then sent the recipes to local newspapers, prompting housewives to cut them out and shop for the ingredients. In the process, it started to position soy sauce not as a Japanese product, but as an "all-purpose seasoning," as a housewife puts it in Kikkoman's 1950s television advertisements. The same words can still be seen emblazoned on its bottles.

In 1961, the company picked up many new customers by introducing teriyaki sauce—a mixture of soy sauce and other ingredients devised specifically for the American market as a barbecue glaze. Kikkoman is now devising products for South American and European tastes, such as a soy sauce that can be sprinkled on rice—something that is not done in Japan. In Europe and Australia, where consumers are suspicious of biotechnology, Kikkoman's sauce is made without genetically modified ingredients. Mr. Mogi is also taking Kikkoman into a foreign market rather close to home: China. It is a more difficult market to enter than America or Europe, because soy sauce is already part of Chinese cuisine and cheap products abound, often chemically synthesized rather than naturally brewed. Mr. Mogi hopes to establish Kikkoman's sauce as a premium product aimed at wealthier buyers. His early recognition of the importance of adapting his firm's product for foreign markets is Kikkoman's real special sauce.

Sources: "Sauce of success," *Economist*, 11 April 2009, 68. © 2009 Economist Newspaper Group.

How can multinational enterprises (MNEs) such as Kikkoman be appropriately structured so that they can be successful both locally and internationally? How can they learn country tastes, global trends, and market transitions that would call for structural changes? How can they improve the odds for better innovation? These are some of the key questions we address in this chapter. The focus here is on relatively large MNEs with significant internationalization. We start by discussing the crucial relationship between four strategies and four structures. Next, we consider how the institution-based and resource-based views shed light on these issues. Then, we discuss worldwide learning, innovation, and knowledge management and look at a debate over whether control should be centralized or decentralized. Managerial implications follow.

for cost reduction and local responsiveness. We then outline the four strategic choices and the four corresponding organizational structures that MNEs typically adopt.

Pressures for Cost Reduction and Local Responsiveness

MNEs confront primarily two sets of pressures: cost reduction and local responsiveness. These two sets of pressures are dealt with in the **integration-responsiveness framework**, which allows managers to deal with the pressures for both global integration and local responsiveness. Cost pressures often call for global integration, while local responsiveness pushes MNEs to adapt locally. In both domestic and international competition, pressures to reduce costs are almost universal. What is unique in international competition is the pressure for **local responsiveness**, which means reacting to different consumer preferences and host-country demands. Consumer preferences vary tremendously around the world. For example, the beef-based hamburgers at McDonald's would obviously find few customers in India, a land where cows are held sacred by the Hindu majority. Thus, McDonald's must change its menu in India. Host-country demands and expectations add to the pressures for local responsiveness. Throughout Europe, Canadian firm Bombardier manufactures an Austrian version of railcars in Austria, a Belgian version in Belgium, and so on. Bomdardier believes that such local responsiveness, although not required, is essential for making sales to railway operators in Europe, which tend to be state owned.

LO1 Describe the relationship between multinational strategy and structure.

Integration-responsiveness framework
An MNE management framework for simultaneously dealing with the pressures for both global integration and local responsiveness.

Local responsiveness
The need to be responsive to different customer preferences around the world.

MULTINATIONAL STRATEGIES AND STRUCTURES

This section first introduces an integration-responsiveness framework centered on the pressures

EXHIBIT 12.1   Multinational Strategies and Structures: The Integration-Responsive Framework

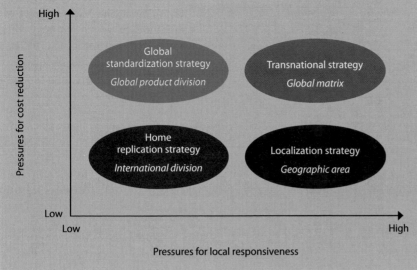

Pressures for cost reduction (vertical axis: Low → High)

- Global standardization strategy — *Global product division*
- Transnational strategy — *Global matrix*
- Home replication strategy — *International division*
- Localization strategy — *Geographic area*

Pressures for local responsiveness (horizontal axis: Low → High)

Note: In some textbooks, "home replication" may be referred to as "international" or "export" strategy, "localization" as "multidomestic" strategy, and "global standardization" as "global" strategy. Some of these labels are confusing because one can argue that all four strategies here are "international" or "global," thus resulting in some confusion if we label one of these strategies as "international" and another as "global." The present set of labels is more descriptive and less confusing.

Taken together, being locally responsive certainly makes local customers and governments happy but unfortunately increases costs. Given the universal interest in lowering cost, a natural tendency is to downplay or ignore the different needs and wants of various local markets and instead market a global version of products and services. The movement to globalize offerings can be traced to a 1983 article by Theodore Levitt: "The Globalization of Markets."[1] Levitt argued that worldwide consumer tastes are converging. As evidence, Levitt pointed to the worldwide success of Coke Classic, Levi Strauss jeans, and Sony color TV. Levitt predicted that such convergence would characterize most product markets in the future.

Levitt's idea has often been the intellectual force propelling many MNEs to globally integrate their products while minimizing local adaptation. Ford experimented with "world car" designs. MTV pushed ahead with the belief that viewers would flock to global (essentially American) programming. Unfortunately, most of these experiments were unsuccessful. Ford found that consumer tastes ranged widely around the globe. MTV eventually realized that there is no "global song." In a nutshell, one size does not fit all. This leads us to look at how MNEs can pay attention to *both* dimensions: cost reduction and local responsiveness.

Four Strategic Choices

Based on the integration-responsiveness framework, Exhibit 12.1 plots the four strategic choices: (1) home replication, (2) localization, (3) global standardization, and (4) transnational. Each strategy has a set of pros and cons outlined in Exhibit 12.2. (Their corresponding structures in Exhibit 12.1 are discussed in the next section.)

Home replication strategy, often known as international (or export) strategy, duplicates home country-based competencies in foreign countries. Such competencies include production scales, distribution efficiencies, and brand power. In manufacturing, this is usually manifested in an export strategy. In services, this is often done through licensing and franchising. This strategy is relatively easy to implement and usually the first one adopted when firms venture abroad.

On the disadvantage side, home replication strategy often lacks local responsiveness because it focuses on the home country. This strategy makes sense when the majority of a firm's customers are domestic. However, when a firm aspires to broaden its international scope, failing to be mindful of foreign customers' needs and wants may alienate those potential customers. For example, when Wal-Mart entered Brazil, the stores had

EXHIBIT 12.2   Four Strategic Choices for Multinational Enterprises

		Advantages	Disadvantages
1	Home replication	• Leverages home country-based advantages • Relatively easy to implement	• Lack of local responsiveness • May alienate foreign customers
2	Localization	• Maximizes local responsiveness	• High costs due to duplication of efforts in multiple countries • Too much local autonomy
3	Global standardization	• Leverages low-cost advantages	• Lack of local responsiveness • Too much centralized control
4	Transnational	• Cost-efficient while being locally responsive • Engages in global learning and diffusion of innovations	• Organizationally complex • Difficult to implement

Home replication strategy
A strategy that emphasizes duplicating home country-based competencies in foreign countries.

exactly the same inventory as its US stores, including a large number of *American* footballs. Considering that Brazil is the land of soccer, having won soccer's World Cup five times—more wins than any other country—nobody (except a few homesick American expatriates in their spare time) plays American football there.

Localization strategy is an extension of the home replication strategy. **Localization (or multidomestic) strategy** focuses on a number of foreign countries/regions, each of which is regarded as a stand-alone local (domestic) market worthy of significant attention and adaptation (see the Opening Case on Kikkoman). While sacri-

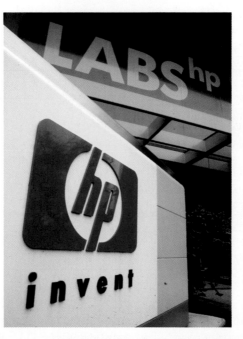

a result, this strategy is only appropriate in industries where the pressures for cost reductions are not significant. Another potential drawback is too much local autonomy, which happens when each subsidiary regards its country as so unique that it is difficult to introduce corporate-wide changes. For example, in the 1980s Unilever had subsidiaries in 17 European countries, and it took four *years* to persuade all 17 subsidiaries to introduce a single new detergent across Europe.

As the opposite of the localization strategy, **global standardization strategy** is sometimes referred to simply as global strategy. Its hallmark is the development and distribution of standardized products worldwide in order to reap the maximum benefits

Given that innovations are inherently risky and uncertain, there is no guarantee that the home country will generate the highest quality innovations.

Localization (or multidomestic) strategy
A strategy that focuses on a number of foreign countries/regions, each of which is regarded as a stand-alone local (domestic) market worthy of significant attention and adaptation.

Global standardization strategy
A strategy that relies on the development and distribution of standardized products worldwide to reap the maximum benefits from low-cost advantages.

Center of excellence
An MNE subsidiary explicitly recognized as a source of important capabilities that can be leveraged by and/or disseminated to other subsidiaries.

Worldwide (or global) mandate
A charter to be responsible for one MNE function throughout the world.

ficing global efficiencies, this strategy is effective when differences among national and regional markets are clear and pressures for cost reductions are low. As noted earlier, MTV started with a home replication strategy when first venturing overseas. It simply broadcast American programming. It has now switched to a localization strategy by broadcasting in local languages.

In terms of disadvantages, the localization strategy has high costs due to duplication of efforts in multiple countries. The costs of producing such a variety of programming for MTV are obviously greater than the costs of producing one set of programming. As

from low-cost advantages. While both the home replication and global standardization strategies minimize local responsiveness, a crucial difference is that an MNE pursuing a global standardization strategy is not limited to its major operations at home. In a number of countries, the MNE may designate **centers of excellence**, defined as subsidiaries explicitly recognized as a source of important capabilities, with the intention that these capabilities be leveraged by and/or disseminated to other subsidiaries. Centers of excellence are often given a **worldwide** (or **global**) **mandate**—namely, a charter to be responsible for one MNE function throughout the world. HP's Singapore subsidiary, for instance, has a worldwide mandate to develop, produce, and market all of HP's handheld products.

In terms of disadvantages, a global standardization strategy obviously sacrifices local responsiveness. This strategy makes great sense in industries where pressures for cost reductions are paramount and pressures for local responsiveness are relatively minor (particularly commodity industries such as semiconductors and tires). However, as noted earlier, in industries ranging from automobiles to consumer products, a one-size-fits-all strategy may be inappropriate. Consequently, arguments such as "all industries are becoming global" and "all firms need

EXHIBIT **12.3** International Division Structure at Starbucks

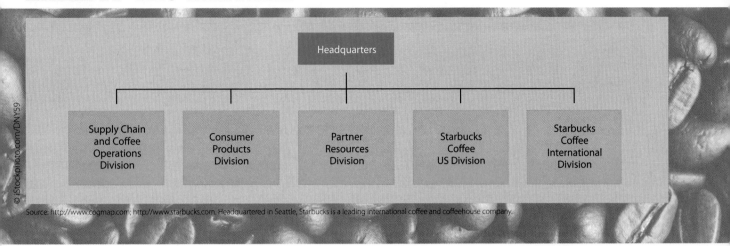

Source: http://www.cogmap.com; http://www.starbucks.com. Headquartered in Seattle, Starbucks is a leading international coffee and coffeehouse company.

to pursue a global (standardization) strategy" are potentially misleading.

Transnational strategy aims to capture the best of both worlds by endeavoring to be both cost efficient and locally responsive.[2] In addition to cost efficiency and local responsiveness, a third hallmark of this strategy is global learning and diffusion of innovations. Traditionally, the diffusion of innovations in MNEs is a one-way flow from the home country to various host countries—the label "home replication" says it all (!). Underpinning the traditional one-way flow is the assumption that the home country is the best location for generating innovations. However, given that innovations are inherently risky and uncertain, there is no guarantee that the home country will generate the highest quality innovations.

MNEs that engage in a transnational strategy promote global learning and diffusion of innovations in multiple ways. Innovations not only flow from the home country to host countries (which is the traditional flow), but also flow from host countries to the home country and flow among subsidiaries in multiple host countries. Kia Motors, for example, not only operates a design center in Seoul, Korea, but also has two other design centers in Los Angeles and Frankfurt, tapping into innovations generated in North America and Europe.[3]

On the disadvantage side, a transnational strategy is organizationally complex and difficult to implement. The large amount of knowledge sharing and coordination may slow down decision making. Trying to achieve cost efficiencies, local responsiveness, and global learning simultaneously places contradictory demands on MNEs (to be discussed in the next section).

Overall, it is important to note that given the various pros and cons, there is no optimal strategy. The new trend in favor of a transnational strategy needs to be qualified with an understanding of its significant organizational challenges. This point leads to our next topic.

Four Organizational Structures

Exhibit 12.1 also shows four organizational structures that are appropriate for each of the strategic choices: (1) international division, (2) geographic area, (3) global product division, and (4) global matrix.

International division is typically used when firms initially expand abroad, often engaging in a home replication strategy. Exhibit 12.3 shows that Starbucks has an international division, in addition to the four divisions that primarily focus on the United States. Although this structure is intuitively appealing, it often leads to two problems. First, foreign subsidiary managers, whose input is channeled through the international division, are not given sufficient voice relative to the heads of domestic divisions. Second, by design, the international division serves as a silo whose activities are not coordinated with the rest of the firm, which is focusing on domestic activities. Consequently, many firms phase out this structure after their initial stage of overseas expansion.

Geographic area structure organizes the MNE according to different geographic areas (countries and regions). It is the most appropriate structure for a localization strategy. Exhibit 12.4 on the next page illustrates such a structure for Avon Products, which is featured in Chapter 1's Opening Case. A geographic area can be a country or a region, led by a **country** (or **regional**) **manager**. Each area is largely

Transnational strategy
A strategy that endeavors to be simultaneously cost efficient, locally responsive, and learning driven around the world.

International division
An organizational structure that is typically set up when a firm initially expands abroad, often engaging in a home replication strategy.

Geographic area structure
An organizational structure that organizes the MNE according to different countries and regions.

Country (or regional) manager
The business leader of a specific country (or geographic region).

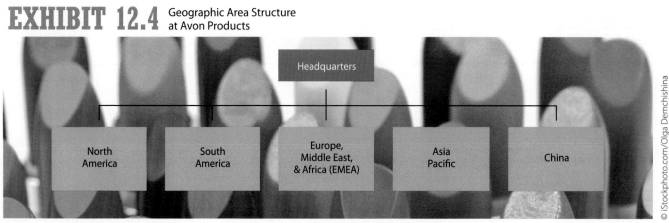

EXHIBIT 12.4 Geographic Area Structure at Avon Products

Headquarters

North America | South America | Europe, Middle East, & Africa (EMEA) | Asia Pacific | China

Source: www.avoncompany.com. Headquartered in New York, Avon is a leading global beauty products company (see Chapter 1 Opening Case).

stand-alone. In contrast to the limited voice of subsidiary managers in the international division structure, country (and regional) managers carry a great deal of weight in a geographic area structure. Interestingly and paradoxically, *both* the strengths and weaknesses of this structure lie in its local responsiveness. While being locally responsive can be a virtue, it also encourages the fragmentation of the MNE into fiefdoms.

Global product division structure, which is the opposite of the geographic area structure, supports the global standardization strategy by assigning global responsibilities to each product division. Exhibit 12.5 shows such an example from the European Aeronautic Defense and Space Company (EADS), whose most famous unit is Airbus. This structure treats each product division as a stand-alone entity with full worldwide responsibilities. This structure is highly responsive to pressures for cost efficiencies, because it allows for consolidation on a worldwide (or at least regional) basis and reduces inefficient duplication in multiple countries. For example, Unilever reduced the number of soap-producing factories in Europe from ten to two after adopting this structure. Recently, because of the popularity of the global standardization strategy (noted earlier), the global product division structure is on the rise. The structure's main drawback is that local responsiveness suffers, as Ford discovered when it phased out the geographic area structure in favor of the global product division structure.

A **global matrix** alleviates the disadvantages associated with both geographic area and global product division structures, especially for MNEs adopting a transnational strategy. Shown in Exhibit 12.6, its hallmark is the coordination of responsibilities between product divisions and geographic areas in order to be both cost efficient and locally responsive. In this hypothetical example, the country manager in charge of Japan—in short, the Japan manager—reports to Product Division 1 and Asia Division, both of which have equal power.

In theory this structure supports the goals of the transnational strategy, but in practice it is often difficult to deliver. The reason is simple: While managers (such as the Japan manager in Exhibit 12.6) usually find dealing with one boss headache enough, they do not appreciate having two bosses who are often in conflict (!). For example, Product Division 1 may decide that Japan is too tough a nut to crack and that there are more promising markets elsewhere, thus ordering the Japan manager to *curtail* her investment and channel resources elsewhere. This makes sense because Product Division 1 cares about its global market position and is not wedded to any particular country. However, Asia Division, which is evaluated by how well it does in Asia, may beg to differ. Asia Division argues that it cannot afford to be a laggard in Japan if it expects to be a leading player in Asia. Therefore, Asia Division demands that the Japan manager *increase* her investment in the country. Facing these conflicting demands, the Japan manager, who prefers to be politically correct, does not want to make any move before consulting corporate headquarters. Eventually, headquarters may provide a resolution. But crucial time may be lost in the process, and important windows of opportunity for competitive actions may be missed.

Despite its merits on paper, the matrix structure may add layers of management, slow down decision speed, and increase costs while not showing significant performance improvement. There is no conclusive evidence for the superiority of the matrix structure. The following quote from the CEO of Dow Chemical, an early adopter of the matrix structure, is sobering:

We were an organization that was matrixed and depended on teamwork, but there was no one in charge. When things went well, we didn't know whom to reward; and when things went poorly, we didn't know whom to blame. So we created a

Global product division structure
An organizational structure that assigns global responsibilities to each product division.

Global matrix
An organizational structure often used to alleviate the disadvantages associated with both geographic area and global product division structures, particularly when adopting a transnational strategy.

EXHIBIT 12.5 Global Product Division Structure at European Aeronautic Defense and Space Company (EADS)

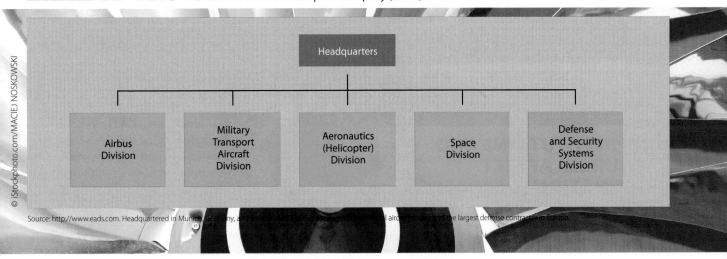

Headquarters

| Airbus Division | Military Transport Aircraft Division | Aeronautics (Helicopter) Division | Space Division | Defense and Security Systems Division |

Source: http://www.eads.com. Headquartered in Munich, Germany, and Paris, France, EADS is the second largest commercial aircraft maker and the largest defense contractor in Europe.

global product division structure, and cut out layers of management. There used to be 11 layers of management between me and the lowest level employees, now there are five.[4]

Overall, the positioning of the four structures in Exhibit 12.1 is not random. They develop from the relatively simple international division through either geographic area or global product division structures and may finally reach the more complex global matrix stage. It is important to note that not every MNE experiences all of these structural stages, and that the movement is not necessarily in one direction. For example, the matrix structure's poster child, the Swedish-Swiss conglomerate ABB, recently withdrew from this complex structure.

The Reciprocal Relationship Between Multinational Strategy and Structure

In one word, the relationship between strategy and structure is *reciprocal*. Three key ideas stand out. First, strategy usually drives structure. The fit between strategy and structure, as exemplified by the *pairs* in each of the four cells in Exhibit 12.1, is crucial. A misfit, such as combining a global standardization strategy with a geographic area structure, may have grave performance consequences.

Second, the relationship is not a one-way street. As much as strategy drives structure, structure also drives strategy. The withdrawal from the unworkable matrix structure at MNEs such as ABB has called into question the wisdom of the transnational strategy.

Finally, neither strategies nor structures are static. It is often necessary to change strategy, structure, or both. In an effort to move toward a global standardization strategy, many MNEs have adopted a global product division structure while de-emphasizing the role of country headquarters. However, unique challenges in certain countries, especially China, have now pushed some MNEs to revive the country headquarters, such as the China headquarters, so that it can coordinate numerous activities within a large, complex, and important host country.[5] A further experimentation is to have an emerging economies

EXHIBIT 12.6 A Hypothetical Global Matrix Structure

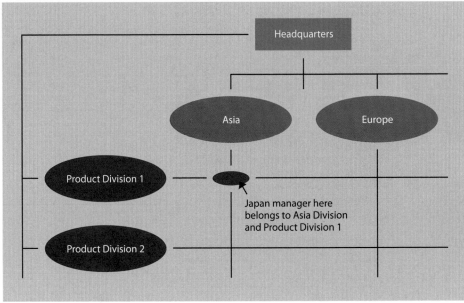

Headquarters

Asia

Europe

Product Division 1

Product Division 2

Japan manager here belongs to Asia Division and Product Division 1

© Cengage Learning 2013

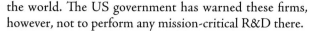

division, which is not dedicated to any single country but dedicated to pursuing opportunities in a series of emerging economies ranging from Brazil to Saudi Arabia. Cisco pioneered this structure, which has been followed by rivals such as IBM.[6]

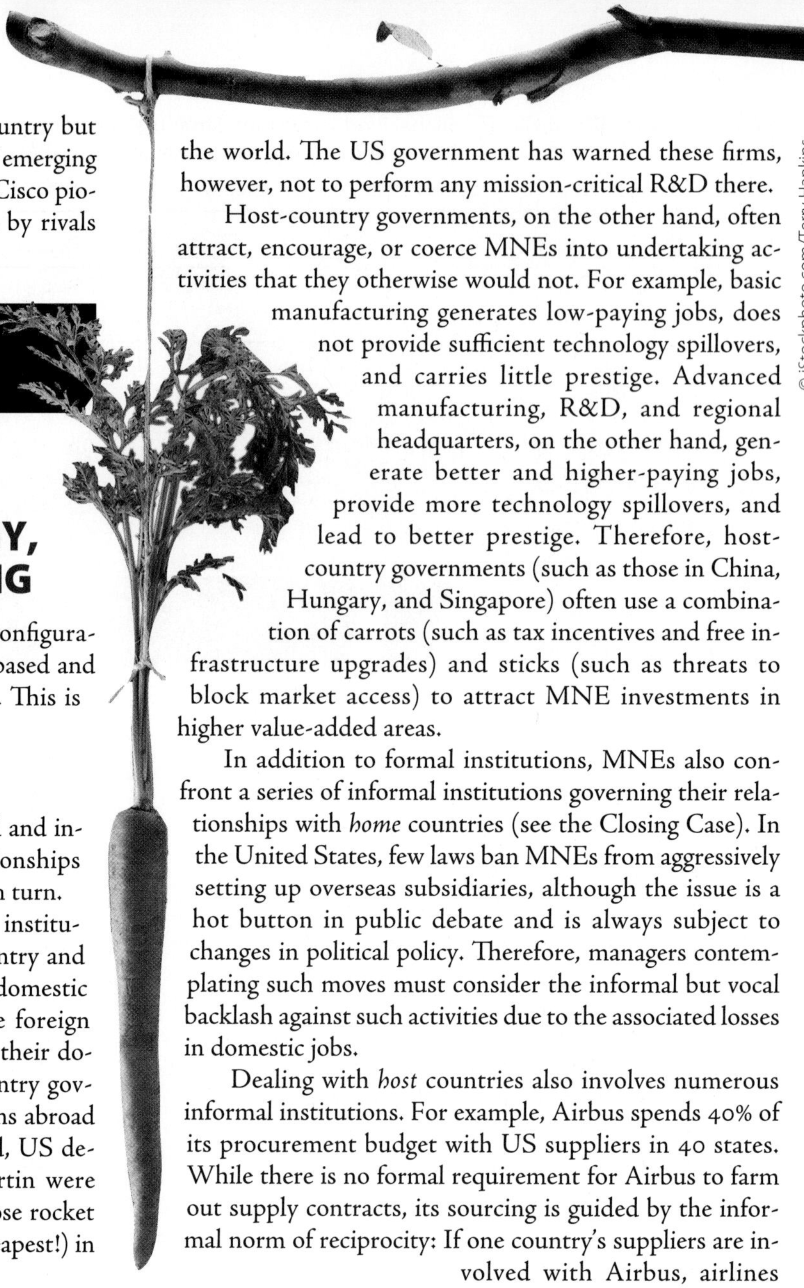

> *Explain how institutions and resources affect multinational strategy, structure, and learning.*

HOW INSTITUTIONS AND RESOURCES AFFECT MULTINATIONAL STRATEGY, STRUCTURE, AND LEARNING

Having outlined the basic strategy/structure configurations, let us now introduce how the institution-based and resource-based views shed light on these issues. This is mapped out in Exhibit 12.7.

Institution-Based Considerations

MNEs face two sets of rules of the game: formal and informal institutions governing (1) *external* relationships and (2) *internal* relationships. Each is discussed in turn.

Externally, MNEs are subject to the formal institutional frameworks erected by various home-country and host-country governments. In order to protect domestic employment, the British government taxes the foreign earnings of British MNEs at a higher rate than their domestic earnings. In another example, home-country governments may discourage or ban MNE operations abroad for political reasons. After the Cold War ended, US defense firms such as Boeing and Lockheed Martin were eager to set up R&D subsidiaries in Russia, whose rocket scientists were some of the best (and certainly cheapest!) in

the world. The US government has warned these firms, however, not to perform any mission-critical R&D there.

Host-country governments, on the other hand, often attract, encourage, or coerce MNEs into undertaking activities that they otherwise would not. For example, basic manufacturing generates low-paying jobs, does not provide sufficient technology spillovers, and carries little prestige. Advanced manufacturing, R&D, and regional headquarters, on the other hand, generate better and higher-paying jobs, provide more technology spillovers, and lead to better prestige. Therefore, host-country governments (such as those in China, Hungary, and Singapore) often use a combination of carrots (such as tax incentives and free infrastructure upgrades) and sticks (such as threats to block market access) to attract MNE investments in higher value-added areas.

In addition to formal institutions, MNEs also confront a series of informal institutions governing their relationships with *home* countries (see the Closing Case). In the United States, few laws ban MNEs from aggressively setting up overseas subsidiaries, although the issue is a hot button in public debate and is always subject to changes in political policy. Therefore, managers contemplating such moves must consider the informal but vocal backlash against such activities due to the associated losses in domestic jobs.

Dealing with *host* countries also involves numerous informal institutions. For example, Airbus spends 40% of its procurement budget with US suppliers in 40 states. While there is no formal requirement for Airbus to farm out supply contracts, its sourcing is guided by the informal norm of reciprocity: If one country's suppliers are involved with Airbus, airlines based in that country are more likely to buy Airbus aircraft.

Institutional factors affecting MNEs are not only external. How MNEs are governed *internally* is also determined by various formal and informal rules of the game. Formally, organizational charts, such as those in Exhibits 12.3 to 12.6, specify the scope of responsibilities for various parties. Most MNEs have systems of evaluation, reward, and punishment in place based on these formal rules.

What the formal organizational charts do not reveal are the informal rules of the

EXHIBIT 12.7 How Institutions and Resources Affect Multinational Strategy, Structure, and Learning

Institution-Based View
External institutions governing MNEs and home-/host-country environments
Internal institutions governing MNE management

Resource-Based View
Value
Rarity
Imitability
Organization

Multinational Strategy, Structure, and Learning

© Cengage Learning 2013

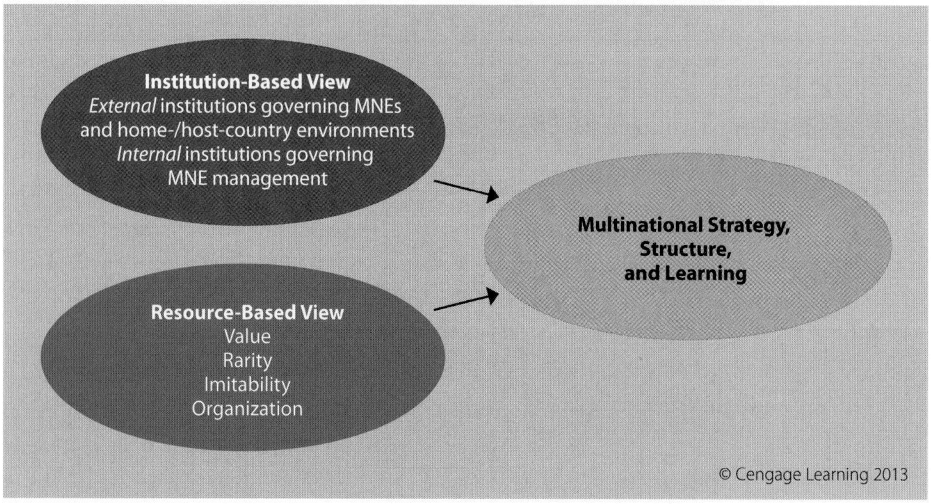

game, such as organizational norms, values, and networks. The nationality of the head of foreign subsidiaries is an example. Given the lack of formal regulations, MNEs essentially can have three choices:

+ a home-country national as the head of a subsidiary (such as an American for a subsidiary of a US-headquartered MNE in India)

+ a host-country national (such as an Indian for the same subsidiary above)

+ a third-country national (such as an Australian for the same subsidiary above).

MNEs from different countries have different norms when making these appointments. Most Japanese MNEs follow an informal rule: Heads of foreign subsidiaries, at least initially, need to be Japanese nationals. In comparison, European MNEs are more likely to appoint host-country and third-country nationals to lead subsidiaries. As a group, US MNEs are somewhere between Japanese and European practices. These staffing approaches may reflect strategic differences. Home-country nationals, especially long-time employees of the same MNE at home, are more likely to have developed a better understanding of the informal workings of the firm and to be better socialized into its dominant norms and values. Consequently, the Japanese propensity to appoint home-country nationals is conducive to their preferred global standardization strategy, which values globally coordinated and controlled actions. Conversely, the European comfort in appointing host-country and third-country nationals is indicative of European MNEs' (traditional) preference for a localization strategy.

Beyond the nationality of subsidiary heads, the nationality of top executives at the highest level (such as chairman, CEO, and board members) seems to follow another informal rule: They are almost always home-country nationals. To the extent that top executives are ambassadors of the firm and that the MNE's country of origin is a source of differentiation (for example, a German MNE is often perceived to be different from an Italian MNE), home-country nationals would seem to be the most natural candidates for top positions.

In the eyes of stakeholders such as employees and governments around the world, however, a top echelon consisting of largely one nationality does not bode well for an MNE aspiring to globalize everything it does. Some critics even argue that this "glass ceiling" reflects "corporate imperialism."[7] Consequently, such leading MNEs as BP, Coca-Cola, Electrolux, GSK, Nissan, PepsiCo, and Sony have appointed foreign-born executives to top posts. Such foreign-born bosses bring substantial diversity to the organization, which may be a plus. However, such diversity puts an enormous burden on these non-native top executives to clearly articulate the values and exhibit behaviors expected of senior managers of an MNE associated with a particular country. For example, Procter & Gamble (P&G) appointed Durk Jager, a native of the Netherlands, to be its chairman and CEO in 1999. Unfortunately, Jager's numerous change initiatives almost brought the venerable company to a grinding halt, and he was quickly forced to resign in 2000. Since then, the old rule is back: P&G is again led by an American executive.

Resource-Based Considerations

Shown in Exhibit 12.7, the resource-based view—exemplified by the value, rarity, imitability, and organization (VRIO) framework—adds a number of insights. First, when looking at structural changes, it is critical to consider whether a new structure (such as a matrix) adds concrete value. The value of innovation must also be considered. A vast majority of innovations simply fail to reach market, and most new products that do reach market end up being financial failures. The difference between an innovator and a *profitable* innovator is that the latter not only has plenty of good ideas but also lots of complementary assets (such as appropriate organizational structures and marketing muscles) to add value to innovation (see Chapter 4). Philips, for example, is a great innovator. The company invented rotary shavers, video cassettes, and CDs. Still, its ability to profit from these innovations lags behind that of Sony and Panasonic, which have much stronger complementary assets.

A second question is rarity. Certain strategies or structures may be in vogue at a given point in time. So, for example, when a company's rivals all move toward a global standardization strategy, this strategy cannot be a source of differentiation. To improve global coordination, many MNEs spend millions of dollars to equip themselves with enterprise resource planning (ERP) packages provided by SAP and Oracle. However, such packages are designed to be implemented

Indra Nooyi, Chairman and CEO of PepsiCo

Corporate Controls Versus Subsidiary Initiatives

One of the leading debates on how to manage large firms is whether control should be centralized or decentralized. In an MNE setting, the debate boils down to central controls versus subsidiary initiatives.

SUBSIDIARY CONTROL Subsidiaries are not necessarily receptive to headquarters' commands. When headquarters requires that certain practices (such as ethics training) be adopted, some subsidiaries may be in full compliance, others may pay lip service, and still others may simply refuse to adopt the practice, citing local differences. In addition to reacting to headquarters' demands differently, some subsidiaries may actively pursue their own, *subsidiary*-level strategies and agendas. These activities are known as **subsidiary initiatives**, defined as the proactive and deliberate pursuit of new opportunities by a subsidiary to expand its scope of responsibility. For example, Honeywell Canada requested that it be designated as a global "center for excellence" for certain Honeywell product lines. Many authors argue that such initiatives may inject a much-needed spirit of entrepreneurship throughout the larger, more bureaucratic corporation.

DEBATE
ETHICAL DILEMMA

CORPORATE CONTROL From corporate headquarters' perspective, however, it is hard to distinguish between good-faith subsidiary initiative and opportunistic empire building on the part of subsidiary managers. Much is at stake when determining whether subsidiaries should be named "centers of excellence" with worldwide mandates. Subsidiaries that fail to attain this status may see their roles marginalized or, worse, their facilities closed. Subsidiary managers are often host-country nationals (such as the Canadian managers at Honeywell Canada) who would naturally prefer to strengthen their subsidiary, if only to protect local (and their own!) employment and not necessarily to be patriotic. However natural and legitimate these tendencies, they are not necessarily consistent with the MNE's *corporate*-wide goals. These tendencies, if not checked and controlled, can surely lead to chaos for the MNE as a whole.

Sources: T. Ambos, U. Andersson, and J. Birkinshaw, "What are the consequences of initiative-taking in multinational subsidiaries?" *Journal of International Business Studies* 41 (2010): 1099–1118; J. Birkinshaw, S. Ghoshal, C. Markides, J. Stopford, and G. Yip (eds.), *The Future of the Multinational Company* (London: Wiley, 2003).

widely and appeal to a broad range of firms, thus providing no firm-specific advantage for the adopting firm.

Even when capabilities are valuable and rare, they have to pass a third hurdle—imitability. Formal structures are easier to observe and imitate than informal structures. This is one of the reasons why the informal, flexible matrix is in vogue now. The informal, flexible matrix "is less a structural classification than a broad organizational concept or philosophy, manifested in organizational capability and management mentality."[8] Obviously imitating an intangible mentality is much harder than imitating a tangible structure.

The last hurdle is organization—namely, how MNEs are organized, both formally and informally, around the world (see Debate). One elusive but important concept is organizational culture. Recall from Chapter 3 that culture is defined by Hofstede as "the collective programming of the mind which distinguishes the members of one group or category of people from another." We can extend this concept to define **organizational culture** as the collective programming of the mind that distinguishes members of one organization from another. China's Huawei, for example, is known to have a distinctive "wolf" culture, which centers on "continuous hunting" and "relentless pursuit" with highly motivated employees who routinely work overtime and sleep in their offices. Although rivals can imitate everything Huawei does technologically, their biggest hurdle lies in their lack of ability to wrap their arms around Huawei's "wolf" culture.

> *Outline the challenges associated with learning, innovation, and knowledge management.*

WORLDWIDE LEARNING, INNOVATION, AND KNOWLEDGE MANAGEMENT

Having outlined how institutions and resources affect multinationals, next let us devote our attention to the crucial issues of learning, innovation, and knowledge management.

Knowledge Management

Underpinning the recent emphasis on worldwide learning and innovation is the emerging interest in knowledge management. **Knowledge management** can be defined as the

Subsidiary initiative
The proactive and deliberate pursuit of new opportunities by a subsidiary to expand its scope of responsibility.

Organizational culture
The collective programming of the mind that distinguishes members of one organization from another.

Knowledge management
The structures, processes, and systems that actively develop, leverage, and transfer knowledge.

EXHIBIT 12.8 Knowledge Management in Four Types of Multinational Enterprises

Strategy	Home replication	Localization	Global standardization	Transnational
Interdependence	Moderate	Low	Moderate	High
Role of foreign subsidiaries	Adapting and leveraging parent-company competencies	Sensing and exploiting local opportunities	Implementing parent-company initiatives	Differentiated contributions by subsidiaries to integrate worldwide operations
Development and diffusion of knowledge	Knowledge developed at the center and transferred to subsidiaries	Knowledge developed and retained within each subsidiary	Knowledge mostly developed and retained at the center and key locations	Knowledge developed jointly and shared worldwide
Flow of knowledge	Extensive flow of knowledge and people from headquarters to subsidiaries	Limited flow of knowledge and people to and from the center	Extensive flow of knowledge and people from the center and key locations to subsidiaries	Extensive flow of knowledge and people in multiple directions

Sources: C. Bartlett and S. Ghoshal, *Managing Across Borders: The Transnational Solution* (Boston: Harvard Business School Press, 1989) 65; T. Kostova and K. Roth, "Social capital in multinational corporations and a micro-macro model of its formation," *Academy of Management Review* 28 (2003): 299.

structures, processes, and systems that actively develop, leverage, and transfer knowledge.

Many managers regard knowledge management as simply information management. Taken to an extreme, "such a perspective can result in a profoundly mistaken belief that the installation of sophisticated information technology (IT) infrastructure is the be-all and end-all of knowledge management."[9] Knowledge management depends not only on IT but also on informal social relationships within the MNE.[10] This is because there are two categories of knowledge: (1) explicit knowledge and (2) tacit knowledge. **Explicit knowledge** is codifiable—that is, it can be written down and transferred with little loss of richness. Virtually all of the knowledge captured, stored, and transmitted by IT is explicit. **Tacit knowledge** is non-codifiable, and its acquisition and transfer require hands-on practice. For example, reading a driver's manual (which contains a ton of explicit knowledge) without any road practice does not make you a good driver. Tacit knowledge is evidently more important and harder to transfer and learn; it can only be acquired through learning by doing (driving in this case). Consequently, from a resource-based view, explicit knowledge captured by IT may be strategically *less* important. What counts is the hard-to-codify and hard-to-transfer tacit knowledge.

Knowledge Management in Four Types of Multinational Enterprises

Differences in knowledge management among four types of MNEs in Exhibit 12.1 fundamentally stem from the interdependence (1) between the headquarters and foreign subsidiaries and (2) among various subsidiaries, as illustrated in Exhibit 12.8.[11] In MNEs pursuing a home replication strategy, such interdependence is moderate and the

role of subsidiaries is largely to adapt and leverage parent-company competencies. Thus, knowledge on new products and technologies is mostly developed at the center and flown to subsidiaries, representing the traditional one-way flow. Starbucks, for example, insists on replicating its US coffee shop concept around the world, down to the elusive "atmosphere."

When MNEs adopt a localization strategy, the interdependence is low. Knowledge management centers on developing insights that can best serve local markets. Ford of Europe used to develop cars for Europe, with a limited flow of knowledge to and from headquarters.

In MNEs pursuing a global standardization strategy, on the other hand, the interdependence is increased. Knowledge is developed and retained at the headquarters and a few centers of excellence. Consequently, knowledge and people typically flow from headquarters and these centers to other subsidiaries. For example, Yokogawa Hewlett-Packard, HP's subsidiary in Japan, won a coveted Japanese Deming Prize for quality. The subsidiary was then charged with transferring such knowledge to the rest of HP, which resulted in a tenfold improvement in *corporate*-wide quality in ten years.

A hallmark of transnational MNEs is a high degree of interdependence and extensive and bidirectional flows of knowledge. For example, Häagen-Dazs developed a popular ice cream in Argentina that was based on a locally popular caramelized milk dessert. The company then took the new flavor and sold it as Dulce De Leche throughout the

Explicit knowledge
Knowledge that is codifiable (that is, can be written down and transferred with little loss of richness).

Tacit knowledge
Knowledge that is non-codifiable, whose acquisition and transfer require hands-on practice.

United States and Europe. Within one year, it became the second most popular Häagen-Dazs ice cream, next only to vanilla. Particularly fundamental to transnational MNEs is knowledge flows among dispersed subsidiaries. Instead of a top-down hierarchy, the MNE thus can be conceptualized as an integrated network of subsidiaries. Each subsidiary not only develops locally relevant knowledge but also aspires to contribute knowledge to benefit the MNE as a whole.

Globalizing Research and Development

R&D represents an especially crucial arena for knowledge management. Relative to production and marketing, only more recently has R&D emerged as an important function to be internationalized—often known as innovation-seeking investment (see Chapter 10). For example, Airbus has a significant R&D presence in Wichita, Kansas. Motorola has R&D units around the world. Intense competition for innovation drives the globalization of R&D. Such R&D provides a way to gain access to a foreign country's local talents.

From a resource-based standpoint, a fundamental basis for competitive advantage is innovation-based firm heterogeneity (that is, being different). Decentralized R&D work performed by different locations and teams around the world virtually guarantees that there will be persistent heterogeneity in the solutions generated. Britain's GSK, for example, began aggressively spinning off R&D units as it became clear that simply adding more researchers in centralized R&D units did not necessarily enhance global learning and innovation.[12] Overall, the scale and scope of R&D by MNE units in host countries has grown significantly in recent years.

LO4 *List three things you can do to make a multinational firm successful.*

MANAGEMENT SAVVY

MNEs are the ultimate large, complex, and geographically dispersed business organizations. What determines the success or failure of multinational strategies, structures, and learning? The answer boils down to the institution-based and resource-based dimensions. The institution-based view calls for thorough understanding and skillful manipulation of the rules of the game, both at home and abroad. The resource-based view focuses on the development and deployment of firm-specific capabilities to enhance the odds for success.

© KRT PHOTO BY JAMES F. QUINN/CHICAGO TRIBUNE/Newscom

Consequently, three clear implications emerge for savvy managers (see Exhibit 12.9). First, understanding and mastering the external rules of the game governing MNEs and home/host-country environments become a must. For example, some MNEs take advantage of the rules that subsidiaries in different countries need to be registered as independent legal entities in these countries, and claim that other subsidiaries do not have to be responsible for the wrongdoing of one subsidiary in one country (see In Focus). Other MNEs abandon their original countries of origin and move their headquarters to be governed by more market-friendly and politically stable laws and regulations in their new countries of domicile (see the Closing Case).

Second, managers need to understand and be prepared to change the internal rules of the game governing MNE management. Different strategies and structures call for different internal rules. Some facilitate and others constrain MNE actions. A firm using a home replication strategy should not appoint a foreigner as its CEO. Yet, as an MNE becomes more global in its operations, its managerial outlook needs to be broadened as well. While not every MNE needs to appoint a foreigner as its head, the foreign-born bosses at Coca-Cola, Nissan, and Sony represent one of the strongest signals about these firms' global outlook.

Finally, managers need to actively develop learning and innovation capabilities to leverage multinational presence. A winning formula is: *Think global, act local.*[13] Failing to do so may be costly. In 1999 and 2000, Ford Explorer SUVs were involved in numerous fatal rollover accidents in the United States. Most of these accidents were blamed on faulty tires made by Japan's Bridgestone and its US subsidiary Firestone. However, before the increase in US accidents, an alarming number of similar accidents had already taken place in warmer-weather countries such as Brazil and Saudi Arabia—tires wear out faster in warmer

EXHIBIT 12.9 Implications for Action

- Understand and master the external rules of the game governing MNEs and home-country/host-country environments.
- Understand and be prepared to change the internal rules of the game governing MNE management.
- Develop learning and innovation capabilities to leverage multinational presence as an asset—"think global, act local."

© Cengage Learning 2013

IN FOCUS

ETHICAL DILEMMA

One Multinational Versus Many National Companies

We often treat each MNE as one firm, regardless of the number of countries in which it operates. However, from an institution-based standpoint, one can argue that a *multinational* enterprise may not exist. Legally, incorporation is only possible under national law, so every so-called MNE is essentially a bunch of *national* companies (subsidiaries) registered in various countries. A generation ago, such firms were often labeled "multi-national companies" with a hyphen. Although some pundits argue that globalization is undermining the power of national governments, there is little evidence that the modern nation-state system, in existence since the 1648 Treaty of Westphalia, is retreating.

This debate is not just academic hair splitting—fighting over a hyphen. It is very relevant and stakes are high. One case in point is the 2009 bankruptcy of General Motors (GM). While the US and Canadian governments bailed out GM by taking over 61% and 8% of its equity, respectively, they technically only bailed out GM's North American operations. GM could not use US and Canadian taxpayer dollars to fund overseas operations. As a result, GM's Opel subsidiary, based in Germany, had to be rescued by the German government, creating a major political firestorm (see Chapter 6 Closing Case).

Another case in point is brought by Indian firm Satyam's recent scandal. Satyam is listed on the New York Stock Exchange (NYSE), and PricewaterhouseCoopers (PwC) endorsed Satyam's books even though $1 billion cash on the books did not exist at all. While such sloppy auditing was done by PwC India, some Satyam shareholders have sued PwC International Limited headquartered in New York. But a PwC International spokesman argued in interviews that "there is no such thing as a global firm because we are a membership organization." That is to say: PwC India, registered in India, is a legally independent firm whose conduct has nothing to do with other nationally registered firms such as PwC International or PwC Hong Kong. On PwC India's website, it is noted that PwC "refers to the network of member firms of PricewaterhouseCoopers International Limited, each of which is a separate and independent legal entity." In 2011, the Securities and Exchange Commission (SEC) and the Public Company Accounting Oversight Board in the United States fined PwC India $7.5 million in what was described as "the largest American penalty ever against a foreign accounting firm." Meanwhile, former client Satyam agreed to pay $125 million to settle US

AP Images

shareholder litigation and another $10 million to settle a fraud case with the SEC. Together with the pending lawsuits from dismayed Satyam shareholders, some observers estimate that claims against PwC may reach $1 billion. In court battles, whether the argument that PwC International is not responsible for PwC India's misconduct and can repel the pending lawsuits remains to be seen.

Sources: "For accounting giants, nowhere to hide?" *BusinessWeek*, 16 February 2009: 56–57; S. Kobrin, "Sovereignty@bay," in A. Rugman (ed.), *The Oxford Handbook of International Business* (New York: Oxford University Press, 2009) 183–204; http://www.pwc.com/in/en/index.jhtml; "Satyam of India and PricewaterhouseCoopers settle accounting fraud case," *New York Times*, 5 April 2011; "Satyam Computer agrees to pay $125 million to settle US suit," *Bloomberg Businessweek*, 17 February 2011.

---

weather. Local Firestone managers dutifully reported the accidents to headquarters in Japan and the United States. Unfortunately, these reports were dismissed by the higher-ups as due to driver error or road conditions. Bridgestone/Firestone thus failed to leverage its multinational presence

as an asset. It should have learned from these reports and proactively probed into the potential for similar accidents in cooler-weather countries. In the end, lives were lost unnecessarily, and informed car buyers abandoned the Bridgestone/Firestone brand.

ETHICAL DILEMMA
MOVING HEADQUARTERS OVERSEAS

While many MNEs have been moving operations around the world, a small number of them have also moved headquarters (HQ) overseas. In general, there are two levels of HQ: *business unit HQ* and *corporate HQ*. At the business unit level, examples are numerous. In 2004, Nokia moved its corporate finance HQ from Helsinki, Finland, to New York. In 2006, IBM's global procurement office moved from New York to Shenzhen, China. In 2009, Nomura moved the HQ of its investment banking division from Tokyo to London. Examples for corporate HQ relocations are fewer, but they tend to be of higher profile. In 1992, HSBC moved corporate HQ from Hong Kong to London. Similarly, Anglo American, Old Mutual, and SAB (later to become SABMiller after acquiring Miller Beer) moved from South Africa to London. In 2004, News Corporation moved corporate HQ from Melbourne, Australia, to New York. In 2005, Lenovo set up corporate HQ in Raleigh, North Carolina, home of IBM's former PC division that Lenovo acquired. The question is: Why?

If you have moved from one house to another in the same city, you can easily appreciate the logistical challenges (and nightmares!) associated with relocating HQ overseas. A simple answer is that the benefits must significantly outweigh the drawbacks. At the business unit level, the answer is straightforward: the "center of gravity" of the activities of a business unit may pull its HQ toward a host country. See the following letter to suppliers from IBM's chief procurement officer informing them of the move to China:

IBM Global Procurement is taking a major step toward developing a more geographically distributed executive structure . . . By anchoring the organization in this location, we will be better positioned to continue developing the skills and talents of our internal organization in the region . . . Clearly, this places us closer to the core of the technology supply chain which is important not only for IBM's own internal needs, but increasingly for the needs of external clients whose supply chains we are managing via our Procurement Services offering. As IBM's business offerings continue to grow, we must develop a deeper supply chain in the region to provide services and human resource skills to clients both within Asia and around the world.

At the corporate level, there are at least five strategic rationales. First, a leading symbolic value is an unambiguous statement to various stakeholders that the firm is a global player. News Corporation's new corporate HQ in New York is indicative of its global status, as opposed to being a relatively parochial firm from "down under." Lenovo's coming of age is no doubt underpinned by the establishment of its worldwide HQ in the United States.

Second, there may be significant efficiency gains. If the new corporate HQ is in a major financial center such as New York or London, the MNE can have more efficient, more direct, and more frequent communication with institutional shareholders, financial analysts, and investment banks. The MNE also increases its visibility in a financial market, resulting in a broader shareholder base and greater market capitalization. As a result, three leading (former) South African firms, Anglo American, Old Mutual, and SABMiller, have now joined FTSE 100—the top 100 UK-listed firms by capitalization.

Third, firms may benefit from their visible commitment to the laws of the new host country. By making such a commitment, firms benefit from the higher quality legal and regulatory regime they now operate under. These benefits are especially crucial for firms from emerging economies where local rules are not world-class. A lack of confidence about South Africa's political stability drove Anglo American, Old Mutual, and SABMiller to London. By coming to London, HSBC likewise deviated from its Hong Kong roots at a time before the 1997 handover when the political future of Hong Kong was uncertain.

Fourth, moving corporate HQ to a new country clearly indicates a commitment to that country. In addition to political motivation, HSBC's move to London signaled its determination to become a more global player instead of being a regional player centered on Asia. HSBC indeed carried out this more global strategy since the 1990s. However, in an interesting twist of events, HSBC's CEO relocated back to Hong Kong in 2010. Technically, HSBC's corporate HQ is still in London, and its chairman remains in London. However, the symbolism of the CEO's return to Hong Kong is clear. As China becomes more economically powerful, HSBC is interested in demonstrating its commitment to that part of the world, which was where HSBC started (HSBC was set up in Hong Kong in 1865 as Hongkong and Shanghai Banking Corporation).

Finally, by moving (or threatening to move) HQ, firms enhance their bargaining power vis-à-vis that of their (original) home-country governments. Tetra Pak's 1981 move of its corporate HQ to Switzerland was driven primarily by the owners' tax disputes with the Swedish government. A few years ago, Seagate Technology, formerly registered in Silicon Valley, changed its incorporation to the Cayman Islands in search of lower taxes. More US firms may follow such a move. Having already paid overseas taxes, US-based MNEs naturally resented the Obama administration's proposal to extract from them $109 billion in additional US taxes. "Doesn't the Obama administration recognize that most big US companies are multinationals that happen to be headquartered in the United States?" asked Duncan Niederauer, CEO of NYSE Euronext in a *BusinessWeek* interview. Likewise, as three of Britain's large banks—Barclays, HSBC, and Standard Chartered, the three that didn't need bailouts—now face higher taxes and more government intervention, they too have threatened to move their HQ out of London. The message is clear: If the home-country government treats us harshly, we will pack our bags.

The last point, of course, is where the ethical and social responsibility controversies erupt. Although the absolute number of jobs lost is not great, these are high-quality (and high-paying) jobs that every government would prefer to see stay. More alarmingly, if a sufficient number of HQ move overseas, there is a serious ramification that other high-quality service providers, such as lawyers, bankers, and accountants, will follow them. In response, proposals are floating to offer tax incentives for these "footloose" MNEs to keep HQ at home. However, critics question why these wealthy MNEs (and executives) need to be subsidized (or bribed), while many other sectors and individuals are struggling.

Sources: J. Birkinshaw, P. Braunerhjelm, U. Holm, and S. Terjesen, "Why do some multinational corporations relocate their headquarters overseas?" *Strategic Management Journal*, 27 (2006): 681–700; "NYSE chief Duncan Niederauer on Obama and business," *BusinessWeek*, 8 June 2009, 15–16; "Las Vegas leaving," *Economist*, 4 December 2010, 71; IBM, "IBM Procurement headquarters moves to Shenzhen, China," 22 May 2006, available online at http://www-03.ibm.com; "HSBC re-emphasizes its 'H,'" *Wall Street Journal*, 26 September 2009, available online at http://www.wsj.com.

USE THE TOOLS.

- Rip out the Review Cards in the back of your book to study.

Or Visit CourseMate to:

- Read, search, highlight, and take notes in the Interactive eBook
- Review Flashcards (Print or Online) to master key terms
- Test yourself with Auto-Graded Quizzes
- Bring concepts to life with Games, Videos, and Animations!

Go to CourseMate for GLOBAL to begin using these tools.
Access at **www.cengagebrain.com**

Complete the Speak Up survey in CourseMate at
www.cengagebrain.com

f Follow us at
www.facebook.com/4ltrpress

©iStockphoto.com/A-Digit | © Cengage Learning 2013

Managing Human Resources GLOBALLY

CHAPTER 13

OPENING CASE

Managing Human Resources in Recession

During the 2008–2009 recession, the world economy faced the greatest rise in unemployment in decades. In China, 20 million employees, mostly migrant workers, lost their jobs. In India, about ten million were let go. As bad as the US unemployment level of 9% was (which broke a record), Spain's 18% unemployment, the highest in the EU, was double the US level. As the recession intensified its grip on the world, the role of human resource management (HRM) also intensified. HR managers occupied the center stage of the recession's bad news. Armed with the sympathetic box of tissues, HR managers frequently attended tearful layoff meetings. While they often played no role in layoff decisions (which were typically made by line managers), HR managers fielded angry calls about broken promises and did the dirty work of managing termination details. "If there was ever a time to underscore the importance of HR," *BusinessWeek* announced, "it has arrived."

As unemployment numbers skyrocketed around the world, how to manage layoffs and how to manage survivors remained at the heart of HRM challenges during the recession. Experts suggested that firms needed to treat laid-off employees with dignity, fairness, and respect. For plant closures and large-scale layoffs, key milestones and dates needed to be communicated well in advance. The business case needed to be explained in detail. Affected employees would preferably be given options for finding other jobs inside the company or resources to hunt for jobs outside. HR managers were advised to show compassion and understanding. This could be done not only in words, but also in concrete ways, such as offering to serve as a reference to prospective employers.

Unfortunately, too many firms did not do it right. Many line managers did not have the guts to face laid-off employees, and hid

LEARNING OBJECTIVES
After studying this chapter, you should be able to:

LO1 *explain staffing decisions, with a focus on expatriates.*

LO2 *identify training and development needs for expatriates and host-country nationals.*

LO3 *discuss compensation and performance appraisal issues.*

LO4 *list factors that affect labor relations in both home and host countries.*

LO5 *discuss how the institution-based and resource-based views shed additional light on human resource management.*

LO6 *identify the five Cs of human resource management.*

©iStockphoto.com/YinYang

behind HR managers who had to deliver the bad news. Losing one's job is dehumanizing in any event, but many employees left feeling alienated and unfairly treated. Further, a lot of firms gave in to the temptation to short change employees on severance when downsizing. As a result, employee lawsuits for unlawful termination skyrocketed. Around the world, different countries have different rules for severance arrangements. In France, employees are entitled to 30 days of severance pay for each year—an employee with 20 years of service can walk away with 20 months of pay. In Germany and India, the severance is two weeks pay per year of service. In Britain, it is a minimum of $470 per year of service. In China and Russia, workers can be fired with only one month of wages. In the United States, there is no legal requirement for severance pay.

In addition to the stress of managing layoffs, managing surviving employees was no less challenging. Even when jobs were relatively safe, employees still asked: When would the layoffs come? Survivors often saw their salaries and hours cut, budgets shaved, and perks gone. Many employees were preemptively organizing unions or calling hotlines for suspected corporate wrongdoing. Per US law, once employees reported any corporate wrongdoing (whether real or bogus), they would become a protected class ("whistleblowers"), and employers firing them could be easily dragged into court as evidence for retaliation against them. As a result, the outspoken and the litigious often ended up

becoming an influential group among the surviving rank and file, undermining firms' ability to get the real job done.

Not all HR news was bad in this tough time. One innovative practice emerging out of the recent recession was to tell laid-off employees: "You're fired—but please stay in touch." From Dow Chemical to JPMorgan Chase, many firms now labeled laid-off, former employees "alumni," and cultivated alumni networks online as a forum for opportunities in networking and for possible future rehiring. When the economy recovers, firms hope to recruit some of these "alumni" back. Such hire-back cases are now called "boomerangs" in the new HR jargon. By showing compassion and understanding to laid-off employees, such firms hope to preserve some goodwill in a tough time. Advising CEOs, two experts wrote: "HR matters enormously in good times. It defines you in bad times."

Sources: "Human resources: They're human, too," *BusinessWeek*, 27 July 2009, 19; "The hidden perils of layoffs," *BusinessWeek*, 2 March 2009, 52–53; "You're fired— but stay in touch," *BusinessWeek*, 4 May 2009, 54–55; "When jobs disappear," *Economist*, 14 March 2009, 71–73; R. Sutton, "How to be a good boss in a bad economy," *Harvard Business Review*, June 2009: 42–50; US Department of Labor, eLaws: FLSA advisor, 2011, http://www.dol.gov; J. Welch and S. Welch, "Layoffs: HR's moment of truth," *BusinessWeek*, March 23 & 30 2009, 104.

HR matters enormously in good times. It defines you in bad times.

How can firms select, retain, reward, and motivate the best employees that they can attract? How can they link the management of people with firm performance? During a recession, how can they manage both the surviving employees and laid-off workers? These are some of the crucial questions we will address in this chapter. This chapter is devoted to **human resource management** (HRM)—activities that attract, select, and manage employees. As a function, HRM used to be called "personnel" and before that "records management." Few of you are HRM experts, but everyone can appreciate HRM's rising importance just by looking at the evolution of the terminology. The term "HRM" clearly indicates that people are key resources of the firm to be actively managed and developed. From a lowly administrative support function, HRM has now

increasingly been recognized as a strategic function that, together with other crucial functions such as finance and marketing, helps accomplish organizational goals and financial performance.[1]

This chapter first reviews the four main areas of HRM: (1) staffing, (2) training and development, (3) compensation and performance appraisal, and (4) labor relations. Then, we use the institution-based and resource-based views to shed light on these issues. We will also consider whether it is better in a crisis to lay off employees or cut pay—a major debate in HRM. To conclude, we will outline the five Cs of HRM.

> **LO1** *Explain staffing decisions, with a focus on expatriates.*

STAFFING

Staffing refers to HRM activities associated with hiring employees and filling positions. In multinational enterprises (MNEs), there are two types of employees. **Host-country nationals (HCNs)** are from the host country and are often known as "locals." First introduced in Chapter 1, expatriates (expats for short) are individuals working in a foreign country. **Parent-country nationals (PCNs)** come from the parent country of the MNE and work at its local

---

Human resource management (HRM)
Activities that attract, select, and manage employees.

Staffing
HRM activities associated with hiring employees and filling positions.

Host-country national (HCN)
An individual from the host country who works for an MNE.

Parent-country national (PCN)
An employee who comes from the parent (home) country of the MNE and works at its local subsidiary.

EXHIBIT 13.1 Parent-, Third-, and Host-Country Nationals

	Advantages	Disadvantages
Parent-country nationals (PCNs)	• Control by headquarters is facilitated • PCNs may be the most qualified people • Managers are given international experience	• Opportunities for HCNs are limited • Adaptation may take a long time • PCNs are usually very expensive
Third-country nationals (TCNs)	• TCNs may bridge the gap between headquarters and the subsidiary (and between PCNs and HCNs) • TCNs may be less expensive than PCNs	• Host government and employees may resent TCNs • Similar to disadvantages for PCNs
Host-country nationals (HCNs)	• Language and cultural barriers are eliminated • Continuity of management improves, since HCNs stay longer in positions • Usually cheaper	• Control and coordination by headquarters may be impeded • HCNs may have limited career opportunities • International experience for PCNs are limited

Source: P. Dowling and D. Welch, *International Human Resource Management*, 4th ed. (Cincinnati: Thomson South-Western, 2005) 63.

© Howard Grey/Stone/Getty Images

subsidiary. **Third-country nationals (TCNs)** come from neither the parent country nor the host country.

The majority of an MNE's employees would be HCNs. For example, of Siemens's 400,000 employees worldwide, only a small cadre of 300 executives are expatriates and another 2,000 executives are short-term assignees abroad. Of these 2,300 executives, about 60% are PCNs (Germans) and 40% are TCNs (from countries other than Germany and the host country). A leading concern is how to staff the *top* positions abroad, such as the subsidiary CEO, country manager, and key functional heads such as CFO and CIO. The three choices for top positions—PCNs, TCNs, and HCNs—all have their pros and cons (see Exhibit 13.1). The staffing choices are not random and are often a reflection of the strategic posture of the MNE, as discussed next.

Ethnocentric, Polycentric, and Geocentric Approaches in Staffing

There are three primary approaches for making staffing decisions for top positions at subsidiaries. An **ethnocentric** approach emphasizes the norms and practices of the parent company (and the parent country of the MNE) by relying on PCNs. Not only can PCNs ensure and facilitate control and coordination by headquarters, they may also be the best qualified people for the job because of special skills and experience. A perceived lack of talent and skills among HCNs often necessitates an ethnocentric approach. In addition, a cadre of internationally mobile and experienced managers, who are often PCNs, can emerge to spearhead further expansion around the world.

As the opposite of an ethnocentric approach, a **polycentric approach** focuses on the norms and practices of the host country. In short, "when in Rome, do as the Romans do." Who would be the best managers in Rome? Naturally, Roman (or Italian) managers—technically, HCNs. HCNs have no language or cultural barriers. Unlike PCNs who often pack their bags and move after several years, HCNs stay in their positions longer, thus providing more continuity of management. Further, placing HCNs in top subsidiary positions sends a morale-boosting signal to other HCNs who may feel they can reach the top as well (at least in that subsidiary).

Disregarding nationality, a **geocentric approach** focuses on finding the most suitable managers, who can be PCNs, HCNs, or TCNs. In other words, a geocentric approach is color-blind—the

Third-country national (TCN)
An employee who comes from neither the parent country nor the host country of the MNE.

Ethnocentric approach
A staffing approach that emphasizes the norms and practices of the parent company (and the parent country of the MNE) by relying on PCNs.

Polycentric approach
A staffing approach that emphasizes the norms and practices of the host country by relying on HCNs.

Geocentric approach
A staffing approach that focuses on finding the most suitable managers, who can be PCNs, HCNs, or TCNs.

EXHIBIT 13.2 Multinational Strategies and Staffing Approaches

MNE strategies	Typical staffing approaches	Typical top managers at local subsidiaries
Home replication	Ethnocentric	Parent-country nationals
Localization	Polycentric	Host-country nationals
Global standardization	Geocentric	A mix of parent-, host-, and third-country nationals
Transnational	Geocentric	A mix of parent-, host-, and third-country nationals

© Cengage Learning 2013

color of a manager's passport does not matter. For a geographically dispersed MNE, a geocentric approach can help create a corporate-wide culture and identity. This can reduce the typical us-versus-them feeling in firms that use either ethnocentric or polycentric approaches. On the other hand, molding managers from a variety of nationalities is a lot more complex than integrating individuals from two (parent and host) countries.

Overall, there is a systematic link between the strategic posture of an MNE (see Chapter 12) and its staffing approaches (see Exhibit 13.2). MNEs pursuing a home replication strategy usually use an ethnocentric approach, staffing subsidiaries with PCNs. MNEs interested in a localization strategy are typically polycentric in nature, hiring HCNs to head subsidiaries. Global standardization or transnational strategies often require a geocentric approach, resulting in a mix of HCNs, PCNs, and TCNs.[2]

The Role of Expatriates

Expatriation is leaving one's home country to work in another country. Shown in Exhibit 13.3, expatriates play four important roles. First, expatriates are *strategists* representing the interests of the MNE's headquarters. Expatriates, especially PCNs who have a long tenure with a particular MNE, may have internalized the parent firm's values and norms. They may not only enable headquarters to control subsidiaries, but also facilitate the socialization process to bring subsidiaries into an MNE's global orbit.

Second, expatriates are *daily managers* who run operations and build local capabilities where local management talent is lacking. Third, expatriates are *ambassadors.*[3] Representing headquarters' interests, they build relationships with host-country stakeholders such as local managers, employees, suppliers, customers, and government officials. Importantly, expatriates also serve as ambassadors representing the interests of the *subsidiaries* when interacting with headquarters.

Finally, expatriates are *trainers* for their replacements. Over time, some localization in staffing is inevitable, calling for expatriates to train local employees.[4]

Expatriate Failure and Selection

Few expatriates can play the challenging multidimensional roles effectively.[5] It is not surprising that expatriate failure rates are high. Expatriate failure can be defined several ways, including (1) premature (earlier-than-expected) return, (2) unmet business objectives, and (3) unfulfilled career development objectives. Using the easiest-to-observe measure of premature return, studies in the 1980s reported that 76% of US MNEs had expatriate failure rates of more than 10% and that 41% and 24% of European and Japanese MNEs, respectively, had comparable failure rates.[6] More recent studies find that the failure rates may have declined slightly. However, given the much larger number of expatriates now (1.3 million from the United States alone), expatriate failure rates are still high enough to justify attention. Since expatriates typically are the most expensive group of managers, the cost of each failure is tremendous—between a quarter of a million and one million dollars.

Expatriation can fail for a variety of reasons. Surveys of US and European MNEs find that the leading cause is the spouse and family's inability to adjust to life in a foreign country. In the case of Japanese MNEs, the leading cause is the inability to cope with the larger scope of responsibilities overseas. It usually is a *combination* of work-related and family-related problems that leads to expatriate failures.

Given the importance of expatriates and their reported high failure rates, how can firms enhance the odds for

Expatriation
Leaving one's home country to work in another country.

EXHIBIT 13.3 The Roles of Expatriates

MNE headquarters in parent country ↔

Expatriate Roles
- Strategist
- Daily manager
- Ambassador
- Trainer

↔ Subsidiary in host country

© Cengage Learning 2013

EXHIBIT 13.4 Factors in Expatriate Selection

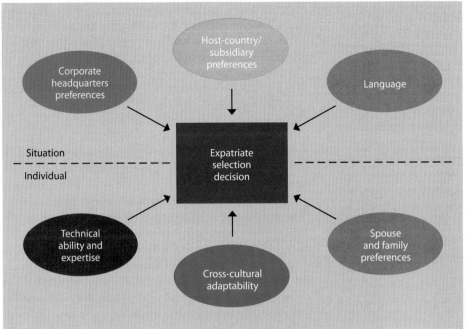

Source: P. Dowling and D. Welch, *International Human Resource Management*, 4th ed. (Cincinnati: South-Western Thomson, 2005) 98.

expatriate success? Exhibit 13.4 outlines a model for expatriate selection, with six underlying factors grouped along situation and individual dimensions. In terms of situation dimensions, the preferences of both headquarters and the subsidiary are important. The subsidiary may also have specific requests, such as "Send a strong IT person." It is preferable for expatriates to have some command of the local language.

In terms of individual dimensions, both technical ability and cross-cultural adaptability are a must. Desirable attributes include a positive attitude, emotional stability, and previous international experience. Last (but certainly not least), spouse and family preferences must be considered. The accompanying spouse may leave behind a career and a social network. The spouse has to find meaningful endeavors abroad, but many countries protect local jobs by not permitting the spouse to work. It is not surprising that many families find expatria-

tion frustrating and that this frustration often leads to expatriate failure.

Expatriates are expensive and failure rates are high in general, but middle-aged expatriates (forty-somethings) are the most expensive. This age group typically has children still in school, so the employer often has to provide a heavy allowance for the children's education. High-quality schools can be expensive. In places such as Manila, Mexico City, and Moscow, international or American schools cost $10,000 to $30,000 per year. Unfortunately, these expatriates also have the highest percentage of failure rates in part because of their family responsibilities. In response, many MNEs either select expatriates in their fifties, who are less likely to have school-age children, and/or promote younger expatriates in their late twenties and early thirties who may not yet have children. Younger expatriates typically do not need a large home or education allowance. Further, given the importance of international experience, many younger managers are eager to go overseas. This development has strong implications for students studying this book now: Overseas opportunities may come sooner than you expect. Are *you* ready?

Identify training and development needs for expatriates and host-country nationals.

TRAINING AND DEVELOPMENT

Training is specific preparation to do a particular job. **Development** refers to longer-term, broader preparation to improve managerial skills for a better career. Training and development programs focus on two groups: expatriates and HCNs. Each is discussed in turn.

Training
Specific preparation to do a particular job.

Development
Longer-term, broader preparation to improve managerial skills for a better career.

© iStockphoto.com/Anthony Rosenberg

Training for Expatriates

The importance and cost of expatriates and their reported high failure rates make training necessary. Yet, about one third of MNEs do not provide any pre-departure training for expatriates. Even for firms that provide training, many offer short, one-day programs that are inadequate. Not surprisingly, many MNEs and expatriates get burned by such underinvestment in preparation for what are arguably some of the most challenging managerial assignments.

Ideally, training length and rigor should correspond to the expatriate's expected length of stay. For a short stay, training can be short and less rigorous. Sometimes survival-level language training—such as how to say "Where is the lady's room?" and "I'd like a beer"—would suffice. However, for a long stay of several years, it is imperative that more in-depth and rigorous training be provided, especially for first-time expatriates. Preparation should involve more extensive language as well as sensitivity training, preferably with an immersion approach (training conducted in a foreign language/culture environment). Enlightened firms concerned about failure rates now often involve the spouse in expatriate training as well.

Development for Returning Expatriates (Repatriates)

Many expatriate assignments are not one-shot deals; instead, they are viewed as part of a manager's accumulated experience and expertise and enhance a long-term career in the firm. Thus, at some point, expatriates may become **repatriates**, individuals who return to their home countries to stay after working abroad for a length of time. While the idea to develop a repatriate's long-term career sounds good in theory, in practice, many MNEs do a lousy job managing **repatriation**, which is the process of returning to the expatriate's home country after an extended period overseas.

Chief among the problems experienced by repatriates is career anxiety. A leading

Repatriate
A manager who returns to his or her home country to stay after working abroad for a length of time.

Repatriation
Returning to an expatriate's home country after an extended period overseas.

Psychological contract
An informal understanding of expected delivery of benefits in the future for current services.

concern is "What kind of position will I have when I return?" Prior to departure, many expatriates are encouraged by their boss: "You should take (or volunteer for) this overseas assignment. It's a smart move for your career." Theoretically, this is known as a **psychological contract**, an informal understanding of expected delivery of benefits in the future for current services. A psychological contract is easy to violate. Bosses may change their minds. Or they may be replaced by new bosses. Violated psychological contracts naturally lead to disappointments.

Many returning expatriates find readjusting to the domestic workplace to be a painful experience. Ethnocentrism continues to characterize many MNEs. Many employees at headquarters have a bias when it comes to knowledge transfer, which typically moves from headquarters to subsidiaries via expatriates. Consequently, they are not interested in learning from returning expatriates, which would mean knowledge moving from subsidiaries to headquarters. This attitude typically leads repatriates to feel that their international experience is not appreciated. After being a big fish in a small pond at the subsidiary, repatriates often feel like a small fish in a big pond at headquarters. While many MNEs are growing operations in emerging economies that come with more opportunities, opportunities are more limited back home in developed economies, thanks to the downturn and shrinking headcount. Thus, instead of being promoted, many repatriates end up taking comparable (or lower-level) positions.

Repatriates may also experience a loss of status. Overseas, they are big shots, rubbing shoulders with local politicians and visiting dignitaries. They often command lavish expatriate premiums, with chauffeured cars and maids. But most of these perks disappear once they return to the home country.

Lastly, the spouse and the children may also find it difficult to adjust back home. The feeling of being a part of a relatively high-class, close-knit expatriate community is gone. Instead, life at home may now seem lonely, dull, and in some cases, dreadful. Children, being out of touch with current slang, sports, and fashion, may struggle to regain acceptance into peer groups back home. Having been brought up overseas, (re)adjusting back to the home-country educational system may be especially problematic. Some returning Japanese teenagers have committed suicide after failing to make the academic grade back home.

Overall, if not managed well, repatriation can be traumatic not only for expatriates and their

IN F●CUS

Expatriation Versus Inpatriation

Addressing the expatriation problem, one solution is **inpatriation**—relocating employees of a foreign subsidiary to the MNE's headquarters for the purposes of (1) filling skill shortages at headquarters and (2) developing a global mindset for such inpatriates. The term "inpatriation" of course is derived from "expatriation," and most inpatriates are expected to eventually return to their home country to replace expatriates. Examples would include IT inpatriates from India working at IBM in the United States and telecom inpatriates from China working at Alcatel in France. Technically, these inpatriates are expatriates from India and China, who will experience some of the problems associated with expatriation discussed earlier in this chapter.

In addition, some inpatriates, being paid by the going rate of their home (typically developing) countries, are upset after finding out the compensation level of colleagues at headquarters doing equivalent work—the cost of an Indian IT professional is approximately 10%–12% of that of an American one. Some inpatriates thus refuse to go back and decide to find work in their host countries. Other inpatriates go back to their home countries but quit their sponsoring MNEs—they jump ship to rival MNEs willing to pay more.

Of inpatriates who return to assume leadership positions in subsidiaries in their home countries (as planned), unfortunately, many are ineffective. In China, inpatriated ethnic Chinese often struggle with an ambiguous identity: Western headquarters views

them as "us," whereas HCNs also expect them to be "us." When these managers favor headquarters on issues where headquarters and locals conflict (such as refusing to pay HCNs more), HCNs view them as traitors of sorts. These problems erupt in spite of these inpatriates' Chinese roots— or perhaps *because* of their Chinese roots. Overall, one lesson is that there will be no panacea in international staffing. Inpatriates, just like expatriates, have their fair share of headaches.

Sources: Economist Intelligence Unit, *Up or Out: Next Moves for the Modern Expatriate* (London: The Economist, 2010); M. Kulkarni, M. Lengnick-Hall, and R. Valk, "Employee perceptions of repatriation in an emerging economy: The Indian experience," *Human Resource Management* 49 (2010): 531–548; M. W. Peng, "Making M&As fly in China," *Harvard Business Review* March (2006): 26–27.

© iStockphoto.com/rpphotos

---

families but also for the firm. Unhappy returning expatriates do not stay around long. Approximately one in four repatriates leave the firm within one year. Since a US MNE spends on average approximately $1 million on each expatriate over the duration of a foreign assignment, losing that individual can wipe out any return on investment. Worse yet, the returnee may end up working for a rival firm.

The best way to reduce expatriate turnover is a career development plan. A good plan also comes with a mentor. The mentor helps alleviate the out-of-sight, out-of-mind feeling by ensuring that the expatriate is not forgotten at headquarters and by helping secure a challenging position for the expatriate upon return. Another way to reduce expatriate turnover is to send more expatriates on short-term or commuter-type assignments, and rely more on local staff. The skill gap of the local staff can be overcome through inpatriation (see In Focus).

Overall, despite the numerous horror stories, many expatriates do succeed. Carlos Ghosn, after successfully turning around Nissan as a PCN, went on to become CEO of the parent company, Renault. To reach the top at most MNEs today, international experience is a must. Therefore,

despite the drawbacks, aspiring managers should not be deterred from taking overseas assignments. Who said being a manager was easy?

Training and Development for Host-Country Nationals

While most international HRM practice and research focus on expatriates, it is important to note that the training and development needs of HCNs deserve significant attention as well. In the ongoing war for talent in China, a key factor in retaining or losing top talent is which employer can provide better training and development opportunities. To slow turnover, many MNEs in China now have formal career development plans and processes for HCNs. GE, for example, has endeavored to make promising managers in China stimulated, energized, and recognized. This has resulted in a managerial turnover rate of "only" 7% per year,

Inpatriation
Relocating employees of a foreign subsidiary to the MNE's headquarters for the purposes of filling skill shortages at headquarters and developing a global mindset for such inpatriates.

substantially lower than the nationwide average of 40% for HCNs at the managerial rank working at multinationals in China.

COMPENSATION AND PERFORMANCE APPRAISAL

As part of HRM, **compensation** refers to salary and benefits. **Performance appraisal** is the evaluation of employee performance for the purpose of promotion, retention, or ending employment. Three related issues are: (1) compensation for expatriates, (2) compensation for HCNs, and (3) performance appraisal.

Compensation for Expatriates

A leading issue in international HRM is how to properly compensate, motivate, and retain expatriates. Exhibit 13.5 shows two primary approaches: going rate and balance sheet. The **going rate approach** pays expatriates the prevailing (going) rate for comparable positions in a host country. When Lenovo acquired IBM's PC division, it sent Chinese expatriates to New York and paid them the going rate for comparable positions for HCNs and other expatriates in New York. The going rate approach fosters equality among PCNs, TCNs, and HCNs within the same subsidiary. It also makes locations where pay is higher than the home country a more attractive place to work for PCNs and TCNs. Overall, this approach excels in its simplicity and fosters strong identification with the host country.

However, the going rate for the same position differs around the world, with the United States leading in managerial compensation. The typical US CEO commands a total compensation package of over $2 million, whereas a British CEO fetches less than $1 million, a Japanese CEO $500,000, and a Chinese CEO $200,000. According to the going rate approach, returning Lenovo expatriates, accustomed to New York-level salaries, will have a hard time accepting relatively lower Beijing-level salaries, thus triggering repatriation problems.

A second approach is the **balance sheet approach**, which balances the cost of living differences relative to parent-country levels and adds a financial inducement to make the package attractive. This method is the most widely used in expatriate compensation. Historically, this approach has been justified on the grounds that a majority of expatriates were coming from higher-pay, developed economies and going to lower-pay locations. Under these conditions, the going rate approach would not work because an expatriate from New York probably would not accept the lower going rate in Beijing. The balance sheet approach essentially pays Beijing-bound expatriates "New York Plus."

Compensation
Salary and benefits.

Performance appraisal
The evaluation of employee performance for the purposes of promotion, retention, or ending employment.

Going rate approach
A compensation approach that pays expatriates the prevailing (going) rate for comparable positions in a host country.

Balance sheet approach
A compensation approach that balances the cost-of-living differences based on parent-country levels and adds a financial inducement to make the package attractive.

EXHIBIT 13.5 Going Rate Versus Balance Sheet Approaches to Expatriate Compensation

	Advantages	Disadvantages
Going rate	• Equality among parent-, third-, and host-country nationals in the same location • Simplicity • Identification with host country	• Variation between assignments in different locations for the same employee • Re-entry problem if the going rate in the parent country is less than that in the host country
Balance sheet	• Equity between assignments for the same employee • Facilitates expatriate re-entry (repatriation)	• Costly and complex to administer • Great disparities between expatriates and host-country nationals

The "Plus" is non-trivial: additional financial inducement (premium), cost of living allowance (for housing and children's education), and a hardship allowance (fewer companies now pay a hardship allowance for Beijing, but many MNEs used to). Exhibit 13.6 shows one hypothetical example. Adding housing and taxation that the MNE pays (not shown in the exhibit), the total cost may reach $300,000.

The balance sheet approach has two advantages (see Exhibit 13.5). First, there is equity between assignments for the same employee, whose compensation is always anchored to the going rate in the parent country. Second, it also facilitates repatriation, because there is relatively little fluctuation between overseas and parent-country pay despite the cost-of-living differences around the world.

However, there are three disadvantages. The first is cost. Using the example in Exhibit 13.6, the cost can add up to $1 million for a three-year tour of duty. The second disadvantage is the great disparities between expatriates (especially PCNs) and HCNs. Such unequal pay naturally causes resentment by HCNs.

Lastly, the balance sheet approach is organizationally complex to administer. For a US firm operating in South Africa, both the American PCNs and Australian TCNs are typically compensated more than the South African HCNs. The situation becomes more complicated when the US firm recruits South African MBAs before they finish business school training in the United States. Should they be paid as locally hired HCNs in South Africa or as expatriates from the United States? What about TCNs from Kenya and Nigeria who also finish US MBA training and are interested in going to work for the US MNE in South Africa? Ideally, firms pay for a position regardless of passport color. However, the market for expatriate compensation is not quite there yet.

Compensation for Host-Country Nationals

At the bottom end of the compensation scale, low-level HCNs, especially those in developing countries, have relatively little bargaining power. The very reason that they have jobs at MNE subsidiaries is often because of their low labor cost—that is, they are willing to accept wage levels substantially lower than those in developed countries (see Exhibit 13.7). The HCNs compare their pay to the farmhands sweating in the fields and making much less, or to the army of unemployed who make nothing but still have a family to feed (see PengAtlas Maps 17 and 18). Despite accusations of exploitation by some social activists, MNEs in developing countries typically pay *higher* wages compared to similar positions in the local market.

On the other hand, HCNs in management and professional positions increasingly have bargaining power. MNEs are rushing into Brazil, Russia, India, and China (BRIC), where the local supply of top talent is limited. Some executives in China reportedly receive calls from headhunters every *day*.[7] It is not surprising that high-caliber HCNs, because of their scarcity, will fetch more pay. The question is: How much more? Most MNEs plan to eventually replace even top-level expatriates with HCNs, in part to save on costs. However, if HCNs occupying the same top-level positions are paid the same as expatriates, then there will be no cost savings. But MNEs unwilling to pay top dollar for local talent may end up losing high-caliber HCNs to competitors that are willing to do so. The war for talent is essentially a

EXHIBIT 13.6 A Hypothetical Annual Expatriate Compensation Package Using the Balance Sheet Approach

Items for a hypothetical US expatriate	Amount (US$)
Base salary	$150,000
Cost-of-living allowance (25%)	$37,500
Overseas premium (20%)	$30,000
Hardship allowance (20%)	$30,000
Housing deduction (–7%)	–$10,500
TOTAL (pretax)	$237,000

Note: The host country has a cost-of-living index of 150 relative to the United States. *Not* shown here are (1) the full cost of housing and (2) the cost to pay the difference between a higher income tax in a host country and a lower income tax in the parent country. Adding housing and taxation, the net cost of the MNE can reach $300,000 in this case.

EXHIBIT 13.7 Compensation for Host-Country Nationals in Asia (Average Monthly Pay in US$)

Dhaka, Bangladesh	Ho Chi Minh City, Vietnam	Jakarta, Indonesia	Shenyang, (north) China	Shenzhen, (south) China	Taipei, Taiwan	Seoul, Korea	Yokohama, Japan
$47	$100	$148	$197	$235	$888	$1,220	$3,099

Source: Extracted from data in "Global inflation starts with Chinese workers," *Bloomberg Businessweek*, 7 March 2011, 10.

Across-the-Board Pay Cut Versus Reduction in Force

Both HR and line managers often have to make tough decisions. One of the most challenging decisions is how to cope with an economic downturn such as the financial market meltdown during 2008 and 2009. Reduction in force (RIF), a euphemism for mass layoffs, is often used in the United States and the United Kingdom. Outside the Anglo-American world, however, mass layoffs are often viewed as unethical. Some critics label mass layoffs as "corporate cannibalism." One alternative is for the entire firm to have an across-the-board pay cut while preserving all current jobs. Which approach is better?

Earlier experiences with across-the-board pay cuts may provide some clue. In 2003, SARS hit Asia. The Portman Ritz-Carlton in Shanghai, a five-star hotel, implemented an across-the-board pay cut. A majority of Chinese HCNs supported this practice, as evidenced by the 99.9% employee satisfaction in that year. However, when US firms experiment with across-the-board pay cuts, the results tend to be very *negative*. To avoid RIF in its US facilities during the post-2001 downturn, Applied Materials implemented an across-the-board pay cut: Executives took a 10% hit, managers and professionals 5%, and hourly production workers 3%. The pay cut lasted for 18 months. An HR executive at Applied Materials commented:

This across-the-board pay cut has a longer lasting and far greater negative impact on morale than an RIF would have. RIFs are very hard on the impacted employees as well as the survivors. However, when managed correctly, impacted employees are able to separate from the company with dignity and in the case of Applied Materials, with a very generous financial package.... I don't know of any surviving employees that appreciated having their paycheck impacted every two weeks for 18 months.... Ultimately, pay levels were restored. However, employee memories are very long and this particular event was pointed to over and over again throughout multiple employee surveys as an indicator of poor leadership and a major cause of employee dissatisfaction.

Applied Materials and other US firms that implemented across-the-board pay cuts lost numerous star performers who found greener pastures elsewhere. This raises serious concerns as to whether such large-scale sacrifice is worth it, at least in an individualistic culture. In the 2008–2009 recession, a small but increasing number of US firms such as FedEx, HP, and The New York Times Company trimmed base pay for all employees—more for senior executives than for the rank and file. While President Obama praised such practices in his inaugural speech in January 2009, some HRM experts complained that these managers are "chicken managers" who did not have the guts to make tough choices and therefore, in their cowardice, chose to inflict equal pain on everybody.

Sources: "Cutting salaries instead of jobs," *BusinessWeek*, 8 June 2009, 48; S. Parker, EMBA student in the author's class, individual assignment 1, University of Texas at Dallas, January 2007; A. Yeung, "Setting the people up for success," *Human Resource Management* 45 (2006): 267–275.

---

bidding war for top HCNs. MNEs may eventually have to pay international rates for qualified individuals in top positions, regardless of nationality.

Performance Appraisal

While initial compensation is determined upon entering a firm, follow-up compensation usually depends on performance appraisal. Performance appraisal helps managers make decisions about pay and promotion, development, documentation, and subordinate expression. In our case, performance appraisal is based on how expatriates provide performance appraisal to HCNs and how expatriates are evaluated.

When expatriates evaluate HCNs, cultural differences may create problems.[8] Western MNEs typically see performance appraisals as an opportunity for subordinates to express themselves. In high power distance countries such as those in Asia and Latin America, however, such an expression may potentially undermine the power and status of supervisors. Employees themselves do not place a lot of importance on self-expression. So Western expatriates who push HCNs in these cultures to express themselves in performance appraisal meetings would be viewed as indecisive and lacking integrity.

Expatriates need to be evaluated by their own supervisors. In some cases, however, expatriates are the top manager in a subsidiary (such as country manager), and their supervisors are more senior executives based at headquarters. Some of these off-site managers have no experience as expatriates themselves. They often evaluate expatriates based on hard numbers (such as productivity and market growth), but sometimes these numbers are beyond the expatriate's control (such as effects from a currency crisis). This is one of the reasons why many expatriates think they are not evaluated fairly. The solution lies in fostering more visits and communication between on-site expatriates and off-site supervisors.

Always sensitive, compensation and performance evaluation are even more important during tough economic times. Facing grave financial situations, should the firm impose an across-the-board pay cut or engage in reduction in force, which is massive layoffs? (See the Debate and the

Closing Case.) If someone has to go, according to what criteria should the firm decide who will receive a pink slip first? (See the Opening Case.) These are crucial questions for which HR managers need to be prepared.

LO4 **List factors that affect labor relations in both home and host countries.**

LABOR RELATIONS

The term **labor relations** refers to a firm's relations with organized labor (unions) in both home and host countries. Each is discussed in turn.

Managing Labor Relations at Home

In developed economies, a firm's key concern is to cut costs and enhance competitiveness to fight off low-cost rivals from emerging economies such as China and India. Labor unions, on the other hand, are organized with the purpose of helping workers earn higher wages and obtain more benefits through collective bargaining. In the United States, unionized employees earn 30% more than nonunionized employees. As a result, disagreements and conflicts between managers and unions are natural.

The bargaining chip of labor unions is their credible threat to strike, slow down, refuse to work overtime, or cause some other form of disruption. The bargaining chip of managers is the threat to shut down operations and move jobs overseas. It is clear which side is winning. In the United States, union membership dropped from 20% of the workforce in 1983 to 12% now.

Unlike MNEs, which can move operations around the world, unions are organized on a country-by-country basis. Efforts to establish multinational labor organizations have not been effective. In the 1990s, US MNEs moved aggressively to Mexico to take advantage of NAFTA. The leading US union, the AFL-CIO, contacted the Mexican government and requested permission to recruit members in Mexico. It was flatly rejected. In 2007, the US House of Representatives passed a new Employee Free Choice Act, which was designed to make it easier to organize unions in the United States. It provoked fierce debates.

Managing Labor Relations Abroad

If given a choice, MNEs prefer to deal with non-unionized workforces. When Japanese and German automakers came to the United States, they avoided the Midwest, a union stronghold. Instead, these MNEs went to the rural South and set up non-union plants in small towns in Alabama (Mercedes and Hyundai), Kentucky (Toyota), and South Carolina (BMW). When MNEs have to deal with unions abroad, they often rely on experienced HCNs instead of locally inexperienced PCNs or TCNs.

Throughout many developing countries, governments typically welcome MNEs and simultaneously silence unions. However, things are changing. In 2010, a series of high-profile strikes took place at plants run by Taiwan's Foxconn and Japan's Honda in China. Instead of cracking down, the Chinese government chose to look the other way. Emboldened workers ended up forcing these MNEs to accept 30%–40% pay increases. The media widely reported that "the days of cheap labor [in China] are gone."[9]

LO5 **Discuss how the institution-based and resource-based views shed additional light on human resource management.**

INSTITUTIONS, RESOURCES, AND HUMAN RESOURCE MANAGEMENT

Having outlined the four basic areas of HRM, let us now turn to the institution-based and resource-based views to see how they shed additional light (see Exhibit 13.8 on the next page).

Institutions and Human Resource Management

Formal and informal rules of the game shape HRM significantly, both at home and abroad. Every country has *formal* rules, laws, and regulations governing the do's and don'ts of HRM. Foreign firms ignoring such rules do so at their own peril. For example, in Japan, firms routinely discriminate against women and minorities. However, when Japanese MNEs engage in such usual practices in the United States, they face legal charges.

On the other hand, foreign firms well versed in local regulations may take advantage of them. For example, the legal hurdles for firing full-time workers in France are legendary. When HP announced a plan to lay off 1,200 employees in France, then-president Jacques Chirac called HP directly and complained. However, it is this very difficulty in firing full-time workers that has made France a highly lucrative market for the US-based Manpower. French firms reluctant or unwilling to hire full-time employees value Manpower's expertise

Labor relations
A firm's relations with organized labor (unions) in both home and host countries.

EXHIBIT 13.8 Institutions, Resources, and Human Resource Management

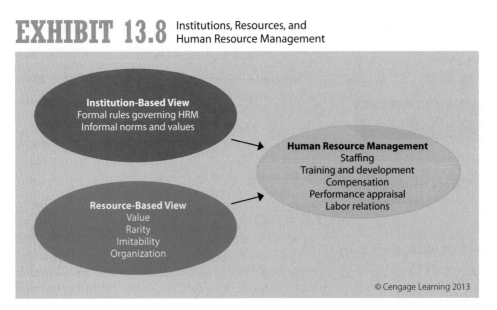

Institution-Based View
Formal rules governing HRM
Informal norms and values

Resource-Based View
Value
Rarity
Imitability
Organization

Human Resource Management
Staffing
Training and development
Compensation
Performance appraisal
Labor relations

© Cengage Learning 2013

in providing part-time workers. France is now Manpower's *largest* market, ahead of the United States.

Informal rules of the game, embodied in cultures, norms, and values, also assert powerful influence (see Exhibit 13.9). MNEs from different countries have different norms in staffing. Most Japanese MNEs follow an informal rule: Heads of foreign subsidiaries, at least initially, need to be PCNs. In comparison, European MNEs are more likely to appoint HCNs and TCNs to lead subsidiaries. There is a historical reason for such differences: Most European MNEs expanded globally before low-cost telephones, faxes, emails, and Skype were available. Thus, a localization strategy relying on HCNs and TCNs was necessary. Most Japanese MNEs went abroad in the 1980s, when modern communication technology enabled more centralized control from headquarters. In addition to technology, the Japanese cultural preference for low uncertainty also translated into a higher interest in headquarters' control. Thus, Japanese MNEs often implemented a home replication strategy that relied on PCNs who constantly communicated with headquarters.

While informal cultures, norms, and values are important, HR managers need to avoid stereotyping and instead consider changes. In the area of compensation, one study hypothesized that presumably collectivistic Chinese managers would prefer a more egalitarian compensation compared to what their individualistic US counterparts would prefer. The results turn out to be surprising: Chinese managers actually prefer *more* merit-based pay, whereas US managers behave exactly the opposite.[10] In other words, the Chinese seem more "American" than Americans! Further digging has revealed that these are not average Chinese; they are HCNs working for some of the most competitive Western MNEs in China. The upshot? Naive adaptation to presumed local norms and values based on outdated stereotypes may backfire. HR managers must do more homework to better understand their HCNs.

EXHIBIT 13.9 Some Blunders in International HRM

A Spanish company sent a team of expatriates to Saudi Arabia. The group included a number of young, intelligent women dressed in current Spanish style. Upon arrival, the Saudi immigration official took one look at the women's short skirts and immediately put the entire team on the next flight back to Spain. The expatriate team and the company belatedly learned that despite the heat, women in Saudi Arabia never show their bare legs.

In Malaysia, an American expatriate was introduced to an important potential client he thought was named "Roger." He proceeded to call this person "Rog." Unfortunately, this person was a "Rajah," which is an important title of nobility. In this case, the American tendency to liberally use another person's first name—and to proactively shorten it—appeared disrespectful and insensitive. The Rajah walked away from the deal.

A Japanese CEO of a subsidiary in New York held a meeting of his staff, all of whom were American, to inform them that the firm had grave financial losses and that headquarters in Japan had requested that everybody redouble their efforts. The staff immediately redoubled their efforts—by sending their resumes out to other employers.

Source: D. Ricks, *Blunders in International Business*, 3rd ed. (Oxford: Blackwell, 1999) 95–105.

One norm that is changing is the necessity to pay extra compensation to attract higher-caliber and more senior expatriates. Since overseas experience, especially in major emerging economies such as China, is now viewed as a necessary step to advance one's career, demand is outstripping supply of such opportunities.[11] Therefore, many firms do not feel compelled to offer financial inducements, because, according to Siemen's HRM chief, "we don't want people to take the job merely for the money."[12] Many Western managers are willing to accept a "local plus" package instead of the traditional expatriate package full of perks. Further, more expatriates are now younger. They may be sent abroad to gain experience—often with more down-to-earth titles such as "assignees" or "secondees." In addition, more expatriates are now sent on short-term, commuter-type assignments for which they do not need to uproot their families—a major source of stress for the families and a cost item for the firm. Overall, the norms and images associated with the stereotypical expatriate, a more senior executive leading a life of luxury to compensate for hardship overseas, are changing rapidly.

Resources and Human Resource Management

As HRM becomes more strategic, the VRIO dimensions are increasingly at center stage.[13] To start, managers need to ask: Does a particular HR activity add *value*? Consider two examples. First, labor-intensive chores such as administering payroll, benefits, and basic training may not add value. They can often be outsourced. Second, training is expensive. Does it really add value? Results pooled from 397 studies find that, on average, training adds value by improving individual performance by approximately 20%.[14] Thus, training is often justified.

Next, are particular HR activities *rare*? The relentless drive to learn, share, and adopt best practices may reduce their rarity and thus usefulness. If every MNE in Russia provides training to high-caliber HCNs, such training, which is valuable, will be taken for granted but not viewed as rare.

Further, how *imitable* are certain HR activities? It is relatively easy to imitate a single practice, but it is much more difficult to imitate a complex HR *system* (or *architecture*) consisting of multiple, mutually reinforcing practices that work together. Consider the five-star Portman Ritz-Carlton Hotel in Shanghai. Its expatriate general manager personally interviews *every* new hire. It selects HCNs genuinely interested in helping guests. It cares deeply about employee satisfaction, which has led to superb guest satisfaction. Each single practice here may be imitable, and the Portman Ritz-Carlton, which has been voted the "Best Employer in Asia," has been studied meticulously by rivals (and numerous non-rivals) in China and around the world. Yet, none has been able to successfully imitate its system.

Finally, do HR practices support *organizational capabilities* to help accomplish performance goals? Consider

teamwork and diversity, especially multinational teams that have members from different subsidiaries.[15] While most firms promote some sort of teamwork and diversity, it is challenging to organizationally leverage such teamwork and diversity to enhance performance. Too little or too much diversity may hurt performance. In teamwork, certain disagreements may help promote learning. But obviously too many disagreements may lead to conflict and destroy team effectiveness. However, few managers (and few firms) know where to draw the line to keep team disagreements from getting out of control.

> **LO6** Identify the five Cs of human resource management.

MANAGEMENT SAVVY

How much does effective HRM impact firm performance? Results from 3,200 firms show that change of one standard deviation in the HR system affects 10%–20% of a firm's market value.[16] Findings from 92 studies suggest that an increase of one standard deviation in the use of an effective HR system is associated with a 4.6% increase in return on assets (ROA).[17] These recent findings validate a long-held belief among HRM practitioners and scholars: HRM is indeed *strategic*. In other words, HRM has become a direct answer to the fundamental question of our field: What determines the success and failure of firms around the world?

Consequently, we identify implications for actions, listed in Exhibit 13.10, that center on the four Cs developed by Susan Meisinger, president of the Society for Human Resource Management.[18] These insights have important implications for HR managers.

First, savvy HR managers need to be *curious*. They need to be well versed in the numerous formal and informal rules of the game governing HRM worldwide. They must be curious about emerging trends in the world and be prepared to respond to these trends. Second, HR managers must be *competent*. Far from its lowly roots as a lackluster administrative support function, HRM is now acknowledged as a strategic function. Many HR managers may have been trained more narrowly and with a more micro (non-strategic) focus. Now, HR managers must be

EXHIBIT 13.10 Implications for Action

For HR managers: The four Cs
• Be *curious*. Know formal and informal rules of the game governing HRM in all regions of operations.
• Be *competent*. Develop organizational capabilities that drive business success.
• Be *courageous* and *caring*. As guardians of talent, HR managers need to nurture and develop people.

For non-HR managers: The fifth C
• Be proactive in managing your (international) *career*.

© Cengage Learning 2013

able to not only contribute to the strategy conversation but also to take things off the CEO's desk as full-fledged business partners.

Finally, HR managers must be *courageous* and *caring*. As guardians of talent, HR managers need to nurture and develop employees. This often means that as employee advocates, HR managers sometimes need to be courageous enough to disagree with the CEO and other line managers, if necessary. GE's recently retired head of HR, William Conaty, is such an example. "If you just get closer to the CEO, you're dead," Conaty shared with a reporter, "I need to be independent. I need to be credible." GE's CEO Jeff Immelt called Conaty "the first friend, the guy that could walk in my office and kick my butt when it needed to be"— exactly how a full-fledged business partner should behave.[19]

In addition, there is a fifth C for non-HR managers: Proactively manage your *career* in order to develop a global mindset. Since international experience is a prerequisite for reaching the top at many firms, managers need to prepare by investing in their own technical expertise, cross-cultural adaptability, and language training. Some of these investments (such as language) are long term in nature. This point thus has strategic implications for students who are studying this book *now*: Have you learned a foreign language? Have you spent one semester or year abroad? Have you made any friends from abroad, perhaps fellow students who are taking classes with you now? Have you put this course on your resume? Arm yourself with the knowledge now, make proper investments, and advance your career. Remember: your career is in your hands.

CLOSING CASE

ETHICAL DILEMMA
CUT SALARIES OR CUT JOBS?

As a Japanese expatriate in charge of US operations of Yamakawa Corporation, you scratch your head, facing a difficult decision: When confronting a horrific economic downturn with major losses, do you cut salaries across the board or cut jobs? Headquarters, in Osaka, has advised you that earnings at home are bad and that you cannot expect them to bail out your operations. Too bad US government bailouts are only good for US-owned firms and are thus irrelevant for your unit, which is 100% owned by the Japanese parent company.

As a person being brought up in a collectivistic culture, you instinctively feel compelled to suggest an across-the-board pay cut for all 1,000 employees in the United States. Personally, as the highest-paid US-based employee, you are willing to take the *highest* percentage of a pay cut (you are thinking of 30%). If implemented, this plan would call for other executives, who are mostly Americans, to take a 20%–25% pay cut, mid-level managers and professionals a 15%–20% pay cut, and all the rank-and-file employees a 10%–15% pay cut. Indeed, in your previous experience at Yamakawa in Japan, you did this with positive results among all affected Japanese employees. This time, most executive colleagues in Japan are doing the same. However, since you are now managing US operations, HQ—being more globally minded and sensitive—does not want to impose any uniform solutions around the world and asks you to make the call.

As a conscientious executive, you have studied all the HRM books that you can get your hands on—in both Japanese and English—in order to research this tough decision. Most recently, you have meticulously studied Chapter 13 in Mike Peng's *GLOBAL* and paid particular attention to the debate on across-the-board pay cut versus reduction in force (RIF). While you understand that US executives rou-tinely undertake RIF, which is a euphemism for mass layoffs, you have also noticed that in the recent recession, even "bona-fide" US firms such as AMD, FedEx, HP, and the New York Times Company have all trimmed the base pay for all employees. If there is a time to shift the norm toward more across-the-board pay cuts in an effort to preserve jobs and avoid RIF, this may be it, according to some US executives quoted in the media.

At the same time, you have also read that some experts note that across-the-board pay cuts are *anathema* to a performance culture enshrined in the United States and taught in virtually all HRM textbooks. "The last thing you want is for your A players—or people in key strategic positions delivering the most value—to leave because you have mismanaged your compensation system," said Mark Huselid, a Rutgers University HRM professor, in an interview. You have also read in a *Harvard Business Review* survey that despite the worst recession, 20% of high-potential players in US firms have voluntarily jumped ship during the 2008–2009 recession, in search of greener pastures elsewhere. Naturally, you worry that should you decide to implement the across-the-board pay cuts, you may lose a lot of American star performers and end up with a bunch of mediocre players who cannot go elsewhere—and you may be stuck with the mediocre folks for a long time even after the economy recovers.

After spending two days reading all the materials you have gathered, you still do not have a clear picture. Instead, you have a big headache. You scratch your head again: How to proceed?

Sources: This case is fictitious. It is inspired by M. Brannen, "Global talent management and learning for the future: Pressing concerns for Japanese multinationals," *AIB Insights* 8 (2008): 8–12; "Cutting salaries instead of jobs, *BusinessWeek*, 8 June 2009, 46–48; "Pay cuts made palatable," *BusinessWeek*, 4 May 2009, 67; N. Carter and C. Silva, "High potentials in the downturn: Sharing the pain?" *Harvard Business Review* September 2009: 25.

WHY CHOOSE?

Every 4LTR Press solution comes complete with a visually engaging textbook in addition to an interactive eBook. Go to CourseMate for GLOBAL to begin using the eBook. Access at **www.cengagebrain.com**

Managing Corporate SOCIAL Responsibility Globally

CHAPTER 14

Zero Emission

Nissan

LEA

the new ca

Launching the Nissan Leaf: The World's First Electric Car

An electric car that does not burn a single drop of gasoline—technically called an "electric vehicle" (EV)—is the dream car of many environmentalists. Known as a "plug-in" vehicle, an EV is totally based on battery power, has no tailpipe, and thus has zero emission. It would be more revolutionary than Toyota's hybrid Prius, which drives on battery power before its gasoline engine kicks in and recharges the battery.

The million-dollar question is: Are car buyers ready for the EV? The environmental benefits are clear, yet the technological, social, psychological, and economic forces working against the EV are formidable. Technologically, the most advanced EV can only run between 60 and 100 miles per charge. It takes about seven hours to fully charge. The EV is clearly not as convenient as the conventional car. Socially, the EV, like the Prius, may be a hit in a niche market, but it is questionable whether the EV can penetrate the mainstream. Psychologically, since public charging stations are few (and nonexistent in many communities), drivers will experience "range anxiety"—will the EV run out of battery before it reaches the next charging station? Finally, the economic implications of the EV are not too enticing. Hybrids such as the Prius cost about $4,000 more than a comparable conventional car. The EV is likely to cost $10,000 to $20,000 more. Owners preferably will also need special chargers installed at home, which would cost another $2,000. Simply plugging into a standard household power outlet is advised for emergency charging only; the local utility circuit may collapse if so much electricity is suddenly sucked out by an EV.

100% electr

LEARNING OBJECTIVES
After studying this chapter, you should be able to:

LO1 articulate a stakeholder view of the firm.

LO2 apply the institution-based and resource-based views to analyze corporate social responsibility.

LO3 identify three ways you can manage corporate social responsibility.

Against such significant odds, Nissan, in December 2010, launched a mid-size five-door hatchback, the Leaf, which is the world's first mass-produced EV. The world's very first customer, in San Francisco, drove home the Leaf on December 11, 2010. The first delivery in Japan took place in Kanagawa Prefecture on December 22, 2010. Portugal, Ireland, and the UK are the first European markets the Leaf entered. While Americans may be shocked by the $32,780 list price, the Nissan Leaf in the United States is the least expensive globally (see Exhibit 14.1). Elsewhere, the EV costs between $44,600 to $49,800 (!). Even considering all the incentives dished out by governments, the Leaf is still not a cheap car. So what did Nissan do to prepare the launch of this pioneering car?

EXHIBIT 14.1 The Nissan Leaf's Prices and Launch Times

	List price (US$)	Net price after incentives (US$)	Market launch
United States	$32,780	$25,000	December 2010
Japan	$44,600	$35,500	December 2010
Portugal	$45,500	$39,325	January 2011
Ireland	$45,100	$39,000	February 2011
United Kingdom	$49,800	$38,400	March 2011

At least three areas of Nissan's preparation stand out. First, from an institution-based view, Nissan has a sharp awareness of the emerging regulatory requirements that would necessitate the EV. While the car industry fought the tightening emission standards for years, the 2007 Energy Independence and Security Act raised fuel economy averages of all cars made by any single automaker to 35 miles per gallon by 2020, a 40% improvement over current levels. Instead of shying away from the EV, having a zero-emission car like the Leaf has become a smart way to balance out the fuel-thirsty gas guzzlers such as SUVs. All of a sudden, most automakers are rushing to develop the EV, but none—not even Prius' maker, Toyota—can beat Nissan in the race to introduce the first EV.

Second, from a resource-based view, Nissan has accumulated significant capabilities in the crucial lithium-ion battery technology. As early as 1997, it introduced its first prototype EV. In 1999, when Renault took over Nissan and Carlos Ghosn took charge, Nissan was dangerously close to bankruptcy. In the gut-wrenching restructuring initiated by Ghosn, 60% of R&D projects were slashed. Yet, the costly and uncertain battery project was kept and nurtured, which ultimately led to the Leaf.

Third, to ensure a successful launch, Nissan embraced a stakeholder approach by meticulously working with a variety of stakeholders, such as government officials, utilities, activists, and customers, in highly innovative ways. In 2008, Nissan set up a Zero Emission Mobility Team, and team members were not only executives from sales and marketing, but also from government affairs, product planning, and communications. In the United States, the team looked for environmentally progressive states as possible first launch markets and decided to focus on seven states: Arizona, California, Hawaii, Oregon, Tennessee, Texas, and Washington. By limiting the launch geographically, Nissan can achieve a critical mass of charging stations. The team visited government officials to urge them to offer more incentives to buyers, to push utilities to install public charging stations, and to streamline the permitting and installation process for home chargers. The team also called on the utilities to get ready, and made presentations at utility conferences, which was something automakers had never done before. Additionaly, the Nissan team reached out to activists. It invited a total of 1,400 people in 307 cities in 27 states to participate in focus group meetings. Leading activists were invited to Yokohama, Japan, where the Leaf was being built, to test-drive the EV.

The moment of truth came in April 2010, when Nissan invited interested buyers to pre-order by putting down a refundable $99 fee. Within the first 24 hours, Nissan received 6,000 (!) reservations. By September, Nissan no longer accepted reservations for the remainder of 2010. Customers had to wait four to seven months. It seems that Nissan will have no problem selling the first 50,000 Leafs produced in its Yokohama factory. Production will ramp up, involving Nissan's Smyrna, Tennessee, plant in 2012 and then its Sunderland, UK, plant in 2013.

Officially ranked as the most fuel-efficient vehicle (99 miles per gallon gasoline *equivalent*) in the United States, the Leaf costs about 2 cents per mile to drive, far more economical than the 13 cents per mile for an average conventional car. While the Chevy Volt and the Toyota Prius Plug-In will enter the foray soon, they remain hybrids. As the only full EV, the Leaf has enjoyed the world's attention and grabbed numerous awards, such as the 2011 World Car of the Year, 2011 European Car of the Year, and 2011 Eco-Friendly Car of the Year. While the Leaf earns a lot of kudos for its contributions to a cleaner environment, from a competitive standpoint, Nissan is especially pleased that so much of the "green car" conversation now revolves around the Leaf instead of the Prius.

Sources: "Charged for battle," *Bloomberg Businessweek*, 3 January 2011, 49–56; "Green cars still need training wheels," *Bloomberg Businessweek*, 6 December 2010, 37–38; http://www.2011nissanleaf.net; http://www.nissanusa.com.

Corporate social responsibility (CSR)
Consideration of, and response to, issues beyond the narrow economic, technical, and legal requirements of the firm to accomplish social benefits along with the traditional economic gains that the firm seeks.

Why is an EV the dream car for many environmentalists? Why do many automakers not bother to offer it? Why does Nissan, the first firm that has mass produced an EV, earn so many kudos? The simple answer is that Nissan's decision to take the risk to develop the first EV is indicative of Nissan's interest in **corporate social responsibility (CSR)**, which refers to "consideration of, and response to, issues beyond the narrow economic, technical, and legal requirements of the firm to accomplish social benefits along with the traditional economic gains which the firm seeks."[1] Historically, CSR issues have been on the back burner for managers, but these issues are increasingly being brought to the forefront of corporate agendas. Although this chap-

EXHIBIT 14.2 A Stakeholder View of the Firm

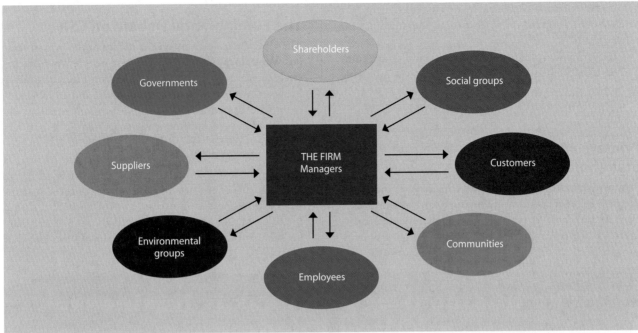

Source: T. Donaldson and L. Preston, "The stakeholder theory of the corporation: Concepts, evidence, and implications," *Academy of Management Review* 20 (1995): 69.

ter is positioned as the last in this book, by no means do we suggest that CSR is the least important topic. Instead, we believe that this chapter is one of the best ways to *integrate* all previous chapters concerning international trade, investment, strategy, and human resources. The comprehensive nature of CSR is evident in our Opening Case.

At the heart of CSR is the concept of the **stakeholder**, which is any group or individual who can affect or is affected by a firm's actions. Shown in Exhibit 14.2, shareholders are important but are not the only group of stakeholders. Other groups include managers, non-managerial employees (hereafter "employees"), suppliers, customers, communities, governments, and social and environmental groups (see the Opening Case). This chapter focuses on *non-shareholder stakeholders*, which we will call "stakeholders" here for simplicity. A leading debate on CSR is whether managers' efforts to promote the interests of these other stakeholders are at odds with their fiduciary duty to safeguard shareholder interests. To the extent that firms are *not* social agencies and that their primary function is to serve as economic enterprises, it is certainly true that firms should not (and are not able to) take on all of the social problems of the world. However, failing to heed certain CSR imperatives may be self-defeating in the long run.

The remainder of this chapter first introduces a stakeholder view of the firm. Next, we discuss how the institution-based and resource-based views inform the CSR discussion. We will then consider a debate on CSR in both domestic and overseas contexts. Finally, we will consider how savvy managers can best manage CSR.

A STAKEHOLDER VIEW OF THE FIRM

A Big Picture Perspective

A stakeholder view of the firm, with a quest for global sustainability, represents a big picture. A key goal for CSR is **global sustainability**, which is defined as the ability "to meet the needs of the present without compromising the ability of future generations to meet their needs."[2] It refers not only to a sustainable social and natural environment but also to sustainable capitalism. Globally, the urgency of sustainability in the 21st century is driven by at least three concerns. First, increasing population, poverty, and inequity require new solutions. The repeated protests around the world since the 1999 Seattle protests (see Chapter 1) are but the tip of the iceberg of anti-globalization sentiments. Second, the relative power of national governments has eroded in the wake of globalization, but the influence of nongovernmental organizations (NGOs) and other civil society stakeholders has increased. Finally, industrialization has created some irreversible effects on the environment. Global warming, air and water pollution, soil erosion, deforestation, and

Stakeholder
Any group or individual who can affect or is affected by a firm's actions.

Global sustainability
The ability to meet the needs of the present without compromising the ability of future generations to meet their needs around the world.

over-fishing have become problems that demand solutions (see the Opening and Closing Cases). Because firms contribute to many of these problems, many citizens believe that firms should also take on at least some responsibility for solving them.

Drivers underpinning global sustainability are complex and multidimensional. This bewilderingly complex big picture forces managers to *prioritize*.[3] To be able to do that, primary and secondary stakeholders must be identified (see the Opening Case).

Primary and Secondary Stakeholder Groups

Primary stakeholder groups are constituents on which the firm relies for its continuous survival and prosperity. Primary stakeholders typically refer to shareholders, managers, employees, suppliers, customers, and governments and communities whose laws and regulations must be obeyed and to whom taxes and other obligations may be due.

Secondary stakeholder groups are groups or individuals who can indirectly affect or are indirectly affected by a firms's actions. Examples include environmental groups (such as Greenpeace) and labor practice groups (such as the Fair Labor Association). While the firm does not depend on secondary stakeholder groups for its survival, such groups may have the potential to cause significant embarrassment and damage to a firm. Think of Nike in the 1990s.

A key proposition of the stakeholder view is that firms should not simply pursue the economic bottom line (such as profits and shareholder returns). Instead, firms should pursue a more balanced **triple bottom line**, consisting of *economic*, *social*, and *environmental* performances that simultaneously satisfy the demands of all stakeholder groups. The key reason that Nissan has earned so many kudos for its Leaf is its exemplary efforts to enhance the triple bottom line (see the Opening Case). To the extent that some competing demands obviously exist, it seems evident that the CSR proposition represents a dilemma. In

fact, it has provoked a fundamental debate, which is introduced next.

The Fundamental Debate on CSR

The CSR debate centers on the nature of the firm in society. Why does the firm exist? Most people would intuitively answer: "to make money." Milton Friedman was a former University of Chicago economist and a Nobel laureate who passed away in 2006. In an influential article published in 1970, he eloquently suggested: "The business of business is business."[4] The idea that the firm is an economic enterprise seems to be uncontroversial. At issue is whether the firm is *only* an economic enterprise.

One side of the debate argues that "the social responsibility of business is to increase its profits." In fact, that is the title of Friedman's article quoted above. The free market school of thought goes back to Adam Smith's idea that

> ## "The business of business is business." —Milton Friedman

pursuit of economic self-interest (within legal and ethical bounds) leads to efficient markets. Free market advocates such as Friedman believe that the firm's first and foremost stakeholder group is the shareholders, and managers have a fiduciary duty (required by law) to look after shareholder interests. To the extent that the hallmark of our economic system remains capitalism, the providers of capital—namely, capitalists or shareholders—deserve a commanding height in managerial attention. In fact, since the 1980s, *shareholder capitalism* explicitly places shareholders as the single most important stakeholder group and has become increasingly influential around the world.

Free market advocates argue that if firms attempt to attain social goals such as providing employment and social welfare, managers will lose their focus on profit maximization (and its derivative, shareholder value maximization).[5] Consequently, firms may lose their character as capitalistic enterprises and become *socialist* organizations. The idea of a socialist organization is not a pure argumentative point but is derived from the accurate characterization of numerous state-owned enterprises (SOEs) throughout the pre-reform Soviet Union, Central and Eastern Europe, and China as well as other developing countries in Africa, Asia, and Latin America. Privatization, in essence, removes the social function of SOEs and restores their economic focus through private ownership. Overall, the free market school has also provided much of the intellectual underpinning for globalization spearheaded by multinational enterprises (MNEs).

It is against such a formidable and influential school of thought that the CSR movement has emerged. A free market

Primary stakeholder groups
Constituents on which the firm relies for its continuous survival and prosperity.

Secondary stakeholder groups
Groups or individuals who can indirectly affect or are indirectly affected by a firms's actions.

Triple bottom line
Economic, social, and environmental performance that simultaneously satisfies the demands of all stakeholder groups.

DEBATE

ETHICAL DILEMMA

Domestic Versus Overseas Social Responsibility

Given that corporate resources are limited, devoting resources to overseas CSR often means fewer resources left to devote to domestic CSR. Consider two primary stakeholder groups: domestic employees and communities. Expanding overseas, especially into emerging economies, may not only increase corporate profits and shareholder returns but also increase employment in host countries and help develop those economies at the base of the economic pyramid, all of which have noble CSR dimensions. However, this expansion is often done at the expense of domestic employees and communities. The devastation that job losses can have on employees and communities is vividly portrayed in the movie *The Full Monty*. The movie takes place in Sheffield, England, which was the former steel capital not only of Europe but of the world. In the film, the local economy has been so decimated by closures that laid-off steel mill workers end up taking up an alternative line of work—male strip dancing. To prevent such a possible fate for their members, in the mid-2000s, Daimler's German unions had to scrap a 3% pay raise and endure an 11% increase of work hours (from 35 to 39 hours) with no extra pay in exchange for promises that 6,000 jobs would be kept in Germany for eight years; otherwise, the jobs would go to the Czech Republic, Poland, and South Africa. But such labor deals will probably only slow down, not stop, the outward flow of jobs from developed economies.

To the extent that few (or no) laid-off German employees would move to the neighboring Czech Republic or Poland to seek work (South Africa would be even less likely), most of them would end up being social welfare recipients in Germany. Thus, one may argue that MNEs shirk their CSR by increasing the social burdens in their home countries. Executives who make these decisions are often criticized by the media, unions, and politicians. Defenders, however, argue that MNEs are doing nothing wrong by maximizing shareholder returns.

Although framed in a domestic versus overseas context, the heart of this debate boils down to a fundamental point that frustrates CSR advocates: In a capitalist society, it is shareholders (otherwise known as *capitalists*) who matter at the end of the day. According to Jack Welch, General Electric's former CEO:

Unions, politicians, activists—companies face a Babel of interests. But there's only one owner. A company is for its shareholders. They own it. They control it. That's the way it is, and the way it should be.

When companies have enough resources, it would be nice to take care of domestic employees and communities. However, when confronted with relentless pressures to cut costs and restructure, managers have to prioritize. Given the lack of a clear solution, this politically explosive debate is likely to heat up in the years to come.

Sources: M. W. Peng, *Global Strategy*, 2nd ed. (Cincinnati: South-Western Cengage Learning, 2010); J. Welch and S. Welch, "Whose company is it anyway?," *BusinessWeek*, 9 October 2006, 122.

---

system is, in theory, constrained by rules, contracts, and property rights. But CSR advocates argue that a free market system that takes the pursuit of self-interest and profit as its guiding light may in practice fail to constrain itself, thus often breeding greed, excesses, and abuses. Firms and managers, if left to their own devices, may choose self-interest over public interest. The financial meltdown in 2008–2009 is often fingered as a case in point. While not denying that shareholders are important stakeholders, CSR advocates argue that all stakeholders have an *equal* right to bargain for a fair deal. Given stakeholders' often conflicting demands, a couple of thorny issues in the debate are whether all stakeholders indeed have an equal right and how to manage their (sometimes inevitable) conflicts (see Debate).

Starting in the 1970s as a peripheral voice in an ocean of free market believers, the CSR school of thought has slowly but surely become a more central part of management discussions. There are two

United States

driving forces. First, even as free markets spread around the world, the gap between the haves and have-nots has *widened*. While 2% of the world's children live in America and enjoy 50% of the world's toys, one quarter of the children in Bangladesh and Nigeria are in the workforces of these two countries. Even within developed economies such as the United States, the income gap between the upper and lower echelons of society has widened. In 1980, the average American CEO was paid 40 times more than the average worker. The ratio is now above 400. Although American society accepts a greater income inequality than many others do, aggregate data of such widening inequality, which both inform and numb, often serve as a stimulus for reforming a leaner and meaner capitalism. Such sentiments have become especially strong since the 2008–2009 recession. However, the response from free market advocates is that to the extent there is competition, there will always be *both* winners and losers. What CSR critics describe as "greed" is often translated as "incentive" in the vocabulary of free market advocates.

Second, disasters and scandals also drive the CSR movement. In 2001–2002, corporate

Bangladesh

scandals at Enron, WorldCom, Royal Ahold, and Parma-lat rocked the world. In 2008–2009, excessive amounts of Wall Street bonuses distributed by financial services firms receiving government bailout funds were criticized as being socially insensitive and irresponsible. In 2010, BP made a huge mess in the Gulf of Mexico. Not surpris-ingly, new disasters and scandals often propel CSR to the forefront of public policy and management discussions.

Overall, managers as a stakeholder group are unique in that they are the only group that is positioned at the center of all these relationships. It is important to understand how they make decisions concerning CSR, as illustrated next.

> *Apply the institution-based and resource-based views to analyze corporate social responsibility.*

INSTITUTIONS, RESOURCES, AND CORPORATE SOCIAL RESPONSIBILITY

While some people do not consider CSR an integral part of global business, Exhibit 14.3 shows that the institution-based and resource-based views can inform the CSR dis-cussion with relatively little adaptation. This section articulates why this is the case.

Institutions and Corporate Social Responsibility

The institution-based view sheds considerable light on the gradual diffusion of the CSR movement and the strategic responses of firms. At the most fundamental level, regula-tory pressures underpin *formal* institutions, whereas norma-tive and cognitive pressures support *informal* institutions. The strategic response framework consists of (1) reactive, (2) defensive, (3) accommoda-tive, and (4) proactive strategies, as first introduced in Chapter 3 (see Exhibit 3.5). This frame-work can be extended to explore how firms make CSR decisions, as illustrated in Exhibit 14.4.

A **reactive strategy** is indi-cated by relatively little or no

support by top management of CSR causes. Firms do not feel compelled to act in the absence of disasters and outcries. Even when problems arise, denial is usually the first line of defense. Put another way, the need to accept some CSR is neither internalized through cognitive beliefs nor does it re-sult in any norms in practice. That leaves only formal regula-tory pressures to compel firms to comply. For example, in the United States, food and drug safety standards that we take for granted today were fought by food and drug compa-nies in the early half of the 20th century. The basic idea that food and drugs should be tested before being sold to custom-ers and patients was bitterly contested even as unsafe foods and drugs killed thousands of people. As a result, the Food and Drug Administration (FDA) was progressively granted more powers. This era is not necessarily over. Today, many dietary supplement makers, whose products are beyond the FDA's regulatory reach, continue to sell untested supple-ments and deny responsibility.

A **defensive strategy** focuses on regulatory compli-ance. Top management involvement is piecemeal at best, and the general attitude is that CSR is an added cost or nuisance. Firms admit responsibility but often fight it. After the establishment of the Environmental Protection Agency (EPA) in 1970, the US chemical industry re-sisted the intrusion by the government agency (see Ex-hibit 14.4). The regulatory requirements were at significant odds with the norms and cognitive beliefs held by the industry at that time.

How do various institutional pressures change firm behavior? In the absence of informal normative and cog-nitive beliefs, formal regulatory pressures are the only fea-sible way to push firms ahead. A key insight of the institution-based view is that individuals and organiza-tions make *rational* choices given the right kind of incen-tives. For example, one efficient way to control pollution is to make polluters pay some "green" taxes. These can

Reactive strategy
A strategy that would only respond to CSR causes when required by disasters and outcries.

Defensive strategy
A strategy that focuses on regulatory compliance but with little actual commitment to CSR by top management.

EXHIBIT 14.3 Institutions, Resources, and Corporate Social Responsibility

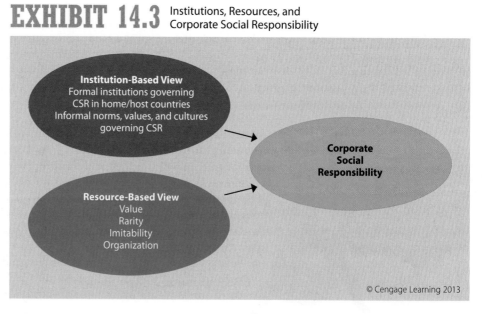

© Cengage Learning 2013

EXHIBIT 14.4 The US Chemical Industry Responds to Environmental Pressures

Phase	Primary strategy	Representative statements from the industry's trade journal, *Chemical Week*
1. 1962–1970	Reactive	Denied the severity of environmental problems and argued that these problems could be solved independently through the industry's technological prowess.
2. 1971–1982	Defensive	"Congress seems determined to add one more regulation to the already 27 health and safety regulations we must answer to. This will make EPA [Environmental Protection Agency] a chemical czar. No agency in a democracy should have that authority." (1975)
3. 1983–1993	Accommodative	"EPA has been criticized for going too slow. . . . Still, we think that it is doing a good job." (1982) "Critics expect overnight fix. EPA deserves credit for its pace and accomplishments." (1982)
4. 1993–present	Proactive	"Green line equals bottom line—The Clean Air Act equals efficiency. Everything you hear about the 'costs' of complying with CAA [Clean Air Act] is probably wrong. . . . Wiser competitors will rush to exploit the Green Revolution." (1990)

Sources: A. Hoffman, 'Institutional evolution and change: Environmentalism and the US chemical industry,' *Academy of Management Journal* 42 (1999): 351–371 for the phases and statements. Hoffman's last phase ended in 1993; its extension to the present was done by the present author.

range from gasoline retail taxes to landfill charges on waste disposal. How demanding these regulatory pressures should be remains controversial. One side of the debate argues that tough environmental regulation may lead to higher costs and reduced competitiveness, especially when competing with foreign rivals not subject to such demanding regulations. Others argue, however, that "green" taxes simply force firms to pay real costs that they otherwise place on others. If a firm pollutes, it is imposing a cost on the surrounding community that must either live with the pollution or pay to clean it up. By imposing a pollution tax that roughly equals the cost to the community, the firm is forced to account for pollution as a real cost of production. Economists refer to this as "internalizing an externality."

CSR advocates, endorsed by former vice president Al Gore and strategy guru Michael Porter, further argue that stringent environmental regulation may force firms to innovate, however reluctantly, thus benefiting the competitiveness of both the industry and country.[6] For example, a Japanese law set standards to make products easier to disassemble. Although Hitachi initially resisted the law, the company responded by redesigning products to simplify disassembly. The company reduced the parts in its washing machines by 16% and in vacuum cleaners by 30%. The products became not only easier to disassemble but also easier and cheaper to *assemble* in the first place, thus providing Hitachi with a significant cost advantage.

The **accommodative strategy** is characterized by some support from top managers, who may increasingly view CSR as a worthwhile endeavor. Since formal regulations may be in place and informal social and environmental pressures may be increasing, a number of firms themselves may be concerned about CSR, leading to the emergence of some new industry norms. Further, new managers who are passionate about or sympathetic toward CSR causes may join the organization, or some traditional managers may change their outlook, leading to increasingly strong cognitive beliefs that CSR is the right thing to do. In other words, from both normative and cognitive standpoints, it becomes legitimate or a matter of social obligation to accept responsibility and do all that is required. For example, in the US chemical industry, such a transformation probably took place in the early 1980s (see Exhibit 14.4). More recently, Burger King, Kraft, Nestle and Unilever were pressured by Greenpeace to be concerned about the deforestation practices undertaken by their major palm oil supplier

Accommodative strategy
A strategy characterized by some support from top managers, who may increasingly view CSR as a worthwhile endeavor.

Sinar Mas in Indonesia. Eventually, the food giants accommodated Greenpeace's demands and dumped Sinar Mas as a supplier, leading to a new industry norm that is more earth friendly.[7]

Adopting a code of conduct is a tangible indication of a firm's willingness to accept CSR. A **code of conduct** (sometimes called a **code of ethics**) is a set of written policies and standards outlining the proper practices for a firm. The global diffusion of codes of conduct is subject to intense debate. First, some argue that firms adopting these codes may not necessarily be sincere. This *negative* view suggests that an apparent interest in CSR may simply be window dressing. Some firms feel compelled to appear sensitive to CSR, following what others are doing, but have not truly and genuinely internalized CSR concerns. For example, in

that Nike is a more responsible corporate citizen in 2012 than it was in 1990.

From a CSR perspective, the best firms take a **proactive strategy** when engaging in CSR, constantly anticipating responsibility and endeavoring to do more than is required. Top management at a proactive firm not only supports and champions CSR activities, but also views CSR as a source of differentiation. For example, Starbucks has emphasized ethical sourcing, environmental stewardship, and community involvement. In terms of ethical sourcing, Starbucks is one of the world's largest buyers of fair-trade certified coffee. It launched its own Coffee and Farmer Equity (CAFE) guidelines, benefitting more than a million workers employed by 100,000 participating farms. Independent audits found that 99% of school-age children

> # Adopting a code of conduct is a tangible indication of a firm's willingness to accept CSR.

2009, BP implemented a new safety-oriented operating management system.[8] But after the 2010 oil spill, it became apparent that this system had not been seriously implemented, and the result was a huge catastrophe. Second, an *instrumental* view suggests that CSR activities simply represent a useful instrument to make good profits. Firms are not necessarily becoming more ethical. For example, after the 2010 oil spill, BP reshuffled management and created a new worldwide safety division. The instrumental view would argue that these actions did not really mean that BP became more ethical. Finally, a *positive* view believes that (at least some) firms and managers may be self-motivated to do it right regardless of social pressures. Codes of conduct tangibly express values that organizational members view as central and enduring.

The institution-based view suggests that all three perspectives are probably valid. This is to be expected given how institutional pressures work to instill value. Regardless of actual motive, the fact that firms are practicing CSR is encouraging, indicative of the rising *legitimacy* of CSR on the management agenda. Even firms that adopt a code of conduct simply as window dressing open doors for more scrutiny by concerned stakeholders because they have publicized a set of CSR criteria against which they can be judged. Such pressures are likely to transform these firms internally into more self-motivated, better corporate citizens. For example, it probably is fair to say

on participating farms were enrolled in schools, 99% of these farms had not engaged in any deforestation practices to grow coffee since 2004, and the majority of workers earned higher than the legal minimum wage for their country. Since 2001, Starbucks has voluntarily published an annual report on CSR, which embodies its founder, chairman, and CEO Howard Schultz's vision that "we must balance our responsibility to create value for shareholders with a social conscience."[9]

Proactive firms often engage in three areas of activity. First, like Swiss Re (see In Focus), they actively participate in regional, national, and international policy and standards discussions.[10] To the extent that policy and standards discussions today may become regulations in the future, it seems better to get involved early and (hopefully) steer the course toward a favorable direction. Otherwise—as the saying goes—if you're not at the table, you're on the menu. For example, Duke Energy operates 20 coal-fired power plants in five states. It is the third largest US emitter of CO_2 and the 12th largest in the world. But its CEO Jim Rogers has proactively worked with green technology producers, activists, and politicians to engage in policy and legislative discussions. These are not merely defensive moves to protect his firm and the power utility industry. Unlike his industry peers, Rogers has been "bitten by the climate bug" and is genuinely interested in reducing greenhouse gas emissions.[11]

Second, proactive firms often build alliances with stakeholder groups. For example, many firms collaborate with NGOs. Because of the historical tension and distrust, these sleeping-with-the-enemy alliances are not easy to handle. The key lies in identifying relatively short-term,

Code of conduct (code of ethics)
A set of written policies and standards outlining the proper practices for a firm.

Proactive strategy
A strategy that anticipates CSR and endeavors to do more than is required.

Swiss Re's Climate-Smart Strategy

Founded in Zurich, Switzerland, in 1863, Swiss Re is the world's largest reinsurer, operating in more than 20 countries. Reinsurance is a low-profile business that insures the insurance companies. Although Swiss Re has been in the United States for over 100 years and was the lead insurer of the World Trade Center during the 9/11 attacks, few people outside the industry knew what it was. In recent years, Swiss Re's quiet existence has been transformed by its strategic choice to be a vanguard in the climate change battle. This is because climate change poses significant climate-related risks in the form of floods, storms, and tsunamis. While other industries avoid risk, Swiss Re *embraces* risk by offering financial services products that enable risk taking by other firms. As a result, Swiss Re has developed a special interest in understanding more about the risk associated with climate change and played a leading role in disseminating this knowledge and enhancing public awareness.

Since the 1990s, Swiss Re has placed climate change at the core of what it does, sponsoring a series of high-profile public forums, research projects, and TV documentaries. Swiss Re is obviously not totally altruistic. It has deployed its considerable expertise in climate risk modeling to develop innovative products such as weather derivatives and catastrophe bonds, in which it is the world market leader.

Sources: A. Hoffman, *Getting ahead of the curve: Corporate strategies that address climate change* (Arlington, VA: Pew Center on Global Climate Change, 2006) 76–87; "Weathering climate change," 2011, available online at http://www.swissre.com.

manageable projects of mutual interests. For instance, Starbucks collaborated with Conservation International to help enforce CAFE standards.

Third, proactive firms often engage in *voluntary* activities that go beyond what is required by regulations.[12] While examples of industry-specific self-regulation abound, an area of intense global interest is the pursuit of the International Standards Organization (ISO) 14001 certification of the environment management system (EMS). Headquartered in Switzerland, the ISO is an influential NGO consisting of national standards bodies in 111 countries. Launched in 1996, the ISO 14001 EMS has become the gold standard for CSR-conscious firms. Although not required by law, many MNEs, such as Ford and IBM, have adopted ISO 14001 standards in all their facilities worldwide. Firms such as Toyota, Siemens, and General Motors have demanded that all of their top-tier suppliers be ISO 14001 certified.

From an institutional perspective, these proactive activities are indicative of the normative and cognitive beliefs held by many managers on the importance of doing the right thing. While there is probably a certain element of window dressing and a quest for better profits, it is obvious that these efforts provide some tangible social and environmental benefits.

Resources and Corporate Social Responsibility

CSR-related resources can include *tangible* technologies and processes as well as *intangible* skills and attitudes. The value, rarity, inimitability, and organization (VRIO) framework can shed considerable light on CSR.

Do CSR-related resources and capabilities add *value*? Many large firms, especially MNEs, can apply their financial, technological, and human resources toward a variety of CSR causes. For example, firms can choose to appease environmental groups by purchasing energy only from power plants utilizing green sources, such as wind-generated power. Or firms can respond to human rights groups by not doing business in or with countries accused of human rights violations. These activities can be categorized as **social issue participation**, which refers

Social issue participation
Firms' participation in social causes not directly related to the management of primary stakeholders.

to a firm's participation in social causes not directly related to the management of its primary stakeholders. Research suggests that these activities may actually *reduce* shareholder value.[13] Overall, although social issue participation may create some remote social and environmental value, it does not satisfy the economic leg of the triple bottom line, so these abilities do not qualify as value-adding firm resources.

CSR-related resources are not always *rare*. Remember that even a valuable resource is not likely to provide a significant advantage if competitors also possess it. For example, both Home Depot and Lowe's have NGOs such as the Forest Stewardship Council certify that suppliers in Brazil, Indonesia, and Malaysia use only material from renewable forests. These complex processes require strong management capabilities such as negotiating with local suppliers, undertaking internal verification, coordinating with NGOs for external verification, and disseminating such information to stakeholders. Such capabilities are valuable. But since both competitors possess capabilities to manage these processes, they are common (but not rare) resources.

Although valuable and rare resources may provide some competitive advantage, the advantage will only be temporary if competitors can *imitate* it. Resources must be not only valuable and rare but also hard to imitate in order to give firms a sustainable (not merely temporary) competitive advantage. At some firms, CSR-related capabilities are deeply embedded in idiosyncratic managerial and employee skills, attitudes, and interpretations. The socially complex way of channeling their energy and conviction toward CSR cannot be easily imitated. For example, the enthusiasm and energy that Starbucks devotes to CSR are very difficult to imitate.

Does the firm have *organizational* capabilities to do a good job on CSR? Is the firm organized to exploit the full potential of CSR? Numerous components within a firm, such as formal management control systems and informal relationships between managers and employees, may be relevant. These components are often called complementary assets (see Chapter 4), because, by themselves, they typically do not generate advantage. However, complementary assets, when combined with valuable, rare, and hard-to-imitate capabilities, may enable a firm to fully utilize its CSR potential.

For example, assume that Firm A is able to overcome the three hurdles mentioned above (V, R, I) by achieving a comprehensive understanding of some competitors' best practices in pollution prevention. Although Firm A has every intention to implement such best practices, chances are that they may not work unless Firm A also possesses a number of complementary assets. Process-focused best

© Steven May/Alamy

practices of pollution prevention are not in isolation and are often difficult to separate from a firm's other activities. These best practices require a number of complementary assets, such as a continuous emphasis on process innovation, an uncompromising quest to reduce costs, and a dedicated workforce. These complementary assets are not developed as part of new environmental strategies; rather, they are grown from more general business strategies, such as differentiation. If such complementary assets are already in place, they can be leveraged in the new pursuit of best environmental practices. Otherwise, single-minded imitation is not likely to be effective.

The resource-based view helps solve a major puzzle in the CSR debate: the CSR-economic performance puzzle. The puzzle—a source of frustration to CSR advocates—is why there is no conclusive evidence on a direct, positive link between CSR and *economic* performance such as profits and shareholder returns. Although some studies do indeed report a *positive* relationship,[14] others find a *negative* relationship[15] or *no* relationship.[16] Viewed together, "CSR does not hurt [economic] performance, but there is no concrete support to believe that it leads to supranormal [economic] returns."[17] While there can be a number of explanations for this intriguing mess, a resource-based explanation suggests that because of the capability constraints discussed above, many firms are not cut out for a CSR-intensive (differentiation) strategy. Since all studies have some sampling bias (no study is perfect), studies that over-sample firms not yet ready for a high level of CSR activities are likely to report a negative relationship between CSR and economic performance. Likewise, studies that over-sample firms ready for CSR may find a positive relationship. Also, studies with more balanced (more random) samples may fail to find any statistically significant relationship. In summary, since each firm is different (a basic assumption of the resource-based view), not every firm's economic performance is likely to benefit from CSR.

LO3 *Identify three ways you can manage corporate social responsibility.*

MANAGEMENT SAVVY

Concerning CSR, the institution-based and resource-based views suggest three clear implications for action (see Exhibit 14.5). First, savvy managers need to understand the formal and informal rules of the game, anticipate changes, and seek to shape such changes. Although the US government refused to ratify the 1997 Kyoto Protocol and only signed the nonbinding 2009 Copenhagen Accord (see the

Closing Case), many US firms (such as Duke Energy) voluntarily participate in CSR activities not (yet) mandated by law, in anticipation of more stringent environmental requirements down the road.

Second, savvy managers need to pick CSR battles carefully. The resource-based view suggests an important lesson, which is captured by Sun Tzu's timeless teaching: "Know yourself, know your opponents." While your opponents may engage in high-profile CSR activities that allow them to earn bragging rights and contribute to their triple bottom line, blindly imitating these practices without knowing enough about yourself as a manager and the firm/unit you lead may lead to some disappointment. Instead of always chasing the newest best practices, firms are advised to select CSR practices that fit with their *existing* resources, capabilities, and especially complementary assets.

Third, given the increasingly inescapable responsibility to be good corporate citizens, managers may want to integrate CSR as part of the core activities of the firm instead of faking it and making only cosmetic changes. For example, instead of treating NGOs as threats, Home Depot, Lowe's, and Unilever have their sourcing policies certified by NGOs. Dow Chemical has established community advisory panels in most of its locations worldwide. Many managers traditionally treated CSR as a nuisance, involving regulation, added costs, and liability. Such an attitude

EXHIBIT 14.5 — Implications for Action

- Understand the rules of the game, anticipate changes, and seek to shape and influence changes.
- Pick your CSR battles carefully. Don't blindly imitate other firms' CSR activities.
- Integrate CSR as part of the core activities and processes of the firm. Faking it doesn't last very long.

© Cengage Learning 2013

may underestimate potential business opportunities associated with CSR.

What determines the success and failure of firms around the world? No doubt, CSR will increasingly become an important part of the answer. The best-performing firms are likely to be those that can integrate CSR activities into their core economic functions while addressing social and environmental concerns (see the Opening Case). In the post-9/11 and post-2008-bailouts world (see Chapter 1), managers, as a unique group of stakeholders, have an important and challenging responsibility to safeguard and advance capitalism.[18] From a CSR standpoint, this means building more humane, more inclusive, and fairer firms that not only generate wealth and develop economies, but also respond to changing societal expectations concerning CSR around the world.

CLOSING CASE

ETHICAL DILEMMA

FROM KYOTO TO COPENHAGEN: CUT EMISSIONS OR CUT JOBS?

Lately, the world has been hit by more droughts, more floods, more storms, and more heat waves than ever before. It seems clear that global warming and climate change caused by greenhouse gas (GHG) emissions require decisive actions to stem the trend. The scale of the problem and the uncertainty associated with it demand extraordinary ingenuity and cooperation among governments, firms, and consumers around the world. Unfortunately, since the United Nations Framework Convention on Climate Change (UN-FCCC) was signed in 1992, global emissions of carbon dioxide (CO_2), the most potent GHG, have *risen* by a third (see PengAtlas Map 19).

Stimulated by UNFCCC, the Kyoto Protocol signed in 1997 was a hard-fought attempt to do something immensely difficult. Under Kyoto, developed countries pledged to cut emissions by 6% from 1990 levels by 2012. Each country was permitted to emit a certain quantity of CO_2. Governments issued emission permits to polluting firms within their borders, and such permits (essentially rights to pollute) could be bought and sold by firms worldwide. Through this carbon trading system, polluting firms in developed countries could pay someone else (at home or abroad) to cut emissions and claim credit.

While the EU and Japan took Kyoto most seriously, the United States, which had been the world's number one emitter of GHG until recently, refused to ratify

it. China (the current world champion in GHG emissions), India, and many developing countries essentially argued: "Sorry, we have to develop our economy first—and have to forget about Kyoto now." Not covering the world's top two emitting countries, Kyoto, despite noble intentions, did not seem to have any noticeable effect in achieving its goals. Since Kyoto's first commitment period would run out in 2012, the 15th UNFCCC conference in December 2009, popularly known as the Copenhagen Climate Conference, thus became extremely important in reaching a more effective, more inclusive, and more equitable global deal.

By the time of the Copenhagen conference, the scientific evidence about climate change became stronger. Thanks to the burning of fossil fuels, the average temperature on Earth has increased by 1° C since the Industrial Revolution. A decade after Kyoto, GHGs in the atmosphere are still increasing. Worse, they are increasing at an accelerating rate. Because GHGs stay in the atmosphere for decades (and often centuries), continuous and accelerated pumping of GHGs is likely to lead to global warming of 5° C by the end of this century, with disastrous ramifications. How dangerous is 5° C of warming? To put things in perspective, this is the difference between today's climate and the last ice age's—when glaciers reached Central Europe and northern United States. In addition to more droughts, storms, and heat waves, global warming and rising sea levels on this scale will cause the permanent flooding of a lot of low-lying coastal areas (such as central Bangladesh and south Florida), famine, and possibly wars. Clearly, climate change is a global problem. No country is immune. The solution has to be global.

While the global community convening in Copenhagen, in principle, agreed with the necessity to do something (the goal was to control the level of global warming to 2 °C by century's end), countries strongly disagreed with what each of them needed to do. The timing was also unfortunate, because few governments would agree to major cuts on their CO_2 emissions when their countries had not recovered from the 2008–2009 crisis and the army of unemployed was proliferating.

Since there is no "free environmental lunch," the debate boils down to who is going to pay most of the cost to combat climate change. Although developed countries have been pumping more GHGs to the atmosphere on a per capita and cumulative basis, 1.6 billion people in the developing world still suffer from poverty and lack access to electricity, which will most likely be generated by old-tech, high-carbon technologies. The World Bank in the *World Development Report 2010*, released before the Copenhagen conference, urged developed countries to take aggressive action to reduce their own emissions, which "would free some 'pollution space' for developing countries, but more importantly, it would stimulate innovation and the demand for new technologies so they can be rapidly scaled up."

A crucial bone of contention is coal-fired power plants. Relative to oil, gas, nuclear, wind, solar, and biofuel sources, coal is not only the cheapest and the dirtiest, but also the most widely used energy source in Australia, China, Germany, India, and the United States. Displacing a third of power generation from coal in the United States by 2015 will put 1.2 million Americans out of work, and displacing two-thirds will result in 2.7 million lost jobs. Of course, the new wind, solar, and biofuel industries generate new jobs. However, these new sources of energy are so expensive that for now, they stand little chance in the absence of subsidies, and the jobs they create are far fewer than the jobs that will be lost if coal is drastically reduced. Not surprisingly, few politicians in coal-dependent countries are politically suicidal enough to advocate the aggressive displacement of coal in power plants.

Proposals are numerous but solutions are few, because every new proposal generates new loopholes. In the same spirit of Kyoto, the "cap and trade" legislation discussed in the United States in 2009 called for polluters to pay for permits ("caps") and buy and sell them ("trade"). However, critics argued that this would be a stealth tax that would be a job killer, encouraging US firms to shift more production abroad. Then the next proposal called for import duties on goods from countries that have laxer rules on emissions. Not surprisingly, China and other developing countries vehemently opposed such "climate protectionism."

It is clear that with so much at stake, no solution will be perfect and trade-offs will be inevitable. The *Economist* suggested that climate change "is a prisoner's dilemma, a free-rider problem, and the tragedy of the commons all rolled into one." Until the last day of the Copenhagen conference, no deal had been in sight and countries were locked into bitter arguments because no one wanted to pay the "sucker's cost." While the United States, despite its skyrocketing

Leaders of Brazil, China, India, and the United States in negotiations on the last day of the Copenhagen Climate Conference, December 18, 2009.

national debt, offered $100 billion in long-term financing to help developing countries adapt to climate change on the condition of verification of efforts, China disagreed with the notion of verification, claiming this to be an affront to national sovereignty. Of course, China's real concerns were economic slowdown and job losses given the need to continuously find jobs for the world's largest population. The choice boils down to this: cut emissions or cut jobs?

However, inaction was not an option, because the longer the world waited, the more drastic future actions would have to be, and greater future sacrifices would have to be endured. It was in this spirit of urgency that leaders of Brazil, China, India, South Africa, and the United States reluctantly agreed, on the last day of the conference, December 18, 2009, to reach a very weak, nonbinding Copenhagen Accord. The Accord agreed to limit the level of global warming to no more than 2° C by century's end. Developed countries committed to reducing their GHG emissions by 80% by 2050. Developing countries committed to reducing GHG emissions but with no specific targets, and agreed in broad terms some sort of reporting and verification—again with no specifics. In essence, countries agreed to keep talking. While some politicians such as Obama called the Copenhagen Accord "a meaningful first step," other politicians and numerous activists were deeply disappointed by the lack of a binding agreement.

Although the impact of proposed actions is uncertain, they can be regarded as investing in an insurance policy for the future health of our planet. The World Bank and the *Economist* estimate the cost to be between 0.5% and 1% of global GDP and argue that this amount should be socially acceptable. In comparison, the world spends 3% of GDP on (traditional) insurance, and governments recently burned 5% of GDP to bail out failed banks. Overall, deals such as Kyoto and Copenhagen are clearly flawed and do not make every country happy, but, given the risk, they seem better than nothing.

Sources: "Why Copenhagen will be good for business," *BusinessWeek*, 14 December 2009, 65; "Cooling the earth," *The World in 2011* (London: The Economist, 2011) 26; "Getting warmer," *Economist*, 5 December 2009, 22; "Stopping climate change," *Economist*, 5 December 2009, 11; "The grass is always greener," *Economist*, 24 April 2009, 81; "Climate deal announced, but falls short of expectations," *New York Times*, 18 December 2009, available online at http://www.nytimes.com; World Bank, *World Development Report 2010* (Washington: World Bank, 2010).

Notes

Chapter 1

1   J. Dunning, *Multinational Enterprises and the Global Economy* (Reading, MA: Addison-Wesley, 1993) 30.

2   J.-F. Hennart, "Down with MNE-centric models!" *Journal of International Business Studies* 40 (2009): 1432–1454.

3   M. W. Peng, "Institutional transitions and strategic choices," *Academy of Management Review* 28 (2003): 275–296; M. Wright, I. Filatotchev, R. Hoskisson, and M. W. Peng, "Strategy research in emerging economies," *Journal of Management Studies* 42 (2005): 1–33.

4   T. London and S. Hart, "Reinventing strategies for emerging markets," *Journal of International Business Studies* 35 (2004): 350–370.

5   "Developing your global know-how," *Harvard Business Review* (March 2011): 71–75.

6   "The changing talent game," *BusinessWeek*, 20 August 2007, 68–71.

7   J. Cantwell, J. Dunning, and S. Lundan, "An evolutionary approach to understanding international business activity," *Journal of International Business Studies* 41 (2010): 567–586.

8   M. W. Peng, "Identifying the big question in international business research," *Journal of International Business Studies* 35 (2004): 99–108.

9   K, Meyer, S. Estrin, S. Bhaumik, and M. W. Peng, "Institutions, resources, and entry strategies in emerging economies," *Strategic Management Journal* 30 (2009): 61–80.

10 M. W. Peng, D. Wang, and Y. Jiang, "An institution-based view of international business strategy: A focus on emerging economies," *Journal of International Business Studies* 39 (2008): 920–936.

11 M. W. Peng, "The resource-based view and international business," *Journal of Management* 27 (2001): 803–829.

12 "The happiest man in Detroit," *Bloomberg Businessweek*, 7 February 2011, 67–71.

13 J. Johanson and J. Vahlne, "The Uppsala internationalization process model revisited: From liability of foreignness to liability of outsidership," *Journal of International Business Studies* 40 (2009): 1411–1431.

14 K. Moore and D. Lewis, *The Origins of Globalization* (New York: Routledge, 2009).

15 D. Yergin and J. Stanislaw, *The Commanding Heights* (New York: Simon & Schuster, 2002) 385.

16 J. Stiglitz, *Globalization and Its Discontents* (New York: Norton, 2002) 9.

17 M. W. Peng, R. Bhagat, and S. Chang, "Asia and global business," *Journal of International Business Studies* 41 (2010): 373–376.

18 N. Taleb, D. Goldstein, and M. Spitznagel, "The six mistakes executives make in risk management," *Harvard Business Review* (October 2009): 78–81.

19 S. Lee and M. Makhija, "The effect of domestic uncertainty on the real options value of international investments," *Journal of International Business Studies* 40 (2009): 405–420.

20 P. Ghemawat, "Semiglobalization and international business strategy," *Journal of International Business Studies* 34 (2003): 138–152.

21 J. Bhagwati, *In Defense of Globalization* (New York: Oxford University Press, 2004).

22 M. Kotabe, "Global security risks and international competitiveness," *Journal of International Management* 11 (2005): 453.

23 United Nations (UN), *World Investment Report 2010* (New York and Geneva: UN, 2010) 10.

24 M. W. Peng, "The global strategy of emerging multinationals from China," *Global Strategy Journal* (2012, in press).

25 T. Friedman, *The World is Flat* (New York: Farrar, Straus, & Giroux, 2005); R. Rajan, *Fault Lines* (Princeton, NJ: Princeton University Press, 2010).

26 M. W. Peng, S. Sun, and D. Blevins, "The social responsibility of international business scholars," *Multinational Business Review* 19 (2011): 106–119; D. Rodrik, *The Globalization Paradox* (New York: Norton, 2011).

Chapter 2

1   M. W. Peng, "Institutional transitions and strategic choices," *Academy of Management Review* 28 (2003): 275.

2   M. W. Peng, S. Sun, B. Pinkham, and H. Chen, "The institution-based view as a third leg for a strategy tripod," *Academy of Management Perspectives* 23 (2009): 63–81; M. W. Peng, D. Wang, and Y. Jiang, "An institution-based view of international business strategy," *Journal of International Business Studies* 39 (2008): 920–936.

3   D. North, *Institutions, Institutional Change, and Economic Performance* (New York: Norton, 1990) 3.

4   W. R. Scott, *Institutions and Organizations*, 3rd ed. (Thousand Oaks, CA: Sage, 2008).

5   O. Williamson, *The Economic Institutions of Capitalism* (New York: Free Press, 1985) 1–2.

6   "Dancing with the bear," *Economist*, 3 February 2007, 63.

7   M. W. Peng, *Business Strategies in Transition Economies* (Thousand Oaks, CA: Sage, 2000).

8   M. Beaulieu, J. Cosset, and N. Essaddam, "The impact of political risk on the volatility of stock returns," *Journal of International Business Studies* 36 (2005): 701–718.

9   R. La Porta, F. Lopez-de-Silanes, A. Shleifer, and R. Vishny, "Law and finance," *Journal of Political Economy* 106 (1998): 1118.

10 H. de Soto, *The Mystery of Capital* (New York: Basic Books, 2000).

11 T. Khoury and M. W. Peng, "Does institutional reform of intellectual property rights lead to more inbound FDI? Evidence from Latin America and the Caribbean," *Journal of World Business* (2011, in press).

12 Heritage Foundation, available online at http://www.heritage.org [accessed 21 July 2009].

13 D. North, *Understanding the Process of Economic Change* (Princeton, NJ: Princeton University Press, 2005) 48.

14 "Doing business in Africa," *Economist*, 2 July 2005, 61.

15 D. North, *Structure and Change in Economic History* (New York: Norton, 1981) 164.

Chapter 3

1   G. Hofstede, *Cultures and Organizations* (New York: McGraw-Hill, 1997) xii.

2   Hofstede, *Cultures and Organizations* 5.

3   K. Leung, R. Bhagat, N. Buchan, M. Erez, and C. Gibson, "Beyond national culture and culture-centricism," *Journal of International Business Studies* 42 (2011): 177–181.

4   R. McCrum, *Globish: How the English Language Became the World's Language* (New York: Norton, 2010).

5   D. Ricks, *Blunders in International Business*, 3rd ed. (Oxford, UK: Blackwell, 1999).

6   E. Hall and M. Hall, *Hidden Differences* (Garden City, NY: Doubleday, 1987).

7   S. Ronen and O. Shenkar, "Clustering countries on attitudinal dimension," *Academy of Management Review* 10 (1985): 435–454.

8   M. W. Peng, C. Hill, and D. Wang, "Schumpeterian dynamics versus Williamsonian considerations," *Journal of Management Studies* 37 (2000): 167–184.

9   R. House, P. Hanges, M. Javidan, P. Dorfman, and V. Gupta, (eds.), *Culture, Leadership, and Organizations: The GLOBE Study of 62 Societies* (Thousand Oaks, CA: Sage, 2004).

10 S. Huntington, *The Clash of Civilizations and the Remaking of World Order* (New York: Simon & Schuster, 1996) 43.

11 *World Development Indicators* (2004), The World Bank, http://www.worldbank.org.

12 H. Berry, M. Guillen, and N. Zhou, "An institutional approach to cross-national distance," *Journal of International Business Studies* 41 (2010): 1460–1480; T. Fong, "Asian management research needs more self-confidence," *Asia Pacific Journal of Management* 27 (2010): 155–170; B. McSweeney, "Hofstede's model of national cultural differences and their consequences," *Human Relations* 55 (2002): 89–118; R. Tung and A. Verbeke, "Beyond Hofstede and GLOBE," *Journal of International Business Studies* 41 (2010): 1259–1274.

13 Hofstede, *Cultures and Organizations* 94.

14 M. W. Peng, *Global Strategy*, 2nd ed. (Cincinnati: South-Western Cengage Learning, 2009) 10.

15 C. Fombrun, "Corporate reputations as economic assets," in M. Hitt, R. E. Freeman, and J. Harrison, (eds.), *The Blackwell Handbook of Strategic Management* (Cambridge, UK: Blackwell, 2001) 289–312.

16 This section draws heavily from T. Donaldson, "Values in tension," *Harvard Business Review* (September–October 1996): 4–11.

17 "How to grease a palm," *Economist*, 23 December 2006, 116.

18 S. Lee and K. Oh, "Corruption in Asia," *Asia Pacific Journal of Management* 24 (2007): 97–114.

19 S. Wei, "How taxing is corruption on international investors?" *Review of Economics and Statistics* 82 (2000): 1–11.

20 "Bribery is losing its charm in China," *Bloomberg Businessweek*, 12 July 2010, 11–12.

21 J. Hellman, G. Jones, and D. Kaufmann, "Far from home: Do foreign investors import higher standards of governance in transition economies," Working paper (2002), World Bank, www.worldbank.org [accessed 21 July 2009].

22 C. Kwok and S. Tadesse, "The MNC as an agent of change for host-country institutions," *Journal of International Business Studies* 37 (2006): 767–785.

23 "Toyota recalls 1.7 million vehicles for fuel leaks," *Clear Politics*, 28 January 2011, available online at http://www.realclearpolitics.com.

Chapter 4

1   J. Barney, "Firm resources and sustained competitive advantage," *Journal of Management* 17 (1991): 99-120; M. W. Peng, "The resource-based view and international business," *Journal of Management* 27 (2001): 803–829.

2   J. Barney, "Is the resource-based view a useful perspective for strategic management research?," *Academy of Management Review* 26 (2001): 54.

3   D. Teece, "Explicating dynamic capabilities," *Strategic Management Journal* 28 (2007): 1319–1350.

4   J. Barney, *Gaining and Sustaining Competitive Advantage*, 2nd ed. (Upper Saddle River, NJ: Prentice Hall, 2002) 157.

5   M. Porter, *Competitive Advantage* (New York: Free Press, 1985).

6   A. Pande, "How to make onshoring work," *Harvard Business Review* (March 2011): 30.

7   D. Boehe, "Captive offshoring of new product development in Brazil," *Management International Review* 50 (2010): 747–773.

8   D. Levy, "Offshoring in the new global political economy," *Journal of Management Studies* 42 (2005): 687.

9   This section draws heavily from Barney, *Gaining and Sustaining Competitive Advantage*, 2nd ed., 159–174.

10 "IBM is (still) the patent king in the US," *Fast Company*, 10 January 2011, available online at http://www.fastcompany.com.

11 S. Godin, "To win, create what's scarce," *Harvard Business Review* (November 2010): 46.

12 M. Kotabe, R. Parente, and J. Murray, "Antecedents and outcomes of modular production in the Brazilian automobile industry," *Journal of International Business Studies* 38 (2007): 84–106.

13 J. Barney, *Gaining and Sustaining Competitive Advantage* (Reading, MA: Addison-Wesley, 1997) 155.

14 The author's paraphrase based on T. Friedman, *The World Is Flat* (New York: Farrar, Straus, & Giroux, 2005) 237.

Chapter 5

1   I. Colantone and L. Sleuwaegen, "International trade, exit, and entry," *Journal of International Business Studies* 41 (2010): 1240–1257.

2   M. W. Peng, "The resource-based view and international business," *Journal of Management* 27 (2001): 803–829.

3   B. Cassiman and E. Golovko, "Innovation and internationalization through exports," *Journal of International Business Studies* 42 (2011): 56–75; M. Czinkota, "How government can help increase US export performance," testimony before the House Committee on Small Business, US Congress, Washington, DC, 28 April 2010; R. Salomon and B. Jin, "Do leading or lagging firms learn more from exporting?" *Strategic Management Journal* 31 (2010): 1088–1113.

4   "Obama: Venture capitalist-in-chief," *Bloomberg Businessweek*, 9 August 2010, 28–31.

5   M. Porter, *Competitive Advantage of Nations* (New York: Free Press, 1990).

6   D. Bernhofen and J. Brown, "An empirical assessment of the comparative advantage gains from trade," *American Economic Review* 95 (2005): 208–225.

7   "Don't go to Rio for a deal on an iPad," *Bloomberg Businessweek*, 13 December 2010, 13–14.

8   Tire Industry Association (TIA), "Tire Industry Association expresses disappointment with President's decision concerning Chinese tire tariff," Bowie, MD: TIA, 14 September 2009, available online at http://www.tireindustry.org.

9   "Electoral reform in Japan," *Economist*, 29 January 2011, 40–41.

10 "A row over cows," *Economist*, 17 February 2011, available online at http://www.economist.com.

11 "DHL will pay $9.4M fine to settle shipping dispute," *USA Today,* 7 August 2009, 2A.

12 US-China Business Council, "US exports to China," *China Business Review* (July 2010): 46–49.

Chapter 6

1 T. Khoury and M. W. Peng, "Does institutional reform of intellectual property rights lead to more inbound FDI? Evidence from Latin America and the Caribbean," *Journal of World Business* (2011, in press).

2 United Nations (UN), *World Investment Report 2010* (New York and Geneva: UN, 2010).

3 J. Dunning, *Multinational Enterprises and the Global Economy* (Reading, MA: Addison-Wesley, 1993).

4 "Vietnam: An Asian-tiger wannabe (again)," *Bloomberg Businessweek,* 21 June 2010, 12–13.

5 R. Tasker, "Pepperoni power," *Far Eastern Economic Review,* 14 November 2002, 59–60.

6 B. Kogut and U. Zander, "Knowledge of the firm and the evolutionary theory of the multinational corporation," *Journal of International Business Studies* 34 (2003): 516–529.

7 S. Chen, "A general TCE model of international business institutions," *Journal of International Business Studies* 41 (2010): 935–959.

8 K. Gordon and J. Pohl, "The response to the global crisis and investment protection," *Columbia FDI Perspectives* 25 (2010): 2.

9 K. Meyer and E. Sinani, "When and where does FDI generate positive spillovers," *Journal of International Business Studies* 40 (2009): 1075–1094.

10 UN, *World Investment Report 2010* 17.

11 UN, *World Investment Report 2010* 57.

12 "More car jobs shift to Mexico," *Bloomberg Businessweek,* 28 June 2010, 10–11.

13 "Venezuela: You are working for Chavez now," *BusinessWeek,* 15 May 2006, 76–78.

14 "Bolivia: Now it's the people's gas," *Economist,* 6 May 2006, 37–38. Throughout the socialist world, May 1 (May Day) is typically celebrated as the International Workers' Day against capitalism. President Morales deliberately chose this day to seize MNE oil fields in Bolivia.

Chapter 7

1 "McCurrencies," *Economist,* 27 May 2006, 74.

2 "Behind the yen's paradoxical strength," *Bloomberg Businessweek,* 28 March 2011, 15.

3 R. Lyons, *The Microstructure Approach to Exchange Rates* (Cambridge, MA: MIT Press, 2001) 1.

4 "Bretton Woods II," *Guardian,* 14 November 2008, available online at http://www.guardian.co.uk [accessed 24 July 2009].

5 "Life amid the ruins," *Bloomberg Businessweek,* 28 June 2010, 52–60.

6 R. Carbaugh, *International Economics,* 11th ed. (Cincinnati: South-Western Cengage Learning, 2007) 360.

7 S.-H. Lee and M. Makhija, "The effect of domestic uncertainty on the real options value of international investments," *Journal of International Business Studies* 40 (2009): 405–420.

8 "A mixed blessing," *Economist,* 20 May 2010, 68.

9 R. Faff and A. Marshall, "International evidence on the determinants of foreign exchange rate exposure of multinational corporations," *Journal of International Business Studies* 36 (2005): 539–558.

10 M. W. Peng and K. E. Meyer, *International Business* (London: Cengage Learning EMEA, 2011) 200–202.

Chapter 8

1 World Trade Organization (WTO), *10 Benefits of the WTO Trading System* (Geneva: WTO, 2005) 3.

2 D. Xu, Y. Pan, C. Wu, and B. Yim, "Performance of domestic and foreign-invested enterprises in China," *Journal of World Business* 41 (2006): 268.

3 "The future of globalization," *Economist,* 29 July 2006, 11.

4 "A deadline for Doha," *Economist,* 29 January 2011, 75.

5 "In the twilight of Doha," *Economist,* 29 July 2006, 63.

6 P. Bustos, "Trade liberalaization, exports, and technology upgrading," *American Economic Review* 101 (2011): 304–340.

7 H. Van Rompuy, "Europe in the new global game," *The World in 2011* (London: Economist Newspaper Group, 2011) 97. Herman Van Rompuy is the first President of the European Council.

8 Delegation of the European Commission to the USA, *The European Union: A Guide for Americans* (Washington: Delegation of the European Commission to the USA, 2005) 2.

9 "No easy exit," *Economist,* 7 December 2010, 87–88.

10 "A club in need of a new vision," *Economist,* 1 May 2004, 26.

11 "Babelling on," *Economist,* 16 December 2006, 50.

12 "Mexico: Was NAFTA worth it?" *BusinessWeek,* 22 December 2003, available online at http://www.businessweek.com [accessed September 30, 2006].

13 A. Farrell, "'Giant sucking sound,' part deux," *Forbes.com,* 15 July 2008, available online at http://www.forbes.com [accessed 29 May 2009].

14 "Happy birthday, NAFTA," *BusinessWeek,* 22 December 2003, available online at http://www.businessweek.com [accessed 24 July 2009].

15 J. Sargent and L. Matthews, "The drivers of evolution/upgrading in Mexico's maquiladoras," *Journal of World Business* 41 (2006): 233–246.

16 A. Rugman, *The Regional Multinationals* (Cambridge, UK: Cambridge University Press, 2005) 215.

17 G. Qian, T. Khoury, M. W. Peng, and Z. Qian, "The performance implications of intra- and inter-regional geographic diversification," *Strategic Management Journal* 31 (2010): 1018–1030.

Chapter 9

1 M. Hitt, R. D. Ireland, S. M. Camp, and D. Sexton, "Strategic entrepreneurship," *Strategic Management Journal* 22 (2001): 480.

2 S. Shane and S. Venkataraman, "The promise of entrepreneurship as a field of research," *Academy of Management Review* 25 (2000): 218.

3 P. McDougall and B. Oviatt, "International entrepreneurship," *Academy of Management Journal,* 43 (2000): 903.

4 D. Kelley, N. Bosma, and J. Amoros, *Global Entrepreneurship Monitor 2010 Global Report* (Wellesley, MA: Babson College/GEM, 2011).

5 M. W. Peng, Y. Yamakawa, and S. Lee, "Bankruptcy laws and entrepreneur-friendliness," *Entrepreneur Theory and Practice* 34 (2010): 517–530.

6 "Son also rises," *Economist*, 27 November 2010, 71–72.

7 "In Russia, Facebook is more than a social network," *Bloomberg Businessweek*, 3 January 2011, 32–33.

8 S. Lee, Y. Yamakawa, M. W. Peng, and J. Barney, "How do bankruptcy laws affect entrepreneurship development around the world?" *Journal of Business Venturing* (2011, in press).

9 Y. Lu, L. Zhou, G. Bruton, and W. Li, "Capabilities as a mediator linking resources and the international performance of entrepreneurial firms in an emerging economy," *Journal of International Business Studies* 41 (2010): 419–436.

10 "The Megabus effect," *Bloomberg Businessweek*, 11 April 2011: 62–67.

11 M. W. Peng, "Private military companies," *Global Business*, 2nd ed. (Cincinnati, OH: South-Western Cengage Learning, 2011) 445–448.

12 D. Ahlstrom, G. Bruton, and K. Yeh, "Venture capital in China," *Asia Pacific Journal of Management* 24 (2007): 247–268.

13 N. Coviello, "The network dynamics of international new ventures," *Journal of International Business Studies* 37 (2006): 713–731.

14 M. W. Peng and A. York, "Behind intermediary performance in export trade," *Journal of International Business Studies* 32 (2001): 327–346.

15 R. Tesker, "Pepperoni power," *Far Eastern Economic Review*, 14 November 2002: 59–60.

16 M. W. Peng, C. Hill, and D. Wang, "Schumpeterian dynamics versus Williamsonian considerations," *Journal of Management Studies* 37 (2000): 167–184.

Chapter 10

1 K. Meyer, S. Estrin, S. Bhaumik, and M. W. Peng, "Institutions, resources, and entry strategies in emerging economies," *Strategic Management Journal* 30 (2009): 61–80.

2 "Europe's rush to grab US stimulus cash," *BusinessWeek*, 4 May 2009: 52.

3 M. Guillen and E. Garcia-Canal, "How to conquer new markets with old skills," *Harvard Business Review* November (2010): 118–122; M. W. Peng, "The resource-based view and international business," *Journal of Management* 27 (2001): 803–829.

4 S, Newman, C. Rickert, and R. Schaap, "Investing in the post-recession world," *Harvard Business Review* (January 2011): 150–155.

5 "Rulers of the new silk world," *Economist*, 5 June 2010, 75–77.

6 "Short takes: Autos," *China Business Review* (January–March 2011): 8.

7 M. W. Peng and D. Wang, "Innovation capability and foreign direct investment," *Management International Review* 40 (2000): 80.

8 D. Xu and O. Shenkar, "Institutional distance and the multinational enterprise," *Academy of Management Review* 27 (2002): 608.

9 "Don't mess with Russia," *Economist*, 16 December 2006, 11

10 J. G. Frynas, K. Mellahi, and G. Pigman, "First mover advantages in international business and firm-specific political resources," *Strategic Management Journal* 27 (2006): 321–345.

11 M. W. Peng, S. Lee, and J. Tan, "The *keiretsu* in Asia," *Journal of International Management* 7 (2001): 253–276.

12 "Land of war and opportunity," *Bloomberg Businessweek*, 10 January 2011: 46–54.

13 "Cisco's brave new world" (p. 68), *BusinessWeek*, 24 November 2008: 56–68.

14 G. Gao and Y. Pan, "The pace of MNEs' sequential entries," *Journal of International Business Studies* 41 (2010): 1572–1580; Y. Luo and M. W.

Peng, "Learning to compete in a transition economy," *Journal of International Business Studies* 30 (1999): 269–296.

15 M. W. Peng, Y. Zhou, and A. York, "Behind make or buy decisions in export strategy," *Journal of World Business* 41 (2006): 289–300.

16 A. Chintakananda, A. York, H. O'Neill, and M. W. Peng, "Structuring dyadic relationships between export producers and intermediaries," *European Journal of International Management* 3 (2009): 302–327.

Chapter 11

1 Z. Lin, M. W. Peng, H. Yang, and S. L. Sun, "How do networking and learning drive M&As? An institutional comparison between China and the United States," *Strategic Management Journal* 30 (2009): 1113–1132.

2 M. W. Peng, "Making M&As fly in China," *Harvard Business Review* (March 2006): 26–27.

3 "The surprising strength of Spain's Santander," *Bloomberg Businessweek*, 5 July 2010: 41–42.

4 "Open skies and flights of fancy," *Economist*, 4 October 2003, 67.

5 T. Tong, J. Reuer, and M. W. Peng, "International joint ventures and the value of growth options," *Academy of Management Journal* 51 (2008): 1014–1029.

6 L. Mesquita, "Starting over when the bickering never ends," *Academy of Management Review* 32 (2007): 72–91.

7 C. Christensen, R. Alton, C. Rising, and A. Waldeck, "The new M&A playbook," *Harvard Business Review* (March 2011): 49–57.

8 G. Andrade, M. Mitchell, and E. Stafford, "New evidence and perspectives on mergers," *Journal of Economic Perspectives* 15 (2001): 103–120.

9 G. Lee and M. Lieberman, "Acquisition versus internal development," *Strategic Management Journal* 31 (2010): 140–158.

10 M. W. Peng and O. Shenkar, "Joint venture dissolution as corporate divorce," *Academy of Management Executive* 16 (2002): 92–105.

11 A. Arino and J. Reuer, "Designing and renegotiating strategic alliance contracts" (p. 44), *Academy of Management Executive* 18 (2004): 37–48.

12 "Pepsi's Russian challenge," *Economist*, 11 December 2010: 75–76.

13 "China's lucky man bags Volvo," *Economist*, 7 August 2010: 64.

14 H. Moore, "Bank of America-Merrill Lynch: A $50 billion deal from hell," *Wall Street Journal*, 22 January 2009, available online at http://blogs.wsj.com [accessed 1 June 2009].

Chapter 12

1 T. Levitt, "The globalization of markets," *Harvard Business Review* (May–June 1983): 92–102.

2 C. Bartlett and S. Ghoshal, *Managing Across Borders* (Boston: Harvard Business School Press, 1989).

3 "Kia Motors: Still cheap, now chic," *BusinessWeek*, 1 June 2009, 58.

4 R. Hodgetts, "Dow Chemical CEO William Stavropoulos on structure," *Academy of Management Executive* 13 (1999): 30.

5 X. Ma and A. Delios, "Host country headquarters and an MNE's subsequent within-country diversification," *Journal of International Business Studies* 41 (2010): 517–525.

6 "Cisco's brave new world," *BusinessWeek*, 24 November 2008, 56–66.

7 C. K. Prahalad and K. Lieberthal, "The end of corporate imperialism," *Harvard Business Review* (August 1998): 68–79.

8 Bartlett and Ghoshal, *Managing Across Borders* 209.

9 A. Gupta and V. Govindarajan, *Global Strategy and Organization* (New York: Wiley, 2004) 104.

10 P. Gooderham, D. Minbaeva, and T. Pedersen, "Governance mechanisms for the promotion of social capital for knowledge transfer in multinational corporations," *Journal of Management Studies* 48 (2011): 123–150.

11 M. Kotabe, D. Dunlap-Hinkler, R. Parente, and H. Mishra, "Determinants of cross-national knowledge transfer and its effect on firm innovation," *Journal of International Business Studies* 38 (2007): 259–282.

12 A. Witty, "Research and develop," *The World in 2011* (London: The Economist, 2011) 140. Witty is CEO of GSK.

13 P. Ghemawat, "The cosmopolitan corporation," *Harvard Business Review* (May 2011): 92–99.

Chapter 13

1 C. Fey, S. Morgulis-Yukushev, H. Park, and I. Bjorkman, "Opening the black box of the relationship between HRM practices and firm performance," *Journal of International Business Studies* 40 (2009): 690–712; L. Wei and C. Lau, "The impact of market orientation and strategic HRM on firm performance," *Journal of International Business Studies* 39 (2008): 980–995.

2 E. Farndale et al., "Context-bound configurations of corporate HR functions in multinational corporations," *Human Resource Management* 49 (2010): 45–66.

3 D. Vora and T. Kostova, "A model of dual organizational identification in the context of the multinational enterprise," *Journal of Organizational Behavior* 28 (2007): 327–350.

4 Y. Chang, Y. Gong, and M. W. Peng, "Expatriate knowledge transfer, subsidiary absorptive capacity, and subsidiary performance," Working paper, University of Texas at Dallas, 2011.

5 "A tale of two expats," *Economist*, 31 January 2011, 62–64.

6 R. L. Tung, "Selection and training procedures for US, European, and Japanese multinationals," *California Management Review* 25 (1982): 57–71.

7 C. Schmidt, "The battle for China's talent," *Harvard Business Review* March (2011): 25–27.

8 F. Chiang and T. Birtch, "Appraising performance across borders," *Journal of Management Studies* 47 (2010): 1365–1392.

9 "A new labor movement is born in China," *Bloomberg Businessweek*, 14 June 2010, 8.

10 C. Chen, "New trends in allocation preferences," *Academy of Management Journal* 38 (1995): 408–428.

11 Economist Intelligence Unit, *Up or Out: Next Moves for the Modern Expatriate* (London: The Economist, 2010).

12 "Developing your global know-how," *Harvard Business Review* (March 2011): 72.

13 D. Holtbrugge, C. Friedmann, and J. Puck, "Recruitment and retention in foreign firms in India," *Human Resource Management* 49 (2010): 439–455.

14 W. Arthur, W. Bennett, P. Edens, and S. Bell, "Effectiveness of training in organizations," *Journal of Applied Psychology* 88 (2003): 234–245.

15 D. Zoogah, D. Vora, O. Richard, and M. W. Peng, "Strategic alliance team diversity, coordination, and effectiveness," *International Journal of Human Resource Management* 22 (2011): 510–529.

16 B. Becker and M. Huselid, "Strategic HRM," *Journal of Management* 32 (2006): 907.

17 J. Combs, D. Ketchen, A. Hall, and Y. Liu, "Do high performance work practices matter?," *Personnel Psychology* 59 (2006): 501–528.

18 S. Meisinger, "The four Cs of the HR profession," *Human Resource Management* 44 (2005): 189–194.

19 "Secrets of an HR superstar," *BusinessWeek*, 19 April 2007, 66.

Chapter 14

1 K. Davis, "The case for and against business assumption of social responsibilities," *Academy of Management Journal* 16 (1973): 312.

2 World Commission on Environment and Development, *Our Common Future* (Oxford: Oxford University Press, 1987) 8.

3 B. Husted and D. Allen, "Corporate social responsibility in the multinational enterprise: Strategic and institutional approaches," *Journal of International Business Studies* 37 (2006): 838–849.

4 M. Friedman, "The social responsibility of business is to increase its profits," *New York Times Magazine*, 13 September 1970, 32–33.

5 A. Karnani, "The case against corporate social responsibility," *Wall Street Journal*, 23 August 2010.

6 A. Gore, *An Inconvenient Truth* (Emmaus, PA: Rodale Press, 2006); M. Porter and M. Kramer, "Strategy and society," *Harvard Business Review* (December 2006): 78–92.

7 "The other oil spill," *Economist*, 26 June 2010: 71–73.

8 "Nine questions (and provisional answers) about the spill," *Bloomberg Businessweek*, 14 June 2010: 62.

9 "Message from Howard Schultz," *Starbucks Global Responsibility Report 2010*, 2011, www.starbucks.com.

10 G. Unruh and R. Ettenson, "Winning in the green frenzy," *Harvard Business Review* (November 2010): 110–116.

11 "The smooth-talking king of coal—and climate change," *Bloomberg Businessweek*, 7 June 2010: 65.

12 P. Christmann and G. Taylor, "Firm self-regulation through international certifiable standards," *Journal of International Business Studies* 37 (2006): 863–878; M. Delmas and M. Montes-Sancho, "Voluntary agreements to improve environmental quality," *Strategic Management Journal* 31 (2010): 575–601.

13 A. Hillman and G. Keim, "Shareholder value, stakeholder management, and social issues," *Strategic Management Journal* 22 (2001): 125–139.

14 P. Godfrey, C. Merrill, and J. Hansen, "The relationship between CSR and shareholder value," *Strategic Management Journal* 30 (2009): 425–445; B. Lev, C. Petrovits, and S. Radhakrishnan, "Is doing good good for you?" *Strategic Management Journal* 31 (2010): 182–200.

15 S. Ambec and P. Lanoie, "Does it pay to be green?" *Academy of Management Perspectives* (November 2008): 45–62; D. Vogel, "The low value of virtue," *Harvard Business Review* (June 2005): 26.

16 S. Brammer and A. Millington, "Does it pay to be different?" *Strategic Management Journal* 29 (2008): 1325–1343; A. McWilliams and D. Siegel, "CSR and financial performance," *Strategic Management Journal* 21 (2000): 603–609.

17 T. Devinney, "Is the socially responsible corporation a myth?" *Academy of Management Perspectives* (May 2009): 53.

18 M. Porter and M. Kramer, "Creating shared value," *Harvard Business Review* (January 2011): 62–77.

4LTR Press solutions are designed for today's learners through the continuous feedback of students like you. Tell us what you think about GLOBAL and help us improve the learning experience for future students.

YOUR FEEDBACK MATTERS.

Index

culture and, 41, 165
defense industry, 74
EU and, 117, 118, 119, 120, 124
film industry, 63–64
foreign exchange market, 103
HR, 195–196
informal investment, 133
inpatriation vs. expatriation, 191
inshoring, 54
laissez faire, end of, 20
Libya and, 31
mixed economy, 28
pragmatic nationalism, 88
severance pay, 186
Toyota in, 107
trade, 62
Venezuela and, 89
venture capital investment, 132
franchising, 136, 151
freedom of expression and organization, 24
free float policies, 100
free market principles, 19, 204–205
free market view on FDI, 87
free trade. *See also* trade, international
absolute advantage and, 64
defined, 64
economic arguments against, 74
political arguments against, 74–76
tariff and non-tariff barriers to, 72–74
Free Trade Area of the Americas (FTAA), 122
free trade areas (FTAs). *See also* regional economic integration
ACFTA, 122–123
AFTA, 122
CAFTA, 122
CER, 122
defined, 116
NAFTA, 120–121
Friedman, Milton, 204
Friedman, Thomas, 59
FTAs. *See* free trade areas
The Full Monty (film), 205

G

G-20 (Group of 20), 6, 102, 104
GATS (General Agreement on Trade in Services), 114
GATT (General Agreement on Tariffs and Trade), 112, 114
GAZ, 92
Gazprom, 31
GDP. *See* gross domestic product

Geely, 157, 163, 165
General Agreement on Tariffs and Trade (GATT), 112, 114
General Agreement on Trade in Services (GATS), 114
General Electric (GE), 16–17, 35, 59, 160, 166, 198
General Motors (GM), 29, 56, 84, 91–92, 145, 147, 181
geocentric approach to staffing, 187–188
geographic areas structure, 173–174
Georgia, 104, 143
Germany
aerospace industry, 69, 146
alliances and acquisitions, 161, 167
anti-corruption legislation, 46
automobile industry, 145, 181
BOT power-generation project in Iran, 151
climate change and, 211
corporate bankruptcy and, 138
corruption and, 43
culture and, 39, 40
entrepreneurship, 129, 131
EU and, 111–112, 117, 118, 119, 120, 124
executive nationalities and, 177
exports, 12, 61–62
FDI, 81, 82
foreign exchange, 102
foreign exchange market, 103
informal investment, 133
inshoring, 54
Kia in, 173
labor relations, 195, 205
Libya and, 31
location-specific advantages, 145
Opel case, 91–92
outsourcing, 76–77
Ritmüller, 142, 144
severance pay, 186
Siemens and, 46–47
staffing, 187
"take-back" auto policy, 44–45, 46
Transparency International, 42
venture capital investment, 132
Wal-Mart in, 153
Wintershall, 31
Ghosn, Carlos, 191, 202
gift giving, 42
Giscard d'Estaing, Valéry, 108
global business
definition and importance of, 5–8
united framework for, 8–10

global economic crisis of 2008–2009. *See* Great Recession
global economic integration
defined, 112
Doha Round, 115
economic benefits, 113
evolution of GATT and WTO, 112–113, 114
management implications, 123
political benefits, 113
trade dispute settlement, 114
global economic pyramid, 6–7
global economy, size of, 14–15
globalization
debate over, 13–16
defined, 10
financial crisis blamed on, 11–12
as historical, 10
language and, 35
local responsiveness and, 171
opposition to, 10, 11–12, 13–14
pendulum view on, 10–13
semiglobalization, 13
global mandate, 172
global matrix structure, 174–175
global product division structure, 174
global standardization strategy, 172–173, 179
global sustainability, 203–204
GLOBE clusters, 38
GNI (gross national income), per capita, 28
going rate approach, 192
Goldman Sachs, 20
gold standard, 101
Google, 130, 132, 146
government-sponsored enterprises (GSEs), 29
Grameen Project, 134
Great Britain. *See* United Kingdom (Britain)
Great Depression (1929–1933), 29
Great Recession (global economic crisis of 2008–2009)
corporate bankruptcy and, 138–139
direct selling and, 4
FDI and, 91
globalization blamed for, 11–12
IMF reforms and, 104
layoffs and, 185–186
pragmatic nationalism and, 88
private vs. state ownership and, 29
Russia and, 143
symptoms of, 13

Greece
ancient, 24
financial crisis and bailout, 119, 120, 124
foreign exchange, 107
GDP, 14
IMF and, 103, 104
informal investment, 133
PIGS countries, 120, 124
Siemens and, 46–47
uncertainty avoidance, 40
venture capital investment, 132
green-field operations, 152
greenhouse gas (GHG) emissions, 211–212
Greenpeace, 207–208
"green" taxes, 206–207
Greyhound, 147, 153
gross domestic product (GDP)
BRIC and, 11
defined, 6
informal investment as percentage of, 133
PPP vs., 6
venture capital as percentage of, 132
gross national income (GNI), per capita, 28
Group of 20 (G-20), 6, 102, 104
Grove, Andy, 59
GSK, 180
Guatemala, 122

H

Häagen-Dazs, 179–180
Hasina, Sheikh, 134
HCNs. *See* host-country nationals
headquarters, 175, 182
Heckscher, Eli, 67
Heckscher–Ohlin theory, 67
Hess, 31
high-context cultures, 37
Hindi language, 35
Hitachi, 207
Hofstede, Geert, 35, 39, 40, 178
Home Depot, 210, 211
home replication strategy, 171–172, 179
Honda, 147
Honduras, 122
Honeywell, 166
Hong Kong
economic freedom in, 27–28
entrepreneurship, 131
foreign exchange, 97, 109
foreign exchange market, 103
formal institutions, 9
in Four Tigers, 11
HQ moves, 182

Hong Kong (*cont.*)
investment in China, 38
location-specific advantages, 144
Nomura in, 167
Pearl River Piano Group in, 141–142
PwC in, 181
Stagecoach Group in, 153
WTO meeting, 115
horizontal FDI, 80–81
host-country nationals (HCNs).
See also human resources management (HRM)
compensation, 193–194
defined, 186
informal rules and, 177
labor relations, 195
norms, 196
performance appraisal, 194–195
staffing, 186–188
training and development for, 191–192
HP, 164, 166, 179, 194, 195
HR. *See* human resources management (HRM)
HSBC, 26, 182
Huawei, 35, 178
hubristic motives for acquisitions, 163–164
human dignity and rights, respect for, 42
human resources and capabilities, 51
human resources management (HRM)
across-the-board pay cuts vs. reduction in force, 194, 198
compensation and performance appraisal, 192–195
defined, 186
inpatriation vs. expatriation, 191
institutions and, 195–197
labor relations, 195
management implications, 197–198
recession and layoffs case, 185–186
resources and, 197
staffing, 186–189
training and development, 189–192
Hungary
currency risk, 107
EU and, 119
exchange rate policy, 100
FDI, 87
IMF and, 103, 104
informal investment, 133

mixed economy, 28
Russian FDI, 143
Siemens and, 46–47
strategies to attract MNEs, 176
venture capital investment, 132
Huntington, Samuel, 38
Huselid, Mark, 198
Hyundai, 147, 152–153, 195

I

IB (international business), 4–5
IBM, 54–56, 59, 165, 166
Iceland
capital flight, 101
English language and, 35
euro and, 118
IMF and, 103, 104
informal investment, 133
interest rates, 98–99
IKEA, 22, 23, 35
IMF (International Monetary Fund), 102–103, 104
imitability
acquisitions and, 160–161
alliances and, 160
CSR and, 210
entrepreneurship and, 130–131
HR and, 197
management implications, 58
multinational structures, 178
in VRIO framework, 56–57
imitation effect, 88
Immelt, Jeff, 16, 198
import quotas, 73
imports, defined, 62. *See also* trade, international
import tariffs, 72
India
alliances and acquisitions, 161, 162, 165
automobile industry, 152–153
CAFTA and, 122
climate change and, 211
Coca-Cola in, 9
compensation, 193
culture and, 38
as democracy, 24
discrimination, 142
dumping and, 150
entrepreneurship, 131
ethics and, 42
executive nationalities and, 177
FDI, 87, 143
foreign exchange, 95–96
formal institutions, 9
GDP growth, 11
GE in, 17
household income, 23
IMF and, 104

inpatriation vs. expatriation, 191
institutional constraints, 22
investment in, 21
IT industry, 71, 145, 151, 191
labor relations, 195
McDonald's in, 170
microfinance, 133
offshoring, 54, 55, 59
privatization in, 29
PwC in, 181
resource-based view on, 9
severance pay, 186
subcultures, 35
terrorism and, 14
trade, 75–76
as transition economy, 22
unemployment, 185
WTO and, 115
after WWII, 11
indirect exports, 137, 150–151
individualism
convergence and, 44
defined, 39
as dimension of culture, 39–40
global management and, 41
informal institutions and, 9
Indonesia
CAFTA and, 122
compensation, 193
CSR, 208, 210
FDI, 82
foreign exchange, 109
GDP, 14
IMF and, 103
Nike and, 43
Siemens and, 46–47
subcultures, 35
terrorism and, 14
trade, 73
industrial policy, 59
infant industry argument, 74
informal institutions
alliances, acquisitions and, 158–159
culture, 35–41
defined, 9
ethics, 41–43
market-supporting institutions and, 30
normative and cognitive pillars and, 21
norms, 43–45
sources of, 34–35
uncertainty and, 22
information technology (IT)
in India, 71, 145, 151, 191
knowledge management and, 179
market responsiveness and, 22
offshoring and, 55
patent licensing and, 56
Silicon Valley, 145

initial public offerings (IPOs), 134
initiators, 162
innovation
developing capabilities, 180–181
entrepreneurship and, 132
location and innovation-seeking strategy, 145
transnational strategy and, 173
value of, 177
innovation resources and capabilities, 51
inpatriation, 191
inshoring, 54
institutional distance, 145–146, 164
institutional framework, 9
institutional transitions, 20, 22, 23
institution-based view
alliances and acquisitions, 158–159, 163–164, 166
bankruptcy, 138
core propositions, 22–24
CSR, 202, 206–209
cultural intelligence and, 45
currency management, 107
defined, 8–9
economic integration, 112, 123
entrepreneurship, 129–130, 137–138
FDI, 80, 82, 87, 91
foreign exchange, 96, 103
foreign market entry, 152
HR, 195–197
internalization and, 86
IPR and, 27
liability of foreignness, 143
management savvy and, 30–31
multinational strategy, structure, and learning, 176–177
multinational vs. multi-national, 181
rational action and, 44
trade and, 62–64
institutions ("rules of the game").
See also formal institutions; informal institutions; institution-based view
defined, 9, 20
market-supporting institutional frameworks, 30
regulatory, normative, and cognitive pillars, 20–21
trade and, 63–64
uncertain reduction, 21–22
intangible resources and capabilities, 51
integration-responsiveness framework, 170

M

Maastricht Treaty, 117
Magna, 91–92
Malawi, 28, 153
Malaysia
  captive sourcing, 54
  CSR, 210
  electronics industry, 68
  foreign exchange, 109
  GDP, 14
  HR, 196
  migration of jobs to, 12
  trade, 76
Malta, 124
managed float policies, 100
management and managers. *See specific topics, such as* ethics
management control rights, 80
management savvy
  alliances and acquisitions, 165–166
  cross-cultural literacy, 45–46
  CSR, 210–211
  economic integration, 123
  entrepreneurship, 137–138
  FDI, 91
  foreign exchange, 107
  foreign markets, 152–153
  HR, 197–198
  institution-based view and, 30–31
  multinational structure and strategy, 180–181
  resource-based view, 58–59
managerial motives for acquisitions, 163–164
Mandatory Country of Origin Labeling (COOL), 77
Manpower, 195–196
manufacturing, outsourcing of, 59
Marathon, 31
market economies, 27
market entry. *See* foreign market entry
market failure, 83, 86–87
market imperfections, 83
marketing, 36
market-seeking firms, 145
market-supporting institutional frameworks, 30
Marshall, Alfred, 144
M&As. *See* acquisitions
masculinity, 40, 41
matrix structure, 174–175
Matsushita, 41
Mattel, 56–57
McDonald's, 11, 26, 136, 151, 160, 170
McGraw-Hill, 5
Medvedev, Dmitry, 23

Megabus, 130, 147, 153
Meisinger, Susan, 197
mercantilism, 64
Mercedes, 107, 145, 195
merchandise trade, 62
Merck, 47
Mercosur, 121–122
mergers and acquisitions (M&As). *See* acquisitions
Merkel, Angela, 92
Merrill Lynch, 24, 164
Metallurgical Corporation of China, 147
Mexico
  APEC and, 123
  automobile industry, 145
  China compared to, 120
  Coca-Cola in, 10
  corruption and, 42
  exchange rate policy, 100
  expatriates, 189
  Ford in, 89
  foreign exchange, 95, 99
  IMF and, 103
  informal investment, 133
  labor relations, 195
  NAFTA, 120–121
  outsourcing, 55
  Russia compared to, 23
  Siemens and, 46–47
  US Hispanics and, 36
  WOSs, 158
  WTO meeting, 115
  after WWII, 11
MFA (Multifiber Arrangement), 114
MGA, 57
microfinance, 132–133, 134
microfinance institutions (MFIs), 134
Microsoft, 166
Miller Beer, 79–80, 157
Mitsubishi Motors, 41
mixed economies, 27–28
MNEs. *See* multinational enterprises
modes of entry, 148–152
Mogi, Yazaburo, 169–170
Mohammed, 26
monetary unions, 117
money supply, 98–99
Mongolia, 115
Morales, Evo, 89
moral hazard, 29, 104
Morgan Stanley, 20
Morocco, 31
Motorola, 180
movie industry, 57, 63–64, 70
Mozambique, 28, 38
MTV, 171, 172
multidomestic (localization) strategy, 172

Multifiber Arrangement (MFA), 114
multilateral trading system, 113
multinational enterprises (MNEs)
  defined, 4–5
  equity modes through FDI, 149
  FDI and, 82
  joint ventures and, 151
  Latin American anti-MNE events, 89
  multinational vs. multinational, 181
  proliferation of, 82
  Russian, 143
  semiglobalization and, 13
  size and location of, 14–15
multinational structure and strategy
  cost reduction and local responsiveness, 170–171
  global standardization strategy, 172–173, 179
  home replication strategy, 171–172, 179
  institution-based considerations, 176–177
  Kikkoman case, 169–170
  knowledge management, 178–180
  localization strategy, 172, 179
  management implications, 180–181
  moving HQ overseas, 182
  multinational vs. multinational, 181
  organization structure types, 173–175
  reciprocal relationship between, 175–176
  resource-based considerations, 177–178
  transnational strategy, 173, 179
Murdoch, Rupert, 142

N

NAFTA (North American Free Trade Agreement), 120–121
nationalism, pragmatic, 88
National Oil Corporation (NOC), Libya, 31
national security, 74
natural resources and economic development, 28. *See also* oil and gas industry
natural-resources-seeking firms, 145
NEC, 152
Neeleman, David, 127–128, 137
nepotism, 42

Nestle, 207–208
Netherlands
  alliances and acquisitions, 167
  English language and, 35
  flower industry, 84
  informal investment, 133
  Maastricht Treaty, 117
  per capita income, 28
  P&G and, 177
  Rotterdam as hub, 144
  Shell, 31
  venture capital investment, 132
New York Times Company, 194
New Zealand
  CER and, 122
  dumping and, 150
  GDP, 14
  informal investment, 133
  Siemens and, 46–47
  Stagecoach Group in, 153
  venture capital investment, 132
NGOs. *See* nongovernmental organizations
Nicaragua, 122
Niederauer, Duncan, 182
Niger, 28
Nigeria
  compensation, 193
  income gap, 205
  oil industry, 86–87
Nigerian National Petroleum Corporation (NNCP), 86–87
Nike, 43, 53
Nissan, 147, 157, 191, 201–202, 204
Nixon, Richard, 102
Nokia, 182
Nomura, 164–165, 167, 182
non-discrimination, 113
non-equity-based alliances, 156–157
non-equity modes, 149
nongovernmental organizations (NGOs)
  collaborations with, 208–209
  CSR and, 210, 211
  globalization debate and, 15
  influence of, 203
non-tariff barriers (NTB), 73–74, 114
normative pillar, 21, 159
norms and values
  alliances, acquisitions, and, 159
  defined, 43
  ethical challenges and, 43–45
  HR and, 196
North America, 6. *See also* Canada; Mexico; United States

CHAPTER SUMMARY

LO1 Explain the concepts of international business and global business.

- International Business (IB) is typically defined as (1) a business (firm) that engages in international (cross-border) economic activities or (2) the action of doing business abroad.
- Multinational enterprises (MNEs) are firms that engage in foreign direct investment (FDI).
- Global business is defined in this book as business around the globe.
- Emerging economies contribute close to 50% to global gross domestic product (measured by purchasing power parity, PPP).
- Viewed as a pyramid, the global economy has one billion people at the top and another billion in the second tier. The majority of humanity, approximately five billion people, makes up the base of the pyramid.

LO2 Give three reasons why it is important to study global business.

- Studying global business is important in order to better compete in the corporate world that will require global expertise.
- Be better prepared for possible expatriate assignments abroad.
- Studying global business will help you possess stronger competence in interacting with foreign suppliers, partners, and competitors, and in working for foreign-owned employers in your own country.

LO3 Articulate the fundamental question that the study of global business seeks to answer and two perspectives from which to answer it.

- Our most fundamental question is: What determines the success and failure of firms around the globe?
- The two core perspectives are (1) the institution-based view and (2) the resource-based view.
- The institution-based view suggests that the success and failure of firms are enabled and constrained by different rules of the game.
- The resource-based view says that successful firms have certain valuable and unique firm-specific resources and capabilities that are not shared by competitors in the same environments.
- We develop a unified framework by organizing materials in every chapter according to the two perspectives guided by the fundamental question.

LO4 Identify three ways of understanding what globalization is.

- The three views of globalization are (1) that it is a recent phenomenon, (2) that it is a one-directional evolution since the dawn of human history, and (3) that it is a process similar to the swing of a pendulum.
- Advocates of globalization say that it increases economic growth, standards of living, and technology sharing and contributes to more extensive cultural integration.
- Critics argue that globalization undermines wages in rich countries, exploits workers in poor countries, and gives

KEY TERMS A[...]

International business (IB)
(1) A business (or firm) that engages in international (cross-border) economic activities or (2) the action of doing business abroad.

Multinational enterprise (MNE)
A firm that engages in foreign direct investment and operates in multiple countries.

Foreign direct investment (FDI)
Investment in, controlling, and managing value-added activities in other countries.

Global business
Business around the globe.

Emerging economy (or emerging market)
A developing country.

Group of 20 (G-20)
The group of 19 major countries plus the European Union (EU) whose leaders meet on a regular basis to solve global economic problems.

Gross domestic product (GDP)
The sum of value added by resident firms, households, and governments operating in an economy.

Purchasing power parity (PPP)
A conversion that determines the equivalent amount of goods and services different currencies can purchase. This conversion is usually used to capture the differences in cost of living in different countries.

Triad
Three regions of developed economies (North America, Western Europe, and Japan).

Base of the pyramid
The vast majority of humanity, about five billion people, who make less than $2,000 a year on a per capita basis.

Expatriate manager (expat)
A manager who works outside his or her native country.

International premium
A significant pay raise commanded by expatriates when working overseas.

Institution-based view
A leading perspective in global business that suggests that firm performance is, at least in part, determined by the institutional frameworks governing firm behavior around the world.

Institutions
Formal and informal rules of the game.

Institutional framework
Formal and informal institutions that govern individual and firm behavior.

Formal institutions
Institutions such as laws, regulations, and rules.

Informal institutions
Institutions such as norms, cultures, and ethics.

MNEs too much power.
- Semiglobalization is more complex than extremes of total isolation and total globalization and provides a more accurate picture of the current global economy.

LO5 State the size of the global economy and its broad trends.
- MNEs, especially large ones from developed economies, are sizeable economic entities.
- Emerging economies have numerous MNEs in the *Fortune Global 500* as well.
- Current and would-be business leaders need to be aware of their own hidden pro-globalization bias.
- The rapid globalization of the 1990s saw significant backlash around the turn of the century marked by protests and terrorist attacks, largely attributed to a sense of powerlessness in the face of rapid global change.
- Much of the opposition to globalization comes from nongovernmental organizations (NGOs) and raises valid points about how MNEs' actions affect various stakeholders around the world.

Resource-based view
A leading perspective in global business that suggests that firm performance is, at least in part, determined by its internal resources and capabilities.

Liability of foreignness
The inherent disadvantage that foreign firms experience in host countries because of their non-native status.

Globalization
The close integration of countries and peoples of the world.

BRIC
A newly coined acronym for the emerging economies of Brazil, Russia, India, and China.

Risk management
The identification and assessment of risks and the preparation to minimize the impact of high-risk, unfortunate events.

Scenario planning
A technique to prepare and plan for multiple scenarios (either high or low risk).

Semiglobalization
A perspective that suggests that barriers to market integration at borders are high but not high enough to completely insulate countries from each other.

Nongovernmental organizations (NGOs)
Organizations that are not affiliated with governments. Such organizations include environmentalist groups, human rights activists, and consumer groups.

REVIEW QUESTIONS

1. What is the difference between international business and global business, as defined in this chapter?
2. Why are you studying global business? How does it affect your future?
3. What is the most fundamental question driving global business? Why is it important?
4. How would you describe an institution-based view of global business?
5. How would you describe a resource-based view of global business?
6. After comparing the three views of globalization, which seems the most logical and sensible to you?

CRITICAL DISCUSSION QUESTIONS

1. A classmate says: "Global business is relevant for top executives such as CEOs in large companies. I am just a lowly student who will struggle to gain an entry-level job, probably in a small domestic company. Why should I care about it?" How do you convince her that she should care about it?
2. *ON ETHICS:* What are some of the darker sides (in other words, costs) associated with globalization? How can business leaders make sure that the benefits of their various actions (such as outsourcing) outweigh their drawbacks (such as job losses in developed economies)?
3. *ON ETHICS:* Some argue that aggressively investing in emerging economies is not only economically beneficial but also highly ethical, because it may potentially lift many people out of poverty. However, others caution that in the absence of reasonable hopes of decent profits, rushing to emerging economies is reckless. How would you participate in this debate?

CLOSING CASE DISCUSSION QUESTIONS

1. What are the similarities and differences between GE's traditional innovation and reverse innovation?
2. Why is GE so interested in reverse innovation?
3. What are the main concerns that prevent Western MNEs from aggressively investing in emerging economies? What are the costs if they choose not to focus on emerging economies?
4. Why is a leading US MNE such as GE afraid of emerging multinationals from emerging economies?

Understanding Politics, LAWS, & Economics

CHAPTER SUMMARY

LO1 Identify two types of institutions.

LO2 Explain how institutions reduce uncertainty.
- Institutions are commonly defined as the "rules of the game."
- There are two types of institutions: formal and informal. Each has different supportive pillars.
- Their key function is to reduce uncertainty, curtail transaction costs, and combat opportunism. Institutions accomplish these things by reducing the range of acceptable actions.

LO3 Identify the two core propositions underpinning an institution-based view of global business.
- Proposition 1: Managers and firms *rationally* pursue their interests and make choices within formal and informal institutional constraints in a given institutional framework.
- Proposition 2: When formal constraints are unclear or fail, informal constraints will play a *larger* role.

LO4 List the differences between democracy and totalitarianism.
- Democracy is a political system in which citizens elect representatives to govern the country.
- Freedom of expression is a fundamental aspect of democracy.
- Totalitarianism is a political system in which one person or party exercises absolute political control.
- Totalitarian systems can be communist, right-wing, theocratic, or tribal.
- Totalitarian systems generally carry a greater degree of political risk than democracies do.

LO5 List the differences among civil law, common law, and theocratic law.
- Civil law uses comprehensive statutes and codes as a primary means to form legal judgments and as such is less confrontational.
- Common law is shaped by precedents and traditions from previous judicial decisions and is more confrontational as plaintiffs and defendants argue the relevance of precedent to specific cases.
- Theocratic law is a legal system based on religious teachings, such as Islamic law.

LO6 Articulate the importance of property rights and intellectual property rights.
- Protection of property rights by a functioning legal system is fundamental to economic development.
- Patents, copyrights, and trademarks are the three primary ways that intellectual property is recognized and protected.
- The intangible nature of intellectual property rights makes enforcement difficult, and weak enforcement makes counterfeiting a rational choice for certain firms.

LO7 List the differences among market economy, command economy, and mixed economy.
- A pure market economy is characterized by *laissez faire* and total control by market forces.

KEY TERMS AND DEFINITIONS

Institutional transitions
Fundamental and comprehensive changes introduced to the formal and informal rules of the game that affect organizations as players.

Regulatory pillar
The coercive power of governments exercised through laws, regulations, and rules.

Normative pillar
The mechanisms through which norms influence individual and firm behavior.

Cognitive pillar
The internalized, taken-for-granted values and beliefs that guide individual and firm behavior.

Transaction costs
The costs associated with economic transactions or, more broadly, the costs of doing business.

Opportunism
The act of seeking self-interest with guile.

Political system
The rules of the game on how a country is governed politically.

Democracy
A political system in which citizens elect representatives to govern the country on their behalf.

Totalitarianism (or dictatorship)
A political system in which one person or party exercises absolute political control over the population.

Political risk
Risk associated with political changes that may negatively impact domestic and foreign firms.

Legal system
The rules of the game on how a country's laws are enacted and enforced.

Civil law
A legal tradition that uses comprehensive statutes and codes as a primary means to form legal judgments.

Common law
A legal tradition that is shaped by precedents from previous judicial decisions.

Theocratic law
A legal system based on religious teachings.

Property rights
Legal rights to use an economic property (resource) and to derive income and benefits from it.

Intellectual property
Intangible property that results from intellectual activity (such as the content of books, videos, and websites).

Intellectual property rights (IPR)
Legal rights associated with the ownership of intellectual property.

- A pure command economy is defined by government ownership and control of all means of production, distribution, and pricing.
- Most countries operate mixed economies, with a different emphasis on market versus command forces.

LO8 Explain why it is important to understand the different institutions when doing business abroad.
- Have a thorough understanding of the formal institutions before entering a country.
- Recognize when informal relationships must be developed before business can be conducted due to generally weak formal institutions.

REVIEW QUESTIONS

1. Name the one pillar that supports formal institutions and the two additional pillars that support informal institutions.
2. Explain the two core propositions underpinning the institution-based view of global business.
3. How does political risk affect global business?
4. Describe the differences among the three types of legal systems.
5. Name and describe the three economic systems. Which economic system is the most common?
6. Generally, what is the result of strong, effective, market-supporting formal institutions?

CRITICAL DISCUSSION QUESTIONS

1. Without looking at any references, please identify the top three countries with the most significant change in political risk in the last five years. Why do you think so?
2. *ON ETHICS:* As a manager, you discover that your multinational firm's products are counterfeited by small family firms that employ child labor in rural Bangladesh. You are aware of the corporate plan to phase out the products soon. You also realize that once you report to the authorities, these firms will be shut down, employees will be out of work, and families and children will be starving. How do you proceed?
3. *ON ETHICS:* Your multinational is the largest foreign investor and enjoys good profits in (1) Sudan, where government forces are reportedly cracking down on rebels and killing civilians, and (2) Vietnam, where religious leaders are reportedly being persecuted. As a country manager, you understand that your firm is pressured by activists to exit these countries. The alleged government actions, which you personally find distasteful, are not directly related to your operations. How would you proceed?

Patents
Exclusive legal rights of inventors to derive income from their inventions through activities such as manufacturing, licensing, or selling.

Copyrights
Exclusive legal rights of authors and publishers to publish and disseminate their work.

Trademarks
Exclusive legal rights of firms to use specific names, brands, and designs to differentiate their products from others.

Piracy
The unauthorized use of intellectual property rights.

Economic system
The rules of the game on how a country is governed economically.

Market economy
An economy that is characterized by the "invisible hand" of market forces.

Command economy
An economy in which theoretically all factors of production are state-owned and state-controlled, and all supply, demand, and pricing are planned by the government.

Mixed economy
An economy that has elements of both a market economy and a command economy.

Washington Consensus
A view centered on the unquestioned belief in the superiority of private ownership over state ownership in economic policy making, which is often spearheaded by two Washington-based international organizations: the International Monetary Fund and the World Bank.

Moral hazard
Recklessness when people and organizations (including firms and governments) do not have to face the full consequences of their actions.

CLOSING CASE DISCUSSION QUESTIONS

1. What lessons can be learned about political risk in countries run by totalitarian regimes such as those in the Middle East?
2. As an executive at ENI or ConocoPhillips, what are your plans for the future of your operations in Libya?
3. As an executive at BP, Gazprom, or Sinopec, given this traumatic experience in Libya, would you recommend that in the future, your firm enter another oil-rich country with a similar political system with its typical problems (such as dictatorship, corruption, and nepotism) that provoke mass unrest in the Middle East?

Emphasizing Cultures, ETHICS, & Norms

CHAPTER SUMMARY

LO1 Explain where informal institutions come from.
- Informal institutions are a pervasive feature of every economy.
- Societies tend to perceive their own culture, ethics, and norms as "natural, rational, and morally right"—a self-centered mentality known as ethnocentrism.

LO2 Define culture and articulate its two main manifestations.
- Culture is the collective programming of the mind that distinguishes one group from another.
- Managers and firms ignorant of foreign languages and religious traditions may end up with embarrassments and, worse, disasters when doing business around the globe.
- English is the *lingua franca* because of the need in a global market for a common language.
- The four leading religions in the world are Christianity, Islam, Hinduism, and Buddhism.

LO3 Articulate three ways to understand cultural differences.
- The context approach differentiates cultures based on the high- versus low-context dimension.
- The cluster approach groups similar cultures together as clusters and civilizations.
- Hofstede and colleagues have identified five cultural dimensions: (1) power distance, (2) individualism/collectivism, (3) masculinity/femininity, (4) uncertainty avoidance, and (5) long-term orientation.

LO4 Explain why understanding cultural differences is crucial for global business.
- A great deal of global business activity is consistent with the context, cluster, and dimension approaches to cultural differences.

LO5 Explain why ethics is important.
- Ethics refers to the principles, standards, and norms of conduct governing individual and firm behavior.
- When managing ethics overseas, two schools of thought are ethical relativism and ethical imperialism.

LO6 Identify ways to combat corruption.
- The fight against corruption around the world is a long-term, global battle.
- Corruption distorts the basis for competition.
- High levels of corruption and low levels of economic development are strongly correlated.
- Legislation criminalizing corruption must not only be institutionalized but must be enforced to be effective.

LO7 Identify norms associated with strategic responses when firms deal with ethical challenges.
- When confronting ethical challenges, individual firms have four strategic choices: (1) reactive, (2) defensive, (3) accommodative, and (4) proactive strategies.
- Using a reactive strategy, a firm is passive and does not feel compelled to act even when problems arise.

KEY TERMS AND DEFINITIONS

Ethnocentrism
A self-centered mentality held by a group of people who perceive their own culture, ethics, and norms as natural, rational, and morally right.

Culture
The collective programming of the mind which distinguishes the members of one group or category of people from another.

Lingua franca
A global business language.

Context
The background against which interaction takes place.

Low-context culture
A culture in which communication is usually taken at face value without much reliance on unspoken conditions or assumptions.

High-context culture
A culture in which communication relies heavily on the underlying unspoken conditions or assumptions, which are as important as the words used.

Cluster
A group of countries that have similar cultures.

Civilization
The highest cultural grouping of people and the broadest level of cultural identity people have.

Power distance
The extent to which less powerful members within a culture expect and accept that power is distributed unequally.

Individualism
The idea that the identity of an individual is fundamentally his or her own.

Collectivism
The idea that an individual's identity is fundamentally tied to the identity of his or her collective group.

Masculinity
A relatively strong form of societal-level sex-role differentiation whereby men tend to have occupations that reward assertiveness and women tend to work in caring professions.

Femininity
A relatively weak form of societal-level sex-role differentiation whereby more women occupy positions that reward assertiveness and more men work in caring professions.

Uncertainty avoidance
The extent to which members of a culture accept or avoid ambiguous situations and uncertainty.

Long-term orientation
A perspective that emphasizes perseverance and savings for future betterment.

Ethics
The principles, standards, and norms of conduct that govern individual and firm behavior.

Code of conduct
A set of guidelines for making ethical decisions.

- Using a defensive strategy, a firm fights informal pressure and is only concerned with required regulatory compliance.
- Using an accommodative strategy, a firm accepts responsibility and will act beyond what is simply required.
- Using a proactive strategy, a firm anticipates institutional changes and does more than required by current regulations.

LO8 Explain how you can acquire cross-cultural literacy.
- It is important to enhance cultural intelligence, leading to cross-cultural literacy.
- Acquisition of cultural intelligence passes through three phases: (1) awareness, (2) knowledge, and (3) skills.
- The most effective way to acquire cultural intelligence is through total immersion in a foreign culture.
- It is crucial to understand and adapt to the changing norms globally.

Ethical relativism
A perspective that suggests that all ethical standards are relative.

Ethical imperialism
The absolute belief that "there is only one set of Ethics (with a capital E), and we have it."

Corruption
The abuse of public power for private benefits, usually in the form of bribery.

Norms
The prevailing practices of relevant players that affect the focal individuals and firms.

Reactive strategy
A response to an ethical challenge that often involves denial and belated action to correct problems.

Defensive strategy
A response to an ethical challenge that focuses on regulatory compliance.

Accommodative strategy
A response to an ethical challenge that involves accepting responsibility.

Proactive strategy
A strategy that anticipates ethical challenges and addresses them before they happen.

Cultural intelligence
An individual's ability to understand and adjust to new cultures.

REVIEW QUESTIONS

1. Where do informal institutions come from?
2. What is the difference between a low-context culture and a high-context culture?
3. Describe the three systems for classifying cultures by clusters.
4. Describe the differences among the five dimensions of Hofstede's framework.
5. What is the difference between ethical relativism and ethical imperialism?
6. How would you define corruption in a business setting?

CRITICAL DISCUSSION QUESTIONS

1. Suppose that you are on a plane and the passenger sitting next to you tries to have a conversation with you. You would like to be nice but don't want to give too much information about yourself (such as your name). He or she asks: "What do you do?" How would you answer the question?
2. *ON ETHICS:* Assume that you work for a New Zealander company exporting a container of kiwis to Azerbaijan or Haiti. The customs official informs you that there is a delay in clearing your container through customs, and it may last a month. However, if you are willing to pay an "expediting fee" of US$200, he will try to make it happen in one day. What would you do?
3. *ON ETHICS:* Most developed economies have some illegal immigrants. The United States has the largest number with between 10 and 11 million. Without legal US identification (ID) documents, they cannot open bank accounts or buy houses. Many US firms have targeted this population, accepting the ID issued by their native countries and selling them products and services. Some Americans are furious with these business practices. Other Americans suggest that illegal immigrants represent a growth engine in an economy with relatively little growth elsewhere. How would you participate in this debate?

CLOSING CASE DISCUSSION QUESTIONS

1. What are the costs and benefits of bribery?
2. Is the FCPA unnecessarily harsh or do its provisions dispense the appropriate level of punishment?
3. In your view, how heavy should Siemens be fined? In addition to fines, what else can be done?
4. Are some of Siemens' employees "bad apples," or is Siemens a "bad barrel"? Can its organizational culture be changed?

Leveraging Resources & CAPABILITIES

CHAPTER SUMMARY

LO1 Define resources and capabilities.
- Resources and capabilities are tangible and intangible assets a firm uses to choose and implement its strategies.
- Although scholars define resources and capabilities differently, in practice the distinctions become blurred.
- Tangible resources and capabilities can be financial, physical, and technological.
- Intangible resources and capabilities can be human, innovation, and reputational.

LO2 Explain how value is created from a firm's resources and capabilities.
- A value chain consists of a stream of activities from upstream to downstream that add value.
- A SWOT analysis engages managers to ascertain a firm's strengths and weaknesses on an activity-by-activity basis relative to rivals, a process known as benchmarking.
- If a firm's particular activity is unsatisfactory, the manager uses a two-stage decision model to remedy the situation.

LO3 Articulate the difference between keeping an activity in-house and outsourcing it.
- Outsourcing is defined as turning over all or part of an organizational activity to an outside supplier.
- An activity with a high degree of industry commonality and a high degree of commoditization can be outsourced.
- An industry-specific and firm-specific (proprietary) activity is better performed in-house.
- On any given activity, the four choices for managers in terms of modes and locations are (1) offshoring, (2) inshoring, (3) captive sourcing/FDI, and (4) domestic in-house activity.

LO4 Explain what a VRIO framework is.

LO5 Explain how to use a VRIO framework to understand a firm's resources and capabilities.
- A VRIO framework suggests that only resources and capabilities that are valuable, rare, inimitable, and organizationally embedded will generate sustainable competitive advantage.
- Non-value-adding resources and capabilities may become weaknesses instead of strengths.
- Valuable but common resources and capabilities will lead to competitive parity but no advantage.
- Valuable and rare resources and capabilities can be a source of competitive advantage only if they are difficult for competitors to imitate.
- Causal ambiguity is the difficulty of identifying the actual cause of a firm's successful performance.
- Only valuable, rare, and hard-to-imitate resources and capabilities that are organizationally embedded and exploited can possibly lead to persistently above average performance.

KEY TERMS AND DEFINITIONS

SWOT analysis
An analytical tool for determining a firm's strengths (S), weaknesses (W), opportunities (O), and threats (T).

Resources (or capabilities)
The tangible and intangible assets a firm uses to choose and implement its strategies.

Tangible resources and capabilities
Assets that are observable and easily quantified.

Intangible resources and capabilities
Assets that are hard to observe and difficult (if not impossible) to quantify.

Value chain
A series of activities used in the production of goods and services that make a product or service more valuable.

Benchmarking
Examining whether a firm has resources and capabilities to perform a particular activity in a manner superior to competitors.

Commoditization
A process of market competition through which unique products that command high prices and high margins gradually lose their ability to do so, thus becoming commodities.

Outsourcing
Turning over an organizational activity to an outside supplier that will perform it on behalf of the focal firm.

Offshoring
Outsourcing to an international or foreign firm.

Onshoring (or inshoring)
Outsourcing to a domestic firm.

Captive sourcing
Setting up subsidiaries abroad so that the work done is in-house but the location is foreign. Also known as foreign direct investment (FDI).

VRIO framework
The resource-based framework that focuses on the value (V), rarity (R), imitability (I), and organizational (O) aspects of resources and capabilities.

Business process outsourcing (BPO)
The outsourcing of business processes such as loan origination, credit card processing, and call center operations.

Causal ambiguity
The difficulty of identifying the actual cause of a firm's successful performance.

Complementary assets
The combination of numerous resources and assets that enable a firm to gain a competitive advantage.

Social complexity
The socially intricate and interdependent ways that firms are typically organized.

LO6 Identify four things you need to do as part of a successful career and business strategy.

- Managers need to distinguish resources and capabilities that are valuable, rare, hard-to-imitate, and organizationally embedded from those that do not share these attributes.
- Relentless imitation or benchmarking, while important, is not likely to be a successful strategy.
- Managers need to build up resources and capabilities for future competition.
- Students are advised to make themselves into "untouchables" whose jobs cannot be outsourced, by nurturing valuable, rare, and hard-to-imitate capabilities indispensable to an organization.

REVIEW QUESTIONS

1. Describe two types of tangible resources and capabilities, and describe two types of intangible resources and capabilities.
2. What is commoditization?
3. What are the components of VRIO?
4. Why is imitation difficult?
5. How do complementary assets and social complexity influence a firm's organization?
6. Outline the two positions in the debate on offshoring versus non-offshoring.

CRITICAL DISCUSSION QUESTIONS

1. Pick any pair of rivals (such as Samsung/Sony, Nokia/Motorola, and Boeing/Airbus) and explain why one outperforms the other.
2. Conduct a VRIO analysis of your business school relative to the top three rival schools in terms of (1) perceived reputation (such as rankings), (2) faculty strength, (3) student quality, (4) administrative efficiency, (5) IT, and (6) building maintenance. If you were the dean and had a limited budget, where would you invest precious financial resources to make your school number one among rivals? Why?
3. *ON ETHICS:* Ethical dilemmas associated with offshoring are plenty. Pick one of these dilemmas and make a case either defending your firm's offshoring activities or arguing against such activities. (Assume that you are employed at a firm headquartered in a developed economy.)

CLOSING CASE DISCUSSION QUESTIONS

1. From a resource-based view, what resources and capabilities do Asian firms involved in the production of Amazon Kindle have that US-based firms do not have?
2. What are the differences between the production of PCs and the production of Amazon Kindle?
3. From an institution-based view, what should the US government do to foster US competitiveness?

For more great resources, especially interactive maps that can help you grasp GLOBAL geography, log in to CourseMate at www.cengagebrain.com.

CHAPTER SUMMARY

LO1 Use the resource-based and institution-based views to explain why nations trade.

- The resource-based view suggests that nations trade because firms in one nation generate valuable, unique, and hard-to-imitate exports that firms in other nations find it beneficial to import.
- The institution-based view argues that as rules of the game, different laws and regulations governing international trade determine how the gains from trade are shared or not shared.

LO2 Outline the classical and modern theories of international trade.

- Classical theories include (1) mercantilism, (2) absolute advantage, and (3) comparative advantage.
- Mercantilism was widely practiced during the 17th and 18th centuries, viewed international trade as a zero-sum game, and is the forerunner of modern protectionism.
- The theory of absolute advantage was proposed by Adam Smith and advocates specialization and trade as a win-win game for all.
- David Ricardo developed the theory of comparative advantage in 1817 as an explanation for how countries can benefit from trade even when one of them does not have an absolute advantage.
- Modern theories include (1) product life cycles, (2) strategic trade, and (3) national competitive advantage of industries or "diamond."
- The product life cycle theory was developed in 1966 by Raymond Verson to explain the changes in trade patterns over time.
- The strategic trade theory was developed in the 1970s to address the question of whether government intervention can actually add value.
- Developed by Michael Porter, the theory of national competitive advantage of industries is presented in a diamond-shaped diagram to show why nations are competitive internationally in some industries but not in others.

LO3 Explain the importance of political realities governing international trade.

- The net impact of various tariffs and non-tariff barriers is that the nation as a whole is worse off while certain special interest groups (such as specific industries, firms, and regions) benefit.
- Economic arguments against free trade center on (1) protectionism and (2) infant industries.
- Political arguments against free trade focus on (1) national security, (2) consumer protection, (3) foreign policy, and (4) environmental and social responsibility.

LO4 Identify factors that should be considered when your firm participates in international trade.

- Be aware of the comparative advantage of certain locations, and leverage their potential.
- Monitor and nurture the current comparative advantage, and take advantage of new locations.
- Be politically active to demonstrate, safeguard, and advance the gains from international trade.

KEY TERMS AND DEFINITIONS

Export
To sell abroad.

Import
To buy from abroad.

Merchandise trade
Tangible products being bought and sold.

Service trade
Intangible services being bought and sold.

Trade deficit
An economic condition in which a nation imports more than it exports.

Trade surplus
An economic condition in which a nation exports more than it imports.

Balance of trade
The country-level trade surplus or deficit.

Mercantilism
A theory that holds that the wealth of the world (measured in gold and silver) is fixed and that a nation that exports more than it imports will enjoy the net inflows of gold and silver and become richer.

Protectionism
The idea that governments should actively protect domestic industries from imports and vigorously promote exports.

Free trade
The idea that free market forces should determine the buying and selling of goods and services with little or no government intervention.

Theory of absolute advantage
A theory that suggests that under free trade, each nation gains by specializing in economic activities in which it is the most efficient producer.

Absolute advantage
The economic advantage one nation enjoys because it can produce a good or service more efficiently than anyone else.

Theory of comparative advantage
A theory that suggests that a nation gains by specializing in production of one good in which it has comparative advantage.

Comparative advantage
The relative (not absolute) advantage in one economic activity that one nation enjoys in comparison with other nations.

Opportunity cost
The cost of pursuing one activity at the expense of another activity.

Factor endowments
The extent to which different countries possess various factors of production such as labor, land, and technology.

Factor endowment theory (or Heckscher–Ohlin theory)
A theory that suggests that nations will develop comparative advantages based on their locally abundant factors.

Product life cycle theory
A theory that suggests that patterns of trade change over time as production shifts and as the product moves from new to maturing to standardized stages.

REVIEW QUESTIONS

1. Why do nations trade? Why do some people argue that this question may be a bit misleading?
2. Summarize the three classical theories of international trade.
3. Compare and contrast the three modern theories of international trade.
4. What are the major political and economic arguments against free trade?
5. Are theories of international trade still valid given the new realities of world trade?

CRITICAL DISCUSSION QUESTIONS

1. Is the government of your country practicing free trade, protectionism, or something else? Why?
2. *ON ETHICS:* As a foreign policy tool, trade embargoes are meant to discourage foreign governments. Examples include US embargoes against Cuba, Iraq (until 2003), and North Korea. But embargoes also cause a great deal of misery among the population of the affected countries (such as shortages of medicine and food). Are embargoes ethical?
3. *ON ETHICS:* While the nation as a whole may gain from free trade, there is no doubt that certain regions, industries, firms, and individuals may lose their jobs and livelihood due to foreign competition. How can the rest of the nation help the unfortunate ones cope with the impact of international trade?

CLOSING CASE DISCUSSION QUESTIONS

1. Why do Canada and the United States have the largest bilateral trading relationship in the world?
2. Why do Canadian products have such a large market share in the United States?
3. While 98% of Canada–US trade flows smoothly, trade disputes affect the remaining 2%. Some argue that the Canadians have overreacted in this case. What do you think?

Strategic trade theory
A theory that suggests that strategic intervention by governments in certain industries can enhance their odds for international success.

First-mover advantage
Advantage that first entrants enjoy and do not share with late entrants.

Strategic trade policy
Economic policy that provides companies a strategic advantage through government subsidies.

Theory of national competitive advantage of industries (or diamond theory)
A theory that suggests that the competitive advantage of certain industries in different nations depends on four aspects that form a diamond when diagrammed.

Resource mobility
The assumption that a resource used in producing a product in one industry can be shifted and put to use in another industry.

Tariff barrier
A means of discouraging imports by placing a tariff (tax) on imported goods.

Import tariff
A tax imposed on imports.

Deadweight costs
Net losses that occur in an economy as the result of tariffs.

Non-tariff barrier (NTB)
A means of discouraging imports using means other than taxes on imported goods.

Subsidy
A government payment to domestic firms.

Import quota
A restriction on the quantity of goods that may be brought into a country.

Voluntary export restraint (VER)
An international agreement that shows that an exporting country voluntarily agrees to restrict its exports.

Local content requirement
A rule that stipulates that a certain proportion of the value of a good must originate from the domestic market.

Administrative policy
A bureaucratic rule that makes it harder to import foreign goods.

Antidumping duty
A cost levied on imports that have been "dumped," or sold below cost to unfairly drive domestic firms out of business.

Trade embargo
A politically motivated trade sanction against foreign countries to signal displeasure.

For more great resources, especially interactive maps that can help you grasp GLOBAL geography, log in to CourseMate at www.cengagebrain.com.

Investing Abroad DIRECTLY

CHAPTER SUMMARY

LO1 Identify and define the key terms associated with foreign direct investment (FDI).

- The resource-based view suggests that *direct* is the key word in FDI, which reflects firms' interest in directly managing, developing, and leveraging their firm-specific resources and capabilities abroad.
- The institution-based view argues that recent expansion of FDI is indicative of generally more friendly formal policies and informal norms and values associated with FDI (despite some setbacks).

LO2 Use the resource-based and institution-based views to explain why FDI takes place.

- FDI takes place due to the quest for ownership, location, and internalization (OLI) advantages.

LO3 Explain how FDI results in ownership advantages.

- MNEs generally prefer ownership over licensing because ownership reduces dissemination risks, provides greater control over foreign operations, and makes firm-specific know-how easier to implement.

LO4 Identify the ways your firm can acquire and neutralize location advantages.

- Location refers to certain advantages that can help MNEs attain strategic goals, whether it is access to labor, natural resources, or markets.

LO5 List the benefits of internalization.

- Internalization refers to the replacement of a cross-border market relationship with a single firm (the MNE) with locations in two or more countries.
- Internalization helps combat market imperfections and failures.

LO6 Identify different political views on FDI and understand its benefits and costs to host and home countries.

- The radical view, with its roots in Marxism, is hostile to FDI, and the free market view calls for minimum intervention in FDI.
- Since the 1980s, many countries, including Brazil, China, Hungary, India, Ireland, and Russia, have moved from radical to more FDI-friendly policies.
- Most countries practice pragmatic nationalism, weighing the costs and benefits of FDI.
- FDI brings a different (and often opposing) set of benefits and costs to host and home countries.
- Host-country benefits include capital inflow, technology spillover, improved management know-how, and job creation; costs include loss of sovereignty, adverse competition, and capital outflow.
- Home-country benefits include repatriated earnings, increased exports of components and services, and knowledge gains from operations abroad; costs include capital outflow and job losses.

KEY TERMS AND DEFINITIONS

Foreign portfolio investment (FPI)
Holding securities, such as stocks and bonds, of firms in other countries but without a controlling interest.

Management control rights
The rights to appoint key managers and establish control mechanisms.

Horizontal FDI
A type of FDI in which a firm produces the same products or offers the same services in a host country as at home.

Vertical FDI
A type of FDI in which a firm moves upstream or downstream in different value chain stages in a host country.

Upstream vertical FDI
A type of vertical FDI in which a firm engages in an upstream stage of the value chain.

Downstream vertical FDI
A type of vertical FDI in which a firm engages in a downstream stage of the value chain.

FDI flow
The amount of FDI moving in a given period (usually a year) in a certain direction.

FDI inflow
FDI moving into a country in a year.

FDI outflow
FDI moving out of a country in a year.

FDI stock
The total accumulation of inbound FDI in a country or outbound FDI from a country across a given period of time (usually several years).

OLI advantages
The advantages of ownership (O), location (L), and internalization (I) that come from engaging in FDI.

Ownership
Possessing and leveraging of certain valuable, rare, hard-to-imitate, and organizationally embedded (VRIO) assets overseas in the context of FDI.

Location
Advantages enjoyed by a firm that derive from the places in which it operates.

Internalization
The replacement of cross-border markets (such as exporting and importing) with one firm (the MNE) located in two or more countries.

Licensing
Buying and selling technology and intellectual property rights.

Market imperfections (or market failure)
The imperfect rules governing international market transactions.

Dissemination risk
The possibility of unauthorized diffusion of firm-specific know-how.

LO7 **List three things you need to do as your firm considers FDI.**

+ Carefully assess whether FDI is justified, in light of other options such as outsourcing and licensing.
+ Pay careful attention to the location advantages in combination with the firm's strategic goals.
+ Be aware of the institutional constraints governing FDI, and enhance legitimacy in host countries.

Agglomeration
The clustering of economic activities in certain locations.

Knowledge spillover
The diffusion of knowledge from one firm to others among closely located firms that attempt to hire individuals from competitors.

Oligopoly
An industry populated by a small number of players.

Intrafirm trade
International trade between two subsidiaries in two countries controlled by the same MNE.

Radical view on FDI
A political view that sees FDI as an instrument of imperialism and a vehicle for foreign exploitation.

Free market view on FDI
A political view that holds that FDI, unrestricted by government intervention, will enable countries to tap into their absolute or comparative advantages by specializing in the production of certain goods and services.

Pragmatic nationalism view on FDI
A political view that approves FDI only when its benefits outweigh its costs.

Technology spillover
The domestic diffusion of foreign technical knowledge and processes.

Demonstration effect (or contagion or imitation effect)
The effect that occurs when local rivals recognize the feasibility of foreign technology and imitate it.

Sovereign wealth fund (SWF)
A state-owned investment fund composed of financial assets such as stocks, bonds, real estate, or other financial instruments funded by foreign exchange assets.

REVIEW QUESTIONS

1. Explain the differences between horizontal and vertical FDI.
2. What distinguishes an MNE from a non-MNE?
3. Can you summarize each of the OLI advantages?
4. How can FDI be used to overcome high transaction costs and prevent market failure?
5. Compare and contrast the three political views on FDI.
6. What are the costs and benefits of inbound FDI to host countries and of outbound FDI to home countries?

CRITICAL DISCUSSION QUESTIONS

1. Identify the top five (or ten) *source* countries of FDI into your country. Then identify the top ten (or 20) foreign MNEs that have undertaken inbound FDI in your country. Why do these countries and companies provide the bulk of FDI into your country?
2. Worldwide, which ten countries were the largest recipient and source countries of FDI *last year*? Why? Will this situation change in five years? How about 20 years down the road? Why?
3. *ON ETHICS:* Undertaking FDI, by definition, means not investing in the MNE's home country (see the Closing Case). What are the ethical dilemmas here? What are your recommendations as (1) MNE executives, (2) labor union leaders of your domestic (home-country) labor forces, (3) host-country officials, and (4) home-country officials?

CLOSING CASE DISCUSSION QUESTIONS

1. What are the costs and benefits of FDI inflows for a host country such as Germany?
2. Will foreign firms such as GM make decisions in the best interest of Germany?
3. What would you vote if you were a member of the GM board regarding the fate of Opel?

Dealing with Foreign EXCHANGE

CHAPTER SUMMARY

LO1 List the factors that determine foreign exchange rates.

+ Currency is a commodity, and its price is fundamentally determined by supply and demand.
+ A foreign exchange rate is the price of one currency expressed in terms of another.
+ Basic determinants of foreign exchange rates include (1) relative price differences and purchasing power parity (PPP), (2) interest rates, (3) productivity and balance of payments, (4) exchange rate policies, and (5) investor psychology.
+ The theory of PPP, the "law of one price," suggests that in the absence of trade barriers (such as tariffs), the price for identical products sold in different countries must be the same.
+ Variations in interest rates have a powerful effect in the short run, with a high domestic interest rate increasing the demand for a country's currency and a low interest rate decreasing demand.
+ A country's rate of inflation, relative to that in other countries, affects its ability to attract foreign funds and thereby its exchange rate. Thus exchange rates are highly sensitive to changes in monetary policy.
+ A rise in a country's productivity, relative to other countries, will improve its competitive position and in turn, more foreign direct investment will be attracted to the country, fueling demand for its home currency and affecting its balance of payments.
+ Most countries practice a dirty (or managed) float, with selective government interventions.
+ Short-run movements in the exchange rate are largely determined by investor psychology and are thus difficult to predict.

LO2 Articulate and explain the steps in the evolution of the international monetary system.

+ The gold standard (1870–1914) pegged the value of each country's currency to gold, providing a predictable and stable system but forcing countries to maintain gold reserves.
+ The Bretton Woods system (1944–1973) emerged after World War II and pegged all currencies to the US dollar, which in turn was convertible to gold at a fixed $35 per ounce.
+ The current post–Bretton Woods system (1973–present) has various floating and fixed rates, making it a flexible and diverse exchange system. However, the current system is also turbulent and uncertain.
+ The International Monetary Fund (IMF) serves as a lender of last resort to help member countries correct balance-of-payments problems.

LO3 Identify strategic responses firms can take to deal with foreign exchange movements.

+ The three foreign exchange transactions are (1) spot transactions, (2) forward transactions, and (3) swaps.

KEY TERMS AND DEFINITIONS

Foreign exchange rate
The price of one currency in terms of another.

Appreciation
An increase in the value of the currency.

Depreciation
A loss in the value of the currency.

Balance of payments
A country's international transaction statement, which includes merchandise trade, service trade, and capital movement.

Floating (or flexible) exchange rate policy
The willingness of a government to let demand and supply conditions determine exchange rates.

Clean (or free) float
A pure market solution to determine exchange rates.

Dirty (or managed) float
Using selective government intervention to determine exchange rates.

Target exchange rates (or crawling bands)
Specified upper or lower bounds within which an exchange rate is allowed to fluctuate.

Fixed rate policy
Setting the exchange rate of a currency relative to other currencies.

Bandwagon effect
The effect of investors moving in the same direction at the same time, like a herd.

Capital flight
A phenomenon in which a large number of individuals and companies exchange domestic currencies for a foreign currency.

Gold standard
A system in which the value of most major currencies was maintained by fixing their prices in terms of gold.

Common denominator
A currency or commodity to which the value of all currencies are pegged.

Bretton Woods system
A system in which all currencies were pegged at a fixed rate to the US dollar.

Post–Bretton Woods system
A system of flexible exchange rate regimes with no official common denominator.

International Monetary Fund (IMF)
An international organization that was established to promote international monetary cooperation, exchange stability, and orderly exchange arrangements.

Quota
The weight a member country carries within the IMF, which determines the amount of its financial contribution (technically known as its "subscription"), its capacity to borrow from the IMF, and its voting power.

- Firms' strategic responses to the risk of losses from fluctuations in the foreign exchange market include (1) currency hedging, (2) strategic hedging, or (3) both.

LO4 Identify three things you need to know about currency when doing business internationally.
- Fostering foreign exchange literacy is a must.
- Risk analysis of any country must include an analysis of its currency risks.
- A currency risk management strategy is necessary, be it via currency hedging, strategic hedging, or both.

Foreign exchange market
The market where individuals, firms, governments, and banks buy and sell currencies of other countries.

Spot transaction
The classic single-shot exchange of one currency for another.

Forward transaction
A foreign exchange transaction in which participants buy and sell currencies now for future delivery.

Currency hedging
A transaction that protects traders and investors from exposure to the fluctuations of the spot rate.

Forward discount
A condition under which the forward rate of one currency relative to another currency is higher than the spot rate.

Forward premium
A condition under which the forward rate of one currency relative to another currency is lower than the spot rate.

Currency swap
A foreign exchange transaction between two firms in which one currency is converted into another at Time 1, with an agreement to revert it back to the original currency at a specified Time 2 in the future.

Offer rate
The price at which a bank is willing to sell a currency.

Bid rate
The price at which a bank is willing to buy a currency.

Spread
The difference between the offer price and the bid price.

Currency risk
The potential for loss associated with fluctuations in the foreign exchange market.

Strategic hedging
Spreading out activities in a number of countries in different currency zones to offset any currency losses in one region through gains in other regions.

REVIEW QUESTIONS

1. What are the five major factors that influence foreign exchange rates?
2. What are the differences between a floating exchange rate policy and a fixed exchange rate policy?
3. Describe the IMF's roles, responsibilities, and challenges.
4. Describe the three primary types of foreign exchange transactions made by financial companies.
5. Why is the strength of the US dollar important to the rest of the world?

CRITICAL DISCUSSION QUESTIONS

1. Suppose that US$1 equals €0.7778 in New York and US$1 equals €0.7775 in Paris. How can foreign exchange traders in New York and Paris profit from these exchange rates?
2. Should China revalue the yuan against the dollar? If so, what impact might this have on (1) US balance of payments, (2) Chinese balance of payments, (3) relative competitiveness of Mexico and Thailand, (4) firms such as Wal-Mart, and (5) US and Chinese retail consumers?
3. *ON ETHICS:* You are an IMF official going to a country whose export earnings are not able to pay for imports. The government has requested a loan from the IMF. In which areas would you recommend the government make cuts: (1) education, (2) salaries for officials, (3) food subsidies, and/or (4) tax rebates for exporters?

CLOSING CASE DISCUSSION QUESTIONS

1. Why is the value of the yuan relative to the dollar so important?
2. If you were the CEO of Wal-Mart and were prepared for a meeting with the most vocal members of the US Congress on China's currency "manipulation," what would you say to them?
3. Assuming the yuan will appreciate further against the dollar, what should Wal-Mart do?
4. If you were an exporter from Argentina, Indonesia, Malaysia, or South Korea and selling to China, would you accept payment in yuan (instead of dollars)?

Capitalizing on Global & Regional INTEGRATION

CHAPTER SUMMARY

LO1 Make the case for global economic integration.
- There are both political and economic benefits for global economic integration.
- The biggest expected political benefit is peace.
- The three economic benefits of global integration are constructive dispute settlement, streamlined trade policies, and increased worldwide income through job creation and economic growth.

LO2 Explain the evolution of the GATT and the WTO, including current challenges.
- The GATT (1948–1994) significantly reduced tariff rates on merchandise trade.
- The WTO (1995–present) was set up not only to incorporate the GATT but also to cover trade in services and intellectual property, settle trade disputes, and provide a peer review of trade policy.
- The Doha Round was intended to promote more trade and development but has so far failed to accomplish its goals.

LO3 Make the case for regional economic integration.
- Political and economic benefits for regional integration are similar to those for global integration.
- Regional integration may undermine global integration and lead to some loss of countries' sovereignty.
- The five levels of regional economic integration are (1) free trade area, (2) customs union, (3) common market, (4) economic union, and (5) political union.

LO4 List the accomplishments, benefits, and costs of the European Union.
- The EU has delivered more than half a century of peace and prosperity, launched a single currency, and constructed a single market.
- The EU's challenges include internal divisions and enlargement concerns.

LO5 Identify the five organizations that promote regional trade in the Americas and describe their benefits and costs.
- Despite initial misgivings, NAFTA has significantly boosted trade and investment among members.
- The two South American customs unions, the Andean Community and Mercosur, have not been effective because only a relatively small part of any member's trade is within the union and their largest trading partner, the United States, is outside the union.
- The FTAA strove to unite all of the Americas, but the refusal of some countries to join meant that it was never established. USAN/UNASUR was established instead. Its goal is to make the Americas EU-like with a common currency, parliament, and passport.

LO6 Identify the three organizations that promote regional trade in the Asia Pacific and describe their benefits and costs.
- Regional integration in Asia Pacific centers on CER, ASEAN, and APEC.

KEY TERMS AND DEFINITIONS

Regional economic integration
Efforts to reduce trade and investment barriers within one region.

Global economic integration
Efforts to reduce trade and investment barriers around the globe.

General Agreement on Tariffs and Trade (GATT)
A multilateral agreement governing the international trade of goods (merchandise).

World Trade Organization (WTO)
The official title of the multilateral trading system and the organization underpinning this system since 1995.

Multilateral trading system
The global system that governs international trade among countries—otherwise known as the GATT/WTO system.

Non-discrimination
A principle that a country cannot make distinctions in trade among its trading partners.

General Agreement on Trade in Services (GATS)
A WTO agreement governing the international trade of services.

Trade-Related Aspects of Intellectual Property Rights (TRIPS)
A WTO agreement governing intellectual property rights.

Doha Round
A round of WTO negotiations to reduce agricultural subsidies, slash tariffs, and strengthen intellectual property protection that started in Doha, Qatar, in 2001. Officially known as the "Doha Development Agenda," it was suspended in 2006 due to disagreements.

Free trade area (FTA)
A group of countries that remove trade barriers among themselves.

Customs union
One step beyond a free trade area, a customs union imposes common external policies on non-participating countries.

Common market
Combining everything a customs union has, a common market additionally permits the free movement of goods and people.

Economic union
Having all the features of a common market, members also coordinate and harmonize economic policies (in areas such as monetary, fiscal, and taxation) to blend their economies into a single economic entity.

Monetary union
A group of countries that use a common currency.

Political union
The integration of political and economic affairs of a region.

European Union (EU)
The official title of European economic integration since 1993.

Schengen
A passport-free travel zone within the EU.

Euro
The currency currently used in 17 EU countries.

- APEC is the largest regional integration by both geographic area and GDP.

LO7 Articulate how regional trade should influence your thinking about global business.
- Think regional, downplay global.
- Understand the rules of the game and their transitions at both global and regional levels.

Euro zone
The 17 EU countries that currently use the euro as the official currency.

North American Free Trade Agreement (NAFTA)
A free trade agreement among Canada, Mexico, and the United States.

Andean Community
A customs union in South America that was launched in 1969.

Mercosur
A customs union in South America that was launched in 1991.

Free Trade Area of the Americas (FTAA)
A proposed free trade area for the entire Western Hemisphere.

Union of South American Nations (USAN/UNASUR)
A regional integration mechanism integrating two existing customs unions (Andean Community and Mercosur) in South America.

United States–Dominican Republic–Central America Free Trade Agreement (CAFTA)
A free trade agreement between the United States and five Central American countries and the Dominican Republic.

Association of Southeast Asian Nations (ASEAN)
The organization underpinning regional economic integration in Southeast Asia.

Asia-Pacific Economic Cooperation (APEC)
The official title for regional economic integration involving 21 member economies around the Pacific.

REVIEW QUESTIONS

1. What are some of the political and economic benefits of global economic integration?
2. What happened to the Doha Development Agenda at the WTO?
3. Should the EU remain an economic union, or should it move to become a political union?
4. What achievements do NAFTA supporters point to as evidence of NAFTA's success?
5. What are the leading examples of regional integration in South America and the Asia Pacific?

CRITICAL DISCUSSION QUESTIONS

1. The Doha Round collapsed because many countries believed that no deal was better than a bad deal. Do you agree or disagree with this approach? Why?
2. *ON ETHICS:* Critics argue that the WTO single-mindedly promotes trade at the expense of the environment. Therefore, trade—or, more broadly, globalization—needs to slow down. What is your view on the relationship between trade and the environment?
3. *ON ETHICS:* Critics argue that thanks to NAFTA, a flood of subsidized US food imports wiped out Mexico's small farmers. Some 1.3 million farm jobs disappeared. Consequently, the number of illegal immigrants in the United States skyrocketed. What is your view on NAFTA, CAFTA, and FTAA?

CLOSING CASE DISCUSSION QUESTIONS

1. What are the benefits and costs of using a common currency for Greece, Germany, and the EU?
2. How do the austerity programs imposed by the bailouts help a Greek firm that exports olive oil?
3. While Greece needs help, the German economy has also suffered a major recession itself and a budget deficit. Would you advise the chancellor to bail out or not to bail out Greece? As a German taxpayer, are you willing to pay higher taxes to help Greece (bear in mind, after Greece, there will be Ireland, Portugal, and possibly Spain)?
4. For the €750 billion European Stability Mechanism, even Sweden and Poland (EU members that do not use the euro) felt they had enough at stake to contribute. But Britain (another EU member that does not use the euro) decided not to contribute any funds. As a British official, how do you defend this decision?

CHAPTER SUMMARY

LO1 Define entrepreneurship, entrepreneurs, and entrepreneurial firms.

- Entrepreneurship is the identification and exploitation of previously unexplored opportunities.
- Entrepreneurs may be founders and owners of new businesses or managers of existing firms.
- In this chapter, we use the term "entrepreneurial firms" when referring to small- and medium-sized (SMEs).

LO2 Identify the institutions and resources that affect entrepreneurship.

- Institutions—both formal and informal—enable and constrain entrepreneurship around the world.
- The more entrepreneur friendly the formal institutional requirements are, the more flourishing entrepreneurship is and the more developed the economies become.
- Resources and capabilities largely determine entrepreneurial success and failure.

LO3 Identify three characteristics of a growing entrepreneurial firm.

- Growth of an entrepreneurial firm is an attempt to more fully utilize currently under-utilized resources and capabilities, particularly entrepreneurial vision, drive, and leadership.
- Innovation is at the heart of entrepreneurship and allows for a more sustainable basis for competitive advantage.
- The primary sources of entrepreneurial financing are founders, family, friends, and strategic investors.
- The extent to which entrepreneurs draw on resources from outside investors versus family and friends varies from country to country.
- Microfinance has emerged in response to the lack of financing for entrepreneurial opportunities in many developing countries.

LO4 Describe how international strategies for entering foreign markets are different from those for staying in domestic markets.

- Compared with domestic transaction costs (the costs of doing business), international transaction costs are qualitatively higher, so entrepreneurial opportunities exist where innovation can lower transaction costs and bring distant groups of people, firms, and countries together.
- Entrepreneurial firms can internationalize by entering foreign markets through entry modes such as (1) direct exports, (2) licensing and franchising, and (3) foreign direct investment.
- Direct exports are attractive because entrepreneurial firms are able to reach foreign customers directly, but SMEs may not have enough resources to turn overseas opportunities into profits.
- With licensing and franchising, the SME can expand abroad while risking relatively little of its own capital but may suffer a loss of control over how its technology and brand names are used.
- Foreign direct investment gives a firm better control over how its proprietary technology and brand name are used but requires both a non-trivial sum of capital and a signifi-

KEY TERMS AND DEFINITIONS

Small- and medium-sized enterprises (SMEs)
Firms with fewer than 500 employees in the United States and with fewer than 250 employees in the European Union.

Entrepreneurship
The identification and exploitation of previously unexplored opportunities.

Entrepreneurs
Founders and owners of new businesses or managers of existing firms who identify and exploit new opportunities.

International entrepreneurship
A combination of innovative, proactive, and risk-seeking behavior that crosses national borders and is intended to create wealth in organizations.

Microfinance
Lending small sums ($50–$300) used to start small businesses with the intention of ultimately lifting the entrepreneurs out of poverty.

Born global firm
A start-up company that attempts to do business abroad from inception.

Direct exports
The sale of products made by firms in their home country to customers in other countries.

Sporadic (or passive) exporting
The sale of products prompted by unsolicited inquiries from abroad.

Letter of credit (L/C)
A financial contract that states that the importer's bank will pay a specific sum of money to the exporter upon delivery of the merchandise.

Licensing
Firm A's agreement to give Firm B the rights to use A's proprietary technology (such as a patent) or trademark (such as a corporate logo) for a royalty fee paid to A by B. This is typically done in manufacturing industries.

Franchising
Firm A's agreement to give Firm B the rights to use A's proprietary assets for a royalty fee paid to A by B. This is typically done in service industries.

Stage model
Model of internationalization that involves a slow step-by-step (stage-by-stage) process a firm must go through to internationalize its business.

Indirect exports
A way for SMEs to reach overseas customers by exporting through domestic-based export intermediaries.

Export intermediary
A firm that acts as a middleman by linking domestic sellers and foreign buyers that otherwise would not have been connected.

- cant managerial commitment.
- Entrepreneurial firms can also internationalize without venturing abroad by (1) exporting indirectly, (2) supplying foreign firms, (3) becoming licensees/franchisees of foreign firms, (4) joining foreign entrants as alliance partners, and (5) harvesting and exiting through sell-offs to foreign entrants.

LO5 Articulate what you should do to strengthen your entrepreneurial ability on an international level.
- Push for both formal and informal institutions that facilitate entrepreneurship development.
- When internationalizing, be bold but not too bold.

REVIEW QUESTIONS

1. How do you define entrepreneurship?
2. From an institution-based view, to what extent do government regulations affect the start up of new firms in developed countries as opposed to developing countries?
3. From a resource-based view, how important are entrepreneurial resources and capabilities in determining the performance of SMEs?
4. Summarize the three modes that SMEs can use to enter foreign markets.
5. Name the five ways that SMEs can internationalize without leaving their home countries.
6. We know it is possible for SMEs to rapidly internationalize. Do you think this is wise?

CRITICAL DISCUSSION QUESTIONS

1. Given that most entrepreneurial start-ups fail, why do entrepreneurs found so many new firms? Why are (most) governments interested in promoting more start-ups?
2. Some suggest that foreign markets are graveyards where entrepreneurial firms over-extend themselves. Others argue that foreign markets represent the future for SMEs. If you were the owner of a small, reasonably profitable domestic firm, would you consider expanding overseas? Why?
3. *ON ETHICS:* Your former high school buddy invites you to join an entrepreneurial start-up that specializes in cracking the codes of protection software, which protect CDs, VCDs, and DVDs from being copied. He has developed the pioneering technology and lined up financing. The worldwide demand for this technology appears to be enormous. He offers you the job of CEO and 10% of the equity of the firm. How would you respond to his proposition?

CLOSING CASE DISCUSSION QUESTIONS

1. What are the pros and cons for entrepreneur-friendly bankruptcy laws?
2. Why can bankruptcy laws become entrepreneurial firms' exit barriers? And entry barriers?
3. Having studied this case, how do you now respond to a friend's comment: "Recent news about the boom in bankruptcies is so depressing"?

© Cengage Learning 2013

For more great resources, especially interactive maps that can help you grasp GLOBAL geography, log in to CourseMate at www.cengagebrain.com.

Entering Foreign MARKETS

CHAPTER 10

CHAPTER SUMMARY

LO1 Identify ways in which institutions and resources affect the liability of foreignness.
- When entering foreign markets, firms confront a liability of foreignness.
- The institution-based view suggests that firms need to undertake actions deemed legitimate and appropriate by the various formal and informal institutions governing market entries.
- The resource-based view advises foreign firms to deploy *overwhelming* resources and capabilities to offset the liability of foreignness in order to achieve competitive advantage.

LO2 Match the quest for location-specific advantages with strategic goals.
- Where to enter depends on the location-specific advantages of certain foreign countries and the strategic goals of firms involved.
- Firms seeking natural resources have to go to particular foreign locations where those resources are found.
- Market-seeking firms go to countries that have a strong demand for their products and services.
- Efficiency-seeking firms often single out the most efficient locations featuring a combination of scale economies and low cost factors.
- Innovation-seeking firms target countries and regions renowned for generating world-class innovations.
- Firms must also consider cultural and institutional distance when considering foreign locations.

LO3 Compare and contrast first-mover and late-mover advantages.
- First movers may gain advantages through proprietary technology, preemptive investments, erecting barriers to entry, and building relationships with key stakeholders.
- First movers may be disadvantaged when late movers free ride on their investments as well as by technological and market uncertainties and being locked into fixed assets or existing product lines.
- Late-mover advantages may include free riding on the investments of first movers, resolution of technological and market uncertainties, and leapfrogging the first mover's fixed assets or existing products.
- Late movers may be disadvantaged by lack of access to proprietary technology, barriers to entry, and difficulty in building relationships with key stakeholders who are already loyal to the first mover.
- Each has pros and cons, and there is no conclusive evidence pointing to one direction.

LO4 List the steps in the comprehensive model of foreign market entries.
- How to enter depends on the scale of entry, whether large scale or small scale.
- A comprehensive model of foreign market entries first focuses on the equity (ownership) issue.

KEY TERMS AND DEFINITIONS

Liability of foreignness
The inherent disadvantage that foreign firms experience in host countries because of their non-native status.

Location-specific advantages
The benefits a firm reaps from the features specific to a place.

Cultural distance
The difference between two cultures along identifiable dimensions such as individualism.

Institutional distance
The extent of similarity or dissimilarity between the regulatory, normative, and cognitive institutions of two countries.

First-mover advantages
Benefits that accrue to firms that enter the market first and that later entrants do not enjoy.

Late-mover advantages
Benefits that accrue to firms that enter the market later and that early entrants do not enjoy.

Scale of entry
The amount of resources committed to entering a foreign market.

Modes of entry
Method used to enter a foreign market.

Non-equity mode
A mode of entering foreign markets through exports and/or contractual agreements that tends to reflect relatively smaller commitments to overseas markets.

Equity mode
A mode of entering foreign markets through joint ventures and/or wholly owned subsidiaries that indicates a relatively larger, harder-to-reverse commitment.

Dumping
Exporting products at prices that are below what it costs to manufacture them, with the intent to raise prices after eliminating local rivals.

Turnkey project
A project in which clients pay contractors to design and construct new facilities and train personnel.

Build-operate-transfer (BOT) agreement
A non-equity mode of entry used to build a longer-term presence by building and then operating a facility for a period of time before transferring operations to a domestic agency or firm.

Research and development (R&D) contract
Outsourcing agreements in R&D between firms.

Co-marketing
Efforts among a number of firms to jointly market their products and services.

Joint venture (JV)
A new corporate entity created and jointly owned by two or more parent companies.

- The second step focuses on making the actual selection within each mode, be it exports, contractual agreements, joint ventures (JVs), or wholly owned subsidiaries.

LO5 Explain what you should do to make your firm's entry into a foreign market successful.
- Understand the rules of game—both formal and informal—governing competition in foreign markets.
- Develop overwhelming resources and capabilities to offset the liability of foreignness.
- Match efforts in market entry with strategic goals.

Wholly owned subsidiary (WOS)
A subsidiary located in a foreign country that is entirely owned by the parent multinational.

Green-field operations
Building factories and offices from scratch (on a proverbial piece of "green field" formerly used for agricultural purposes).

REVIEW QUESTIONS

1. What does the institution-based view indicate about how a firm should deal with the liability of foreignness? What does the resource-based view suggest?
2. What are some of the location-specific advantages found in agglomeration?
3. What are the advantages and disadvantages for first movers? What are the advantages and disadvantages for late movers?
4. Summarize the pros and cons for each of the non-equity and equity modes of entry.
5. Do you support or oppose antidumping restrictions? Explain your answer.

CRITICAL DISCUSSION QUESTIONS

1. During the 1990s, many North American, European, and Asian MNEs set up operations in Mexico, tapping into its location-specific advantages such as (1) proximity to the world's largest economy (the United States); (2) market-opening policies associated with NAFTA membership; and (3) abundant, low-cost, and high-quality labor. None of these has changed much. Yet, by the 15th anniversary of NAFTA (2009), a significant number of MNEs were starting to curtail operations in Mexico and move to China (see Chapter 8). Use institution- and resource-based views to explain why this is the case.
2. From institution-based and resource-based views, identify the obstacles confronting MNEs from emerging economies interested in expanding overseas. How can such firms overcome the obstacles?
3. *ON ETHICS:* Entering foreign markets, by definition, means not investing in a firm's home country. For example, since 2000, GN Netcom shut down some operations in its home country of Denmark while adding head counts in China. Nissan closed factories in Japan and added a new factory in the United States. What are the ethical dilemmas here? What are your recommendations?

CLOSING CASE DISCUSSION QUESTIONS

1. As a late mover into the US intercity bus market, what advantages and disadvantages does Megabus have?
2. Does Megabus have any overwhelming resources and capabilities?
3. As a college student, among choices of private car, train, airplane, Greyhound, and Megabus between Chicago and Columbus, which one would you choose?

For more great resources, especially interactive maps that can help you grasp GLOBAL geography, log in to CourseMate at www.cengagebrain.com.

Making Alliances & ACQUISITIONS Work

CHAPTER SUMMARY

LO1 Define alliances and acquisitions.

LO2 Articulate how institutions and resources influence alliances and acquisitions.
- Formal institutions influence alliances and acquisitions through antitrust and entry mode concerns.
- Informal institutions affect alliances and acquisitions through normative and cognitive pillars.
- The impact of resources on alliances and acquisitions is illustrated by the VRIO framework.
- Alliances and acquisitions must create value.
- The abilities to successfully manage interfirm relationships may be rare.
- Imitability can occur at the firm level or at the alliance level.
- The organization of a successful alliance relationship or an acquisition may be difficult to replicate.

LO3 Describe how alliances are formed.
- Managers typically go through a three-stage decision process when considering alliances.
- Stage one is the decision to cooperate with another firm or to grow purely by market transactions (not cooperate).
- Stage two is the decision whether to use a contract or equity mode.
- Stage three is specifying which type of relationship to pursue.

LO4 Outline how alliances are dissolved.
- The phases of dissolution are initiation, going public, uncoupling, and aftermath.
- Managers need to combat opportunism and, if necessary, manage the dissolution process.

LO5 Discuss how alliances perform.
- Alliance performance may be affected by (1) equity, (2) learning, (3) nationality, and (4) relational capabilities.

LO6 Explain why firms undertake acquisitions and what performance problems they tend to encounter.
- Acquisitions are often driven by synergistic, hubristic, and/or managerial motives.
- Many acquisitions fail because managers fail to address pre- and post-acquisition problems.
- Pre-acquisition problems include managers over-estimating their ability to create value; inadequate pre-acquisition screening; poor strategic fit; a lack of familiarity with foreign cultures, institutions, and business systems; or nationalistic concerns.
- Post-acquisition problems include poor organizational fit, failure to address multiple stakeholder groups' concerns, clashes of organizational cultures and/or national cultures, and nationalistic concerns.

LO7 Articulate what you can do to make global alliances and acquisitions successful.
- Understand and master the rules of the game governing alliances and acquisitions around the world.

KEY TERMS AND DEFINITIONS

Strategic alliances
Voluntary agreements of cooperation between firms.

Contractual (non-equity-based) alliance
An association between firms that is based on a contract and does not involve the sharing of ownership.

Equity-based alliance
An association between firms that is based on shared ownership or financial interest.

Strategic investment
A business strategy in which one firm invests in another.

Cross-shareholding
A business strategy in which each partner in an alliance holds stock in the other firm.

Acquisition
The transfer of the control of operations and management from one firm (target) to another (acquirer), the former becoming a unit of the latter.

Merger
The combination of operations and management of two firms to establish a new legal entity.

Real option
An investment in real operations as opposed to financial capital.

Relational (or collaborative) capability
The ability to successfully manage interfirm relationships.

Learning race
A situation in which alliance partners aim to learn the other firm's "tricks" as fast as possible.

Acquisition premium
The difference between the acquisition price and the market value of target firms.

Strategic fit
The effective matching of complementary strategic capabilities between two or more firms.

Organizational fit
The similarity in cultures, systems, and structures between two or more firms.

Initiator
The party who begins the process of ending the alliance relationship.

Hubris
Exaggerated pride or overconfidence.

Managerial motives
A manager's desire for power, prestige, and money, which may lead to decisions that do not benefit the firm overall in the long run.

- When managing alliances, pay attention to the soft relationship aspects.
- When managing acquisitions, do not over-pay. Focus on both strategic and organizational fit.

REVIEW QUESTIONS

1. What are the two broad categories of strategic alliances?
2. Which is more common, mergers or acquisitions? Why?
3. Outline the three stages of alliance formation.
4. Outline the process of alliance dissolution.
5. What are three of the most common motives for acquisition?
6. How does a manager avoid pre-acquisition and post-acquisition problems?

CRITICAL DISCUSSION QUESTIONS

1. *ON ETHICS:* Some argue that engaging in a learning race in alliance management is unethical. Others contend that a learning race is part and parcel of alliance relationships. What do you think?
2. *ON ETHICS:* During the courtship and negotiation stages, managers often emphasize equal partnerships and do not reveal (or they try to hide) their true intentions. What are the ethical dilemmas here?
3. *ON ETHICS:* As a CEO, you are trying to acquire a foreign firm. The size of your firm will double, and it will become the largest in your industry. On the one hand, you are excited about the opportunity to be a leading captain of industry and the associated power, prestige, and income. You expect your salary, bonus, and stock option to double next year. On the other hand, you have just read this chapter and are troubled by the fact that 70% of mergers and acquisitions reportedly fail. How would you proceed?

CLOSING CASE DISCUSSION QUESTIONS

1. What is the strategic fit between Nomura and Lehman?
2. Is there any organizational fit? How can the gaps between the cultures of these two firms be bridged?
3. How does Nomura alleviate the concerns of multiple stakeholders?
4. How would you predict the effectiveness of Nomura's transformation after this acquisition?

© Cengage Learning 2013

For more great resources, especially interactive maps that can help you grasp GLOBAL geography, log in to CourseMate at www.cengagebrain.com.

CHAPTER SUMMARY

LO1 Describe the relationship between multinational strategy and structure.

- An integration-responsiveness framework governs multinational strategy and structure.
- Strategy and structure work in four pairs.
- Home replication strategy duplicates home-country strengths in foreign countries and adds an international division to the existing company structure.
- Localization strategy focuses on a number of foreign countries, each of which is regarded as a stand-alone local market supported by a geographic area structure.
- Global standardization strategy relies on the development and distribution of standardized products worldwide in order to reap the maximum benefits from low cost advantages by organizing each product division as a stand-alone entity with full worldwide responsibilities.
- Transnational strategy, which is often supported by a global matrix structure, seeks to be simultaneously cost efficient, locally responsive, and learning driven around the world.

LO2 Explain how institutions and resources affect multinational strategy, structure, and learning.

- "Rules of the game" for multinational enterprises (MNEs) are set by both formal and informal institutions governing (1) external relationships and (2) internal relationships.
- According to the resource-based view, management of MNE structure, learning, and innovation must be handled within the VRIO framework.

LO3 Outline the challenges associated with learning, innovation, and knowledge management.

- Knowledge management should primarily focus on tacit knowledge, which is more important than explicit knowledge but also harder to transfer and learn.
- Differences in knowledge management among four types of MNEs fundamentally stem from the interdependence (1) between the headquarters and foreign subsidiaries and (2) among various subsidiaries.
- Globalization of research and development (R&D) calls for capabilities to combat a number of problems associated with knowledge creation, retention, outflow, transmission, and inflow.

LO4 List three things you can do to make a multinational firm successful.

- Understand and master the external rules of the game from home/host-country environments.
- Understand and be prepared to change the internal rules of the game governing MNE management.
- Develop learning and innovation capabilities around the world: "Think global, act local."

KEY TERMS AND DEFINITIONS

Integration-responsiveness framework
An MNE management framework for simultaneously dealing with the pressures for both global integration and local responsiveness.

Local responsiveness
The need to be responsive to different customer preferences around the world.

Home replication strategy
A strategy that emphasizes duplicating home country-based competencies in foreign countries.

Localization (or multidomestic) strategy
A strategy that focuses on a number of foreign countries/regions, each of which is regarded as a stand-alone local (domestic) market worthy of significant attention and adaptation.

Global standardization strategy
A strategy that relies on the development and distribution of standardized products worldwide to reap the maximum benefits from low-cost advantages.

Center of excellence
An MNE subsidiary explicitly recognized as a source of important capabilities that can be leveraged by and/or disseminated to other subsidiaries.

Worldwide (or global) mandate
A charter to be responsible for one MNE function throughout the world.

Transnational strategy
A strategy that endeavors to be simultaneously cost efficient, locally responsive, and learning driven around the world.

International division
An organizational structure that is typically set up when a firm initially expands abroad, often engaging in a home replication strategy.

Geographic area structure
An organizational structure that organizes the MNE according to different countries and regions.

Country (or regional) manager
The business leader of a specific country (or geographic region).

Global product division structure
An organizational structure that assigns global responsibilities to each product division.

Global matrix
An organizational structure often used to alleviate the disadvantages associated with both geographic area and global product division structures, particularly when adopting a transnational strategy.

Subsidiary initiative
The proactive and deliberate pursuit of new opportunities by a subsidiary to expand its scope of responsibility.

Organizational culture
The collective programming of the mind that distinguishes members of one organization from another.

REVIEW QUESTIONS

1. What are the four strategic choices in the integration-responsiveness framework?
2. What are the four corresponding organizational structures?
3. Why is the relationship between strategy and structure reciprocal?
4. What are some of the informal rules of the game governing the selection of subsidiary managers in MNEs headquartered in different countries?
5. How is knowledge developed and disseminated in each of the four types of MNEs?

CRITICAL DISCUSSION QUESTIONS

1. In this age of globalization, some gurus argue that all industries are becoming global and that all firms need to adopt a global standardization strategy. Do you agree? Why or why not?
2. *ON ETHICS:* You are the manager of the best-performing subsidiary in an MNE. Because bonuses are tied to subsidiary performance, your bonus is the highest of all subsidiary managers. Now headquarters is organizing managers from other subsidiaries to visit and learn from your subsidiary. You worry that if performance at other subsidiaries catches up, your subsidiary will no longer be the star unit and your bonus will go down. What are you going to do?
3. *ON ETHICS:* You are a corporate R&D manager at Boeing and are thinking about transferring some R&D work to China, India, and Russia. Reportedly the same work performed by a US engineer who makes $70,000 can be done by an engineer in China, India, or Russia for less than $7,000. However, US engineers at Boeing have staged protests against such moves. US politicians are similarly vocal concerning job losses and national security hazards. What are you going to do?

CLOSING CASE DISCUSSION QUESTIONS

1. What are the drawbacks and benefits associated with moving a business unit and corporate HQ to another country?
2. If you were a CEO or a business unit head, under what conditions would you consider moving HQ?
3. If you were a government official in the MNE's home country, what can you do to discourage such moves of multinational HQ out of the country?

© Cengage Learning 2013

For more great resources, especially interactive maps that can help you grasp GLOBAL geography, log in to CourseMate at www.cengagebrain.com.

Review Card

CHAPTER 13

CHAPTER SUMMARY

LO1 Explain staffing decisions, with a focus on expatriates.
- International staffing primarily uses one of three approaches: ethnocentric, polycentric, or geocentric.
- Expatriates (primarily parent-county nationals [PCNs] and to a lesser extent third-country nationals [TCNs]) play multiple challenging roles and often have high failure rates, defined by either premature return or unmet business objectives.
- Expatriates need to be carefully selected, taking into account a variety of factors in terms of both the individual and the situation.

LO2 Identify training and development needs for expatriates and host-country nationals.
- Training length and rigor should correspond to the expatriate's expected length of stay.
- Expatriates need to be properly trained and be cared for during repatriation.
- Training and development of host-country nationals (HCNs) is now an area of differentiation among many multinational enterprises (MNEs).

LO3 Discuss compensation and performance appraisal issues.
- Expatriates are compensated using the going rate and balance sheet approaches.
- The going rate approach fosters equality among PCNs, TCNs, and HCNs within the same subsidiary, but the going rate for the same position differs around the world, making it potentially problematic to attract or possibly repatriate talent.
- The balance sheet approach balances the cost-of-living differences relative to parent-country levels and adds a financial inducement to make the package attractive. But this approach can be expensive, create disparities between expatriates and HCNs, and is organizationally complex to administer.
- Top talent HCNs now increasingly command higher compensation.
- Performance appraisal needs to be carefully provided to achieve its intended purposes.

LO4 List factors that affect labor relations in both home and host countries.
- Despite revival efforts, unions have been declining in developed countries.
- MNEs prefer to deal with non-unionized workforces, but the power of unions in developing countries deserves some attention.

LO5 Discuss how the institution-based and resource-based views shed additional light on human resource management.
- Formal and informal rules of the game shape human resource management (HRM) significantly, both at home and abroad.

KEY TERMS AND DEFINITIONS

Human resource management (HRM)
Activities that attract, select, and manage employees.

Staffing
HRM activities associated with hiring employees and filling positions.

Host-country national (HCN)
An individual from the host country who works for an MNE.

Parent-country national (PCN)
An employee who comes from the parent (home) country of the MNE and works at its local subsidiary.

Third-country national (TCN)
An employee who comes from neither the parent country nor the host country of the MNE.

Ethnocentric approach
A staffing approach that emphasizes the norms and practices of the parent company (and the parent country of the MNE) by relying on PCNs.

Polycentric approach
A staffing approach that emphasizes the norms and practices of the host country by relying on HCNs.

Geocentric approach
A staffing approach that focuses on finding the most suitable managers, who can be PCNs, HCNs, or TCNs.

Expatriation
Leaving one's home country to work in another country.

Training
Specific preparation to do a particular job.

Development
Longer-term, broader preparation to improve managerial skills for a better career.

Repatriate
A manager who returns to his or her home country to stay after working abroad for a length of time.

Repatriation
Returning to an expatriate's home country after an extended period overseas.

Psychological contract
An informal understanding of expected delivery of benefits in the future for current services.

Inpatriation
Relocating employees of a foreign subsidiary to the MNE's headquarters for the purposes of filling skill shortages at headquarters and developing a global mindset for such inpatriates.

Compensation
Salary and benefits.

Performance appraisal
The evaluation of employee performance for the purposes of promotion, retention, or ending employment.

- While informal cultures, norms, and values are important, HR managers need to avoid stereotyping and instead consider changes.
- As HRM becomes more strategic, VRIO dimensions are now more important.

LO6 Identify the five Cs of human resource management.
- HR managers need to be *curious*, *competent*, *courageous*, and *caring* about people.
- Non-HR managers need to proactively develop their *careers*.

Going rate approach
A compensation approach that pays expatriates the prevailing (going) rate for comparable positions in a host country.

Balance sheet approach
A compensation approach that balances the cost-of-living differences based on parent-country levels and adds a financial inducement to make the package attractive.

Labor relations
A firm's relations with organized labor (unions) in both home and host countries.

REVIEW QUESTIONS

1. What are the three main approaches to staffing?
2. What are the four key roles that expatriates typically play?
3. Why do a high percentage of expatriates fail abroad?
4. In expatriate compensation, what are the differences between the going rate approach and the balance sheet approach?
5. Why have efforts to establish multinational labor organizations been unsuccessful?
6. How do HR managers benefit from the four Cs? What is the fifth C for non-HR managers?

CRITICAL DISCUSSION QUESTIONS

1. You have been offered a reasonably lucrative expatriate assignment for the next three years, and your boss will have a meeting about the assignment with you next week. How would you discuss the assignment with your boss?
2. *ON ETHICS:* If you were an HCN, do you think pay should be equal between HCNs and expatriates in equivalent positions? Suppose that you were president of a subsidiary in a host country, and as a PCN your pay was five times higher than that for the highest-paid HCN (your vice president). What do you think?
3. *ON ETHICS:* As HR director for an oil company, you are responsible for selecting 15 expatriates to go to work in Iraq. However, you are personally concerned about their safety. How do you proceed?

CLOSING CASE DISCUSSION QUESTIONS

1. What are the benefits of across-the-board pay cuts?
2. What are the benefits of reduction in force (mass layoffs)?
3. How would you advise this Japanese expatriate working in the United States?

© Cengage Learning 2013

For more great resources, especially interactive maps that can help you grasp GLOBAL geography, log in to CourseMate at www.cengagebrain.com.

Managing Corporate SOCIAL Responsibility Globally

Review Card

CHAPTER 14

CHAPTER SUMMARY

LO1 Articulate a stakeholder view of the firm.

- A stakeholder view of the firm urges companies to pursue a balanced triple bottom line consisting of economic, social, and environmental performance.
- Despite the fierce defense of the free market school, especially the shareholder capitalism variant, the corporate social responsibility (CSR) movement has now become a more central part of management discussions.
- The CSR debate centers on the nature of the firm in society.
- Free market advocates argue that the social responsibility of business is to increase its profits, and, if firms attempt to attain social goals, such as providing employment and social welfare, managers will lose their focus on profit maximization.
- CSR advocates argue that a free market system that takes the pursuit of self-interest and profit as its guiding light—although in theory constrained by rules, contracts, and property rights—may in practice fail to constrain itself, thus often breeding greed, excesses, and abuses.

LO2 Apply the institution-based and resource-based views to analyze corporate social responsibility.

- The institution-based view suggests that when confronting CSR pressures, firms may employ (1) reactive, (2) defensive, (3) accommodative, or (4) proactive strategies.
- A code of conduct (sometimes called a code of ethics) is a tangible indication of a firm's willingness to accept CSR.
- CSR-related resources can include *tangible* technologies and processes as well as *intangible* skills and attitudes.
- The resource-based view argues that not all CSRs satisfy the VRIO requirements.
- The resource-based view suggests that because of capability constraints, many firms are not cut out for a CSR-intensive (differentiation) strategy.

LO3 Identify three ways you can manage corporate social responsibility.

- Understand the rules of the game, anticipate changes, and seek to influence such changes.
- Pick your CSR battles carefully. Don't blindly imitate other firms' CSR activities.
- Integrate CSR as part of the core activities and processes of the firm.

KEY TERMS AND DEFINITIONS

Corporate social responsibility (CSR)
Consideration of, and response to, issues beyond the narrow economic, technical, and legal requirements of the firm to accomplish social benefits along with the traditional economic gains that the firm seeks.

Stakeholder
Any group or individual who can affect or is affected by a firm's actions.

Global sustainability
The ability to meet the needs of the present without compromising the ability of future generations to meet their needs around the world.

Primary stakeholder groups
Constituents on which the firm relies for its continuous survival and prosperity.

Secondary stakeholder groups
Groups or individuals who can indirectly affect or are indirectly affected by a firm's actions.

Triple bottom line
Economic, social, and environmental performance that simultaneously satisfies the demands of all stakeholder groups.

Reactive strategy
A strategy that would only respond to CSR causes when required by disasters and outcries.

Defensive strategy
A strategy that focuses on regulatory compliance but with little actual commitment to CSR by top management.

Accommodative strategy
A strategy characterized by some support from top managers, who may increasingly view CSR as a worthwhile endeavor.

Code of conduct (code of ethics)
A set of written policies and standards outlining the proper practices for a firm.

Proactive strategy
A strategy that anticipates CSR and endeavors to do more than is required.

Social issue participation
Firms' participation in social causes not directly related to the management of primary stakeholders.

REVIEW QUESTIONS

1. How do the concerns for primary stakeholders differ from those for secondary stakeholders?
2. What does triple bottom line mean?
3. What are the four types of strategies underpinning CSR decisions?
4. Using a resource-based view, explain why some firms improve their economic performance by adopting a CSR-intensive strategy, whereas others achieve no or damaging results.
5. Do you think "green" practices should be voluntary or mandatory for businesses? Why?

CRITICAL DISCUSSION QUESTIONS

1. In the landmark *Dodge v. Ford* case in 1919, the Michigan State Supreme Court decided whether or not Henry Ford could withhold dividends from the Dodge brothers (and other shareholders of the Ford Motor Company) to engage in what today would be called CSR activities. Returning a resounding "No," the court opined that "a business organization is organized and carried on primarily for the profits of the stockholders." If the court in your country were to decide on this case this year (or in 2019), what do you think would be the likely outcome?
2. *ON ETHICS:* Some argue that investing in emerging economies greatly increases the economic development and standard of living at the base of the global economic pyramid. Others contend that moving jobs to low-cost countries not only abandons CSR for domestic employees and communities in developed economies but also exploits the poor in emerging economies and destroys the environment. If you were (1) CEO of a multinational (MNE) headquartered in a developed economy moving production to a low-cost country or (2) the leader of a labor union in the home country of the same MNE and about to lose lots of jobs, how would you participate in this debate?
3. *ON ETHICS:* Hypothetically, your MNE is the largest foreign investor in (1) Vietnam, where religious leaders are reportedly being persecuted, or (2) Estonia, where ethnic Russian citizens are being discriminated against by law. As the country manager there, you understand that the MNE is being pressured by nongovernmental organizations (NGOs) of all stripes to help the oppressed groups in these countries. But you also understand that the host government could be upset if your firm is found to engage in local political activities deemed inappropriate. These alleged activities, which you personally find distasteful, are not directly related to your operations. How would you proceed?

CLOSING CASE DISCUSSION QUESTIONS

1. From an institution-based view, how can firms play the game when the rules are uncertain?
2. From a resource-based view, identify potential first mover advantages in climate-smart strategies.
3. As CEO of a coal-fired utility in Australia, Germany, or the United States, how can your firm reduce greenhouse gas emissions? As CEO of a similar utility in China or India, what are your options?

For more great resources, especially interactive maps that can help you grasp GLOBAL geography, log in to CourseMate at www.cengagebrain.com.

MAP 1

pengAtlas Map

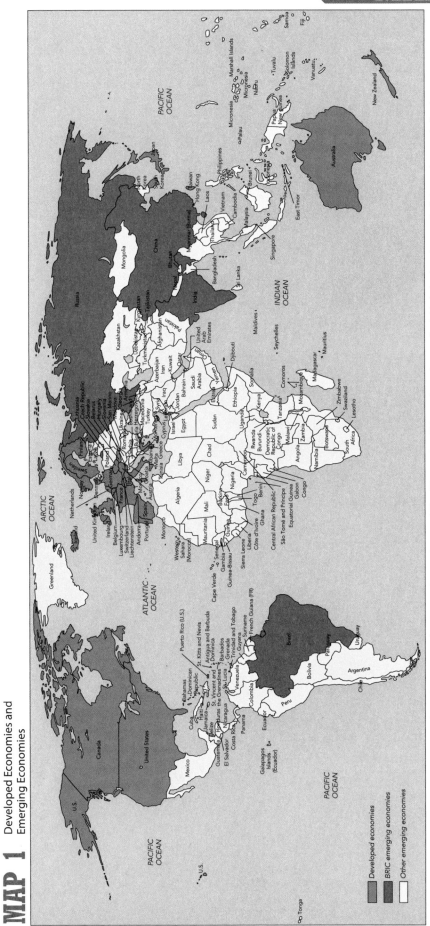

MAP 1   Developed Economies and Emerging Economies

Developed economies

BRIC emerging economies

Other emerging economies

Source: International Monetary Fund (IMF), available online at http://www.imf.org [accessed 16 October, 2009]. The IMF recognizes 184 countries and economies. It labels developed economies "advanced economies," and labels emerging economies "emerging and developing economies."

MAP 2

MAP 2
The Group
of 20 (G-20)

PACIFIC
OCEAN

ARCTIC
OCEAN

PACIFIC
OCEAN

INDIAN
OCEAN

ATLANTIC
OCEAN

Canada
pop. 33,487,208

United States
pop. 307,212,123

Mexico
pop. 111,211,789

U.K.
pop. 61,113,205

Germany
pop. 82,329,758

France
pop. 64,057,792

Italy
pop. 58,126,212

European Union
pop. 501,259,840

Russia
pop. 140,041,247

Turkey
pop. 76,805,524

China
pop. 1,338,612,968

South Korea
pop. 48,508,972

Japan
pop. 127,078,679

Indonesia
pop. 240,271,522

Australia
pop. 21,262,641

India
pop. 1,166,079,217

Saudi Arabia
pop. 28,686,633

South Africa
pop. 49,052,489

Brazil
pop. 198,739,269

Argentina
pop. 40,913,584

Source: U.S. Census Bureau, International Database; *The World Factbook 2009* (Washington, DC: Central Intelligence Agency, 2009). See PengAtlas Map 9 for a map of EU member countries.

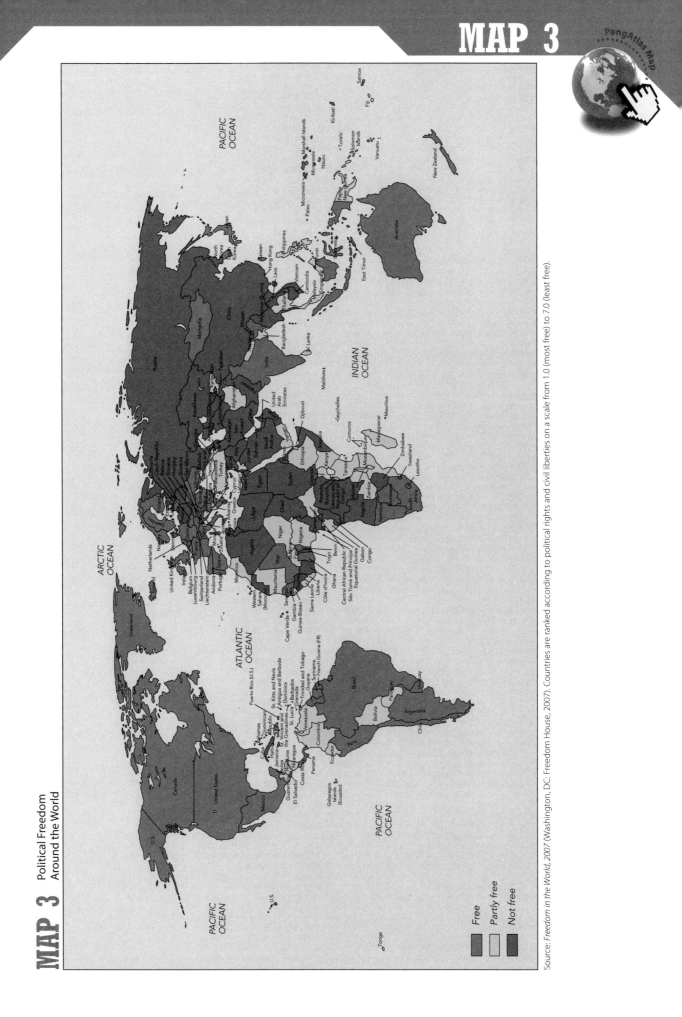

MAP 3

MAP 3 Political Freedom Around the World

Free
Partly free
Not free

Source: Freedom in the World, 2007 (Washington, DC: Freedom House, 2007). Countries are ranked according to political rights and civil liberties on a scale from 1.0 (most free) to 7.0 (least free).

MAP 4

MAP 4 Top Ten and Bottom Ten Countries by Per Capita Income

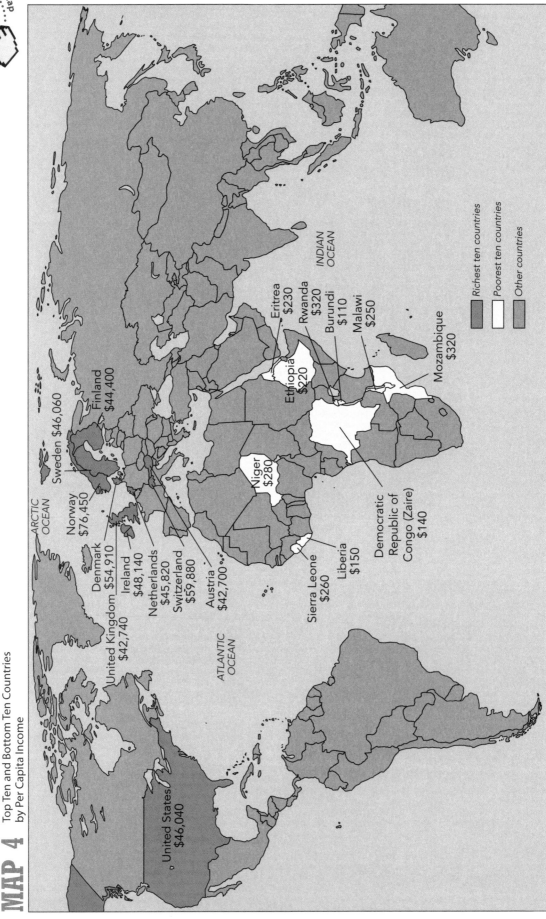

United States $46,040

Sweden $46,060

Finland $44,400

Norway $76,450

Denmark $54,910

Ireland $48,140

Netherlands $45,820

Switzerland $59,880

Austria $42,700

United Kingdom $42,740

ARCTIC OCEAN

ATLANTIC OCEAN

INDIAN OCEAN

Eritrea $230

Rwanda $320

Burundi $110

Malawi $250

Ethiopia $220

Mozambique $320

Niger $280

Sierra Leone $260

Liberia $150

Democratic Republic of Congo (Zaire) $140

Richest ten countries

Poorest ten countries

Other countries

Source: The World Bank, *World Development Report 2009: Reshaping Economic Geography* (Washington, DC: The World Bank, 2009). "Income" here refers to per capita gross national income (GNI), which is gross domestic product (GDP) plus net receipts of income from nonresident sources. GNI is also known as gross national product (GNP).

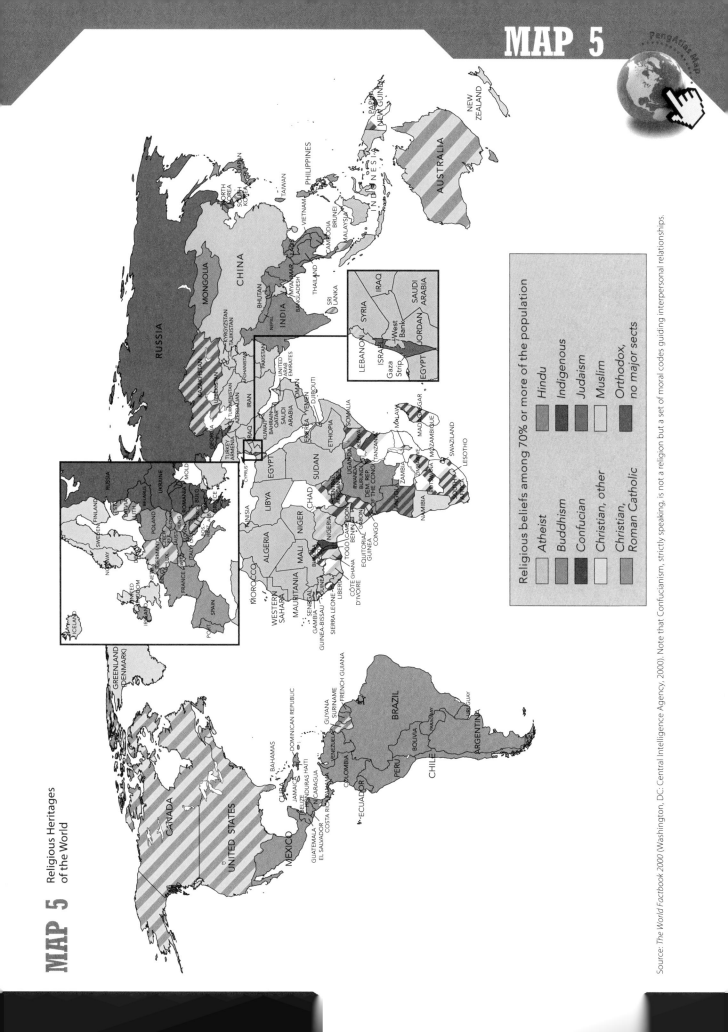

MAP 5

MAP 5

Religious Heritages
of the World

Religious beliefs among 70% or more of the population

Atheist	Hindu
Buddhism	Indigenous
Confucian	Judaism
Christian, other	Muslim
Christian, Roman Catholic	Orthodox, no major sects

Source: *The World Factbook 2000* (Washington, DC: Central Intelligence Agency, 2000). Note that Confucianism, strictly speaking, is not a religion but a set of moral codes guiding interpersonal relationships.

MAP 6

MAP 6 Top Ten Merchandise
Importers and Exporters

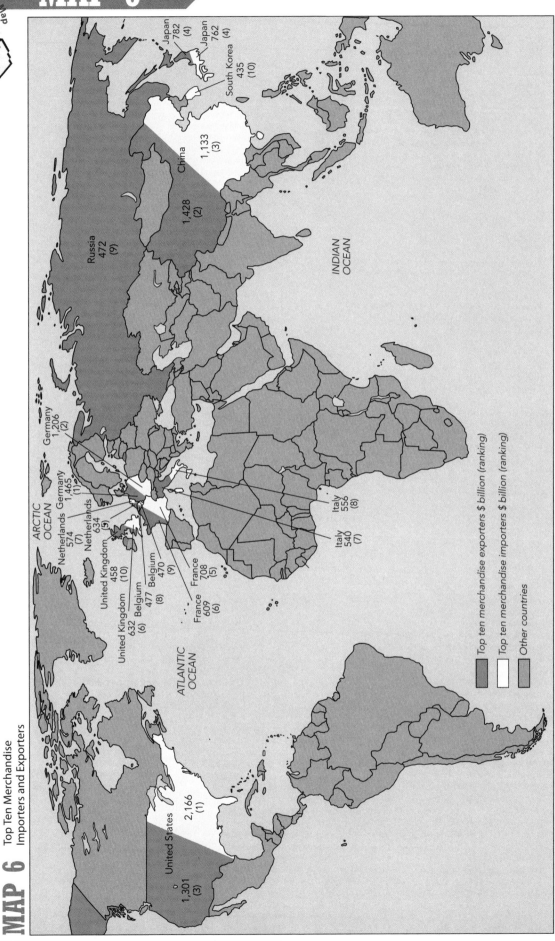

Japan
782
(4)

Japan
762
(4)

South Korea
435
(10)

China
1,133
(3)

China
1,428
(2)

Russia
472
(9)

INDIAN
OCEAN

Germany
1,206
(2)

Germany
1,465
(1)

ARCTIC
OCEAN

Netherlands
574
(7)

Netherlands
634
(5)

United Kingdom
458
(10)

United Kingdom
632
(6)

Belgium
477
(8)

Belgium
470
(9)

France
708
(5)

France
609
(6)

Italy
540
(7)

Italy
556
(8)

ATLANTIC
OCEAN

United States
2,166
(1)

United States
1,301
(3)

Top ten merchandise exporters $ billion (ranking)

Top ten merchandise importers $ billion (ranking)

Other countries

Source: World Trade Organization, *World Trade Report 2009* (Geneva: WTO, 2009) Appendix Table 5 and Table 3. All data are for 2008.

MAP 7

MAP 7 Top Ten Service Importers and Exporters

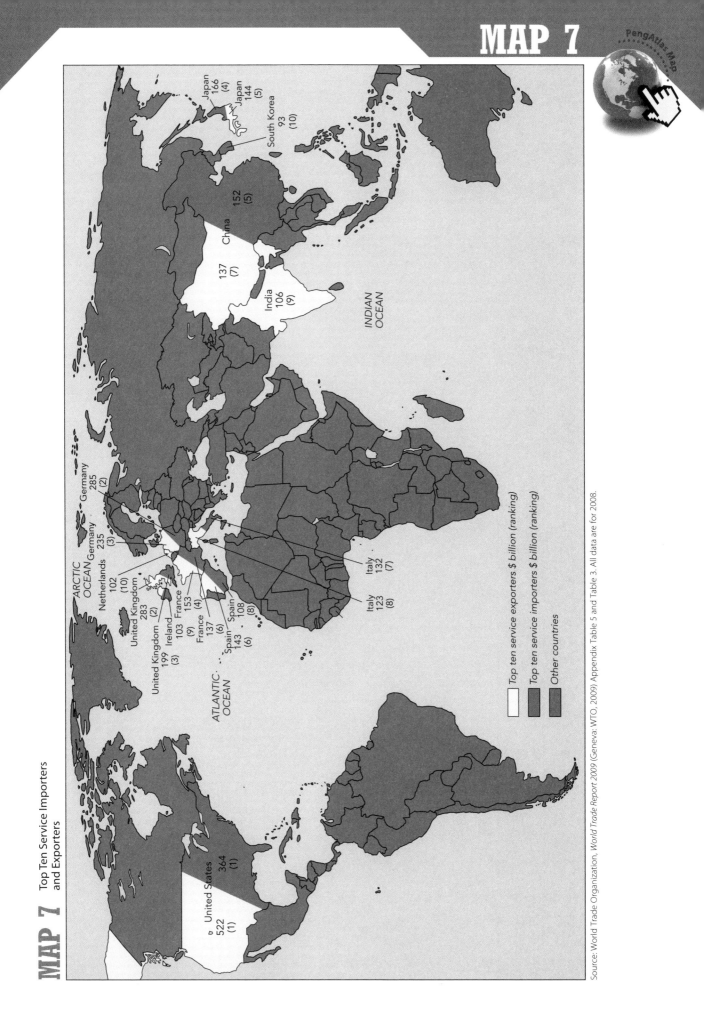

Japan 166 (4)

Japan 144 (5)

South Korea 93 (10)

China 152 (5)

China 137 (7)

India 106 (9)

INDIAN OCEAN

Germany 285 (2)

Germany 235 (3)

ARCTIC OCEAN

Netherlands 102 (10)

United Kingdom 283 (2)

United Kingdom 199 (3)

Ireland 103 (9)

France 153 (4)

France 137 (6)

Spain 143 (6)

Spain 108 (8)

Italy 132 (7)

Italy 123 (8)

ATLANTIC OCEAN

United States 364 (1)

United States 522 (1)

Top ten service exporters $ billion (ranking)

Top ten service importers $ billion (ranking)

Other countries

Source: World Trade Organization, *World Trade Report 2009* (Geneva: WTO, 2009) Appendix Table 5 and Table 3. All data are for 2008.

MAP 8

MAP 8 Top Ten Economies for FDI
Inflows and Outflows

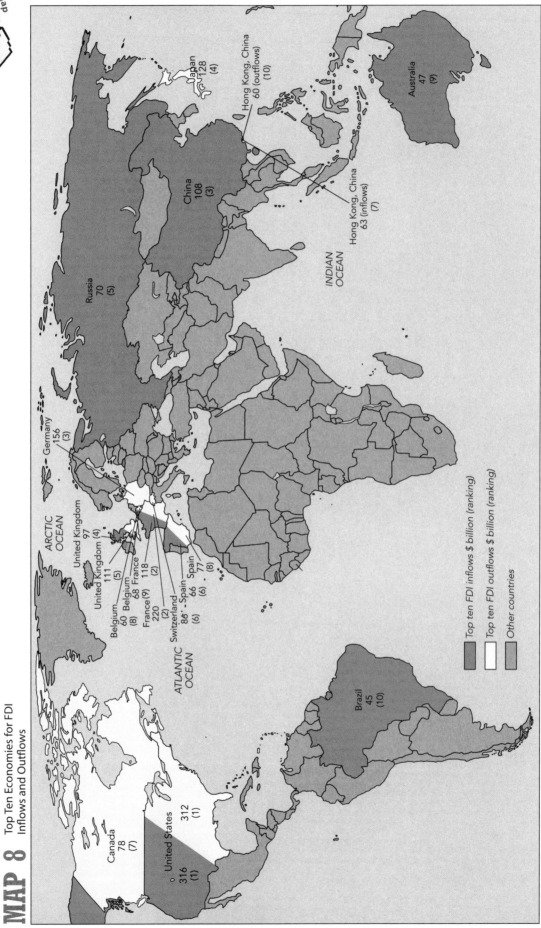

Japan
128
(4)

Hong Kong, China
60 (outflows)
(10)

Australia
47
(9)

China
108
(3)

Hong Kong, China
63 (inflows)
(7)

INDIAN
OCEAN

Russia
70
(5)

Germany
156
(3)

ARCTIC
OCEAN

United Kingdom
97

United Kingdom
111
(5)

Belgium
60
(8)

Belgium
68
(8)

France
118
(2)

France
220
(2)

Switzerland
86
(6)

Spain
66
(6)

Spain
77
(8)

ATLANTIC
OCEAN

Top ten FDI inflows $ billion (ranking)

Top ten FDI outflows $ billion (ranking)

Other countries

Brazil
45
(10)

Canada
78
(7)

United States
312
(1)

United States
316
(1)

Source: United Nations, *World Investment Report 2009* (New York: UN, 2009) Annex Table B.1, 247–250. All data are for 2008.

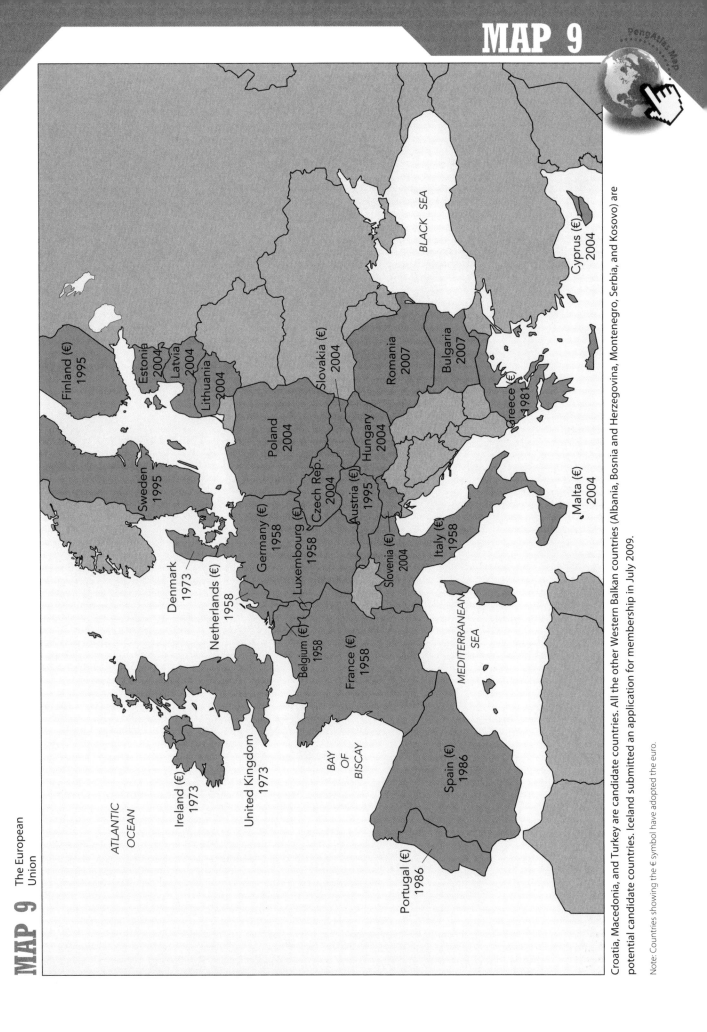

MAP 9

The European Union

Croatia, Macedonia, and Turkey are candidate countries. All the other Western Balkan countries (Albania, Bosnia and Herzegovina, Montenegro, Serbia, and Kosovo) are potential candidate countries. Iceland submitted an application for membership in July 2009.

Note: Countries showing the € symbol have adopted the euro.

ATLANTIC OCEAN

Finland (€) 1995

Sweden 1995

Estonia 2004

Latvia 2004

Lithuania 2004

Denmark 1973

Netherlands (€) 1958

Ireland (€) 1973

United Kingdom 1973

Belgium (€) 1958

France (€) 1958

BAY OF BISCAY

Portugal (€) 1986

Spain (€) 1986

Germany (€) 1958

Luxembourg (€) 1958

Czech Rep. 2004

Poland 2004

Slovakia (€) 2004

Austria (€) 1995

Hungary 2004

Slovenia (€) 2004

Italy (€) 1958

MEDITERRANEAN SEA

Romania 2007

Bulgaria 2007

Greece (€) 1981

BLACK SEA

Cyprus (€) 2004

Malta (€) 2004

MAP 10

MAP 10 Regional Integration in South America

Dominican Republic

Honduras

Guatemala

Nicaragua

El Salvador

Costa Rica

Venezuela

Colombia

Ecuador

Peru

Brazil

PACIFIC
OCEAN

Bolivia

Paraguay

Argentina

Uruguay

ATLANTIC
OCEAN

■ Mercosur members
□ Andean Community members
▨ CAFTA members

In May 2008, Andean Community and Mercosur agreed to merge to form the Union of South American Nations (USAN, more commonly known by its Spanish acronym, UNASUR, which refers to *Unión de Naciones Suramericanas*).

MAP 11

MAP 11 Regional Integration in the Asia Pacific

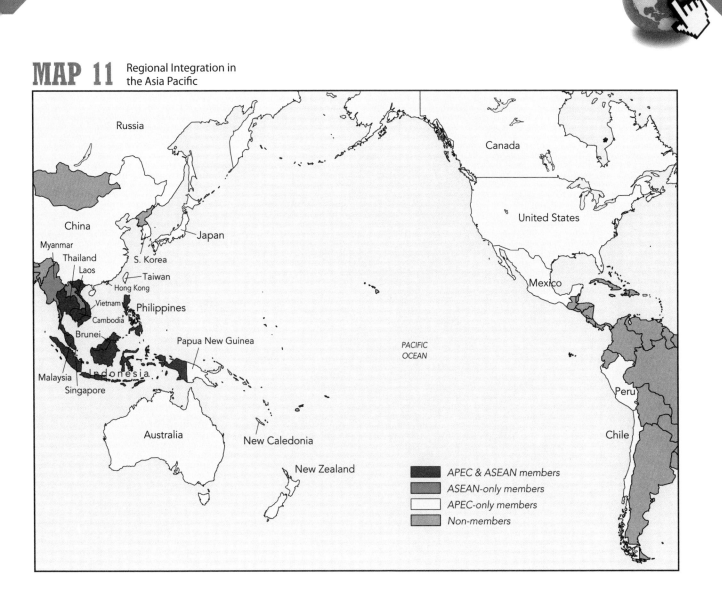

Russia

Canada

China

United States

Myanmar
Thailand
Laos

Mexico

S. Korea
Japan
Taiwan
Hong Kong

Vietnam
Philippines

Cambodia

Brunei

Papua New Guinea

Malaysia
Indonesia

PACIFIC
OCEAN

Singapore

Peru

Australia

New Caledonia

Chile

New Zealand

APEC & ASEAN members
ASEAN-only members
APEC-only members
Non-members

MAP 12

MAP 12 Ease of Doing Business: Top Ten and Bottom Ten

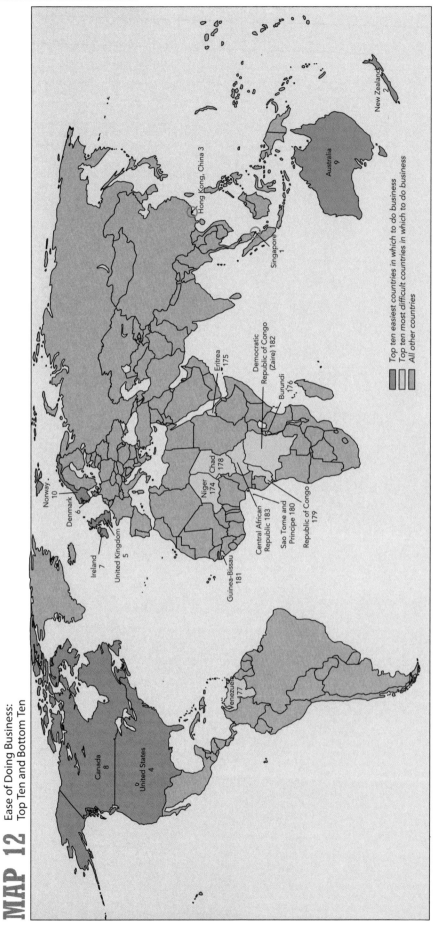

New Zealand 2

Australia 9

Hong Kong, China 3

Singapore 1

Eritrea 175

Democratic Republic of Congo (Zaire) 182

Burundi 176

Niger 174

Chad 178

Central African Republic 183

Sao Tome and Principe 180

Republic of Congo 179

Guinea-Bissau 181

Norway 10

Denmark 6

Ireland 7

United Kingdom 5

Venezuela 177

Canada 8

United States 4

Top ten easiest countries in which to do business
Top ten most difficult countries in which to do business
All other countries

Source: Data extracted from World Bank, 2010, *Doing Business*, database available online at http://www.doingbusiness.org.

MAP 13 PengAtlas Map

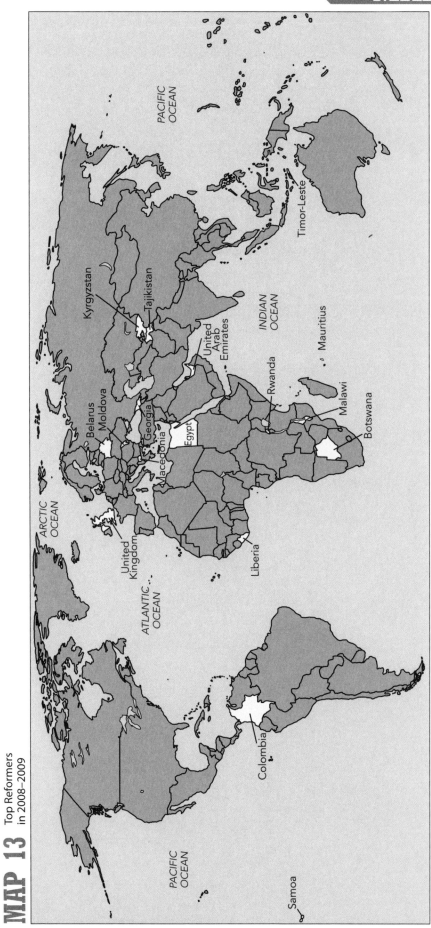

MAP 13 Top Reformers in 2008–2009

Source: World Bank, 2010, *Doing Business*, database available online at http://www.worldbank.org.

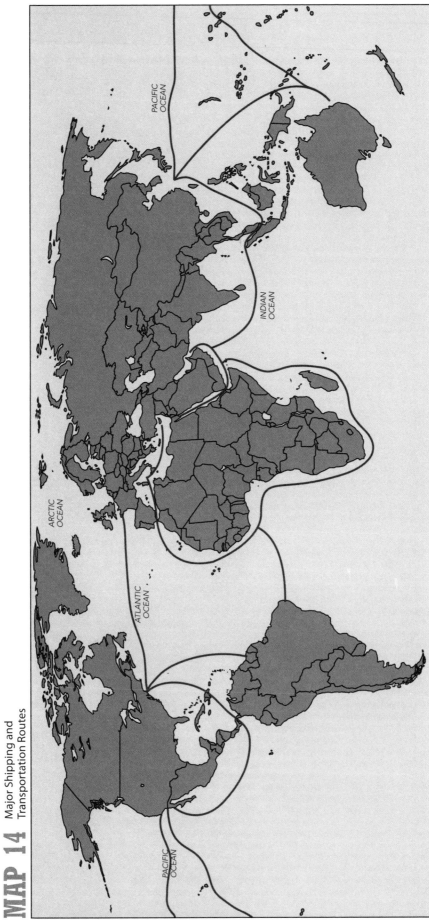

MAP 14

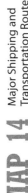

MAP 14 Major Shipping and Transportation Routes

PACIFIC OCEAN

INDIAN OCEAN

ARCTIC OCEAN

ATLANTIC OCEAN

PACIFIC OCEAN

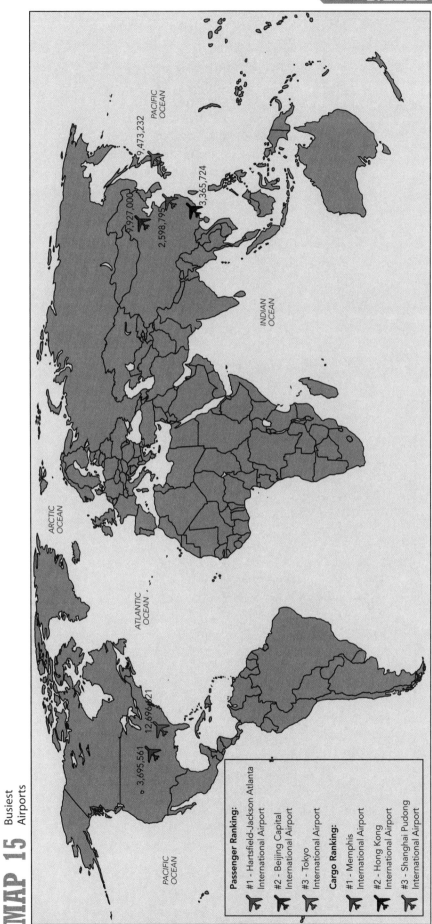

MAP 15

MAP 15 Busiest Airports

PengAtlas Map

PACIFIC
OCEAN

9,473,232

3,365,724

2,598,795

INDIAN
OCEAN

ARCTIC
OCEAN

ATLANTIC
OCEAN

12,696,621

3,695,561

PACIFIC
OCEAN

Passenger Ranking:

#1 - Hartsfield-Jackson Atlanta
International Airport

#2 - Beijing Capital
International Airport

#3 - Tokyo
International Airport

Cargo Ranking:

#1 - Memphis
International Airport

#2 - Hong Kong
International Airport

#3 - Shanghai Pudong
International Airport

Source: http://encarta.msn.com/media_46153297//major_shipping_trade_routes.html.

MAP 16

MAP 16 Rotterdam—Centrally Located in the EU

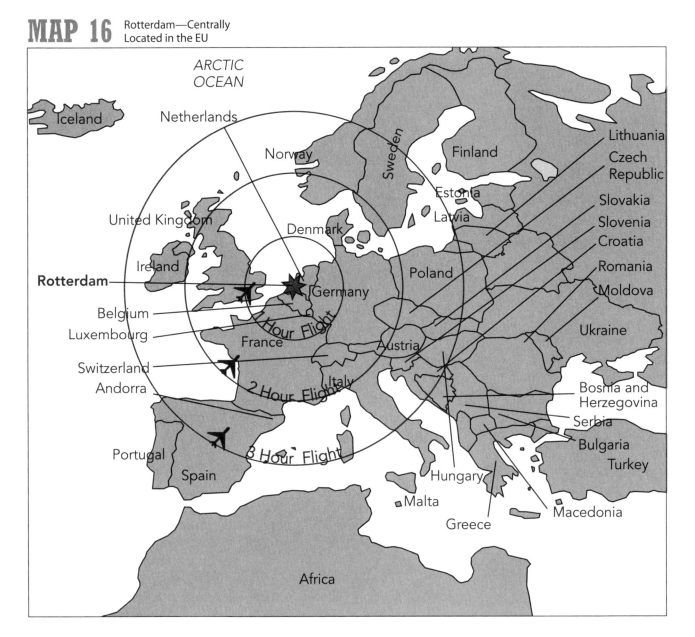

MAP 17

PengAtlas Map

MAP 17

Countries with the
Largest Labor Forces

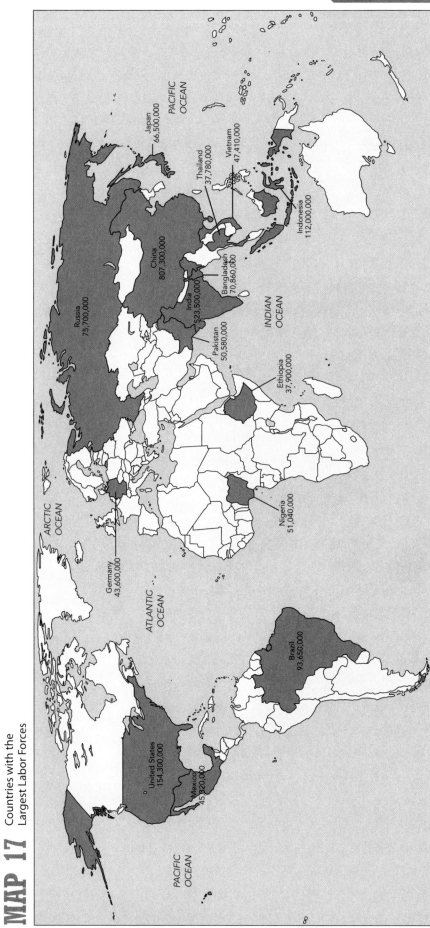

PACIFIC
OCEAN

Japan
66,500,000

Vietnam
47,410,000

Thailand
37,780,000

Indonesia
112,000,000

China
807,300,000

Bangladesh
70,860,000

India
523,500,000

Russia
75,700,000

Pakistan
50,580,000

INDIAN
OCEAN

Ethiopia
37,900,000

Nigeria
51,040,000

ARCTIC
OCEAN

Germany
43,600,000

ATLANTIC
OCEAN

Brazil
93,650,000

United States
154,300,000

Mexico
45,920,000

PACIFIC
OCEAN

8

Source: http//world.bymap.org/LaborForce.html, 2008.

MAP 18

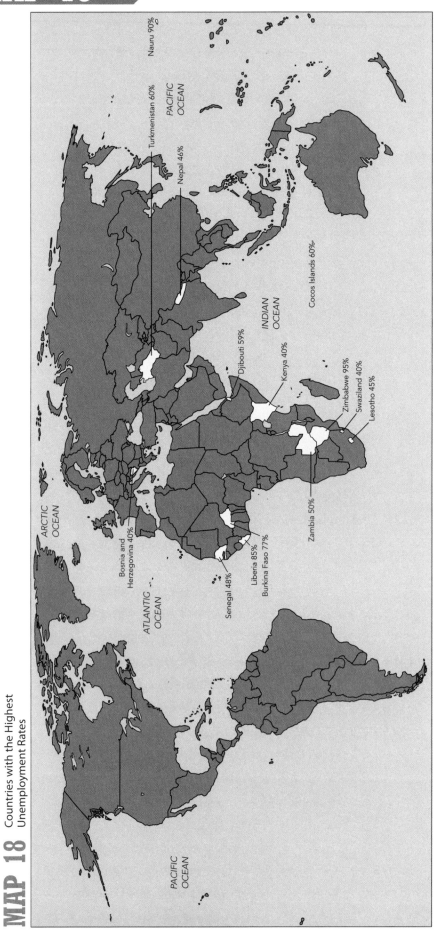

MAP 18 Countries with the Highest Unemployment Rates

Nauru 90%

Turkmenistan 60%

PACIFIC OCEAN

Nepal 46%

Cocos Islands 60%

INDIAN OCEAN

Djibouti 59%

Kenya 40%

Zimbabwe 95%

Swaziland 40%

Lesotho 45%

Zambia 50%

ARCTIC OCEAN

Bosnia and Herzegovina 40%

ATLANTIC OCEAN

Senegal 48%

Liberia 85%

Burkina Faso 77%

PACIFIC OCEAN

Source: *The World Factbook 2009* (Washington, DC: Central Intelligence Agency, 2009).

MAP 19

MAP 19 Top 20 Countries in CO_2 Emissions (in mio tonnes)

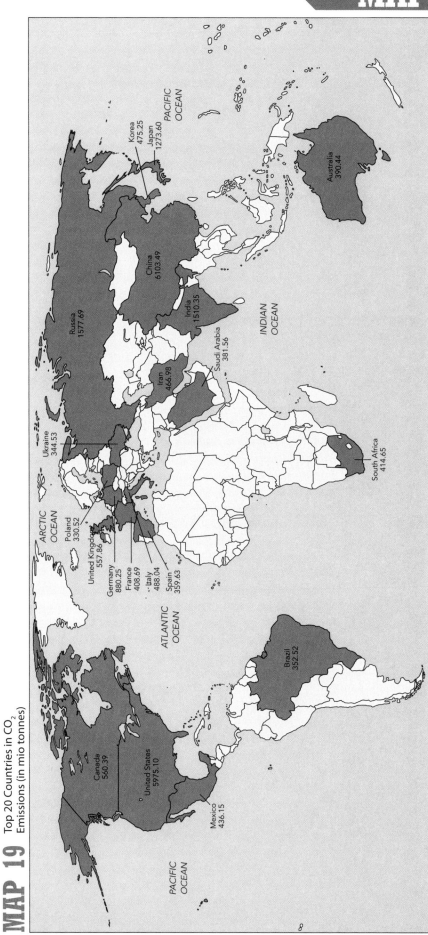

Korea 475.25
Japan 1273.60
Australia 390.44
China 6103.49
India 1510.35
Russia 1577.69
Saudi Arabia 381.56
Iran 466.98
Ukraine 344.53
South Africa 414.65
Poland 330.52
United Kingdom 557.86
Germany 880.25
France 408.69
Italy 488.04
Spain 359.63
Canada 560.39
United States 5975.10
Mexico 436.15
Brazil 352.52

PACIFIC OCEAN
ARCTIC OCEAN
ATLANTIC OCEAN
INDIAN OCEAN

Source: http://unstats.un.org/unsd/environment/air_co2_emissions.htm, 2009.

More Maps at the CourseMate for GLOBAL

In addition to the 19 PengAtlas maps in these cards, a set of four interactive maps are available at the CourseMate for GLOBAL. These engaging maps let you delve more deeply into key concepts presented in the book and enhance your grasp of GLOBAL geography.

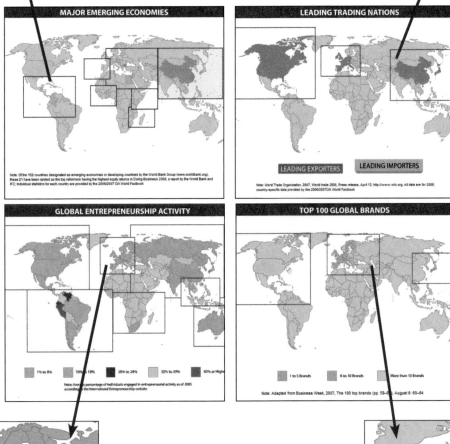

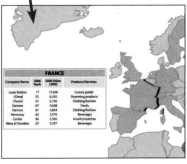

For even more great resources such as videos, e-lectures, games, interactive flashcards, and quizzes, log in to the CourseMate for GLOBAL at www.cengagebrain.com.